CW00422030

Patrick White and God

Patrick White and God

By

Michael Giffin

Cambridge
Scholars
Publishing

Patrick White and God

By Michael Giffin

This book first published 2017

Cambridge Scholars Publishing

Lady Stephenson Library, Newcastle upon Tyne, NE6 2PA, UK

British Library Cataloguing in Publication Data
A catalogue record for this book is available from the British Library

Copyright © 2017 by Michael Giffin

All rights for this book reserved. No part of this book may be reproduced,
stored in a retrieval system, or transmitted, in any form or by any means,
electronic, mechanical, photocopying, recording or otherwise, without
the prior permission of the copyright owner.

ISBN (10): 1-4438-1750-3
ISBN (13): 978-1-4438-1750-9

DEDICATED TO

Benedict XVI
logos philosopher

and

Patrick White
mythos poet

CONTENTS

Acknowledgements ix

Introduction 1
   Continental Australian 1
   Historicized Rhetorician 7
   Perspectivist Disclosures 10
   Romantic Performances 13
   Interconnected Relationships 15

Chapter One 27
Shadow
   Rationalism and Empiricism 27
   Myths and Metaphors 35
   Fatalism and Humanism 46
   Transcendence and Immanence 59
   Tragedy and Comedy 68

Chapter Two 82
Riders
   Logos and Mythos 82
   Mary Hare 89
   Mordecai Himmelfarb 94
   Ruth Godbold 103
   Alf Dubbo 107
   Rosenbaums–Rosetrees 115

Chapter Three 124
Mandala
   Apollonian and Dionysian 124
   The Brown Family 132
   The Feinstein Family 158
   The Poulter Family 169

Chapter Four... 177
Vivisector
    Author as Painter 177
    Discovering Rhoda 191
    Losing Rhoda.. 199
    Absent Rhoda.. 206
    Finding Rhoda... 219

Chapter Five 230
Storm
    Nature and Civilization.. 230
    Parents... 236
    Children 246
    Acolytes 263

Future Directions... 287

Appendix 299
    Iris Murdoch 299
    Muriel Spark 308
    William Golding 330
    Robertson Davies... 343
    Margaret Atwood 359

Bibliography.. 372

Index.. 389

ACKNOWLEDGEMENTS

A debt of gratitude is owed to Emeritus Professor Ann McCulloch for issuing necessary challenges and enlarging my intellectual frame. Thanks are also due to my three first readers—Therese Milham, Grahame Reynolds, and Craig Willcox—each of whom made important insights and offered strategies for improvement. There is a reason why I took on board much but not all of their advice. There comes a time, when writing and editing any critical work, when too much reworking threatens to undermine what little coherence the author's original arguments may have had. The flaws in this book are therefore all mine. I trust I am allowed to recognize that fact as forcefully as any future reader.

INTRODUCTION

Continental Australian

In mid-1985, I wrote to Patrick White, on hearing he was ill, offering the pastoral care of what is—indelibly—his Church by Baptism and Confirmation. His answer, dated 12 August 1985, said:

> I'm ashamed not to have answered your message before, but I have had a lot more illness since returning from hospital. Thank you for offering to bring us Communion to the house. If I refuse the offer it is because I cannot see myself as a true Christian. My faith is put together out of bits and pieces. I am a believer, but not the kind most "Christians" would accept (Marr 1994, 603–604).

White's emphasis—which Marr's book underlines differently from the original letter—raises questions about White's withdrawal from the Church and how it is expressed in his novels.

White believed in God. This much is irrefutable. From *Flaws in the Glass* (1981) we know that, in December 1950, as he was approaching his middle age, he fell in the mud at his Castle Hill property, Dogwoods, and realized there is a God (144). The experience humbled him and brought him back to the Church for a lengthy but unknown period (Marr 1991, 281–285). We do not know when White stopped going to Church, regularly, but he was still occasionally attending High Mass at my parish—Christ Church St Laurence—with Kylie Tennant, around the time *The Solid Mandala* was published.

Our parish priest 1964–1996, Father Austin Day AM, wrote to White on 13 August 1985 inviting him to our 140th Dedication Festival. White's reply, dated 18 August 1985, said:

> I don't like to say outright that I can come to your celebrations. Every time I say "Forgive us our trespasses as we forgive those who trespass against us" I realize I am a hypocrite and un-Christian. Manoly Lascaris, my friend of 45 years, an ingrained Christian (Greek Orthodox), is the reason I have managed to stay afloat (CCSL Archives).

The reason White gave for his ultimate lapse, in *Flaws*, was the rector of the Castle Hill parish banning a guessing game, at a fête, of how many beans were in a jar (145). Clearly his parish did not nurture his adult faith—a measure of its failure rather than his—but at least he gave the Church another go before withdrawing into the "mystical circus" of an "Anglican egotist agnostic pantheist occultist existentialist would-be though failed Christian Australian" (102). In spite of White's final lapse, Manoly remained secure within the Orthodox Church, which White always admired and took an interest in.

The truth of White's relationship with the Church lies somewhere between falling in the mud and shunning the Castle Hill rector. His struggle with his faith will resonate with many who continue to struggle with their faith from within the Church. According to him, one of the problems was that his family's relationship with the Church was tribal rather than spiritual. Apparently this did not nurture his adult faith. This is common. Many lapsed Christians blame others—particularly their parents—for their unwillingness to remain in and struggle with an institution that is as human as it is divine.

The story of the extended White family's relationship with the Anglican Church—as patrons of the Sydney and Newcastle Dioceses—is interesting yet not widely known. On the whole, Marr avoided the subject in *Patrick White: A Life* (1991) which, in spite of its strengths, did not take White's faith seriously. Perhaps this was because of Marr's own hostility towards the Church as a former adherent who once toyed with the idea of ordination before coming out and seeing the light (Marr 1999, xi).

In February 1993, on *The Search for Meaning*, ABC Radio aired a talk Marr gave to the Eremos Institute. The talk was meant to be about White's spirituality but struck me as more of a comic monologue by someone outside the Church, affecting inside knowledge, who wanted to entertain. Marr told his audience that White was not a Christian but until his death he was passionately concerned for the Church's welfare. Evidently he identified as "tarred with the brush" of the Low Church. This fuelled his tribal antipathy towards the Catholic Church and prevented him from joining the Orthodox Church.

A few minutes later, however, Marr said White was devoted to the Virgin Mary. He acknowledged her intercessory power and influence over world affairs: for example in relation to communism. Also, he observed the Orthodox calendar in his home until his death. The talk raises more questions than it answers, since it is hard to imagine someone tarred with a Low Church brush being devoted to the Virgin Mary, or acknowledging her intercessory power, or observing the Orthodox calendar. Either Marr was confused, or White was confused, or both were confused.

It is easy to take White's tribal anti-Catholicism out of context.

Catholicism has been a soft target—and the subject of false witness—for centuries (Stark 2016). But there is always another side to the story. In *Patrick White: A Tribute* (Joyce 1991), Father Edmund Campion tells a charming story about White hosting two dozen young Christian Brothers just out of training and about to start teaching. One January afternoon they went to Dogwoods with their Master of Scholastics, at some point after *Riders in the Chariot* had begun to win acclaim, before *The Solid Mandala* was published, during the period White was writing plays and short stories. They were given a tour of the house. The walls were crowded with Greek icons and the paintings of well-known Australian painters:

> Going through the house, the Brothers noticed how spick and span the two bachelors kept everything. They were led outside, where afternoon tea, with several Greek dishes, was laid on a table under the trees.
>
> Then it was time for talk. Patrick White told the Brothers how he wrote his novels, starting with the characters who grew in his mind until they found a story they were able to inhabit. He said he didn't "enjoy" writing, it was more of a personal compulsion. Here Manoly Lascaris chimed in with the information that the novelist sometimes spent weeks polishing a single phrase. When he flagged he sought refreshment in music. Although later novels had greater commercial success, he thought his best novel to date was *The Aunt's Story* (1948). He claimed not to read much fiction.
>
> Patrick White showed exquisite courtesy to his at times gauche questioners. No, he had had few associations with Catholics, although he had observed them closely. No, he had not made a special study of Aboriginal psychology; indeed, he had never met an Aborigine. What did he think of A.D. Hope's charge that he wrote "illiterate verbal sludge"? He smiled faintly but ... tolerantly (9).

According to White's autobiography, which in some ways is more informative than Marr's biography, his formative religious experiences came from St James King Street, Sydney, which has never been a Low Church parish.[1] The autobiography gives an engaging account of the Reverend Dr Philip Micklem, rector of St James between 1917 and 1937, the period that includes White's childhood and adolescence:

> Mr, or Dr, Micklem was an ascetic, celibate Englishman who conducted a service considered "very high". Mr Micklem could have been the reason why so many ladies fainted on steamy Sunday mornings, and were supported, and in some cases even carried out by vergers, and sat on

---

[1] The terms High Church and Low Church tend to be confused with the terms Anglo-Catholic and Evangelical but they are quite different. The High Church liturgies of St James King Street are English Cathedral style. The Anglo-Catholic liturgies of Christ Church St Laurence are Use of Salisbury (Sarum Rite).

upright chairs in the porch. I was overawed by Mr Micklem's raven notes.
He had the head, I realized later in life, of a saint in an Orthodox icon, or
one of those Greek or Coptic heads painted on wood in the National
Gallery London. I was fascinated by the whole production at St James's:
the Greek head, the voice, the ascetic cheekbones and blue chin, the
fainting ladies (you waited for the next) and Ruth tiptoeing back, hands
folded over her stomach, after drinking the communion wine. I never
fainted, but was terrified if ever a lady called Una de Burgh in charge of
the choristers approached after the service (she had a club foot) to ask
Ruth, "When are we going to have him for the choir?" I used to pray my
voice would crack there and then. But my mother knew enough to protect
me from Una (145).

At this time, the Whites lived at Lulworth, their home in Rushcutters
Bay. They also had Withycombe, their summer home in the Blue
Mountains. The autobiography tells another story about the rector of St
James visiting Withycombe:

Actually Dr Micklem was a human being. My mother invited him to
Mount Wilson, and told me to take him for a walk, for the good of my soul
and to get him off her hands before lunch. He was tall, not so gaunt as
when performing at St James's, and his gravity had a twinkle in it. I was
soon in love. I decided to take Dr Micklem to the cave I had never shown
anybody, and where I kept a cardboard box full of secrets. The cave was
on a track to one of those tedious Australian, would-be tourist attractions
called Chinaman's Hat. Hidden in the scrub below the cave was the
rudimentary ladder I had made by nailing lengths of sapling together. I led
the way up the rickety ladder, the doctor wobbled perilously behind me.
When I produced the cardboard box and shared my secrets he was graver
than ever. He treated me, not as a child, but a conspirator. As he sat in the
shallow cave, his knee-caps almost under his chin, I stood a little to one
side and behind. I looked down at his bald patch surrounded by cropped
pepper-and-salt, almost a tonsure. I would have loved to touch it. Instead
we went back to lunch, stowing the ladder in the scrub above the track to
Chinaman's Hat. I felt hot, and finally disenchanted (72).

The autobiography also gives an account of White's revelatory
experience at Dogwoods in December 1950:

The seasons we experienced ran through every cliché in the Australian
climatic calendar: drought, fire, gales, floods along the roads at Windsor
and Richmond. During what seemed like months of rain I was carrying a
trayload of food to a wormy litter of pups down at the kennels when I
slipped and fell on my back, dog dishes shooting in all directions. I lay
where I had fallen, half blinded by rain, under a pale sky, cursing through
watery lips a God in whom I did not believe. I began laughing finally, at
my own helplessness and hopelessness, in the mud and the stench from my

filthy old oilskin.

It was the turning point. My disbelief appeared as farcical as my fall. At that moment I was truly humbled.

We both began an exercise in organized humility. There is nothing remoter from Greek Orthodoxy than Sydney Evangelical C. of E., but in its hatred of Rome the Eastern Church had accepted Protestant overtures. A Greek living at a distance from a church of his own faith might attend the local C. of E., as Manoly did during our years of trial and error.

Every Sunday we set out for early communion [BCP Holy Communion] as it did not interfere with our activities about the "farm". Built in the early days, the church at Castle Hill had accumulated the kind of Victorian and Edwardian bric-à-brac with which prosperous Australians express their gratitude for God's recognition. Kneeling in this church, under a succession of worthy and not so worthy rectors, in winter frost or the cool before a summer blaze, perhaps I was awaiting unconsciously one of the miracles which had not occurred after confirmation. Secure in a more elaborate tradition Manoly was less expectant or more sceptical. Like any expatriate he was not responsible for the farce he had dropped into. I could not protect myself as he did from the bigotry we found. We withdrew after the rector of the day declared it sinful to guess the number of beans in a jar at the annual church fête.

For a brief space we tried driving to Sydney to the service at Christchurch St Lawrence, unintelligible to both of us, though there were some nice moments of theatre as the acolytes, including a young Chinese, strolled among the faithful weaving veils of incense. Surprisingly, it was the esoteric element which caused our withdrawal—and the presence of the Bad Fairy [Una de Burgh] from my childhood at St James's, now in charge of vestments at Christchurch. So each of us retreated into his private faith, and there we have remained. Each respects what the other believes, though Manoly, I think, disapproves of my erratic spirit, chafing free, rejecting tradition. Is it ever possible to believe entirely in someone one knows by heart, who is, at the same time, the one it is impossible to know? (144–145)

That last sentence, about knowing and unknowing, is worth reflecting upon.

This book attempts to locate Patrick White's fiction within a 200-year phase in western philosophy and aesthetics beginning with romanticism in the late 18th century. The attempt is ambitious because his fiction is a critique of western consciousness, in particular its understanding of reason;[2] however, his critique looks like a metaphysics—and perhaps a

---

[2] As Alasdair MacIntyre reminds us, in *Whose Justice? Which Rationality?* (1988), the terms reason and rationality have never been defined objectively. There are only

metapsychology—now challenged by an unstable marriage of promethean science and intersectional politics. Because of this, his religious frame—which remained remarkably consistent during his career—is harder to recognize in the 21st century.

According to the Nobel Prize website, White became a Nobel Laureate in 1973 for an "epic and psychological narrative art which has introduced a new continent to literature". He first appeared on the Nobel short-list in 1969. He would have become a Laureate in 1972 had one judge not strongly objected to *The Vivisector* (1970) (Marr 1991, 532–534). Before he did become a Laureate, another judge said 1973 would be his last chance. So, there was obviously a symbiosis between what he wrote and what the judges thought important at the time. Had he lived in another period, and been shaped by other influences, his fiction might have been different, and the symbiosis might not have existed.

Time moves on. Time influenced the religious festivals that shaped the theatrical culture of ancient Greece. Even in the secularizing festivals of our apparently post-Christian age, time still influences the way writers write, readers read, and critics critique. It separates the ephemeral from the enduring. Is White ephemeral or enduring? We do not know. It is too early to tell. If curriculum developers and the reading public still take their cues from literary critics, a lot will depend on the state of literary criticism.

In the 20th century, many Australians liked White's work having read all of it. Many disliked it, preferring to judge it without having read it. Most were in between. To some he was a great novelist who held up the mirror. Others were more sceptical about his greatness and turned the mirror back on him. Before the Nobel, his work was better understood overseas. After the Nobel, Australian critics wrote perceptive studies interpreting him in his own terms. Yet there were some who suggested—implicitly when not explicitly—that his literary vision was the incoherent rambling of a disordered mind.

I was introduced to White in the 1980s not as an Australian novelist but as part of a broader literary tradition, the British and Commonwealth novel from romanticism to the present, an extended period of overlapping genres between the late-18th and late-20th centuries. As a result, I have

---

subjective theories—all contested—about what they mean to particular movements or individuals. One of the fundamental problems westerners face is our tendency to presume their meaning, as universal or self-evident givens, when there is no consensus over what they mean. One person's rationality is another person's irrationality and vice versa. Yet the west still needs a consensus over what these terms mean, because they are often said to define the west. Westerners must do more than wave these terms around like a fetish—or point them like a witchdoctor's bone—at anyone they disagree with.

always compared and contrasted him with his postwar contemporaries from England, Scotland, and Canada: Iris Murdoch, Muriel Spark, William Golding, and Robertson Davies. After the war, because of the war, these authors worked with a shared pattern of archetypes, or tropes, which allowed each of them to explore the metaphysical dimension of western consciousness, individual and collective, and the civilization that consciousness has produced. This book hopes to shed light on how and why that pattern evolved.

In the 20th century, White's metaphysics was too close to be noticed in its entirety. As his novels are studiously encoded with "bits and pieces" of western philosophy and aesthetics, explaining the sum of its parts was hard. Even in the 21st century it is easier to avoid his metaphysics entirely or refer to it vaguely. Also, since David Marr's *Patrick White: A Life* (1991), with its wealth of biographical detail, the majority of White's critics are unable to discuss his texts without making an issue of his class, sexuality, whiteness, personality, or private life. He is dead when we need him dead, in the Barthean sense. He is alive when we need him alive, as a god who fills our critical gaps.

Historicized Rhetorician

Every author mentioned in this book is a rhetorician whose rhetoric mirrors their period; as a mixture of the timeless and the timebound. Their novels are performative topoi where backgrounds, characterizations and dialogues are aspects of each performance. White's performances, and those of his contemporaries, are therefore historicized. Each of these authors looks to the past, speaks to the present, and points to the future. Margaret Atwood offers two observations about this manoeuvre. First, authors adopt their terms of discourse early in their reading and writing lives. Second, authors have a double consciousness within the shadow of romanticism or its fragments (Atwood 2002, xxvi).

These observations, which Atwood applies to herself, also apply to White, his predecessors, and his contemporaries. They operate across two spheres. First, the sphere of the changing role of the artist since romanticism began. Second, the sphere of the changing message that evolved with the changing role. Her point is that, in both spheres, romanticism has influenced both the author's consciousness and her or his terms of discourse. Understanding this phenomenon requires a general sense of the Greek origins of the dream of reason (Gottlieb 2016), a general sense of the philological origins of the modern humanities (Turner 2014), a general sense of how different authors thought and wrote at different points over a 200-year period, and a general sense of how trends in literature parallel trends in philosophy.

Atwood is wary of the perception of the artist as inspired and set apart, in the way Kermode describes in *Romantic Image* (1957). She therefore avoids the drastic mythologies of the author as self-dedicated "priestess of the imagination" dedicated to creating the "perfect work". But if authors do not acknowledge some loyalty to this romantic ideal, she believes they are unlikely to achieve "more than mediocrity" or perhaps "glaring insignificance" (Atwood 2002, 96). If she avoids the role of priest, she is happy to accept the role of shaman, who descends to the forbidden places, struggles with the dark forces, wrests a story from them, and returns to the world, while trying to avoid being killed in the process (175–176).

Atwood cannot control how her message is received but controls what she writes. She has studied and taught literary fiction as well as written it. Her favourite teaching method is blackboard analysis (Ingersoll 2006, 219). She could no doubt do a blackboard analysis of most novelists discussed in this book. She understands how literature operates and is aware of the distinctive roles of author and critic:

> Literary critics start with an already-written text. They then address questions to this text, "What does it mean?" being both the most basic and the most difficult. Novelists, on the other hand, start with the blank page, to which they similarly address questions. But the questions are different. Instead of asking, first of all, "What does it mean?" they work at the widget level; they ask, "Is this the right word?" "What does it mean?" can only come when there is an "it" to mean something. Novelists have to get some actual words down before they can fiddle with the theology. Or, to put it another way: God started with chaos—dark, without form and void—and so does the novelist. God made one detail at a time. So does the novelist. On the seventh day, God took a breath to consider what he'd done. So does the novelist. But the critic starts on Day 7 (Ingersoll 2006, 187).

Notice Atwood's admission that, after struggling to create an "it" to mean something, she "fiddles with the theology". The text can never be completely unconscious to her. Like White, she is a sub-creator, a created being who creates, and there is a mysterious yet unknown level of intentionality about creating. Like White, her creations are the result of a human need to transform chaos into some order shaping narrative. The "consonance" of this kind of story, its "coherent pattern", is often an attempt to mirror the west's past, present, and future (Kermode 1966; Kermode 1979).

Given the trajectory of Atwood's career, particularly her journey into speculative fiction (Atwood 2011), she seems to be suggesting that, for the post-romantic artist, including the modernist and postmodernist artist, the unchartered future will owe increasingly less to the romantic past, once the fragments of the romantic shadow have been reabsorbed by the aether. Her novels have always questioned the canonical roles of classicism and romanticism. Her questioning intensified during her middle age—the period of her literary maturity—in her desire to focus on the current challenges facing the socially-conscious and globally-aware author: the dangers of promethean hubris, the consequences of science and technology, the existential threats to civilization, and the environmental threats to nature. One cannot help feel, when reading her later work, that humanity is heading for a reckoning.

Critics have noticed a tension in Atwood's work—also found in White's work—which mirrors a struggle between two concepts of western narrative:

> One of these is the concept of apocalypse that permeates the Hebrew-Christian *Heilsgeschichte*, the story of the salvation of God's people. The other is the concept of mimesis from Aristotle's discussion of tragedy in his *Poetics* (Detweiler 1990, 2).

The American Academy of Religion has published an intriguing collection of essays, *The Daemonic Imagination* (Detweiler and Doty 1990), focused on this tension as it appears in Atwood's short story "The Sin Eater" and Mark's pericope of the Gerasene demoniac (Mark 5:1–17). This collection of essays demonstrates how Atwood and Mark are excellent examples of apocalypse struggling with mimesis. In White, perhaps the first example of mimesis struggling with apocalypse is his short story "The Twitching Colonel" (1937). The mimesis is the story of the Colonel's poor physical and mental health, the result of his colonial service in India. The apocalypse is what happens after his immolation and the Indian rope trick, an Oriental version of Jacob's Ladder (Shepherd, 1978, 28–33).

While apocalypse is focused on an ever receding end, and is often associated with eschatology, there are non-religious ends to write about and even the formation of race and gender can be apocalypse rather than mimesis (Ledbetter 1993, 79–90). In *MaddAddam* (2013) the apocalypse has already happened and Atwood describes why it happened. The trace of a classical trope, Glenn–Crake, destroys the world. The trace of a romantic trope, Jimmy–Snowman, is powerless to save it. All that is left are a few humans, and genetically-modified humanoids, flora, and fauna, all existing within a permanently altered ecosystem absorbing the ruins of what was once western civilization.

The novel is about the beginning of a post-apocalyptic, post-western, post-human world. The future belongs to the genetically-modified humanoids, who have no creation story and, being blank slates, are unable to make one up. This is why Atwood assigns Toby, one of the novel's remnant female protagonists, the role of new Hesiod. Toby narrates a new Theogony or creation story for the humanoids. This is necessary, since even a post-human culture needs a creation story and existing creation stories are no longer relevant. They have vanished, along with all the real and imagined tensions within western philosophy and aesthetics, including the influential tension between classicism and romanticism.

Atwood's career began when the careers of Patrick White and Roberston Davies were at their height. Her first novel *The Edible Woman* (1969) appeared between White's *The Solid Mandala* (1966) and *The Vivisector* (1970), just before Davies's *Fifth Business* (1970), the first novel in the Deptford Trilogy. Atwood was clearly the newcomer signalling the next generation. As her career progressed, she gradually became more focused on our next apocalypse. Hence the stark contrast between *The Handmaid's Tale* (1985) and Davies's masterpiece *What's Bred in the Bone* (1985), both short-listed for the 1986 Booker Prize (see Appendix).

Perspectivist Disclosures

Other changes were happening to narrative modes, apart from shifting tensions between apocalypse and mimesis. During the neoclassical and romantic periods, philosophical and aesthetic perceptions of knowledge and truth were given form and content through theories of analogy (or analogical theories); through correspondence theories associated with Socrates, Plato, Aristotle, and Aquinas; through coherence theories associated with Spinoza, Kant, and Hegel (DiCenso 1990). After neoclassicism and romanticism, analogical theories of knowledge and truth became less congruent, less idealistic, and more relativistic and fragmented. For this reason, many post-romantic novelists moved away from correspondence and coherence theories. Following the fashion of their period, they adapted to the new non-analogical or anti-analogical perspectivist theories associated with Nietzsche (Young 1992; Tanner 2000) or disclosure theories associated with Heidegger (Young 2001; Inwood 2000). White was a creature of his period. To understand his texts in their context, it is necessary to understand this transition from correspondence–coherence theories to perspectivist–disclosure theories.

As a romantic, White de-trancendentalized religion by critiquing classical aesthetics and aristocratic–bourgeois norms, by replacing rational theological doctrine with feeling and metaphor, and by locating the divine within nature and the soul (Ferber 2010). As a modernist, he was an innovator who deviated from 19th century realism and naturalism, with their stable intellectual frameworks narrated by "authoritative" reporters (Butler 2010) such as George Eliot and Thomas Hardy. As a postmodernist, he maintained an interrogatory, sceptical attitude towards the metanarratives of historical progress and human emancipation contained in or implied by in the philosophies of Kant, Hegel, and Marx (Butler 2002).[3]

We know he was hostile towards realism and naturalism (White 1989, 13–17 and 19–23). We also know many influential 20th century critics regarded romanticism as a turning point or definitive break with the past (Auerbach 1953; Abrams 1953; Berlin 1999) which would evolve into modernism and postmodernism. Such critics presumably took this view because they regarded classicism—in its neoclassical form—as closer to the Enlightenment and its obsession with reason. This (neo)classicism represented the past being broken from, as romanticism had claimed the future on behalf of feeling rather than reason. Theoretically, there could be no going back.

There are problems with this break-from-the-past logic, however, as classicism and romanticism are siblings. They are obverse sides of the same metaphysical coin. They are interdependent aspects of a single dialectic. They are inseparable siblings, like the Dashwood sisters in *Sense and Sensibility* (1811) and Brown brothers in *The Solid Mandala* (1966). Although the line between classicism and romanticism "has been constantly drawn and redrawn", it represents binary thinking that has "hovered for two centuries over discussions of the cultural history of Europe and North America". While these two modes are cultural "imaginaries", many believe that, because there is "so much smoke" surrounding them, "there must have been a real fire somewhere: a real difference between two cultural styles" (Ferber 2010, 14).

So, if romanticism, modernism, and postmodernism critique classical metaphysics, the critique was simply a variation on an ancient theme. Also, paradoxically, the logic of the reaction against classicism depended upon the continuation of classicism (Honour 1968, Honour 1979). When situating White within this 19th and 20th century milieu, as a variation on an ancient theme, it is useful to notice how his fiction operates across two interdependent spheres.

The first sphere revolves around a hypothetical tension within the pagan imagination of ancient Greece, between its philosophy and its

---

[3] This book accepts the axiom that "one person's postmodernism is another person's modernism" and vice versa.

poetry–drama–rhetoric, which presents itself in a variety of archetypal or dialectical ways. The second sphere revolves around a hypothetical tension between the mind of ancient Greece (Athens) and the mind of ancient Israel (Jerusalem). During White's "religious" phase he moved between both spheres simultaneously. Like most westerners, he treated them as interchangeable, which they are not.

Throughout the 19th and 20th centuries, the tension between reason and feeling (within the Greek mind) was often confused with the tension between reason and revelation (between the Greek and Jewish minds). After Kant, there was a tendency to consign revealed religion to the realm of feeling and alienate it from the realm of reason. This tendency is no longer fashionable, as recent developments in classical studies, talmudic studies, diaspora studies, and church history are challenging many of our inherited assumptions about the role of reason in ancient Greece, ancient Israel, and early Christianity.

In *Process and Reality* (1929), A.N. Whitehead suggests the European philosophical tradition is a series of footnotes to Plato. This also applies to the west's literary tradition. The model of mind underpinning White's vision, and the vision of every novelist mentioned in this book, is part of the west's inheritance from ancient Greece. In Book IV of *The Republic* (c.380 BC), Plato tells us the mind has a tripartite structure (rational, spirited, and appetitive), analogous with different parts of the body (head, heart, and lower abdomen), analogous with different classes of society (guardians, auxiliaries, and producers). The difference between these parts becomes obvious as he describes what his ideal society looks like while referring to the "old quarrel" between philosophy and poetry. As the quarrel was already old, when Plato refers to it, it must have existed in some form within Presocratic philosophy, Sophist rhetoric, or their equivalent in ancient Greek poetry and drama.

Plato believed philosophy has the highest truth-claims, because it comes from the rational mind (analogous with the head). He believed poetry has lesser truth-claims, because it comes from the spirited mind (analogous with the heart) and therefore poetry can easily be corrupted by the appetitive mind (analogous with the lower abdomen).[4] He banned the poets from his ideal republic because their poetry comes from the mind's spirited part, not its rational part, and therefore it does not represent the highest form of truth. As he applied the same logic to rhetoricians, whether he would ban the authors mentioned in this book depends on

---

[4] Polynesians believe "the abdomen is the realm of thought as well as of emotion" (Brown 1924, 131). This is more optimistic than Plato's view of the mind–body dualism.

whether he agreed or disagreed with the form and content of their stories, as rhetoric and as poetry.

Plato's student Aristotle moved from Platonic rationalism towards his own form of empiricism. The resulting dialectic of rationalism and empiricism profoundly influenced the trajectory of Jewish and Christian theology, and formed the basis of what, until relatively recently, was regarded as science (McCrone 1993). For a Renaissance example, consider Raphael's famous fresco *The School of Athens* (1509–1511) in the Vatican's papal apartments. In the fresco, Plato points to the heavens, to his realm of Forms and Ideas, while Aristotle extends his hand horizontally, suggesting that while the knowledge of philosophy and science is the knowledge of universal essences (rationalism) we should look towards the earth (empiricism).

While understanding the rationalism–empiricism dialectic is essential to understanding White's contribution to the western literary tradition, it is also essential to notice how the debate changed after the Renaissance, particularly after the Enlightenment. Humanists of the Renaissance and the Enlightenment both looked back to ancient Greece, but they did so in different ways and for different reasons. The debate White participated in was a deviation from the one on the walls of the papal apartments. Particularly on the Continent, the debate gradually evolved, away from a dialectic of Plato and Aristotle, towards a wide-ranging "immanent" or "emancipatory" critique of classical philosophy and aesthetics,[5] and a nostalgia for their supposedly "holistic" Presocratic forebears. Also, White was not an expert on the past. Like his contemporaries, and like us, he absorbed the critique of classical philosophy and aesthetics secondhand. Occasionally that may make him an unreliable witness.

Romantic Performances

Winckelmann's *History of Ancient Art* (1764) was the beginning of an influential period of looking back at ancient Greece and seeing parallels with modern Europe which were regarded as theoretically true, or psychologically true, when not historically true (Butler 1935; Williamson 2004). In *Flaws in the Glass* (1981) White admitted to being influenced by the assumptions behind Germany's romantic reconstruction of the past (39). Within this context, Nietzsche announced God's death, which Heidegger saw as the end of metaphysics, in its classical form. and the

---

[5] The terms immanent or emancipatory critique are associated with the Frankfurt School. They are always rooted in, and always convey, Hegelianism or Marxism.

beginning of post-Kantian alternatives—existential, phenomenological, hermeneutical—all focused on the idea of "being".

White's fiction is a consistent and persistent commentary on God's death; however, to appreciate the complexity of his commentary, it is necessary to distinguish the postmetaphysical from the anti-metaphysical, and to understand existentialism, phenomenology and hermeneutics as different ways of "doing" metaphysics. White was part of a tradition that critiqued the purpose of things (teleology) while championing the nature of being (ontology). As an extension of the rationalism–empiricism debate within philosophy and aesthetics, there was also a shift from the idea of transcendence to the idea of immanence. As a result, questions about God's existence, and his relationship with creation, became philosophically complex and politically contentious.

White knew the announcement of God's death did not prove atheism with language. Rather than "killing" God, the announcement was about replacing classical assumptions about God with a range of assumptions that all involved impasses and aporias beyond language. The announcement therefore presented him with the impossible task of reimagining the God who "died"—through language—using language as his only means of communication.

Each critic approaches the announcement of God's death with their own assumptions about what it meant to him, what it means to them, and how they see it performed in his novels. The announcement has been interpreted in antithetical ways: as atheistic or theistic, as secular or religious, as humanistic or fatalistic, or as different combinations of these. After Nietzsche the nostalgia became—and in many quarters still is—a desire to replace the Torah and the Christ with some reification or embodiment of dionysian man.

White issues difficult challenges. He forces us into uncomfortable territory. Like Nietzsche and Heidegger, he has always been and continues to be a screen on which strong, ambivalent thoughts and emotions are projected. Occasionally he has been used as a kind of scapegoat. His novels and short stories still fascinate me, as I struggle to interpret them, yet they remain just beyond my reach. Is this the function of great art?

As Marr 1991 points out:

> Had White been able to act, he might not have written a word. He still dreamed of *his* Lear, *his* Hedda and the vaudeville routines he would perform—if he had the knack. His imagination was essentially theatrical, and the best of White's characters are not only astonishing inventions but great performances. At his desk he acted all the roles. When he spoke of the creative process he used the language of the theatre. Characters wandered across the stage of his imagination for years—the spinster, the

artist, the dame, the boy, the laundress—but not until a couple of them came face to face and began to speak did a novel begin. They put on costume; the air smelt of hot lights and greasepaint. "There are moments when you have *no* control over it. One's characters are part of one's consciousness but they do take control and you haven't much say in the matter." His writing life was dotted with complaints of his characters keeping him awake at night. When he could not stop their dialogues, it was time to put them down on paper. The performance continued until the last words were written, with White as cast, director and audience in the theatre of his mind (495).

Interconnected Relationships

White said many things about the religious nature of his novels. About being a novelist who "lifted bits and pieces from various religions in trying to come to a better understanding". About using religious themes and symbols to lead his readers towards religion "a different way" (White 1989, 19–23). About conveying "a religious faith through symbols and situations which can be accepted by people today" (Marr 1991, 284). Through Alex Gray, the protagonist of *Memoirs of Many in One* (1986), he confessed the religious aspects of these performances "won't be known until after I'm dead" (157).

Readers who approach White as a religious author, or those who want to advance convincing secular arguments, may find it useful to associate him with several interwoven relationships that, individually and collectively, tell us something significant, and occasionally contradictory, about his agon. If he is a creature of his period, we are obliged to understand that agon as best we can.

Logos and Mythos

While the logos–mythos dialectic has existed as an influential "imaginary", throughout the history of western philosophy and aesthetics, a powerful view emerged—after the proto-romantic Sturm und Drang movement—which revolved around the notion that at some point "mythos was replaced by logos, the desouled Word" (Waterfield 2000, xi). The desoulment was thought to have occurred during the classical Greek Enlightenment of the 4th and 5th century BC. Romanticism's goal was finding a way of reclaiming the hypothetical *Weltanschauung* of the Presocratic philosophers, Sophist rhetoricians, and pre-classical poets–playwrights. If that reclamation was not possible, the options were to continue lamenting the desoulment or continue theorizing it in a range of postromantic ways which all involve the Frankfurt School somewhere.

The desoulment idea was slippery in practice. Logos and mythos continued to be constructed or deconstructed by different individuals, in different ways, for different purposes, across the humanities and the social sciences. Whatever form this took, in whatever discipline it occurred, the unifying idea was a perceived shift in Greek intellectual history with Socrates, Plato and Aristotle. As most of what is known about Socrates is refracted though Plato—and as Aristotle was Plato's student—this is what Whitehead means by "footnotes to Plato". In the neoclassical period, the authoritative "footnotes" promoted the self-evident truth of logos. In the romantic period, which overlaps the neoclassical period, the footnotes began to question Plato's logos and ask whether other forms of logos, or some forms of mythos, might be better means to arrive at knowledge and truth. In this way, the footnotes reimagined ancient territory as part of an ongoing agon within the western mind.[6]

What is logos? The Presocratic philosopher Heraclitus believed it was the "systematic structure that underlies every aspect of our experience" through which we can understand "the true significance of the world" (Osborne 2004, 91–95). As this definition is broad, narrower ones have been offered. Logos can mean language, theory, reason, ratio, proportion, and definition; from logos "we derive our word logic, and the endings of science and knowledge words such as biology, geology, theology, and anthropology" (92); also, there is the ultimate Logos of John 1:1 (92). Logos can also mean word, speech, argument, formula, principle, reason as rationality, or as explanation, and an account as story or value–amount (Waterfield 2000). Its full range of meanings are rarely considered because logos is usually associated, in unfortunately narrow terms, with Nietzschean assumptions about Socrates disunifying philosophy and Euripides disunifying tragedy.

What is mythos? The glib answer is everything one happens to believe post-Presocratic logos has desouled, which is what makes the task of resouling the desouled world, or word, such a difficult thankless task. Among White's influences, mythos has been described as the world from which the gods have departed or God has died (Nietzsche) or from which God has chosen to conceal himself (Heidegger). Since the Sturm und Drang period, logos and mythos are thought to be dialogical when not anithetical; however, this view is too simplistic, because there are many different myths, and many different cultures in which they function, and

---

[6] So the story goes, the older footnotes embody ideological, hegemonic, logocentric, and patriarchal–phallocentric biases which the newer footnotes are struggling to revise.

because God is also logos. We have been conditioned to see science as logos but science is as much mythos as any other mythos. It has not banished the old gods, or God, it has merely created new scientific gods. One person's mythos is another person's logos. In *Gorgias* 523a, Plato has Socrates saying exactly that: "I want to tell you a story. You may think it's a mythos but to me it's a logos" (Waterfield 2000).

In his immensely useful study *The Longing for Myth in Germany* (2004), Williamson notes that:

"Myth" was originally a Greek word (μύθος). While scholars dispute its exact meaning for Homer and Hesiod, by the fourth century BC it had come to signify a kind of authoritative speech that philosophers like Plato criticize as immoral and at the same time exploit for their own purposes. "Mythology", as a coherent system or narratives that legitimate the religious and political traditions of the polis, was a retrospective invention, born of an era in which pious and impious skepticism had already begun to undermine belief in the old tribal stories. The Greek origins of "myth" are crucial to its career in Germany, because it is largely through the study of Greek literature and philosophy that scholars developed an image of what myth was and how it functioned in ancient societies. Indeed the rise of a discourse on myth coincided more or less directly with the establishment of the institutions of neohumanist *Bildung* in the second half the eighteenth century. For intellectuals like Goethe, Schiller, and Wilhelm von Humboldt, Greek art represented an absolute standard of beauty, as well as the foundation of individual self-cultivation. In subsequent years, these neohumanist ideals of beauty as well as *Bildung* would be preserved through the institutions of the gymnasium and the philological seminar, which encouraged a regimen of study and scholarship that Suzanne Marchand has aptly characterized as "aesthetic asceticism" (7).

In ancient Greece, logos and mythos were thought to be different; however, in spite of much romantic and post-romantic theorizing, we still do not know how, precisely, or in what way. In *The Republic* Plato distinguishes between philosophy, rhetoric, and poetry. He seems to treat philosophy as logos and poetry–rhetoric as mythos but we can only guess what these terms meant to him. More important, in spite of much desoulment theory, we can only guess what philosophy and poetry–rhetoric meant in the centuries preceding Plato. The methodological problem here is how 19th and 20th theories about the logos–mythos dialectic are used, as they relate to the Presocratics, and whether those theories are still worth taking seriously in the 21st century. Irrespective of whether we take a hegemonic or counter-hegemonic view of the logos–mythos dialectic, each side is methodologically constrained.

As far as the Sophists are concerned, contemporary scholars of rhetoric such as Jarratt (1991) use feminist theory to challenge traditional views of logos and mythos, particularly the orality–literacy thesis popularised Dodds (1951), Havelock (1963), and Ong (1982). However, Jarratt faces the same or similar methodological constraints as the Presocratic scholars. As long as these methodological constraints exist, theories about the Sophists are guesswork.

A lot depends on what the original sources allow us to conclude. There are complete texts to provide an evidence base for interpreting Socrates, Plato, and Aristotle. For the Presocratics there are only fragments of original papyri and a range of second-hand testimonia from later centuries, much of which is hostile. In the 21st century, Presocratic scholarship has "expanded out of all recognition". Old paradigms and models "have come under heavy attack". In some cases new material has rendered most previous interpretations obsolete. Sophisticated computer modelling is now being used to test the internal validity of the second-hand testimonia, to see if convergences exist, which might allow an academic consensus to emerge (McKirahan, 2010). In other words, there might not be much of an evidence base to support the influential 19th and 20th century theorizing about the Presocratics that has dominated so much literary-cultural theory.

Science and Religion

Critical attitudes towards neoclassicism as reason–logos and romanticism as feeling–mythos reinforce the assumption that the former is linked with science and the latter is linked with religion. While White agreed with this science–religion binary, it becomes unstable if science is actually a form of mythos and religion is actually a form of logos, since it challenges our arbitrary distinction between rational fact and irrational fiction. More important, Jewish and Christian revelation come from quite different conceptual domains, neither of which can be assigned to one or another half of the logos–mythos or science–religion binary. The acceptance of revelation on the part of the believer—whether on Sinai or in Christ—involves an assent from the rational and spirited minds not one or the other (1 Corinthians 1:22–23). If White understood this in principle, his romanticism and modernism made it difficult for him to accept in practice.

Protestantism and Roman Catholicism

White accepted the Blakean idea of solitary poetic genius and shared Blake's hostility towards institutional–clericalized religion. Directly or indirectly, Blake and White participated in the anti-Catholic Protestant agenda of their period, which had been bearing false witness about Roman Catholicism for centuries (Stark 2016). Blake's ideas and antipathies are paradoxical, however. He clearly identified as a solitary poetic genius—a romantic view of the artist no longer encouraged—and he clearly believed this solitary poetic genius did not require the mediation of any church or synagogue. However, he was inspired by the Old and New Testaments, and he was under the impression that canonical scripture, both Jewish and Christian, was the product of solitary poetic genius.

This is not true. Divine inspiration may have been given, originally, to solitary individuals, some of whom may have been poetic geniuses, but the final canonical result—the Bible as we know it—was the product of centuries of collaborative editorial formation by religious functionaries within similar hierarchies to the ones Blake and White were both hostile towards.[7]

Athens and Jerusalem

As mentioned earlier, White moved between two spheres: the philosophical tension between reason and feeling (in the Greek mind), and the theological tension between reason and revelation (between the Greek and Jewish minds), and the latter tension includes the original Jesus movement. Athens and Jerusalem are cosmologically different. They have different senses of what it means to be a person and different understandings of the relationships between mind–body and matter–spirit. As far as Judaism is concerned, White tended to confuse philosophy and theology. He took the typically romantic and post-romantic view that ancient Greek reason was logos, Jewish revelation was mythos, and therefore Athens and Jerusalem have little or nothing in common.

The way White portrays his Jewish characters reinforces this view. For him, the worst thing a Jew could do was align himself with Athens, as doing so would compromise his covenental relationship with the God of Israel. While this view is understandable—in its historical specificity—it has dated. Also, it is unclear whether White's view of Judaism was part of his critique of the Enlightenment, or whether he was aware of the Jewish Enlightenment, the Haskalah, as a phenomenon in its own right (Feiner 2004; Litvak 2012).

White's characterization of his Jewish characters does not account for

---

[7] There is another paradox here too. Being Anglican is different from being Protestant. While it is no longer fashionable to use the term *via media* to describe Anglicanism's balance between Protestantism and Roman Catholicism, Anglican polity is still different from Protestant polity. And that polity has never been Blakean.

the ways in which the Jewish mind was influenced by the Greek mind during the Hellenistic Period before Christ (Boyarin 2009; Boyarin 2011; Satran 2011). Or the role of logos in Rabbinic Judaism (Boyarin 2003; Boyarin 2011). Or the insights of diaspora studies, which now tell us that in the ancient world there were many more Jews outside Israel, throughout the Graeco-Roman world, than there were within it, and each diaspora community inculturated itself differently (Barclay 1996; Williams 1998; Collins 2000; Barclay 2004; Goodman 2007). Judaism, including the Jesus movement, has never been a fossil in amber. From the beginning, it has remained a living faith engaging with the different cultures in which it exists.

Judaism and Christianity

If Nietzsche's passionate aphorisms have been influential—in philosophy and aesthetics—they are not a sound basis for understanding Judaism and Christianity. He believed the west could not achieve its full potential until it was freed from the bondage of revealed religion. According to him, biblical values had universalized a negative "slave morality" that opposed the positive "master morality" of Graeco-Roman civilization (Nietzsche 1887). He also believed that, in its classical form, Christianity had become an oppressive "Platonism for the people" (Nietzsche 1886). If White did not agree with Nietzsche's negative view of Judaism, Nietzsche's negative view of Christianity must have resonated with him as part of the influential anti-Platonic spirit of his milieu. Once White finally withdrew from the Church, during his middle age, it would have been impossible for him to write about Christianity without a Nietzschean as well as a Blakean underpinning.

White's critics do not need to be Jewish or Christian to understand how he portrays Judaism and Christianity in his novels; however, in addition to being honest about their secular biases, they should place Nietzsche's influence on White in a broader context. If we want to approach White as a religious author, and consider whether his religious critique is accurate, in its historical specificity, or inaccurate given what we currently know, we must consider academic developments that neither Nietzsche nor White knew about. This includes a general understanding of the Jesus movement as one of the many varieties of Judaism in the Late Second Temple Period (Saldarini 1988; Neusner and Chiltern 2007; Schwartz 2011; Levenson 2011; Vermes 2011), of Jesus as a rabbi or pharisee who understood and used midrashic techniques (Levine 2006; Levine 2014), of Paul's rabbinic or pharisaic role in the politics of religious identity (Davies 1948; Boyarin 1994; Sanders 2015), of the New Testament as Jewish literature (Brettler 2011; Stern 2011, Boyarin 2012), and of the complex processes through which mainstream Judaism and Christianity evolved, gradually and in parallel, after the destruction of the Temple in 70 AD (Galambush 2005).

Patristics and Rabbinics

Before 70 AD, when the Jesus movement was still wholly within the fluid structure of First Century Judaism, intra-faith conflict could be understood as a halachic debate among Jews, not as a debate between two faiths whose future identities had yet to be formed. After the destruction of the temple in 70 AD, Christianity and Judaism grew in parallel, over several centuries, each defining the other as different as a way of defining itself as unique. Both religions adapted or developed different forms of logic, rhetoric, and hermeneutics which have remained powerful throughout western history. Christianity became more Aristotelian. Judaism became more Rabbinic.

The degree to which these differences existed before 70 AD is not known, precisely, although some varieties of First Century Judaism would have been more Hellenized than others, and some Jewish academics are now even arguing that Christianity retained theological and liturgical aspects of First Century Judaism which later Rabbis chose to discard (Boyarin 2004; Schäfer 2012). While this is a hot topic within the current generation of Jewish and Christian academics—with strong levels of agreement and disagreement—there is an increasing awareness that many of the differences between the two faiths, as they evolved after 70 AD, cannot be projected anachronistically onto the Jesus movement without distorting its relationship within the rest of First Century Judaism. The point being made here is that, like most Christians, White's understanding of Christianity was historicized and often anachronistic.

How far can the paradigmatic differences between Patristics and Rabbinics, or Athens and Jerusalem more generally, be attributed to linguistic differences between the ancient Greek and ancient Hebrew languages? In *The Slayers of Moses* (1982), Handelman provides insights into how contemporary schools of literary theory, particularly the psychoanalytical and deconstructionist schools, are influenced by Rabbinic interpretation: its patterns of organising reality; its structures of language. By contrast, in *Ruin the Sacred Truths* (1987), Bloom argues that most attempts to contrast Greek and Hebrew thought, on the supposed differences of Greek and Hebrew as languages, are illusory; however, he believes the intellectual and spiritual conflict between Greek and Jew is definitely real: "Western conceptualization is Greek; and yet Western religion, however conceptualized, is not" (147).

Wholeness and Salvation

The Christian definition of wholeness comes from the noun σωτηια (soteria) in common or κοινη (koine) Greek, the lingua franca of the Mediterranean world, including ancient Israel and early Christianity, during the Hellenistic and Roman periods. As Nobbs 1986 points out:

> The spread of Christianity in the Roman Empire during the first four centuries AD was a gradual process, one of "assimilation, adaptation and improvisation". This process of adaptation extended to the realm of religious terminology where, too, we find Christianity borrowing and appropriating. As we would expect, Christianity used ideas and concepts which were already familiar, and it was only gradually that these ideas came to be found more and more within a Christian framework.
>
> One such example is the Greek word σωτηια which referred originally to wholeness, then to health and preservation from disease. In Christian usage σωτηια (or σωτηιον) means the salvation offered in Christ. The Old Testament background to the Christian usage represents a movement from the more physical aspects of salvation (for instance, deliverance from enemies), towards moral and spiritual deliverance. The Greek σωτηια, with its basic sense of wholeness, viewed salvation from a different perspective from the Hebrew, where the basic sense was breadth or enlargement (59).

The Christian understanding of salvation comes from soteria and the theological study of salvation is called soteriology. As with logos, we need a basic understanding of how ancient Greece and ancient Israel understood soteria, in the full range of its rational and empirical senses, and worldly and other-worldly senses, in addition to the sense conferred by God in Christ (John 20:25–28). Soteria has always been contentious within philosophy and aesthetics. Is soteria a chameleon, a lizard which changes its colour to fit in with its surroundings, rather than something inalterable like the laws of the Medes and Persians? (O'Sullivan 1986, 43) What does soteria look like within rationalism and empiricism? Can it be a physical reality as well as metaphysical idea? Can it occur in the "now" as well as the "not yet"? Can it only be expressed through philosophy or can it also be expressed through aesthetics. In other words, can we be "saved" through art: including the art of literary fiction?

The latter question is central to the relationship between literature and life; hence to the relevance of writing, reading, and studying literature. The question must be asked by anyone who believes in the transformative power of the word, the human logos, or the Word, the divine Logos. Words are important, even to those who contest their truth-claims. It is easy to dismiss the truth-claims of John 1:1–4, and the theology flowing from it, but when we become seriously ill, it is difficult to dismiss the truth-claims of a physician's prescription for the treatment that will "save" us. Prescriptions are words. Words are logos.

Structuralism and Poststructuralism

In the early 19th century, Wilhelm von Humboldt suggested that different languages, as rule-governed systems, determined the worldviews of each language. Nietzsche continued this line of thinking by proposing that all ideations take place from particular perspectives, and suggesting there are many perspectives from which judgments of knowledge and truth can take place. Freud and Jung advanced Nietzsche's thinking by systematizing the unconscious, in ways that led "the French Feud", Lacan, to declare "the unconscious is structured like a language" (Johnston 2014). Gadamer continued to develop this view in *Truth and Method* (1960) by proposing that we are defined by the prejudices we inherit from our historically and culturally conditioned language. In *La Symbolique du Mal* (1960) Ricoeur takes this proposal further by proposing an archaeology of the west's symbolic language, grounded in the west's creation myths as the origin of its metaphysical metaphors. Derrida 1982 develops Ricoeur's thinking but cautions us against over-determining the meanings we attach to this symbolic language—whether as a culture or as individuals—because no meaning is absolute and all meaning is indeterminate.

Secularism and Modernity

In *The Theological Origins of Modernity* (2008), Gillespie reminds us of the two images that have shaped our understanding of our times: the fall of the Berlin wall, as a totalitarian symbol, and the collapse of the Twin Towers, as a globalization symbol conceived as the spead of western values to the rest of the world. "As a result, we ceased to look forward to a new golden age and glanced instead over our shoulders and sideways into the out-of-the-way places we imagined to be filled with dark figures waiting to attack us" (ix). The attack on the World Trade Center has called the whole Enlightenment project into question in a new and unsettling way.

We still live with a widespread but simplistic narrative: that modernity is synonymous with the Enlightenment, both of which are, or were, about overcoming superstition and asserting the claims of a secularism that takes the "truth" of reason for granted. Against this simplistic narrative, Gillespie reminds us that: "The concept of the 'modern' arose in context of the twelfth century reform in the Church, although it had a different signification than it has today" (3). While we take modernity for granted, and think we know what it is, we still do not know what it means to be modern. The underlying assumption of modernity is that God does not exist and religion is a human construction:

> The idea that modernization produces secularization rests on the notion that modernization produces enlightenment, that enlightenment reveals the truth, and that the truth is that there is no God (or at least there is no God that matters for the conduct of human life). A philosophically astute believer might see the process in a radically different way. Heidegger, for example, argued in opposition to this point of view that what appears to be a process of secularization that ends in the death of God is in fact only God's withdrawal and concealment. Christians of various persuasions have developed similar explanations to account for this phenomenon. It is clear that there is no possible way of deciding which of these explanations is correct. The secularization thesis depends on the belief that God is a human construct, the notion of God's withdrawal on the view that the world and everything in it are divine creations. Whether one or the other is correct cannot be empirically determined and thus rests on the faith that God does or does not exist (272).

What actually occurs in the course of modernity is not simply the erasure or disappearance of God but the transference of his attributes, essential powers, and capacities to other entities or realms of being:

> While on the surface the Enlightenment in general is positively hostile to religion, this hostility did not prevent (and in many instances facilitated) this transference. Indeed, Enlightenment thinkers repeatedly "discovered" powers and capacities in man and nature that had previously been ascribed to God (274).

As far as White is concerned, this exaltation of man as God, of man "getting out of hand" like Frankenstein's monster (White 1989, 19), led to the kind of hubris that flows naturally and inevitably from modernity's blessings and curses.

Iconography and Iconoclasm

To White, symbolism was a necessary part of his reaction against realism and naturalism:

> Characters, images situations and themes are repeated so insistently that

they must surely be constant and unchanging components of White's temperament and world-view. He seems, in fact, to invite the reader to regard the various works as different manifestations of the same continuous vision by the way he links them together into an unbroken chain. Each novel contains a seed that unfolds in time to become the dominant preoccupation of the next. Holstius, the "tree walking" of *The Aunt's Story*, grows into The Tree of Man. Stan Parker's lonely vigils in stony places are transformed into Voss's obsession with the desert. The Comet that appears at the end of *Voss* emerges as the Chariot in the next novel, and its fourfold conjunction of the Riders surrounded by the Whirlwind is, in turn, metamorphosed into the key symbol of *The Solid Mandala*. Arthur Brown's passing reference in this novel to "the Viviseckshunist" swells into Hurtle Duffield's Vivisector, while the "Mad Eye" that Hurtle paints as a boy becomes the growing point of *The Eye of the Storm*. As well as these overt signs of continuity we find explicit thematic utterances in the early novels illuminating obscure corners of the later ones, while symbols and concepts that have risen to consciousness in the later works organize and elucidate in retrospect much that was only latent in the earlier years. In spite of the manifold forms into which Patrick White has incarnated his vision, there has been no basic change of direction (Beatson 1976, 4).

This description, published before *The Twyborn Affair*, also applies to that novel, but not all critics will agree, especially those who are suspicious of the meanings White was pointing to—or looking beyond—and those who see his last novel as a radical departure from his earlier work. His career paralleled a range of structuralist and/or poststructuralist theories about language: its operations, its significance, its boundaries, its limitations. If it seems somewhat counterintuitive to be iconographic and iconoclastic at the same time, the simultaneous creation and destruction of meaning is an essential aspect of what he tried to achieve.

Sceptics of White's performances are suspicious of his tendency to look beyond words for meaning. Kramer 1973 complains about his pointing to "a wordless revelation at the heart of which meaning might be found" (9). In the same vein, Mitchell 1978 complains about White's habit, when alluding to mystical experience, of forcing his readers to "play a game of linguistic and narrative detection" hoping they will find meaning in "the crevices and arcs between the words" or "perhaps behind them". Asking a reader to do that, he says, "is to ask quite a lot; more, perhaps, than a novelist ought to ask" (12).

Ultimately, to believe that all mystical experience can be expressed in words is to be the kind of rationalist that ignores or misunderstands the post-Enlightenment critique of logos. Are Kramer and Mitchell suggesting that, if White's religious performances are to be meaningful, he must communicate their absolute meaning in words, since it is unconvincing or unacceptable to point beyond words? The question is important because the limitation of language was his chief frustration. With White everything returns sooner or later to what language can and cannot do. This major source of his insecurity was the gift that made his work complex.

Bulman-May begins *Patrick White and Alchemy* (2001)—surely the best study on White and Jung to date—with a description of this complexity:

> The pleasure in reading Patrick White derives not only from the high degree of stylistic perfection which characterizes his oeuvre, but to a great extent from the author's mythological and literary erudition. The multi-dimensional logic of White's myths forms a textual body of concerted symbolism, a hieroglyphic landscape inviting exploration. In White's texts universal mythical entities and archetypes from classical and modern literature appear and fade in kaleidoscopic fields of signification. The continual metamorphosis engendered in the promiscuous networks of White's myths qualify the author as a challenging modernist interlocutor whose technique, often referred to as eclecticism, forms the basis of a complex personal mythology (1).

While the mythology is complex, and may be personal, it is also religious. White wanted to communicate it, as a religious mythology, which means it must also be universal in some way. He once admitted that Manoly seemed secure inside the structure of Eastern Orthodoxy but he could not share that security as a lapsed Anglican searching for soteria outside the church (White 1981, 146). This is why it is important to consider the different relationships he and Manoly had with Christianity as adults.

Because the Orthodox churches never experienced an equivalent of the Enlightenment, or the post-Enlightenment critique of logos, they maintain a positive, Patristic, Trinitarian understanding of logos. But the Anglican Church did experience the Enlightenment, and post-Enlightenment critique of logos, which provided it with a range of opportunities and threats, which only a strong faith or a blind faith could negotiate. This was White's problem, as a religious author, but it was not of his making. It was a problem he inherited and responded to. It was the problem of the Reformation gone astray (Gregory 2012). It was the problem of the Enlightenment misconceived or unfinished (Horkheimer and Adorno 2002). In the west, these problems are still with us, yet to be resolved.

Who is God? Where is God? White cared about these questions. By the end of this book the reader will hopefully link them with the ten relationships described above, as each relationship tells us something important about White's agon, and about our different critical responses to his fiction.

CHAPTER ONE

SHADOW

Rationalism and Empiricism

White's contribution to the west's literary tradition is a unity of aesthetics (form) and rhetoric (content), both of which are integral to his work's meaning.[1] He participated in a wide-ranging romantic and post-romantic critique of neoclassicism and its Enlightenment (Ferber 2010; Butler 2002; Butler 2010). This involved adapting a Continental tradition into an Australian milieu—of his period and his class—influenced more by an Anglophone or Analytical tradition. Kant is said to be the final great figure common to both traditions (Critchley 2001; Scrunton 2001).

Although there was a parting of the ways after Kant (Marckie 2015), both traditions continued the debate between rationalism and empiricism:

> Rationalists claim that there are significant ways in which our concepts and knowledge are gained independently of sense experience. Empiricists claim that sense experience is the ultimate source of all our concepts and knowledge (Critchley 2001).

Like his contemporaries in the visual and performing arts, White translated this debate into fiction, while pointing to what lay beyond it. As words are the only medium available to an author, this was a constant struggle for him, hence his frustration with the "rocks and sticks" of words, and his desire to use words in the same way a painter uses paint and a musician uses sound (White 1989, 16).

In *Patrick White, Painter Manqué* (2002), Hewitt describes the role of painters in his reaction against literary realism and naturalism. "White read the modernist writers" but "it was modernist painters whom he observed and lived with" and "discussed modern art" (13). This is evident in his attempt to translate the images from a wide range of painters into words: Roy de Maistre in *Happy Valley* (1939); Walter Sickert et al. in

---

[1] "The relationship between form and content is paradoxical. Form is made possible by content, just as content takes shape through form" (Randisi 1991, 18).

The Living and the Dead (1941); Klee et al. in *The Aunt's Story* (1948); Van Gogh et al. in *The Tree of Man* (1955); Blake, Delacroix, and Nolan in *Voss* (1957); Redon in *Riders in the Chariot* (1961); Daws et al. in *The Solid Mandala* (1966); Bacon et al. in *The Vivisector* (1970).

In *The Articles and the Novelist* (1983), Heltay provides a linguistic parallel to Hewitt by describing what White does with words and can make words do. Heltay sees him as a non-conformist, a system-opponent, whose passion for painting provoked a rebellion against language, which drove an alienating wedge between his urge for self-expression and his medium of self-expression. His need to "push against the limitations of language", to "force the barriers of tradition and convention", to "make language do what it has not done before and perhaps does not willingly do", defines what "author" means in the original sense of *augere* (to augment).

Heltay finds White's understanding of authorship close to that of Wilhelm von Humboldt (1767–1835) whose views on the creativity of language posits Aristotle's *energeia* (potency) in relation to *ergon* (act), distinguishes between an inner-form and an outer-form of language, and insists that language is never static but always involved in the process of becoming. To Heltay, White's use of language places him in a Humboldtian context of linguistic worldviews, how they are maintained and transformed, and also in a Saussurean context among a series of semiotic relationships: sign, signifier, signified; *la langue* and *la parole*; synchrony and diachrony; anaphoric and cataphoric reference.[2]

White once admitted something important about his form and content: "Characters interest me more than situations. I don't think any of my books have what you call plots". In the same interview he admitted his fiction was:

> … an attempt to come close to the core of reality, the structure of reality, as opposed to the merely superficial. The realistic novel is remote from art. A novel should heighten life, should give one an illuminating experience; it shouldn't set out what you know already (White 1989, 21).

He wanted to achieve something more complex: to imagine the real (177) and to explore the deep end of the unconscious (White 1981, 104).

These admissions beg questions. Can art represent reality, life, imagination, or the unconscious? Does art tell truths or lies? Does the artist's inspiration come from rationalism or empiricism? Which parts of

---

[2] Hollier follows a similar path in *The Rocks and Sticks of Words* (1992), the abridged version of his doctoral dissertation on *The Solid Mandala*.

the mind or body are involved? Is art's function theoretical or does it advocate a practical program of social–economic and/or ethical–moral change? These open-ended questions are central to western philosophy and aesthetics. They have been debated since Plato and perhaps before Plato.

Our answers to these questions will depend on how we understand romanticism in relation to its older sister, neoclassicism, and also in relation to its descendents modernism and postmodernism. Auerbach 1953 promoted the influential view that romanticism was unique in emancipating literature, once and for all, from a received tradition of classical mimesis, opening the way for the "increasingly rich" forms of modern realism (554–557). Halliwell 2002, relieved to not be competing with Auerbach (vii), points out that Auerbach barely touches on the theory of mimesis, and argues against the simplistic idea of a received tradition of classical mimesis.

Although Austen is often thought a romantic, and in some senses is a romantic (Harris 2007), she was aware of romanticism's dangers. Her relationship with the Enlightenment was more neoclassical (Giffin 2002; Knox-Shaw 2005). Her novels are a good example of what Auerbach means by classical mimesis. Like White, she relied on Plato's tripartite structure of mind, although her form and content are different from White's. While his novels are driven by character, her novels are driven by plot; they have a symmetry that owes much to Aristotle's *Poetics* (335 BC). She is faithful to the classical formula of exposition, rising action, climax, falling action, and resolution. Within this classical structure, each of her published novels provides a sudden reversal of fortune or change in circumstance (peripeteia), a fatal flaw leading to the downfall of the hero (hamartia), the moment the hero makes a critical discovery (anagnorisis), and the purging of strong or repressed emotions (catharis).

While White also relied on Plato's tripartite structure of mind, his character-driven novels are a good example of what Auerbach means by the increasingly rich literature of romantic emancipation, which gave birth to the varieties of modernism and its posts. Deleuze 1997, who seems to agree with Auerbach, sees five inter-related effects within this emancipated modernism: the destruction of the world, the dissolution of the subject, the disintegration of the body, the stuttering of language, and the minorization of politics (xxv–li).[3] While Deleuze's interrelated effects are useful to understanding White—and how he differs from Austen—

---

[3] Apart from the fifth effect—the minorization of politics—*The Aunt's Story* (1948) is a superb example of how White reified or embodied modernism's interrelated effects.

they should be adopted with a proviso. In one sense White was creating something new. In another sense, he was adapting or repackaging something old.

In his autobiography, *Flaws in the Glass* (1981), White sheds light on his formative influences. In Australia, his godmother Gertrude Morrice introduced him to Aldous Huxley and D.H. Lawrence at a young age. The wife of his cousin, Mariamne Wynne, introduced him to an unknown edition of *Myths of Ancient Greece*. Later in England, at boarding school, he developed a passion for Chekov, Ibsen, and Strindberg. Between 1932 and 1935, he studied French and German literature at Cambridge (White 1981). From Marr 1991, we are told he was strongly influenced by Spengler's cyclic model of civilization in *The Decline of the West* (151), which was influenced by Nietzsche, who influenced Heidegger.

During White's Cambridge years, Frazer's *The Golden Bough* (1890), Harrison's *Prolegomena to the Study of Greek Religion* (1903), and Cornford's *From Religion to Philosophy* (1912) were still influential. Also, Leavis was becoming influential at Cambridge. The first issue of his journal *Scrutiny* appeared in 1932 during White's first undergraduate year. Even if he was not directly influenced by Frazer, Harrison, Cornford, or Leavis they were part of his zeitgeist.

From his autobiography we know that during the 1930s White spent most of his holidays on the Continent. Although he loved Germany, and its romantic literature, like many uncommitted Germans he only stopped his "romantic reconstruction of the past" when his nose was rubbed in the reality of what was happening under the Nazis (39). He went to the United States where on 3 September 1939, the day Britain declared war on Germany, he was in a cinema in Maine watching *The Wizard of Oz*, an American myth he found more convincing than a real world he did not want to participate in (74). Perhaps he could have avoided the war, by remaining in the United States.[4] Instead, he chose to return to that real world unfolding in the United Kingdom. No one could explain why. Neither could he (75).

Living in London during the Blitz made White feel nervous and rootless. It forced him to reassess his status as an expatriate and his achievements as the author of two novels, *Happy Valley* (1939) and *The Living and the Dead* (1941); each accomplished in its own way; both different from his postwar work. While the bombs were falling around him, he "reached rather often for the bottle", read Eyre's *Journal*, and

---

[4] While White was in the USA, April to September 1939, he visited Lawrence's Taos for three weeks and felt he could have remained there forever (Marr 1991, 182–193).

thought about the Australian landscape (83). He joined the R.A.F. as an operational intelligence officer and served in North Africa, Palestine, and Greece for five years. While in North Africa he read the Bible from cover to cover, was powerfully influenced by Dostoevsky, and rediscovered Dickens during the siege of Tobruk:

> Detesting, misunderstanding Dickens when I was a boy, I had suddenly cottoned onto him. As blood flowed, and coagulated in suppurating wounds, as aircraft were brought down in flames and corpses tipped into the lime-pits of Europe, I saw Dickens as the pulse, the intact jugular vein of a life which must continue, regardless of the destructive forces Dickens himself recognized (96).

Clearly, his old influences were being challenged. He was exposed to new influences without having the time, space, or motivation to work them through:

> Throughout the war I seemed to exist on several levels: in the higher reaches a swinging trapeze set in motion by Spengler's predictions which I had been faced with in London as an idler of the Nineteen-Thirties, later my discovery of Dostoevsky's *The Possessed* in a transport plane out of Jules Verne above the jungles and deserts of Africa, farther down there were the ironed-out press and radio announcements, while at the lowest level, one clung to Judy Garland's Technicolor rainbow and, as the Stukas flew overhead in the desert, that other voice with the catch in it, assuring us that we'd meet again (74).

White's experience of life between two world wars, and his first-hand experience of World War II, seemed to vindicate Spengler's predictions of western decline. These experiences were central to his literary development.[5]

Austen knew romanticism had done nothing to prevent the French Revolution, the Reign of Terror, or the Napoleonic Wars, and may have even contributed to them. This is an important sub-text in her novels. White and his contemporaries knew modernism had done nothing to prevent World War II and may have even contributed to it (Bauman 1989; Bauman 2004). This is an important sub-text in their novels. Atwood knows there is something wrong with the direction the west is heading in. This is an important sub-text in her novels. If we no longer take the romantic view of the artist, as priest or prophet, we must allow him or her the freedom to encode ethical–moral visions in their commentaries on the

---

[5] If the story of the 1930s idler in "knockabout" London is well-described (Marr 1991; Marr 2015), literary critics have a curious tendency to draw a veil over his war service, as if it does not matter. In fact, his war service was a large part of his literary development.

human condition, even if we do not agree with them.

By the time White was de-mobbed, and began writing *The Ham Funeral* (1947) and *The Aunt's Story* (1948), he was still under the influence of modernism but knew what its limitations were. Pinpointing those limitations is difficult, particularly as one person's modernism can be another person's postmodernism (Butler 2002) and vice versa. In *Waiting for Godot* (1949), first performed in 1953, Beckett created a topos, placed particular tropes within it, and wrote the dialogues those tropes have. For specific reasons, which some would call modernist and others would call postmodernist reasons, he reduced his topos, tropes, and dialogues to their barest minimum.

Vladimir and Estragon are two characters with a discrete relationship. Pozzo and Lucky are two characters with another discrete relationship. Each pair represents a dialectic, which occasionally shares the stage with the other dialectic, along with a messenger boy who may or may not be an angel. These two pairs of four characters are waiting for someone or something called Godot who may or may not be God. If Godot is God, they are left with the dilemma of what kind of God, and this unknown God might never arrive, or perhaps has already arrived but is different from the God they are waiting for (Acts 17:23–25). If Godot is not God—or is the God who has "died"—they are left with the dilemma of there being no God, or a God who has concealed himself in the Heideggerian sense.

It is possible to interpret the topos as modernism–postmodernism itself. Vladimir and Estragon could be a minimalist variation of the neoclassicism–romanticism dialectic. Pozzo and Lucky could be a minimalist variation of the master–slave dialectic. In this interpretation, the philosophical and aesthetic concerns of the postwar period are on view, and we are invited to consider whether the play is metaphysical, post-metaphysical, or anti-metaphysical.

White's play *The Ham Funeral* (1947), revised in the late 1950s and first performed in 1961, is an interesting contrast to *Waiting for Godot*. The play is set in London just after World War I. The story unfolds in a house with two floors, each containing its own dialectic. The first dialectic lives upstairs, which is analogous with the rational mind. A young man and a young girl live in separate rooms with a locked door between them. He is an aspiring poet. She is his anima: his soul, inner self, or conscience. The door represents the divide between them. He lives on the side that represents the conscious. She lives on the side that represents the unconscious. He would like the door to be opened, so he can be united with her, but it is never opened, except at the end of the play, when he breaks it down and finds she has disappeared into thin air. It is important they never meet. If they did meet, they could not fulfil their rhetorical function as tropes for the conscious and the unconscious.

Notice how White mixes metaphysics and metapsychology here; reminding us that metapsychology is an attempt to map the conscious and unconscious in ways that pretend to be new but are actually grounded in Plato's tripartite model of mind. That mapping was a major temptation in the post-romantic period, which seduced Freud, Jung, and many authors. Spark offers a warning to those who theorize or systematize what is behind the locked door:

> I think the best thing is to be conscious of everything that one writes, and let the unconscious take care of itself, if it exists, which we don't know. If we knew it, it wouldn't be the unconscious (Spark 1962, 31).

White is to be commended for realizing—at this early stage of his career—that the door must remain locked. Authors who became overly attached to Freud or Jung found themselves hostage to fortune when these men went out of fashion.

The second dialectic lives in the basement, which is analogous with the spirited and appetitive minds. This is significant in Platonic and Nietzschean terms as well as in Freudian and Jungian terms. There is a landlord and a landlady. They have eponymous names: Will Lusty (will + lusty) and Alma Lusty (alma = nourishing–kind + lusty). If the reader considers the dynamics of their relationship, it looks rather Lawrencian, which makes sense as Lawrence was an early influence on White. As fictional characters, they are as much archetypally masculine and feminine as they are biologically male and female. As such, they should be regarded in a particular 19th and 20th century way, across a spectrum of disciplines, when archetypes were increasingly used to describe human characteristics.

In both plays, each dialectic is different, in itself, and each dialectic relates to the other dialectic differently. In Beckett's play, the two dialectics share the stage now and again but their internal dilemmas, between Vladimir and Estragon, and between Pozzo and Lucky, are only indirectly related to each other and are part of a larger dilemma within the human condition. In White's play, the two dialectics are more directly related as aspects of his "dissociation of sensibility", "loss of wholeness", or "sense of alienation" rhetoric.

The action of *The Ham Funeral* revolves around the young poet's dilemma in relation to his anima (within the first dialectic) and his landlady (within the second dialectic). Just as the feminine Anna wins an archetypal victory over the masculine Will in *The Rainbow* (1915), the feminine Alma wins an archetypal victory over the masculine Will in *The*

Ham Funeral. Lawrence's Anna has many children, which tells us something about her relationship with her weaker husband and his metaphysical aspirations. White's Alma has lost her only child, which tells us something about her relationship with her weaker husband and his physical aspirations. Lawrence's Will is defeated but still lives. White's Will dies. Alma does not die but White leaves a question mark over her life.

This is the difference between Lawrence and White. They have different takes on the "flesh versus spirit" and "nature versus civilization" struggles. In this respect, White seems closer to Hardy than to Lawrence, particularly if *Jude the Obscure* (1895) is used as a comparison. In that novel, the tensions between Jude (an aspiring young man), Arabella (flesh), and Sue (spirit) can be usefully contrasted with the tensions within *The Ham Funeral* between the poet (an aspiring young man), his landlady (flesh), and his anima (spirit).

In *The Ham Funeral*, White's young man is the only character who moves between upstairs and downstairs, agonizing over his role as a poet and the source of his creativity. Whenever he goes downstairs, he witnesses the archetypal clash between Will and Alma but only as an observer. After Will dies, Alma attempts to involve him in her archetypal world, as a replacement for her lost child. There is a struggle. He resists and wrestles free; however, when he returns upstairs, his anima reminds him that his victory is pyrrhic, as his maturity—as a person and as a poet—depends on coming to terms with his landlady's archetypal significance. While the victory is pyrrhic, White presents it as necessary, as Alma would have destroyed the young poet, just as she destroyed her husband, and just as Arabella destroyed Jude.

Of course, Sue Bridehead also destroyed Jude, but that is another story. While Hardy is often thought of as a naturalistic author, and many readers experience *Jude the Obscure* as realistic, there is nothing natural or real about Sue Bridehead. He thinks he is writing a tragedy, but it is really a melodrama, and his moral is something like this: When a "tragic" hero, Jude, consummates his relationship with his anima, Sue, against her inclination and will, things will fall apart, as this is against the natural order, or fate, or the gods. It is always a difficult manoeuvre, portraying a character as a person, when the character represents an aspect of the mind–soul, or is an archetype in the unconscious, or is part of a dialectic, or is a cosmic force.

The rhetoric of *The Rainbow* and *Jude the Obscure*, like so much of the literature of western consciousness, originates in Plato's tripartite structure of mind. Both novels rework the "old quarrel" between philosophy and poetry. White inherited this rhetoric from his influences and the zeitgeist generally. It represents a fundamental dilemma in all his novels. As we can see in *The Ham Funeral*, he clearly understood why the young poet's anima belongs on the other side of the locked door, which divides the conscious and the unconscious minds, and why the door cannot be opened. While he accepted the existence of the unconscious, he knew, like Spark, that all attempts to systematize it are provisional—when not erroneous—as once it is systematized it ceases to be the unconscious. If he accepted aspects of Freud's theories, he thought they were too much about sex (Marr 1991, 151). If he also accepted aspects of Jung's theories, his did not do so systematically (Marr 1991, 451–452). Apart from that, his purposes were different from Jung's (Morley 1972, 9–11).

White's thinking about the unconscious resembles Lawrence's. In two essays, *Psychoanalysis and the Unconscious* (1921) and *Fantasia of the Unconscious* (1922), Lawrence was initially responding to psychoanalytic criticism of *Sons and Lovers* (1913); however, both essays turned out to be counterproposals to psychoanalytical theory itself. If White might not have agreed with everything Lawrence says in these essays, he might have agreed with Lawrence's position on the sundering of science and religion, the attempt to equate religious impulses with sexual desires, and the attempt to pathologize the author's relationship with his mother. As Lawrence was one of White's many influences, and as White may have been familiar with both essays, they are useful to his critics.

Myths and Metaphors

White's frustration with the "rocks and sticks of words", and the limits of linguistic systems, was not unique to him. Within the romantic and post-romantic period, there was an influential hypothesis that logos (defined here as word or reason) had created a civilization that, through its subjugation of mythos, resulted in a dissociation of sensibility, loss of wholeness, or sense of alienation (Steven 1983). If Nietzsche inherited rather than invented this hypothesis, he popularized the idea that Platonic idealism and Socratic reason were to blame. Conversely, the idea that the Presocratics had a more connected, whole, grounded, or unified sense of logos became widespread. There was a symbiosis between author and critic here. Authors encoded this discourse, with varying degrees of agreement or suspicion. Critics decoded it in a similar spirit. Without this symbiosis, the trajectory of 19th and 20th century western literature would have been different.

Within Continental philosophy and aesthetics, the critique of logos and mythos was performed on many levels, from asserting the priority of romantic feeling over classical reason, empiricism over rationalism, and immanence over transcendence. Humboldt believed language constructs worldviews, since language forms thought and knowledge. After Humboldt, Nietzsche developed a non-idealistic or anti-idealistic version of Humbolt's worldviews thesis, perspectivism, the relativistic theory that there are no objective truths in the conscious only subjective views in the unconscious (Southwell 2009, 16–34). After Nietzsche, Heidegger continued to question the subject–object distinction and the epistemology that supported it. Instead of epistemology, he explored the nature of "being", ontology, asking "primordial" questions about "being".

As his career progressed, Heidegger's theories about "primordial" disclosure were increasingly focused on the Presocratics. However, his 1916 habilitation thesis *Duns Scotus's Doctrine of Categories and Meaning* focused on the mediaeval Franciscan theologian John Duns Scotus (Seidel 1964, 18; Tonner 2010, Witham 2008). There is still debate as to whether Scotus, known as the Subtle Doctor, heralded a change in thinking about the nature of "being", which in some quarters has become a debate over the mediaeval origins of modernity, postmodernity, secularism, and the idea of "being" itself. Scotus's "univocity of being"— the idea that words used to describe God mean the same thing when applied to persons or things—has influenced a range of secular philosopher and "radical orthodoxy" theologians (Horan 2014). In this way, the univocal idea that "being in all its senses is affirmed in one voice" continued to be influential after Heidegger.[6]

Humboldt, Nietzsche, Heidegger, Freud and Jung all have something to contribute to how we understand White's frustration with language.[7] Given the way his four "religious" novels operate—in their historical specificity—it is useful to approach them through the lenses of two postwar contemporaries: Hans-Georg Gadamer and Paul Ricoeur (DiCenso 1990). Gadamer (1900–2002) developed a "practical" dialogical approach to hermeneutics grounded in Platonic, Aristotelian, and Heideggerian thought (Malpas 2014). Ricoeur (1913–2005) thought through the relationship between the subjective self and the objective

---

[6] Secular critics often invoke Duns Scotus when defining and defending ontological arguments that are anti-teleological. One even goes so far as to, somewhat weirdly, regard Scotus as a libertarian whose ontology of being "offers resources for the Foucaultian dissatisfied with the limitations of Foucault's anthropology" (Nielsen 2013).

[7] In *The Sovereignty of Good* (1967) Murdoch writes: "most existentialist thinking seems to me either optimistic romancing or something positively Luciferian. (Possibly Heidegger is Lucifer in person.)" (70).

semiotic structures through which we communicate meaning and gain understanding (Zimmermann 2015; Pellauer and Dauenhauer 2016).

In *Truth and Method* (1960), Gadamer proposes that our understanding is historically determined and linguistically conditioned: each individual has a horizon that circumscribes his or her ability to understand self, world, and other. Within this matrix of history and language there is no understanding without prejudice. However, the term prejudice has negative connotations Gadamer wants to overcome. It simply means an individual's horizon is shaped by viewpoints that are neither wholly conscious nor fully chosen. Therefore, he argues: "the prejudices of the individual, far more than his judgments, constitute the historical reality of his being" (289).

Gadamer does not believe prejudice is a bad thing, as some prejudices are true, others are false, and it is the task of reason to distinguish whether a prejudice is legitimate. He questions the Enlightenment's attempt to discredit prejudice, in its desire "to understand tradition correctly", by which it means "rationally and without prejudice" (284). He believes the Enlightenment tried to do this by subjecting western philosophy and aesthetics to the "judgment seat of reason" (285), because it believes there is no authority higher than reason. However, like White, Gadamer believes the western tradition has an authority that cannot be verified by reason alone, and those who share this belief participate in what he calls "romantic hermeneutics". Apart from romanticism, this includes every discipline in which reason plays a role.

Gadamer sees a paradox in romantic hermeneutics. He believes movements that critique the claims of reason paradoxically develop and extend those claims. The paradox emerges with romanticism, which describes the "conquest" of mythos by logos and desires the "restoration" of what logos has suppressed (285). This is Gadamer's comment on the ambiguous Yes–No relationship romanticism has with the Enlightenment, since attempts to reverse neoclassicism perpetuate rather than overcome the abstract contrast between myth and reason. In other words, the prejudice that imagines a pre-classical wholeness, whether prior to the classical Enlightenment in ancient Greece (the supposed *Weltanschauung* of the Presocratics) or prior to the neoclassical Enlightenment in modern Europe (the supposed *Weltanschauung* or Magian worldview of the Middle Ages) is as abstract and dogmatic as the prejudice that imagines reason to be the highest authority.

Romantic hermeneutics illuminates the central frame of White's novels. He gives his protagonists Gadamerian horizons, which is why understanding the historical and linguistic conditioning of those horizons

—their truths and lies; the way they relate or fail to relate to other horizons—is fundamental to understanding how White develops the complex inner lives of his characters. Also, he was not the only literary novelist of the postwar period to do this. Murdoch, Spark, Golding, and Davies did as well. So did many of their contemporaries. Although each of them asks different questions, and answers their questions differently, their tropes for logos and mythos have similar characteristics.

Protagonists identified with logos represent reason, are males associated with the apollonian-cum-socratic, the ego, and the conscious mind, have difficulty relating to the archetypal feminine, and are often but not always celibate or homosexual or both. Protagonists identified with mythos represent feeling, are mostly but not always females associated with the dionysian-cum-chthonic, the id, and the unconscious, have difficulty relating to the archetypal masculine, and usually but not always have red hair. There are far too many of these archetypes or tropes for logos and mythos in the postwar novel to ignore their presence or the consistency with which they are employed.

These horizons can be called Gadamerian, because they complement his hermeneutics in *Truth and Method*. Some critics call them Platonic, because they signify the different parts of Plato's tripartite structure of the mind, or the "old quarrel" between philosophy and poetry. In some novels, male homosexuality is shorthand for Platonism. Other critics call them Nietzschean, Freudian, or Jungian, depending on the particular context in which a postwar novelist uses them. What they are called depends on what each novelist is trying to achieve and how critics choose to interpret them using the range of critical lenses available to them. The critical question is why these horizons should appear so consistently in postwar novels.

In *Mysticism and the Mid-Century Novel* (2012), Clements locates White among his postwar contemporaries Iris Murdoch, William Golding, and Saul Bellow, while excluding other contemporaries such as Muriel Spark and Graham Greene (Robertson Davies never made it onto Clements's radar). His purpose was to explore his chosen authors' understanding of mysticism:

> as a pure phenomenon untouched by dogma—"no (conventional God), no Church"—as well as their attempts to find new symbols and structures to clothe it; Spark and Greene's religious background (both were converted Catholics) was entrenched in an established and complex theology which did not allow them the same freedom. This is not to say that Spark and Greene were unquestioning or conventional in their beliefs, only that their religious background invites particular theological questions that do not

usually resonate with the other writers under consideration (189).[8]

Clements's study reassesses Lodge's "crossroads" theory of the postwar novel "occupying an ambiguous intermediary period, lost somewhere in the no-man's-land between modernism and postmodernism" (22) and Bradbury's "ruins" theory of the postwar novel huddled in the ruins "of a collapsed civilization, awaiting but not contributing to, the establishment of the next":

> They are in the middle, and middleness is middling. The middle, however, is where decisions are pondered, where deliberation is done, before a stance is finally taken. The mid-century novelist can, to some degree, be correctly understood as occupying a period of reflection rather than decision, of humility rather than confidence. The question is whether this should be seen as contributing to their lack of definition, or as a definitive quality in itself (1).

The desire of mid-century novelists is metaphysical:

> they wished to return what they considered to be the increasingly interior novel to the world, but not to a dry world of empirical facts and events; instead, they sought to unveil a world of inherent moral value. This was not a return to nineteenth century realism, but a new form of realism; one that refused to ignore the philosophical ideas that had led to the novel's apparent impoverishment—the opacity of language, and the loss of stable external cources of meaning—and sought new techniques and structures to overcome them (3).

While neither logos nor mythos feature in Clements' study, their existence and relationship with each other—as real imaginaries—is a common currency (or perhaps a battleground) which allowed mid-century authors to explore the metaphysical and metapsychological aspects of our consciousness, individual and collective.

Like Spark, White investigated logos and mythos in all his novels, but not the same way in each novel, which is why the differences between the novels need to be noticed along with the similarities. Also, while his protagonists represent logos or mythos, or a hybrid of the two, there is another phenomenon operating in the background. If there are echoes of this phenomenon in the Standish family in *The Living and the Dead*, it becomes more noticeable in the postwar novels, as archetypal protagonists

---

[8] It is an obvious necessity for Clements to limit his study in this way, by putting Spark and Greene in a too hard basket and then calling the basket religious dogma. The idea that authors outside the Church have more freedom than those within it tends to be invoked as a universal given; although, in Spark's case, it is ludicrous to argue that she was less free than her contemporaries outside the Church.

are increasingly portrayed as products of archetypal marriages, between apollonian–socratic civilization and dionysian–chthonic nature (Paglia 1990). None of White's child protagonists is his contemporary. He was born in 1912. Most of them were born in the last decade of the 19th century, during the fin de siècle period, construed as a period of degeneration but with the possibility of renewal.

In each of these families, White draws our attention to the child protagonist's "natural" ability to "see" and the ways in which this ability has been denatured, distorted, or deformed by their parents' archetypal marriage (Giffin 1989). What White does here is buy into the dissociation of sensibility, loss of wholeness, and sense of alienation rhetoric that was so influential in romantic and post-romantic literature. The rhetoric can be understood in a variety of philosophical and aesthetic ways, each of which is a variation on an influential theme. The tension between logos and mythos is an important clue, as White considers the questions: When was sensibility dissociated or wholeness lost? Can they be found or reassociated? Is a sense of alienation inevitable?

It is necessary to notice the rhetoric White offers, as he considers these questions. It is also necessary to think carefully before buying into its compelling mixture of truths and lies. We have to ask ourselves how or in what way his rhetoric functions as metaphysics, and/or metapsychology, and what our answers tell us about his search for meaning and perhaps our own. This is because humans are neither archetypes nor tropes. Beyond the world of literary fiction, male homosexuals are not logos and red-haired females are not mythos.

The tension between logos and mythos has been expressed in different ways, most of which take us inevitably back to ancient Greece. In *The Greeks and the Irrational* (1951), Dodds is motivated by the question: "Were the Greeks in fact quite so blind to the importance of nonrational factors in man's experience and behaviour as is commonly assumed both by their apologists and by their critics?" (1). His influential study, still in print, provides an overview of how irrationalism was accepted as part of the Presocratics' "inherited conglomerate" before it was subsumed by the rationalism of the Greek Enlightenment. On reading Dodds—whose arguments are variations on a well-recognized and commonly-accepted theme—it is possible to see a parallel between the critique of the Greek Enlightenment and the critique of the European Enlightenment. Both critiques are critiques of reason.

If Gadamer dismantled aspects of the grand tradition of aesthetics, inherited from teleological, or analogical, correspondence and coherence theories, he reconstructed the tradition's central insights to demonstrate their continuing relevance to the west. His focus was the cognitive dimension of aesthetic experience, what art addresses, what art puts at issue, hence what the relevance of our experience of art might be. He believed art is dialogical, conversational, and has the potential to disclose truth. However, any truth disclosed is never analogical, in a teleological way, instead, it is a flickering of revealing and concealing, in an ontological way. It asks rather than answers questions. He was primarily concerned with the place of art in our experience of being in the world, and he attempted to re-acquaint us with traditional or received meanings and preoccupations that underlie our experience of art (Davey 2011, 1–2).

For Gadamer, art has the role of an interlocator that speaks directly and immediately to us (3); although we can be surprised, shocked or dismayed at being forced to reflect on its claims (4). His aesthetics is anti-Kantian. He rejects phenomenalist disinterestedness for the sake of phenomenological involvement (5). He believes the symbols within art can connote explicitly what we recognise implicitly. They can refer to their signs; however, if a sign's conscious intention is to refer to its referent, it is self-cancelling (15).

The symbol does not refer to something outside itself. It presents its own meaning. The symbol is the place where meaning becomes present. It suggests meaning because it is constantly invoking what is not immediately given. This not-given does not exist apart from the given but is within it (16). In this way, Gadamer's account of the symbol establishes art as presentational rather than representational. The representational view relegates art to a secondary status where it brings to mind something other than itself: an original state of affairs, a specific meaning or reality, which includes the yet-to-be. The presentational view sees art as an occasion to experience the meanings it invokes; however, the meanings are not independent of the art itself (18). As far as knowledge and truth are concerned, Gadamer is against teleological correspondence–coherence theories and in favour of ontological perspectivist–disclosure theories.

While the first novel in this book—*Riders in the Chariot*—has a Gadamerian frame, something else is happening in the frame that broadens it considerably. The novel represents a methodological shift for White, from an early phase (*Happy Valley*, *The Living and the Dead*, *The Aunt's Story*, *The Tree of Man*, and *Voss*) to a middle phase (*Riders in the Chariot*, *The Solid Mandala*, *The Vivisector*, and *The Eye of the Storm*), to a late phase (*A Fringe of Leaves*, *The Twyborn Affair*, *Memoirs of Many in One*, *Three Uneasy Pieces*, and the posthumous nachlass *The Hanging Garden*). In the four novels of his middle phase he investigated not just logos and mythos but the broader varieties of western religious experience. This interrogation, remarkably systematic wherever it occurred, was absent from the earlier novels and disappeared from the later novels.

At the same time White was researching *Riders in the Chariot*, Ricoeur was making a similar methodological shift in *La symbolique du mal* (1960), which would later appear in English as *The Symbolism of Evil* (1969). How do we account for this intriguing postwar phenomenon? In Ricoeur's case, the answer has something to do with the ways in which he kept evolving within romantic hermeneutics, as he continued to refine his thinking and process the antimonies he saw in Kant, the impasses he saw in Heidegger, and the aporias he saw in Gadamer (DiCenso 1990, 113–143). For example, Ricoeur believed that Heidegger and Gadamer had "circumvented the necessary explanatory moment demanded by the linguistic structures we inhabit" (Zimmermann 2015). In White's case, his link with Ricoeur may be an example of multiple discovery or simultaneous invention, since Ricoeur was also influenced by Humboldt's theory of linguistic worldviews, which White would have absorbed indirectly.

In the postwar period, different authors and philosophers regarded myth differently.[9] Their pre-war counterparts tended to "de-mythologize" myth in order to arrive at unmediated knowledge and truth, on the assumption that myth was synonymous with superstition and untruth. The ancient Greeks were different in this regard, in ways that are still not fully understood. In *Self-Knowledge in Plato's Phaedrus* (1986), Griswold describes myth in Phaedrus:

> Socrates orients himself from the start toward human experience, refusing to rationalize myths about human beings in terms of subhuman principles

---

[9] For example, Murdoch is not a literary realist, in the sense that realism is opposed to myth, which is why she chooses to work with mythic backgrounds (see Appendix). In explaining her choice, Murdoch makes several points paraphrased here: it is difficult for an author to be existential and work, as Hemingway did, without the background myths provide, and still keep her head; it is hard to hold to a metaphysics or a morality, in literature or in life, without the drama and personalities myths allow; the author cannot just manufacture myths, she needs to remain within a body of "valid" myths; the author needs to be aware of the myths she uses as a "prop", lest they become an obstacle or barrier and "close the mind against the acceptance of fresh truth". The way Murdoch uses myths is to give her protagonists what hermeneuts call horizons, and through her critique of these horizons she exposes what she believes true or false about them (John Wilkins, "Christ and Myth: A Conversation with Iris Murdoch", *Frontier* 8(III), Autumn 1965, 219–221). For Murdoch, myths were necessary to create order out of chaos. In her fiction, they provide explanatory structure or points of reference.

or events (for example, materialistic ones). Our ordinary self-understanding serves as the basis and touchstone of our explanation of experience. An analysis of *what* we are cannot but proceed on the basis of our understanding of *who* we are. A myth, unlike a syllogism, has the capacity to act as a complex mirror in which people can recognize not just who they are but who they might become at their best. Platonic myth is a mirror that cannot only reflect one's hopes but also seek to realize them. While it preserves contact with our ordinary self-understanding, it also deepens it (147).

Williamson's immensely useful study *The Longing for Myth in Germany* (2004) reminds us of the contributions of some of Ricoeur's contemporaries:

> Horkheimer and Adorno's engagement with a version of the "Homer question" is one more indication that the roots of myth discourse lie in the problems and assumptions of eighteenth century neohumanism, The belief that ancient Greece represented a universal norm for European culture and that its art and philosophy were uniquely in touch with the fundamental qualities that defined the "human" was so widely accepted among the intellectual classes in Germany that scholars have only recently begun to treat it as a contingent, historically conditioned phenomenon (294).

In looking beyond ancient Greece, and by including Babylonian and Akkadian myths, Ricoeur's anthropology of myth and metaphor is dedicated to exploring this contingent, historically conditioned phenomenon.

In *The Symbolism of Evil*—the middle stage of a life project of combining phenomenology with hermeneutics—Ricoeur suggests the metaphors that describe classical metaphysical concepts such as defilement, sin, guilt, the "fall", freedom, and constraint, have sub-texts the great creation myths try to express. However, because these myth-laden metaphors convey more than a single meaning—as they mingle within the western imagination—they always need to be re-interpreted. If philosophy and aesthetics are to address the "fullness" of these myths and metaphors—because "the symbol gives rise to thought" (347–357)—he believes they should be deconstructed within phenomenology and hermeneutics, not simply demythologized as a reaction against classical metaphysics. In articulating his anthropology of myths and metaphors, he located them within distinct paradigmatic categories.

First, the myths of chaos and creation describe the birth of the gods who struggle to create order from chaos. In this category, because the origin of order and chaos are coextensive, like the origin of good and evil, the victory of the gods will always be temporary, since chaos and evil are older than the gods. Liberation comes from the cultural re-enactment of the myths; however, any liberation is temporary, because a new act of creation is always followed by a new act of destruction (175–210). The myths of chaos and creation, as they are described by Ricoeur, have affinities with Nietzsche's dionysian, Paglia's chthonic, Freud's id, and Jung's unconscious mind.

Second, the myths of the tragic hero pit humans against wicked gods or blind fate. The tragic hero is guilty, and will always fail, because of his very existence not because he has committed any fault. As gods and men oppose each other, the divinity of the gods cannot be distinguished from the diabolical, and the virtue of men cannot be distinguished from hubris. Within this category of myth, soteria comes vicariously from an experience of terror, which results in a catharsis that provides a compassionate understanding of the human condition (tragic pity). This catharsis will always be temporary, as the myths of the tragic hero are anti-humanistic, since they have no understanding of a freedom apart from fate (211–231). The myths of the tragic hero, as described by Ricoeur, have affinities with Nietzsche's apollonian–socratic, Paglia's civilization, Freud's ego, and Jung's conscious mind.

Third, the myths of the exiled soul divide man into body and soul and focus on the destiny of the soul. This distinct, solitary category of myth has had a considerable role in defining western culture, because it has presided if not over the birth then over the growth of Greek philosophy:

> The Orphics, says Plato, "named" the body; in naming the body, they named the soul. Now the act in which man perceives himself as soul, or, better, makes himself the same as his soul and other than his body—this purifying act *par excellence* is knowledge. In this awareness, in this awakening to itself of the exiled soul, all "philosophy" of the Platonic and Neo-Platonic type is contained. If the body is desire and passion, the soul is the origin and principle of any withdrawal, of any attempt to put a distance between the λογος on the one hand and the body and its πάθος on the other; and all knowledge of anything, every science, whatever its object, is rooted in the knowledge of the body as desire and of oneself as thought in contrast with desire (300–301).

In what looks like a Nietzschean manoeuvre, Ricoeur says the myths of the exiled soul "contaminated" early Christianity, as a variety of First Century Judaism. These myths are therefore responsible for the shift in Christianity towards what Nietzsche calls Platonism for the people; a shift that made Christianity seem like an invention of later history (279–305). Also, the myths of the exiled soul are responsible for an extra-biblical or non-biblical story of the "fall" of a divine soul into an earthly body through which man understands himself as the same as his soul and other than his body (279).[10]

Within this category of myth, and story of the "fall", there is an inner dualism, an alienation of body and soul, where soteria is understood to come at death, when the soul is released from its bodily prison and returns to the divine soul. The myths of the exiled soul, and story of the "fall", as they are described by Ricoeur, have several affinities with Nietzsche's apollonian–socratic, Paglia's civilization, Freud's ego, and Jung's conscious mind. The myths of tragic hero and exiled soul, and the story of a "fall", are important to understanding White critique of logos.

Fourth, the adamic myth is unique in distinguishing the origin of good from the origin of evil and making good prior to evil. "Adam", which means "man", is humanity symbolized. In the biblical account of creation, God is good and humanity is made in God's image. Evil enters the world through humanity, as a historical and existential event which should not be confused with the myths of the tragic hero, the myths of the exiled soul, or the story of a "fall", none of which are biblical, although these myths and stories have become attached to the adamic myth over time (232–278). While the adamic myth, as it is described by Ricoeur, has no parallel in Nietzsche, and one struggles to see it anywhere in Freud, Jung, and Paglia, it does have several affinities with White's sense of the Jewish horizon— in its Ashkenazi or Hasidic form—and his sense of the Christian horizon, the christological nucleus of which belongs to the adamic myth rather than to any other category of myth.

Ricoeur regards the myths of chaos and creation, tragic hero, and exiled soul as "speculative", because they narrate the origin of evil before the history of human agency begins. He regards the adamic myth as "existential", because it narrates the origin of evil within the history of human agency, which means the adamic myth gives humans a greater power to act. Through this anthropology, he distinguishes the fatalistic myths of constraint (chaos and creation, tragic hero, and exiled soul) from the humanistic myth of freedom (adamic). Also, he groups these four categories of myths into three types of metaphor: Theogonic (representing chaos and creation), Hellenic (representing the tragic hero and exiled soul), and Hebraic (representing the adamic myth).

Although he is a Christian, Ricoeur studiously avoids attaching truth-claims to one category of myth over another, when articulating this anthropology, since he believes it is more important to notice their existence and come to terms with them as "imaginaries". As a theoretical

---

[10] It may surprise the reader to hear that the mythological–metaphorical origin of the "fall of humanity" story is not biblical. It originates in Greek rather than Hebrew cosmology.

exercise, he attempted to view all the creation myths in relation to a dominant myth, given the hegemony of Christianity within the western mind, but found the exercise unsatisfactory. "The universe of the myths is a broken universe", he admits, and the inability to unify that universe is simply to acknowledge the dynamism of myths, within themselves, and among their relationships with each other (345).

It is important to acknowledge this admission of Ricoeur's, as White was often criticized for being a failed visionary, in both a philosophical and an aesthetic sense, because he could not describe a vision of life that suited his readers. This kind of criticism is naïve, as it assumes literary visions ought to reflect how we want to see life rather than life as it truly is. Also, it overlooks what White was attempting to accomplish, and actually did accomplish, as an Australian author working within a romantic and post-romantic kaleidoscope.

Much of our difficulty with White stems from our desire to fit external assumptions into his texts rather than working outwards from the texts themselves. Mark Williams ends his useful study *Patrick White* (1993) with a significant observation about this:

> In the end terms like modernism, postmodernism, realism and so forth are inadequate to a writer on White's scale. They account for the impulses within his writing but never for the whole thing. He escapes the categories. John Berger's words, speaking of the sculptor, Ernest Neizvestney, are relevant: "His profoundest works defy explanation by resort to any established concept. They remain—like the experiences they express— mysterious" (168–169).

These are wise words, since it is always unhelpful to confine White to influences from which he has obviously escaped. However, it is still important to locate him within an era—to a context or a movement—that took a particular attitude towards the languages of myth and metaphor.

Fatalism and Humanism

White's form and content, with its myths and metaphors, could involve a series of interconnecting philosophical–aesthetic binaries, differences, opportunities to compare or contrast, ways of ordering or disrupting thought. A selection of these could include, in no particular chronology:

> Fatalism–humanism, socratic–presocratic, apollonian–dionysian, ego–id, mind–body, spirit–flesh, conscious–unconscious, reason–feeling, male– female, philosophy–poetry, metaphor–metonymy, word–thing, language– silence, self–other, rationalism–empiricism, master–slave, colonizer– colonized, logos–mythos, masculine–feminine, reason–revelation, unity–

disunity, disembodiment–embodiment, freedom–necessity, life–art, civilization–nature, eschatology–scatology, divinity–humanity, language–silence, subject–object, signifier–signified, tragedy–comedy, presence–absence, event–process, transcendence–immanence, teleology–ontology, telos–techne, mimetic–apocalyptic, nomos–physis, chronos–kairos, eros–agape, eros–thanatos, apophatic–kataphatic, noesis–noema, being–becoming, Athens–Jerusalem, Patristics–Rabbinics, Platonism–Aristotelianism, etcetera.

During White's lifetime, he was often criticized for failing to reconcile the sub-set of these binaries that concerned him, although no one else has succeeded.

It would become more difficult to criticize his failure, philosophically and aesthetically, after his death, once the progressive cultural establishment promoted the influential theory (or anti-theory) of non-binary thinking, after the splintering of post-Lacanianism into a range of subjectivities and relativities including: transcendental empiricism (Deleuze), nomadic theory (Braidotti), post-analytic philosophy (Rorty), cynical subjectivity (Sloterdijk), populist critiques of false consciousness wherever they occur (Žižek), and the attempt to resurrect communism (Badiou).

The success of these thinkers has been mixed because traditional binaries, powerful currencies for thousands of years, do not lose their currency with progressive reframing. Also, White's success or failure is not the point. In fact, to succeed is to miss the point:

> In his failure, he approaches doing justice to his sense of being in the world.
>
> This is not to argue that White is praiseworthy *because* he fails, but rather that these deliberate technical failures represent the successful incorporation of philosophical vision with fictional technique. The concept of necessary failure which permeates White's vision also shapes its thematic, structural, stylistic and generic expression, thereby providing the novels with an enigmatic unity which mirrors, although it distorts, that which obtains in the full world of being. Our glass is flawed, the glass of the novels more so; but in both cases the marred reflections gesture toward the more real and more perfect.
>
> Failure thus becomes felicitous … In "what we have not yet become" lie the mysterious possibilities with which Patrick White sees life so richly furnished. His work confirms that the paradox of fortunate failure entails the most profound of these possibilities (Bliss 1986, 207).

Fortunate failure, particularly when an author offers it deliberately, is a difficult concept to accept, although it is a (logically illogical) part of what White was doing. In a literary sense, fortunate failure can mean a series of unfortunate events leading to a happy outcome. In a theological sense, it can imply a theodicy: a vindication of providence in the face of evil (such as the felix culpa). However, White does not function on, and seems to actively reject, these literary or theological senses. In his novels, fortunate failure is more about attempting to look beyond humanism and fatalism.

White is often called a humanist by critics who never explain what the term means. The term is originally linked with the Renaissance rediscovery of ancient Greece. By one definition, it emphasizes human value and agency and chooses critical thinking and evidence (rationalism and empiricism) to dogma and superstition (shorthand for ancient Israel or the religious worldview more generally). By a simpler definition, it is the belief that humans can change their condition for better and for worse. Fatalism, on the other hand, is the belief that all human changes are pointless as all human actions are subject to fate: that is, humanity cannot change its condition. Problems arise when humanists present themselves as fatalists and vice versa. For example, Hardy regarded himself as a meliorist—someone who believed in human progress—but in *Jude the Obscure* he foredooms the protagonist for having opposed the natural order, and this is not humanism. Did White believe we can change the human condition? If so, what are the limits? Or was he really a fatalist?

For Rutherford 2010, writing about White's pessimism and melancholy gave her "a way of speaking about the normative traits of the white Australian imaginary" (48):

> Patrick White was the first Australian writer to draw parallels between white Australian racism and the genocidal practices of the European fascist movements of the twentieth century. This was a "thought out of season" in the white world of 1960s and 1970s Australia … He wrote [about] women that were sexually voracious, active, and hungry, presaging as Elizabeth Webby wrote recently, the three great challenges to Australian identity: multiculturalism, the women's movement, and Aboriginal activism.[11] And he wrote in a language that had you stumbling after its meaning, stalling in thick, congested quagmires of words or spellbound by passages gloriously filled with light and space. Reading White is never comfortable. White wrote a white Australian self still unconscious of its own history, a self that had not yet been charged by Stanner to redress the silences of colonization. And as he disparaged, lampooned, and tormented this white self he incited his readers to—*identify outside the circumference of the white imaginary* (49).

Because humans are linguistically defined beings, questions about fatalism

---

[11] Webby "Our Invisible Colossus"," *Australian Literary Review* (May 2007): 10.

and humanism are asked by and answered within language. In his anthropology of language, Ricoeur allocated the western myths to fatalistic and humanistic categories of metaphor. Theogonic and Hellenic metaphors are fatalistic. Hebraic metaphors are humanistic. They give humans more agency. Did White agree with Ricoeur? Do the Theogonic, Hellenic, and Hebraic metaphors act in Ricoeurean ways in his novels? They do in *Riders in the Chariot* and *The Solid Mandala* and—to a lesser extent—in *The Eye of the Storm*.

White's binaries only exist if we perceive them. This has always been difficult, as they can often seem like the tree in Berkeley's forest. Even if we do perceive them, noticing the gaps between his terms of discourse and ours is not easy. He used his binaries to explore the light and dark aspects of the western mind, its psychology of consciousness, its linguistic turn, and the civilization it has produced. He was influenced by Spengler's cyclic model of decay and renewal. He believed the west was sliding into decay. He saw it happening. It was happening. Depending on one's perspective, it is still happening. He tried to fill a broad human condition canvas with ambitious and ambiguous portraiture, not restricted by identity-based caricatures. If he were alive today, he would question our current obsession with intersectional identity politics. To focus on his explorations of human identity, without giving equal weight to his explorations of the human condition, is to distort his literary vision.

In White's last novel, *The Twyborn Affair* (1978), the protagonist moves between male and female personae, while exploring the boundaries of each. The term personae means mask or role. It is the face of a person perceived by the other. Or the mask of an actor perceived by the audience. Or the role of a protagonist perceived by the reader. Eddie (Eadie–Eadith) Twyborn changes his–her clothes, wears make-up when female, and, depending on the man–woman he–she is sleeping with at the time, assumes different roles in the bedroom. We know this identity crisis is a rhetorical construct in a work of fiction, the logic of which belongs to White's literary context. When his overseas contemporaries, such as Murdoch and Spark, did something similar, they always reminded their readers that the rhetoric within their novels was about a mental or a metaphysical world not a physical one.

If White is read alongside his contemporaries he is obviously—yet perhaps unconsciously—manoeuvring himself within a postwar genre where Plato, Nietzsche, Freud, and Jung were influential in providing different authors with a shared terms of discourse. Male protagonists, who are often but not always homosexual, had evolved into tropes for logos, civilization, the ego, and the conscious mind. Red-haired protagonists, who are often but not always female, had evolved into tropes for mythos, nature, the id, and the unconscious mind.

This manoeuvre, where logos and mythos are tropes within an overarching frame, is fundamental to White's literary vision. Given his sexual orientation, the manoeuvre was particularly fearless, and is easily misinterpreted, as there seems to be a widespread inability among his critics to distinguish between his life as a male homosexual and how male homosexuals function in his fiction. Whenever he assigns a male homosexual a role, in his mythological–metaphorical scheme, it is a philosophical–psychological role rather than a biographical–autobiographical role. In this world, gender fluidity was a mental phenomenon not a medical process.

The relationship White performs in *The Eye of the Storm* (1973), between an old matriarch Elizabeth Hunter and her young nurse Flora Manhood, is a good illustration of White's archetypal manoeuvre, as it relates to the red-haired female trope for mythos. Elizabeth's marriage to Alfred was unsuccessful, as a marriage between nature and civilization, although Elizabeth regrets this—as much as nature is capable of regret—but redeems herself while nursing Alfred as he dies from cancer. Flora is being courted by the chemist Col—a trope for logos, who reads books and listens to classical music, neither of which her mythos understands—and she resents his desire to possess her. Although Elizabeth keeps her motives hidden, she wants Flora to marry Col, to demonstrate that a marriage between nature–mythos and civilization–logos can be successful, even if hers has failed.

Flora spends the entire novel resisting this destiny, exploring alternative relationships with her lesbian bus-conductor cousin, Snow Tunks, and her employer's famous actor son, Sir Basil Hunter. She finally accepts it after Elizabeth dies and her soul has a dark night on Anzac Parade. White's performance here is Gadamerian and Ricoeurean. Elizabeth and Flora are tropes for mythos, complete with red hair and everything it signifies. Elizabeth represents the trope as its Theogonic or chthonic power is waning. Flora is still a confused fledgling. Both Alfred and Col are tropes for logos: the Hellenic civilization that desires to possess and control nature but does not succeed. The fact that Flora will never fulfil the role of bitch goddess, which Elizabeth Hunter excels in, does not change her archetypal function.

This literary scheme belongs to a fictional landscape; metaphysical rather than physical; immaterial rather than material. Outside that fictional landscape, humans are neither logos nor mythos, nor any combination of the two; however, the archetypes logos and mythos represent have been attributed to humans for a long time. For better or for worse—depending on where one stands—White's terms of discourse are remarkably similar, here and in other novels, to the terms Paglia describes in *Sexual Personae* (1990).

Paglia has been accused of advocating a biological determinism of sex, as one form of fatalism, which sits uncomfortably alongside the social constructionism of gender, as one form of humanism. White could be accused of a similar tension; sometimes he comes across as a social constructionist, as could appear the case with Eddie (Eadie–Eadith) Twyborn; at other times he comes across as a biological determinist, as can appear the case with Elizabeth Hunter and Flora Manhood. Then again, he might be attempting to look beyond these categories.

As long as we read texts to suit our own purposes, rather than those of the author, White will remain at the wrong end of the sex–versus–gender debate, or the fatalism–vesus–humanism debate, or the intersectional politics inspired by third-wave feminism, depending on whether or not he serves our ideological or anti-ideological needs. Some read him to promote a literary or cultural theory. Others studiously ignore him. He is fertile ground for postcolonial and queer theorists, who project their theories onto him. He is barren ground for feminists, who probably regard him in the same way they regard Lawrence and/or Paglia, although Paglia is a feminist herself.

In White's case, critical attitudes towards his homosexuality have always been, and continue to be, a complicating factor. For much of his life as a male homosexual, male–male sex was a criminal activity and a diagnostic criterion for mental disorder. One of the paradoxes in White criticism is that, not long after his sexuality was decriminalized, ceased to be a criterion for mental disorder, and gained public tolerance, his critics began using contemporary Freudian and Jungian prisms to psychoanalyze homosexuality in his fiction, and in him, even though they were never clinically qualified to do so, and never operated in a clinical setting.

Some critics adopted psychoanalytical poses that were never appropriate. They were never his analyst. He was never their analysand. In *Patrick White: Fiction and the Unconscious* (1988), Tacey diagnoses the trajectory of White's supposed literary failure, as a progressive decline, by arguing that individuated male homosexuals have difficulty achieving mental integration within the Jungian system.[12] In *Patrick White* (1996), During gave Tacey's diagnosis a Freudian twist, investing White's life and fiction with a "double Oedipal relation". In the late 1990s, Leonie Kramer

---

[12] An account of the fascination critics had for the Jungian aspects of his work can be found in Marr 1991, 451–452. White's reaction to Tacey, and their correspondence, can be found in Marr 1994.

commented privately that White had tilted at the metaphysical windmill, but got mangled in its big picture, because he was homosexual. Her meaning seemed clear to me at the time: as homosexuals are not whole persons, they do not have access to the big picture.

If the theories driving these attempts to pathologize White and his fiction are no longer hegemonic in the sciences, the situation is different in the humanities, where Lacan applied Freud's discovery of the unconscious beyond psychoanalysis to philosophy, phenomenology, existentialism, structuralism, poststructuralism, feminism and "just about every discipline represented in the university" (Johnston 2014, 5). Also, the post-Lacanian philosophers who came of age in the 1960s and 1970s—including Hyppolite, Foucault, Deleuze, Irigaray and Kristeva—all absorbed Freudian analysis in one way or another via Lacan's seminars (ibid.).

If the present generation of White's critics is no longer wedded to Freud, or Jung, post-Lacanian assumptions still dominate many of their critiques. Also, there is a curious tendency among 21st century critics to distinguish the fiction he wrote in "the closet" from the fiction he wrote after "coming out". This distinction is erroneous. There never was a "before" or an "after". He never "came out" (Marr 1991, 526–527). He explains this in the autobiography:

> Homosexual society as such has never had much appeal for me. Those who discuss the homosexual condition with endless hysterical delight as though it had not existed, except in theory, before they discovered their own, have always struck me as colossal bores. So I avoid them, and no doubt I am branded a closet queen. *I see myself not so much a homosexual as a mind possessed by the spirit of man or woman according to actual situations of the characters I become in my writing.* This could make what I write sound more cerebral than it is. I don't set myself up as an intellectual. What drives me is sensual, emotional, instinctive. At the same time I like to think *creative reason* reins me in as I reach the edge of disaster (italics added) (80–81).

While there is a discussion about creative reason, and what it means, his sexuality is not as definitive as his humanity. He stated the significance of male homosexuality in *Riders in the Chariot* (1961), written around the time Ricoeur was situating his anthropology of myths and metaphors within Gadamer's romantic hermeneutics, and continued to state it for the rest of his career.

In the repressed British expatriate clergyman—the Reverend Timothy Calderon—White presents an "unnatural" logos figure uncomfortable within the "natural" mythos of the Australian landscape. In Calderon, White was critiquing many things. He associates Calderon with John's

Gospel, with its high christology, and its focus on Christ as the logos. This is part of his colonial critique. Along with his widowed sister, Mrs Pask, Calderon is raising the Irish–Aboriginal half-caste Alf Dubbo, who occupies a liminal place between logos and mythos. The failure of this "great experiment"—and particularly the role of classical or logos religion in it—is an early example of White assigning the male homosexual a role, as logos, within his critique of colonialism (and the metaphysics attached to it).

White's postcolonial critics are diverse and fall into groups.[13] Most postcolonialists approach him benignly, simply locating him in the transition from commonwealth to postcolonial literature, and simply comparing his constructions of colonizer–colonized identities with those in other postcolonial fictions (Alonso-Breto 2009, 302–318; Kaur 2014, 339–353; Mehta 2014, 368–381). Some refer to him and his work obliquely, as an opportunity to discuss the history of native title (de Soyza 2014, 400–412; Dolin 2014, 413–428), why Australia did not become a republic in 1999 (Alomes 2014, 470–485), why Australians feel threatened by the Muslim other in the 21st century (Ali 2014, 486–495), and guessing his grazier family's relations with the indigene, including gratuitously assuming that his father, Dick, would have had power-tainted sex with the victim–other (Grieves 2014, 429–432).

In the oblique category, while White's attitude towards the Muslim "other" is hypothetical, we can assume it would have been informed by his Greek influences. He referred to "the Castastrophe" of 1922 a few times in his work. We can assume he would have taken the Greek view of Ottoman Turkish genocides. Before making judgments about White's attitude on this subject, reading Giles Milton's book *Paradise Lost: Smyrna 1922—The Destruction of Islam's City of Tolerance* (2008) is useful.

Some postcolonialists still revere and follow Edward Said, the once influential but now dated polemicist who describes the world in dualistic terms of hegemonic west versus counter-hegemonic non-white other. The explicit motivation here is to reverse White's critique of colonialism, making it look like another form of colonizing, and making him look like a complicit member of a hegemonic elite, describing and inscribing the indigene as other within a totalizing white mythology (Leane 2014, 257–267; Mehta 2014, 241–256).

Rutherford 2010 offers an opposing view, which argues that, like his

---

[13] The most comprehensive and nuanced postcolonial study of White is still vanden Dreisen 2009.

contemporaries, White unpicked the triumphal narratives of white colonial cultures to "undercut the readers' identification with cultural chauvinism and white mythology" (47–64). The relationship between Calderon and Dubbo operates on this level. Calderon's horizon is deliberately described as sterile, philosophically, because he represents logos, while Dubbo's horizon is deliberately described as fertile, aesthetically. Whether Alf represents mythos is another question. He is more fertile than logos but logos gave him something important that it could not give other archetypes–tropes more clearly aligned with mythos. So it is useful to regard Dubbo as occupying a liminal space between mythos and logos.

The transition from colonialism to postcolonialism is only one aspect of a larger story. In White's novels, not all male homosexual tropes function in the same way as Calderon, but each is related to logos in some way. Elsewhere in *Riders in the Chariot* there is Humphrey Mortimer, a sterile seller of art not a fertile creator of art, who covets Alf Dubbo's paintings. In *The Solid Mandala*, the apollonian-cum-socratic Waldo is another failed artist, who uses reason to deflect and never to create. In *The Vivisector* there is Maurice Caldicott, another art seller rather than art creator. And, of course, there is the iconic masturbating grocer, Cecil Cutbush, one of the novel's redemptive characters.

Apart from these male homosexual tropes, other male characters are bisexual, in a purely archetypal sense. Like Dubbo, Arthur Brown occupies a liminal place between logos and mythos, although he has the red-hair of mythos, as do Eddie Twyborn and Don Prowse in *The Twyborn Affair*. Lord Gravener's status as a homosexual or a bisexual is difficult to discern. He may instead represent the heterosexual norm Eadith aspires to, hence her fear of what might happen should he ever discover her male genitalia.[14] Norman Fussell is harder to classify, as White presents him as little more than a "poof" ambiguously involved with Dubbo's female prostitute landlady, Hannah.

There are obvious critical challenges to understanding the meaning of male homosexuality and bisexuality in relation to what White's contemporaries were attempting to achieve, in their historical moment, which is not our historical moment. As the language we use to describe these attempts is significant, up until this point the terms gay, queer, or transgender have been avoided, in relation to White or his fiction. These are our terms not his. They have contemporary meanings for us that cannot be applied to him, or to anyone in the past, without introducing

---

[14] It is easy to assume Gravener knew Eadith was a biological male, but we cannot be so sure. Much of what White tries to achieve in the novel depends on that ambiguity.

presentism and/or anachronism into our literary–historical analyses. To be a male homosexual in White's period was to be mentally defined and physically confined in particular ways. To be gay, queer, or transgender in our period is quite different, mentally and physically. This then–now distinction is important to maintain.

Before the term homosexual was first used as a noun—in the late 19th century—there were homosexual acts not homosexual persons. Since then, we have been encouraged to define persons in terms of their sexual and/or sensual feelings. However, the category of homosexual person has since fragmented, intersectionally, moving from male–male and female–female to a bewildering array of alternatives. As many of these alternatives now depend on the promethean hubris of social constructionism, in collusion with the craven opportunism of science and technology, they blur the boundaries between humanism and fatalism or freedom and constraint White explored in his fiction.

Today's LGBT identity politics is the intersectional fragmentation of norms which were still on the horizon, and were invisible, in White's lifetime. How White might have felt about this development is hypothetical; however, in *Flaws in the Glass* he admitted to having "unequivocal male genes" (154). This suggests he identified as a cisgendered male whose forays into gender fluidity were purely archetypal and never intended to be biological or genetic. Also, as his mental and physical reality as a male homosexual was different from ours, we can assume Bruce (Caitlyn) Jenner or Bradley (Chelsea) Manning are not the rhetorical equivalent of what he was trying to achieve in Eddie (Eadie–Eadith) Twyborn as a "twice-born" or "born again" trope.

Lang 2015 alludes to White's queer modernism (193–204), which she wants to see merged with what she calls mainstream modernism. Graham-Smith 2010 reminds us of the primordial androgyny in Aristophanes' speech in Plato's *Symposium*, how it was translated into psychoanalytical terms by Freud, and how Lacan disseminated Freud's terms throughout the humanities in ways that reinforced heterosexual norms. To correct this, he wants to reclaim the "silenced homosexual aspect" of Plato's story, so its queerness can exert a subversive influence on hegemonic heterosexist assumptions (163–179). Taking his cue from Beatson's *The Eye of the Mandala* (1976), Henderson 2015 sees White's central subject as the "almost moribund" theological doctrine of the Incarnation or Word made Flesh. He wants to "inject new and urgent meaning" into the moribund doctrine, or what he sees as White's version of it, while preserving its "negative capability" by rendering it a "solid" object with a comic twist: cartography in drag = (in)cartography (181–192).

The relevance of these queer approaches is not self-evident, beyond queer theory's desire to remake the world in its image. Lang never tells us what queer modernism looks like, or how it is similar to, or different from, the modernism White and his contemporaries performed in the decades before queer theory emerged. Graham-Smith alludes to Lacan's negative effect on the humanities, which is arguably true, although Lacan's legacy is intimately related to Freud's legacy. Both men became irrelevant around the same time and for the same reasons. The relevance of Aristophanes' speech is difficult to measure, since it does not have the status of a creation myth. Also, the concept of the Godhead's androgyny is not radical. It is well known to, and well tolerated by, Judaism and Christianity. What is meant by the "silenced homosexual aspect" is unclear, since the LGBT lobby has been noisy and militant for quite some time now. Henderson's belief that Christians are waiting for their doctrines to be rescued by queer theory, by making them "cartography in drag", is about as far from reality as one can get.

What queer theory shares with postcolonial theory—and any other form of literary or cultural theory inspired by third wave feminism—is the tendency to use White as a vehicle to discuss something other than his life or his fiction. He was not interested in the identity politics of gay liberation. This suggests that, in all probability, he would not have been interested in the identity politics of queer theory or any other intersectional politics.

McMahon 2010 does not declare herself as a queer theorist or explain why she uses queer theory to critique White. She simply assumes he is queer and therefore that queer theory applies to him. She proposes the queer specificities "of White's homographesis need to be addressed in their no doubt complex relationship to the aesthetic of modernist universalism that underpins White's fiction" (77–91). This manoeuvre is difficult, as "homographesis" already implies queer theory, which did not emerge until after his death in 1990.

If the term "homographesis" is applied to White's modernism, an artificial gulf is created between his male homosexual archetypes or tropes, in their historical specificity, and the imperatives of what she calls "national graphesis". When this jargon is unpacked, it seems that "writing the individual" and "writing the nation" are mutually exclusive. The logic here is that any story of individual identity cannot legitimately participate in or speak on behalf of national identity (or, by analogy, universal identity). She suggests that, when he outed himself in *The Twyborn Affair*, he compromised his relationship with his readers, who had been conditioned by the closeted nature of his earlier work, and this breach of an unspoken contract nullified his right to speak about the human condition.

McMahon argues that, like David Malouf, White adopted a mode of writing that neither denied nor explicated sexual identity but deployed a style, sensibility, and aesthetic which is both recognizable and induced the reader into a contract of "knowing unknowing" (86):

> It is this contract that is threatened by *The Twyborn Affair*. Up until this novel there appears to be a tacit contract between text and reader: the text will not insist on the specific terms of its claims to difference (which may unsettle the reader's homophobia and suggest distinctions within the category of the universal) if the reader agrees to acknowledge the universalist terms of its project (which validate this novel and shore up the validity of those previous). But what is the content and quality of this knowledge that is already known? That White was a homosexual? That he has always written as/of the homosexual? That his writing is homographetic?
>
> There is a profound contradiction in the assumption of this knowledge. If we already know about the relationship between White, homosexuality, and writing, then we must have gained the knowledge from White's earlier work, which means that all that he wrote has always been recognized as a homographesis. Further, if we accept this claim to knowledge at face value, then the overt declarations of homosexuality in *The Twyborn Affair* are being heard by a readership skilled in the deflection of homosexuality according to the terms of this kind of gentlemanly contract (86–87).

If we apply McMahon's argument to the central argument of this book, she seems to be saying that the male homosexual trope is allowed to appear in modernist or postmodernist novels about the human condition; however, she assumes readers will misunderstand (or deny the universal significance of) that trope, especially if they know the author is also a male homosexual. Further, she seems to be doing two other things. Perhaps unintentionally, she is segregating White from his contemporaries —heterosexual and bisexual— who work with similar male homosexual tropes. Hopefully unintentionally, she is advocating a cultural–critical apartheid revolving around an author's sexuality.

McMahon associates White's "queer specifics", which she believes are explicitly played out in *The Twyborn Affair*, with what Adorno and Said have to say about the "paradox of unproductive productiveness" of an author's late style (84). Apparently, in the history of art, late works are "catastrophes", especially if an author like White uses his earlier work as an origin or generative source, and particularly if the ending of his final quest-narrative is over-determined (84).[15] She then associates his supposed queerness and lateness with Sedgewick's supposed contradiction between minoritizing views, where homo–hetero definitions are important to a minority, and universalizing views important to "people across the spectrum of sexualities" (84–85). Following Derrida, she then warns of the dangers in foregrounding any "queer ontology or aesthetic", in a "narrativization of the human condition", for *"to be homosexual is not to be fully human or, for that matter, fully Australian or even fully real or material"* (italics added) (85).

McMahon never explains her motives. If they are to warn of the dangers of equating "the queer specifics of White's writing" with a "universalized mode of reading", her warning is between herself and queer theorists not between White and his readers. If they are about White's hypothetical "queerness", a theoretical category invented after he died, she needs to explain how White is queer rather than human, and why she does not believe he is fully human, fully Australian, fully real, or fully material.

How do lesbian and bisexual female tropes function in White's overarching Gadamerian frame of logos and mythos? The news is not good for cisgendered lesbians, as *Riders in the Chariot* describes Snow Tunks in undesirable terms: an alcoholic butch dyke incapable of maintaining a relationship. He tells a more positive story in *The Vivisector*, where a female bisexual trope, Olivia Davenport (a.k.a. Boo Hollingrake) is the novel's hidden force, operating in the background, sponsoring Hurtle's career as an artist and putting him in touch with his deformed red-haired sister Rhoda, the Pythoness at Tripod, the oracle who does not speak.

What White does with this bisexual female trope can be contrasted with what his postwar contemporaries do with the same trope. To give one example, Robertson Davies used his novels of the 1970s and 1980s to develop Jung's assumptions about psychological individuation and integration, and his own assumptions about a rare authentic romanticism versus a more prevalent inauthentic romanticism. In these novels, there is always a pattern of traumatic individuation, and a process of gradual integration within the Jungian system, translated into literature.

The psychic damage is always caused by logos. Mythos is always the victim. Davies assigns the female bisexual trope a special role, as an agent of soteria, because her female bisexuality gives her a unique ability to reconcile the archetypal male conscious and archetypal female unconscious

---

[15] Many regard Said's views as either subjective or erroneous. Surely not all late works are "catastrophes". Are Spark's late novels catastrophes? Or Atwood's?

minds, which apparently male homosexuals and male bisexuals do not have. In *World of Wonders* (1975), the third volume of *The Deptford Trilogy*, bisexual female Liesl facilitates the integration of Paul, who was damaged as young boy. In *The Lyre of Orpheus* (1988), the third volume of *The Cornish Trilogy*, bisexual female Gunilla facilitates the integration of Hulda, who was damage as a young girl. While this Jungian manoeuvre is logical within romantic hermeneutics, as part of an exploration of dissociated sensibility or lost wholeness, it is dated and has risks.

In the 20th century, there was no precedent for reading White's literary homosexuality comparatively against his contemporaries. Even if one had existed, it would have seemed farfetched. In the 21st century, a precedent like the one offered in this book may still seem farfetched, even among those who read him as queer rather than human. A common challenge, across the generations, is the complexity of his metaphysics. It is much simpler to ignore it completely, focus on one aspect of it, or refer to it obliquely for other purposes. The way we approach White is always an indication of the way we approach the world.

Transcendence and Immanence

In mid-1930s London, White reworked the naturalistic draft of *Happy Valley* (1939) after Roy de Maistre showed him the expressive power of abstractionism (Hewitt 2002, 13). In early-1960s Sydney, he admitted that abstracting the final version of his first novel expanded his creative ability and allowed him to "weave about freely on different levels at one and the same time" (Marr 1994, 170). What are these levels, precisely? Why was naturalism undesirable? What did abstractionism add? Throughout the history of western art, form and content keep changing, and the change is supposed to serve a purpose. In explaining the change and purpose, Hewitt reminds us that:

> White was, first and foremost, a romantic; romanticism was the part of his cultural heritage to which his spirit and nature responded most deeply. He was also drawn to those modernist and abstract expressionist painters whose work retained the mystic or transcendental strain of northern romanticism, while fully absorbing the devastation of the World Wars. Revelation and revulsion go hand in hand throughout White's work. "The blow-fly on its bed of offal is but a variation of the rainbow"; all it takes is a shift of time, or light.
>
> White worked from within romantic European traditions in both art and literature. His familiarity with those traditions allowed him to understand their progressions into modernism and abstract art, and to seek to foster their development in a Euro-Australian context. He had a

profound desire to see develop an Australian culture that would wrench
itself free from overwhelming British influence. He wanted to see it spring
from the whole rich European inheritance, in conjunction with the
Aboriginal spirit of the land (3).

Everything we can say about White's novels comes back to this
observation, and of course to his attempt to look beyond. He was always
looking beyond. We are always looking at him looking (Battye 2014).
This is not easy, as the similarities between romantic–modernist painting
and romantic–modernist music are easier to visualize or hear than the
parallel similarities in romantic–modernist literature. White wants his
readers to visualize his novels as a series of paintings, or hear them as a
series of sonatas, with many different styles. Is this too much to ask?

When romanticism claimed the future on behalf of feeling rather than
reason it was making a judgment about the model of mind classical
metaphysics inherited from Plato. The rational mind is analogous with the
head, the spirited mind is analogous with the heart, and the appetitive
mind is analogous with the lower abdomen. This logic depended on
Plato's theory of Forms and Ideas, which has been critiqued since
Aristotle. Romanticism's focus on feeling evolved into modernism's
attempts to make the immaterial material (reification) and the intangible
tangible (embodiment). During this evolution there emerged, post-Kant,
an immanent or emancipatory critique of classical metaphysics,
constitutionally opposed to all forms of "transcendental" metaphysics prior
to Kant. In this way, the rationalism–empiricism debate was repackaged as
the transcendence–immanence debate.

When White returned to Australia after World War II he brought with
him what Hughes 1991 calls the shock of the new. While he was on the
voyage home, *The Aunt's Story* (1948) was being published in New York
to positive reviews (Marr 1991, 253). He was disappointed that the novel,
one of his three favourites, was not read locally (White 1981, 143–144).
Australians were clearly unprepared for a self-reflexive modernist novel
that attempted a literary version of Klee's surrealism and expressionism.
That used a mixture of mimetic and apocalyptic modes to represent the
decline of the west. That reified or embodied four of Deleuze's five interrelated effects of modernism: the world's destruction, the subject's
dissolution, the body's disintegration, and the stuttering of language, but
not the minorization of politics.

When Australians began reading White in the 1950s they found him
challenging. Before the Nobel Prize, local critics censured him for being
too foreign, misrepresenting the national character, not writing their Great
Australian Novel, disobeying the reference conventions of language,

straining the expressive power of words, telling rather than showing, using an omniscient narrator to tell, creating bad art, promoting poor rhetoric, blurring the distinction between prose and poetry, merging aesthetics with philosophy, being obscure, experimental, and provocative. After the Prize, local critics began taking him seriously, because he was being taken seriously overseas, but some chose to remain sceptical.

If there are no correct approaches to experiencing the breathtaking range of White's performances, there are baseline measures when interpreting them. I believe his critique of logos is one of those measures. As his view of logos was conditioned by romantic hermeneutics, understanding his performances means coming to terms with the assumptions, strengths, and weaknesses of romantic hermeneutics. One way of doing this is comparing his negative view of logos with Benedict XVI's positive view of logos, described in the pope's Regensburg Lecture of September 2006.

Comparing Benedict and White is not as challenging as it may seem. In different ways, they were reacting to the challenges of romantic hermeneutics: Benedict from the outside, White from the inside. In Platonic terms, the former is a philosopher, the latter is a poet. Together they represent an updated version of an "old quarrel" which has always revolved around the differences between logos and mythos. In this sense, Benedict and White are contemporaries, obverse sides of the same metaphysical coin, like the Dashwood sisters or the Brown brothers, and it would be misleading to label one conservative and the other progressive. Such labels are meaningless and do neither of them justice. If Benedict's vision of logos seems antithetical to White's, and irreconcilable by comparison, both visions exist in parallel.

If we assume Benedict has a Platonic–Aristotelian understanding of logos, and White has a Presocratic understanding of logos, we limit ourselves to Frankfurst School-type assumptions about classicism and romanticism, rationalism and empiricism, and transcendence and immanence. This will not promote a meaningful dialogue between the two men. The first step to any dialogue is acknowledging that a working definition of logos is needed. The second step is acknowledging the Hegelian or Marxist assumptions that accompany immanent or emancipatory critiques.

According to Osborne 2004, the Heraclitan definition of logos is the "systematic structure that underlies every aspect of our experience" which needs to be noticed in order to understand "the true significance of the world" (91–95). Other possible meanings include: language, theory, reason, ratio, proportion, definition, word, speech, argument, formula, principle, reason as rationality or explanation, and account as story or value–amount (Waterfield 2000; Osborne 2004). As one person's logos is another person's mythos, the scope for logos is broad.

Benedict is aware of the problem of defining logos. He would probably approve of the Heraclitan definition in spite of its broadness. In the Regensburg Lecture, he explains how romantic hermeneutics began and why it has led to: first, a self-limiting understanding of logos; second, a distorted perception of the roles Judaism and Christianity have played in the development of western civilization. He begins by reminding his audience that Christianity, like Judaism, is the religion of logos not mythos. He describes the rapprochement between Jewish revelation and Greek reason, during the Hellenistic period (323–31 BC), after which rationality was seen as part of, and irrationality was seen as contrary to, God's revealed nature. As Christianity inherited this understanding of God as logos from Judaism, traditional claims that it obtained the understanding from Athens on its own, during its slow disentanglement from Judaism, are no longer tenable.

For the sake of honesty and completion, Benedict admits that trends in theology in the high Middle Ages set the scene for what would gradually become, after Kant, an undermining of the rapprochement between reason and revelation. In reaction against the alleged intellectualism of Augustine and Aquinas, there arose with Duns Scotus a voluntarism which, in its later developments, led to the claim that God's freedom allows him to do anything he wishes. In other words, that God is free to change his mind and do the opposite of everything he has done. Benedict believes this voluntarism allows for images of a capricious God, not bound to truth and goodness, which breaks the traditional Jewish and Christian nexus between humanity and God by proposing that human reason—including the human sense of what is true and good—is no longer an authentic mirror of God. He believes this voluntarism is untenable, since the truly divine God is the God who has revealed himself as logos and continues to act as logos on our behalf.

While this position, of God as logos, and of humanity as the image and likeness of logos, is still the mind of the Church, Benedict says it was challenged, within romantic hermeneutics, by a call for the de-Hellenization of Christianity. He believes the first stage of this call emerged in the 16th century, when the Reformers looked at Catholic theology, in its Scholastic form, and saw a faith system totally conditioned by Greek thought. To the Reformers, the Catholic expression of biblical faith no longer seemed a living historical word but merely one element of an overarching system of Greek reason; hence their desire to return to scripture alone: *sola scriptura*. In other words, metaphysics appeared to the Reformers as a premise derived from another source, an extra-biblical source, from which biblical faith had to be liberated so it could become fully itself once again.

Benedict believes that, when Kant said he needed to set thinking aside to make room for faith, he carried the reformation program forward with a radicalism the Reformers could never have foreseen. In anchoring faith in "practical" reason, Kant denied reason access to reality as a whole, and things got worse after Kant. Modernist theologies of the 19th and 20th century, Protestant and Catholic, ushered in a second stage in the de-Hellenization process, by distinguishing the God of philosophy from the God of scripture. The goal of these modernist theologies was to return to the simple message of Jesus, the historical man with a moral message, hidden beneath the accretions of Hellenized theology, liberating it and harmonizing it with "practical" reason. Unfortunately, this manoeuvre had the opposite effect. Instead of liberating theology, it colluded with modernism's self-limiting reason, expressed in Kant's critiques and radicalized by developments after Kant.

White's negative view of reason, which echoes his post-Kantian influences, opposes Benedict's positive view of reason, which echoes his pre-Kantian influences. A great deal flows from this difference in their terms of discourse. The issue for critics is not whether Benedict is right and White is wrong, or vice versa, it is noticing White's critique of reason and how Benedict gives us the means to critique the critique. I believe the possibility of an open-ended dialogue, between the logos philosopher and the mythos poet, is an essential measure of White's enduring significance.

White is a theist not a deist and a panentheist not a pantheist,[16] but his theism and panentheism are different from Benedict's. He said he believed in a creator God, a Higher Power, a Divine Presence, who created us and we got out of hand, like Frankenstein's monster (White 1989, 19). He also believes this creator God can make mistakes, as we can. However, this God does influence, and does intervene, if we are open to him through prayer (19). In White's understanding of God we see the voluntarism Benedict tells us originates in Scotus, which leads to a distorted view of logos. This is not to be taken as a judgment against White, as his understanding of God was determined by and consistent with his literary context.

Benedict's Regensburg Lecture is essential reading for religious critics who want to situate White's critique of reason within a Jewish and Christian context. This will never be easy, as his performances can have

---

[16] Pantheism believes nature and God are identical. Panentheism believes God's immanence in the world does not exhaust his reality. It is a form of theism that criticizes traditional theism "for depicting the world as external to God" (Cobb 1984, 423).

atheistic meanings for non-believers as well as religious meanings for believers. While he wanted to challenge Australian secularism, his religious performances can be experienced as secular performances, and many critics interpret them that way. How we interpret White's performances always depends on our religious or anti-religious beliefs. Also, we must acknowledge that not many secular critics will agree with Benedict's positive view of logos. Many will object to it in principle simply because it is his view.

Murdoch puts it thus in *The Sovereignty of Good* (1970):

> It seems to me that the idea of the transcendent, in some form or another, belongs to morality: but it is not easy to interpret. As with so many of these large elusive ideas, it readily takes on forms which are false ones. There is a false transcendence, as there is a false unity, which is generated by modern empiricism: a transcendence which is in effect simply an exclusion, the relegation of the moral to a shadowy existence in terms of emotive language, imperatives, behaviour patterns, attitudes. "Value" does not belong inside the world of truth functions, the world of science and factual propositions. So it must live somewhere else. It is then attached somehow to the human will, a shadow clinging to a shadow. The result is the sort of dreary moral solipsism which so many so-called books on ethics purvey. An instrument for criticizing false transcendence, in its many forms, has been given to us by Marx in the concept of alienation. Is there, however, any true transcendence, or is this idea always a consoling dream projected by human need on to an empty sky? (57)

In other words, the critique of transcendence is never apolitical, since it arises from terms which began in Hegelian or Marxist assumptions and continue to be shaped and disseminated by the cultural and political Left.

As an empiricist, Deleuze is an example of what Benedict means by a philosopher with a negative view of logos. Deleuze believes Plato's rationalism was a calculated response to an Athenian democracy in which anyone could make truth claims about anything. As Plato's project was supposedly about restoring a "criteria of selection among rivals", Deleuze believes:

> It will be necessary for him to erect a new type of transcendence, one that differs from imperial or mythical transcendence (although Plato makes use of myth by giving it a special function). He will have to invent a transcendence that can be exercised and situated *within* the field of immanence itself. This is the meaning of the theory of Ideas. And modern philosophy will continue to follow Plato in this regard, encountering transcendence at the heart of immanence as such. The poisoned gift of Platonism is to have introduced transcendence into philosophy, to have

given transcendence a plausible philosophical meaning (the triumph of the judgment of God). This enterprise runs up against numerous paradoxes and aporias, which concern, precisely, the status of the *doxa* (*Theataetus*), the nature of friendship and love (*Symposium*), and the irreducibility of an immanence of the earth (*Timaeus*).

Every reaction against Platonism is a restoration of immanence in its full extension and in its purity, which forbids the return of any transcendence. The question is whether such a reaction abandons the project of a selection among rivals, or on the contrary, as Spinoza and Nietzsche believed, draws up completely different methods of selection. Such methods would no longer concern claims as acts of transcendence, but the manner in which an existing being is filled with immanence (the Eternal Return as the capacity of something or someone to return eternally). Selection no longer concerns the claim, but power: unlike the claim, power is modest. In truth, only the philosophies of pure immanence escape Platonism, from the Stoics to Spinoza or Nietzsche (Deleuze 1997, 137).

We need to recognize what is happening here. Deleuze is rehearsing his script while patrolling his boundaries. This kind of criticism is always a sneer at Plato's theory of Forms and Ideas, and the reference to "the triumph of the judgment of God" is a sneer at Judaism and Christianity. The script, the boundaries, and the sneer are what one expects from this kind of theorist. Their starting point is always an assumption of the wrongness of classical metaphysics. Yet questions must be asked: Why is escaping Platonism so important? Why is Plato's transcendence a "poisoned gift" from which only philosophies of pure immanence can escape? And what are the "philosophies of pure immanence", exactly? Finally, how can classical metaphysics be so resilient when we are constantly told it is so wrong?

Academic responses to Deleuze are varied. From the Right, Scrunton 2015 argues that Deleuze "is explicitly challenging the distinction between sense and nonsense, showing that the true use of language is expressive, not representational, so that nonsense is as much a part of communication as what is normally called sense". As a result, Scrunton believes, the Deleuzean text "continues to pile abstraction upon abstraction with no real hint of a real question, still less an answer". The problem with Deleuze, as Scrunton sees it, is "an endless stream of abstractions, from which all reference to concrete reality and the flow of human life has been excised. He does not argue, but encloses his key words in fortified boxes, which he firmly locks against all questioning before throwing the key away". From the Left, Culp 2016 argues against the "canon of joy" school that celebrates Deleuze as an "affirmative thinker of connectivity" (1). Instead,

Culp seeks to repackage Deleuze's dark negativity, in order to promote a necessary revolutionary agenda: "The Death of God, the Death of Man, and now the Death of this World" (65).

For Deleuze, what may be "out there"—in White's "beyond"—is always illusory within the rational forms of transcendence. Instead, he believes transcendence can be embodied or reified in empirical forms. This manoeuvre is clever but can only ever be theoretical within Deleuze's popularized version of immanent critique theory. If White's religious performances can be located within Deleuze's transcendental empiricism, transcendental illusions cannot be manoeuvred away so easily. They continue in both rational and empirical forms. This is the dilemma of Waldo's rational transcendence, which has no immanence, and Arthur's empirical immanence. The twins cannot live without each other. They are two aspects of a single whole. Also, immanence implies transcendence. Without transcendence there is nothing to immanate. This is why the doctrine of the Incarnation is crucial to Christian belief.

In the four novels of White's middle phase, protagonists associated with logos search for but are never given access to "authentic" religious experience, because that experience is only assigned to protagonists associated with mythos. This is because White's concept of logos is framed by Continental influences that describe logos in negative terms. The central assumption revolves around the idea that logos was originally unified under the Presocratics, but Socratic reason destroyed this unity, hence the dissociation of sensibility, loss of wholeness, and sense of alienation that concerns romantic hermeneutics.

We keep returning to the question: What is logos? That question, standing at the centre of western self-understanding, is asked by many schools of thought. While each school has its own descriptive terms, there is still no consensus over how reason and rationality are defined and measured. There are only influential opinions, each invoking rationality and reason—like a god of the gaps—to serve whatever purpose each school wants it to serve. Also, the relationship between them is apparently circular. Rationality is the quality of being reasonable. Being reasonable is based on reasons as facts. This circularity does not take us far.

Benedict is willing to discuss the breadth of logos and how it can be restored to its pre-Kantian grandeur. This discussion can only begin once the post-Kantian embargo on logos is lifted. If there might be more common ground between Benedict and White than we imagine, we cannot explore that common ground without engaging the pope and the poet in a conversation that, traditionally, has both defined and limited western consciousness.

What does White offer the rationalism–empiricism and transcendence–immanence debates? Is it fair to label Benedict a rationalist who advocates transcendence (and excludes immanence), and label White an empiricist who advocates immanence (and excludes transcendence), or are these labels unhelpful and self-limiting? Each time White points to transcendence, like Plato, he counters it with a reminder about immanence, like Aristotle. How do we interpret White's pointing–reminding manoeuvre?

Around the time White was refining his use of the male homosexual trope to signify logos, rationalism, and transcendence, he was also refining his use of the excremental vision to strengthen the claims of mythos, empiricism, and immanence. After Stan Parker points to a gob of spittle and says "That is God", White's novels of the 1960s and 1970s increasingly refer to bodily fluids, waste matter, and flatulence. He was not unique in doing this. In the Deptford Trilogy of the 1970s and Cornish Trilogy of the 1980s, Davies was also refining his use of the male homosexual trope and the excremental vision, at the same time, and for similar reasons (see Appendix).

Encouraged by their different influences, all of which critiqued the Enlightenment, White and Davies held logos responsible for the west's individual and collective dissociation of sensibility, loss of wholeness, and sense of alienation. For Davies, the answer was reclaiming the hypothetical *Weltanschauung* or Magian worldview of the Middle Ages, which could still be found in the excremental vision of Rabelais the French monk (1494–1553) and Swift the Anglo-Irish priest (1667–1745). What was at stake, for Davies, was the possibility of soteria through art, which depended on realizing an "authentic" romanticism rather than a "superficial" romanticism.

White's influences were more focused on the hypothetical *Weltanschauung* of the Presocratics, or rather on the German longing for it. The parallels with Rabelais and Swift still stand, however, which is why Mikhail Bakhtin's grotesque realism and Norman O. Brown's excremental vision are still relevant to understanding White.[17] The major difference between White and Davies is that Davies was more systematically Jungian, which may date his novels more quickly. If White found Jungianism compelling, like Freudianism, he suspected all systems: "He took on board not the whole cargo but only what was needed for the voyage" (Marr 1991, 451–452).

When Augustine of Hippo (354–430) wrote "We are born between

---

[17] Bakhtin: *Rabelais and His World* (1968), *The Dialogic Imagination* (1981), and *Problems of Dostoevky's Poetics* (1984). Brown: *Life Against Death* (1959), *Love's Body* (1966), *Apocalypse and/or Metamorphosis* (1991).

faeces and urine" (Brown 1959, 188), he was reminding us of a physical reality that happened to Jesus and his followers as well as to White and his readers. When Julian of Norwich (1342–1416) wrote of the human rectum and sphincter as "a well-made purse", which God made "for love of the soul which he made in his likeness", she was reminding us that Jesus, the Word made Flesh, passed wind and had bowel movements, all according to "the goodness of God" (Llewelyn 1982, 45). The point being made here is simple yet complex. As long as Rabelais the monk and Swift the priest exist within Christian orthodoxy, White's excremental vision cannot be heterodox.

Take Elizabeth Hunter's stream of consciousness fragment from *The Eye of the Storm*:

> As light as unlikely probably as painful as a shark's egg the old not body rather the flimsy soul is whirled around sometimes spat out anus-upward (souls have an anus they are never allowed to forget it) never separated from the brown the sometimes tinted spawn of snapshots the withered navel string still stuck to what it aspires to yes at last to be past the dream life will allow (194).

Immanence is not a denial of transcendence. This aspect of White's vision is not contrary to Christian orthodoxy. Benedict's vision of logos embraces it.

Tragedy and Comedy

There are two broad approaches to tragedy: the performative exemplified by *The Greek Sense of Theatre* (Walton 2015) and the philosophical or rhetorical exemplified by *The Fragility of Goodness* (Nussbaum 2001). The performative approach focuses on what the ancient Greeks might have expected or experienced when they went to the theatre, which Walton believes was less about the rhetoric projected by the monologues or dialogues and more about what the protagonists might act out on the stage. The philosophical approach focuses on the rhetoric projected by the protagonists' speech. While both approaches complement each other, and need to be held in creative tension, the philosophical or rhetorical approach has been vastly more influential within the history of ideas.[18]

What is White's relationship with tragedy? The question is important because his career parallels, and mirrors, an ongoing debate about the

---

[18] Irrespective of approach, ancient Greek tragedy was formulaic. The playwright had conventions to obey and little room to move. Greek comedy, on the other hand, was less formulaic, more inventive, and characterized by a taxing, arduous creative freedom.

possibility or impossibility of modern tragedy. In searching for provisional answers, which always beg further questions, it is useful to locate White's wide-ranging signals about tragedy and place them in their broadest possible context. In *The Tragic Vision* (1983), McCulloch was the first critic to describe the density and complexity of tragic themes running through White's fiction: particularly Nietzsche's amor fati, will to power, superman, eternal recurrence, socratic man, the apollonian–dionysian dichotomy, and the death of God.

While Nietzsche inherited and adapted these themes rather than invented them, there are other post-Kantian themes in White's fiction: themes from Goethe, Hegel, and Schopenhauer; themes from Freud, Jung, and Spengler; themes from Heidegger, Gadamer, and Ricoeur. As White's fiction is intentionally ambiguous, what these themes mean is unclear. His kaleidoscope had many facets.

In one short story from *The Burnt Ones* (1964), "The Letters" (1962), he alludes to Freud's Oedipus complex with a Ferenzian twist at the end. In another from the same anthology, "Miss Slattery and Her Demon Lover" (1963), he alludes to Hegel's master–slave dialectic. In one short story from *The Cockatoos* (1975), "The Night the Prowler" (1978), Felicity Bannister, having emancipated herself from her parents' neurotic attempts to construct her identity, explores her freedom and her constraint. At the end of the story, she discovers an old man with advanced prostate cancer dying in a derelict, rat-infested house. Moved by his plight, she asks if he needs anything:

> "No rats," he sighed, "and an easy pee."
> For he had begun to urinate; and as she watched it trickle over the withered thighs, her own being was flooded with pity.
> "That's something, isn't it?" She was so grateful for their common release from the myths to which they had been enslaved, she only slowly realized the hand she was holding in hers had died" (168).

We are never told what the narrator means by "their common release from the myths to which they had been enslaved". We do know White used myth for specific purposes. He was never a naïve de-mythologizer.

White's themes can be construed as "tragic", depending on how tragedy is defined and measured, how an author uses them, and how a critic interprets them, but their presence does not automatically make literature "tragic" unless tragedy is a catch-all term that includes every representation of, or commentary on, the human condition, and is regarded as the supposed benchmark for the ultimate possibilities of art.

McCulloch's baseline argument is stated early in her book:

> Although it is correct to identify White's artistic method as following

classical and/or romantic lines, it would be misleading to classify his work as romantic or classical. In terms of thematic content his philosophy, for example, would be in opposition to Plato's doctrine of the relationship between the phenomenal world and the realm of Ideas or Forms. White follows Plato in believing there is "another world" but, whereas Plato believes the real world is transcendent to the lesser reality of sights and sounds, White believes it is immanently present within the phenomenal world. White and Plato, however, have more in common than we might first suppose. In identifying differences between the two conceptions of life and art, it is more revealing to note that White construes his art in a post-Christian desanctified world which, unlike Plato's Divinely imbued one, must ascertain its God within man, matter and finally art, than to exaggerate Plato's position as a rationalist and White as the intuitive visionary. White is an artist who, in his later novels, becomes a "philosopher" of the artistic attitude; although starting from his own artistic experiences, he develops within his experiment the philosophical implications of the artist's outlook on life, employing the classical and the romantic artist's method and technique (2).

This brings us to the heart of White's context and offers specific challenges to White studies. Its implications are large, as the pursuit of "immanence", in philosophy and aesthetics after Kant, is associated with Hegel, Marx, and their influential descendents. The immanent or emancipatory critique cannot be separated from an ideology hostile towards "transcendence": a term that I believe has become a sneering code word for Platonism and Christian theology.

White clearly explores tragedy in his work but what that exploration means is unclear. Judging from the way his fiction operates, his position on tragedy is equivocal. Given his first-hand experience of World War II, is his postwar fiction questioning if not subverting the conventions of pre-war tragedy? Or is he giving those conventions new form and content? Or is he doing both? As his career evolved in stages—and as these questions can be approached from different angles—there are no unequivocal answers.

White is a creature of a 19th and 20th century zeitgeist. His themes are often German and mostly Continental. They originate in Winckelmann's homoerotic Hellenism which influenced the proto-romantic Sturm und Drang movement of the late 18th century and everything that came after it in the 19th and 20th centuries. The influence was not all good, however. During White's last year at university, Cambridge University Press published Butler's *The Tyranny of Greece over Germany* (1935), which suggests that beginning with Winckelmann the Germans had "too much exposure" to ancient Greek literature and art, which resulted in "the tyranny of an ideal". This "emboldened the Nazis to remake Europe in their image":

> It seems to me that Winckelmann's Greece was the essential factor in the development of German poetry throughout the latter half of the eighteenth century and the whole of the nineteenth century. It was the renaissance all over again, but this time in a country which takes such movements differently from the rest of Europe. If the Greeks are tyrants, the Germans are predestined slaves. Greece has profoundly modified the whole trend of modern civilization, imposing her thoughts, her standards, her literary forms, her imaginary, her visions and dreams wherever she is known. But Germany is the supreme example of her triumphant spiritual tyranny. The Germans have imitated the Greeks more slavishly; they have been obsessed by them more utterly, and they have assimilated them less than any other race. The extent of the Greek influence is incalculable throughout Europe; its intensity is at its highest in Germany.
>
> There is another side to the picture. Tyranny of any sort always engenders rebellion; and a sturdy resistance to the alien beauty of Greek poetry has also left its mark on European literature. The *Querrelle des Anciens et des Modernes* had repercussions in many countries. Shakespeare's hatred of Homer's heroes, so defiantly manifest in *Troilus and Cressida*, was a spirited answer to the spiritual challenge inherent in the devastating glory of the Greeks. But the Germans outdid the rest of Europe in the violence of their rebellion. The romantic poets and the naturalistic writers went to the utmost to free themselves from the Greeks, only to see the enemy return in power and vigour as they fell into decay. And if such poets as Milton and Racine have been too deeply influenced by the Greeks for mere analysis to reveal, the Germans are unique in having suffered an impact so terrific that it took the form of fate. …
>
> I have come to the conclusion that it was Heine and not Nietzsche who gave the *coup de grâce* to Winckelmann's Greece; and that Nietzsche was the first victim to a new ideal introduced by Heine … And if this book seems sensational, the subject and not the writer must be blamed. The Germans create sensations because they ignore obstacles and appear unaware of danger where ideas or ideals are involved.
>
> Those solitary children on the imaginary island drew together at last and rose in a body to play with the others. They dug deeper, but built less securely; they swam faster but not so far; they made larger boats which capsized sooner; they grew angry and created confusion and uproar; they either could not or would not assimilate the rules of the various games. And yet they knew something the others did not, something about the nature of the sea (6–8).

Of course, Butler's book was banned in Germany, but it was also controversial in Britain, where Winckelmann's homoerotic Hellenism had also influenced neoclassicism and romanticism. Also, while Butler does not mention Heidegger's obsession with the ontology of the Presocratics, which he was theorizing as she was publishing, it must be included as an example of the "tyranny" she describes. If White did not read Butler or Heidegger, their arguments were still part of his zeitgeist, informing the unfolding reality around him, forcing him to reassess his and Germany's "romantic reconstruction of the past" (*Flaws* 39).[19] Perhaps this included a reassessment of the neoclassical–romantic view of ancient tragedy and the modernist–postmodernist view of modern tragedy (Young 2013).

Those who argue the No case against modern tragedy believe the logic that gave tragedy philosophical–aesthetic coherence belongs to ancient Greece or to a pre-Enlightenment west. They do not believe ancient tragedy is necessarily a benchmark for the ultimate possibilities of art or commentary on the human condition. They do not believe modern tragedy is possible, after the war, because of the war. They believe the visual, performing, and literary arts can mirror the human condition without being tragic.

In *Tragedy Is Not Enough* (1952), Jaspers suggests that Christianity cannot be subsumed within the "tragic knowledge" of ancient Greece. In *The Symbolism of Evil* (1960), Ricoeur contextualizes tragedy as a myth among myths or metaphor among metaphors.[20] In *The Death of Tragedy* (1961), Steiner offers the mainstream view of tragedy among Jewish and Christian theologians struggling with the Holocaust and Hiroshima. The Judaic spirit, he says, "is vehement in its conviction that the order of the universe and of man's estate is accessible to reason" (4). The problem of Christian tragedy, he says, is not of historical distance or of a mythology gone stale:

> There has been no specifically Christian mode of tragic drama even in the noontime of the faith. Christianity is an anti-tragic vision of the world. This is as true today as it was when Dante entitled his poem a *commedia* or Corneille wrestled with the paradox of sainthood in *Polyeucte*. Christianity offers to man an assurance of final certitude and repose in God. It leads the soul towards justice and resurrection. The Passion of Christ is an event of unutterable grief, but it is also a cipher through which is revealed the love of God for man (331).

The No case will resonate with those who read White as a religious

---

[19] While Butler is useful to understanding White's re-evaluation of Germany's romantic reconstruction of the past, critics may find Williamson's *The Longing for Myth in Germany* (2004) more useful, particularly his chapter "Nietzsche's *Kulturekampf*".

[20] Ricoeur is adamant that the adamic myth is "anti-tragic"; however, he says the myth has several "tragic" aspects, which fall short of making it a "tragic" myth (311).

author, those who distinguish between the gods of paganism and the God of Judaism and Christianity, and those who do not have a problem with mainstream Christian theology. Beatson believes White's religious vision is more aligned with Christianity than any other religion, although his readers must be prepared for departures from dogma: "White's range of mythical and cultural reference is too wide, his spiritual and psychological awareness too deep, to be bound by any one body of doctrine" (2).

The No case may also resonate with secular readers, as Paglia 1990 argues:

> The tragic sense of life is a partial response to experience. It is a reflex of the west's resistence to and misapprehension of nature, compounded by the errors of liberalism, which in its Romantic nature–philosophy has followed the Rousseauist Wordsworth rather than the daemonic Coleridge.
>
> Tragedy is the most western literary genre. It did not appear in Japan until the late nineteenth century. The western will, setting itself up against nature, dramatized its own inevitable fall as a human universal, which it is not …
>
> Female tragic protagonists are rare. Tragedy is a male paradigm of rise and fall, a graph in which dramatic and sexual climax are in shadowy analogy. Climax is another western invention. Traditional eastern stories are picaresque, horizontal chains of incident. There is little suspense or sense of an ending …
>
> Tragedy is a western vehicle for testing and purification of the male will. The difficulty in grafting female protagonists onto it is a result not of male prejudice but of instinctive sexual strategies. Woman introduces untransformed cruelty into tragedy because she is the problem that the genre is trying to correct.
>
> Tragedy plays a male game, a game it invented to snatch victory from the jaws of defeat. It is not flawed choice, flawed action, or even death itself which is the ultimate human dilemma. The gravest challenge to our hopes and dreams is the messy biological business-as-usual that is going on within us and without us at every hour of every day. Consciousness is a pitiful hostage of its flesh-envelope, whose surges, circuits, and secret murmurings it cannot stay or speed. This is the chthonian drama that has no climax but only and endless round, cycle upon cycle … Tragedy's inhospitality to woman springs from nature's inhospitality to man (6–7).

Those who argue the Yes case for modern tragedy tend to subsume within tragedy any attempt to create "great" art or reflect on the human condition. In 1949, just after *Death of a Salesman* opened on Broadway, Miller published two essays: "Tragedy and the Common Man" and "The Nature of Tragedy" (Miller 1996). In these essays, he promotes the romantic vision of the artist as an inspired priest of the imagination who not only intends to create a perfect work of art but tells his audience how they should interpret it. More seriously, and without a trace of irony, he offers Willy Loman's life as a modern tragedy at the same time the west was processing the Holocaust and Hiroshima.

In *The Vision of Tragedy* (1959), Sewall subsumes Judaism and Christianity within the "tragic knowledge" of ancient Greece, strangely equates the author of Job with Aeschylus, and strangely assigns the secular Miller the rabbinic role of Jewish theologian. In *The Tragic Vision* (1960), and its sequel *The Classic Vision* (1971), Krieger distinguishes tragedy from classicism, perhaps motivated by a vague dissatisfaction with the assumptions of the Yes case, and an equally vague awareness of a No case unfolding around him.

In *Modern Tragedy* (1966), Williams takes square aim at Steiner, while attempting to argue the Yes case, presumably to advance tragedy as a means of promoting the New Left's cultural critique. In *Sweet Violence: The Idea of the Tragic* (2003), Eagleton picks up where Williams leaves off, in advocating a Leftist program for tragedy that is not purely aesthetic and brings with it a program of political engagement. He chastizes the Left from within the Left. The Leftist who writes about tragedy today, he says, "usually takes for granted a highly reactionary version of the form, which he or she then proceeds to reject" (ix). In a similar vein, he is critical of postmodernism, some of which is too shallow for tragedy, and the kind of poststructuralism that reinterprets tragedy rather than changes it (xi).

In *Tragedy and Philosophy* (1968), Kaufmann offers an overview of tragedy from the Presocratics to the present. He suggests the question of whether tragedy is still possible is paradoxical, as we still live in tragic times, but that does not explain why tragedy is no longer written. He points to an obstacle here. The most distinctive and universal feature of Greek tragedy, without exception, was the immense and overwhelming suffering presented to the audience, who were led to believe that existence is agony and terror. This is no longer fashionable in an age of mixed genres where unadulterated tragedy is out and black comedy is in. The problem is one of excellence, as tragedy is hard to do well, but he believes untried possibilities abound in comedy. What Kaufman does—which few do apart from McCulloch—is link the possibility of contemporary tragedy with Nietzsche's critique of socratic reason. This is crucial to White's novels with their pervasive critique of reason.

In *The Greek Sense of Theatre*, Walton notes that dramatized Greek myth has gone global, as the recoding of myth serves new political and cultural contexts: the Greeks "spawned all manner of bastards from Racine to Dryden, O'Neill to TS Eliot". If bastard seems a harsh term, Walton explains why it is appropriate: "alongside Greek tragedy as a wonderful inspiration is a less reputable history of claiming the authority of the Greeks for the inappropriate personal agenda" (156).

In *The Fragility of Goodness*, Nussbaum warns about this tendency:

> We should not confuse Greek religion with Judaeo-Christian religion, where it is generally true that the actions of God are to be received as the mysterious doings of a basically moral order. Job is right to renounce his attempt to accuse God of wrongdoing, and to accept the inscrutible mysteriousness of His actions. In the Greek world, by contrast, the morality of the gods' actions is regularly impugned, and it is frequently suggested that the gods lack full awareness of and sensitivity to moral norms, not being in the position of neediness and incompleteness that gives rise to the need for them. Aristotle takes this perspective to one extreme, denying that the gods have the moral virtues at all. Because it would be ridiculous to imagine the gods making contracts and returning deposits, they cannot be said to have justice. While the tragic poets do not go this far, there is a tendency, from Homer on, to portray the gods as callous and selfish in their dealings with mortals. But this means that even tragedies that are caused by divine scheming may be caused by obtuseness, laziness, and moral failure, not by mysterious necessity (xxxii).

But what about comedy? Comedy has been described as a way of resolving ambiguity and White is an intentionally ambiguous author.

Bevis 2013 points out that, in the festivals of ancient Greece, comic dramatists were not permitted to recycle plots from myths, but tragedians were. Because of this, Antiphanes (408–334 BC) suggests the comic plot is, in fact, logos rather than mythos. He called tragedy a "cushy art". Comedy was harder to do, he believed, since "we have to invent everything: new names, setup, action, second act curtain, opening" (9). Comedy's chorus was twice the size of tragedy's chorus, and it took liberties of *parabasis*—addressing the audience directly—which the tragic chorus would never allow itself. Even outside *parabasis*, there were frequent ruptures in theatrical illusion which, in Bevis's words, "announce not only comedy's fascinated interest in the process of its own creativity, but also its hope that the audience members might be somehow in on the act—participators as well as spectators" (10).

In *Comic Relief* (2009), Morreall quotes de Bono: "Humour is by far the most significant behaviour of the human brain … Humour … shows how perceptions set up in one way can suddenly be reconfigured in another way. This is the essence of creativity" (112). This creativity is not possible in tragedy, as a "cushy art", which explains why comedy is much harder. In *Comedy, Tragedy, and Religion* (1999), Morreall develops Antiphanes' views by describing the cognitive differences between the tragic vision and the comic vision, both of which share the belief that "life is full of incongruities, discrepancies between the way things ought to be and the way they are" (21).

In psychological terms, tragedy is mentally rigid, tragic heroes approach life with relatively simple concepts they wish to apply neatly to every experience. They also crave order, need closure, prefer the familiar or routine, have a low tolerance for cognitive dissonance, use convergent thinking, shun ambiguity, search for the "truth" with an emphasis on what is past and real, are not good at questioning inherited thought processes, respond to challenges with emotions, are single minded, stubborn, idealistic, serious, and are focused on the spirit rather than the body. On the other hand, comic protagonists deal with (or are allowed) "more complex, messier sets of concepts", are comfortable with disorder, do not need closure, "reframe" situations from new and unusual perspectives, seek out the unfamiliar, accept ambiguity, are critical thinkers, keep an emotional clear-headedness, are willing to change their minds, are pragmatic, look for second chances, and are focused on the body rather than the spirit (21–32).

In social terms, the tragic vision is heroic, militaristic, vengeful, hierarchical, sexually unequal, respects authority and tradition, obeys rules, and is socially isolated. By contrast, the comic vision is antiheroic, pacifist, forgiving, egalitarian, sexually equal, questions authority and tradition, uses situation ethics, and is socially integrative (33–39). If these observations about the contrasts between tragedy and comedy are true, they can be applied to White's characterizations to measure his relationship with tragedy and comedy.

In White's first postwar play, *The Ham Funeral* (1947), tragedy is implied. In Act One, Scene Four, the young man–poet wonders aloud whether the downstairs drama of the landlord and landlady is a tragedy or simply "two fat people in a basement, turning on each other". It is also worth asking whether the four male relatives are the equivalent of a chorus. Is that their function?

In his first postwar novel, *The Aunt's Story* (1948), tragedy is also implied. In Part One, "Meroë", set in Australia, he explores the tension between the Old World and the Antipodes, through the mind of the protagonist Theodora Goodman. In Part Two, "Jardin Exotique", set in late 1930s France, he explores the disintegration of the protagonist's mind, which parallels the disintegration of Europe on the eve of war, in ways that echo Spengler's cyclic model of civilization. Are *The Ham Funeral* and *The Aunt's Story* tragedies? The question is left open and we must decide for ourselves. In *The Aunt's Story*, he may be associating tragedy with Europe and questioning its relevance within Australia's physical and metaphysical landscapes.

Is *Riders in the Chariot* (1961) a tragedy? The answer depends on how tragedy is defined. The novel is perspectivist in a Nietzschean sense and disclosive in a Heideggerian sense. It revolves around four protagonists, each of whom has a horizon with mythical–metaphorical parallels in Ricoeurean anthropology. Rather than being plot-driven, it is about the characteristics of each protagonist's horizon and the ways it relates—or fails to relate—to the horizons of other protagonists. In this matrix of Theogonic, Hellenic and Hebraic metaphors, the myths of tragic hero and exiled soul have no primacy. They compete with other myths. Could this be White's commentary on modern tragedy's lack of primacy in any anthropology of myth?

After *Riders in the Chariot* (1961), before *The Solid Mandala* (1966), White focused on writing plays and short stories. One of these is *Night on Bald Mountain* (1964) where the theme of tragedy is more explicit than in *The Ham Funeral*. As tragedy meant "goat song"—and tragedies were performed during religious festivals that often involved goat sacrifices and laments—it is significant that *Night on Bald Mountain* is framed by a goat lady and her goats. The tragedy—if it is a tragedy—unfolds within this "goat song" frame.

The action revolves around two representatives of logos and mythos, the eponymous Hugo and Muriel Storm, husband and wife, whose surname has obvious Sturm und Drang connotations. They are similar to, yet different from, the landlord and landlady of *The Ham Funeral*. Hugo is a frustrated, unfulfilled English Professor who bears the weight of White's critique of contemporary literature academics—socratic individuals with diseased and life-denying attitudes—who use reason to deflect and never to create. By contrast, Miriam, whose name echoes Mary Hare's—and is the ancient Hebrew form of the English Mary—embodies the dionysian Yes that overcomes the socratic No. Unfortunately, Miriam has become a self-destructive alcoholic, because her creative power threatens the rational Hugo (she once wrote a play which he found challenging and therefore destroyed). Hugo and Muriel prefigure Waldo and Arthur Brown.

Is *The Solid Mandala* (1966) a tragedy? The question is deceptive, as the novel explores—quite densely—the central theme of *The Birth of Tragedy* (1872). There is no public record of White having read it, although he must have known it well. In 1958 White wrote: "Of Nietzsche

I read *Also Sprach Zarathustra* when I was an undergraduate without being drawn to it" (Marr 1991, 317). To Nietzsche, the success of ancient Greek tragedy depended on the fusion of an apollonian principle (a dream world where reality is ordered and differentiated) and a dionysian principle (an intoxicated world where reality is disordered and undifferentiated) into a unity or whole. A downhill slide supposedly began under Euripides, who supposedly introduced socratic rationalism to his tragedies. After Socrates, because of Socrates, the fusion of apollonian and dionysian became impossible and therefore the perfect tragedy became impossible. This logic depends upon a "romantic reconstruction of the past" (*Flaws* 39) which White had been reassessing since the 1930s.

The novel is about twin brothers. As they age, apollonian Waldo becomes increasingly socratic and resentful of Arthur's dionysian powers.[21] Waldo eventually dies of spite. Arthur goes mad. While this is certainly a commentary on Greek tragedy—or at least Nietzsche's view of it—there are two non-tragic or anti-tragic protagonists to consider. There is the Jewish Dulcie Feinstein, who makes a gradual journey away from her liberated father's obsessive attachment to the Enlightenment and eventually embraces her destiny as an Orthodox wife and mother. There is the Christian Mrs Poulter, who comes to "believe" in Arthur after Waldo dies. This "belief" can be understood in two ways: as the "death" of her God, or as a shift from "high" christology (a focus on Christ's divinity) to "low" christology (a focus on Christ's humanity). The latter is a post-Vatican II way of expressing her shift from transcendence to immanence.[22]

Is *The Vivisector* (1970) a tragedy? The innately artistic Hurtle is born into a poor family and adopted by a wealthy family. While he finds inspiration in his new home, he eventually becomes disillusioned. He serves in World War I. After the war, he reclaims his birth name, but avoids his birth family, and is obsessed with becoming an artist. At different times, he has relationships with a prostitute (Nance), with an heiress (Olivia–Boo), with the eponymous wife ("tragic" Hero) of a Greek magnate (Cosma), and with a talented teenager (Kathy). Finally, he is reunited with his adopted sister (Rhoda); a pythoness–oracle who does not speak; a dionysian–chthonic archetype he loves and hates.

Beneath their child-like, good-natured, and benevolent exteriors, Hero and Cosma are selfish fatalists who treat others as a disposable commodity.

---

[21] At some point in his life, Waldo went from being an apollonian trope to being a socratic trope, after which his future was fated. When was that turning point?

[22] Vatican II (1962–1965) caught many metaphysical or "religious" authors offguard, as it was trying to address many of their concerns. In this case, Vatican II was unfolding at the same time *The Solid Manadala* was being conceptualized and written.

While living in Sydney they adopt then discard an Aboriginal child, have cats drowned in bags, and keep alive a suffering dog dying of cancer. Hero leaves Cosma for Hurtle. The couple make a kind of pilgrimage to Greece, where "tragic" Hero hopes to reclaim a spiritual connectedness, nurtured by the idea of Greek soteria, which turns out to be a transcendental illusion. Is Hurtle's relationship with "tragic" Hero White's commentary on tragedy? If he were to stay with "tragic" Hero, rather than leave her in Greece, she would have destroyed him, in the same way Arabella Don destroyed Jude Fawley. He would never have returned home to be reunited with Rhoda.

Is *The Eye of the Storm* (1973) a tragedy? Again, the question is deceptive. In the novel, White obviously adapts themes from *King Lear*; however, just as a No case can be made for *The Solid Mandala*'s reworking of *The Birth of Tragedy*, a No case can be made for *The Eye of the Storm*'s reworking of Shakespeare. The action of the novel flows from an unhappy marriage between Elizabeth (nature = mythos) and Alfred (civilization = logos) which produces two Hellenic metaphors; Basil, the tragic hero, who leaves Australia and becomes a famous actor, and Dorothy, the exiled soul, who leaves Australia and becomes a failed princess. In *The Eye of the Storm*—as in *The Solid Mandala*—White follows Paglia in presenting tragedy as a male apollonian construction that will always fail against the dionysian, chthonic, female power of nature. Nature cannot be tragic. It can only be nature.

Is *The Twyborn Affair* (1978) a tragedy? In his last novel, White continues to comment on tragedy through recurring themes: Deleuze's interrelated effects of modernism, Jung's archetypal masculine and feminine, the tension between the Old World and the Antipodes, Spengler's cyclic model of civilization, and the disintegration of Europe. Part I is set in France, on the eve of World War I, where the Australian protagonist is living as a young woman (emblematic of the antipodean version of the new world) "married" to a dying geriatric Greek (emblematic of the Old World). She tries to escape from this "existential" dilemma by diving into the ocean, intending to swim to her death, but laughs at her tragic pose. Realizing she is a strong swimmer, and an "amateur suicide", she returns to shore snoozing "through healing water". The war approaches, her "husband" dies, she becomes a man again, and enlists as a soldier.

Part II is set in Australia, after the war, where the protagonist, now a decorated soldier, tries to live as a man again without success. Part III is set in England—during the 1930s—where the protagonist is living as a woman again, now the madam of a brothel. Towards the end of the novel she visits a country estate, where the shallowness of the dying Old World is on display, and where she "blew a fart" at "every spurious work of art", including herself. Near the end of the novel, she meets her estranged Australian mother on a bench outside an English cathedral.[23] They resolve to return to Sydney, and work on their relationship, but this is not to be. After changing her sexual personae once again, the protagonist is killed by a bomb, during the Blitz, on his way to his mother's hotel. Is this tragedy or something else? The question is open.

If White is ambiguous about tragedy, and if he uses comedy to resolve that ambiguity, there needs to be as much discussion about his relationship with comedy as tragedy. This is particularly important for Jewish and Christian readers, for whom the question of tragedy is often confused with the question of theodicy: the attempt to answer the question of why a God who is good permits evil and suffering. After World War II, there is no longer a consensus that tragedy, God, and theodicy are interchangeable.

Among many Jewish theologians, theodicy is regarded as blasphemous and immoral, and perhaps the source of all immorality, since humans are not called upon to justify God in the face of evil; rather, they should concentrate on loving God while living according to the Torah. Many Christian theologians hold similar views, which propose that speculating about theodicy merely legitimates evil and suffering and may even add to them. Karl Barth took the view that—as the evil of human suffering is ultimately a matter of divine providence—only the Crucifixion establishes the idea of God's goodness.

If this territory is foreign to the majority of White's critics, it is the territory we need to explore if we want to understand his work. White's agon is not whether God exists—since he was a believer—it is how to describe God through art in an age where God's death is widely assumed and language—the "rocks and sticks of words"—is a limited means of communication.

There seems to be an assumption, particularly among those who argue the Yes case in favour of modern tragedy, that before God's death was proclaimed, the truth-claims of art driven by analogical theories—or correspondence and coherence theories—were accepted as an influential cultural currency. For example, the frescoes of Giotto and Michaelangelo were compelling because they represented an age of belief that either made them compelling or allowed them to be compelling. We do not live

---

[23] Significantly, White reconciles mother and son outside a Church. They communicate through a 1662 *Book of Common Prayer*. In a sense, their reunion is an answer to prayer.

in this age. The question of White and tragedy–comedy is always a question about his agon, within the genres he moved among, and the limits of what those genres allowed him to accomplish.

CHAPTER TWO

RIDERS

Logos and Mythos

In May 1959, White wrote to Ben Huebsch, his loyal Jewish publisher in New York, advising he had completed about three-quarters of an early draft of *Riders in the Chariot*. In writing the draft, he was beginning to wonder whether it was a mistake attempting to portray a Jew in any depth; however, drawing the other three protagonists was helping him to understand Himmelfarb, as was studying the Talmud, Kabbalah, and other Jewish texts:

> What I want to emphasize through my four "Riders"—an orthodox refugee intellectual Jew, a mad Erdgeist of an Australian spinster, an evangelical laundress, and a half-caste aboriginal painter—is that all faiths, whether religious, humanistic, instinctive, or the creative artist's act of praise, are in fact one. The half-caste aboriginal, who is diseased and degraded as a human being, will perhaps be the real test—whether I can make his creative genius strong and convincing enough. That is something—and nothing of the book! Even so, it is more than I like to tell, so I would rather you keep it to yourself (Marr 1994, 152–153).

Notice how White links the terms faith and religion with humanism, instinct, and the creative artist's "act of praise". While he sees these terms as part of the same oneness or unity, his understanding of what they mean is selective. He excludes definitions that, if they are not anti-romantic, are nevertheless cautious about the claims romanticism makes on behalf of faith, religion, humanism, instinct, and the romantic image of the artist as inspired.

As *Riders in the Chariot* is a perfect example of what Atwood means by the shadow of romanticism, it is best understood in relation to what Gadamer means by romantic hermeneutics. One clue about White's relationship with romantic hermeneutics comes from the novel's epigraph, an excerpt from Blake's *The Marriage of Heaven and Hell* (1790–1793), where Isaiah admits to experiencing the infinite in everything, and Ezekiel admits to a desire to raise humanity to a perception of the infinite. Notice White has chosen an excerpt where Blake puts words in the mouths of two prophets for his own rhetorical purposes. They are not the words of the scriptural Isaiah and Ezekiel. This distinction is necessary. Scripture is interpreted by living faith communities not by an inspired artist who thinks he or she knows more than the Church.

Blake's poem offers a theory of contraries, divine and human, which immediately places him at odds with Benedict XVI. He takes the voluntarist view,[1] one that allows God the freedom to have a contrary nature if he chooses to. Blake believes each person reflects God's contrary nature and their progression in life depends upon these contraries. This is a personal and highly idiosyncratic take on the traditional Jewish and Christian belief that humanity is made in the divine image (*imago dei*).

Because of his view of God's contrary nature, Blake believes there are two types of persons, rational organizers (angels) and energetic creators (devils), who have clearly assigned roles within the rationalism–empiricism debate. In this scheme of things, it is presumably more urgent that the angel type gets in touch with its inner devil (reason needs to be balanced by feeling), and less urgent that the devil type gets in touch with its inner angel (feeling needs to be balanced by reason), since Blake's argument, and the whole thrust of romantic hermeneutics, revolves around the idea that reason's hegemony has had a negative effect on the western mind and the civilization it has produced.

In *All Religions Are One* (1794), Blake offers the notion of poetic genius, "which by the Ancients was call'd an Angel and Spirit and Demon", where the imagination becomes an all-purpose replacement for the systematic theology, ecclesiological structures, and clerical mediation of institutional religion. He believes that all humans are alike in their poetic genius; and, as all religions originate with poetic genius, even the Jewish and Christian Testaments, all religions are therefore one and the same. This logic, which is fallacious, argues for the primacy of the poetic imagination over metaphysical and moral systems, especially those mediated by institutional religion and its clerics.

In *There Is No Natural Religion* (1794), Blake offers two series of aphorisms that intentionally contradict each other. In Series A, which advocates an extreme or one-sided empiricism, he says man is purely physical and limited to that physicality. In Series B, he refutes this

---

[1] For different reasons, Benedict and his influential non-binary opponents, such as Deleuze, both trace the rise of this voluntarism to Duns Scotus.

extreme empiricism, by proposing a form of rationalism: "the ratio of all we have already known", whereby humans can perceive what lies beyond immediate empirical experience. Also, he argues against the contemporary idea of "natural" religion, as a contradiction in terms, since religion must be "revealed" not by the senses but by an imaginative "revelation" of poetic genius. He never tells us the proportions he assigns to rationalism and empiricism in this poetic "revelation" but we know they are not an equal 50:50. Guessing these proportions is important, as they would allow us to know where to locate him along the neoclassicism–romanticism spectrum.

Some critics believe Blake's concession to reason, as part of the "ratio" of "all we have already known", makes him proto-romantic rather than romantic. This suggests that the boundaries between neoclassicism and romanticism are fluid and cannot be dogmatically defined. The two movements are obverse sides of the same metaphysical coin. Both are extensions of the "old quarrel" between philosophy and poetry, transformed into dialectical–archetypal tensions between neoclassicism's focus on rationalism (reason) and romanticism's focus on empiricism (feeling).

Within romantic hermeneutics, the "old quarrel" has always been about the respective truth claims of Plato's rational mind (analogous with the head), and spirited mind (analogous with the heart), and the ever present danger of corruption by the appetitive mind (analogous with the lower abdomen). It was within this mental territory that rationalists and empiricists conducted their 19th and 20th century debates over spirit and matter, transcendence and immanence, or good and evil. These debates were always complex, because the traditional domains of rational mind, spirited mind, and appetitive mind were mental parts of Plato's tripartite model of the mind, in which "the mind" is synonymous with "the soul". Further, their relationships with the physical body and the material world were always understood to be analogous within correspondence and coherence theories of knowledge and truth.

Blake uses the "old quarrel" to conduct a wide-ranging critique of conventional morality, similar to the critique Nietzsche would later conduct under the banner of revaluation (transvaluation) of values, and both men were involved in a similar beyond good and evil manoeuvre (Southwell 2009, 104). Blake believes we need to balance our rational angels and our empirical devils; however, he uses the term "devil" in a positive "daemonic" sense, rather than a negative "demonic" sense. Like many of his contemporaries, and successors, he believes Christianity is responsible for "demonizing" the "daemonic". This is one reason why he was reverent towards the Bible but hostile towards institutional religion. Nietzsche was of a similar view, but his atheistic critique of reason was more radical than Blake's theistic critique, as was his rejection of objective truth and western religion. Jung was of a similar view as Blake, which may explain why he psychologized the Trinity as a quaternity and made the Devil (Evil) its fourth person (Jung 2009).[2]

White's religious sense owes more to Blake, as both men were theists rather than deists and panentheists rather than pantheists. He grew up in the Anglican Church. Like many people, he maintained a passionate interest in the Church, even after lapsing. Ultimately, however, his attitude towards reason was much more Nietzschean. This heightens the conflict we see in his work, between Blake's positive understanding of authentic religious experience and Nietzsche's negative understanding of reason.

Patricia Morley begins *The Mystery of Unity* (1972) thus:

> The view of man and his world which underlies White's novels is religious in its basic orientation. His heroes are seeking the true permanence or unchanging structure beneath the illusory flux, the true freedom which is valid even beyond physical death. All his novels testify to the reality of another world, not outside this one but inside, "wholly within," as stated in the first two epigraphs to *The Solid Mandala*. And essential to White's vision is the affirmation that this other or spiritual world is immanent in our natural one, *as well as* transcendent to it. William Blake found God in a grain of sand; White finds him in a gob of spittle, or a table. Like Pierre Teilhard de Chardin, White views matter as something good, something inherently spiritual, not opposed to spirit, as the ancient Greeks conceived it to be …
>
> His novels examine such problems as the meaning of suffering and the possibilities of salvation and atonement for evil. His basic concerns, that is, are theological, but existential rather than dogmatic in approach. Like Dostoyevsky, White believes that suffering is a necessary route to spiritual progress, beneficial both to the individual who suffers and to those involved in the suffering. The idea of the movement into the world and back to faith which we find in White's novels also underlies much of Dostoyevsky's writing. Indeed, much of White's work shows the influence of both Dostoyevsky and Tolstoy; and, like the works of these writers, it has received more recognition outside his own country than within. His vision is not original but traditional, an expression of the Judaeo-Christian cultural heritage from which it flowers (italics added) (1972, 1–2).

---

[2] This is one reason why Jungianism is incompatible with Christianity. Many critics have attempted "religious" readings of White but failed. Some of them, on discovering Jung, found what they thought to be the perfect substitute for religion and master key to White. However, their Jungian interpretations are ultimately psychological rather than religious. Even within psychology, Jung is mythopoeic rather than "scientific".

Morley, a Canadian, expressed this view before *The Eye of the Storm* (1973) and *The Twyborn Affair* (1978), but I believe it applies to those novels as well as to *Memoirs of Many in One* (1986) and *Three Uneasy Pieces* (1987).

For many reasons, the view that White's religious vision is compatible with the west's Judaeo-Christian cultural heritage is difficult for most critics to accept. Such a view challenges a range of influential assumptions about the secularizing character of romanticism, modernism, and postmodernism. His affirmation that the spiritual world is immanent within the natural world, as well as transcendent to it, is not easily understood. It has tended to be approached through the work of non-binary thinkers, such as Deleuze, and is therefore difficult to disentangle from critiques of binary thought. Also, there is a powerful but erroneous assumption that Judaism and Christianity are pro-transcendence and anti-immanence. As a result, secular critics tend to pit transcendence and immanence against each other in ways that are false. What this adds up to is a widespread inability to understand the theological implications of God's death, and negative (apophatic) theology generally.

McCulloch makes an important point about White's romanticism:

> White's elected characters are poet-seers, gifted with a peculiar insight into the nature of reality. His symbolist experiment consists in exploring the possibilities for the ideal poet-seer who may perhaps, at last, be the vehicle towards perfect artistic expression, thus rescuing man from the metaphysical void of his culture. White's process towards "knowledge" becomes not primarily a process of the artist's making, but rather a process of the artist's discovering the ultimate frontiers of human existence. White becomes a kind of "priest". Indeed, said Riviere, when commenting on twentieth century romanticism, this whole literature is "a vast incantation towards the miracle".
>
> White is attempting to celebrate this world which is within the visible one as well as to discover that ultimate symbol or language that could unlock and penetrate the mere appearance of things. Like Blake, White believes that, if the doors of perception were cleansed, everything would appear to man as it is, that is infinite (4).

The doors of perception cannot be cleansed, and the infinite in everything cannot be perceived, until Blake and White realize their shared philosophical and aesthetic concerns. Although Blake is more positive about the possibility of cleansing, and White is more negative, they both face a similar problem. The logic of their shared concerns belongs within the shadow of romanticism as a particular phase of western consciousness. As Benedict reminds us, however, the shadow of romanticism—which is essentially a post-Kantian fragmentation of subjectivities and relativisms—

does not have a monopoly on universal significance.

There is a connection between the novel's epigraph from *The Marriage of Heaven and Hell* and the novel's title, which refers to Ezekiel's two throne–chariot visions in the Hebrew Bible (Ezekiel 1:4–28 and Ezekiel 10:1–22). The context here is an ancient historical event that occurred during the 6th century BC. Jerusalem has fallen, the First Temple has been destroyed, and a large proportion of Israel—but not all of Israel—has been exiled to Babylon. These two throne–chariot visions are part of Ezekiel's prophetic purpose. First, to explain why God did not keep his promise to protect the earthly Zion, because Israel had failed to fulfil her covenantal obligations. Second, to remind Israel that, in spite of this, God will keep his eternal promises to her in exile.[3]

Both visions of the throne–chariot represent transcendent realities. They are revelations of God's glory within a heavenly Zion. Also, the visions are twice mediated. The prophet sees them through an imaginative veil and then conveys them to the people. Because the visions are doubly veiled—not given to the prophet directly, not given to the people directly—they are beyond the purview of the rationalism–empiricism debate. This is a feature of revelation generally.

Instead of being plot-driven, *Riders in the Chariot* is about the interior lives of its four protagonists, which are determined by the horizons White gives them. These horizons qualify them to be riders, because he sees them as genuine representatives of the varieties of religious experience, as he understood them. The novel is not only about the protagonists, however; it is a snapshot of the battle between good and evil within secular, materialistic Australia at a specific historical moment. The snapshot was not always recognizable to—or appreciated by—the novel's first generation of readers and critics. It was not the Australia they identified with and wanted to see portrayed in literature. Also, because Australia has changed dramatically, the snapshot has become less recognizable over time. Nevertheless, it is a faithfully realized picture of the Australia White saw and understood.

In giving the novel form and content, White bought into the influential romantic idea that authentic religious experience is located within the realm of feeling (mythos) rather than the realm of reason (logos). As romanticism evolved, this idea has come to us systematized in many overlapping ways, all of which describe the "conquest" of mythos by logos and desire the "restoration" of what logos is supposed to have

---

[3] Himmelfarb was not a Zionist. He reminds us of the different covenant promises God makes to his chosen people, with regard to the Diaspora, and the Holy Land.

suppressed (Gadamer 1960, 285). Noticing White's attempt to reclaim the religious authority of mythos is not to judge his attempt as right or wrong—although Benedict reminds us that logos also has a strong claim to religious authority—it is simply locating him within his context.

Unfortunately, critics tend to treat all of White's "visionaries"—or what McCulloch calls his "poet-seers"—as the same and make no mythological or metaphorical distinction between them. This approach is self-limiting, as each poet-seer is paradigmatically different from the others. White intended these differences to be noticed, which is why we should notice them. Also, in his "religious" novels, he narrates the different stories of these paradigmatic horizons chronologically, as they appeared in history. Mary Hare's Theogonic horizon comes first, Norbert Hare's Hellenic horizon comes second,[4] Mordecai Himmelfarb's Jewish version of the adamic horizon comes third,[5] and Ruth Godbold's Christian version of the adamic horizon comes fourth.

Alf Dubbo's horizon comes last, as he is half-Aboriginal and half-Celtic. His hybrid horizon presents a challenge for postcolonial critics. Questions about this must be asked. Is there an ontologically distinct indigenous horizon, standing apart from logos and mythos or from the Theogonic, Hellenic, and Hebraic metaphors? Is Dubbo's portrayal a flaw in White's attempt to articulate a universal discourse? These questions will be discussed later in this chapter.

The novel is set in and around White's iconic Sarsaparilla and nearby Barranugli (barren + ugly). Sarsaparilla was called Durilgai towards the end of *The Tree of Man* but the landscape had no name when the Parkers first settled there early in the novel. While this landscape was once indigenous—and while White anticipated aspects of postcolonialism—it was never his intention to critique the displacement of an indigenous horizon from Sarsaparilla. It was to critique the European horizons that colonized the landscape, which came to be called Durilgai, then Sarsaparilla, on its journey from bush to suburb. Without intending disrespect to the original inhabitants of the land, this is a mental landscape in a metaphysical novel—an imaginative topos—where White's characters conduct their rhetorical dialogues.

---

[4] Norbert is not a rider for the same or a similar reason Waldo is excluded from Arthur's dream and dance in *The Solid Mandala*.

[5] In this genre, there is a tendency to treat the horizon of ancient Greece as older than the horizon of ancient Israel, although both horizons evolved in parallel.

Mary Hare

The "mad Erdgeist of an Australian spinster", Mary Hare, is central to the novel's Gadamerian frame, and to the Ricoeurean anthropology within the frame. White begins her story just after World War II, with an already old and frail Mary posting a letter, before describing her early life. Her story ends several years later, not long after her disappearance into the aether. Notice that she does not die. An Erdgeist cannot die. It can only be reabsorbed.

What does Mary signify? Given her red hair, we can say with certainty that she signifies mythos at its most elemental level; however, mythos is an expansive category that signifies many things, and red-hair comes in many shades, including strawberry blond, pink, and lilac. She has precursors and successors in the earlier and later novels. Most noticeably these are Theodora Goodman in *The Aunt's Story*, Arthur Brown in *The Solid Mandala*, Rhoda Courtney in *The Vivisector*, Elizabeth Hunter and Flora Manhood in *The Eye of the Storm*, and all red-haired protagonists in White's novels up to and including Eddie Twyborn in *The Twyborn Affair*. If there is an overarching mythos across his novels, it varies from novel to novel. While they have shared characteristics, each of these protagonists is unique. No single explanation describes them all. Also, while I often call them tropes, I do not associate them with any particular theory of tropes (Maurin 2014).

There are many comparisons as well as contrasts between Mary and other red-haired protagonists in the postwar novels of White's contemporaries: including Dora Greenfield in Murdoch's *The Bell* (1958), January Marlow in Spark's *Robinson* (1958), and Mary Dempster in Davies's *Fifth Business* (1970). As we consider what these novelists are doing with these red-haired protagonists—and they are doing similar but not the same things—we are entitled to ask an obvious question: Does Mary represent a variety of religious experience? The answer is yes if we accept the logic of White's rhetoric and no if we do not. If he tells us a mixture of truths and lies, like Spark, his truths may be lies and his lies may be truths.

Why is Mary thought to be "mad"? If not all red-haired tropes are mad, each has the potential to go mad, like the submerged red-haired Pre-Raphaelite subject of Millais's *Ophelia*. And this madness—or potential for madness—has a particular significance in the novel where logos signifies the word or reason and mythos signifies the irrational or non-rational. In his influential *Madness and Civilization* (1961), Foucault proposes that madness is a social construct. In his scheme, before the

Enlightenment, the mad were thought to bear holy fool wisdom or subjugated knowledges. However, during the Enlightenment, with its emphasis on reason, the mad were understood as irrational and therefore in need of confinement and correction. Similarly, in *The Politics of Experience* and *The Bird of Paradise* (1967), Laing takes a romantic view and sees the "mad" as explorers of an inner world. He presents psychosis not as clinical disorder but as social difference: "a psychedelic voyage of discovery in which the boundaries of perception were widened, and consciousness expanded". Likewise, as part of his *critique et clinique* project, Deleuze 1997 draws a long bow, arguing that certain literary authors—such as Lawrence, Miller, Kerouac, Burroughs, Artaud, and Beckett—know more about schizophrenia than psychiatrists and psychoanalysts (xxi).

The literary tradition of madness supports Foucault, Laing, and Deleuze. Mad characters are defined by a romantic–modernist view of irrational mythos. Sane characters are defined by a classical–neoclassical view of rational logos. This tradition can only be influential, in and beyond literature, as long as the cause of madness is located within Plato's tripartite model of the mind, which we see in both *The Republic* and *Phaedrus*. Until relatively recently, this model of mind underpinned the psychoanalytical tradition—of the Freudian and Jungian schools—and the Platonic view of madness generally (Griswold 1986, 74–137; Nussbaum 1986, 200–233).

However, the literary view, the model of mind, and the psychoanalytical tradition, are no longer relevant in contemporary brain science. Clinical views of mental illness have broadened. So, as far as madness is concerned, the gap between literature and life is widening. In the 21st century, Foucault is not used as a diagnostic tool, and Deleuze is irrelevant to the clinical treatment flowing from brain science.

Within contemporary psychiatry the term "madness" is vague, emotive, and no longer appropriate. The broad categories of mental illness are now described in more concrete terms, including bipolar disorder, schizophrenia, psychosis, depression, and anxiety disorders. Some of these illnesses may have a cultural component. Some may be socially-constructed. For example, neuroses and phobias occur some societies but not in others. However, most mental illness is understood to have biological and/or genetic causes, rather than sociological and/or metaphysical causes. Bipolar disorder and schizophrenia are not socially constructed.

As mythos, Mary's Theogonic dilemma is her father's logos, specifically her inability to understand his Hellenic metaphors. In Norbert, who belongs to what White calls "That Class" (17), White is questioning a neoclassical–romantic civilization where mythos had been idealized to the point where it no longer represented Mary's archetypal–metaphysical reality. Norbert built an estate, Xanadu, a stately pleasure-dome like the one decreed by Coleridge's *Kubla Khan* (1816). While it is stately and pleasing, to Norbert, it is a folly not in harmony with the surrounding landscape (nature). In an archetypal sense, this landscape belongs to the deformed and ugly Mary, because of who she is and what she represents.

By simply existing, Theogonic Mary is constantly reminding her Hellenic father of the "shadow" he has been "dogging" all his life. Rather than engage with this reminder, of what he does not want to acknowledge, and rather than effectively manage his estate, he prefers to squander his substantial inheritance. Whenever his imaginative order is challenged, he buys another symbol of neoclassical–romantic civilization, which he installs at Xanadu: "In that way he was fortified", the narrators says, and "not unlike a traveller walking into a landscape which may prove a mirage" (30).

As Theogonic mythos, Mary has illumination but no language; that is, she does not have the language to describe her affinity with nature or her unified vision of matter and spirit. As Hellenic logos, Norbert has language but no illumination. He suspects his daughter has glimpses of things he cannot see, like the chariot and its riders. She becomes a constant reminder that his Hellenic metaphors, with their myths of tragic hero and exiled soul, are failing to protect him. He gradually descends into madness, but this descent is comic rather than tragic, as White was of the view that tragedy could always be given the red nose of a clown.

In subverting the conventions of tragedy, by giving them a red nose, White is revealing his tragicomic sense, which is widely recognized but difficult to place in a particular theoretical frame; there being many such frames. In *Poetics* (c.335 BC), Aristotle kept tragedy and comedy in separate domains. He regarded tragedy as "a representation of an action of a superior kind—grand, and complete in itself—presented in embellished language, in distinct forms" with six parts: the story or plot, the moral element, the style, the ideas, the staging, and the music (23). He regarded comedy as the "representation of people who are inferior but not wholly vicious" (22), the ridiculous being one category of the embarrassing, and what is ridiculous is "some error or embarrassment that is neither painful nor life threatening" (22).

Norbert fits Aristotle's definition of comic, as he is inferior without being vicious and ridiculous without being painful or life-threatening. He does not fit Aristotle's definition of tragedy, since his story is comic rather than tragic, and because he is not a tragic hero, even though the myths of the tragic hero and exiled soul are behind his Hellenic metaphors. His life is misguided, without being tragic, as his pragmatic pastoralist cousin Ted observes when visiting the beautiful but useless Xanadu, which was never intended to be a going concern: "What becomes of all this flummery when Bert has blown the cash?" (25) If we are meant to see Norbert as absurd, which brings the tragicomic into the modernist and postmodernist realm, elsewhere in White's novels, we find comic characters who are inferior and vicious as well as ridiculous and life-threatening.

Mary offers to take the blame for her Theogonic metaphors, and for the failure of her father's Hellenic metaphors, but he knows he will never be free, having long since regarded her with hate "for what she saw and understood". So, Norbert tries to commit suicide by jumping into a cistern. He cries for help but refuses to be saved by Mary, who is holding out a pole to him: "Although rigid, her pole was merciful, but he warded it off with his hands."

In Freud's typology of ego differentiation as a defence mechanism, the parent–child relationship is "represented in countless dreams by pulling out of the water or rescue from the water" signifying amniotic fluid (Freud 1964, 12). White seems to have known about this motif. Norbert is a failed hero, in the tragic sense. Could Mary become another kind of hero, as according to Freud "a hero is someone who has had the courage to rebel against his father and has in the end victoriously overcome him"? (12) No, she cannot, as there are no heroes in White's novels, tragic or otherwise. As she looks at her dead father, she sees herself reflected in his "gaze", to use an existentialist term, and realizes for the first time "how very similar his expression was to her own" (73). So, father and daughter belong to the same metaphysical as well as physical family. Logos and mythos are related, as opposites, in dialectical and archetypal senses.

Mary, the economically poor but archetypally rich mythos, inherits the decaying metaphor of Xanadu, and lives among the dilapidations of her father's logos, supported by a small annuity from her Cousin Eustace in Britain. In her old age, after World War II, she is forced to advertise for a live-in companion, as she is frail and cannot care for herself. The position is filled by the eponymous Mrs Jolley, a widow with no sense of humour, through whom White satirizes a range of what are to him negative aspects of the Australian character. She is a typical example of what he sees as a shallow Australian who shies away from "the deep end of the unconscious". She lacks self-awareness, is anti-intellectual, non-spiritual, and bigoted. She goes to Church but is not authentically "religious" in White's terms. She is also evil, having somehow facilitated her husband's death, which her family suspects, hence she is forced to live apart from them in exile. They do not want her around.

Once Mrs Jolley is installed at Xanadu, White begins to populate his Gadamerian frame with the kind of Ricoeurean anthropology we find in *La Symbolique du Mal*. Mary meets Alf Dubbo, for the first time, fleetingly, in the bush. While they rarely encounter each other during the novel, their first encounter establishes their communion as similar horizons, fleeting though it is:

> Both the illuminates remained peacefully enfolded inside the envelopes of their flesh. Each knew it was improbable they would ever communicate in words. Yet they had exchanged a token of goodness which would remain for ever in each other's keeping. From behind closed eyelids each would have recognized the other as an apostle of truth. And that was enough (80).

Soon after this fleeting encounter, Mary recalls her first encounter with Mrs Godbold, who saved her life one winter, during the war, nursing her through a bout of pneumonia (82). After Mary recovered, she ventured to ask Mrs Godbold whether they had shared any confidences about the chariot while she was delirious. Mrs Godbold is shy and evasive: "Some people," she said, "get funny ideas when they are sick" (85). Mary is not deceived, however, "and remained convinced they would continue to share a secret, after her friend had returned to carry out her life sentence of love and labour in the shed below the post office" (85).

After the story of Mary's horizon is told, White segues, neatly and schematically, to the next horizon in his chronology, which belongs to Himmelfarb. These two protagonists meet in Mary's garden, under a tree, similar to Arthur's dream–tree in *The Solid Mandala*. Although this is their first encounter, she makes "little grunting sounds of happiness and recognition" (113) while gesturing to her garden: "This," she said, "is what I am really interested in … All these things … are what I understand" (117). Himmelfarb is empathic and polite. However, as his Hebraic metaphors and their adamic myth are paradigmatically different from her Theogonic metaphors and their myths of chaos and creation, he admits "it is still difficult" for Jews to appreciate her horizon "except in theory" (117).

Hence their different perspectives of a dying plum blossom, which for Himmelfarb is "almost finished" yet for Mary "is only beginning" a cycle of birth and death and rebirth, as the flower dies to bear fruit, which will sometimes be "full of worms". Mary accepts "the essential mystery and glory" of decay, even decay of "the putrid human kind", as decay does "not necessarily mean an end" (122). The God of Israel has led Himmelfarb to another paradigm entirely. What separates Himmelfarb from Mary is revelation, which some refer to positively as the revealed-in-language, and others refer to negatively as logocentrism. Although they are paradigmatically distinct, there is a high level of goodwill between them. He acknowledges they are "mathematically and morally" equal (121), thus he is simultaneously attracted to and repelled by "this mad, botched creature" who "might subject him to the thumbscrews and touch him with feathers at one and the same time" (121). This is one of many examples where White has a higher view of Jewish revelation than Nietzsche.

Later in the novel, Mary expresses concern for Himmelfarb's safety, after Mrs Jolley leaves Xanadu and moves in with Mrs Flack. She senses the evil these two women represent will converge, which is true. The result is an antisemitic mission, which ends in Himmelfarb's mock crucifixion in Barranugli and death in Sarsaparilla. When Mary discovers Himmelfarb is untroubled by this looming danger, she becomes upset and remonstrates with him: "I am responsible for you!" (395).

To what is White alluding, when Mary claims to be responsible for Himmelfarb? Is it an allusion to the primacy of process metaphysics over event metaphysics, or the superiority of oral culture over written culture, or to the polytheistic origins of monotheism, or the Theogonic origins of Judaism, as those origins were understood within romantic hermeneutics? If so, how does the allusion fit in with White's claim to be non-theoretical? In Mary we can see an evolving inheritance through a broad range of contributors to White's zeitgeist: Blake's *The Marriage of Heaven and Hell*, Nietzsche's *The Birth of Tragedy*, Frazer's *The Golden Bough*, Harrison's *Prolegomena to the Study of Greek Religion*, Cornford's *From Religion to Philosophy*, Heidegger's *Being and Time* (1927), Whitehead's *Process and Reality*, and a host of others. There is a bit of this, a bit of that, but it adds up to a kind of theory, a kind of system.

Mordecai Himmelfarb

As White made what he called a "thorough" study of Judaism before writing *Riders in the Chariot* (White 1989, 19), the novel's Jewish horizon did not erupt from his unconscious, against his will, or beyond his control. His description of the Jewish horizon must have been successful, as it has been the subject of Jewish scholarship in Israel (Ben-Bassat 1990) and praise from Jewish readers: one of whom has commented "How does this man know it all? He has written what I thought nobody but me and my kind could possibly know and with the understanding of a god" (Joyce 1991, 125).

Mordecai Himmelfarb represents the adamic myth and its Hebraic metaphors. However, White wants us to know that for much of Mordecai's life he was disconnected from those myths and metaphors. Why? To answer that question, we need to be aware of the historical specificity of White's Jewish characters in relation to a significant tension within European Judaism for much of the 19th and 20th century.

White's Jewish characters are always Ashkenazim. The most consistent and significant feature of his attitude towards them is his sense of their folly should they embrace the neoclassical Enlightenment. Whether he knew much about the Haskalah, the Jewish Enlightenment, and its relationship with neoclassicism (Feiner 2004) and romanticism (Litvak 2012), is not directly relevant here. Both movements were focused on reason. His critique was a critique of reason.

The Haskalah was a major driver in the secularization of Jewish culture and the kind of Zionism—focused on the Holy Land rather than the Torah—which eventually led to the creation of the State of Israel (Boyarin 2015). As far as White was concerned, the Enlightenment threatened Jewish identity as a covenant people. If this threat does not seem logical to us, from a 21st century perspective, including a 21st century Jewish perspective, it was an organic part of his critique of reason within romantic hermeneutics.

White's Jewish characters of the 1960s and 1970s do have a precursor in *The Living and the Dead* (1941). In an archetypal sense, Muriel Raphael is associated with "Jerusalem", just as Elyot Standish is associated with "Athens"; however, their archetypal associations, including their initial attraction and eventual separation, are vaguely implied and have nothing of the religious intensity of the later novels (Giffin 1999, 130–134). Like his contemporaries, White did not refine his archetypal sense of the varieties of religious experience until the postwar period, around the time Ricoeur was developing his anthropology in *The Symbolism of Evil*.

Himmelfarb's dilemma, prefigured in Muriel's relationship with Elyot, was logical to White, and logical within romantic hermeneutics generally. If the dilemma is harder for us to recognize, in the 21st century, it is because the dilemma is increasingly foreign to us on an academic as well as a cultural level. On the academic level, Jewish and Christian academics now have a much stronger (Maimonidean) sense of the ways in which the Jewish mind was influenced by the Greek mind during the Hellenistic Period (323–31 BC). As a result of this scholarship—in biblical studies, systematic theology, and religious history—it is no longer useful to make rigid or antithetical distinctions between reason and revelation.

Bloom 1989 was right when he suggested that:

> Western conceptualization is Greek, and yet Western religion, however

conceptualized, is not (147).

Bloom proposes that the west has always lived with a distinction between the Greek sphere of philosophy and the Jewish sphere of religion. This seductive and influential proposal operates on many levels; from assuming that Jerusalem was always hostile to Athens; to assuming that Christianity was only able to become a universal religion once it left the confines of Jerusalem and embraced the universalizing potential of Greek thought; to assuming that the sociopolitical character of the west owes more to Athens than it owes to Jerusalem; to assuming that the modern Enlightenment was a gift from Athens, imposed unwillingly upon Jerusalem, rather than a gift from Jerusalem itself. While all of these assumptions are now moot, Bloom is expressing a view that was influential in the 20th century.

Because White associates revelation with mythos rather than logos, he makes romantic distinctions between reason and revelation that, because of advances in Jewish and Christian scholarship, are neither fashionable nor feasible. Judging from the way his "Jewish" novels operate, he could not see the Enlightenment as a viable option for religious Jews, just as he could not see the Enlightenment as a viable option for committed Christians. Was he right or wrong? We cannot answer that question conclusively, as long as the drama of the Enlightenment is still being acted out. We can only say he had a particular attitude towards reason consistent with romantic hermeneutics. His critique of reason led him to emphasize the Jewish diaspora tradition, and the Babylonian Talmud that articulates–interprets that tradition (Boyarin 2015), in ways that outweighed more recent Zionist emphases on the Holy Land.

Ben-Bassat (1990) believes White uses a multi-faceted ironic strategy, to present a vast array of seemingly contradictory ideas, and Himmelfarb's "quest for healing the rift between earth and spirit by ultimately realizing his spiritual ideals in acts of flesh and blood" is the leitmotif that unifies that strategy. She demonstrates this with an analysis of Himmelfarb's development as a protagonist which focuses on two points.

First, more than the Old and New Testament sources, Kabbalistic texts account for the novel's central imagery; the insistent myth of the exile and ingathering of the sparks, the implied allegory of the four who entered the orchard (Pardes in Hebrew), the symbols of the cutting of the shoots and the archetype of Adam Kadmon (Primordial Man). Second, Hasidic Kabbalistic models furnished White with a time-honoured way of fusing the mystic layer of the quest for integrating the sparks with the moral layer of the quest for reconstructing human relations.

This makes sense. Of the four riders, White makes Himmelfarb's development the strongest—philosophically and aesthetically—strong enough to unite the four riders. As Ben-Bassat argues: "From the perspective of Christianity, imprisonment within the finite can only be viewed as a failure"; as a result, "The novel forces on the reader the riddle of how its protagonists nevertheless reconcile their infinite yearnings with finite fulfilment." This is certainly true, as long as we accept the "infinite yearnings" of each poet-seer as paradigmatically different, mythically and metaphorically. To say Himmelfarb unites them is not to suggest they are the same.

The novel chronicles Himmelfarb's life from his youth in Germany to his death in Australia. For much of his adult life he goes through the motions of being an observant Ashkenazi Jew; however, right up until the eve of the Holocaust (Shoah), he is intellectually and emotionally absent from Orthodoxy. Why? Because as a young man he embraced the Enlightenment's belief in reason. According to White's logic, and the logic of romantic hermeneutics generally, he lost a sense of God's immanence, a sense of the Creator's relationship with his creation, and he was therefore unable to recognize what was unfolding around him in Germany during the 1930s. As that decade advanced, everything physical and metaphysical was gradually taken from him: his career, wife, and possessions; his belief in reason and enlightenment. Once he is naked in every sense—metaphysical, phenomenological, existential, hermeneutical—he is transported to a concentration camp, and arrives at the door of a gas chamber, but is inexplicably saved.

Finding himself alive, mysteriously, his life becomes a journey of atonement, for his sins and for the sins of the world, as he returns to the spirit of Orthodoxy, and finally accepts his vocation as a zaddik; a vocation of saintliness and righteousness a poor dyer once predicted for him; a vocation he had earlier eschewed in Germany. He travels to Palestine as a refugee but refuses an invitation to join his late wife's relatives—who are participating in the secular Zionist experiment there—because he does not believe it is God's will for him, as a diaspora Jew, now focused completely on covenant identity and the texts that created that identity.

Himmelfarb travels to Australia where he settles in Sarsaparilla and obtains a humble job, in nearby Barranugli, in a bicycle factory owned by an apostate Jew. He becomes part of an assembly line that makes bicycle lamps. His job is to create the hole in the centre of the metal plate, so the light of the lamp, the light of Judaism, can illuminate the darkness. The distinction between enlightenment and illumination is important, here and elsewhere in White. Illumination means shining a light in the darkness and is associated with Plato's *Allegory of the Cave* (Republic VII, 514a–520a).

Enlightenment occurs outside the cave and is associated with Plato's *Allegory of the Sun* (Republic VI, 508b–509c). The *Allegory of the Divided Line* (Republic VI, 509d–511e) explains the boundaries between the two.

As a child and an adolescent, Himmelfarb was caught between his father's affinity with the Enlightenment and his mother's affinity with Orthodoxy. Moshe was a good man, a reasonable man, a "worldly Jew of liberal tastes" (125) who "would laugh and chatter with him as required, or listen gravely as the beauties of Goethe or the other poets were pointed out" (128). Malke, who "made rather a sombre impression, stiff and given to surrounding herself with certain dark, uncouth, fanatically Orthodox Jews, usually her relatives" (127), "had given him her character" and insisted he received religious instruction in "our own tongue". This tension "made him proud, shy, exalted, indifferent, explosively hilarious and uncommunicative of his true feelings—if he was conscious of what they were" (133). By the time he enters university, he is a highly conflicted young man.

As Moshe wants Mordecai to adopt a gentile persona, he starts calling him Martin, to Malke's disdain and embarrassment. Martin starts moving within a gentile world. He befriends the Stauffers, a gentile family, with whom he plays the game he "had learned how to play", the game of ridiculing himself and his religion as unenlightened; the game of trying to win acceptance. But any acceptance is frail and conditional. The friendship is brought to an abrupt end when the Stauffer's daughter confesses to being attracted to him as "a kind of black *buck*" (138). At that point: "Frau Stauffer apparently decided to bring down the curtain on the comedy they had been enacting in their relationship with the young Jew" (139).

As Himmelfarb withdraws from this gentile rejection, he also finds himself rejecting his mother's family and the collection of ragged and unwashed Jews at her Sabbath table. An assortment of "unenlightened" Jews who disgust him. Including "a little dyer, whose skin was bathed in indigo; the palms of his hands were mapped indelibly in purple" (140).[6] He withdraws into his books; "He did, in fact, cling to them, like fingers to a raft" (141). However, the books he clings to are not Jewish. They are English, his preferred language. Hebrew he would read only intermittently "late at night, both for instruction, and for the bitter pleasure of it" (142).

The fruits of this withdrawal from his unconscious—and any reality

---

[6] The blue spectrum is always symbolic in White's novels; also, indigo happens to be an anagram for the immanent God-in-I. He repeats this in *The Vivisector*.

within it—are a doctorate in English and admission to Oxford as a post-doctoral researcher. This is a triumph for Himmelfarb's conscious mind (his father) and a failure for his unconscious mind (his mother). This parental tension is best summed up in Moshe's desire that in Martin "the world should recognize a good man" and Malke's desire that in Mordecai "God will recognize a good Jew" (143). According to White's logic, this is the essential difference between Athens and Jerusalem. The Hellenized mind is teleological. It pursues the good. The individual is a citizen of the polis. The Hebraic mind is deontological. It pursues its covenantal obligations. The community follows God's commands.

The tension between Athens and Jerusalem, or rather White's romantic understanding of it, creates a problem for Martin–Mordecai. Moshe's hope is that someday Jews will be seen to be no different to all humankind; Malke's hope is that someday, on the Day of the Lord, "the Jews will remain distinct from men" (143). Martin–Mordecai cannot reconcile these antithetical views, which involve him more deeply than ever "in the metaphysical thicket from which he was hoping to tear himself free" (144). He remains lost between Athens and Jerusalem, clinging to his hopes as a literary academic, and the prospect of Oxford for deliverance. This is logical, as he is a literature academic and White tends to consign literature academics to Gehenna.

Himmelfarb achieves academic distinction at Oxford. While in England, his father converts to Christianity, as the ultimate "reasonable step" (148), and hopes his son will follow him, while Malke internalizes her husband's apostasy, which becomes the tumour that eventually kills her. On hearing of his father's apostasy, Himmelfarb "never felt emptier": "great fissures were beginning to appear, besides, in what he had assumed to be the solid mass of history". Up until now, his crisis of identity has been lived out in a manageable tension within the capacious structure of Ashkenazi Judaism; however, his father's conversion, and the approaching clouds of World War I, remind him that he was "scarcely, Jew and scarcely German" (150).

The call of Malke's Orthodoxy, dominating Himmelfarb's unconscious, brings him back to Germany, but on arriving home he discovers she has died, according to Moshe: "from an internal malady she had been hiding from us" (151). Living in his father's house, now, he felt "an outcast" in the Jewish community, living in a no-man's land. The narrator tells us this is not really so: "He only failed to realize that neither his father's apostasy, nor his own spiritual withdrawal was the true cause of their suspicion, and that almost every soul must endure the same period of probation before receiving orders" (152).

During World War I, Himmelfarb serves as a private in the German army. After the war, he feels unable to return to his father's house, where Moshe now lives with his new wife, a young blond Roman Catholic girl. He accepts a readership at the University of Bienenstadt, following an intuitive prompting "that he had been directed to this far from lucrative post at a minor university for reasons still obscure" (155). Before his departure, many "homely Jews" insisted on "offering him introductions to others, probably of their own kind", including the "disgusting dyer of his youth" who still repels him. The dyer encourages him to make contact with a man called Liebmann (love + man) "who will receive you with lovingkindness, such as you were accustomed to in childhood" (155).

Himmelfarb moves to Bienenstadt and spends months alone, not unloved but inaccessible, "withdrawn for the moment too far into himself to be reached" (156). He destroys his introductions and lives in isolation. However, after some months, "he began to be tormented" and "suddenly, on a certain afternoon, he stood up knowing that he must go in search of Liebmann the printer. He could not have been more relieved" (156). He has partly overcome some of his enlightened inhibitions, enough to be re-absorbed into an Orthodox family; with a father whose "yellow skin remained tinged with the faint glow of lovingkindness" (159); with a daughter who has the same characteristics as his mother Malke.

Eventually Himmelfarb asks Reha to marry him. She accepts. When she tells him her people "know you will bring us honour" (161) he professes to be ashamed, and, in a tone reminiscent of his false humility of old, admits to being "the lowest of human beings" (162). If his tone is insincere it is because he is insecure about his re-entrance into the Orthodox world. He is still radically conflicted, between a conscious he senses to be false and an unconscious he is drawn to but remains ambivalent about.

This tension is reflected at his wedding feast, attended by the repulsive dyer from his past. The dyer, whose name is Israel, suggests that Himmelfarb's "heart has been touched and changed" but he denies this is so: "I am, as always, myself, I regret to tell you" (164). The dyer tries to convince him there is still a zaddik within him; that he could well be "a light that will reflect out over the community—all the brighter from a bare room" (165). There are images of sparks throughout *Riders in the Chariot*. They are intrinsic to the novel's densely woven Kabbalistic elements (Ben-Bassat 1990). Here the dyer is prophesying Himmelfarb's future of "gathering the sparks" which fell in a cataclysm, according to one Jewish account of creation. It is a hope Himmelfarb is currently unable to realize, as the seeds sown within him will only germinate after much delusion, suffering, and finally, illumination.

In the course of his married life Himmelfarb does not follow the path chosen by his mother or hoped for by his wife's family. He clings to his gods of reason and enlightenment. He pursues his career as an academic in English Literature, specializing in 19th and early 20th century literature and its relationship with English and German culture. In spiritual terms, this preoccupation does nothing to meet the hopes and expectations of the Liebmann family, the dyer Israel, or his wife. The couple remains childless and Reha "began to suffer from breathlessness" (169). Like the blue spectrum, and asthma, childlessness and breathlessness are symbolic in White's novels. He was a childless asthmatic himself.

Reha uses a ruse, of wanting a recipe book, to steer Himmelfarb into a bookshop where he discovers the Kabbalah. At first he dismisses them as books which "deal with magic" (171) but is interested enough to buy "several of the more interesting old volumes of Hebrew, and one or two loose, damaged parchments" (173). He takes them home but does not tell Reha he has bought them; however, he suspects she might secretly know, as he was "never certain with Reha: to what extent perception was revealed in her words and her behaviour, or how far she had accompanied him along the inward path" (175).

Himmelfarb's encounter with the Kabbalah is a wrenching confrontation to "his rational self" (175). He has a mystical experience, a dark night of the soul, which causes a nervous collapse; however, he withdraws from this call from his unconscious to integration and wholeness. He puts the Kabbalistic texts aside, and goes on a rest cure at a Baltic resort, where he and Reha personally experience antisemitism—for the first time—in the dining room of their resort. While they were "trembling, shaken" (177) by this experience, a prevailing liberal ambience at the resort lets them put the matter aside. By the time they return home, where he finds he has been offered the Chair of English at his home-town university, his conscious mind is repressing his mystical experience, and his experience of antisemitism, along with the other sublimated aspects of his Orthodox affinities.

In Holunderthal, Himmelfarb lives a life of successful inauthenticity, oblivious to the sociopolitical tensions around him, unaware of his disintegrating psyche, unable to "gather the sparks". The zaddik in him is still dormant because his delusions of reason and enlightenment have yet to be stripped away. In this non-Orthodox environment, the Orthodox Reha is buried uncomfortably in the Greco-German metaphor of their house (178), childless and breathless, but content to be her husband's "suffering servant" within the neoclassical–romantic setting he desires.

While she is usually meek, however, she rises to great emotion on one occasion, where she is called upon to stand up for the promise of soteria (182–183). So far, she has not admitted to guiding her husband to the Kabbalistic texts, but she now asks him what he has done with them. Angry at this encroachment upon his reasonable and enlightened "world", guilty because he has left the texts behind, and not brought them into their new home, he remonstrates with her. In their ensuing argument, the clash of horizons is profound, as Jerusalem fights for its survival against Athens.

Still dominated by his false humility, Himmelfarb cannot read the signs of the times. He cannot see the approaching Holocaust. He chooses to remain in Germany along with all those who "could not detach themselves from the ganglion of Europe" (184). He is dismissed from his position at the university, but still refuses to engage with the reality unfolding around him, and ignores all offers of escape. Eventually, however, there came "a night when comfort is not to be found"; when "faith will spill out of the strong like sawdust" (189). Gripped by an "ungovernable fear" and a need "to be accepted, rather, by those who stood on the right side of the grave" (190), he runs to the home of Konrad Stauffer, his childhood friend. The Stauffers are sympathetic but remind him of the present dangers. He runs home to Reha but it is too late. The Nazis came for him and took her. He must now live with the knowledge that he facilitated her death and denied her hope of salvation.

Losing Reha plunges Himmelfarb into an abyss, a "whimpering, directionless" descent into darkness (197). Now that his illusions are destroyed he is free to pursue his vocation as a zaddik, to gather the sparks. The pattern is set for the rest of his pilgrimage, armed with nothing more than a small case containing his tallith and tephillin, and a desire to seek a state of being he "had not yet arrived at"; a "state of equanimity, of solitariness, or disinterest, from which, it had been suggested by the dyer, he might illuminate the vaster darkness" (212). Himmelfarb does not achieve this state in Mandatory Palestine, which will soon become the State of Israel, with its emphasis on the Holy Land. Its Zionist hopes. Its promise of earthly fulfilment. He only achieves this state in his dilapidated hut in Sarsaparilla, and in the factory in Barranugli, where he bores the holes in bicycle lamps, as one of the hidden zaddikhim. In Australia, his vocation is not recognized by other Jews, or by gentiles. It is only recognized by the other three riders in the chariot.

Through this manoeuvre, White remains loyal to the spirit of Ezekiel's throne–chariot prophecy, in both its biblical and Blakean senses. God has honoured his promise to protect Himmelfarb in exile, but suffering in exile is apparently a condition of God's protection, for him, and for all four riders. The role of White's poetic geniuses is to witness to this fact. While this is not a message the contemporary west wishes to hear, whether in Europe, North America, Australia, or Israel, the message may still be relevant.

Ruth Godbold

In White's novels, Christianity appears in many forms. He depicts a broad spectrum of Christians, from holy saints embodying great faith, to deluded sinners embodying great evil, to those in between. This is the fruit of his remarkable powers of observation, since the spectrum has always existed within the Church and always will. However, his depiction of saints and sinners can also be explained more systematically within romantic hermeneutics.

In Ricoeurean terms, Christianity does not have a symbolic language of origin or end unique to itself. The revelation of God in Christ originates within Judaism, within the adamic myth and its Hebraic metaphors, as Ricoeur 1960 explains:

> The bond that unites the Adamic myth to the "Christological" nucleus of the faith is a bond of suitability; the symbolic description of man, in the doctrine of sin, suits the announcement of salvation (307).

This is where White's challenge and our challenge begins. If Christianity does not have its own symbolic language, independent of Judaism, and if any language we imagine as distinctively Christian actually describes a variety of First Century Judaism, we need to contextualize where White's sense of a Christian horizon comes from.

What emerges is a picture of White's complex struggle with the Church which resists simplistic and cavalier explanation. This struggle might explain why later, in *The Solid Mandala*, Arthur Brown dreamed Mrs Poulter would be smooth to the touch when in fact she was rough and prickly bark at the base of the tree. The Christian mind is not a static thing. Different myths and metaphors mingle within the Christian mind. What Ricoeur identifies as the humanistic quality of the adamic myth competes and coexists with the fatalistic quality of the myths of chaos and creation, tragic hero, and exiled soul. At its core, Christianity is metaphorically Hebraic, but the influence of Theogonic and Hellenic metaphors also acts upon the Christian imagination. White's persistent send-up of Christian Science, as an extreme form of Hellenism, demonstrates his awareness that any sect that believes in "mind over matter" cannot represent Christian orthodoxy.

Chronologically, White was consistent. He narrated the story of Ruth Godbold's horizon after those of Mary Hare and Mordecai Himmelfarb. This makes sense, as Christianity came after Judaism, which came after Theogony. While she is Christian, her faith is instinctive and not subject to systematic theology, ecclesial structures, or clerical authority. In this way she fulfils Blake's criteria for an authentic religious experience as a kind of solitary poetic genius. She is described in New Testament language that suggests the Pauline contradiction of her faith: "For one so strong, it must be admitted she was regrettably weak. Or else kind" (2 Corinthians 12:10).

But Ruth's faith was not "less persuasive for its fluctuations; rather, it becomes a living thing, like a child fluttering in the womb" (301). As childbirth is painful, and all creation is a perpetual "groaning like a woman in labour" (Romans 8:22), her life is an extended labour on many levels: physically, in terms of her fertility; economically, in terms of the consequences of that fertility; sociologically, in terms of her abusive marriage; metaphorically, in terms of her faith, which "would stir and increase inside the grey, gelatinous envelope of morning, until, at last, it was delivered, new-born, with all the glory and confidence of fire" (301).

No other woman in White's novels suffers as much physical and emotional abuse as Ruth. Her husband Tom hated the "almost biological aspect" of her faith (301), which allowed her to cope with the social and economic reality of their lives. He could not bear a faith that allowed his wife to accept his limitations as a man and their poverty as a family. In spite of her life of domestic violence, Ruth continued to turn the other cheek (Matthew 5:39), an aspect of Christianity Nietzsche despised because it embodied a slave mentality rather than a master morality. She is always rising above her fallen condition; always rising from the floor, to her feet, to concentrate on the minutiae of living. Although she:

… would have liked to talk to somebody about the past, even those occasions which had racked her most, of emigration, and miscarriages, not to mention her own courtship; she longed to dawdle amongst what had by now become sculpture (304).

Ruth's horizon constantly projects her forward, into the contradictory mystery of Christian soteria, with its tension between a realized eschatology (the now) and an unrealized eschatology (the not yet), and its dilemmas of freedom and constraint:

For present and future are like a dreadful music, flowing and flowing without end, and even Mrs Godbold's courage would sometimes falter as she trudged along the bank of the one turbulent river towards its junction with the second, always somewhere in the mists (304).

Although Ruth never dwells on the statuary of her past, the narrator tells her story for her. She emigrated from England; "her folk were chapel" (305); a rural family, dutiful and devout, who understood the world in scriptural terms. She was a strong girl who worked like a man:

> Her capacity for physical exertion was, it must be admitted, enormous. At haymaking, for example, she would never falter, or on pitching up the hay to load, like a man. At the end of the day, when women and boys were leaning exhausted and fiery, her normal pallid, nondescript skin would seem at last to have come alive, like a moist, transparent brier rose, as she continued to pitch regularly into the drays (309).

Her brother Rob "liked to stand on the load, to receive. He always had to climb to where it was highest and most awkward." One day he slipped and fell from the dray into the thresher:

> Then the girl, whose strong back could formerly have held off the weight of the whole world, was tearing at iron, wood, stubble. She was holding in her hands the crushed melon that had been her brother's head … Several people ran to help … But it was she, of course, who had to carry her brother. It was not very far, her blurry mouth explained. From that field. To the outskirts of the town … She brought the body to their father, who did not look at her straight, she saw, then, or ever again. He would sometimes look at her boots, that strong pair, which he himself had made, and on which blood had fallen (310).

Ruth was also weak, however, and in one instance, unforgiving. As the principal female in her family, she could not accept her widowed father's decision to remarry, or his new wife: "You should learn to forgive, Ruth," he tells her. "That is what we have been taught" (313). In her weakness, her inability to forgive, or make way for her step-mother, she decides to migrate to Australia, clinging to her faith: the means through which her weakness becomes a vocation in a Pauline sense. On the voyage out, she would say her prayers on deck looking out to sea:

> Released finally from the solid body, her soul was free to accept its mission, but hesitated to trust its own strength. And hovered, and hovered in the vastness, until recognizing that the rollers were folded into one another, and the stars were fragments of the one light (313).

Not long after arriving in Sydney, Ruth enters the service of a socialite, Mrs Chalmers-Robinson. This was a period that "remained within her memory as the most significant phase of her independent life" (314). It was a period of comparisons, as White contrasts Ruth's substance with her mistress's lack of substance as "the flimsiest of women" (314). Ruth had never met anyone "quite so dazzling, or so fragmentary" (315) before. She sees Mrs Chalmers-Robinson as someone who could "never emerge from her own distraction to receive" (319). Her vocation to serve is challenged by the sheer strength of her mistress's distraction; her selflessness is tested by the selfishness of a socialite who disguises her futility and lack of fulfilment by pursuing, in a desultory way, what White understood to be the heterodoxy of Christian Science: "Mrs Chalmers-Robinson read and studied" the Science to transform "hard, unloving thoughts", and become a "new creature" (338), but her attempts are half-hearted and always unsuccessful.[7]

Perhaps it was Ruth's pursuit of her vocation to serve which drove her away from her mistress into the arms of Tom Godbold, who is simultaneously attracted and repelled by her apparently unassailable character, and whom she resisted at first. They are destined to live with the difficult reality of their lives: their fertility, their social position, their poverty, his drinking problem, their domestic violence, and the suffering this will bring them. Ruth's faith gives her the grace to cope with these impossible circumstances. However, according to the novel's logic, Tom never shares his wife's faith and therefore never receives soteria. He is never given the grace to cope with his sins or harsh life.

Ruth, who lives out her Christian vocation with an extraordinary saintliness, does experience soteria, which gives her the grace to move forward in a cycle of birth and re-birth, physically and spiritually. This is why, at the end of the novel, she "continued along a road which progress had left rather neglected" (638). It is a road that might be on a separate plane, a plane of higher love, on which she travelled throughout all the difficulties of her life. She always accepted the central axiom of hermeneutics—that "everybody saw things different" (640)—and at the end of the novel she accepts there might be other views of the chariot apart from her own. She accepts the difference of Mary Hare, Mordecai Himmelfarb, and Alf Dubbo without compromising the uniqueness of her experience of soteria within her own Christian horizon.

In a final vision Ruth looks at Xanadu, now torn down and turned into a living and thriving suburban development:

> When she opened her eyes again, there, already, was the new settlement of Xanadu, which they had built on the land Mr Cleugh, the relative [of Mary's], had sold. Mrs Godbold could not help admiring the houses for their signs of life: for the children coming home from school,

---

[7] Throughout his novels, White takes a dismissive but orthodox approach to Christian Science—a sect rather than a church—which believes in "mind over matter". Mainstream Christianity believes in the unity of matter and spirit not mind over matter.

for a row of young cauliflowers, for a convalescing woman, who had stepped outside in her dressing gown to gather a late rose.

"It is too cold, though! Too cold!" Mrs Godbold called, wrapped up her own throat, to illustrate.

"Eh?" mumbled the woman, as she stood tearing the stalk of the resistant rose.

You will catch cold!" Mrs Godbold insisted.

She could have offered more love than was acceptable (640).

Her memory combines with her vision; her vivid historicity blends into her experience of the moment, creating a mosaic, an imaginative picture of her life on which she can look upon and judge: "as an artist, after an interval, will approach and judge his work of art" (642). Having made this lofty assessment, of her unconscious relationship with Blake's and White's sense of poetic genius, "she was content to leave then, since all converged finally upon the Risen Christ, and her own eyes had confirmed that the wounds were healed" (642). She has been given another glimpse of soteria—transcendent and immanent—before continuing her earthly journey, her feet "still planted firmly on the earth", walking on while "breathing heavily, for it was a stiff pull up the hill, to the shed in which she continued to live" (643).

Alf Dubbo

While White wrote his novels and short stories before postcolonial, poststructural, and intersectional theory became entrenched in literary criticism, his fiction is now interpreted through their various lenses. During his career he did not characterize Aborigines often but when he did there was no pattern to his characterization. While his view of Aboriginality is clearly a non-Aboriginal view, the debate among postcolonial critics is whether it is accurate, coherent, and empathic; whether it is truly postcolonial, or whether it continues to colonize Aboriginals by describing and inscribing them as other.

Some of them notice that Alf Dubbo seems to anticipate what is currently referred to as the "stolen generation", although White characterized Alf before the term was coined, and he did not seem concerned with the life or culture Alf was allegedly "stolen" from. In other words, if he anticipated postcolonialism, he would not have recognized the form it would take. It is difficult to use this against him without being presentist or anachronistic. The most neutral observations we can make about Alf is that he is a solitary poetic genius, in White's Blakean sense, and that he lives the life of a suffering servant or exile, as all four riders must.

Why is Alf a rider? What vision does he share with the other riders? What vision is unique to him? These are difficult questions, as it is challenging to distinguish a specifically indigenous horizon from the romantic Theogony White assigns to Mary Hare. Apart from that, Alf is a half-caste, so a white imaginary is also his by birth. White always knew it would be a test for him to make Alf's creative genius convincing: first, because of the ambiguity surrounding Alf's horizon, since he is clearly not a mad Erdgeist like Mary Hare; second, because we never really know what his painting looks like.

White will face a similar dilemma later, when describing Hurtle Duffield's horizon in *The Vivisector* (1970). It is always important to compare and contrast Alf and Hurtle, as a similar rhetoric surrounds both artists. In both cases, what their drawings and paintings look like is hypothetical, as we cannot see them, but White gives us enough language to visualize them. Both Alf and Hurtle have innate talent, both are raised by couples—one brother and sister, the other husband and wife—who represent a seductive but deficient symbolic order; however, both benefit from that order in similar ways.

While Alf and Hurtle move away from that order, as emerging adults, it has an indelible effect upon them and becomes an integral part of who they are as adult artists. In terms of White's rhetoric, they therefore occupy a liminal space between logos and mythos: neither fully one nor the other. While neither has been professionally trained, neither can be called naïve, although there is a degree of primitivism about their similar modernist and postmodernist responses to neoclassical and romantic art. In Alf's case, he is always trying to "improve" the art that attracted him as a child. Again, we cannot see his drawing and paintings, and do not know what they look like, but we assume they move between modernism and postmodernism in eclectic ways. Perhaps they involve abstracting representational art and, perhaps occasionally, making non-representational art more symbolic.

Hewitt 2002 reminds us that the post-impressionist French artist Odilon Redon "gave White the central unifying symbol for *Riders in the Chariot*" (55). Alf paints the chariot in which he and the other three riders sit. The novel clearly tells us he adapted his vision of the chariot from a painting from Redon's Chariot of Apollo series:

> … which had haunted White ever since he saw it in a Bond Street window as a young man. It was probably *Apollo's Sun Chariot with Four White Horses*, exhibited in London in 1938. The chariot appears in ancient mythology and literature, in the Book of Ezekiel (1:4–28), in Blake's famous hymn *Jerusalem* and in Jungian mandala symbolism. White also found the Jewish Merkabah ("throne-chariot") mystical traditions in

Gershom Scholem's *Major Trends in Jewish Mysticism* (56).

The novel carefully describes Alf's encounter with the painting in a book, as a boy and again as an adult. From the moment he first saw it, he knew he could improve on it.[8]

Alf's encounter with Redon's Chariot, and his lifelong desire to reconceptualize it, is part of White's post-Enlightenment critique of the Enlightenment. As this critique is both philosophical and aesthetic, we need to consider the philosophical parallel of what Alf can see, aesthetically, because as far as White is concerned that is what qualifies him to be a rider in the chariot he paints. What he can see situates him within romantic hermeneutics, somewhere within Gadamer's frame of logos and mythos, and Ricouer's anthropology of Theogonic, Hellenic and Hebraic metaphors.

At the most fundamental level, Alf has an artistic genius that comes from somewhere other than his conscious mind. This relates him to mythos rather than logos, although he is attracted to and absorbs something from logos, which a pure trope for mythos such as Mary Hare never does. He can see things Mary cannot see. This makes him an archetypal hybrid. We are told he is half Celtic and—in the postwar novels of White and his contemporaries—Celtic archetypes are usually mythos with red hair. Within the novel, however, the dominant culture treats him as an outcast: "Propriety alone made them reduce Alf's Irish ancestors to the mythical status of the Great Snake" (409). This tells us nothing about the horizon Alf might have inherited, hypothetically, from his Aboriginal forebears. That creates a problem for postcolonial critics.

By Alf's own admission he is not a Christian, as he tells Ruth, while she is wiping the blood from his consumptive mouth. He is drunk, on the floor of Mrs Khalil's brothel, where she has come to fetch her husband: "I was educated up to it. But gave it away. Pretty early on, in fact. When I found I could do better, I mean," he mumbled, "a man must make use of what he has. There is no point in putting on a pair of boots to walk to town, if you can do it better in your bare feet" (370). What does Alf "have"? What does "bare feet" mean here?

The Christianity Alf gave away is quite different from Ruth's. In White's terms, it was logos Christianity, not mythos Christianity, although that is a Blakean distinction White made which is no longer fashionable to make. Also, in spite of giving away the boots of this logos Christianity,

---

[8] When Alf saw the printed reproduction he could not have seen true colours. Contemporary print technology did not allow that. Dobell experienced the same problem—as a youth in Australia—which is why he was blown away when he moved overseas and saw original paintings. White had a similar experience in the 1930s.

Alf acknowledged his indebtedness to those boots throughout his life: he
continued to read the Bible, paint biblical themes, and generally behave in
a Blakean solitary poetic genius way. When Ruth tells him he should go
home, and asks where he lives, his answer is surprising for someone who
had long since abandoned Christianity. At first he says "along the river at
the parson's" (367) before remembering that time had long past.[9]

As a youth, Alf was the "Great Experiment" of the Reverend Timothy
Calderon and his widowed sister, Emily Pask; expatriates from England
who seek to impose their foreign vision on a half-caste child. A foreign
vision which, according to White's logic, sits uncomfortably within an
inhospitable Australian landscape. They perceive him to be an
"exceedingly bright boy" (409), and, to be fair to them, they are the only
white people in early 20th century rural Australia who do. They see him as
a blank slate, a tabula rasa,[10] upon which they can project and perpetuate
the image and likeness of their logos Christianity. Calderon and Pask think
he is bright but lazy; simply because he does not fit their mould; simply
because his motivations are directed elsewhere. He tells them candidly: "I
don't think I can be that kind of character" (410). He can only be himself.

Alf is bright enough to learn Latin but he cannot see the point. His
medium of expression is visual rather than written. He uses paint rather
than words. He loves to draw. He would "scribble on the walls of the shed
where he milked the rector's horny cow" (410). To Pask, this suggests Alf
has hidden talent; however, as he has noticed from early on, she "preferred
to avert her eyes from nature" (410), she wants his talent for expressing
immanence to conform to her transcendent logos ideology. She tries to
convince Alf that art is a moral force. But for her morals rather than his.

The symbolism of colour is important in this novel, as it is in White's
other novels, since colour signifies particular things, and the symbolism of
colour differs within cultures and across cultures. Pask tries to convince
Alf of "the possibilities of white as a livener of unrelieved surfaces" (411)
but he wants other colours to predominate: reds and blues to demonstrate
the divinity of sensuality. He makes red images that "stand up stiff and
solid" (411) like phalluses. In one painting he circumscribes each
immanent red image in transcendent blue so "they were forever contained"
(411). As her logos Christ is risen and glorified, she accepts the classical
symbolism of white, and she has sublimated the reality of the crucifixion

---

[9] Christianity was important to Alf—in a way it could never be important to Mary—and
in a way he could never articulate, just as White could never articulate why Christianity
was important to him even after he stopped going to Church. In some senses, Christianity
was the only religious home Alf and White ever had, even if they both left home.

[10] None of White's protagonists is tabula rasa. Each is born with a horizon (Giffin 1989).

which the colour red brings to mind. He embraces the reality of Christ's passion and death—its cruelty and its suffering—and he is able to circumscribe this reality with blue, the colour of eternity and heaven. As he understands Christ better than she does—at least in White's scheme of things—he will not allow her white to dominate his reds and blues: the colours of creation and matter taking form.

Alf and Pask clash whenever his growing confidence in his creativity challenges her aesthetic ideology. With each clash his inner strength wins over her inner weakness and imagined superiority. Whenever he expresses his nature—his horizon—she is censorious. Why? Because his expressions, and their essence, remind her of her frailty, of what she needs to conceal about her inner self. Her reaction is to shame him, to censure his nature as "unnatural" scribble, just as the young Hurtle's "unnatural" drawings on walls are censured in *The Vivisector* (1970). She laughs at Alf's early attempt to give expression to an unconscious that "cannot resist colour". She warns him "you must learn in time … it is delicacy that counts" (412).

He paints a tree with fruit that represent "dreams that haven't been dreamt yet" (413).[11] While smiling kindly—in that disturbing Christian way—she tells him his painting is "unnatural" and "peculiar":

> "I am afraid it is something unhealthy," Mrs Pask confided in her brother. "An untrained mind could not possibly conceive of anything so peculiar unless".
> "But the boy's mind is not totally untrained. Since you have begun to train it," the parson could not resist (413–414).

Alf discovers some tubes of oil paints which Pask no longer uses. He is immediately attracted to them, as a medium of expression, for their sensual possibilities. She forbids him from using them, as oil paintings "lead to so much that is undesirable in art" (420). Eventually she relents, seduced by his shrewd promise to paint Jesus, whom he says he can only paint in oils. However, she turns her deepest shade of purple when—having just dismissed a painting he calls "My Life"—she is faced with his unfinished portrait of Jesus.

White encourages us to suspect this portrait contains a penis. This challenges her image of Christ as divine rather than human. What Alf sees as beautiful—the humanity of Christ; the crucified and risen Lord who, as the earthly Jesus, definitely had a penis—Pask must forever regard as blasphemous and filthy:

---

[11] Given the period being written about—the early 20th century—this may be a gesture to an indigenous dreamtime that is sensed without being understood.

"It is downright madness. You must not think this way. My brother must speak to you," she said. "Oh dear! It is dirty! When there is so much that is beautiful and holy!"

She went away nearly crying.

And he called after her, "Mrs Pask! It is beautiful. It is all really, beautiful. It is only me. I am learning how to show it. How it is. In me. I'll show you something that you didn't know. You'll see. And get a surprise." (425).

Mrs Pask must reject any suggestion that Alf has something to teach her.

Alf has a different relationship with Calderon, a relationship that is still frail, and does not speak to his inner nature, but is less damaging to his psyche. This is because the priest is more aware of his own limitations and failings. If he cannot embrace Alf's horizon, he is more open to it than his sister. This is because, throughout his life: "Imagination, just a little, was his own misfortune, for it had never been enough to ferment the rest of him" (414).

In White's scheme, Calderon's limited imagination is emblematic of his logos horizon. He is also impotent—physically and/or metaphysically —like White's other logos characters. Alf senses this impotence, hence his intuitive vision of "the white worm stirring and fainting in the reverend pants" (424). Calderon is a character in a novel, though, not a person in real life. As such, his homosexuality needs to be understood in a dialectical or archetypal way. He is not only an Anglo-Catholic cliché—a pervasive trope among postwar characters who represent logos—like the eponymous Father Watts-Watt in Golding's *Free Fall* (1959). He represents reason (or what Paglia would call civilization). He is associated with the ego and the conscious mind. If he is not as afraid of mythos as his sister is, he still finds mythos incomprehensible.

Alf's horizon is much larger in the way it imagines the relationship between humanity and divinity, matter and spirit, transcendence and immanence. He senses this largeness while still a boy, looking at a book of paintings with Calderon: "Then the boy stopped at a picture he would always remember, and criticize, and wish to improve on," the narrator says (417).

It was the work, he read, of some French painter … In the picture the chariot rose, behind the wooden horses, along the pathway of the sun. The god's arm—for the text implied it was a god—lit the faces of the four figures, so stiff, in the body of the tinny chariot. The rather ineffectual torch trailed its streamers of material light.

"The arm is not painted good," Alf explains, "I could do the arm better. And horses. My horses," the boy claimed, "would have the fire flowing from their tails. And dropping sparks. Or stars. Moving. Everything would move in my picture. Because that is the way it ought to be" (418). Calderon finds Alf's illumination painful. It reminds him of his own sterility. He tries to draw Alf away from the painting—one of Odilon Redon's paintings of Apollo's chariot—back to the Bible, specifically to the logos Christ, the Hellenized Jesus, of the Gospel of John (the Beloved Disciple): "The parson told of spiritual love and beauty, how each incident of Our Lord's life had been illuminated by those qualities. Of course the boy had heard it all before, but wondered again how he failed continually to appreciate" (418).

White is leading up to something inevitable, here. The encounter between Alf's solitary poetic genius and Calderon's clerical impotence will reach its (anti)climax in bed. White does not portray their sexual encounter as we would: as an abuse of power; as a colonizer molesting the colonized; as an oppressor dominating the oppressed. In their sexual encounter, which is metaphysical rather than physical—it occurs in a novel not in life—we do not know who led whom to the bedroom, or who initiated what act, we only know that, by the time they ended up in bed, Alf had become a young man whose "nostrils awaited experience"; who "was puzzled to feel that perhaps he was the one who led"; that Calderon "seemed in particular need of the youth's attention and understanding" (428). However, given their antithetical status as poetic genius and impotent cleric, a relationship between them is impossible. So the "Great Experiment" of a white priest, his white sister, and a half-caste boy, comes to a sudden end, when Mrs Pask discovers them together in bed.

Alf leaves town. The rest of his life is an outsider's journey. He is taken in by Mrs Spice, a filthy promiscuous older woman, who lives in a rubbish dump on the outskirts of another rural town, collects bottles for a living, introduces him to alcohol, and gives him syphilis. When her sexual hold over him becomes unbearable, he goes bush, "figuratively at least" (443), but "avoided his own people, whatever the degree of colour". Because of a particular delicacy and squeamishness acquired from Mrs Pask. Because of his awareness of his "secret gift" for painting which, like his disease, he would no more have confessed to a black than a white. These two poles became "the negative and positive side of his being: the furtive, destroying sickness, and the almost as furtive, but regenerating, creative act" (444).

Alf moves to Sydney in the late 1930s, lives in dilapidated rooms, does menial jobs, saves up for oil paints, and reads the Bible. He goes to the library and looks up Apollo's chariot once again:

He realized how differently he saw this painting since his first acquaintance with it, and how he would now transcribe the Frenchman's limited composition into his own terms of motion, and forms partly transcendental, partly evolved from his struggle with daily becoming, and experience of suffering (446).

Just before World War II begins, Alf meets a prostitute, Hannah, who recognizes the symptoms of his syphilis and points him in the direction of treatment.[12] During the war he rents a room in her house, keeps to himself, goes on the occasional bender, reads the Bible, and tries to pursue his vocation as an artist. Hannah has a homosexual boyfriend, Norman, who gives a drag party near the end of the war, which is attended by an art collector, Humphrey Mortimer. When Humphrey sees Alf's paintings, he recognizes Alf's genius, but Alf refuses to sell his paintings to Humphrey, because by his own measure—the only measure that counts—his secret gift is still unformed and his artistic vision is incomplete. Hannah sells the paintings to Humphrey behind Alf's back. When he discovers what she has done, he becomes enraged, attacks her, and leaves her home for good.

Alf moves into a room in Barranugli on the outskirts of Sydney. After the war ends, he becomes a cleaner at the factory where Himmelfarb works. They are aware of each other—there is a mystical connection between them—but they do not speak. Himmelfarb goes to the washroom one day and is surprised to find a Bible there, open at Ezekiel, which Alf admits is his. Their meeting launches Alf into the final stage of his life, one of recognition, of knowing how to improve on Apollo's chariot, as a Hellenic vision, by making it more biblical, more Hebraic, more like Himmelfarb. With this increasing creative maturity, which depends on Himmelfarb, Alf comes to a whole vision of himself and the world.

During that final year—in which Passover and Easter coincide—Alf instinctively knows something has "happened" to Himmelfarb, who was "crucified" (hoisted upon a tree) at the factory in Barranugli before being taken to Mrs Godbold's shack in Sarsaparilla. He travels to Sarsaparilla, where he witnesses Himmelfarb's "deposition" through Mrs Goldbold's window. (Notice how he remains an outsider to the end, even among the other riders.) Within this frame, he sees Himmelfarb as a kind of Christ, Ruth as a kind of Virgin Mary, and Mary as a kind of Mary Magdalene. Having witnessed this "deposition" he returns home to paint it in "emotional whirlpools" of colour that neither Mrs Pask nor convention would have approved of (592).

Once he has painted his "deposition" he is free. He is now inspired to

---

[12] This is interesting. What cure for syphilis was available in prewar Sydney before penicillin started to be used to treat infections later in the war?

complete his painting of Ezekiel's chariot with its four riders. This is quite different from the painting of Apollo's chariot that excited him as a youth. He is given the strength to "restate his conception" of the chariot and to paint it from memory "as he originally intended". His chariot is more earthbound or immanent than Apollo's chariot. While painting it:

> One curious fact emerged. From certain angles the canvas presented a reversal of the relationship between permanence and motion, as though the banks of a river were to begin to flow alongside its stationary waters. The effect pleased the painter, who had achieved more or less by accident what he had discovered years before while lying in the gutter. So he encouraged an illusion which was also a truth, and from which the timid might retreat simply by changing their position (597–598).

Having painted his vision of truth, Alf finally succumbs to tuberculosis: "The sharp pain poured in crimson tones into the limited space of room", and overflowed upon his hands, which were "gilded, he was forced to observe, with his own gold" (599). The gold of his viscosities, as immanence, blend with the deepest blue he has seen, as transcendence, through which he achieves soteria. After his death, his masterpieces are sold at auction for unknown sums, then disappear, and "still wait to be discovered" (602).

Rosenbaums–Rosetrees

Harry Rosetree is the Roman Catholic convert—the apostate Jew—who owns the Brighta Bicycle factory where Himmelfarb makes lamps holey–holy in its "infernal" depths.

Harry is not as successful at disguises as his wife. Whenever he tries to fling away the persona of Haim, "it stuck to him, like discarded chewing-gum" (262). It is Harry who begs his wife for torte, as he refuses to "assimilate the epple pie" (264). And while Harry professes to hate Himmelfarb, and all Jewish intellectuals, "Freud, and Mozart, and all that *Kaffeequatsch*" (265),[13] the reader is told he could never hate the whole Jewish race because, according to White's logic, hatred is not the essence of the Jewish story of loving-kindness:

> he was essentially a loving man, and still longed to be loved in a way that can happen only in the beginning. But there, his childhood was burnt down, not a trace of it left, except that the voices of the dark women continued to vibrate inside him (265).

---

[13] Those who gossip (quatsch) over coffee (kaffee).

As a sign of his cognitive dissonance, at this point Harry displays a limp, and he "stamped to bear it out" (265). Limps signify impediments in White's novels. They are metaphors that signal a character's psychic affliction, like George Brown's oedipus, or limp, transferred to his son Waldo.

The conjunction of Passover and Easter is portentous in the novel. Harry's discomfort increases with the proximity of Passover–Easter, a season which "always brought confusion" to his disenfranchised soul:

> Which he overcame by overwork, by blasphemy, and by tearing at his groin. There the pants would ruck up regularly, causing him endless discomfort during rush orders and humid weather" (487).

Here is another sign of his cognitive dissonance, for in some modern novels the image of constrained genitals signify how a particular horizon has become distorted. Harry's unhappy crotch is symptomatic of his frustration that Easter is preventing him from fulfilling his orders, which would help him forget the Passover as the commemoration of Israel's deliverance.

Living out this denial of the Torah and the Kabbalah through a work ethic—and an unconvincing conversion to Roman Catholicism—does not make Harry happy or comfortable. His secretary suggests that perhaps his religion should be discarded as harmful to his personal integration, but the essentially loving Harry is still dominated by a sense of law and covenant. Thus he explains with a joking seriousness "You gotta be religious, Miss Whibley. Otherwise you will go to hell, and how will you like that?" (489). But this hell is not the fiery furnace of the medieval or gothic imagination. It is the hell of separation and alienation. It is the existential hell of not living with the God of Israel. It is a hell Harry fears but is already living in.

So with characteristic anti-intellectualism he condemns his secretary's atheism, and that of her dialectical materialist boyfriend, just as he earlier condemned intellectual Jews including Himmelfarb, Freud, Mozart and those who gossip over coffee. Harry needs religion as a substitute for faith, to prop up his essential honesty, yet his attitude towards Roman Catholicism is expressed in the Jewish language of covenant obligation "If you signed a contract, you had to abide by the clauses. And religion is like any other business" (491).

Soon Harry is alone in his office, where the lingering smell of his secretary's decongestant rub reminds him of cinnamon:

> Haim Rosenbaum, the boy, had never cared for the stuff, but long after he had become a man, even after he was supposed, officially, to have stripped

the Ark of its Passover trappings, and dressed his hopes in the white robe of Easter, the scent of cinnamon remained connected with the deep joy of *Pessach* (492).

This smell also evokes a memory of his father's annual homily:

> our history is all we have, Haim, and the peaceful joys of the Sabbath and feast days, the flavour of cinnamon and the scent of spices, the wisdom of Torah and the teaching of the Talmud (492).

At this point Himmelfarb comes past his office and looks at him through the hatchway, reminding Harry with his "one great archetypal face" of all he is seeking to reject (493).

The recognition of his shadow in Himmelfarb's gaze makes Harry tremble "whether from anger" or "from joy at discovering familiar features transferred from memory to the office hatchway, he would not have been the one to decide" (493). In disclosive terms, their encounter continues to be a flickering of anger and joy, of recognition and denial, as Harry resists the faith he has been trying to escape from for so long. Gazing upon what he feared most, the contents of Himmelfarb's brown case, "the fringes of the *Tallith*, the black thongs of the *Tephillin*, wound round and round the Name", Harry "could have been in some agony" (494). Trembling, he begs Mordecai to put it away, declaring it to be "a lot of *Quatsch*. Will you Jews never learn that you will be made to suffer for the next time also" (494).

Harry does not admit his own suffering, his own dilemma, his own existential hell. With a lack of discretion he tries to buy off Himmelfarb with five pounds, "*Für Pessach*" (495), just as he tries to buy off the nuns at St Aloysius. He asks Himmelfarb to take two days off—"for the *Seder* business"—but insists that Himmelfarb observe the Passover in secret, under the cover of sick leave.[14]

Harry has another motive for wanting Himmelfarb out of the factory on Good Friday. The Easter season is in no sense a religious festival in his factory. It is an excuse for gambling and drinking. Also, there is another dynamic occurring on the factory floor, where a culture of antisemitism is about to explode. A pagan antisemitism that associates Good Friday with the accusation of deicide. A pagan antisemitism made more atavistic and irrational because, here, it is divorced from any religious context. However, as the denial of his shadow self has become part of Harry's reason for living, it must now be defended at all costs. So, as Himmelfarb

---

[14] Notice how Orthodox faith—whether Jewish or Christian—is regarded as sickness by the reasonable and enlightened Australian ideology the Rosetrees have embraced.

did not take his advice, and stay away for two days over Passover, he is now able, and willing, to allow Himmelfarb to become a scapegoat: "If there was an enemy of reason, it was the damned Jew Himmelfarb, who must now accept the consequences" (531).

When the mock crucifixion takes place, Harry refuses to become personally involved, lest he be branded a Jew. Instead, he gets his foreman to stop the persecution. However the crucifixion does confront Harry, who loses his desire to "go away at Easter" (574). The Rosetrees had planned on avoiding their own Church at the very time it was due to commemorate the paschal mystery. Harry, the failed Jew and failed Christian, becomes tired and neurotic. He begins to identify his wife's distorted will as part of their problem and rejects both her, "You let me alone, Shirl" (576), and the adopted disguise through which she "could not see by the light of reason and the shadowy room what was devouring Haim" (575).

Aware of Himmelfarb's death and his participation in it, "Haim ben Ya'akov found himself abandoning the controls of reason, not to say the whole impressive, steel-and-plastic structure of the present, for the stuffy rooms of memory" (578). He remembers his father telling him of his own Messianic hopes. A belief in an imminent earthly deliverance. A belief repeated for thousands of years, always expected, always unrealized, while remaining the focus of Hebraic eschatology. A belief that defies all Hellenic reason:

> Listen, Haim, because this is what concerns you. You will be amongst the first to receive our Saviour. I have prayed for it, and prayed, and know. That you. YOU. It was written on the whitest scrap of sky. Then they called to the father from the shop, to attend to business. Soon there was the sound of hardware, and the shattered boy was left saddled with the greatest wonder, the greatest terror of all (579).

For Harry this incredible, revealed promise, this truth of faith in an imminent and earthly soteria now focuses upon Himmelfarb who, as a Zaddik, becomes the subject of Harry's hope for the renewal of his covenant faith.

This is why Harry's tone, when speaking with Mrs Godbold, is one of hopelessness, and why he reacts with confusion and prickling flesh when she tells him that Himmelfarb has died and was buried "like any Christian" (580). Christian burial is different from Jewish burial. Harry's mental crisis needs to be understood in this context, as Himmelfarb's burial, in earth not consecrated according to Jewish custom, with his body not touching the ground, is the final reflection of Haim Rosenbaum's failure to become Harry Rosetree, and his ultimate realization that he has damned himself forever. By not participating in Himmelfarb's ritual passage through death and burial in consecrated ground, Haim loses his last link with and hope for his own soteria. For in his pragmatic conversion to Roman Catholicism Harry never embraces the internal logic of Christian soteria and could never really disengage from the internal logic of his unconscious Hebraic horizon. Now unable to hold Minyan, or to give Himmelfarb a Jewish burial, he discovers it is too late to reclaim his own hope of soteria.

Knowing he cannot give Himmelfarb a Jewish burial leaves Harry bereft, with a sense of his own damnation. Abandoned by his wife, alone, stripped of his false identity, cut adrift from the only myth which could give him a sustaining identity in salvation history, Harry Rosetree hangs himself in the bathroom, his final vision an image of himself with bared teeth "and the least vein in his terrible eyeballs" (584).

In an ironic way Shirley Rosetree—or Shulamith Rosenbaum—ultimately triumphs in the novel, her life being "a series of disguises, which she had whisked on, and off" (632) as circumstances demanded, in an attempt to avoid being seen as Jewish. Her husband commits suicide because he is haunted, by the shadow of his myth, by his failure to abandon his Hebraic horizon. But Shulamith Rosenbaum—like most women in White's novels—has an indomitable character. She lives to become, first Shirley Rosetree, then Sheila Wolfson, the only secularized and "liberated" Jewish character in White's oeuvre who survives to experience the fruits of her self-determination.

Newly rich, wearing a satin bon-bon hat, and lunching with her two socialite friends—one wearing a lacquered crab-shell hat, the other wearing a felt volcano that cunningly emitted smoke (627)—they find themselves "in the depths of the obscure purgatory in which they sat" (635). In this purgatory, Sheila–Shirley–Shulamith contemplates "her plateful of forbidden sauce. Food had made her melancholy" (629). For Sheila, who to the crab-shell looks "both vulgar and predatory" (629), choosing to eat shellfish is a sign of her liberation. But there is no getting away from ingrained food laws, no release from the horizon given to her by the author. Sheila cannot completely discard Shulamith. She is still confronted by food laws, with their unconscious powers of totem and taboo, and their evocation of Moses and the wilderness.

Sheila is confronted by the suspicions of her fellow diners. She may have abandoned Judaism and Roman Catholicism, and finally arrived at St Mark's Darling Point, an Anglican parish White occasionally satirizes, but she is still in essence a Jewish matriarch, a lost soul among the incredulous and suspicious world of social Anglicanism within—what she hopes will be—the Anglo-Celtic power elite. In this world, to which she aspires, she is not comfortable, because she can never pull off her disguise convincingly.

When the extinct volcano, Jinny Chalmers-Robinson, says she no longer goes to St Marks, since she became interested in "Science", Sheila senses another social disguise she may have to soon adopt to be accepted.

> Now Mrs Robinson could not believe.
> "Christian Science, Jinny means," Mrs Colquhoun explained.
> Everyone listened to the word drop. Mrs Wolfson might by this time have called out: All right, all right, it dogs you like your shadow, but you get used to it at last, and a shadow cannot harm.
> Instead she said:
> "You don't say!" (631)

While Sheila's shadow does not harm her it does remind her. In a palindromic sense, it "dogs" her. The God of Israel is still within her, reminding her of what she continues to deny.

Wanting to be whatever Australians are, as long as it is non-Jewish, Sheila–Shirley–Shulamith is fated to discover that this always eludes her. Her Roman Catholic cross, bought in Europe, once gave her the comfort of a convert, but once she discovers the existence of a Protestant elite in Australia: "the little cross from the Rotenturmstrasse bumped less gaily on Shirl's breasts" (270). In her materialistic suburban home in Persimmon Street, Paradise East, Shirley and Harry would cling to each other "with almost fearful passion" (270), memory always threatening to change them "mercilessly back into Shulamith and Haim Rosenbaum"; the security of their new personae so frail "a mouse could have severed the lifeline with one Lilliputian snap". Even in her sleep, "that other deceiver", Shirley–Shulamith "for all the dreamy validity of her little Cross, would suffer her grandmother" announcing the memory of a Jewish childhood; the celebration of family, identity and community at Passover: "the stars were out, and the Bride had already come" (271).

Shirley–Shulamith's most tangible link with the past is food. In the conscious and relatively safe world of daylight, Sheila and Harry "would sometimes even dare indulge a nostalgia" for Jewish food, "they would stuff it in, as though it might be taken from them. Their lips grew shiny from the fat meat, their cheeks tumid from an excess of *Knockerl*", after which Sheila loved to sit and pick her teeth "with a perfect, crimson finger-nail. And dwell on past pleasures". However, the smell of food also evokes in her the "*smell* of the Orthodox" and causes the regretted remark to slip from her lips "you can't get away from it, Harry, the blood draws you" (272):

> she would have loved still to watch the hands lighting the *Chanukah*

candles. The Scrolls themselves were not more closely written than the faces of some old waxen Jews (272).

Her kindred affinity with the Jewish story threatens to draw Shirley back into Shulamith—insecure, frowning, nervous—unconvinced by the "rightness" of her conversion, the "right ideas" of her own brand of Christianity; ideas that were "true, of course. But the truth was always only half the truth".

While Shirley's insecurity is equal to Harry's, her determination and stamina are greater, so it is Shirley who ruthlessly perpetuates the Rosetree delusion. She rejects Himmelfarb when he arrives at her home, as a timely reminder at Passover, of the shadow she is running from. In him she sees the archetypal image of all Jewishness, images of her father, grandmother, cousins, and "the cousins of cousins", images of "the foetus she had dropped years ago, scrambling into the back of a cart, in darkness, to escape from a Polish village" (501). So she rejects Himmelfarb with a hysterical acclamation, "I will not be persecuted. First it was the *goy*, now it is the Jew. All I want is peace, and a nice home" (501).

Himmelfarb's threatening presence evokes a tirade in which "she could have shocked herself". Shirley and Harry "stood looking at each other, but so immersed in the situation, they did not observe that the sweat was streaming from every pore of their skins. They had turned yellow, too" (502). But while Shirley would have barred him admission to the house, her husband intervenes and allows Himmelfarb a seat in the hallway near the front door:

> "You had better sit there for a bit, and relax. You are pretty well flogged," Mr Rosetree said, using a word he did not seem to remember ever having used before (503).

It is the week before Passover–Easter. Here Harry and Shirley are playing Pilate and his wife, with Harry trying to wash his hands of the Jew, while listening to his wife's counsel to have nothing to do with him.

It is Shirley who explains—peremptorily—that they are leaving for the weekend and cannot extend Himmelfarb any hospitality. She does not even offer the obviously exhausted, hot, old man a drink of water, thus gaining her husband's approval:

> Harry Rosetree had to admire his wife for an unfailing ruthless materialism, such as he himself had been able to cultivate for use in business only. But to Shirl, of course, life was business (504).

So husband and wife retreat and leave Himmelfarb alone in their hallway:

> which was less a room than a means of protecting the owners from the

unwanted; their strength could not be questioned while they remained hidden (505).

In denying hospitality to a traveller, especially a Zaddik, Shirley and Harry are breaching the covenant they are running away from.

After Himmelfarb leaves, Shirley seeks refuge in the kitchen, in the comfort of kosher food: chicken soup, chopped liver, and *Kneidlach*. She calls to her husband:

> Har-ry? All this good soup will be getting cold. You don't wanta be afraid. He's gone. Tt tt! Har-*ry*! The night air is gunna play hell with you (509).

Food is not going to save either Harry or Shirley, and ultimately it is Shirley's desire for self-preservation that over-rides her love for her husband. For she "had a secret longing for hard, blond men, in sweatshirts that revealed their torsos. Not this soft sister, whom she had loved, however, by contract, and even, she could swear, by impulse" (583). When Harry realizes his new persona has ultimately failed him he breaks down and cries over the death of Himmelfarb and his inability to give him a Jewish burial. For Haim, this failure destroys not only the promise of Himmelfarb's bodily resurrection but Harry's last link with his Jewishness. Shirley, who is better at denial and sublimation than her husband, leaves him in his misery to "go to some nice picture. To forget" (584). It is a film, like most of the films she watches, with "no story much, but it made you feel good". For Shirley "feeling good" has something to do with whatever helps her forget.

Yet at the cinema she cannot forget, her friend Marge "kept on not exactly looking at her. Somehow side-ways. Sort of peculiar. All through that lousy picture" (585), thus reminding Shirley that her refuge is a frail one, creating for her a fear of transparency. And transparency has always been a nagging fear of Shirley, along with the fear of exposure: "Mrs Rosetree would like very much to know whether the house in Persimmon Street conveyed an impression of abnormality from the outside" (575). But she need not worry, as:

> normality alone was recognized in Paradise East, tragedy, vice, retribution would remain incredible until the Angel of the Lord stepped down and split the homes open with his sword, or the Bomb crumbled their ant-hill texture, violating the period suites (575).

On returning from the cinema, she is weighed down with shopping, "trailing the fox cape as if the bull had been too much for her" (584). She walks through the garden "in which she had never really felt at home" (585), into the house whose bricks seemed to be crumbling, for the moment becoming "her version of the stuffy, felted tents" (585) of the

Exodus tribes. Her home in paradise East—outside of paradise—is a frail, ephemeral, nomadic construct that cannot reassure "when her spirit craved for reassurance" (585).

On discovering her husband's hanging body she "began to scream, right down, it seemed, to the source of breath" (586), as she is confronted with the embodiment of her guilt and her shame, and her short-lived remembrance of "the power of evil, that they tell us about in the beginning—oh, long! long!—and we forget, because we are leading this modern life—until we are reminded" (587). With the depth of emotion that White's secular Puritan characters do not share, Shulamith runs screaming to a neighbour who "was shocked by such lack of control" (586). However, she immediately corrects her behaviour and becomes Shirley again, controlled and calculated, to the point of fleetingly fearing her husband's suicide "might have been a lapse of taste" (587). Her remembrance of evil recedes. She "was jolted back into reason" and felt "rejuvenated by some power unidentified". Perhaps it is the power of her own distorted will.

Quickly Shulamith recedes into the unconscious, Conscious Shirley recommences the "right" and "practical" business of getting on with life. Having repressed her grief, Shirley immediately begins her transformation to Sheila, preparing to don the next persona from her wardrobe of disguises. Yet she is never comfortable, or secure. Within White's scheme, this is the fruit of her self-determination, consigned forever to sit in the "obscure purgatory" of an inauthentic existence, engaging in social gossip that masks the banality of evil, trying to communicate with the hostile and unhappy socialites, the crab-shell, Mrs Colquhoun, and the volcano Mrs Chalmers-Robinson.

CHAPTER THREE

MANDALA

Apollonian and Dionysian

The Solid Mandala was published five years after *Riders in the Chariot*, halfway through White's middle or religious period. The novels are similar yet different. He continues to use a Gadamerian frame, Ricoeurean anthropology continues to populate that frame, and his critique of logos (defined here as word or reason) continues to revolve around protagonists with Theogonic, Hellenic, and Hebraic horizons. He continues to judge his Jewish characters by their relationship with the Enlightenment.

The dominant symbol of the novel—a mandala—is not the same kind of symbol as Ezekiel's chariot. Occasionally, White's mandala symbolism has been understood as a movement towards eastern religion, or a movement away from religion altogether, but the evidence does not support either view. Whatever meaning we attach to the mandala comes from within western metaphysics, and western metapsychology, neither of which can exclude western religion. Also, this symbol, like all his symbols, does not have a fixed meaning. We are meant to question it while contemplating it. The mandala is an icon, a window. But if White was iconic in a Patristic sense he was also iconoclastic in a Rabbinic sense. This is what Ricoeur means by "the symbol gives rise" to an "occasion for thought" or "something to think about" (Ricoeur 1969, 348). What lies beyond the mandala–window lies beyond language.

In *Riders in the Chariot* White considers the question: Who is allowed to be a rider and who is not? In *The Solid Mandala* he considers the question: Who is allowed to receive a mandala and who is not? The answer is paradoxical. Waldo, who represents half the mandala, never receives one, and never wanted one, although Arthur always wanted him to want and have one. Sadly, this is why Waldo is excluded from both Arthur's dream and Arthur's dance. So, White offers a symbol of unity, and a formula for unity, while reminding us that unity is impossible. If accepting this manoeuvre is difficult, it is important to understand what it means. In *Patrick White's Fiction* (1986), Bliss calls this "the paradox of fortunate failure", which takes a different form in each novel.

What do Waldo and Arthur represent? First, they are meant to be two halves of one whole. Neither can be whole in himself. They also symbolize a dialectical or archetypal reality. What is this reality? How is it real? In philosophy, it appears in Plato's "old quarrel" between philosophy and poetry, which became the reason–feeling dialectic of neoclassicism and romanticism, which became Hegel's master–slave dialectic, then became Nietzsche's apollonian–dionysian dialectic. In metapsychology, it became Freud's model of the psyche (ego, id, super-ego) and Jung's variation of it (the conscious mind, personal unconscious, collective unconscious). The "reality" we are asked to consider here involves two contrasting ciphers: on the one hand, there is the domain of philosophy as logos (reason, neoclassicism, apollonian, ego, and conscious mind); on the other hand, there is the domain of poetry as mythos (feeling, romanticism, the dionysian, id, and unconscious mind). In objective and subjective terms, these two ciphers, and the tension between them, are both true and false.

In 19th and 20th century literature, the tension can be seen in the reason–feeling dialectic in Austen's *Sense and Sensibility* (1811) and the master–slave dialectic in Brontë's *Jane Eyre* (1847). Of course, White is not the same as Austen and Brontë. Waldo and Arthur are not the same as Elinor and Marianne or Jane and Rochester. But all three couples coexist within romantic hermeneutics. Austen lived in a different world from White, and Nietzsche lived between them, but Nietzsche inspired White's contemporaries Freud and Jung.

The essential difference, apart from logos and mythos being an extension of reason and feeling, is that Waldo and Arthur can never become whole as individual characters while Elinor and Marianne can. Austen knows both sisters need to mature before that can happen and she has a formula for what maturity looked like in her period. However, in order to fulfil their function as archetypes or tropes, White knows Waldo and Arthur must die or go mad. In this sense, his lose–lose situation is a perfectly logical aspect of his discourse. In this novel, he is internally consistent.

Austen's position on the reason–feeling dialectic owes much to the philosophy of John Locke (1632–1704). In all her novels, she relies on Locke's formula for maturity as "correct" knowledge—reason, revelation, and reflection on experience—described in *An Essay Concerning Human Understanding* (1690). Maturity was how the hero fulfilled his–her role within Austen's social contract, which looks remarkably like the one Locke describes in *First and Second Treatises of Government* (1689–

1690). While she is located within the romantic period, and is often thought to be a romantic author, her position on reason aligns her more closely with neoclassicism.

Brontë's position on the reason–feeling dialectic is closer to the romantic critique of neoclassicism. She gives the dialectic a makeover in *Jane Eyre* by viewing it, perhaps unconsciously, through the master–slave dialectic Hegel (1770–1831) describes in *The Phenomenology of Mind* (1807). This makes sense as Hegel was part of Brontë's zeitgeist not Austen's. By the time White began reworking the "old quarrel" it had been through a range of post-Kantian prisms in philosophy and post-Winckelmann prisms in aesthetics. One suspects Austen and Brontë were fortunate in not being influenced by the three German speaking men who blessed and cursed White: Nietzsche, Freud, and Jung.

What is unique about *The Solid Mandala* compared with *Riders in the Chariot*, and White's novels generally, is how the dialectical or archetypal relationship between Waldo's logos and Arthur's mythos presents itself as a commentary on *The Birth of Tragedy* not found in his other novels. The question is why, in this particular novel, White should have deconstructed the theme of Nietzsche's book, and deconstructed it as carefully as he did, after withdrawing into his private faith.

As McCulloch reminds us, in *Riders in the Chariot*, Alf Dubbo "projects the divine quaternity onto canvas" and "attempts to beatify" the "souls of his four living creatures" not in life but in art. Despite Alf's failure, White will continue—until *The Eye of the Storm*—to look within the artistic process for the means–technique to express his religious vision:

> White's exploration necessitated the discovery of a model for the perfect whole art form. A close analysis of the structure and subject matter of [*The Solid Mandala*] suggests that he may have found this model in Nietzsche's *The Birth of Tragedy*. Nietzsche's aim in his study was to trace the birth, the death and possible rebirth of tragedy in modern times. He, in learning that the Greeks "developed their mystical doctrines of art through *plausible embodiments*, not through purely conceptual beings", chose to study the significance that the Gods, Apollo and Dionysos, had as artistic forces or sources in Greek art … One learns that Apollo is the god of individuation, dream and illusion, and that Dionysos is the god of intoxication and the forces of nature: Apollo creates form, Dionysus is that out of which form is created. Nietzsche explores how the "Apollonian Greek", the creator of aesthetic forms which still stand as the paradigm of "beauty", is to be understood as the self-conquest of the "Dionysian Greek", whose characteristic mode of expression is the ritual orgy. When these two forces unite the tragic drama is an "Apollonian embodiment of Dionysiac insights and powers". Waldo and Arthur become for White the plausible embodiments of the Apollonian and Dionysian duality. These gods and

their intrinsic artistic forces are appropriate "ciphers" to use *in a secular age when former embodiments of transcendence produced by religions have been abolished by science.*[1] But transcendent ideas still remain in the ciphers, and White is primarily interested in finding an art that can express the "transcendence" he knows exists in the world. It is because "transcendent" ideas still remain in the ciphers that White chooses them to form a part in discovering the necessary literary tools that will enable the artist to express in art the meaning, illumination and Divinity inherent in life. This process also involves a quest for the rebirth of tragedy in this secular age. *The Solid Mandala* is a very complex novel postulating the question of whether or not art is able to constitute the religious activity of man … White's purpose is to attempt to recreate the conditions peculiar to Greek times, prior to the advent of Euripides' drama and Socratic thought, when a marriage between Apollo and Dionysos resulted in the birth of a perfect art form (italics added) (27–28).

This is a useful, concise summary of what Nietzsche and White were both attempting to do—questioning whether or not art is able to constitute the religious activity of man—and it took a particular genius to translate the philosophy of *The Birth of Tragedy* into the art of *The Solid Mandala*.

McCulloch's crucial observation, here, is "attempt to recreate the conditions peculiar to Greek times" prior to the "advent of Euripides' drama and Socratic thought" when "a marriage between Apollo and Dionysos resulted in the birth of a perfect art form".[2] This was not an original idea. Nietzsche did not invent the apollonian–dionysian dichotomy. It was part of his homoerotic post-Winckelmann inheritance. But through him it became, to him and to subsequent generations, an influential base-level assumption of—and often a master key offered by—the humanities and the social sciences. Further, Nietzsche's assumptions were part of Germany's "romantic reconstruction of the past" which White had been reassessing since the late 1930s.

The influence Nietzsche had on White is difficult to contextualize, because White said he was not drawn to the little Nietzsche he had read (Marr 1994, 129 and 413), and because Nietzsche is still a contentious figure. Like Plato, Nietzsche was a large part of White's zeitgeist, so

---

[1] Is this true? Did White believe this? Is it drawing a long bow to state that the "former embodiments of transcendence produced by religions have been abolished by science"? The subject is still debated. It is one thing to acknowledge how Darwin's theories challenged Biblical literalism. It is another thing entirely to declare that—because of this challenge—religious embodiments of transcendence have been abolished by science. The Incarnation has not been abolished by science. Neither has the Resurrection.

[2] The idea that the Presocratic marriage of Apollo and Dionysus resulted in "perfect art" has been highly influential but may be specious.

White may have been influenced by Nietzsche indirectly through other influences including Freud, Jung, and Spengler. Freud believed Nietzsche's "premonitions and insights often agree in the most amazing manner with the laborious results of psychoanalysis" and he believed Nietzsche "had a more penetrating knowledge of himself than any other man who ever lived or was likely to live" (Kaufmann 1992, 266). Nietzsche also influenced Spengler's *The Decline of the West*, which gave White "the gooseflesh" in his youth (Marr 1991, 151). Lawrence, an influence on White's early phase, was also influenced by Nietzsche.

Nietzsche has inspired a broad range of people: "anarchists, feminists, Nazis, religious cultists, Socialists, Marxists, vegetarians, avant-garde artists, devotees of physical culture, and archconservatives" (Tanner 1994, 1) and the list does not stop there. Within the Anglosphere, poor translations of his work ensured he was misunderstood, neglected, disgraced, until Kaufmann began retranslating his key works in 1950, which led to a re-evaluation of his work in the English speaking world (Tanner 1994, 1). Within Europe, where he had never been in disgrace, he became after World War II:

> a continued object of study and appropriation for existentialists, phenomenologists, and then increasingly, during the 1960s and 1970s, a cynosure for critical theorists, poststructuralists, and deconstructionsists. When the latter two movements first gained a foothold in the United States, then took the country over, it was Nietzsche who once more was acknowledged as the major source of their inspiration. Some analytical philosophers, too, found that he was not so remote from their interests as they had assumed, and, in that reciprocal motion that is so characteristic of academic life, congratulated him on having had, in embryonic fashion, some of their insights, while at the same time reassuring themselves about those insights by invoking his authority. There is now a flourishing Nietzsche industry, and almost certainly more books appear on him each year than on any other thinker, thanks to the appeal he has for so many disparate schools of thought and anti-thought (Tanner 1994, 2–3).

Green 2000 even attempted to "articulate a properly Christian hermeneutic of the cross, using Nietzsche's table of virtues and vices as a guide".

Nietzsche's university lectures on the Presocratic philosophers have now appeared as *The Pre-Platonic Philosophers* (1995). Also, at the same time he was writing *The Birth of Tragedy* he was also writing notes for another book, unpublished in his lifetime, which appeared posthumously as *Philosophy in the Tragic Age of the Greeks* (1962). While that book is unfinished, in it we see him warming to his obsession. In *The Birth of Tragedy*, he finds a golden age of pre-Euripidean tragedy in pre-classical Greece, subsequently disrupted by Socratic logos or reason. In *Philosophy in the Tragic Age of the Greeks*, he finds a golden age of philosophy in pre-classical Greece, also disrupted by Socratic logos or reason.

Nietzsche was obsessed with Socrates as a negative turning point. He was preoccupied with what was supposedly lost to Socratic reason during the classical Enlightenment in ancient Greece. And, by analogy, also lost to the neoclassical Enlightenment in modern Europe. This rhetoric reinforced a pre-existing and an ongoing critique of reason. While his speculations about Presocratic tragedy and philosophy have influenced metapsychology and critical theory, questions must be asked. Was he right about Presocratic tragedy? Was he right about Presocratic philosophy? Can we continue to equate, as he does, the problem of tragedy with the problem of philosophy, or are they two separate problems? As the answers to these questions will be determined by our sociopolitical beliefs, Tanner's point about reciprocity is worth considering, since critics will agree with Nietzsche whenever he appears to agree with them.

We need to consider what White took from Nietzsche and what he left behind. *The Solid Mandala* appears to accept Nietzsche's thinking about the creative potential of the apollonian and dionysian principles, provided they are integrated into a single whole, as Nietzsche believed they were in the tragedies of Aeschylus and Sophocles. It also accepts Nietzsche's thinking about the fate of tragedy—or the tragedy of fate—when Euripides introduced Socratic rationalism into his tragedies. Nietzsche is left with an inescapable dilemma in *The Birth of Tragedy*, where apollonian and dionysian are never allowed integration into a philosophical–aesthetic whole, because of Socratic logos–reason. White is left with an inescapable dilemma in *The Solid Mandala*, where apollonian and dionysian are never allowed integration into a philosophical–aesthetic whole, also because of Socratic logos–reason.

When he was a boy, Waldo wanted to write a tragedy and act it out for his family's benefit. Arthur knew there was something wrong with Waldo's tragedy so he proposed an alternative—a more "natural" tragedy of a cow and her stillborn calf—which his family found unbearably confronting. Is Waldo's hypothetical tragedy more apollonian and Euripidean? Is Arthur's hypothetical tragedy more dionysian, as the tragedies of Aeschylus and Sophocles supposedly were (Kaufmann 1966)? We do not know. Each critic will answer these questions differently. If what we see here is not the exact same logic of *The Birth of Tragedy*, the logic still comes from *The Birth of Tragedy*, as White understood it.

In *Flaws in the Glass*, White said: "I see the Brown brothers as my two halves" (146). A few sentences later he admitted that, in his case, he hated what he loved, while Manoly "loved more deeply, because there is less hate in him." Traditionally, when someone says they have two halves, they are referring to the binaries of conscious and unconscious, light and dark, good and evil, mind and heart, love and hate. It is of course understandable to see the apollonian and dionysian binary as extensions of these binaries.

Waldo's tragedy represents the dilemma of an individuated apollonian archetype not integrated with his dionysian twin. Arthur's tragedy represents the dilemma of an individuated dionysian archetype not integrated with his apollonian twin. Waldo represents the west's reigning logos. Arthur represents its subjugated mythos. A similar logic is offered by a lot of 19th and 20th century fiction written within the shadow of romanticism. Like Nietzsche, White believes logos to be problematic, in itself, because it fears mythos (Dodds 1951). Such a belief is not unique to Nietzsche or White. It is characteristic of romantic hermeneutics. It represents problems or pseudo-problems as irreconcilable as they are hypothetical.

Leaving the Church, at some point in his middle age, created a dilemma for White, as he still had to reconcile a range of influential dialectics. If he never succeeded in reconciling the logos–mythos dialectic, in the same way Austen succeeded in reconciling the reason–feeling dialectic, this does not mean he was a failure, it means the discourse he bought into and reworked went awry, somewhere after Austen, during the evolution of romantic hermeneutics. Also, it may be that, if the reason–feeling dialectic has remained true, some of its successor dialectics have turned out to be false. But they were still influential, so reconciling them cannot be a measure of White's success. Being a creature of the 20th century, he may have taken some of his influences more seriously than he should have, or more seriously than we do in the 21st century, but that does not diminish the value of what he was trying to achieve and did achieve.

If the novel is more Nietzschean than his other novels—it contains many references to Greek mythology and Wagnerian opera—we also know he had read and was inspired by Jung while writing it (White 1981, 146; Marr 1991, 451). In the novel, Nietzsche's thinking about tragedy in *The Birth of Tragedy* is clearly inseparable from Jung's thinking about individuation in *Psychology and Alchemy* (1944).

As Jungian psychology was more of an influence in *The Solid Mandala* than it was in *Riders in the Chariot*, it is a point of entry to the novel's combination of post-Kantian philosophy and Nietzschean dramaturgy. As Morley suggests:

> The mandala and the quaternity are the two predominating images in the

novel. These forms and their variants have been extensively explored by Carl Jung, through his studies of dreams, of European and Eastern iconography, and of the writings of mystics. The mandala, as an image of divine perfection and harmony, is of particular importance in Jung's theory of the archetypes of the collective unconscious. But while there is evidence within White's novels that he is familiar with Jung's work, it does not follow that his mystical and visionary material is necessarily derived from the writings and observations of Jung. Contextual evidence also indicates that White has a direct acquaintance with many of the mystical and alchemical writings and much of the religious iconography known to Jung, as well as with the work of many artists whose experiences have led them to formulate a vision of life not unlike White's own. Jung considers that the mandalic visions of modern man, unlike those of past ages, do not contain a deity at the centre, but we should not assume that White is necessarily using the mandala in the same way it has occurred in Jung's twentieth century patients. While man himself seems to be at the centre of White's mandala images, their circumference connotes some aspect of transcendence or divine love. And in Arthur's four-cornered mandala-dance the two basic images of square and circle, man and God, come together and *coalesce* (187).

Behind Jung there is Freud, and behind Freud there is Nietzsche, so we must ask an obvious question: What is behind Nietzsche? The simple answer is whatever Nietzsche inherited from his forebears, adapted, and bequeathed to Freud and Jung.

Plato is behind all of these thinkers and behind Plato the Presocratic philosophers are lurking alongside the Presocratic tragedians. This is where things get murky, as our knowledge of the Presocratic philosophers is based on fragments and second-hand testimonia, but the murkiness must be negotiated because—irrespective of whether White was theoretical or systematic—the milieu that influenced him, and the milieu that interpreted him, *had* theorized and systematized what was supposedly Platonic and positioned it against what was supposedly Presocratic.

Characters identified with logos represent reason (what Paglia would call civilization), are males associated with the apollonian (or the socratic), the ego, and the conscious mind, who have difficulty relating to the archetypal feminine, and are often celibate, or homosexual, or celibate homosexuals. In the fiction of White and his postwar contemporaries, the presence of the male homosexual trope in literature is often shorthand for socratism–platonism. Characters identified with mythos represent feeling (what Paglia would call nature), are females associated with the dionysian, the id, and the unconscious mind, who have difficulty relating to the archetypal masculine, and invariably have red hair, in one of its many shades, or grey hair that was once red.

The Brown brothers are not identical twins. While both are male, we know Arthur has inherited his mother's red hair and other characteristics of mythos (including the archetypal feminine). While we do not know the colour of Waldo's hair, we do know he has inherited his father's affinity with logos (including the archetypal masculine). Waldo is sterile in a celibate, or homosexual, or celibate homosexual way which is socratic. Arthur is fertile in a dionysian way, although his sexuality is unclear, and he does sleep with and often "comforts" Waldo, who is needy without understanding or accepting his neediness.

We must understand what this "comforting" means, as some critics have accused White of "affirming" incest (During 1996). This is mischievous, as White never "affirmed" incest between humans in the real world. It is misleading to suggest he does. There are references to inbreeding among isolated rural families with low IQs in *The Twyborn Affair* (1979)—in that novel one rural father does have a child by his daughter—but White does not "affirm" this incest. If there is incest in *The Solid Mandala*, as there almost is in *The Vivisector*, and there clearly is in *The Eye of the Storm*, it is usually part of White's borrowing from Jung. It relates to individuation and the reconciliation of opposites he found in *Psychology and Alchemy*, a book full of dialectical and archetypal incest. Halfway through *Sense and Sensibility*, Elinor "comforts" her sister, in bed, when Marianne suffers a nervous breakdown on being forced to recognize the truth about Willoughby. That is not incest. It is reason and feeling accepting their need of each other.

Apart from these variations, White makes the same kind of dialectical and archetypal distinctions between logos and mythos made by other literary novelists of his period. So the reader will develop a better sense of what is happening in *The Solid Mandala* if they read a range of similar novels from his literary milieu. Both *The Bell* (1958) and *Robinson* (1958) are summarized in the Appendix, so we can compare what Murdoch and Spark are doing in their novels with what White is doing in this novel.

The Brown Family

In the early 1890s, in fin de siècle England, George Brown married Anne Quantrell. They become atheists and Fabian socialists and have twin sons. Arthur arrives first and is healthy. Waldo arrives second and is sick, having been born with his "innards twisted" (32). In Part III—"Arthur"— we learn of Arthur's earliest memories of the Old World. On one occasion, while sick Waldo is at home with his parents, Anne's wealthy relatives take Arthur to the opera. While sitting in their box, they wonder what the young fellow is making of Wagner's Götterdämmerung, and joke about what his father would make of it, since "Irony is not for Baptist-rationalists even when it kills off a few more unacceptable gods" (217).

We never discover what George Brown thinks of the mimetic possibilities of Wagnerian opera or Nietzsche's views on Greek tragedy. Being a Fabian socialist, he has other obsessions. He escapes to Australia, with his wife and two sons, so his little nuclear family will be free from the myths of the Old World, free from his poor family's Baptist myths, free from her wealthy family's Anglican myths. They end up in what they hope will be an existential or de-mythologized setting, Terminus Road (terminus + road = the end of the road) on the fringes of White's iconic Sarsaparilla, then a rural place.

Unfortunately for George, they can never really be myth-free, because the myths of western religion have preceded them, and because he has brought his own myths with him, although he never recognizes them as myths. George builds a weatherboard house and paints it brown to blend in with the surrounding houses. To remain distinctive within this landscape, he insists on giving his house a classical pediment, making it a "little, apologetic, not quite proportional temple" to reason "standing in the trampled grass" (37). No one in Sarsaparilla understands it. He does not understand it either, or accept the mythos within it.

There is a veranda under the pediment. This is the proscenium on which the Brown brothers act out their götterdämmerung, at the end of the road, in an inhospitable, uncomprehending landscape, because Australia is neither ancient Greece nor the Old World. When Waldo is a little older, he wants to write and stage a tragedy on this veranda, although he is too young to know what tragedy is. He has merely heard about it from his father's storytelling. Already, as an apollonian boy, he is linked with the myths of the tragic hero, struggling to make sense of his unjust fate. As he is uncomfortable being in the world, and always wishes to be in a transcendent place, he is also identified with the myths of the exiled soul.

As Arthur's role in the novel is to continually drag his brother "behind the line where knowledge didn't protect" (46, 47), he intuitively knows Waldo's tragedy will not confer soteria. He tries to distract them. He proposes a more "natural" tragedy of a cow with her stillborn calf, which to him is not really tragic, as the cow can go on to have other calves. While his mother agrees with this proposition, ironically—"Yes," sighed Mother. "Cows often last for years, and lead very useful lives" (40)—his father tries to stop him from shaking "the whole framework of their stage" (40). When George finds he cannot stop Arthur, he retreats from the stage into the house.

If this is a commentary on *The Birth of Tragedy*, how is Arthur's play different from Waldo's play? Does Waldo's play echo Euripides? Does Arthur's play echo Aeschylus and Sophocles? These questions are important when considering the degree to which this passage may be part of White's commentary on the possibility or the impossibility of modern tragedy.

While Waldo was officially his red-haired mother's favourite, and the red-haired Arthur her duty, Anne's affinities with mythos were passed on to Arthur, who had robust health and a certain beauty as a child. Arthur was his father's favourite, in the beginning, but George's affinities with logos were passed on to Waldo, who had frail health as a child, a small head, a withered-looking face, and thin lips that tended to disappear in bitterness and suffering. George also has these characteristics, plus a limp, an Oedipus or swollen foot, symbolically transferred to his logos son:

> He put his hand on Waldo's shoulder, through which the limp transferred itself. They were limping and struggling, as if in the one body, all the way to the front veranda (34).

George wore a special boot, which the rest of the family hardly noticed, as it "fell into the same category as inherited furniture" (33). He also has asthma.

The novel's götterdämmerung, carefully described and densely woven, ends several decades later, when Waldo dies and Arthur is taken into custody and probably committed to residential care. Shall we call this literary scheme philosophy, drama, or psychology? It can be all three. White wore his philosopher's hat when exploring the Platonic model of mind, his dramaturgist's hat when exploring the Nietzschean theory of mimesis, and his analyst's hat when exploring the Jungian psychology of consciousness. These hats were more interchangeable in the 20th century than now. It would be much harder, if not impossible, for a 21st century author to do what he did.

Jung's individuation no longer has the cultural currency it once had. However, individuation does not only refer to Jung's conscious and unconscious minds. Before Jung, it represented a criterion of identity, which included a range of opposites within metaphysics, beginning with Aristotle's belief that "real" identity was located in the individual and not solely in Plato's world of Forms and Ideas. The principle of individuation is associated not only with Jung but with western speculation more generally.

Waldo is half of a whole. He cannot be whole, as a person, because he is a character. He cannot be whole, as a character, because logos can only be half of a whole, and because White, as literary creator, has decided he cannot become whole as long as he is never fully integrated with Arthur's mythos. We need to be clear about what is happening here. If mimesis means an imitation of life then we must evaluate the ways in which *The Solid Mandala* imitates life. This is not straightforward. It depends on how an act of literature can be said to imitate life. Literary characters are not human beings.

Is there a problem with imposing Jungian schemes onto literary schemes? Are literary schemes self-limiting once they become too Jungian or can only be understood through a Jungian prism? While Jungian schemes can result in great fiction, one thinks of Robertson Davies's dazzling performances in the Deptford Trilogy of the 1970s and Cornish Trilogy of 1980s, psychoanalysis pertains to human beings not to literary characters. But if literary characters are not human beings, what is the mimetic relationship between the two? And if we must be wary of Jungian characters then why not be wary of Freudian characters, Nietzschean characters, Platonic characters, and all characters that have metaphorical associations? We can use this against White, if we choose to, but that would be arguing against a lot of literature, and against the possibility of mimesis itself.

If Waldo's death is one symbolic aspect of a larger götterdämmerung, questions must be asked. What is the götterdämmerung and his role within it? What is supposed to be dying with him? Is his death a statement about logos within the Platonic model of mind, or Nietzschean tragedy, or Jungian psychology, or the end of a Spenglerian cycle of civilization, or all these? Although this götterdämmerung idea claims to be timeless, does its logic, and his symbolic death within it, begin somewhere in the 19th century and end somewhere in the 20th century? Are the götterdämmerung and the symbolic death still relevant in the 21st century? Again, this brings us back to the relationship between literature and life, to the question of verisimilitude, or truthlikeness in art, and to the possibility of mimesis itself.

Throughout his adulthood, Waldo pretends to be a writer; however, apart from a few essays, he never finishes what he writes. He is not creative because something is missing that White feels essential to creativity. Waldo remains a dissociated, vicarious, and alienated voyeur. His Socratic No is always negating his brother's Dionysian Yes. Throughout the novel, he hides behind words, the only ejaculations he has, but he is neither a philosopher nor a novelist, because he remains half of a whole, because his logos is nothing by itself and requires the addition of mythos in order to be creative.

We need to be clear about what this means, within the terms of

White's post-Kantian discourse, which Benedict XVI has critiqued. In spite of the assumptions White makes about logos, Waldo is not the final word on logos. He does not represent a living Christian understanding of logos, which belongs to the Hebraic category of metaphor that lies beyond rationalism and empiricism, reason and feeling, transcendence and immanence, philosophy and poetry.[3] He represents a particular kind of 19th and 20th century discourse about logos which begins with romanticism, continues with modernism, and ends with postmodernism.

Waldo's character, as logos, gradually changes from apollonian to socratic, during his journey from childhood to adulthood, while Arthur's character, as mythos, remains consistently dionysian throughout his life. White keeps returning to the idea, central to *The Birth of Tragedy*, that Waldo's increasing identification with socratic man—hence with philosophy and the logocentrism it produces—destroys the primal oneness of the cosmos, the original unity of Presocratic art, and the possibility of psychological integration. Nietzsche did not invent the idea or the dialectic–archetype it represents. He reworked an inheritance which goes back to Winckelmann, who directed Germany's gazed towards ancient Greece. Further, Nietzsche rendered the dialectic problematic, in a way it had not previously been problematic—by offering a hypothetical formula for wholeness while simultaneously declaring wholeness to be impossible. Nietzsche passed this discourse on to Freud, who turned it into the dialectic of ego–id–superego. Freud passed it on to Jung, who turned it into the dialectic of conscious–unconscious–collective unconscious.

It is worth noticing an irony here, as novelists such as White used the mediating terms of logos to critique those same terms. This brings us to the dilemma of critiquing logos while remaining dependent upon logos. This is the irony Gadamer noticed when he said movements which critique the Enlightenment develop and extend the Enlightenment's claims. If romanticism described the "conquest" of mythos by logos, and desired the "restoration" of what logos is supposed to have suppressed, the attempt to reverse the inheritance of classical Greece and neoclassical Europe perpetuates rather than overcomes the "abstract contrast" between logos and mythos. Throughout history, logos and mythos have been invoked for a wide range of purposes. Whether ancient or modern, the prejudice which equates mythos with a pre-Enlightenment wholeness—whether ancient or modern—is just as abstract and dogmatic as the prejudice which imagines logos to have a higher authority than mythos (Gadamer 1960).

---

[3] It tends to be forgotten that, in the post-Kantian context, Christianity has engaged with every philosophical and aesthetic movement—including phenomenology, existentialism, and hermeneutics—while maintaining the intellectual integrity of its Biblical mission.

In *The Solid Mandala*, White presents logos and mythos as a psychic conflict. For White, the original conflict, which was caused by logos, led to the loss of wholeness, and many of his forebears and contemporaries agreed with him, as they reworked Plato's "old quarrel" between philosophy and poetry. Ultimately, Waldo and Arthur are a particular version of the "old quarrel", a quarrel between philosophy and poetry, conscious and unconscious, reason and feeling, and a range of similar dialectics and archetypes. The quarrel was an essential element of White's creativity and the creativity of other novelists inspired by romantic hermeneutics. Whether the quarrel represents truths or lies is moot, as is whether the quarrel is still relevant to us in the 21st century.

Early in the "Waldo" section, while the two retired brothers are taking one of their daily walks, Arthur raises the subject—always elusive and delicate within the Brown family and their acquaintance—of Waldo's "writing". Arthur suggests Waldo might want to write about Leonard Saporta. This startles Waldo, who says there is nothing about Saporta "that anyone could possibly write about". But what startles Waldo even more is Arthur's suggestion that "simple people" like Saporta are "more transparent":

> I mean, you can see right into them, right into the part that matters. Then you can write about them, if you can write, Waldo—can't you? I mean, it doesn't matter what you write about, provided you tell the truth about it (29).

Waldo is deafened by Arthur's use of the terms "transparent" and "truth", and by the hint that he might not be much of a writer. This is because, according to Waldo's logos, Arthur's mythos should not be able to understand the concepts of transparency and truth, or what it takes to be a writer.

White does not agree with Waldo. He has a highly-defined sense of how philosophy–poetry, conscious–unconscious, and reason–feeling each contribute to literary creativity, as different mental processes. At some stage of Waldo's adolescence, he realizes his father—the reader in the family—is a failure. The irony here is that, while Waldo "cultivated his gift for distinguishing failures" (82) until the end of his life he never acknowledged himself as his father's failure. When the realization finally comes, that he is the same kind of failure, it ends his life. Arthur is the agent of that realization; its constant reminder.

Waldo has always been secretive about his writing, which everyone wondered about but few dared to ask about. A major turning point occurs during his middle age, around the time of the Peace and his malicious doll–gift to Mrs Poulter (184–186). After this malicious gift, he began to resent her, and hate everyone associated with a mystery, including Arthur, the "thread of continuity" and the "core of truth" (187). As he feels more exposed and threatened, he is forced to find a new hiding place for his private papers: the evidence of his inability to write. Thereafter, White arranges for Arthur's mythos to make a range of assaults on Waldo's logos.

When one of Waldo's private papers—a transcript of someone else's poem not his own original work—drops to the floor, Arthur picks it up, reads it, and says "Tennyson wrote some pretty good poetry" (195), whereupon the blood drains from Waldo's lips and his hands start trembling. When Arthur admits to reading Shakespeare, Waldo refuses to believe Arthur can understand Shakespeare—especially Shakespeare's language—to which Arthur replies: "Yes. Language is difficult. But a word will suddenly flash out, won't it, Waldo?—for somebody who doesn't always understand" (196).

Now, more than ever, on discovering that logos cannot define and limit mythos, Waldo found it necessary to withdraw, into his territory, into the world of books, into his job at the state library where, theoretically, Arthur does not belong and cannot follow. One day, however, two years before his retirement, a female colleague draws his attention to a quaint old man who occasionally comes to the library to explore extraordinary subjects: the *Bhagavad Gita*, the *Upanishads*, books about Japanese Zen, erotological works, *Through the Looking-Glass*, and *The Brothers Karamazov* (196). As Waldo approaches the reading room—where the old man is sitting in a raincoat, even though it is a fine warm day—he sees it is his brother. On this particular day, Arthur has come to "get on with" *The Brothers Karamazov* (198), which is why, during their conversation in the reading room: "All the loathing in Waldo was centred on *The Brothers Karamazov* and the glass marble in Arthur's hands" (199).

Arthur particularly wants to re-read the parable of the Grand Inquisitor which, although it furthers the character development within *The Brothers Karamazov*, is a philosophical work in its own right, about the ambiguity of human nature and human freedom, which questions the possibility of a personal and benevolent God. On hearing that Arthur wants to understand this parable, Waldo could have laid his head on the table, as their lifetime together has exhausted him: "What will it do for you?" he asks his brother wearily, "To understand? The Grand Inquisitor?" (199) Arthur says it may allow him to help people such as Mrs Poulter, and Waldo himself, but not the Saportas, who no longer need his help. It would also fulfil the need to find somebody to worship: "Everybody's got to concentrate on something. Whether it's a dog. Or," he babbled, "a glass marble. Or a brother, for instance. Or Our Lord, like Mrs Poulter says" (200).

Sweat breaks out on Waldo's forehead as Arthur taps into his fear:

> "Afraid." Arthur was swaying in his chair. "That is why our father was afraid. It wasn't so much because of the blood, however awful, pouring out where the nails went in. He was afraid to worship something. Or body. Which is what I take it this Dostoevski is partly on about."
>
> Suddenly Arthur burst into tears, and Waldo looked around at all the opaque faces waiting to accuse him, him him, not Arthur. But just as suddenly, Arthur stopped.
>
> "That's something you and I need never be, Waldo. Afraid. We learned too late about all this Christ stuff. From what we read it doesn't seem to work, anyway. But we have each other."
>
> He leaned over across the table and appeared about to take Waldo's hands.
>
> Waldo removed his property just in time (200).

Waldo disengages from this crazy old man, Arthur, and ejects his brother from the library. While he is congratulated by his colleagues, for his presence of mind, he was not quite in focus for the rest of the day. While he experiences his public rejection of Arthur as a personal triumph, and while they avoid each other on the train going home, they are reunited, equitably and silently, on the bus from Barranguli to Sarsaparilla. Children follow them, as they walk down Terminus Road, shouting or singing:

> "One a one makes two,"
>   the children seemed to scream.
> *Screeeeee* they went on the evening air damp with nettles.
>   "One a one a one,"
>   they sang,
> "Two a two is never one" (202).[4]

When the children leave them, Arthur takes Waldo by the hand: "Whatever happens," Arthur said, "we have each other" (202). Waldo agrees, because he is too weary to disagree, or to cry, as his brother leads him home. This is the conflict within Waldo: his need of Arthur, his resentment of that need, his inability to love, his belief that his logos is self-sufficient and autonomous. The conflict will only end with his death, which he originally intended to be Arthur's death.

What triggers this death? Arthur confronts Waldo, asking him whether he understands love and has ever been in love. Waldo says he supposes he

---

[4] Each reader will have to decide whether these children function as a chorus, perhaps like the four relatives in *The Ham Funeral*. The answer will depend on the reader's attitude towards the idea of modern tragedy.

has, "as much as any normal person" (207), but he is suspicious of his own reply. He asks Arthur whether *he* has ever been in love. Arthur's answer is "all the time", but he is not sure he loves enough. Apart from that, he believes love is too big a subject for him to understand, however: "If we loved enough … then perhaps we could forget to hate."

Waldo's death is the result of a struggle between what has become Arthur's propensity to love and his own propensity to hate. He discovers a crumbled piece of paper, on which Arthur has written a poem, which he reads aloud "not so menacing as he would have liked, because he was, in fact, menaced":

my heart is bleeding for the Viviseckshunist
Cordelia is bleeding for her father's life
all Marys in the end bleed
but do not complane because they know
they cannot have it any other way.

Arthur's poem is Waldo's ultimate and final challenge. He calls it that "disgusting *blood* myth";[5] a "blood myth"—which includes the Incarnation and the Crucifixion—his logos vehemently rejects; a "blood myth" Arthur's mythos accepts. As he has never loved or suffered—as Cordelia had in *King Lear*; as the Marys had at the foot of the Cross—he has never understood the relationship between love and suffering. He cannot live with the poem's sentiments. He cannot accept that Arthur wrote it. The fact that it might not be a great poem is irrelevant. It still comes from a place that inspires great poetry, a place Waldo's logos has never been, and refuses to acknowledge.

The fact of the poem's existence renders Waldo bloodless and drains all pretense of creativity from him. He is enraged by the possibility of Arthur's creativity, albeit small: the "drop of unnatural blood" which "continued to glitter, like suspicion of an incurable disease" (212). He takes the dress box filled with his private papers and burns them, just as his frustrated father burned his copy of *The Brothers Karamazov* not long before he died (213).

After the burning, Waldo feels free of practically everything except Arthur. He goes and lays on his bed, the bed he shares with Arthur, wondering how he might disembarrass himself of Arthur—quickly, cleanly, subtly—as freeing himself from his brother is now an urgent problem, a final constraint. Arthur enters the bedroom, afraid at last, and Waldo wonders whether Arthur "noticed the hurt which was intended for

---

[5] The "blood myth" refers to any myth or metaphor that accepts the unity of matter and spirit. Arthur's parents and brother reject this unity. He accepts it.

him" (213). There follows a struggle, but we cannot tell who is attacking, and who is defending himself from attack:

> He was entranced by Arthur's great marigold of a face beginning to open. Opening. Coming apart. Falling.
>   "Let me go! Wald! Wald-o!"
>   As dropping. Down. Down (214).

Has the hate-filled Waldo fallen into the love-filled Arthur's open mouth? Has his logos been absorbed by mythos? Or has he simply evaporated? At this point in the novel, we do not know where he has gone. We only know that at the end of "Waldo" he is no longer *there*.

Part III—"Arthur"—is a mixture of Arthur's perspective and the narrator's. It is much shorter than "Waldo" because, theoretically, Arthur's mythos does not have access to the language of Waldo's logos, and because the function of "Arthur" is to provide a different perspective on events already described in "Waldo". Curiously, "Arthur" is a straightforward, ordered, linear narrative compared with "Waldo", which weaves back and forth across time. Also curiously, White uses the language of the conscious mind to describe it. Given what the dionysian is meant to signify, this is somewhat anomalous. When the language of logos is used to theorize– systematize mythos, mythos becomes logos. The unconscious is made conscious and is no longer the unconscious.

Arthur's horizon is quite rational, although it is described as non-rational or irrational. This paradox is unavoidable, as language is dependent upon words. "Arthur" is an example of what Gadamer means when he says movements that critique reason develop and extend the claims of reason. It is also an example of what Nietzsche and Heidegger mean by a Presocratic wholeness theoretically sundered by western speculation since Socrates. Whether or not this idea is a flaw in White's rhetoric, or in the rhetoric of romantic hermeneutics generally, his depiction of Arthur as a dionysian character is still brilliant and coherent. It is great art. It has moral purpose. It may represent a fundamental truth. Although any truth it may represent belongs to the realm of belief. Of course, it may also be a lie.

"Arthur" begins with Arthur's voyage to Australia as a young boy. He is on deck with his mother. Waldo has gone with his father to make friends with the Chief Engineer, so Anne believes, although: "neither George nor Waldo like engines; but perhaps they feel it is manly to try" (216). Everything about the opening scene establishes Arthur as mythos. He has red hair and is linked with his red-haired mother. He is strong and healthy: "Waldo was the sick one, they said, Arthur had always been strong. So he must continue to be" (215). Unlike Waldo, he is fearless, and does not care for his safety, as he climbs over the rails of the ship to reach something he sees that makes him happy: "the red-gold disc of the sun" (215). Screaming ladies snatch him back. His mother tells him he must never climb over the rails. He might fall into the sea and be lost forever. But the prospect of dying does not concern this budding übermensch.

Arthur falls asleep on the deck, whereupon he has an earlier memory, back in England, of attending the opera with his wealthy Quantrell relatives. His grandmother asks him whether he likes being in a box: being confined within a frame, being a spectator rather than an actor, gazing at a representation of life rather than life itself. He is sleepy, excited, and floating in a sea of music:

> … lapped so deliriously in linings of dark red velvet, sleep was carrying him off. Or music. Who and where were the gods? He could not have told, but knew, in his flooded depths. Tell Waldo about the lady in the brass helmet. The primrose pomp. If the crimson flood of music had been of Waldo's world (217).

Like mathematics, this romantic music is part of Arthur's world not Waldo's. Music is also part of Waldo's world—he develops a fine tenor voice as an adult—but his music is not romantic and it does not have romantic feeling.

Arthur "knew from the beginning he was protected. Perhaps it was Waldo. Not everyone has a twin. He must hang on to Waldo" (218). The qualifier here is "perhaps". We never sure who is protecting whom. Both twins are lacking but judgments are made in favour of Arthur, who is given moral weight.

"Arthur" moves quickly. Suddenly the Browns are in Barranugli, where the young family is lodging with a joiner and his wife and George finds work as a bank teller. The boys go to school a couple of blocks away:

> … where nobody understood them until they managed to learn the language. Even so, Waldo, then and always, preferred to speak English because, he said, it had a bigger vocabulary. Arthur did not care. Or he did. He developed the habit of speaking mostly in Australian. He wanted to be understood. He wanted them to trust him too. Waldo, he knew, was suspicious of men, though Waldo was inclined to call them Australians (218).

White wrote of a period in which speech still mediated class, even in Australia.

Sometimes they went see their father at the bank, where Arthur, always curious about other lives, would go upstairs to explore the manager's residence:

> He loved other people's houses, it shocked Mother terribly, of opening cupboards and drawers to look inside. Mother continued shocked even after he pointed out it was the best way of getting to know about the owners (219).

When Anne tells him this is dishonest, he could "feel inside him the rush of words which wouldn't come" (219). He gets excited when defending himself against a charge of dishonesty—which he believes is unjust—but he does not have the language to do so. "Don't excite yourself, dearest," Anne tells him. "It isn't good for you. We do know that" (219). Even at this early age, Arthur's irrational tendencies are recognized and feared. His family encourages him to suppress his feelings, because they fear the irrational, because they signify a world that fears the irrational (Dodds 1951).

"Arthur loved the classical façade of their brown weatherboard house. He learned there was something about the Classical which Dad called 'sacrosanct—in a manner of speaking'" (223). Behind this façade, George would read his sons the Greek myths:

> While pausing every few weeks to remind them: none of this is real, none of this is true.[6] Whatever he meant by that … Arthur could not even care. He loved Demeter for her fullness, for her ripe apples, he loved Athene for her understanding … They would laugh to be told how shocked he was for Tiresias when Zeus took away his sight at the age of seven—*seven*—for telling people things they shouldn't know. So Arthur kept quiet. He was only surprised they didn't notice how obviously his heart was beating when Zeus rewarded Tiresias with the gift of prophecy and a life seven times as long as the lives of ordinary men. Then there was that other bit, about being changed into a woman, if only for a short time. Time enough, though, to know he wasn't all that different (224).

In Sarsaparilla, the Browns come to be regarded as an eccentric family of pagan loners. Through an amusing exchange of letters, between George and the headmaster of his sons' primary school, Waldo and Arthur are exempt from Scripture class (224). Mrs Allwright, wife of the local shop owner, has a feeling the Browns will be on their hands for always: "Mind you", she said, "I've got nothing against the English in general, the decent, church-going ones who you wouldn't mind sitting down at table with. But *these*!" (225) However, as she is a Christian Scientist, she is beyond the pale of what White regards as authentically Christian. Her husband,

---

[6] George is happy to retell the Greek myths, as stories, but does not believe they are "true". He despises Christianity because it is not "true". So what is his "truth" criteria?

however, is one of the novel's authentic Christian characters. He is kinder and more charitable than she is.

Arthur is first exposed to Christianity when he looks through the Allwright's bedroom window one day: "and there was Mr Allwright down on his knees in a blaze of yellow furniture. Arthur was fascinated, if not actually frightened, by his friend's face sunk on his chest, by the hands which he held out in front of him, pressed straining together as stiff as boards. It puzzled Arthur a lot" (226). When Mrs Allwright tells him her husband is praying: "If Arthur did not altogether understand, the wooden man [on the cross] began to put on flesh." After that:

> Arthur eventually added Mr Allwright to what he knew as truest: to grain in wood, to bread broken roughly open, to cow-pats, neatly, freshly dropped. If he did not add Mrs Allwright it was because she did not fit into that same world of objects, she never became distinct, she was all ideas, plots, and tempers. In myth of life, he never looked to Hera (227).

Around this time, Arthur's classmates discover that, although he is a "dill", he can solve their mathematical problems. His idiot savant gift for calculating numbers becomes the means through which he began earning his glass marbles, four of which he considered his permanencies:

> There were the speckled gold and the cloudy blue. There was the whorl of green and crimson circlets. There was the taw with a knot in the centre, which made him consider palming it off, until, on looking long and close he discovered the knot was the whole point.
>   Of all these jewels or touchstones, talismans or sweethearts, Arthur Brown got to love the knotted one best, and for staring at it, and rubbing at it, should have seen his face inside (228).

Waldo scoffs at Arthur's marbles. He cannot see their point, their symbolism. There is a paradigmatic difference between the brothers. Arthur gazes into his marbles–mandalas as symbols of wholeness—and sees his reflection. Waldo gazes into his vanity mirror and kisses his reflection (228). When Arthur catches Waldo in the act, and challenges him, Waldo vehemently denies his narcissism. These differences matter little while they are a youthful apollonian–dionysian unity:

> … they would lie together, and the dark bed was all kindness, all tenderness towards them … As Venus said, in the old book Arthur came across years later: I generate light, and darkness is not of my nature; there is therefore nothing better or more venerable than the conjunction of

myself and my brother (229).[7]

But this conjunction is frail, "darkness could descend suddenly by daylight, in one black solid slab" (229), and the frailty is Waldo's rather than Arthur's.

Arthur sensed he would have to protect his brother, "who was too clever by half, who read essays aloud in class, who liked books … Because of it all, Waldo needed defending from himself and others" (229). Waldo needs defending because he neither recognizes nor understands his frailty. Arthur does not mix with the other boys, apart from solving their mathematical problems and earning his glass marbles. The other boys "accepted Waldo by fits and starts, because they were deceived, from some angles, into seeing him as another of themselves" (229). Hence Waldo's illusion of being "normal".

"Arthur" provides a different gloss on an episode previously described in "Waldo". The boys who "went behind the dunnies to show what they'd got" (229) would occasionally let Waldo come with them. The difference between Waldo and the boys is that, where the boys want to do what normal boys do, Waldo is nonsexual and prefers vicarious sublimations. One day, after a class in which Waldo read aloud a story he wrote—with elements of gothic horror, blood, and murder—Johnny Haynes and another boy walk him down to the pepper trees and begin acting out a "prick" fantasy ("Waldo" 44–45). Haynes takes out a knife and begins to prick Waldo around the gills. While the scene is a send up of Waldo's gothic prick fantasy, with its sublimations—he fears real blood as well as "blood myths"—Waldo begins whimpering. Suddenly, Arthur appears like an avenging angel, threatening to kill anyone who hurts Waldo, and splits open Haynes's lip.

Waldo is furious at Arthur's interference, for trying to make a fool of him, but Arthur believes the boys were in fact making a fool of Waldo. The broader issue here is not so much Arthur's interference, which is understandable, but Waldo's reaction to it, and the way it promotes the legend of Arthur's irrationality. An angry Mr Haynes confronts Mr and Mrs Brown and tells them they must admit to having a loopy son who is likely to become a psychosocial menace as he gets older. While the ineffectual Mr Brown maintains a stunned silence, Mrs Brown brings the confrontation to an end: "Mr Haynes," said Mother finally, "parents realize more than you, apparently, believe" ("Waldo" 47). Mr Haynes is shamed into leaving the Browns alone.

---

[7] At some point, Waldo went from being apollonian to being socratic. When did that point occur?

"Arthur" also provides a different perspective on the family's tragedy scene, on the veranda, under the classical pediment. Arthur is on his way to milk the family cow:

> In the meantime there was his family. All the members of his family were frail. As he went down to milk, there they were, sitting on the classical veranda. Mother who knew better than anyone how things ought to be done, had sliced her finger doing the beans; Waldo who knew how to think, was screwed up tighter than his own thoughts; and poor Dad, very little made him sweat under his celluloid collar.
>
> So Arthur had to go carefully. He tried to prevent the bucket from clanking. He was glad of the opportunity to give Jewel's udder a punch—holding up her milk as per usual—and bury his head in her cow's side.
>
> But when he returned along the path of trampled grass, he would have liked to cry. If they wouldn't have seen it. For there they were. Still. With Waldo going to write some old tragedy of a play.
>
> Arthur had by some means to distract.
>
> So he stood the bucket, and said more or less: "I'll act you out my tragedy of a cow."
>
> For nobody would be able to accuse him of not fully understanding a cow. And they sat looking at him, almost crying for his tragedy. As he stamped up and down, pawing and lowing, for the tragedy of all interminably bleeding breeding cows. By that time his belly was swollen with it. He could feel the head twisting in his guts.
>
> Everyone had begun to share his agony, but that, surely, is what tragedy is for.
>
> When Mother suddenly tried to throw the expression off her face, and said: "Oh Arthur, we understand your tragedy without your showing us any more."
>
> And at that moment he felt Dad turn against him. It was some question of afflictions. Except in theory, the afflicted cannot love one another. Well, you couldn't altogether blame Dad. With his aching leg.
>
> "I wish I knew how it felt," said Arthur.
>
> "Why?" asked Dad, biting his moustache.
>
> "It would make things easier, wouldn't it? if I understood."
>
> Dad didn't seem to think it would (229–230).

This scene confirms what Anne, George, and Waldo suspect about Arthur. It is a turning point in their attitude towards his mythos. Critics who believe in modern tragedy might interpret this scene as Arthur trying to restore tragedy's pre-Euripidean focus on Dionysus. Does this scene provide evidence for that?

Anne does make a final attempt to uncover the genius that may be lurking within Arthur, knowing he has a gift for figures, remembering mathematics and music have something in common. She tries to teach him piano but the experiment does not work. She finally gives up. Thereafter, he continues to help her in the kitchen, making butter and kneading bread, which becomes a "vocation" for the rest of his life (231–232).

About the time Waldo begins high school, his parents decide schooling is wasted on Arthur, who begins an apprenticeship at Allwright's store, where he remains for the rest of his working life. His gift for numbers makes him an invaluable asset to the Allwrights, which even Mrs Allwright grudgingly admits. Also, delivering groceries will give his mythos an entry into other people's homes, via the back door, while Waldo's education will give his logos an entry into other people's homes, via the front door. The logic of this never registers with Waldo, who assumes that his brother is (or should be) invisible and that no one knows (or should want to know) him. In fact, Arthur is a highly visible and integrated part of Sarsaparilla. People know him, albeit in a different way from Waldo.[8]

The first relationship we hear of, between Arthur and his customers, is with the candid and comical Mrs Musto of Fairy Flour fortune. While he has become a favourite with her downstairs and kitchen staff, after the grocery items were checked:

> … more often than not Arthur would get up and wander past the green baize door to the inner parts of Mrs Musto's house. He had never been denied access to them … The morning he went so far as to explore an upstairs room Arthur was surprised to find Mrs Musto standing in her bloomers and camisole. Mrs Musto, too, was surprised. It appeared as though she had just finishing having a cry. Her impulse was to scream, until she realized who it was (235).

She has been crying over her chauffeur, Stubbens, who bullies her and looks like her suave womanizing ex-husband. She tells him her tearful story, about her chauffeur and ex-husband. He is then dismissed, as she has other engagements on her mind, but not before announcing her intention to invite Waldo and Dulcie—who she calls a couple of lost souls—to the tennis party she is giving for the local youth.

Arthur meanders off into other parts of Mrs Musto's house and discovers the library, where he finds the definition of a mandala in her ex-husband's encyclopaedia. He becomes excited as he reads aloud to himself the definition which foreshadows his future dream and dance:

> *The Mandala is a symbol of totality. It is believed to be the "dwelling of the god". Its protective circle is a pattern of order super—imposed on—psychic—chaos. Sometimes its geometric form is seen as a vision (either waking or in a dream) or … danced* (238).

---

[8] Perhaps the works of Mikhail Bakhtin and Norman O. Brown help us to understand why and how this is.

After this, Arthur only half-resumed his rounds, preoccupied with the idea that Waldo is about to be introduced to Dulcie. Arthur, who wants to establish his own relationship with the Feinsteins, may have to share them with his brother:

> If the thought didn't grow unbearable, it was because, as Mrs Musto had pointed out, Waldo was in need of a kind. What this need could be, Arthur was not yet certain, much occupied as he was in working out his own needs and relationships (239).

His primary preoccupation, however, is trying to understand the mandala definition he has just read. He wants to know what "totality" means. He knows he cannot ask Waldo, or his mother, so a few days later he asks his father: the family's knowledge bearer. There follows a comical scene in which George makes a show of looking the word up in a dictionary and telling Arthur that "totality" is "the quality of being total", or "that which is a whole", "Spelt with a *w*—naturally". Then Arthur realized his father would never know any more than Waldo: "It was himself who was, and would remain, the keeper of mandalas, who must guess their final secret through touch and light" (240), who must dream them, and dance them, and share them.

White segues to the relationship between Arthur and Mrs Poulter: "The year the Poulters came to live down Terminus Road Mother had gone into hospital at Barranugli for the operation Waldo would not talk about" (256). The year was around 1920. The operation was for breast cancer. As Arthur had no one to talk to, he "had to tell Mrs Poulter". They became friends, even though her husband does not like him. Still looking into the cupboards of people's lives, he asks Mr Poulter about her private life, about why she married her husband, and about other things. She responds to him, because she has a candid and open nature, and because she has no other friends.

Soon after they become friends, he has a dream one Saturday night:

> Once Arthur dreamed the dream in which a tree was growing out of his thighs. It was the face of Dulcie Feinstein lost among the leaves of the higher branches. But Mrs Poulter came and sat on the ground beside him, and he put out his hand to touch what he thought would be her smooth skin, and encountered rough, almost prickly bark. He would have liked to wake Waldo to tell him. In the morning he could barely remember (260).[9]

The following morning, Mrs Poulter said, "What about that walk,

---

[9] Since the 1980s, I have believed that Arthur's dream and dance encapsulate White's (perhaps unconscious) sense of Gadamerian hermeneutics and Ricoeurean anthropology.

Arthur, you and me was going to take?" They set out in the afternoon, after she returns from church, while she is still dressed in her church-going clothes. As they wander aimlessly across paddocks and scrub, visiting a creek neither had seen before, not speaking but never far from each other's thoughts, Mrs Poulter introduces the subject of religion:

> "Funny none of you Browns never ever went to church," she said.
> "I suppose they went in the beginning. Till they found out."
> "Found out what?"
> "That they could do without it."
> "Ah, but it's lovely!" Mrs Poulter said.
> "They began to feel it wasn't true."
> "What isn't true?"
> He saw her raise her head, her neck stiffen.
> "Oh, all that!" said Arthur Brown, spinning a cow-turd. "About virgins. About Him," he said.
> "Don't tell me," said Mrs Poulter, as prim as Waldo, "that you don't believe in Our Lord Jesus Christ?"
> "Don't know all that much about Him."
> For the moment he cared less for her.
> "How do *you* know, anyway?"
> "It's what everyone has always known," she said. Then, looking at the toes of her shoes as they advanced, she said very softly, "I couldn't exist without Our Lord."
> "Could He exist without *you*?" It seemed reasonable enough to inquire.
> But she might not have heard.
> "Mother says Christians are all the time gloating over the blood."
> "Don't you believe they crucified Our Lord?" she said looking at him angrily.
> He had begun to feel exhausted.
> "I reckon they'd crucify a man," he said. "Yes," he agreed, trundling slower. "From what you read. And what we know. Christians," he said, "are cruel."
> "*They* were not Christians," Mrs Poulter said. "Men are cruel" (261).

While Arthur and Mrs Poulter see Christianity differently, the narrator never takes sides. Rather than closing the dialogue down, the narrator leaves it open. If Arthur notices that Christians are cruel, since he has been told they are cruel, the Christians he knows best—his employer Mr Allwright and his neighbour Mrs Poulter—are not cruel. If Mrs Poulter is right in noticing Christians did not crucify Jesus, men did, this can be interpreted in two ways; that males are predisposed towards cruelty specifically; that humans are predisposed towards cruelty generally.

Their conversation ends with an impasse—an aporia—the reader is invited to dialogue with. Their walk ends suddenly, as Arthur and Mrs

Poulter find themselves back in Terminus Road. That night, Arthur:

> ... dreamed he was licking the wounds, like a dog. He wondered whether
> he had been doing right, to lick up non-existent blood. Fortunately Waldo,
> who was sleeping, need never know. He had reached out and touched him
> to make sure. He reached out to feel for the mandala, his own special, on
> top of the po cupboard, but heard it roll, scamper out of reach. It would
> have involved too much to retrieve it, so he lay there miserably conscious
> of the distance between his desire and perfect satisfaction (262).

Arthur is around 28 years old when he dreams this dream, while still
under the influence of his family's rejection of any system of belief that
includes what Waldo calls—towards the end of his life—that "disgusting
blood myth". The family rejection of "blood myth"—the reason why
Waldo is excluded from Arthur's religious dream and dance—creates a
dilemma for Arthur because he is more accepting of "blood myth".

While Arthur's greatest desire is unity with his brother—and his
greatest frustration is the impossibility of that unity—he is also dialoguing
with Judaism and Christianity and coming up against other impasses and
aporias, which White cannot resolve. They are unresolvable, within his
terms of discourse, and within romantic hermeneutics generally. This is
why any further walks Arthur and Mrs Poulter take in the future: "were
not all that satisfactory, because it was only natural to talk, and you kept
on coming up against a wall, if not religion, something else" (262).

While it is self-evident that all human conversations run up against
walls, sooner or later, we must make a distinction between conversations
that are always difficult—say about politics and religion—and conversations
about the personal lives of interlocutors, especially when they are fictional
characters. Within the Brown family Arthur is unique. He wants to look
into other people's cupboards so he can know them better. In most cases
he is successful. In some cases he is not. He asks Mrs Poulter personal
questions; whether she minds being childless; whether her husband likes
her. She answers him as best she can. They communicate as much as two
friends can.

On one walk Mrs Poulter feels comfortable enough to let her hair
down, literally, whereupon Arthur "suddenly realized what was intended
of him". He is to dance a mandala, in the four stages of a Jungian
quaternary, which points to the idea of wholeness beyond it.

> In the first corner, as a prelude to all he had to reveal, he danced the dance
> of himself. Half clumsy, half electric. He danced the gods dying on a field
> of crimson velvet, against the discords of human voices. Even in the
> absence of gods, his life, or dance, was always prayerful. Even though he
> hadn't been taught, like the grocer, to go down on his knees and stick his

hands together. Instead, offering his prayer to what he knew from light or silences. He danced the sleep of people in a wooden house, groaning under the pressure of sleep, their secrets locked prudently up, safe, until their spoken thoughts, or farts, gave them away. He danced the moon, anaesthetized by bottled cestrum. He danced the disc of the orange sun above icebergs, which was in a sense his beginning, and should perhaps be his end.

While Mrs Poulter sat looking, playing with the tips of her dark hair. Sighing sometimes. Then looking down.

In the second corner he declared his love for Dulcie Feinstein, and for her husband, by whom, through their love for Dulcie, he was, equally, possessed, so they were all three united, and their children still to be conceived. Into their corner of his mandala he wove their Star, on which their three-corner relationship was partly based. Flurries of hydrangea-headed music provided a ceremony of white notes falling exactly into place, and not far behind, the twisted ropes of dark music Waldo had forced on Dulcie the afternoon of strangling. There she was, the bones of her, seated on the upright chair, in black. And restored to health by her lover's flesh. The indistinguishable, always more revealing eyes.

Dulcie's secrets, he could see, had been laid bare in the face of Mrs Poulter, who might otherwise have become the statue of a woman, under her hair, beside the blackberry bushes. Though she swayed lightly as he began to weave her figure into the appropriate corner. In Mrs Poulter's corner he danced the rite of ripening pears, and little rootling suckling pigs. Skeins of golden honey were swinging and glittering from his drunken mouth. Until he reached the stillest moment. He was the child she had never carried in the dark of her body, under her heart, from the beat of which he was already learning what he could expect. The walls of his circular fortress shuddered.

Mrs Poulter was at that point so obviously moved, she would have liked to throw the vision off, or stop him altogether, but he would not let her.

He had begun to stamp, but brittlely, rigid, in his withering. In the fourth corner, which was his brother's, the reeds sawed at one another. There was a shuffling of dry mud, a clattering of dead flags, or papers. Of words and ideas skewered to paper. The old, bent, overused, aluminium skewers. Thus pinned and persecuted, what should have risen in pure flight, dropped to a dry twitter, a clipped twitching. He couldn't dance his brother out of him, not fully. They were too close for it to work, closest and farthest when, with both his arms, he held them together, his fingers running with candle-wax. He could not save. At most a little comfort gushed out guiltily, from out of their double image, their never quite united figure. In that corner of the dance his anguished feet had trampled the grass to a desert.

When Mrs Poulter leaned forward. She was holding her hair by handfuls in knots of fists, he could see—waiting.

Till in the centre of their mandala he danced the passion of all their lives, the blood running out of the backs of his hands, water out of the hole in his ribs. His mouth was a silent hole, because no sound was needed to explain.

And then, when he had been spewed up, spat out, with the breeze stripping him down to the saturated skin, and the fit had almost withdrawn from him, he added the little quivering footnote on forgiveness. His arms were laid along his sides. His head hung. Facing her.

He fell down, and lay, the rise and fall of his ribs a relief, to say nothing of her eyes, which he knew could only have been looking at him with understanding for his dance.

Arthur must have dozed, for when he got up, Mrs Poulter was putting the finishing touches to her hair. Her head was looking so neat, though her nostrils were still slightly flared, from some experience recently suffered.

Then Arthur knew that she was worthy of the mandala. Mrs Poulter and Dulcie Feinstein he loved the most—after Waldo of course.

So he put his hand in his pocket, and knelt down beside her, and said, "I'm going to let you have the mandala, Mrs Poulter."

It was the gold one, in which the sparks glinted, and from which the rays shot upward whenever the perfect sphere was struck by its counterpart (265–266).

Soon after this walk, Arthur and Mrs Poulter stop seeing each other. It is what Mr Poulter wants and demands. It is what Mr and Mrs Brown want but do not openly demand. It is necessary to maintain the "ethical rectitude" Waldo irrationally shouts for—"If only you saw the *obscenity* of such a situation! I ask you! And my brother!" (267)—as the forked veins in his forehead were bursting blue. So, their friendship ceases but not their love for each other.

While Dulcie and Mrs Poulter return Arthur's love, Waldo does not, not completely. Although the twin brothers are inseparable and cannot live without each other. Although, we are told, Waldo loves Arthur in an incomplete way. The final section of "Arthur" returns to this theme, of Waldo's inability to love completely, which begs the question: What does White means by love.

Love is a concept central to the Old and New Testaments, where it appears: as lovingkindness (*hesed*), a biblical word White understood and used in *Riders in the Chariot*; as grace (*hen*); as mercy (*raham*); as forgiveness (*salah*); and as fidelity (*emeth*), a concept the ancient Greeks identified in the four forms of kinship or familiarity (*storge*), of friendship (*philia*), of sexual and/or romantic desire (*eros*), and of self-emptying or divine love (*agape*). Theoretically and rhetorically, Arthur is capable of more forms of love than Waldo.

In the original common (*koine*) Greek version of the New Testament, when Jesus was asked which commandment in the Torah was greatest, he answered:

> "You shall [*agape*] the Lord your God with all your heart, and with all your soul, and with all your mind." This is the greatest and first commandment. And a second is like it: "you shall [*agape*] your neighbour as yourself." On these two commandments hang all the law and the prophets (Matthew 22:37–40).

Jesus was referring to love in the sense of self-emptying or divine love. However, as he was not the only Rabbi to say this, Christians cannot claim a monopoly on the insight, which stands at the heart of Judaism. We cannot claim to love God without loving our neighbour; we cannot claim to love our neighbour without loving God. White understood how hard this principle is. He knew he did not live up to it. Yet he still believed in it.

White segues from Arthur and Mrs Poulter—banned from seeing each other—to their father's death in 1922 (268). Waldo walks away from his father's lifeless body, having refused to acknowledge he is dead, which allows Arthur to discover the body and communicate the death to his family. After this, White segues to Mrs Brown's alcoholic widowhood, between 1922 and her death in 1932, and Waldo's refusal to acknowledge the reality of her failing health. During Mrs Brown's final illness, against Arthur's better judgment, he offers Waldo a mandala:

> "Mother is real sick," he said.
> The lamplight seemed to draw them into its circle.
> "Mother is not *sick*," Waldo shouted.
> All this sickness, of their mother's, of the old weatherboard house, with its dry-rotten tremors and wooden tick-tick, seemed to concentrate itself in Arthur's stomach, till from looking at his own hands, soothing rather than soothed by, the revolving marble, he realized that the knot at the heart of the mandala, at most times so tortuously inwoven, would dissolve, if only temporarily, in light.
> And it seemed as though the worst could only happen for the best. It was most important that his brother, shuffling his papers, looking for a sheet mislaid, or just looking—that Waldo, too, should know.
> "If it would help I would give it to you, Waldo, to keep," Arthur said.
> Offering the knotted mandala.
> While half sensing that Waldo would never untie the knot.[10]
> Even before Waldo gave one of his looks, which, when interpreted, meant: By offering me a glass marble you are trying to make me look like a fool, I am not, and never shall be a fool, though I am your twin brother,

---

[10] Note: Lacan did not theorize his Borromean knot—the relationship binding his Imaginary, Symbolic, and Real registers—until after *The Solid Mandala* was published.

so my reply, Arthur, is not shit, but shit!
    As he shouted, "No, Arthur! Go, Arthur!"
    But Arthur was rooted. His hand closed on the icy marble. If he had
not been his twin brother, would Waldo have hated him? (272–273)

There was too little time, in those days, for Arthur to nurse suspicions.
He was busy entertaining–distracting his sick mother. They agree that
Waldo should not know she is dying, as that might prove unbearable for
him. When Mrs Brown does die in 1932—after Mrs Poulter, the doctor,
and the minister have her removed—Arthur is left to cope alone. He
contacts the Saportas, and lets them arrange and pay for his mother's
funeral, which Waldo does not attend. How many kinds of love has Waldo
been incapable of, in these last few pages alone? The rest of "Arthur"
focuses on this theme, Arthur understanding his need of Waldo, Waldo not
understanding his need of Arthur, while providing a gloss from Arthur's
perspective on events narrated in "Waldo".

While reading Jung's *Psychology and Alchemy* one day, Arthur comes
across a message, about the conscious and unconscious minds—the anima
(the male's feminine inner personality) and the animus (the female's
masculine inner personality)—which he pins to the back of his mind,
where it rattled and twitched, painfully and hopefully, if obscure:

> As the shadow continually follows the body of one who walks in the sun,
> so our hermaphroditic Adam, though he appears in the form of a male,
> nevertheless always carries about with him Eve, or his wife, hidden in his
> body (281).

Arthur is confronted with a dilemma here, as a hermaphroditic Adam
who regards each mandala, and each person who has received a mandala,
as an Eve–wife–anima. Because he cannot choose one, he wants to keep
them all. There are other dilemmas also, as Jung is only one of many
contenders for the kinds of meaning Arthur is struggling with. Including
Carroll's *Alice in Wonderland*, and Dostoevsky's *The Brothers
Karamazov*; a book his father burnt, not long before he died, presumably
because its religious message was too confronting for a failed Fabian
atheist. Beyond that, there is the problem of Waldo, very much his father's
son:

> Once, at the height of a storm, when the rain was coming down aslant,
> in slate-pencils, against the roof, the water coming through the rusty iron,
> in that same place, into the basin, in the scullery, and the quince twigs
> squeaking against, the rose thorns scratching on, the panes, Waldo shouted,
> "I wonder what you damn well think about, Arthur!"
>
> "Well," said Arthur slowly, because it was a difficult one to answer,
> "what most people think about, I suppose."

"Nothing!" Waldo shouted back. "That's the answer!"

"Or everything," Arthur mumbled, because Waldo seemed so put out.

"You think about nothing!" Waldo had begun to cry. "No worries on your mind!"

"If you want to know, I was thinking about Tiresias," Arthur said to interest him. "How he was changed into a woman for a short time. That sort of thing would be different, wouldn't it, from the hermaphroditic Adam who carries his wife about with him inside?"

Then Waldo took him by the wrists.

"Shut up!" he ordered. "Do you understand? If you think thoughts like those, keep them to yourself, Arthur. I don't want to hear. Any such filth. Or madness."

Waldo might have wrenched Arthur's hands off at the wrists if only he had been strong enough. But he wasn't.

Instead he sat down rather hard, and Arthur went to him, to comfort him, because they had only each other. Waldo knew this. He put his head on the table, under the falling rain, and cried.

Waldo was such a terrible problem to Arthur, their love for each other, that there were whole visits to the Library when he couldn't bring himself to take down *The Brothers Karamazov*. He preferred *Alice*.

But he had to return to what had become, if not his study, his obsession. There was all this Christ jazz. Something of which Mrs Poulter had explained. But he couldn't exactly relate it to men, except to the cruelty some men practise, in spite of themselves, as a religion they are brought up in. Reading *The Brothers Karamazov* he wished he could understand whose side anyone was one.

Who was the Grand Inquisitor?

Then suddenly one morning at the Library Waldo was sitting at the same table, opposite him, making that scene. Afterwards Arthur could not remember in detail what was said. You couldn't exactly say *they* were *speaking*, because the remarks were being torn out of them helter skelter, between tears and gusts of breathlessness, like handfuls of flesh. The raw, bleeding remarks were such that Waldo kept looking around to see who might be noticing. As for Arthur, he did not care. Their relationship was the only fact of importance, and such an overwhelming one.

"I shan't ask why you've come here, if you're making this scene, to humiliate me," Waldo was saying, "because the answer is too obvious. That has been your chief object in life. If you would be truthful."

"Why hurt yourself Waldo?" Arthur was given the strength to reply.

"Kick a dog, and hurt yourself. That's you all over."

…

"Afraid," Arthur was saying, and now he did begin to feel a kind of terror rising in him. "Like our father. I mean Dad. Not the one they pray to. But Dad putting Dostoevski on the fire."

He knew the flames of argument must be colouring his face in the way which distressed strangers, even Waldo, most. But for the moment he was almost glad he couldn't control himself.

"Afraid of the blood and the nails, which, as far as I can see, is what everyone is afraid of, but wants, and what Dostoevsky is partly going on about. Do you see, Waldo"—he was bursting with it—"what we must avoid?"

Suddenly Arthur burst into tears because he saw that Waldo was what the books referred to as a lost soul. He, too, for that matter, was lost. Although he might hold Waldo in his arms, he could never give out from his own soul enough of that love which was there to give. So his brother remained cold and dry.

Arthur stopped crying almost at once, because the reason for his beginning was so immense it made the act itself seem insignificant. He was ashamed.

"But we've got to keep on *trying*, Waldo, just as we get up every morning and lace our boots up again" (282–284)

This is where the theory of individuation, in its Jungian form, or any other hypothetical form, parts company with Jewish and Christian revelation, neither of which are about the psychological integration of personality, or the recovery of lost wholeness, but about something much larger: the living relationship between creator and creation. It was fashionable, during much of the 19th and 20th century, to promote the idea that Nietzsche and Jung had provided philosophical and psychological answers to what were once religious questions. That time has passed.

Arthur seems to be suggesting that, if only he and Waldo could achieve integration—as an ancient Greek dialectic or archetypes—"all this Christ jazz" would never have been necessary, and all human fear of "the blood and the nails" would no longer exist. This is a romantic idea, refracted through Nietzsche and Jung, which now appears less tenable than it once was, since it is illogical to propose a formula for wholeness while simultaneously declaring wholeness impossible. In this case, the impossibility is because of Waldo, who views his relationship with Arthur in dualistic terms rather than the dialectical or dialogical terms Arthur views his relationship with Waldo.

Within this dualism, Waldo has a highly defended sense of his logos. He refuses to negotiate with Arthur's mythos, even though the Greek temple they represent and inhabit is crumbling around them. As they act out their götterdämmerung, which is slowly drawing to its end in a fatalistic and mechanistic way, Arthur continues to promote integration and Waldo continues to resist it. We see this in "Arthur", in the scene where the ageing Waldo wears his mother's rotting dress and gazes at himself in the vanity mirror, not realizing Arthur can see him through a window. Because Arthur is always trying to protect Waldo, he creates a distraction to preserve his dignity:

> Oh he might have cried, if he hadn't laughed, through the beads and roses, at himself in Waldo's blue dress. Bursting out of it. His breasts were itching.
> So Arthur had begun to scratch, and call.
> "Come here, Runt! Runty?"
> To call or laugh: "Silly old cunt!"
> When he went inside he told how he had delivered the flour, sensing that in the circumstances the return of Mrs Poulter and Waldo's hatred of her might take his brother's mind off other matters (291).

The reader is meant to be contrasting two things here: first, Arthur's identification with the hermaphroditic Adam, who appears in the form of a male while still carrying his Eves–wives–animas within him (his mandalas and those who have earned them); second, Waldo's identification with the Tiresias myth, which encourages him to wear his mother's rotting dress, gaze in a vanity mirror, and hope the dress can become, like his other clothes, a "disguise he had chosen to hide the brilliant truth" (193). The difference between them is that, while Arthur can see himself in the same dress as Waldo, he knows it is an illusion, while Waldo believes his illusion is real.

While the novel has to end, as all novels must, it is hard to imagine how White could have delayed the götterdämmerung; had Waldo and Arthur kept on coexisting; had Arthur not brought things to a head by reminding Waldo of everything he wants to deny: the diarrhoea in the bed—which was Waldo's diarrhoea, although Arthur accepted responsibility for it and cleaned it up—the rotting dress behind the copper, Arthur's poem which reminds Waldo of the "disgusting *blood* myth", the blasphemy of the "always altering face of the figure nailed on the tree". All this forces Waldo to finally realize his lack of creativity; his failure as a writer:

> That his brother continued to suffer from the brutality of their revelation was evident to Arthur when, in the course of the afternoon, he looked through the trees and saw Waldo carrying his boxful of papers towards the pit. Knowing he had probably destroyed his brother did not help Arthur to act. Through the trees he could smell the burning papers. He stood around snivelling, sniffing the fumigatory smell of burning. But he was not in any way cleansed.
> When finally he went into their room, he found Waldo lying on the bed. Waldo raised himself on an elbow.
> And Arthur saw.
> He saw the hatred Waldo was directing, had always directed, at all living things, whether Dulcie Feinstein, or Mrs Poulter, or the

blasphemous poem—because that, too, had a life of a kind—the poem which celebrated their common pain.

"Waldo!" Arthur was afraid at last. "What are you trying to do to me?"

Arthur was afraid Waldo was preparing to die of the hatred he had bred in him. Because he, not Waldo, was to blame. Arthur Brown, the getter of pain.

Then Waldo, in the agony of their joint discovery, reached out and grabbed him by the wrist, to imprint him for ever with the last moment.

"Waldo! Let me go! Wald."

Big and spongy though he was, Arthur, Waldo's big dill brother, could go crumbly as one thing for love and now the death of it.

Waldo was lying still, but still attached to Arthur at the wrist.

When Arthur saw the murder he had committed on his brother he began to try to throw him off. He did not immediately succeed, because the fingers of this dead man were determined, in their steel circlets, to bring him to trial. So he had to fight against it. And finally snapped the metal open.

Then Arthur went stampeding through the house in which their lives, of life, had been lived until the end. It was a wonder the cries torn out of him didn't bring the structure down. Before he slammed a door on the shocked faces of dogs (293–294).

In White, dogs are often a palindrome for the gods. In this case Apollo and Dionysus.

The Feinstein Family

As in *Riders in the Chariot*, White has a story to tell about the Jewish horizon in *The Solid Mandala*. The story is similar in both novels. Mr Feinstein and Mr Himmelfarb are both in thrall to the Enlightenment, and, as far as White is concerned, the Enlightenment's focus on reason led to the creation of a secular Jewish culture that threatened Judaism's covenant identity.

Mrs Feinstein and Mrs Himmelfarb, both matrilineal transmitters of Judaism, defer to their husbands. They have reservations, however, and win in the end, after sacrificing their lives to ensure their families' covenant identity. In their youth and adolescence, Dulcie and Mordecai–Martin share the same dilemma: their fathers' preference for Greek reason over Jewish revelation, although Dulcie's dilemma is more unconscious than Mordecai–Martin's dilemma. This makes sense in a novel influenced by Jung.

The dilemma was logical to White, although it is harder for us to recognize in the 21st century, with our stronger sense of the positive ways in which the Jewish mind was influenced by the Greek mind during the

Hellenistic Period before Jesus. As White associated revelation with mythos rather than logos, he made a stronger distinction between reason and revelation than we now make. He could never see the Enlightenment as a viable option for religious Jews, just as he could never see the Enlightenment as a viable option for committed Christians. Was he right? Was he wrong? We cannot answer that question, conclusively, as long as the drama of the Enlightenment is still being acted out. We can only say he had a particular attitude towards reason consistent with romantic hermeneutics.

The dilemma Waldo and Dulcie share is rhetorical. His dilemma is logos in Athens. Her dilemma is logos in Jerusalem. His dilemma is never solved, since his death is a result rather than a solution. Her dilemma is solved by the combined influence of Arthur and Mrs Feinstein—mythos in Athens and mythos in Jerusalem—which operates rhetorically on an unconscious level. Through that influence, Dulcie is removed from Waldo's influence, and her father's influence, marries an observant Jew, Leonard Saporta, and is happily absorbed into an Orthodox family. This is what White orchestrates, just as he orchestrated Himmelfarb's absorption into the Liebmann family.

In Part 2—"Waldo"—White introduces Waldo's relationship with the Jewish horizon at the end of that relationship, then proceeds to tell the story of the relationship in flashback, because he wants us to know its outcome before we hear about how it began and unfolded. Waldo and Dulcie are both over 40 and meet by chance in Pitt Street, Sydney, during the Depression, around 1934 (63–67). They have not seen each other since he learned of her engagement after World War I. He is alone. She is with her husband and two children. He is badly confronted by this chance meeting, and visibly shocked when he discovers she named her son Arthur after his brother. He runs away, has an accident in the street, falls, breaks his glasses, and is taken to hospital. As he is not seriously injured, he is allowed to go home. In retrospect, after reading the entire novel, his shock may strike the reader as a strange over-reaction, since his adolescent relationship with Dulcie was never more than a fanciful acquaintance on his part. It was solipsistic and never operated on a grounded or emotional level. He was always interested in himself, never in her.

Mr and Mrs Brown (Athens) and Mr and Mrs Feinstein (Jerusalem) know of but never meet each other. Waldo and Dulcie were introduced to each other, before World War I, by Mrs Musto—the candid, comical heiress of Fairy Flour fortune—who "knows" about the Browns and the Feinsteins. She invites Waldo and Dulcie to a tennis party she is giving, for the youths of the district, where they both stand out as loners. While she senses they are loners, whether she intends them for each other, or whether she simply wants to give them the opportunity to come out of themselves, is unknown. Later, in "Arthur", she describes them as "A *couple* of lost souls" (239), but that does not mean she intends them to be a couple, it simply means she can see they are lost.

So begins their fanciful acquaintance, which is a mixture of Waldo's perspective of the Feinsteins, and the narrator's perspective of the Feinsteins, both of which revolve around the rhetorical dilemmas of logos in Athens and logos in Jerusalem. White reinforces this dilemma with many signs and symbols. For example, in Sarsaparilla the Brown's "enlightened" Greek home, with its classical pediment, is at the bottom of the hill at the end of Terminus Road, while the Feinstein's "enlightened" Jewish home, *Mount Pleasant*, is on a hill and other characters must walk up the hill to reach it. The Feinsteins therefore have a loftier perspective of Sarsaparilla than the Browns. This is analogous with Dulcie's lofty position at the top of the tree in Arthur's dream. They also have another home in Centennial Park, Sydney; a mock mediaeval fortress with gargoyles and battlements. These architectural symbols signify what White understood as the dilemma facing contemporary Judaism, whether to embrace the Enlightenment, or whether to remain within the protective walls of the Torah and Kabbalah and receive the soteria they offer.

Mr Feinstein made a choice, as he declares during Waldo's first visit to Mount Pleasant: "no man today of any intellectual honesty, could adopt any but a rationalist stand in view of politico-economic developments and advances in scientific discovery" (103–104). So he confesses, as an ethnic rather than a religious Jew: "we Jews are not always all that enlightened" (104). He is grateful that his own father "had seen the light before reaching these to-some-extent 'enlightened shores'" (104) Born in Australia, Mr Feinstein professes to wearing his *capple* (kippah), not for prayer—or to be "put through any reactionary hoop"—but to "protect my nut from draughts" (104).

Waldo is invited to Mount Pleasant again but is taken aback when Mrs Feinstein insists he brings Arthur with him. He cannot imagine why anyone would want to know his brother, and assumes the Feinsteins do not already know him, although Arthur delivers their groceries (and those of everyone else in Sarsaparilla):

> At the prospect of Arthur's introduction into his relationship with the Feinsteins, Waldo found he cherished that relationship more than he was prepared to admit. It was not the Feinsteins themselves who interested him particularly. Old Feinstein, with more or less his own parent's ideas, was

frankly a bore, but it was at least something to have become a target for the theories of somebody not his parent, and in another way Mrs Feinstein … confirmed his individual existence as comfortably as cake. As for their daughter, he was not yet sure of Dulcie, of what part she was intended to play, or whether she despised and rejected him. But he had received her, jealously, expectantly, into his mind, and allowed her to drift there passively … The Feinsteins were too private an experience, then, to resist Arthur. Arthur would explode into, and perhaps shatter, something which could not be repaired (106).

As the reader has already been told how this story will end—with Dulcie marrying Leonard Saporta and naming her son after Arthur—they should already sense Waldo is wrong. Arthur will have a positive influence on the Feinsteins. Waldo will never understand or accept this because it challenges his identity, and, because of his solipsism, he can only maintain superficial connections with other lives. While he may be right about Mr Feinstein's boring ideas about reason and enlightenment, they are also the central ideas of his logos, and he is misreading Mrs Feinstein, whose life and agenda are quite different from his own.

If Waldo cannot see into Mrs Feinstein's life, it is partly because she chooses to keep it hidden from him, and partly because he would refuse to acknowledge it even if she chose to reveal it to him. In White's scheme of things, reason always refuses to acknowledge revelation.[11] If he cannot be sure of Dulcie, it is because she is not yet sure of herself, caught as she is between her father's conscious desires and her mother's unconscious desires.

Waldo would prefer to ignore Mrs Feinstein's verbal invitation, but he cannot, as she follows it up with a written one:

> Waldo knew there was no escaping something which was being prepared. Mrs Feinstein's formal note deliberately arranged it for the Saturday. *So that you are able to introduce your brother to our circle*, the writing ended underlined (107).

Notice that White arranges for Arthur's first visit to Mount Pleasant to occur on the Sabbath; a day that, traditionally, Jews are to remain apart.

The Feinsteins rejoice at the prospect of having Arthur in their lives, as part of their extended family, but their conscious and unconscious motives are mixed. Mr Feinstein says Arthur's presence is the natural outcome of reason and enlightenment, as once upon a time the Sabbath "was only for a family of Jews mumbling together behind closed doors" (108). While

---

[11] This is the predictable attitude of the atheist. Religion must always be understood as the antithesis of rationality rather than a manifestation of rationality.

Mrs Feinstein defers to her husband's sentiments, she also sees Arthur's visit as an opportunity to influence her daughter's future, which is still unknown or undecided: "We have been working the *planchette* the other evening" she said, looking at her daughter, "and Dulcie asked it what she will become. Afterwards. In life" (102).

Waldo misreads Dulcie's reaction to Arthur. At first, he assumes she is upset and repelled by Arthur, but this is not so. She is being challenged but rises to the challenge: "I think, Arthur," she said, "you may be able to teach me a lot I shall want to hear. We may be able to teach," she said, "to teach each other things" (109). Arthur thinks teaching him piano would be a good place to start. However, as they move towards the upright, Waldo is so fearful of the damage Arthur's "not quite controlled hands" will wreak upon classical music, he has to "get out quickly". He feels an attack of diarrhoea coming on (110). Waldo's logos is afraid of Arthur's mythos just as classical Greek logos is afraid of pre-classical Greek mythos (Dodds 1951). His diarrhoea is a symbolic response to this fear.

When Waldo returns from the lavatory, the threat to classical music has stopped, but the threat to his logos continues, as he is now worried about "the violence of what his twin might say" (111). As he enters the living room, it is apparent that Arthur and Dulcie have been having a conversation about what words mean, in this case the difference between *Amour* and Love, as Dulcie confesses: "You are right," she was saying, in reply to some remark of Arthur's, though speaking rather to herself. "*Amour* is not the same as 'Love'. *Amour* has a different shape—a different meaning" (111). Waldo is horrified because, theoretically, language is his province not Arthur's. The idea that Arthur can understand language better than he does—and, later in the novel, will understand literature better than he does—is the ultimate challenge to his identity, which eventually kills him.

Mrs Feinstein asks Arthur to help her clear the remains of their afternoon tea while Dulcie takes Waldo out into the garden. While they are in the garden, she notices his brother and her mother are enjoying themselves immensely but thinks it will take her some time to understand Arthur. Waldo tries not to shout as he asks: "What is there to understand?" (113) Her reply is: "Though for that matter … I don't understand myself."

It is now obvious that Dulcie's journey into self-understanding involves Arthur rather than Waldo. It also involves Mrs Feinstein taking her to Europe, to visit her relatives and be exposed to Orthodox ways of being Jewish. Mr Feinstein does not accompany them to Europe. He cannot leave his business, and he would not cope with being exposed to so much emotional religiosity. During their trip, World War I begins. They return to their home in Centennial Park not to their Mount Pleasant home in Sarsaparilla.

Towards the end of the war, Waldo walks past Mount Pleasant and is surprised to see signs of habitation, as it has been deserted since the war began: "Daddy couldn't bear to come here," Dulcie explains: "He's been so upset by everything. You remember all those intellectual theories about human progress!" (130) The war, which reason and enlightenment were supposed to prevent but were unable to prevent, has changed everything. Mr Feinstein loses his value system, Mrs Feinstein loses her health, Dulcie learns about Orthodoxy from her European relatives, and has started to wear a Star of David.

During Waldo and Arthur's next visit to Mount Pleasant, Mrs Feinstein "couldn't stop hugging" Arthur (132) and exclaims "I don't know how we can deprive ourselves of the pleasure of seeing you more often". In spite of her enthusiasm "Mrs Feinstein looked sad and grey". She has aged and shrunk into herself, her pseudo-enlightened life in Australia has been confronted by the reality of what is happening in Europe: war, family loss, personal tragedy, and "so much Jewish emotionalism" (138). But, as a matriarch with a specific archetypal function, she is responsible for Dulcie's engagement to Leonard Saporta, and for helping Arthur realize that Judaism is another mandala. In death she triumphs.

On hearing Mrs Feinstein has died, at her home in Centennial Park, Waldo comes up with the strange idea, an extension of his narcissism and solipsism, of proposing an "idealistic marriage" to Dulcie, who has come to Mount Pleasant "to sort out their things before disposing of the house". On his arrival, he finds Arthur already there, offering Dulcie one of his mandala marbles. After Arthur tactfully retreats, Waldo proposes, but Dulcie says she is not in a position to accept, as she admits she cannot love him in the way he wants her to, and, apart from that, she is already engaged to Leonard Saporta. As she explains: "Don't you think it better, for all of us, to accept the past out of which we've grown, out of which we're still growing?" (157) Dulcie now accepts her past and her future are part of some vast, incomprehensible mystery.

Waldo finally walks away from her, after years of attraction, repulsion, and incompatibility, as Elyot Standish finally walked away from Muriel Raphael in *The Living and the Dead*. He believes Dulcie has been "unfaithful to him intellectually" (133), which in a sense she has. So he leaves Mount Pleasant for the last time; recoiling—in what is clearly a gynophobic way—from her transition to Orthodoxy and the fertility it represents. Thereafter, the Feinsteins and the Saportas cease to exist in Waldo's mind.

In Part III—"Arthur"—we read about Arthur's relationship with the Feinsteins from his perspective not Waldo's. It begins with his grocery deliveries, like his other backdoor relationships. As they only live at Mount Pleasant half of the year, they do not have a maid, so Mrs Feinstein receives their groceries herself. Occasionally she gives Arthur a cold drink, but does not encourage him to explore the house, as Dulcie is inside practising her music. Sometimes, as he leaves, he looks through a window, and sees Dulcie's back, as she plays the piano, but she never looks around, intent on what she is doing:

> Once Mrs Feinstein came out and caught him, and looked the other way so as not to appear annoyed. She was determined, it seemed, though politely, to prevent him seeing more of her daughter. Though he had, he thought, once, at the store: a skinny girl with a dark shadow on her upper lip, standing probably having the sulks beside a bag of potatoes. But that was different (242).

Mrs Feinstein is protecting Dulcie who—at that time—was being groomed for a secular, reasonable, and enlightened future: a logos future determined by her father. But this protection will soon dissolve, after Waldo is introduced to the Feinsteins, and, soon after that when Arthur accompanies Waldo to *Mount Pleasant* for:

> ... his meeting, the first official, socially ratified meeting with Dulcie Feinstein, not that she needed to exist more completely than she already did in his mind. It was only that Dulcie, he knew, had to turn around and face whatever it was in Arthur Brown (243).

Why did Mrs Feinstein make a point of inviting Arthur along with Waldo? Was it because, on Waldo's previous visits to Mount Pleasant, she intuited something amiss with his logos? And what is it Dulcie must face in Arthur? Is it the mythos which will, combined with her mother's unconscious influence, lead her to Orthodoxy?

If the logic of White's rhetoric makes this likely, so does Dulcie's initial reaction when she meets Arthur for the first time. As that meeting was described in Part II—"Waldo"—Dulcie enters the room while Mrs Feinstein is explaining the meaning of Mr Feinstein's *capple* to Arthur. His opening remark to Dulcie is "Did you ever pray in a cap?" Her reply is "It's different with women". Waldo believes he knows what she is feeling, on seeing Arthur for the first time:

> She was so obviously upset. She tried to make it look as though the whole idea of prayer-caps, and of superstition generally, repelled her, whereas it was the lumpy look of Arthur Brown slobbering with imbecile excitement. Although Waldo was personally distressed that she should react in this

way to his brother, he was relieved to find she was sincere (109).

In "Waldo", while Waldo's perception is partially true, it is slanted towards what he wants to believe. As his perspective is not completely true, "Arthur" gives us another perception of this first meeting:

> Then she came in. In that white, loosely-embroidered dress, a flurry of white hydrangea heads. If he was at all flustered it was because of her beauty and the movement of her flowery flowing dress. He was, in fact, so overcome he began to babble all that silly rot about her father's old *capple*, a performance which Duclie obviously found distasteful, it was showing so clearly in her face.
>
> He continued babbling, he heard: "Now that I've seen your face. Even if you never want to see me again."
>
> At the same time he knew, of course, that this could not be true: Dulcie herself let him see it. When he went up to examine her more closely, by touch as well, he saw her suddenly closed face open out again as it must in response to music. In spite of the natural shyness of any young girl, she accepted his entry into her thoughts.
>
> "Oh yes," she seemed to be, and was in fact, saying, "we shall have so much to exchange, to share" (244).

What does Dulcie find distasteful here? The reference to prayer? Or to Arthur presence itself? It could be both. Regardless, the narrator's point is that, from this moment, she puts her distaste aside. Arthur begins to be important to her in a way Waldo is not, and cannot be, since the novel intends to guide her towards Orthodoxy, away from her father's and Waldo's logos. As that journey is not easy—religious journeys are never easy—we are told:

> More than anxiety, fear that something precious might escape her, was making her take him by the hand (244).

Dulcie leads Arthur to the piano, to teach him how to play. Waldo finds this so frightening he has that attack of archetypal diarrhoea.

Arthur's relationship with Dulcie and the Feinsteins, through whom he discovers "the world is another mandala" (245), became a private affair which he could not share with his brother or family. Only Arthur knew Mrs Feinstein was planning to take Dulcie overseas. Only Arthur knew they returned, when World War I broke out, not to Mount Pleasant but to:

> … the life which in fact they had never really left, in the house on the edge of [Centennial] park. They came. And they appeared older. It continually amazed Arthur Brown that other people were growing older. Mrs Feinstein was older, and sadder, perhaps for this very fact of age. Dulcie was older, different, unexpected (247).

Dulcie has changed. Experiencing Europe on the eve of war changed her. Meeting her mother's religious relatives changed her. After a reasonable and enlightened childhood and adolescence in Sydney, her trip exposed her to Old World tensions her father thought he had escaped from—and George and Anne Brown thought they had escaped from—but Australia is no escape.

During the war, Arthur visits Dulcie in Centennial Park. As he finds her melancholic, reflective, and not as accessible as she was before the war. He went away:

> … deciding not to admit to Waldo what could only be counted as defeat. In fact, he wouldn't mention the return of Dulcie and Mrs Feinstein. For some reason, for the moment, he was less able to communicate with them, though if he hadn't lost the art, he would not have known exactly what to say.

Later during the war, on a trip to the city, he visits Leonard Saporta in his carpet shop, after Leonard had returned from the war, discharged with "several shrapnel wounds which he did not care to talk about" (249). Around the time of this visit, the narrator tells us four things: first, while on leave in France, Leonard sent Dulcie a Star of David "which she afterwards wore on a chain round her neck, and which would have become a source of mirth to Mr Feinstein, if his wife had not implored him … to desist, for Dulcie's, for everybody's sake"; second, Arthur notices a mandala image at the centre of a rug in Leonard's shop; third, Leonard does not know the meaning of the mandala, but then he does not have to as an observant Jew; fourth, seeing Leonard thus enclosed in a mandala, Arthur "went away soon afterward, and in the street realized for the first time that the Star of David was another mandala, and that Dulcie's marriage to Mr Saporta would be arranged" (251).

After the Armistice, Arthur hears Mrs Feinstein has died: "Although she had been his friend he didn't exactly grieve for her, realizing that she had in fact died on her last trip to Europe. But again he went to the city, this time to the house in Centennial Park" (252). Mr Feinstein was too disconsolate to receive even those he knew intimately. Dulcie was still melancholic, reflective, and inaccessible; as she comes to terms with the trajectory her life is taking, unsure about how interpret events: the trip to Europe, the Star of David, her mother's death. Intuitively, Arthur asks whether she has seen Mr Saporta. She says yes, she thinks so, yes of course so:

> If he had not known her to be genuine, her manner could have appeared false. Perhaps, it now occurred to him, Dulcie herself had not yet realized. Otherwise she must surely have found the means for grief out of her love

for Mr Saporta.

It was then he conceived the idea of giving Dulcie Feinstein one of his solid mandalas (253).

Dulcie is distracted, on her journey into Orthodoxy, which is why, at that moment, she is unable to be the same kind of friend she was before the war. So they make small talk before Arthur leaves. As he leaves, she tells him she will let him know when to come again, probably to Mount Pleasant, which her father will no doubt sell. There is no longer any point to maintaining the house, as a monument to the Enlightenment. As she is preoccupied, she forgets to contact him when she is next in Sarsaparilla, to collect their belongings and sell the house. Not knowing what to make of this neglect, Arthur visits Mount Pleasant uninvited, and finds her there. She is happy to see him, vaguely remembering an arrangement.

At this point, Arthur notices they have the same coloured eyes (254), which suggests an affinity between their religious horizons, whereupon Dulcie's happiness and conversion combine in a startling way. She becomes confident and outward looking. She admits her life is turning out exactly as her mother predicted or expected, with her marriage to Leonard Saporta. Arthur sees this marriage as the uniting of himself with Mrs Feinstein and the engaged couple. Dulcie seems to agree. Dulcie says she wants him to come to her wedding and Leonard has agreed. Arthur is astonished. He says he cannot, because Waldo would be far too shocked. Dulcie suggests Waldo is only his brother and no more to her than his brother. When Arthur says no, Waldo is surely more to her than that, she hung her head and said: "It's necessary to escape from Waldo". His reply is: "Necessary for you. Not for me" (255).

At that point, Arthur gives Dulcie one of his mandalas, just before Waldo arrives—as we already know from "Waldo"—to make his strange idealistic proposal of marriage. Arthur tactfully retreats, leaving the field to his brother, whom he cannot live without. While Waldo will walk away from the Feinstein–Saportas that afternoon, Arthur maintains a private relationship with them, at their home in Centennial Park. They will give their son his name; they will arrange and pay for his mother's funeral; because of what their revelation shares with his mythos.

The narrator tells us that, after Mrs Brown's death, the lives of the twins would not have diverged all that much if Arthur had not developed his sense of responsibility towards the Saportas. While he did not go to Dulcie's wedding in 1922—and had to control his disappointment over that—he maintained his loyalty to Waldo by keeping his relationship with the Saportas to himself. He visited the Saportas regularly, travelling by public transport from Sarsaparilla (on the outskirts of Sydney) to their home, the Feinstein's mock Mediaeval fortress in Centennial Park (near the centre of Sydney):

> Arthur Brown visited them all through the two children and several miscarriages. Sometimes he sat in company with others, elderly Jewish ladies and uncles, who eventually overcame their surprise. They respected Arthur. Perhaps, for some obscure reason, they even valued his presence amongst them.
>
> When he played with his glass marbles, and explained, "These are my two remaining mandalas," they sat forward, expressing the greatest interest and pleasure, and on one occasion one of the elderly uncles remarked, "There, Magdi, I told you this young man is in some way phenomenal."
>
> Naturally Arthur was pleased. Though not deceived. He waited to be alone with Dulcie, when they might resume that life which they alone were permitted to enjoy. His thighs would quiver in anticipation of blissfully joyful union with his love.
>
> For Dulcie's beauty had increased with marriage, was more outflowing, her eyes more lustrous in communication. She would often put her hand in Arthur's, particularly during pregnancy.
>
> "You know," she would say, and laugh, looking down at her swollen figure, "I am a slave to *all this*" (275).

Mr Feinstein, Dulcie's widowed father, still a rationalist, lives with the Saportas in his old home. He has chosen to remain in the attic.[12] Here he spends his final days, between newspapers and tobacco, taking refuge from what he calls the "Jewish Reaction" downstairs, where his family is thriving on superstition and using their religion as an excuse to overeat (276–277).

Arthur visits Mr Feinstein regularly in his attic room, during a period declining health; he has had three strokes and is becoming increasingly paralyzed. One day he arrives to find Dulcie wearing flowing black and sitting on a mattress on the floor:

> "My father died, Arthur," she explained, as though the old man had tottered out only a moment before, into the park. The only unusual part of it was: they couldn't expect him back.
>
> Then, when she had gathered up her knees inside her arms, and laid her face against her shoulder, she began dreaming, as she rocked.
>
> "Oh yes, I've mourned for him, and shall continue to mourn. But my father was always embarrassed by what he used to call 'Jewesses indulging themselves by tearing their clothes and emotions to tatters.' We were only ever allowed to love him on his own terms. I think on the whole that made him unhappy, but any other behaviour would have offended against his

---

[12] "Attic" has a double meaning here. It signifies the horizon of Athens as well as the room under a roof.

principles. A complete surrender to love might have let in God. Of course, in the end, he did. When they were shut up together in a room, he couldn't avoid it. I saw. My father died peacefully."

Dulcie raised her head.

"You, Arthur," she said, "are you, I wonder, the instrument we feel you are?"

Whatever she intended to convey, he was glad not to grasp it, and lowered his eyes to the level of her breast, from which the milk had trickled, through the black dress. She noticed at once, and covered herself with her scarf. With the same slow but natural motion, she covered her head.

As he continued to visit the Saportas over the years with some regularity, Arthur did not particularly notice Dulcie's greyness or her glasses, nor that Mr Saporta was setting in fat, because friends and lovers enjoy a greater freedom than their bodies: they are at liberty to move out of them, and by special dispensation communicate with one another through far-sighted eyes.

It was Waldo who suffered, Arthur regretted, from his meeting with the whole Saporta family in Pitt Street, in middle age [1934]. The shock of recognition had sent Waldo temporarily off his rocker, with the result that he was knocked down farther along, his pince-nez damaged beyond repair. It was not Arthur who had arranged the meeting, though Waldo seemed to think it was (278–279).

During this episode, "Arthur had suffered for Waldo's suffering, more particularly for Waldo's fear of death", which put Arthur in a difficult position, of convincing Waldo he could not afford to let him die:

> Though Arthur continued to blub a little to show his brother he needed him. Love, he had found, is more acceptable to some when twisted out of its true shape (279).

The Poulter Family

In *The Solid Mandala*, the introduction and conclusion both feature Mrs Poulter. In Part I, she is an elderly woman travelling from Sarsaparilla by bus. She looks out the window and sees the elderly Brown brothers walking home. In Part IV, she discovers Waldo's dead body; soon after this she is confronted with Arthur, who believes he is responsible for his brother's death. She does not agree with him, as her experience of Waldo suggests he died from his own spite—slowly—over a long period of time.

This overarching frame—of *The Solid Mandala* beginning and ending with Mrs Poulter—suggests the novel not only about Waldo and Arthur. It is about their place in her mind, just as *The Bell* is about Dora's mind, and *Robinson* is about January's mind (see Appendix). While White is not doing exactly what Murdoch and Spark are doing, he is doing something similar. All three authors arrive at different conclusions about the human condition.

At the end of the novel, Mrs Poulter declares her "belief" in Arthur. We must consider what this declaration of "belief" means, as its logic is located in the different relationships she has with Waldo in Part II and Arthur in Part III. Many critics understand her declaration of "belief" as a development or shift in her relationship with the Christian horizon. Many see it as an abandonment of that horizon altogether. Fewer see it as a theological shift from "high" to "low" christology, since that shift is logical to those who theologize, post-Kant, within romantic hermeneutics after Vatican II. Regardless of whether we see the shift as an abandonment of Christianity, or as a christological shift within Christianity, there is still a commentary on logos happening, and there is still a relationship with mythos involved, since mythos is where White's sense of authentic religious experience is located.

Part I—"In the Bus"—takes place on the eight-thirteen from Sarasparilla, full of suburban commuters on their way to work in Barranugli. Mrs Poulter is taking chrysanthemums from her garden to a florist. She is sitting alongside an acquaintance, the eponymous Mrs Dun, a new neighbour who is not yet a friend and may never become one. White wants to suggest a frailty about their relationship, just as he wants to suggest a frailty about the mental and geographical landscape they are travelling through. As mentioned in Chapter II, Sarsaparilla was once called Durilgai. Before that the area had no name when the Parkers first settled there in *The Tree of Man*. By the mid-1960s, this landscape was becoming familiar to White's readers. In *Riders in the Chariot*, he tried to "imagine" its "reality" in "the unconscious". He was trying to do the same thing in *The Solid Mandala*.

While the two women are sitting in the bus, tentatively negotiating whatever friendship might be available to them, Mrs Poulter attempts to locate herself within Sarsaparilla's meta-history. She has lived in Terminus Road her whole married life, she says, having arrived there in 1920 as a young bride from the country. On cue, she looks out the window, as her husband comes into view, sweeping the gutters for the local council, but he studiously ignores her, since it is against his principles to acknowledge her in public. The subject then turns to life in Terminus Road, whereupon the narrator hints that the characters (and readers) are entering an inward realm:

> The eyes of the two women followed the tunnel which led inward, through
> the ragged greenery and sudden stench of crushed weeds. You could hide

behind a bush if necessary (14).

Mrs Dun admits the isolation in Terminus Road took some getting used to; she once had thoughts of being murdered in broad daylight, as that kind of thing happens. Mrs Poulter is less afraid, since she has her neighbours, the Brown brothers who live opposite. Mrs Dun, who has never heard of them, is immediately suspicious of what she neither knows nor understands.

Mrs Poulter introduces the Brown story in broad strokes, although the early part of the story is legend to her, as Waldo and Arthur were around 28 when she arrived in Sarsaparilla. Their father had retired and was in declining health. Their mother was preparing for what would soon become an alcoholic widowhood. Mrs Poulter tells Mrs Dun the Browns came out from England when the boys were young. Their house was different from the others in Terminus Road. Its veranda had a peak in what someone told her was the classical style. Their father was a bookish white-collar gentleman who worked as a bank teller. Their mother was kind and good but never stopped letting you know "she had thrown herself away" (16). Waldo was bookish like his father and worked in either the city or state library all his life. Arthur was not bright, but good with figures, and worked in Mr Allwright's store all his life.

The narrator takes over at this point, to tell us the Poulters have different views about Waldo and Arthur. Mrs Poulter believes there is more to them than meets the eye. Mr Poulter believes they are a couple of "poofteroos"; no-hopers with ideas about themselves (18). In some genres of postwar novels, references to male homosexuality is often code for ancient Greece, suggesting those "poofteroos" are, in fact, influential archetypes representing Apollo and Dionysus, living in their dilapidated Greek temple across the road.

Again on cue, Mrs Poulter looks out the window and sees the aged brothers walking home, hand-in-hand, accompanied by their two dogs, as old as their owners are in dog age. She says the two brothers are attached to their dogs. At this point, Mrs Dun admits to hating dogs, whereupon Mrs Poulter feels obliged to not like dogs either. The subject of dogs immediately segues to the subject of children, whereupon both women admit to being childless. Mrs Poulter then wonders what the brothers are doing so far from Terminus Road, whereupon Mrs Dun wonders what is going on in their minds (and alludes to something abnormal). Mrs Poulter tries to defend them, as they may simply be walking for their health: "Anyway", she said, "what goes on in other people's minds is private. I wouldn't want to know what goes on inside of my own husband's mind" (21).

As friendship with Mrs Dun apparently depends on Mrs Poulter denying the importance of Waldo and Arthur to her, or to anyone, and since it is obvious Mrs Dun already despises them, or is afraid of them, Mrs Poulter confesses: "They're nothing to me." Yet the narrator goes on to add:

> ... the confession made her want to cry. And Mrs Dun could feel it. She could feel her own gooseflesh rise. As they waited to escape from the suffocating bus the features of their familiar town began fluctuating strangely through the glass. Like that blood-pressure thing was on your arm. Nor did it help either lady to know the other could be involved (21).

Perhaps this is an admission of Waldo and Arthur's importance as imaginaries in the western mind generally, to be denied at our peril.

Part IV, "Mrs Poulter and the Zeitgeist", begins with Mrs Poulter reflecting on her life; on how fortunate she has been in her marriage to Bill, a man's man, a competent lover, an adequate provider, although he is emotionally absent and gives her nothing in the way of emotional support. She is thankful for her life, and for the comforts she has, although those comforts seem modest to us now. (The Poulters have electricity, and a telephone, but still have an outhouse. The Browns have apparently managed without electricity or a telephone and their sanitary arrangements are unclear.) For most of her life, she has remained friendless. Mrs Dun has proven a disappointment but she does not complain. She has remained childless, regrets losing a child at birth, and wonders what Waldo's malicious gift of the "big lump of a rubbery doll" was all about" (see "Waldo" 184–187).[13]

On Sunday mornings Mrs Poulter usually goes to Church, unless she has a sore throat or her leg is hurting:

> At least she had her faith, which Bill didn't altogether approve of, but it was what she was brought up to, if she didn't always understand, but hope to in time, not through the ministers, she would never of dared ask, but somehow. She had her Lord Jesus. Who was a man. By that she meant nothing blasphemous. Humankind. That was what they turned him into, wasn't it? (298)

White re-enforces his Blakean sensibility here. His "authentic" Christian protagonists—Ruth Godbold and Mrs Poulter and Mary de Santis—all have a loose relationship with systematic theology, and the

---

[13] The gift is ambiguous, since it consciously signifies her sterility but unconsciously signifies his sterility.

institutional Church, and a non-existent relationship with the clerical hierarchy. Throughout his novels, designated individuals, even non-practising Christians on the margins of the church, represent a more "authentic" religious experience; the Christianity of the mythos rather than the Christianity of the logos.

What kind of character would Mrs Poulter have become, had she lived in a different kind of society, with a different kind of husband? While this is purely hypothetical—characters exist within novels, they are not persons—White describes a woman who has been habituated to a civilization contrary to her nature. In other words, her mythos has been negatively influenced by the reigning logos, and this is a recurring theme in the literature of romantic hermeneutics. She has a maternal, loving, gentle attitude towards her pigs and used to cry when they were butchered. "Later on she changed," the narrator says. Her husband asks her how she could live without butchers. "There's the vegetarians," she said. "The vegetarians are nuts," he replied. "So, if men could only live normal by butchery, then she accepted it" (298).

White segues from Mrs Poulter's being habituated to killing pigs to killing humans, now viewable from the comfort of her living room:

> She loved the telly. It made her sit forward, holding her elbows, not exactly tense, but waiting, most of all for the *real* programmes, when they let off one of the bombs, or an aeroplane caught fire the moment of crashing, or those guerrillas they'd collared … the news items so real, you only sometimes overheard the squeals of a stuck and bleeding pig … One midwinter evening the squealing got so bad, she went and slammed the window shut, although it had only been open a crack. She broke a nail, they was so brittle, she got the indigestion, she couldn't concentrate on the telly for all that old sadness returning (299).

Television shuts out nature. Her sadness is a mixture of love for her pigs, her "misborn child", and what the "plastic doll on the square of gelatin" represents, but Mrs Poulter's faith kept her going through all this:

> Not that she knew what it amounted to, not all of it, but knew. It was her own breath, her own body, the blood quicker in her own veins. But she wished she could see more clearly. She wished she could *see*. Recognize the face [of the Lord] they spoke about … In the days when she had gone with poor Arthur lovely walks through the paddocks and blackberrying in season as far as the Chinese farm she had almost seen or at least known so intimately so many details vein of leaf blade of grass sound and silence funny enough by Arthur's being there his head a fire amongst the blackberry bushes Arthur got cured of his trouble anyway on that day to dance the thing the mandala she still had the marble but too afraid to take it out for fear of facing what though on the day she had known there was

never no need for fear with her and Arthur cured and all ... she knew he
was a nut. Though he wasn't. They'll say anybody's a nut. They said about
Jesus ... So the bonfire of Arthur's head had never quite gone out for Mrs
Poulter. Even though she never addressed him after. Unless addressed. In
the moments of years. It was the only secret Bill wouldn't ever get out of
her, if Bill was to ask for all. It was too difficult. Unlike their own lovely-
fitting grooved love of the beginning [of their marriage], it could not be
fitted to word or hand. If she and Arthur was answerable for the day in the
blackberry bushes, where in a moment or two they had gone through more
than you live in years, they was answerable only to the Lord God, to who
the last answers are made. She was no know-all, but she did know that
(300).

In spite of what Mrs Poulter "knows" there is a nagging sense, deep within
her, of what she does not know, and a nagging urgency to remember what
she fleetingly experienced with Arthur. On cold evenings "after the telly
had closed down" she:

> ... would roam far and wide through her wooden house and up the yard,
> crying softly, above grief: My darling, my curly pig, there is an end to the
> blood and squealing if only we can remember how ... For she could never
> quite remember what they had seen and understood there below the
> Chinese farm ... But got at last to remembering she had not seen Waldo,
> she had not seen Him—Arthur—since when (301).

Mrs Poulter bakes a custard, crosses the road, and looks through a
window, only to find Waldo dead in bed, his throat torn open, and Scruffy
(Arthur's eponymous dog) pulling at the "old soft perished rubber" of his
penis, while Runt (Waldo's eponymous dog) is crouching on the floor,
swallowing his owner's dead flesh, growling, and glaring out of his almost
blind eyes (301). Arthur is nowhere to be seen.

Mrs Poulter runs away, terror-stricken, as Arthur did. First she runs to
Mrs Dun for understanding. Mrs Dun, terror-stricken herself, refuses to
open the door and tells her to ring the police. She goes home and does
that. As she puts the receiver down, she turns around and finds Arthur
standing in her kitchen, looking like some old hobo "dragged through a
tunnel" (305). She goes to him, and comforts him, wanting to believe in
him and in his innocence.

Where has Arthur been? He fled to the city. After days of living rough,
he eventually made his way to the Feinstein's home, now the Saporta's
home, the mock mediaeval fortress in Centennial Park. He climbs a
network of vines and looks into a window. He sees Dulcie, who has one of
his mandalas, who named her son after him, whose husband quietly paid

for his mother's funeral. Dulcie is now an older woman, surrounded by her Orthodox family. They are celebrating their Sabbath meal (308–309).[14]

Arthur knows they still love him, and would care for him, but he does not have the will to break through the protective covering of their Orthodoxy. So he walks away from the Saporta home "without attempting to storm their fortress" (309). But where can he go now?

> To Mrs Poulter, naturally. Whose need was as great as his. Who had sat with him on the grass, under the great orange disc of the sun, and burned with him in a fit of understanding or charity. So the drowsily revolving wheels, of trains, of buses, carried him back, as he sat twirling the mandala in his pocket (309).

He must go to Mrs Poulter, the third mandala holder, apart from Dulcie and himself.

The novel's last few pages need to be interpreted with caution, because they lend themselves to antithetical interpretations depending on the critic's secular or religious perspective. While she was on the phone, Mrs Poulter told the police Arthur was nowhere to be found but insists he could not be responsible for Waldo's death. When the phone call is over, she finds him in her kitchen. While she is comforting him, the police arrive at the Brown's dilapidated house with the classical pediment and shoot the two dogs, Arthur's eponymous Scruffy and Waldo's eponymous Runt, thus completing the Brown brothers' götterdämmerung.

At this point, Mrs Poulter declares her belief in Arthur, who has become "all the men she had never loved, the children she never had" (311). She is now acutely aware of his religious significance to her, since discovering Waldo's body, since her crucified Jesus "released His hands from the nails. And fell down, in a thwack of canvas, a cloud of dust", since her God "was brought crashing down" (311), since her Lord "destroyed Himself that same day" and she has been given this man–child, the reality of Arthur, as a token of everlasting life (312).

There are different ways of interpreting what this belief means. If the reader is post-Christian, or anti-Christian, he or she can interpret it as the ultimate götterdämmerung, the abandonment of Christianity altogether. If the reader is Christian, he or she can interpret it as a theological shift from high to low Christology, logical to those who theologize within romantic hermeneutics post-Kant and post-Vatican II. Similarly, if we see high christology as apocalyptic and low christology as mimetic, apocalyptic and mimetic being two modes of thought which continue to coexist in the western imagination (Detweiler 1989, 2), Mrs Poulter's belief in Arthur,

---

[14] Or could it be a Passover seder?

rather than being post-Christian or anti-Christian, is the logical conclusion of a religious novelist searching for ontological or immanent meaning, within consciousness, rather than teleological or imminent meaning at the end of time (Kermode 1967).

Arthur is taken into custody. Both he and Mrs Poulter assume he will be cared for in an asylum. She promises to visit him regularly. We do not know whether she does, beyond the end of the novel. We do not know whether the götterdämmerung of Waldo and Arthur has any permanent influence on her life, apart from once declaring her "belief" in Arthur. The novel ends, instead, with a strong division between her inner thoughts and her outward life, as she continues to be the wife of an emotionally absent husband:

> Then she turned, to do the expected things, before re-entering her actual sphere of life (316).

CHAPTER FOUR

VIVISECTOR

Author as Painter

If the Bible offers soteria is there also soteria through art and, by analogy, through literature? Olivia–Boo asks this question in a different way while speaking to the painter Hurtle Duffield two-thirds through *The Vivisector*:

> "Always at my most desperate, or cynical," Olivia said, watching as the sea continued sucking around their ankles, "when I've most hated men for their lies and presumptuousness, and their attempts to reduce love to a grotesque sexual act, I've felt that somewhere there must be some creature, not quite man, not quite god, who will heal the wounds." She raised her head and drew down the corners of her formal mouth. "Perhaps that's why we look to artists of any kind, why we lose our heads over them."
>
> "Possibly!" He took her lightly by the hand. "But better wait till they're dead. What they have to tell or show improves with decontamination—if it doesn't go up in hot air, or sink into a wall" (415).

The key phrase here is "not quite man, not quite god", which gives the question of soteria through art Blakean connotations of solitary poetic genius. Or Nietzschean connotations of amor fati. This places *The Vivisector* within the romantic image of the artist and the romantic function of art (Kermode 1957).

Both *Riders in the Chariot* and *The Solid Mandala* have Ricoeurean anthropologies within Gadamerian frames. This scheme is repeated in *The Eye of the Storm* (1973), in an attenuated form, after which it disappears. White varied the scheme in *The Vivisector* (1970). In this novel, we see nothing of the humanistic Hebraic metaphors, and their adamic myth, so powerfully present in the previous two novels. Instead, we see White focusing on the fatalistic Theogonic and Hellenic metaphors, and their myths of chaos and creation, tragic hero, and exiled soul, as he assigns different protagonists different degrees of freedom and constraint.

In *The Vivisector* the protagonist is driven, obsessively and compulsively, by creative and destructive forces beyond his control. In *The Solid Mandala* the unanswered question is: At what point does Waldo become socratic, in Nietzsche's life-denying sense, rather than apollonian, which has greater creative possibility? In *The Vivisector* the unanswered question is: At what point does Hurtle lose his free will and become a slave to his agon?[1]

As McCulloch reminds us, at its most basic level *The Vivisector*:

> … involves a structured argument by White, the artist, as he dramatizes his own inner dialogues concerning the ultimate possibilities of art. Even as a small child Hurtle knew that "any possible answers were enclosed by the lines of his drawing". Hurtle insists that he was not in love with himself but, instead, with his art which was a projection of life, but when one analyzes the relationship between White and Hurtle, it is evident that *The Vivisector* is an art form that is a projection of an artist's projection of life (McCulloch 1983, 71).

Behind this projection of an art form, itself a projection of Hurtle's (and perhaps White's) projection of life, is the source of Hurtle's artistic inspiration; the source of the different relationships he has with a range of characters. Each relationship inspires a different painting, or series of paintings, or phases in his life–career. What his paintings look like is hypothetical. If we cannot see them, White gives us enough language to visualize what they are supposed to look like if not mean. Even in their rhetorical context, romantic or post-romantic, they are enigmatic.

Like Alf Dubbo, Hurtle has innate talent. Both are raised by couples, one a brother and sister, the other a husband and wife, who represent an attractive but deficient symbolic order. Each is freed–empowered or oppressed–disabled by that environment in different ways. While they move away from that environment, as adults, it has an indelible effect upon them. For better and for worse, it becomes an integral part of who they become as mature artists.

In terms of White's rhetoric, they therefore occupy a liminal space between logos and mythos: neither fully one nor the other. Also, neither Hurtle nor Alf has been professionally trained as painters, beyond a few drawing lessons as boys, yet neither can be called primitive or naïve. Although, by definition, there is a necessary element of primitivism and naïveté embedded, practically and theoretically, within their responses to classical and romantic art.

None of White's novels has a classicist formula of exposition, rising action, climax, falling action, and resolution. Further, unlike the previous two novels, *The Vivisector* has a direct or linear narrative, from Hurtle's childhood to his death. Although the narrative does not shift back and

---

[1] Hurtle's English contemporary, the artist Sammy Mountjoy in Golding's *Free Fall* (1959), asks himself this question throughout the novel.

forth in time, White introduces three "shapely turns" within its linear structure to indicate major shifts in Hurtle's life stages. These shifts occur one-third, halfway, and two-thirds of the way through the novel.

The first turn is indicated by the text: "Suddenly he had begun to live the life for which he had been preparing, *or for which he might even have been prepared*" (italics added) (204). At this point, Hurtle has rejected his adopted name (Courtney) and returned to his birth name (Duffield), has served in World War I, has returned to Australia as an ex-serviceman with the intention of becoming an artist, and is sexually involved with and inspired by a prostitute, Nance Lightfoot. So we should ask: prepared by whom and for what? How much of his life has been determined by his will? How much has been determined by the will of others?

The second turn is indicated by the text: "We must find Rhoda" (301), which occurs exactly halfway through the novel, often a significant place in a structured novel of ideas. It is now early in the 1930s. Hurtle has established himself as an accomplished artist living if not with guilt–shame then with the unanswered question: Was Nance's death due to an accidental fall because she was blind drunk? Or was it an intentional jump because he was unable to give her the relationship she wanted?

This turn is announced, halfway through the novel, by Olivia Davenport (a.k.a. Boo Hollingrake), Hurtle's silent, subtle patroness, or guardian angel–daemon, during one of her visits to his Paddington home–studio. They are in his bedroom and have just had sex (300). She is pondering the psychological significance of, and the motivation for, his *Pythoness at Tripod* series. In the series, Hurtle is attempting to portray the "truth" about Rhoda, whom they both knew as children and adolescents. Now that they are adults, and have lost contact with Rhoda, she feels that finding Rhoda would do them both good. He is not yet convinced, as he has never had a conscious sense of Rhoda's importance to him, to anyone, or to anything.

The third turn is indicted by the text: "But because he needed her—he suddenly realized how desperately—he must use every means to trap her" (435). It is now somewhere after World War II, in Paddington, in the period before trams were replaced by buses. Hurtle has move from being an established and accomplished artist to being a celebrated one. He is now an eccentric bachelor who needs to be protected from forming a dangerous relationship with a child prodigy, Katherine Volkov, a just-turned 13-year-old Lolita figure who turns the tables on him by taking from him what he took from others. Soon after meeting Kathy, he finds Rhoda by accident, feeding cats in a laneway. He wants her to live with him, as he now has an unconscious sense of her importance, to him, if not to everyone and everything. White knows Rhoda's significance is universal even if Hurtle never does.

White accomplishes many things within this linear, tripartite structure with its neatly programed segues between each relationship. First, he describes Hurtle's adoption into the Courtney family in ways that echo Freud's theory of Family Romances (Freud 1959, 235–241) and Lacan's theory of Symbolic Order (Lacan 1966, Paglia 1991; Johnston 2014). Second, he ensures the novel consistently revolves around the mystery of Rhoda, as a variation of the similar-but-different mysteries of Mary Hare, Arthur Brown, and every other red-haired mythos in his novels, although her hair is more pink than red. Third, he describes Hurtle's sexual relationships with four women: two of whom die (Nance Lightfoot and Hero Pavloussi) and two of whom outlive him (Boo Hollingrake a.k.a. Olivia Davenport and Katherine Volkov).

Fourth, he describes Hurtle's adolescent encounter with his adopted mother, Alfreda Courtney, in her bed:

> When he opened his eyes, Maman, who resisted chocolates now on account of her figure, was scratching in a box on the bedside table. She soon heaved back into their former soft position; she stuck the chocolate in her own mouth, and warmed it up till she had it ready to offer; or so he understood, from the bird-noises she began to make. They were like two birds together, feeding on the same food, as they worked the chocolate, neither soft nor hard, neither his nor hers: the chocolate trickled blissfully.
>
> Suddenly Maman went: "Mm—mm—hmmm!: rising to a high note.
> She sucked in the chocolate so quickly his tongue almost followed it.
> She sat up in bed. "Oh dear, what silly things we do! Childish things!"
> When she was the childish one: he wouldn't have thought of the silly trick with the chocolate.
> Gathering up her hair by handfuls, she was smiling; but it was not for him: more for herself, it looked.
> He got out of bed and began feeling for his slippers. He might have been treading on glass instead of the soft carpet. He straightened up, after spreading his hands to hide what he had to hide (116–117).

This scene has incestual overtones, and this is intentional, but the real point is that, from this time on, Hurtle is sexually aroused when he is sensually inspired.

Fifth, he described Hurtle's confessional encounter with Cecil Cutbush: a closeted homosexual grocer trapped within a heterosexual marriage; living in a period where homosexuality was still illegal and classified as a mental disorder. Sixth, he describes the drawings and paintings most of these characters inspire, as part of his search for the elusive and complex "truth" his art tells. What is this "truth"? Is it also lies? Is it a flickering of revealing and concealing: like looking at God "through a glass darkly" (1 Corinthians 13:12)? Is this the God of Nietzsche, who is dead, or the God of Heidegger, who has chosen to conceal himself?

As readers negotiate White's rhetoric in *The Vivisector*, they should notice that the novel often refers to God. White wants his readers to consider, not whether God exists, since both Hurtle and White take his existence as given. but where God might be, as transcendence, as immanence, or beyond transcendence and immanence. Is Rhoda, the novel's symbol of mythos, a manifestation of God? Who is the Vivisector? Is it only Hurtle? Is it also God? Is it "nature"? Is it Mrs Courtney, ostensibly against the vivisection of animals but capable of vivisecting humans herself? Is it the anthropomorphic moon, defecating on creation in *Lantana Lovers*? Who are the vivisected? Who survives their vivisection? Who learns from it? Who does not? These questions are important to White.

The novel invites the reader to consider the eponymous significance of three names. Early in the novel, we are told Hurtle's name is a corruption of Hertel (hert + el = heart of God), which signifies the loss of his wholeness, or the dissociation of his sensibility, at some point in his childhood, as he moves from being God's heart to God's hurt, the God who can be hurt as well as the God who allows hurt (3). The novel also tells us the name Rhoda, which means "a wished for child", is in the Bible (12). Although Mr and Mrs Courtney wished for her, she is not what they wished for: instead, her deformity is a perpetual reminder of what their marriage symbolizes within White's agon.

Hero's name is also significant. She is Greek, and, along with her husband Cosma, White links her with the Hellenic metaphors and their myths of tragic hero and exiled soul. The reader is invited to consider whether, through Hero, and through her relationship with Hurtle, White could be exploring the possibility–impossibility of modern tragedy. If he is, then notice that the entire novel is not a commentary on tragedy, only one section is. That section occurs between the second shapely turn (Rhoda is lost) and the third (Rhoda is found).

The novel's meaning can be distilled in one point: the "truth" of Rhoda is vastly greater than the "truth" of "tragic" Hero. If Hurtle had been seduced by the myth of Hero's "tragedy" he would have been consumed by its "drama" and remained with her in Greece. It is essential for Hurtle's development, as a character and an artist, that he returns to Sydney and is reunited with Rhoda. He must process the source of his creativity and the formative influence of his childhood and adolescence upon it. Rhoda is central to all of this.

Like all White's mature work, *The Vivisector* is highly structured, densely woven, and contains many signals. It can be difficult for readers to manoeuvre their way through the novel and hold its many elements in a creative tension, while maintaining a focus on the overall structure. The temptation here, as in his other novels, is to focus on the parts at the expense of the whole.

If too much is made of the novel as a fictionalized biography of a painter, or of White himself, the less the reader will understand the novel's rhetoric. If too much is made of Hurtle being "sold", and being removed from his "natural" family, the subtleties of his "family romance" within the "symbolic order" will be lost. True, Mr and Mrs Courtney wanted to adopt him, to make up for whatever White believed deficient in their symbolic order. But this was always a two-way street. Hurtle desired that order. He needed it and wanted to be a part of it. Even though it contributed to the loss of his wholeness, the dissociation of his sensibility, and his sense of alienation.

Marr 1991 reminds us that White did not receive the Nobel Prize in 1972 because one of the judges attacked him for demeaning the image of the artist: "He argued that White depicted the painter as a user and consumer of human beings" (534). But if too much is made of Hurtle's supposed use and consumption of human beings, for the sake of his art, the nuances of each character's rhetorical function are lost. Was Hurtle ever immoral or dishonest, in any of his relationships, at any stage of his life? Was it his responsibility to fulfil the needs and desires of each person he met, including Nance and Hero? Were they victims? Did they not have free will and moral agency?

In his paintings, Hurtle wanted to represent the complex, difficult, elusive, and incomplete "truth" he was inspired to tell. Nance and Hero, the two subjects of his paintings who could not cope with this "truth", both died.[2] Those who could cope with the "truth" admired and loved him, albeit from a distance, and stood by him until his death. He experienced as much of their admiration and love as he was capable of receiving.

In White's autobiography, he confesses that his "Sydney novels"—*The Vivisector* and *The Eye of the Storm*—were conceived in Dogwoods, Castle Hill, but he could not realize them until he moved to Martin Road, Centennial Park (149):

The Vivisector, which came first, is about a painter, the one I was not

---

[2] Cosma wrote to Hurtle, telling him that he "killed" Hero. Hurtle believed this for many years. When he finally learns that she died from cancer, he wonders about what causes cancer and whether he was a contributing cause of her cancer.

destined to become—another of my frustrations. I had imagined that if I could acquire the technique I might give visual expression to what I have inside me, and that the physical act of painting would exhilarate me far more than grinding away at grey, bronchial prose. This could be the delusion of a writer who has always resented having to write. Some painters have told me that Hurtle Duffield is not a painter, others that he is. Throughout my writing life I have encountered fiercely contradictory judgments: that Himmelfarb is/is not a Jew; that I know everything/nothing about women; that what I write illuminates, or on the other hand, that my novels are incomprehensible boring rubbish. But I expect any writer who takes risks has had this battle fought out over his body, live or dead (150).

Marr 1991 says Hurtle's paintings are more like Francis Bacon's than those of any other painter (474) and *The Vivisector* is about how White saw himself as an author:

Who is Hurtle Duffield? No other character in White's novels so provokes the search for the actual man. But there was no one child, artist, recluse, lover or celebrity. Hurtle Duffield is one of the great works of White's imagination, a synthesis of many lives beginning with White's own. The painter's early years are saturated with details from White's rich childhood. White believed he was writing the most detailed portrait of Sydney's plutocracy ever attempted. "Australian writers don't seem to have considered it aesthetically desirable to write about the rich. (There is an exception in Martin Boyd, but he came from Victoria and concentrated on Melbourne society.) At least with the rich, who are usually slightly more cosmopolitan, one can get away from what is referred to as 'the Australian image', which no longer interests me".

The Courtneys' house in Rushcutters Bay is another Lulworth, and the Courtneys—Alfreda (Birdie) and her husband Harry—are Ruth and Dick in light disguise. The disfiguring hump on their daughter Rhoda is another—but exaggerated—detail from White family history. "Suzanne had a suspicion of a hump. My mother had one in old age. Uncle Clem told me of my grandmother Cobb's hump that nobody talked about. There were a lot of humps about."

His mother was Hurtle's first subject:

"Oh, darling, how clever of you! But I shouldn't have taken it for me, exactly. Do you see me like that? You've given me a melon chest."

But Hurtle's Duffield's eye is true. Rather than argue, he keeps on working, "any possible answers were enclosed by the lines of his drawing". Alfreda's complaint echoes through Duffield's career. Are you a perv? "I am an artist." Is it honest to make paintings by lumping many real people into a single figure? "Only the painting can answer that—when it is finished." Was it not cruel to paint Rhoda naked with her hump? "How can you say it's cruel? It's the truth!" Why must he paint disgusting images? "I was trying to find some formal order behind a moment of chaos and unreason. Otherwise it would have been too horrible and terrifying."

> The formal order is God's: White was trying once more in *The Vivisector* to show "unbelievers" the faith buried inside them. Duffield's belief follows the pattern of White's loss and rediscovering of faith. "As an old man he realizes that his belief in God has been there all the time 'like a secret relationship'." This God is fallible—"everyone can make mistakes, including God"—and man is one of God's blunders, a kind of Frankenstein monster. This God is also cruel: "Otherwise, how would men come to their cruelty—and their brilliance.[3] Where White believed the churches went wrong was in rejecting so much that is sordid and shocking, "which can still be related to religious experience". An artist who celebrates the world by depicting it in all its squalor and beauty, draws close to God. The pursuit of truth is an act of worship (472–473).

Marr insists *The Vivisector* is an autobiographical novel: however, the idea that Harry is a thinly disguised portrait of Dick is unconvincing, since Harry's obvious masculinity seems more like the photo of White's uncle Frank from "Samaurez" in *Flaws in the Glass* (55). There is a stronger case to argue that Alfreda has elements of Ruth, as she seems more like Ruth than other literary mother in White's novels. Even so, interpreting Alfreda as a fictional portrait of Ruth is a critical cul-de-sac, or dead-end, from which it is difficult to escape.

Hewitt 2002 reminds us that a number of Australian painters contributed to Hurtle, including Roy de Maistre and Sidney Nolan (71). She also points out that *The Vivisector* was written "during the tail end of Sydney abstract expressionism", when the novel's romantic and post-romantic description of the nexus between painting and religious experience was becoming passé:

> While *Voss* had had great impact on the artists of the late 1950s and early 1960s, generating much inspiration and debate about the nature and direction of Australian art, *The Vivisector* probably seemed rather antiquated to the fashionable post-romantic, conceptual and hard-edged young painters of the 1970s, if they read it at all. Modern romanticism and metaphysical pursuits had suffered a rapid decline during the 1960s. *Riders in the Chariot* had coincided with and contributed to the tide of visionary romantic modernism in Australia, but now, as one of the guests at art Duffield's retrospective puts it, "God is dead, anyway. Anyway—thank God—in Australia" (83).

In his 2008 introduction to the novel's Penguin edition, Coetzee acknowledges and develops Hewitt's description by suggesting:

---

[3] There is no simple Jewish or Christian response to White's belief in a voluntaristic God who is fallible, can make mistakes, and is cruel. All we can do is contextualize his belief—in its historical specificity—and place it in dialogue with Benedict XVI.

> The book White was working on in 1967, the book that became *The Vivisector*, was thus fated to be an elegy not only to the school of painting represented by Duffield but also to the school of writing represented by White himself (Coetzee 2008, xix).

Each of these observations is partially but not wholly true. Hurtle is clearly not a painter, as painters are human beings not fictional characters. The drama, of his artistic struggle to create whatever he creates, the drama of his truths and lies, the drama of his failure to form human relationships, tells us little or nothing about the struggle of a real painter to create painterly effects on canvasses. His paintings cannot look like those of real painters. They are words printed in black ink on white pages. Or pixels on computer screens.

While it is true that *The Vivisector* is an excellent example of modern romanticism, and its metaphysical pursuits, and while White may have been composing an elegy to a school of writing as well as a school of painting, this does not mean the rhetorical concerns of romantic and post-romantic artists are passé. If the rhetoric White offers in *The Vivisector* belongs within the shadow of romanticism, it reworks influential thought processes that go back to Plato, and perhaps before Plato, somewhere among the Presocratics.

To suggest Hurtle's art and White's writing are passé is to suggest their philosophical and aesthetic dilemmas are ephemeral rather than enduring. This ignores the ways in which philosophers, poets, and artists inherit, question, rework, and pass on influential cultural themes. The themes that shaped White, which he reshaped, do not disappear with him. They are alive within the history of philosophy and aesthetics.

The Vivisector's linear narrative, with its tripartite structure signalled by its "shapely turns", tells the story of Hurtle's life stages. The first third of the novel tells his story within his biological Duffield family and his adoptive Courtney family. By the novel's first "shapely turn", he has turned his back on the adopted Courtney world; however, while he has chosen to take the name of Duffield again, he has not chosen to return to the Duffield world. He remains isolated from both worlds, and from any *en famille* world. This provides him with both his identity crisis and his agon.

One way of understanding the meaning of Hurtle's adoption—the leitmotiv of the remaining two-thirds of *The Vivisector*—is to notice the way White reworks the theory of Family Romances (Freud 1959, 235–241). This theory is based on the assumption that the liberation of an individual from parental authority is a necessary but painful part of growing up. The liberation must occur, if the individual is to be "normal", since failure breeds neurotics. Of course, Hurtle continues to be neurotic about many things throughout his life.

According to Freud, the conflict surrounding the family romance arises early, as the child's parents are his only authority and source of belief. As the child grows, he gradually compares his parents with other parents. As a result they lose their uniqueness and he becomes dissatisfied, critical, and jealous. Sibling rivalry emerges—if there are siblings—and the biological child often finds release in the idea of being a step-child or adopted. During puberty, his daydreams and fantasies have two aims, erotic and ambitious, as he imaginatively seeks to free himself from his parents, although at this stage he is still unaware of the sexual determinants of procreation.

When the child becomes aware of his parents as sexual beings, an Oedipal triad emerges, complicated by a common theme; in his daydreams and fantasies both parents are replaced, or the father alone is replaced, by grander people; new and aristocratic parents with attributes derived entirely from recollections of his old and humble parents. The efforts of the biological child to replace his real parents with superior ones is an expression of his longing for vanished happy days, when his father seemed to him the noblest and strongest of men and his mother the dearest and loveliest of women. Thus his daydreams and fantasies are informed by a regret for lost wholeness. Eventually, the overvaluation that characterized his early years comes into its own and survives in his dreams as an adult. In *The Vivisector* White reworks this theory in an idiosyncratic way that fitted his pattern rather than Freud's.

For Freud, the progress of society depends on this inter-generational conflict, which Paglia 1991 places at the centre of western civilization:

> The ghost-ridden character of sex is implicit in Freud's brilliant theory of "family romance." We each have an incestuous constellation of sexual personae that we carry from childhood to the grave and that determines whom and how we love or hate. Every encounter with friend or foe, every clash with or submission to authority bears the perverse traces of family romance. Love is a crowded theatre, for as Harold Bloom remarks, "We can never embrace (sexually or otherwise) a single person, but embrace the whole of her or his family romance." We still know next to nothing about cathexis, the investment of libido in certain people or things. The element of free will in sex and emotion is slight. As poets know, falling in love is irrational.
>
> Like art, sex is fraught with symbols. Family romance means that adult sex is always representation, ritualistic acting out of vanished realities. A perfectly humane eroticism may be impossible. Somewhere in every family romance is hostility and aggression, the homicidal wishes of the unconscious. Children are monsters of unbridled egotism and will, for they

spring directly from nature, hostile intimations of immortality. We carry that daemonic will within us forever. Most people conceal it with acquired ethical precepts and meet it only in their dreams, which they hastily forget upon waking. *The will-to-power is innate, but the sexual scripts of family romance are learned.* Human beings are the only creatures in whom consciousness is so entangled with animal instinct. In western culture, there can never be a purely physical or anxiety-free sexual encounter. Every attraction, every pattern of touch, every orgasm is shaped by psychic shadows.

The search for freedom through sex is doomed to failure. In sex, compulsion and ancient Necessity rule. The sexual personae of family romance are obliterated by the tidal force of regression, the backwards movement towards primeval dissolution, which Ferenzi identifies with ocean. An orgasm is a domination, a surrender, or a breaking through. Nature is no respecter of human identity. This is why so many men turn away or flee after sex, for they have sensed the annihilation of the daemonic. Western love is a displacement of cosmic realities. It is a defence mechanism rationalizing forced ungoverned and ungovernable. Like early religion, it is a device enabling us to control our primal fear.

Sex cannot be understood because nature cannot be understood ... We say that nature is beautiful. But this aesthetic judgment, which not all peoples have shared, is another defence formation. Woefully inadequate for encompassing nature's totality. What is pretty in nature is confined to the thin skin of the globe upon which we huddle. Scratch that skin, and nature's daemonic ugliness will erupt.

Our focus on the pretty is an Apollonian strategy. The leaves and flowers, the birds, the hills are a patchwork pattern by which we map the known. What the west represses in its view of nature is the chthonian, which means "of the earth"—but the earth's bowels, not its surface. Jane Harrison uses the term for pre-Olympian Greek religion, and I adopt it as a substitute for the Dionysian, which has become contaminated with vulgar pleasantries. *The Dionysian is no picnic. It is the chthonian realities which Apollo evades*, the blind grinding of subterranean force, the long slow suck, the murk and ooze. *It is the dehumanizing brutality of biology and geology, the Darwinian waste and bloodshed, the squalor and rot we must block from consciousness to retain our Apollonian integrity as persons. Western science and aesthetics are attempts to revise this horror into imaginatively palatable forms.*

The daemonism of chthonic nature is the west's dirty secret. *Modern humanist's made the "tragic sense of life" the touchstone of mature understanding.* They defined man's mortality and the transience of time as literature's supreme subjects. In this I again see evasion and even sentimentality. *The tragic sense of life is a partial response to experience.* It is a reflex of the west's resistance to and misapprehension of nature, compounded by the errors of liberalism, which in its Romantic nature-philosophy has followed the Rousseauist Wordsworth rather than the daemonic Coleridge (italics added) (4).

Many disagree with Paglia, and Freud, but she understands the philosophical and aesthetic drivers of romantic, modernist, and postmodernist art. It is possible to use *Sexual Personae* as a prism to understand White's novels generally and *The Vivisector* specifically.

As we saw in *Riders in the Chariot*—where a daughter offered a pole to her drowning father who refuses to be rescued by her—Freudian motifs appear elsewhere in White. Marr explains White's attitude towards Freud:

> White remained sceptical of Freud. He accepted much that psychoanalysis had to teach but never allowed himself to be analyzed. In Freudian jargon, he was a heavily defended personality. Psychoanalysis, he later remarked, "is a dark cave into which I'd never venture for fear of leaving something important behind". The loss he feared was some part of his creative self ... His dreams did not fit Freud's pattern. Dreams were important all his life. He dreamed vividly nearly every night and remembered his dreams. They fed his work. The casts of his books moved and spoke as he slept. He dreamed through the problems of his writing. But Freud's explanations of dreams seemed to White too much about sex, too systematic. White suspected all systems (Marr 1991, 151).

At this point it is necessary to ask: What are dreams? What do they mean? What function do they serve? Rather than being mythopoeic, are they more like brain defragmentation? Should they be psychoanalyzed?

The psychoanalytical theory of the late-19th and early-20th century, and its precursors, which Atwood brilliantly describes in *Alias Grace* (1996) (see Appendix), systematized the meaning of dreams in ways that have dated badly and were used inappropriately when not abusively. That said, it would have been extremely difficult for any author of White's generation to not be influenced by Freud's and/or Jung's ideas about dreams, indirectly when not directly. Those ideas had infiltrated the humanities, the social sciences, and had filtered down to popular culture. In a range of forms, some positive and some negative, Freud and Jung reinforced several inter-disciplinary hegemonies.

While it is true that White suspected all systems, which was wise, a problem must be noticed. If he regarded Freud's explanations of dreams as too sexual, and too systematic, there is still a form of "sexual personae" rhetoric throughout *The Vivisector*, which is attached to a system of philosophy and aesthetics. The novel presents the reader with a persistent if ambiguous link between sexual arousal and artistic creativity. Sex drives Hurtle's creativity. It drives him towards artistic expression at the expense of personal relationships.

In explaining the tension between White's ambiguous acceptance and suspicion of Freud—what he accepted; what he did not accept—it is necessary to notice the influential link between Freud's psychoanalytical theory and the rest of the humanities and the social sciences. In this regard, the work of Jacques Lacan (1901–1981) acts as a kind of bridge between White, Freud and the broader context of post-Kantian philosophy on the Continent. Although White may not have been familiar with Lacan's work, or aware of its influential legacy, its fundamental concepts were part of White's zeitgeist. Hurtle's creative struggle, as a child and as an adult, is described in broadly Lacanian rather than specifically Freudian ways.

Intriguingly, the key terms White uses to describe his literary vision coincide with Lacan's theory of three registers: Imaginary, Symbolic, and Real (Johnston 2014). For Lacan, the Imaginary register, roughly equivalent to the restricted spheres of consciousness and self-awareness, is associated with the illusions and abstractions of non-psychoanalytic quotidian reality. The Symbolic register, roughly equivalent to Hegel's "objective spirit", is associated with an elaborate, pre-existing and "non-natural" universe of socio-linguistic arrangements and constellations: a "symbolic order" we are thrown into at birth which influences the vicissitudes of our ensuing lives. The Real register, roughly equivalent to Kant's "things-in-themselves", is whatever plenitude or fullness exists beyond, behind, or beneath the restricted spheres of consciousness and self-awareness: the Real is a troubling and thwarting transcendence *as well as* a perturbing and subverting immanence (Johnston 2014). Lacan also describes a "mirror stage" which is more than a stage in the infant's life and becomes a permanent part of a child's subjectivity that continues throughout life.

White's search for God can be partially explained by Lacan's theories of lower case "other" and upper case Other. For Lacan, the little "other" is everything projected by the thoughts, feelings and inclinations of the Imaginary register, and its accompanying ego and alter-egos, making those projections "like me". The big "Other" is everything beyond the control of the Symbolic and Real registers: Nature, History, Society, Party, Science, God, or the analyst as "the subject who is supposed to know" (*suject supposé savoir*) as described in Lacan's account of analytic transference (Johnston 2014).[4]

Within Lacan's scheme, God is simply one Other competing with other Others. If we accept this manoeuvre, all questions about the human

---

[4] Spark was fond of subverting this existential philosophy of *les autres* manoeuvre: for example, in the character of Margaret Damien in *Symposium* (1990).

condition are relativized within romantic hermeneutics, and there is no difference between believing in God or taking an interest in the environment, or belonging to a political party, or trying to be a good citizen of the polis. However, if we approach White through Lacan, which some do, we are obliged to distinguish his sense of God as *the* Other from Lacan's many big Others.

Often called "the French Freud", Lacan is an important postwar figure in the history and reception of psychoanalysis. Under the banner of "return to Freud", he translated Freudianism into structuralism, motivated by his most famous dictum: "the unconscious is structured like a language" (*l'inconscient est structuré comme un langage*):[5]

> Lacan portrayed himself as the lone defender of a Freudian orthodoxy in danger of being eclipsed by its alleged abandonment and betrayal in the post-Freudian analytic universe, particularly Anglo-American ego psychology as consolidated by the troika of Heinz Hartmann, Ernst Kris, and Lacan's former analyst Lowenstein. Lacan adamantly maintained that a Saussurean-assisted recovery of the overriding significance of language for analysis both clinical and metapsychological is the key to faithfully carrying forward Freud's revolutionary approach to psychical subjectivity (Johnston 2014).

A fundamental broadening of Lacan's thinking occurred around 1960, after which his teachings and writings explored "the significance of Freud's discovery of the unconscious both within the theory and practice of analysis itself as well as in connection with a wide range of other disciplines" (Johnston 2014).[6] Hence his importance and influence beyond psychology, in literature, philosophy and throughout the humanities and social sciences generally. As a result, from 1964 onwards:

> Lacan's audience startlingly increased in both sheer numbers and breadth of backgrounds, with artists and academics from various disciplines across academia joining the more clinically-minded attendees ... For instance, such philosophers as Jean Hyppolite, Michel Foucault, Gilles Deleuze, Luce Irigaray, and Julia Kristeva spent time in Lacan's audience. In his seminars, Lacan deftly manoeuvred within and between a multitude of theoretical currents, putting psychoanalysis into conversation with the history of philosophy, phenomenology, existentialism, structuralism, poststructuralism, feminism, and ... just about every discipline represented in the university. All the major French philosophers of the generation that

---

[5] Is the unconscious really structured like a language? Or has this influential idea been responsible for a lot of ephemeral psychology and literary–cultural theory?

[6] Did Freud really discover the unconscious or did he simply colonize it in specious ways which seemed convincing at the time?

came of age in the 1960s and 1970s engaged with Freudian analysis in one way or another, and all of them did so in fashions varying informed by Lacan's teachings (Johnston 2014).

What is unique about Lacan is how he helps us to contextualize the influences that shaped White. Lacan's work is a bridge to understanding Hurtle's development life: as an infant, as a child, and as an adult struggling to relate to characters as little others, and to God as *the* big Other.

Discovering Rhoda

The first third of *The Vivisector*, the three chapters before the first shapely turn, describe Hurtle's journey from the imaginative barrenness but procreative fertility of Cox Street, Surry Hills, to the imaginative fertility but procreative sterility of Rushcutters Bay. The geography of Sydney makes this journey not an ascent into an Arcadian paradise but a descent to a more complex place: mythically and metaphorically.

The novel opens in the Duffield's Surry Hills yard where "the fowls were fluffing in the dust". One of them is a "crook-neck white pullet Mumma said she would hit on the head if only she had the courage to"; but she hadn't. "So the white crook-neck thing … stood around grabbing what and whenever it could, but sort of sideways". Hurtle asks: "Why are the others pecking at it, Pa?" The answer is "Because they don't like the look of it." Because it's different" (1). Through this universal truth, announced on the first page, White is taking the reader to the heart of the human condition, to the problem of evil.

The Duffields are poor. Their lives are full of hardship. Mumma takes in washing and ironing. Pa collects bottles. There are several children. Hurtle's grandfather was a remittance man from England, probably a gentleman, perhaps an aristocrat, who died in a parodic failed Leichhardt–Voss übermensch attempt: "E *borrowed* a mule ter *ride* to the *centre of Australia*. It was 'is dream" (3). He fell from the mule, probably drunk, and died of a seizure in Parramatta Road. The mule disappeared and Pa says he spent a long time compensating its owners.

There is a mystery surrounding Grandfather Duffield's signet ring, which is kept in a small box with other family "mysteries". Hurtle gets to look at the ring, on Sunday afternoons, whenever Pa is pressed to retell the family story. Later, when Hurtle notices a ring on Harry Courtney's little finger, he felt he "had been brought that much closer" and "could fall in love with both the Courtneys" (54).[7] This signals his "family romance".

After Mr Courtney collects Hurtle from Cox Street, while they are driving back to Rushcutters Bay, Hurtle unwraps the ring Pa gave him, "He said I ought to have it" (71):

> Mr Courtney looked more than ever puzzled and shocked though he too was wearing a ring. After taking a look, he seemed to turn away slightly. He gave the horse a cut with the whip it didn't deserve, while the ring was being wrapped again (71).

Through this signet ring, and Harry's reaction to seeing it, the reader could wonder whether Hurtle is biologically related to the Courtneys. White alludes to this possibility in the next paragraph: "There was so much of him that didn't belong to his [biological] family" (7). Hurtle feels this; so do his parents, especially his biological mother: however, White knows Hurtle must leave his biological family if he is to grow as the kind of artist Kermode describes in *Romantic Image* (1957).

We never know whether Harry wearing the same or a similar ring as Hurtle. However, that the Courtneys and Duffields may be biologically related is not unusual. The whole edifice of Australian colonialism was built upon such ambiguities which White exploits. The different Duffield and Courtney worlds are indelible reminders of the kind of society Australia once was. White's work is an important source of that social and economic memory.

Mrs Duffield—Bessie, Ma, or as Hurtle calls her, Mumma—has some affinity with the archetypal Brangwen women in the opening pages of *The Rainbow*, who "look out" from the "heated blind intercourse" of their lives, to the "spoken world beyond", to the "road and the village with church and Hall and the world beyond" (Lawrence 2015, 43), where males perform their Apollonian civilization-building (Paglia 1990, 21).[8] Her desire is for another life, a better life, if not for herself then for her children. As she says: "It's the edgercation that counts" (6).

What kind of education? Education for what? Hurtle is precociously intelligent and talented. Where do these faculties come from? Are they innate (from nature) or learned (from nurture)? Recognizing her son's potential, Mrs Duffield wants to give him a head start. Following an English tradition, and, because she already cleans the parish church, there is an arrangement with the parish priest, Mr Olliphant, to give Hurtle "lessons" until he is old enough to attend primary school.

---

[7] An obvious question emerges here: Closer to *what*? Within the logic of the family romance, closer might mean his *desire* to be a part of the Courtney world.

[8] Apart from the Brangwen males, who are more content and inward-looking.

Because the rector is a busy man, Hurtle spends a lot of time alone in his library. He reads many books, because he can read, which is unusual for a child of pre-school age. "I learned myself, I suppose. At first." he brags, later, to one of his teachers at Infants School, "Then Mr Olliphant showed me some of the finer points" (33). He is also a natural mimic. He learns to imitate the rector's educated accent, which will assist his social mobility in a class-based society, distinguished by widely-accepted codes, all of which were mediated by speech. He does, however, maintain the ability to shift registers when it suits him:

> So you copied Mr Olliphant's voice instead, whether in multiplication or division, in French fables or Latin verbs, and became so successful at it, you could hear yourself, like a book talking.
>
> Of course you never turned the voice on at home; or not unless you wanted to pay somebody out.
>
> Once he said in Mr Olliphant's voice: "Perhaps I shall soon be so well educated I shan't need to go to ordinary school."
>
> "Edgercated! When you can't even learn to stop scribbling on the walls."
>
> "That isn't scribble, it's a droring," he said in … his own voice (9).

Even as pre-schooler, Hurtle is adamant in asserting his artistic integrity. He draws. He does not scribble. He identifies as an artist without knowing what that means. Through White's affinity with Blake, the reader is asked to accept Hurtle as a solitary poetic genius, regardless of whatever level of education he has attained, or whatever "voice" he speaks in.

Mr Olliphant becomes ill, and can no longer assist with Hurtle's education. For some time his parents did not know what to do with him (13). Mumma is not yet ready to let him go to Infants School, hence the reason for his first visit to the Courtney world, Sunningdale, where she works as a laundress. During that visit, the servants make a fuss of him. One of the servants, Lizzie, takes Mumma and Hurtle on a tour of the house, to the world "behind the green baize door", the traditional dividing line between the "upstairs" world of the employing family and the "downstairs" world of the employed staff. During this tour, Hurtle meets Mrs Courtney, briefly. As he recalls later: "The vision of Mrs Courtney made him shiver with joy; he wished he had been in a position to touch her" (22).[9]

Alfreda Courtney is an important development in White's literary mothers. She should be compared and contrasted with her predecessors, beginning with Catherine Standish in *The Living and the Dead*. While she

---

[9] The colour of her dress and her eyes are both blue: the colour of transcendence.

is different from Elizabeth Hunter in *The Eye of the Storm*, she is definitely Elizabeth's precursor. White encourages his readers to ask questions about Mrs Courtney within Sunningdale's symbolic order: whether she is a creator or a creation, sovereign or subject, oppressor or victim, vivisector or vivisected, what her will-to-power looks like and how she exercises it, whether she is secure or insecure, what her relationship with nature is, and her role as a Lacanian big Other (Johnston 2014). Adopting Hurtle was her idea. When she says, "I could eat you up" (41), the reader has a hint of what is in store for him.

Hurtle's first experience of his future medium—oils—was during one of his pre-adoption visits to Sunningdale in Chapter 1. He asks Mrs Courtney:

> "What's that?"
>
> "It's a painting by a Frenchman called Boudin," she explained. "We brought it back with us from Europe."
>
> If she hadn't been there he could have climbed up to feel the smoothness of the paint.
>
> "It's worth a lot of money," Mrs Courtney said rather dreamily; while he was advancing, dreamier, towards the group of dressy ladies huddled halfway between the flat sea and the bathing machines" (42).

On his next visit, he is interviewed by Mr and Mrs Courtney, who assess his suitability to be adopted. During the interview–assessment, Harry and Alfreda signal their respective archetypal roles, his masculine, hers feminine. When they leave the room, he is glad to be alone:

> … so that he could explore the Frenchman's oil painting. So he got a chair, and stood on it. His heart was knocking, more than it had for Mrs Courtney. To touch the smooth, touchable paint (54).

Rhoda arrives, interrupting his exploration, and tells him her parents like him:

> Because you're a boy. And Mummy thinks you're so delightful. You can read better for your age than most grown-up educated people. You're a prodigy. Mummy wants to discover a genius (55).

However, Alfreda has definite ideas about the kind of genius she wants to be attached to—"Children are like puppies, you know. And a new puppy can be attached to its owner by teaching him to recognize the owner's scent. Or so I'm told" (82).The genius must obey certain rules within her symbolic order. His first transgression is painting an image of his tutor's suicide on his bedroom wall in red paint. Alfreda is enraged by this threat to her symbolic order and demands that Hurtle be punished for this transgression:

Presently he heard Harry Courtney let himself in. He heard her go quickly and talk to him fairly loudly, though not yet loud enough, in the hall.

Then he heard her raise her voice, practically shout: "Oh, but you must! As a discipline. For his own good" (93).

Harry whips Hurtle, because Alfreda demands it, but does so against his will. Afterwards he remembers his promise to take his son to one of his properties, Mumbelong.[10] During this trip, Hurtle is inspired by the landscape but knows the life of a stationer is not for him:

Father and Sid were still talking their different language. They seemed to have forgotten you existed, though you joined them together, fitted tightly between Father's oilskin and Sid's smelly old overcoat.

Then Father remembered and said: "Fine sheep country, son. You wanter keep your eyes open, and you'll pick up a wrinkle or two."

He was speaking as though Maman didn't exist, nor the painting by Boudin, nor the shelves of leatherbound books: when you knew all about them. Nor did he realize all the wrinkles you were picking up, not from the boring old sheep country, but from the world of light as the sun rose pale out of the hills, and the streams of liquid light were splashed across the white paddocks: from the sheep too, the wrinkled sheep huddling or trudging, coughing something that wouldn't come up; there were some so close to the road that you could look right into their grey, clotted wool (97–98).

In the novel's Sunningdale section, before the first shapely turn, White carefully describes Rhoda as Hurtle's red-haired opposite, putting her in the same category as his other red-haired archetypes or tropes.[11] When Rhoda was young she was physically frail but archetypally robust. Like Mary Hare's garden at Xanadu, the garden at Sunningdale "belonged" to Rhoda, not to her parents, or to anyone else (78). Also like Mary Hare, who worried about Himmelfarb's health, Rhoda worries about Hurtle's health: "I hope you haven't been overdoing it," she said, later in the novel. "I shall be the one to blame, because I'm responsible for you" (559). What is White alluding to here? Are Rhoda's Theogonic metaphors older than, or gave birth to, Hurtle's Hellenistic metaphors? Is her link with the chthonic older than his link with the apollonian?

Rhoda could protest in her own voice and often did. The arrival of Hurtle, as her adopted brother, is both an opportunity and a threat, making

---

[10] Mumbelong = Mum + belong. In all White's novels females are the archetypal if not the actual owners of the land.

[11] What does Rhoda have in common with Theodora Goodman? How does she differ from Mary Hare and Arthur Brown?

them allies and enemies. For most of his life he denied being related to her. He only realized he needed her, towards the end of his life, after he met Kathy Volkov, who turned the tables on him. Even then, he never understood Rhoda's significance, as Norbert never understood Mary's significance, and Waldo never understood Arthur's significance.

As McCulloch reminds us:

> White's structural deployment of Rhoda is his most brilliant and complex achievement. To a large extent she represents the tentative answers White considers giving to questions concerning the reason for the inevitable failure of the artist (White) to his attempt to discover an art form that is an expression of his perception of life. Hurtle's failure to love Rhoda, and incorporate her truth into his art coincides with White's failure, despite his attempt to unify the contraries he sees in life, to write "tragedy". Without a unified cosmos bound by an immanent Divinity there can be no means by which man can achieve the tragic heights: consequently there is no possibility of being renewed by the kind of celebration of tragedy that once embodied man's overcoming of despair (230).

This is perceptive: however, Hurtle is also another brilliant and complex achievement. We are always meant to consider Hurtle and Rhoda as a binary couple, like Waldo and Arthur, and never as individuals. They are two sides of a metaphysical and/or a metapsychological relationship that haunted White, as it haunted romantic and post-romantic artists (after Kant). It informed western thinking about consciousness and reality (before Kant). McCulloch is alerting us to a traditional tension between the artist's end goal or purpose (his τελοσ–telos) and the rational method involved in producing it (his τεκνη–techne), which she applies generally to White the author and specifically to Hurtle the painter. She seems to take the view that, before the Death of God was proclaimed, tragedy was a telos and, more than that, it was the highest form of telos. While this is an influential view, it is not the only view, and it does not have the status of absolute truth.

The problem here is that, in a Ricoeurean sense, tragedy is always fatalistic; yet it is championed by those who self-identify as humanists. Renaissance humanism was essentially about the rediscovery of ancient Greece and an attraction to its rationalism. This form of humanism occurred wholly within the Church. Enlightenment humanism, which was an extension of renaissance humanism, was focused on four fundamental notions: first, a commitment to reason as the proper tool and final authority for determining issues; second, a stress on "nature" and the appeal to what is "natural"; third, a widespread acceptance of the idea of progress; fourth, a rejection of the authority of tradition unless it could withstand the judgment seat of reason (Pailin 1983, 179). This form of humanism was critical of traditional Christianity but was still identifiably Christian.

Just as Waldo never fully accepts or understands Arthur, Hurtle never fully accepts or understands Rhoda. He has a love–hate relationship with her (mostly hate). Because of this he has, and will always have, trouble accepting and/or visualizing God, as transcendence, as immanence, or as beyond transcendence and immanence.

All White's child protagonists are symbolic products of their parents' marriages. Each marriage, and every child of that marriage, is part of a commentary on the symbolic order that produced them. Rhoda's deformity and ugliness are therefore emblematic. She is a rhetorical device: the product of the Courtney symbolic order, which is essentially the western symbolic order in its historical specificity. The 19th and 20th centuries preserved a strong distinction between nature and nurture, their different domains, and the different degrees of freedom and necessity each allowed the human sphere. Like the Foucaultian–literary view that regards "madness" as the socially–constructed artefact of classical metaphysics, Rhoda's deformity is emblematic in a similar way. If, like the dionysian Arthur, Rhoda is not God, we are supposed to learn something fundamental about God from her, and from White, since he reinvigorated her ancient story and represented it to the world.

The early 20th-century medical profession prescribed a treatment for Rhoda's deformity, which amounted to torture on a rack. She fought against this torture, when she was young, but lost the fight and her deformity never went away. Gradually, she learns to accept her role, as a deformed and ugly character within the symbolic order, and her powerlessness to change it. When her father dies, and her mother remarries a much younger man, Rhoda is taken to Europe, where Alfreda and her new husband squander the Courtney fortune. This forces her into poverty. For a while she becomes a companion, then a cat-lady who relies on the kindness of others.

Despite many attempts, Hurtle was never able to paint the truth of Rhoda's mythos in his art or accept its truth in his life. White offers this as the reason why Hurtle could never describe God or achieve a connectedness in his life. The question of Rhoda's truth is therefore central to understanding *The Vivisector*, just as the question of Arthur's truth is central to understanding *The Solid Mandala*. This understanding is not easy. The mythos "dilemma" has a long history. It either was, and may still be, a fundamental aspect of western self-understanding. It can be theorized away with non-binary thought but it never goes away.

The initial inspiration for Hurtle's lifelong attempts to paint Rhoda's truth came to him during the Courtneys' trip to Europe not long before World War I:

> He had decided to go into Rhoda's room, for no clear reason: he was drawn in that direction. As soon as he began to make the move he tried to stop himself, but couldn't. The loose nob on Rhoda's door was already rattling. Like his voice offering unconvincing excuses in advance. Before he positively burst in.
>
> Rhoda was standing beside one of the spindly iron-legged bidets. She was naked down to the soles of her feet. She was trying to protect her privacy from this too sudden invasion of light. She was holding in front of her thighs a sponge which only half hid the shadow of pink hair.
>
> Because he was too shocked he began to point, to grind his foot into the floor, to laugh his crudest and loudest. Before backing out. The rattling door slammed shut but only thin between them.
>
> He ran into his room and squashed his face into a disgusting eiderdown, to try to blot out what had happened.
>
> At midday they met in the dining-room. Rhoda sat staring from under sponged eyelids at the *gigot aux haricots*. Hurtle had plastered down his watered hair.
>
> Maman looked at them embracingly and couldn't wait to tell: "Tomorrow we are leaving St Yves de Trégor!" (124).

To Hurtle, Rhoda would never again look fully clothed. After the war, while he was having sex with Nance, an image comes to him of "Rhoda's Cranach figure standing beside the iron-legged bidet" (228).

What does Rhoda look like? Is she a deformed, hunchback version of a Cranach painting, perhaps one of the allegorical Venuses or Judiths? There are many reasons to suppose she is, although the title of his Rhoda series, *Pythoness at Tripod*, refers to the Oracle of Delphi rather than to Cranach's milky redheads. Rhoda is a female oracle who remains silent. A prophetess who keeps her prophecy to herself. No one cares about or wants to hear it.

As an older man, Hurtle often wonders what is really going on behind Rhoda's eyes; how much "truth" she might know, about him, and about life in general. He becomes obsessed with this frail, pale-skinned, pink-haired dwarf, with her rodent-like face, and hunchback, which he reworks in paint throughout his life. Sometimes he abstracts it, even as an octopus, using the conventions of modernist and postmodernist art, in attempting to portray its "truth".

Hewitt makes an important link with Bacon here:

> The first time the young Hurtle sees Rhoda's naked body is when he bursts in on her in a French hotel room. She is standing beside the iron

framework of a collapsible bidet. As well as her hunched back, this tripod links Hurtle's portraits of Rhoda with the Fury in Bacon's triptych.[12] It is the sign of the Delphic oracle, the pythoness whom Rhoda becomes in Hurtle's imagination, and which was quite a common subject in Victorian painting. There is a highly dramatic example at the Art Gallery of South Australia, *Priestess of Delphi*, painted by John Collier in the style of Alma-Tadema, in which the priestess is seated on a high tripod over the smoking fissure in the earth, prophesying. Van Gogh, one of White's and Bacon's heroes, wrote in a letter to his brother Theo: "There are moments when I am twisted by enthusiasm or madness or prophecy, like a Greek oracle on the tripod" (74).

Hewitt also mentions the suggestion of the art historian, Heather Johnson, that de Maistre's *Figure by Bath* (c1937) inspired both the first version of Bacon's *Three Studies for Figures at the Base of a Crucifixion* (1944) and Hurtle's *Pythoness at Tripod* series:

> Theatre director Jim Sharman has suggested that one of Bacon's Furies, a crouching, screaming hunchback, could be one of Hurtle's paintings of his foster sister Rhoda;[13] the Bacon and Duffield paintings both have their original source in de Maistre's. As young men, White and Bacon would have seen Figure by Bath as it was created; probably they discussed it. The disturbing image worked subterraneously in both of them—emerging, in White's case, some thirty years later (73).

While Rhoda was physically absent, between the novel's first and third shapely turns, Hurtle kept working on his *Pythoness at Tripod* series. He knew he had failed to paint the "truth" about her but was driven to keep trying. So, there are two parallel agons operating throughout his career, the agon of painting the women he became involved with, each of whom represents a particular problem he faced as an artist, and the agon of painting Rhoda, which is another matter altogether. Once he met Kathy Volkov he suddenly sensed the importance of Rhoda as a person, without ever understanding why.

Losing Rhoda

At the beginning of Chapter 4, Hurtle has returned from serving in World War I, after a year of washing dishes at a restaurant in France. It must be the end of 1919 or perhaps 1920. He is at the end of Millers Point, near where the southern pylons of Sydney Harbour Bridge are now. While he is

---

[12] *Three Studies for Figures at the Base of a Crucifixion,* first version (1944) and second version (1988).

[13] The Courtneys legally adopted Hurtle. Rhoda was his sister not his foster sister.

eating prawns and chips, he reflects not on the war but on his lack of
contact with the Courtneys. This was his doing. He never answered their
letters, two of which informed him of Rhoda's 18th birthday and Harry's
death. He does not wish to return to their world:

> He had gratified at least some of the desires of all three. If he had left them
> bearing him a grudge, it was because total love must be resisted: it is
> overwhelming, like religion. He certainly wasn't religious: he was an
> artist. But didn't this reduce him to the status of little pink-eyed Rhoda
> nibbling around the edges? The association made him focus his mind on
> other, immediate realities (172).

Notice how he consigns Rhoda to "nibbling around the edges", because he
dismisses her capacity for insight, and sees himself in a higher light.

Hurtle does, however, write to one of the old Sunningdale servants,
May Noble, who tells him Harry left everything to Alfreda, who remarried
a much younger man and moved to England with her new husband and
Rhoda. As he was legally adopted, and is the sole surviving male
Courtney, he knows he could make some claim on the Courtney estate, but
ultimately he "lacked the ultimate belief in the efficacy of family ties":

> He was dependent on himself for anything he might become, and when he
> was too tired, too poor, too hungry, too discouraged, self-opinion was his
> consolation: to sign himself "Duffield", not on the half realized paintings
> he almost immediately painted out, but on those he was still only capable
> of painting in his head (175).

On the next page, Hurtle meets an intoxicated prostitute, Nance, who tries
to pick him up. As he is broke she offers him free sex. Later, in her flat, as
he takes in her naked body: "He was staring at the streaming golden
paddocks on which the sun was rising through his boyhood as he sat
between Sid Cupples and Father" at Mumbelong (179).

White begins a pattern here. In the present, during sex, Hurtle is given
fleeting associative images from his past, but he does not have the
capacity to process their meaning:

> He experienced a shock when Rhoda was projected for a moment in
> amongst the other slides: the pink shadow in her little legs. It might have
> ruined everything if Nance hadn't been in control.
> "Not too bad," she kept muttering between her teeth. "Tisn't *bad*."
> Might have been Boo Hollingrake, except that Nance was holding the
> Delicious Monster against the periwinkle of a navel (180).

So, apparently Hurtle is a well-hung, competent lover, a Delicious
Monster, given to associative images during sex. Rhoda is already
intruding; hinting at a reality he needs to accept. Boo Hollingrake is also

intruding, as a memory of his first sexual experience years earlier.

Nance inspires Hurtle to paint *Electric City*. While he is painting:

> It seemed to him that he loved this woman he hardly knew as a person: at least he loved and needed her form. Whether he desired her sexually was a matter of how far art is dependent on sexuality. He remembered with repulsion, if also recurring fascination, the stormy tones of a large bruise on one of her thighs. He had kissed, but could he love the bruise? Could this course, not exactly old, but lust-worn, prostitute, love her new ponce after one drunken encounter? He couldn't believe it. She needed him, though, for some reason she kept hidden behind the forearm shielding her eyes after the throaty confessions of love (184).

Soon after this, Nance makes her often-quoted observation, propelling the words into his ear like bullets:

> "What your sort don't realize," she wasn't saying, she was firing into his brain, "is that other people exist. While you're all gummed up by the great art mystery, they're alive, and breakun their necks for love" (192).

Nance is a prostitute because she does it good. It is her art. It brings in the money. Now she insists she wants "love". But what does she mean by love?

Hurtle already believes that "total love" must be resisted, because it is overwhelming, like religion, and he is an artist. But what does Nance mean by love? A rescuer? A co-dependent? A hero? With a proud, dedicated prostitute, how does one separate love from sex? Hurtle sees himself as the lover of the perjured art "by which he would celebrate the permanence of her rolling belly":

> The following day, in his cramped room, a sense of freedom started him whistling and singing, until he realized the match was on: to recreate the body as he saw it without losing the feel of the flesh. He knew, or thought he knew, how to fix the formal outline; perhaps he had already done so. Now he was faced with laying on the colour: the lettuce tones; Kohlrabi purple; crimson radish; old boiled swede for the shabbier pockets of skin. What he conceived that day was vegetable in form and essence: limbs spongy in substance, though still crisp enough for breaking off; the necklaces around the fibrous throat carved deeper by love-throes. Like all human vegetables she was offering herself to the knife she only half suspected (195).

If Nance is aware of being a source of inspiration for Hurtle, she never realizes the degree to which she will be vivisected in his paintings. Few of his human subjects do.

The contrast between their different expectations is revealed during their trip to the still-silent movies:

That was what she wanted: to be slowly and sadly possessed by a lost marquise in crushed organdie. And what he wanted was not the common possessive pross he loved by needful spasms, but to shoot at an enormous naked canvas a whole radiant chandelier waiting in his mind and balls (203).

She wants romance. He wants the inspiration he needs to create high art. And that chandelier he wants to "shoot at" with his mind or—to use a modernist image—paint with his balls, is the one that influenced him so powerfully as a child at Sunningdale.

After the film, Hurtle suspected "this would be their wedding night" (204). This is true, at least from Nance's perspective. Later that evening, once they achieved orgasm, Nance said "I will never ever let you go, Hurtle. We could die now" (203). Suddenly he wanted to leave, to protect what she had given him, in terms of artistic inspiration:

He gave her a kiss. It tried to be tender, but he himself felt it to be dry; the moisture in him had gone into his marriage of light (204).

He makes a quick exit, to his own flat, where:

He fell on his own bed and dreamed in his clothes about the Boudin above the fireplace in Harry Courtney's study, in which ladies walked over stretches of firm sand tilting their parasols. There were no quicksands, it appeared, to swallow them down (204).

The novel's first shapely turn begins immediately after this quote. Hurtle is now living with a tension, between the artistic vision of the Boudin, which represents a classical–romantic world, where there are no quicksands to swallow the subject, and the artistic vision of the modern–postmodern world, where subjects like Nance can swallow the painter unless he keeps them under control or swallows them first. Jungian critics interpret this as Hurtle's (and White's) fear of being devoured by the Magna Mater, the Great Mother.

Hurtle continues to see Nance but flags his disengagement. His agent Maurice Caldicott has managed to sell *Electric City* and *Marriage of Light* to a rich widow—Mrs Lopez—and gives him an advance on three more paintings. With this money he buys a strip of scrub on the upper North Shore and builds a shack on the edge of a gorge (211):

He liked to scramble down the face of the gorge through the evening light, chocking his boots against the rock, clinging to the hairy trunks of trees, his fingers slithering over the slippery fleshier ones. Once he caught his mouth trying out the response of one of the pinker, smoother torsos. He was never so happy as in the communicative silence of the evening light. Sometimes he remembered he had been a painter before growing

physically exhausted: musclebound, woodenheaded, contented.
He hadn't seen Nance Lightfoot for months (212).

When Nance finally visits him, he soon discovers she is temperamentally unsuited to the kind of life he is living. Worse than that, she is unsympathetic to the kind of painter he is:

> He said: "I want you to stay, Nancy." It was a form of her name he hadn't used at any point in their relationship.
> He fastened his mouth on the target of a breast while listening for an answer.
> She flipped him off.
> One of the oranges which had rolled off the table the afternoon before was lying almost at the edge of their "bed". She took it up, and threw it, not exactly vindictively, at the canvas at the other end of the room.
> "You an' yer old rocks! There's too much I don't understand."
> Then she turned to him and said: "You've got as much out of me as you want for the present."
> He heard himself trying to contradict, but it sounded mumbled, disconnected: to make it more convincing, he returned to stroking her arm.
> "Go on!" she said, pulling away. "You're such a one for looking for the truth in everything, you oughter recognize it by now" (222).

On his next trip to the city, Nance tells him, now that he has delivered the three paintings from the advance, she is going to visit him again:

> This time it'll be a real visit—now that I know what the conditions are. I'm not a fool, you know, though I dare say you won't admit it. Anyway, this time I'll come, and you can paint me—as I am, I mean."

Rather than engage with her, as a person, he is suddenly riveted by a scent bottle on her dressing table: "a version of those which used to stand on Alfreda Courtney's high altar". He leaves Nance, and, over the following days:

> … he did several little studies of her which he would elaborate later on when the inclination took him. The ideas in his head were still too hectic and fragmented. He either saw in colours, and the architecture eluded him, or else he was obsessed by forms: Nance's yellow cheeses; suddenly out of the past Rhoda's Cranach figure standing beside the iron-legged bidet. In desperation he almost settled for the self-portrait he had been for some time considering. But, did he, any more than the others, see himself as he truly was? His doubts drove him to scramble down to the bottom of the gorge, slashed by swords, whipped by wires, trampling on the board-walk of fallen wood, sinking in the mattresses of rotting leaves. Reaching his nadir he lay full length and buried his face in brown water, gulping at it, watching it lap around the pictures of his distorted features.
> Obviously he didn't know himself (228).

But narcissism is still narcissism, even when it is disguised as an artist's search for the "truth". Nance echoes this view later:

> "All you men are in love with yourselves. That's what it amounts to. When a man feels good about 'imself, he has to have a woman, and it's called love. At least the poofs are honest. They look around for another poof." What she visualized gave her the giggles. "To be on the right track, you oughter be, all of you, one big set of poofs!" (233).

If Hurtle represents the apollonian and Nance represents the dionysian–chthonic, neither side achieves a balance, as an imbalance seems to be essential to Hurtle's agon.

Having sex inspires Hurtle, not Nance, and yet—outside the world of fiction—there is no causal connection between having sex and the capacity to create art, or by analogy, no causal connection between having sex and knowing, loving, or visualizing God. One of the unfortunate legacies of the romantic and post-romantic age has been the devaluation of *agape* love and the overvaluation of *eros* love. Under the rubrics of "embodiment", we are now conditioned to regard the former as "inauthentic" and regard the latter as "authentic". But authenticity is a slippery and overworked concept. A cliché.

In this novel, White is attempting to reify or embody, in art, metaphysical–metapsychological concepts that dominated the 19th and 20th century, as part of the rationalism–empiricism and transcendence–immanence debates. When Hurtle returns to his shack his self-portrait "was leering at him out of a distorting mirror" (235). He spends a great deal of time and energy working on the self-portrait, trying to realize the "truth" of himself as an artist:

> He painted at times with a grimness which was flashed back and forth between glass and board. This skeleton *Doppelgänger*, with his armature in greys and blacks, would have no doubt survived outside pressure if it hadn't been for a conspiracy taking place between the necessary and the unknown: reckless purples began to stain the premeditated; pools of virulent green brooded.
>
> He suddenly suspected something else might have been planned; as, indeed, it was (238).

Nance has arrived, drunk. She has brought not food but bottles of brandy. McCulloch provides an invaluable summary of Nance's last scene:

> Nance is not blind to the part she plays in Hurtle's life. She knows that he is using her in order to reach truth. Her final acceptance of this and her full recognition of her irrelevance to Hurtle as a human being lead perhaps

to her suicide. Before her death she imposes her story of life on Hurtle (240–242) who attempts to devour it as he had her body.[14] Instinctively Nance knows that there is no hope for her in her relationship with Hurtle. She accuses him of being the obsessed artist who can only recognize one brand of truth: "the only brand of truth 'e recognizes is 'is own it is inside 'im 'e reckons and as 'e digs into poor fucker you 'e hopes you'll help 'im let it out" (244). She understands Hurtle's self-portrait as derivative from her sexual energy. Her unveiling of truth coincides with his recognition of his failure. He smears excrement over his self-portrait as an extension of its truth. Their last sexual encounter is a celebration of "Dreck", failure and aspects of truth. Nance is seen for the last time in the half light of sleep and lamplight. As she hovers at a narrow untrue table she is reminiscent of the worst superficial aspects of Alfreda Courtney (247) and one recalls Hurtle's realization as he began his self-portrait that Maman had done a better job than either of them realized in forcing his head in among the scents of the wardrobe, though "he hadn't screwed the Maman in Nance" (232).

Hurtle finds Nance crumpled and broken at the bottom of the gorge. His consequent suffering is not for the death of Nance, the person, but for "the inspiration withheld from him" (249). Her death is the symbol of his failure with his self-portrait. He hacks his painting to shreds with an axe and throws it over the gorge. One feels it is the murder of the painting, rather than that of Nance, that Hurtle experiences as a major tragedy. As an old man his rock paintings viewed in the gallery remind him of the fleshy substance of Nance. Even then it is the vision of himself as a young man that consoles him and not the memory of the person, Nance (78).

This is insightful; however, while McCulloch seems to favour the suicide theory, White is ambiguous and allows the reader to form another view.

Even in her most intense desire to be loved, Nance is a street-wise, materialistic prostitute. She always has her eye on reality. When they were at their most degraded, she was still "ticking off an inventory":

> "That ring," she was mumbling and fumbling.
> "What about it?"
> "What's it *for*?"
> He couldn't have explained to Nance it was for poor bloody Pa Duffield. "It's just a ring. A family ring" She couldn't have understood it was connected with the Adam's apple of your incredible, but true, father.
> "But a *ring*!"
> "All right," he shouted back, "we know it's a ring"; there was nothing

---

[14] Whenever I contemplate what Nance's final hours were like, I watch a YouTube clip, the 1998 Woodstock version of Stevie Nicks performing her ballad "Has anyone ever written anything for you?" It is a powerful female-oriented invocation of what may have been going on in Nance's head in the hours leading up to her fall (or jump).

he didn't know without her harping on it.

It was his worst perversion: to have hung on to a ring, long after the money was spent, the five hundred they sold him for. Or pretension: worse than anything Harry and Alfreda Courtney had tried to put across, blazing with brilliantine and diamonds under the chandelier.

"You're right!" He supposed it was one of his selves still shouting at this whore beside him. "What's in a ring?"

He could tell Nance was frightened: he could hear, he could feel her, gibbering, blubbering, her fingers dithering, when all he wanted was to get up off the shuddering bed not to harm anybody but to reach the door to fling the ring.

"There!" he croaked, after his moment of triumph.

"Whadderyerdone?" Seemed to need confirmation of what she had been watching.

"Nothing to hurt anyone living." It was a lie of course: he could feel the wound deepening in himself. "I just wanted—he sighed it—what I should've done long ago—got rid of the ring."

He could hear the shock in Nance: it hissed between her teeth. "Throwun away a valuable ring yer grandad solid gold!" (245–246).

In addition to the suicide theory, it is just as likely that—being true to her materialistic, realistic self—Nance went looking for the ring, as something of value, and fell to her death.

Absent Rhoda

Chapter 5 is short and contains only one scene, between Hurtle and Cecil Cutbush. An unknown period of time has passed since Nance's death. His shed–house overlooking the gorge near Hornsby was destroyed in a bushfire. He moved to Paddington, somewhere near the old tram line between North Bondi and Bellevue Hill, today the 389 bus route. It is the early 1930s. He is sitting on a bench at sunset. The bench he is sitting on, when he meets Cutbush, might be in the real Quarry Street near the tennis courts beneath the Anglican Retirement Village. This street has the right aspect, looking out through a reserve of native trees. There was a sandstone quarry near this bench until the late 1960s. Hurtle and Cutbush may have been overlooking the quarry, now Trumper Park.[15]

Ostensibly, Hurtle is reflecting on the effect of the sunset on the houses

---

[15] Now heritage listed, Paddington is a rare example of a Victorian residential suburb of terrace houses. When Hurtle lived there, from the early 1930s until his death, it was a slum. It is now a gentrified, inner-city suburb. Olivia Davenport helped him to buy the house, on the corner of the fictional Flint and Brecon Streets, which backed on to the fictional Chubbs Lane. White says the surrounding streets have Welsh names.

in the distance (253). He may also be thinking about his life as an artist, while trying unsuccessfully to process the death of Nance and the failure of his self-portrait. Cutbush interrupts him. What does Cutbush symbolize? Is he merely the inspiration for a modernist–postmodernist painting about the vivisected "truth" that Hurtle the vivisector must tell? Is there more to him than that? The iconic seed-spilling image at the end of the chapter can be interpreted in different yet related ways: in the biblical sense of Genesis 38:8–10 or in a more philosophical and aesthetic sense that locates him among the category of White's male homosexual tropes within the apollonian–dionysian, logos–mythos, and reason–feeling binaries.

As many male authors do, when referring to their novels, Hurtle often uses the fertility or birthing metaphor when referring to his painting. He often calls them his children, none of which is perfectly formed, many of which are deformed, but he nevertheless created them, as a mother creates a child. In this scene, Hurtle is fertile. Cutbush is not. Once again we are returned to the dilemma that dominated the 19th and 20th century: of apollonian creativity, its limitations, and the role the dionysian plays in making the work of art whole.

Hurtle's view of Cutbush is not necessarily White's view; both the artist and the grocer are rhetorical tropes. However, from the 21st century reader's perspective, there is something strange about a homosexual author creating a vigorously heterosexual protagonist, a Delicious Monster, who makes negative judgments about a homosexual character. Some may see this as evidence of the author's internalized homophobia, but that ignores White's literary context and plays into the hands of those who want to project pathologies onto him, and those who regard him as some kind of psychosocial problem. Hurtle is a creature of White's period not ours. Also, he is able to shed the light of "truth" about Cutbush's metaphysical condition, in *Lantana Lovers*, which Cutbush acknowledges later in the novel, although Hurtle never fully accepts it.

As McCulloch suggests:

> To a large extent, the painting "Lantana Lovers under Moonfire" comes close to depicting the tragic vision of the artist. Hurtle's meeting with Cutbush, the grocer, gives him the material he needs to form an expression of his failure with Nance. But it is not a conscious celebration. Instead, an unconscious statement is made on the significance of the struggle in spite of its inevitable failure. The painting contains more meaning retrospectively in Hurtle's last painting which reflect himself and Cutbush struggling towards the summit: "Whenever their common sweat fell, the desert didn't flower, but thorns sprang up in celebration of their victory" (94).

If Cutbush is boring and mediocre, is there a core of goodness about him
Hurtle never recognizes? After all, he is the man who rings Triple 0, many
years later, when Hurtle has his stroke in Oxford Street. He is at Hurtle's
final retrospective, as part of the small protective claque Hurtle tries to
ignore and refuses to acknowledge. Apart from that, the Cutbush of
Chapter 5 will eventually become part of an offstage world Rhoda remains
connected with but keeps hidden from Hurtle in Chapters 8–10. This is the
world of Mrs Volkov and Mr and Mrs Cutbush; the sin eaters or wounded
healers who are the closest thing to a family the adult Hurtle has. Hurtle's
attitudes towards them are not White's. One could write novels about
these hidden people, from many different angles. If White chose not to, he
did assemble them in a group for his rhetorical purposes.

Later in the novel, we learn that Cutbush is a man before his time,
trying to sell now-common but then-exotic foreign delicatessen items
before the Australian palate accepted them. As his wife admits to Hurtle:

> "… The unusual lines aren't what you'd call popular," she said.
> To console her, he told her "Keep at it, and they will be."
> "Cecil's too artistic for a man—for a business—a *business* man." Her
> throat swelling turned a confession into an accusation: she couldn't forgive
> poor old Cec his unusual line in *cuissons*. "That's our whole trouble," she
> said.
> Probably a good woman, and the grocer, who had saved your life by
> Triple 0, good also, if "artistic". Two goods could obviously make a bad
> marriage.
> Just then Cecil Cutbush steamed out from behind glass, trying to be a
> grocer, and churchwarden, and the Progress Association and ex-councillor
> all rolled into one (557).

Mrs Cutbush was disgusted, "less with her husband's clumsy appearance,
and more because she would have liked to stay perving undisturbed on a
great man" (557). When she is forced to serve a customer, Cutbush insists
on walking with Hurtle part of the way back to Flint Street. As the narrator
says, "Cutbush could have been waiting all his life to make a declaration
of love":

> "Mr Duffield … I have never had the opportunity to tell you how much
> it has meant to us—to US—our comparatively small, but no less *avid*
> minority—to have you living in our midst … Our confraternity may be
> under privileged, and despised by some, but no one can deny that we
> appreciate the Higher Things. To walk past your home is, for us, a deeply
> moving experience. Flint Street has become a place of pilgrimage."
> O Lord oh lard lard if you could only reach Flint your own pilgrim

seize the cold pure rose by her thorns,[16] before being larded up in homogrocerdom.

"You remember the night we inadvertently met at The Gash? When the moon came up? I was severely troubled at the time, by conflicts between my home life and my—temperament. I often wondered afterwards whether the distinguished, anonymous—and handsome—stranger, had noticed any signs of stress. Then, several years later, a malicious individual I happen to be connected with, explained a certain painting to me. I was horrified—which is what Malice had been hoping for—till suddenly I realized that, unbeknownst to myself, I had been consummated, so to speak!"

Oh Lard!" The grocer's whispers were thunderous, his words working like sheet lightening.

"It was more than that. It was like as if, after attending regular service for years in a not very eyesthetical church, the same surroundings was illuminated by a—*religion!*"

O Lord save us it was the grocer who was going to have the next stroke. Scuttle scuffle away to Rhoda the cold rose a sister.

"Of course I never told anybody that we'd sort of given birth. I never pointed out to the wife that barren ground can sometimes be what the seed needs. I suppose I'm what people would call a coward." The grocer didn't attempt to hide the drops that were beginning to ooze. "I've often thought Judas must have been of a homo-sex-ual persuasion." Poor bugger didn't seem to know the thing had caught on.

Anyway, now that all was said, the unsavoury disciple flapped to a standstill. Murk couldn't obscure Luv: the big dope was shining with it. "Forgive me, Mr Duffield, if any indiscretion on my part has embarrassed you. I wouldn't want—never ever—to be an embarrassment to the one I I I." He couldn't make it.

Piteous what they lay on your altar, itself a rickety affair, so much shoved out of sight, from bottles of cheap port to unconscious putrefying sins (558).

So, Hurtle now knows Cutbush has been carrying a torch for him. If he were so inclined, he could turn this knowledge into more vivisection art; however, by that late stage of his life, he had other things on his mind, such as the God paintings.

It was a different story several years earlier, in Chapter 5, when Cutbush simply represented the conflict between body and soul (McCulloch 1983, 85). As Hurtle explains to Hero in Chapter 6, he thought the grocer, "had something rotten about him, but only slightly, humanly rotten in the light of the Divine Destroyer"(332). Olivia offers a similar interpretation: "Hurtle sees him, I think, as a damned soul in the

---

[16] The phrase "the cold pure rose by her thorns" could be a reference to Rhoda as the Devil, perhaps in the sense of Jung's fourth person of the Trinity (Jung 2009).

body of a solitary masturbator." As her "crimson nail accused the trajectory of milky sperm dribbled across the canvas" (332).

After leaving The Gash, on the night of his first meeting with Cutbush, Hurtle spends much time visualising what *Lantana Lovers* will look like:

> The world of moonlight and lantana was dragging him tonight: the big-arsed moon aiming at dislocated lovers; the cryptoqueer grocer-councillor machine-gunning them from the Council bench. He could now see how his composition would be divided (264).

The encounter with Cutbush, which has confessional overtones, gives Hurtle a kind of rebirth, and "the material he needs to form an expression of his failure with Nance" (McCulloch 1983, 94).

Soon after the encounter, Hurtle receives a letter from Olivia introducing herself and presuming to make his acquaintance: "or perhaps I should say: confirm a friendship which already exists" (265). At this stage of his adult life, he has not met Olivia, and does not know she is also the Boo from his childhood and adolescence.

For much of Hurtle's life, Olivia–Boo acts as a guiding hand, a kind of guardian angel, part-daemonic and part-demonic. Before World War I, as Boo Hollingrake, she provided the adolescent with his first sexual experience at a party for Rhoda in the Sunningdale garden (145–148). During the 1920s, as Mrs Lopez, she becomes his first patron—an early collector of his work—thus putting him on the path to recognition and success. In the 1930s, as Mrs Davenport, she buys more paintings of his and "indirectly" helped him to buy his house in Flint Street, Paddington (261).

Hurtle does not reply to her letter but still turns up at the appointed time. He discovers, from two other lady guests, waiting for their hostess to appear, that she is allegedly a nymphomaniac, that "a nymphomaniac can only be unhappy" (270), and further: "One good authority claims that Olivia's a lesbian" (271). Of course, this is not true; the most she can be is bisexual. This is rhetorically significant, in this novel, and those of other postwar novelists such as Robertson Davies who use female bisexuality in a particular metaphysical or metapsychological way (see Appendix).

The two lady guests leave, not long after Olivia arrives, while according to the narrator: "The nymphomaniac, or lesbian, remained superbly cold, probably frigid enough to have killed off her brace of husbands" (272). As she leads him upstairs, to look at his paintings, "on a half landing there was a strip-lit painting: a Boudin".

"What's this?" He couldn't believe it.

"Can't you tell?"

"Yes, I know. But where did it come from?"

"I bought it at the sale, after Mrs Courtney—Mrs Boileau had left."

Whether the Boudin was a good one, he couldn't have judged at that moment. It was something he has grown up with and out of; its reappearance made him weak at the knees.

"I'm glad you bought it," he said. "I expect you remember it from when we were children. It used to hang in Harry's study."

He would have liked to explain to her how the Boudin had become a reality of his own at St Yves de Trégor, where he had noticed for the first time, flat, firm sand lying like flesh under the white muslin of sea.

But even if he had been able to explain in words, she mightn't have allowed it. "Oh, no. I don't think I ever noticed the Boudin at Sunningdale. I can't remember. Nothing like that interested me as a child. Paintings were only furniture. No. I bought this one later on simply because it appealed to me as a painting" (275).

Sensing their shared private thoughts of Sunningdale, and the Courtney world, Olivia asks the obvious question, "Where is Rhoda?" (275):

I don't know. She went away with Maman," he stammered, "after the remarriage. During the war I lost touch. She isn't my sister, you know," he offered as an unconvincing excuse (276).

The excuse is unconvincing because his adoption was legal and Rhoda is therefore legally (as well as archetypally) his sister. She said "with a sincerity he could not doubt—in fact she barely avoided turning it into a whimper: "My poor darling monkey—Rhoda!" (276).[17]

After they look at her collection of his paintings, including her favourite, *Marriage of Light*:

Mrs Davenport turned to him smiling a smile of deliberate sweetness. "I wonder whether I don't understand your paintings better than you do yourself."

If he wasn't visibly rocking on his heels, she must have smelt his rage, but pretended she hadn't; the social graces were so well developed in her.

Actually Hurtle—I'm going to call you "Hurtle"—I sometimes feel artists are so preoccupied with technical problems they lose sight of what they're trying to achieve. That's why so many paintings, poems, remain technical exercises. Only the great artists," she was observing him closely, "*senses* where he is going, though he may not understand."

She was so clearly convinced, he felt confused in his reactions to what she had been expounding. She had turned him into a clumsy plumber: or Pa Duffield's boy."

"I'd like to discuss that with you," he collected himself enough to say,

---

[17] The term "monkey" is slang for female genitalia.

from inside his imitation of a Bond Street suit, "because I think you may be right."

But Mrs Davenport had finished dispensing her patronage. She was reminded by the chiming of a little crystal clock, perfect in its way.

She said: "I'm sorry. I must turn you out," still smiling with an exquisite clarity and reasonableness (278).

On Olivia's first visit to Flint Street, Hurtle takes her upstairs to see the paintings he is working on:

They pulled up together in front of Rhoda Courtney.

When she had looked, Boo closed her eyes; she began to sway her head; she began to moan convulsively, and with an uncharacteristic lack of restraint. He was reminded of Nance on the occasions when she had reached a true orgasm. So, now, Boo Hollingrake sounded both appeased and shattered by her experience.

In self-defence she cried out: "How could you be so cruel to poor little Rhoda?"

It was his turn to be become emotional; in an attempt to disguise these emotions he heard himself shouting: "How can you say it's cruel? It's the truth!" He heard his strained, boy's voice protesting against unjust accusations; while the glass showed him as a handsome, dissipated, middle-aged man making excuses for his weaknesses (288).

She asks why he made no effort to find her, "when she seems to have meant so much to you?", before beginning to whimper "… why *I* made no effort to get in touch?" She wants to buy the painting of Rhoda on his easel, but he would not sell it "for all the sugar in the world".

"It's not only as a painting that it haunts me," she says, "it's part of my life—yours too—that we've lost, Hurtle."[18]

Once Olivia raises the issue, of why neither of them has made an effort to find Rhoda, she invites Hurtle to parties at her house on several occasions. At one of these parties, Muriel Devereux, the epileptic daughter of one of the guests, has a seizure on the floor.

The next day, Olivia makes an unexpected, unwelcome visit to Flint Street while he was working on "the last figurative and probably final version of the *Pythoness at Tripod*" (299). While she is watching him paint, she says:

"You're losing her. You're giving her something Rhoda never had."

He tried to fend her off:

"Perhaps it isn't—was never intended to be Rhoda," he lied.

"That's how it began," she answered drowsily, "but became too

---

[18] White carefully alludes to a childhood friendship between Rhoda and Olivia–Boo which Hurtle refuses to acknowledge.

hysterical in feeling"

He could have been struck by lightning: he was, in fact, still involved with the incident the night before.

"Well, we know Rhoda was hysterical," Olivia went on. *"But she was always conscious of the reasons for her hysteria.* That was her great virtue—and why you hated her. She was never a human cow driven by something she couldn't see or understand."

Olivia opened her eyes, and dared him to contradict.

"What do you mean—hysterical—a human cow?" Of course he understood, but that didn't prevent him trying to laugh it off; he resented her intuition.

"You know perfectly well—she wouldn't leave it alone—that poor dumb lump of a girl: Muriel Devereux. You're bringing the two of them together—Rhoda and Muriel—to suit your own purposes. Is it honest?"

"Only the painting can answer that—when it's finished."

He could have strangled Olivia. As he approached her he could have shouted: I am what matters; without me that painting couldn't happen. And you and your kind would have that much less to babble about.

Instead he said humbly. "You're right, Boo; but the painter's only human after all, and used uses human means to disguise his shortcomings."

Yes, he could have killed her, but bent over her and touched her hair with this rather admirable humility he had found.

Suddenly she drew down his face, and thrust her tongue into his mouth; when she wasn't lashing at his tongue with hers, she was gouging his eyes with her cheekbones.

"I could show you," she kept gasping, "a trick or two" (italics added) (299–300).

When they are finished having sex, while she is "arranging her hair in front of the original and most naturalistic version of Rhoda", she announces the second shapely turn, from the novel's geographical centre, "We must find Rhoda … I feel she'd do both of us good."

Rather than start looking for Rhoda, Olivia does something else. She goes to great lengths to introduce Hurtle to two friends of hers, the Pavloussis—Cosmas and Hero Pavloussi—because she would like to think she has contributed something "if not to your happiness, to your work" (301). Note that Olivia already knows the encounter will not make him happy, but it may inspire great art, which is more important.

If the novel is a dramatization of Hurtle's "inner dialogues concerning the ultimate possibilities of art" (McCulloch 1983, 71), what ultimate possibilities does Hero represent? Is the relationship between Hurtle and Hero White's interrogation of modern tragedy? Those who believe in the possibility of modern tragedy may interpret the relationship as Hurtle's unsuccessful attempt to create a modern tragedy. Those who do not will not. Further, they may note that Hurtle cannot find Rhoda, or begin to process her significance, until he abandons the idea of modern tragedy.

From the moment they meet, Hurtle is attracted to Hero sexually but not to what she and her husband symbolize. This is at odds with White's own experience, as he saw Greece as "my other country" (White 1989, 133–136). He is acutely aware of the Pavloussis hypocrisy; disposing of life when it is inconvenient or unwanted; having bags of cats drowned; returning their adopted Aboriginal daughter to her family in La Perouse; keeping Hero's terminally ill dog alive because, although it has advanced cancer, and is suffering, Hero is a non-believer who believes in miraculous recoveries (354). She is upset by Hurtle's implied censure of their hypocrisies and attributes it to "not understanding"; which simply means her will has been thwarted.

Hero was also bisexual but not in the archetypal sense Olivia–Boo is. In Chapter 8 Olivia–Boo admits: "There was a time when she couldn't move without me. I wasn't prepared to be possessed to that extent. I couldn't breathe." So she "gave" Hero to Hurtle to "be his mistress" but "not to kill her" He took her by the wrists. "How many murders, Boo, are ever proved?" (414).

When Hero comes to Flint Street, she and Hurtle immediately try to devour each other. They have vigorous, bestial sex, during which she demands "the ultimate in depravity". When this is over, and she returns from the bathroom, he said "You're quite a bit different from what I expected," to which she replies: "I was no different from what I am." She then admits this is a problem in her marriage, as her husband likes to build monuments, but is shocked to find that his monument to her will be "a monument to lust" (347). In fact, her lust disappoints her husband and makes him impotent with her, so he can only have sex with prostitutes. In order to be whole, Hero needs to construct a life around being a madonna with Cosmas and a whore with Hurtle. This is a difficult manoeuvre to maintain, in life, but apparently many try to maintain it.

Hurtle is aware of this dilemma, since his own career has been dedicated to resolving the same dilemma in modernist and postmodernist ways. Hero senses this about Hurtle, with reference to the drowned cats, and says: "You are so wrong, so perverse, to pick on this one deed of my darling Cosma, and pump it up into a big moral issue and theme of art" (354).[19] When Hero discovers Hurtle has attempted to paint the "truth" about her and sees his portrait of her:

"Hero Pavloussi began to cry and cough. "You see? It is worse! It is a

---

[19] There is a case to argue that, as far as Hurtle and White are concerned, Cosmas and Hero represent the dilemma of the transcendence at the heart of classical metaphysics.

pornography! Are you trying to kill me?" … "Ohhhh!" she was moaning like a whole Greek chorus in the airless junk-room" (357).

She immediately runs out of the house, leaving him alone with his paintings, which he says are "neither pathetic nor tragic, neither moral nor, as she continued erupting in his eardrums, 'pornographic'":

> They were, rather, an expression of truth, on that borderline where the hideous and depraved can become aesthetically acceptable. So, in the hot little, dusk-bound room, the man's phallus glowed and spilled, while the woman, her eyes closed, her mouth screaming silent words, fluctuated between her peacock-coloured desires and the longed for death blow" (358).[20]

He is tired and falls asleep, having resolved to explore the artistic possibilities of these thoughts the next day. But he is wakened in the night by Olivia–Boo, dressed as a man, because she occasionally dresses as a man for social occasions, As Mrs Twyborn and Mrs Goldson occasionally do in *The Twyborn Affair*. She tells him Hero has tried to kill herself because of him; however, suicides are usually fake in White's novels. Before driving Hurtle to see Hero, Olivia–Boo is deeply moved by the "pornographic" painting of Hero: "I wonder if you know how good you are? But of course you do! You're too detached, too hateful, not to" (359) … "If Hero had more taste, she might respect you as an artist though she can't love you as a man" (360).

Basically, Hero is drawing attention to herself to get her own way. Having got his attention, Hero now proposes a trip to Greece. He says he cannot go because of his work. She says she *is* his work:

> Though he could feel himself bridle under pressure from Hero's persuasive hand, it was not a matter of vanity. He realized, on the contrary, he had been feeding on her formally all these weeks, and that the least related corners of his vision borrowed her tones of mind, the most putrescent of which were often the subtlest
>
> Hero seemed as unaware of the cynicism of her remark as she was of her lover's attitude. "It is now so long since I have seen the island I have been telling you about—Perialos. You will remember how my husband took me? It is this island I wish—I must visit again." She kept dragging at his hand in search of the encouragement she wasn't receiving. "I feel the devils may be cast out in the holy places of Perialos."
>
> "I wonder whether grace is given as freely as we're asked to believe."
>
> "Why will this not be given," she shouted, "if I am determined?" She

---

[20] The conjunction of Thanatos (the death instinct) and Eros (the life instinct) is one aspect of Frankfurt School theorizing and attempts by metapsychology to systematize the unconscious. Spark plays with this theme in *The Driver's Seat* (1970).

was positively yanking at his hand as though somewhere at the top of his arm a bell existed.

By now they were standing almost in darkness; there were a few last flames licking the leaden masses of the city in the distance, Hero's face was brown and sweaty.

"And what about my devils?" he asked. "What if I want to hang on to them?"

Then you do not love me! If you did you would want us to be one— one being—through every possible experience."

"Like a husband. I'm not your husband—not even an exorcized one."

"Oh, you are so brutal."

"I'm an artist," he had to say, though it sounded like a vulgar betrayal. "I can't afford exorcism. Is that what you've sensed. Is that why you want it?"

"Oh, but you misinterpret! Deliberately! You do not want to understand!

She couldn't spit it contemptuously enough at the darkness surrounding them; while he was tempted by his half-conceived landscape of Perialos, in which the wooden saints were threatened by their own tongues of fire (370).

White is not the only Australian author to perform this returning-to-Greece manoeuvre. The theme of returning to Greece, to investigate, or to achieve a kind of closure from, its metaphysical or metapsychological influence, has been attempted by other 20th century authors. Tim Winton did it most effectively in *The Riders* (1994), where a single father (who is both actually and archetypally "present") is trying to rebuild his dilapidated Celtic home, decaying in an inhospitable Australian landscape. He takes his daughter on a quest–search to Greece to find her mother (who has mysteriously chosen to be both actually and archetypally "absent"). The novel is, perhaps, Winton's attempt to imagine a new myth for Australia, especially for the white Australian male.

The two scenes on the island of Perialos are crucial to Hero's pilgrimage. First, there is an orphanage, the Convent of the Assumption. Second, there is the little Church of St John, where the hermit monk Theodosius lives. These are places Hero has been to before with Cosmas. She is convinced she will be "saved"—whatever that means to her—by her own will, even though she is not a believer. Hurtle has already voiced his scepticism, as he should. He is following her simply to humour her, because she insists, not because he takes Perialos seriously.

The first visit, to the convent, is not successful. The religious inhabitants are real rather than ideal. Nothing about them meets Hero's classical–romantic expectations of what they ought to be, which is why she blames them for her failure. The second visit, to the church, is not successful, because the hermit is not there:

> They were feeling their way back with their feet down the outside steps of the chapel; when she began to blubber hopelessly. "I think we have lost our faith in God because we cannot respect men. They are so disgusting. And cannot address one another—except mumbling.
> … He tried to support her. Hadn't she been his mistress, more than that, his creative source? He would like to have pointed out the scaly sea, like a huge live fish, rejoicing in its evening play, but he might have mumbled like the vanished saint. Perhaps he could have done a drawing, but Hero only understood the vision of her own inferno (387).

The next morning she asks him what his plans are when they return to Athens, and whether he will continue his tour into Europe. "No," he said, shaking his head, half-choking on the swallowed bread. "I shall go back to Flint Street."

"So soon?" She yawned. "It is not practical to come such a distance and waste the fare" (388). Her own intention is remaining independent from God and her husband: "Nobody is responsible for me: least of all those I love—or worship" (388). She drinks her cup to the dregs, literally and metaphorically:

> *Dreck*! *Dreck*! The Germans express it best. Well I will learn to live with such *Dreck* as I am: to find a reason and purpose in this *Dreck*" (389).

Hurtle tries unsuccessfully to interest her in something other than "her own inferno": a little hen stalking, clucking, and pecking at crumbs. As they rush to board the *vaporaki*, White ends the failed pilgrimage, in search of transcendence, with a charming image of immanence:

> The golden hen flashed her wings: not in flight; she remained consecrated to this earth even while scurrying through illuminated dust (389).

Like Chapter 5, Chapter 7 is also short and contains only a handful of short scenes: he buys milk from a corner shop, at the beginning of a very hot day. On returning home he becomes hostile towards his paintings, which seem lifeless and dead, now that "the chopper, in the innocent hands of the smallgoods store, had descended on his own innocence" (392). He sits on the dunny, trying to move his constipated bowels. While on the dunny, he overhears some neighbourhood women talking about him as eccentric if not "crazy as a cut snake" (393). He is now 55. It is the early 1950s. An unknown period of time has passed since he left Hero in Athens during the late 1930s.

After his bowels fail to move, saving him the need to wipe himself, he decides to go on a ferry trip to Manly, during which he meets a printer, the eponymous Mothersole (mother + soul) (396). Their conversation turns out to be confessional for Hurtle. He admits Hero was his mistress, and for a long time he took for granted that he had killed her, simply because Cosmas wrote to tell him he had:

> For a time I accepted my guilt: even though I kept telling myself she had used me as an instrument of self-torture. She was a very beautiful woman when she was least unhinged; but depravity could make her course, brutal.[21] She was the most depraved woman I've ever met. It seemed she had to degrade herself for being unworthy of her husband-God—a rich old satrap, who drowned cats by the sackful—like other gods when they tire of them (398).

A women friend of Hero's wrote to Hurtle, after the war, telling him Cosmas was wrong. Hero spent many years in an asylum and died of cancer: "The shortage of drugs made her death a particularly agonizing one" (399).

Although Hurtle did not kill her, he still wonders about her illness:

> Or does anyone know what sows the seed. Is cancer entirely a physical disease. Did I hclp kill by failing her? You see, we were never lovers. Oh yes, we fucked like animals; and I was fond, very fond of her; but I didn't love her, I can see that now" (399).

The conversation moves to his paintings. As human subjects may have become too difficult for him, he admits to currently painting tables and chairs:

> "What could be more real? I've had immense difficulty reaching the core of that reality, in I don't know how many attempts, but I think I may have done it at last—or thought so until this morning when everything died on me."
>
> "How do you mean 'died'?"
>
> "Exactly that. It no longer—in fact, none of the paintings of a lifetime—had any life."
>
> "But once a picture is painted, how can it alter?" Mothersole was not concerned about paintings: he might never have noticed one; he was distressed by a state of the human mind.
>
> "Paintings die like anything else, a great many with their creators, and this morning I realized, I think, that I'm already dead" (400).

Once his confession is over he chooses to return to the Quay rather than disembark at Manly with Mothersole.

---

[21] Hurtle's sense of Hero's depravity may seem quaint to us, given the human depravity that has been fetishized and normalized since the 1930s and 1940s, and given that he chose to participate in it himself.

As for the outsiders, he no longer needed his Mothersole. His teeth grated as he regurgitated the nonsense he had talked while in the throes of rebirth: Hero's death; his own; that of his paintings. … He remembered another occasion when he had risen from the dead, by seminal dew and the threats of moonlight, in conversation, repulsive, painful, but necessary, with the grocer Cutbush: and now he was born again by the grace of Mothersole's warm middle-class womb (401).

Just as Cutbush gives Hurtle "the material he needs to form an expression of his failure with Nance" (McCulloch 1983, 94), his meeting with Mothersole gives him the material he needs to form an expression of his failure with Hero. He tears up Mothersole's business card and scatters it, like seed, in the wash from the ferry. Some of this seed germinates. He experiences a kind of rebirth, on the return journey, and wonders:

> Apart from Rhoda, who was ageless, why had he never painted a child? … Sitting with his hands locked, he was fidgeting to create this child. Or more than one. Or many in the one. For after all there is only the one child: the one you still have inside you.
> So the light was exploding around him as they reached the Quay.
> He walked home against an afternoon gale, climbing hills with a speed made possible by the impetus of his thoughts. When he let himself into the darkening house, he began at once to drag at switches. He ran, almost, thundering from room to room, bringing them to life. His despairs that morning were vibrating on the walls, even the one he hadn't faced for several months, the cancer growing inside the monstrance of Hero's womb as the wooden saints of Perialos raised her up, the sea coiling and uncoiling round the foreshore in its ritual celebration of renewal.
> How could his unborn child fail to stir amongst these miracles of the risen dead? (402).

Finding Rhoda

Chapters 8–10, the last third of *The Vivisector*, are a complementary bookend to Chapters 1–3. These chapters weave four related themes: the consequences of Hurtle being reunited with Rhoda, the consequences of meeting Kathy Volkov, the limitations of his paintings, and therefore his limitations as an artist. By the end of the novel, its unifying theme, Hurtle's artistic vision, where it comes from, what it means, what it contributes, is not solved.

It cannot be solved as White relies totally on the Blakean idea, proto-romantic or romantic, of the artist's solitary poetic genius. He cannot provide evidence of that genius, he can only be inspired to turn it into art. Beyond that, he can only ask rhetorical questions about this art, whether it has a telos, what kind of telos it has, and the relationship between the telos and his techne.

Hurtle is a great artist, because his art is great, and vice versa. This chicken-or-egg argument goes around in circles, since accepted criteria for defining and measuring greatness no longer exists. Those who accept McCulloch's view of White as a tragic author may agree that: "*The Vivisector* is about the failure of the modern writer to write tragedy"; however, in spite of that failure, it is also "a celebration of the struggle of the artist towards success" (94). For those who do not see White as a tragic author, tragedy cannot be a benchmark of success. The novel is great because it is great. Criteria for greatness are unnecessary.

In Chapter 8, Rhoda says:

> "I think I'm beginning to understand your paintings, Hurtle, after these last two exhibitions. The horrors are less horrible if you've created them yourself. Is that it?"
>
> "No," he said, and it cannoned off the course white kitchen plate. "I'm still trying," already he realized how stupid it would sound, "I'm still trying to arrive at the truth."
>
> "Then perhaps I don't understand after all. The truth can look so dishonest."
>
> "Exactly!" He ricocheted, when he should have shot her straight to the floor. "That's why we're at loggerheads." He was beating the stupid plate with his spoon. "It's not dishonest! It's not! If it were only a question of paint—but is it dishonest to pour out one's lifeblood?" (514).

On the next page, Rhoda asks Hurtle about the "horrible and unnecessary" childhood painting on the wall of his Sunningdale bedroom:

> "I've often wondered about it. It was so bewildering at the time. I'd always seen Mr Shewcroft as unkempt and repulsive, but as soon as he'd killed himself I began to think of him as handsome and brave, though Miss Gibbons tried to convince me his suicide was a dishonest act. But what made you do something so horrible and unnecessary as that painting?"
>
> "I was only a child of course, but I think I was trying to find some formal order behind a moment of chaos and unreason. Otherwise it would have been too horrible and terrifying".
>
> "Don't tell me you're a mystic! At least I can honestly say I believe in nothing. I need never be afraid."
>
> "Of what?"
>
> "That the conjuring trick won't come off. That my 'god' may let me down."
>
> He found himself crushing the empty shell of the egg he had just eaten.
>
> "I really do pity you, my dear," Rhoda pursued, "if you should believe in a 'god'. Whatever I suffered in my childhood and youth from being ugly and deformed, at least it gave me this other strength: to recognize the

order, and peace, and beauty in nothingness."

"I believe," he said, "in art." He would have liked to elaborate, but was only strong enough to add: "I have my painting."

"Your painting. And yourself. But those, too, are 'gods' which could fail you."

This, perhaps the worst truth of all, he had never been able to face except in theory. Had he brought Rhoda into his house to help him too?

"Ah, yes—failing powers!" He laughed. "I hope I may be struck blind." He jibbed at using the word "dead".

Rhoda laughed too. "We shall be a fine pair!"

In the silence which followed he scented a dishonest terror in her. As for himself: he felt curiously calmed by Rhoda's weakness. If critical opinion ever decided before his death that he was worthless as a painter, he might discover in his fingertips some unsuspected gift for expressing himself; he might even calm Rhoda's fears (515).

This is an important passage. Rhoda believes her suffering—as a deformed and ugly child—has given her the strength to recognize the order, peace, and beauty in nothingness. Arthur tells Waldo something similar in *The Solid Mandala*. This view is romantic, modernist, and above all Nietzschean. However, Hurtle senses Rhoda's amor fati is dishonest, and wonders whether his art has a telos, or a transcendent possibility, which might help her. If this is his agon, then there must be a difference between attempting to reify or embody the transcendent and declaring it illusory. The former is romantic; the latter depends on one's position in the transcendence–immanence debate, and whether one subscribes to a literary–critical theory hostile towards any metaphysics grounded in Plato's theory of Forms and Ideas.

As Chapter 8 begins, Hurtle is reflecting on his current state of imaginative sterility. His relationships with his biological and adoptive parents are in the past, but remain part of who he is. His relationships with Nance and Hero, both of which ended in *Dreck*, are also in the past, but also remain part of who he is. The art these individuals inspired no longer inspires him and he now sees his paintings as lifeless or dead (400). After Nance, he continued the phase, already begun before her death, of painting rocks as sensual anthropomorphic forms. After Hero, he went through a phase of painting furniture. In both cases, it seems human subjects had become too painful or dangerous for him.

These thoughts are weighing upon him as he tries to paint a painting that would "convey the joy he knew he was capable of expressing if desire and idea came together in him" (404). He destroyed this attempt because he saw it was becoming autobiographical:

Whatever the accusations, he was not, he never had been, in love with himself: with his art, yes; and that was a projection of life, with the ugliness and cruelties, for which some critics held him personally responsible.[22] He must have waited till now to create his late child because love is subtler, more elusive, more delicate (404).

Hurtle's assumption about the subtle, elusive delicacy of love will soon be tested, when a girl who is still 12 years old rings his doorbell, carrying a billy of hot soup from her mother, intended not for him but for a neighbour she cannot find. Their exchange is brief. He gives her the neighbour's address and she leaves quickly. He then goes upstairs and "began to draw the head of a girl" but it was not a girl:

> ... and at once saw his mistake; he had made her a woman too soon: the eyes which he had left sightless on purpose began to stare with an expression he found offensively knowing. It was the mystery of pure being, of unrealized possibilities which fascinated him in children's eyes.
>
> Come to think of it, there were few children with whom he had been intimately acquainted: only himself—and Rhoda, each of whom was born old (407).

A few days later, Hurtle has another unplanned meeting with the young girl, again on his doorstep. Her name is Kathy Volkov. She turned 13 a few days earlier. During this short meeting, Hurtle is smitten and admits to being spiritually disconnected. His "bliss" at meeting her caused him to make a regrettable slip: "To be truthful, I don't believe the artist can belong to anyone":

> That night he started working on the flowering rosebush. Each of the big scalloped saucers of single roses was given its tuft of glistening human hairs. It was natural that the face should flower at the centre of the bush, humanly radiant amongst the not dissimilar roses, and not all that unnatural for the bush to be growing at the sea's edge, under a livid sky.
>
> When morning came he felt surprisingly refreshed standing in the front of his finished painting: only his eyelids, dry and fragile, might have been segments of ping-pong balls.
>
> After he had rested a little, he began to draw what would become during the days which followed a more abstract version of the "Flowering Rosebush": the face at the heart of the bush reduced to an eye, its remote candour undazzled by its setting of rose-jewels; the original seascape dissolved in space by fluctuations of gelatinous light, in which a threat of crimson was still suspended.
>
> At intervals he made other drawings: one of a cool, naked, fairly naturalistic, though sexless girl, which satisfied him to the extent that he

---

[22] Just has many of White's critics held him personally responsible for the ugliness and cruelties of life he described in his novels.

propped it up against the easel in the back room. The drawing was taking possession of him, he felt, as he walked up and down through the house, alternately dazzled and distressed by details of a painting it might become. He lay down finally, nursing a kind of anxiety along with his restless excitement, and fell into a sleep of opposing influences (421).

He wakens, with an erection, hearing someone calling from the back door.

Up until this point, we have been reading a repeat of the absorb-or-be-absorbed, control-or-be-controlled, vivisect-or-be-vivisected pattern that has driven Hurtle's creativity throughout his life. However, when he meets Kathy, White purposefully subverts the pattern and forces a reversal. If Hurtle's life is first and foremost about his painting Kathy's life is first and foremost about her music. Even as a child, she is training to be a concert pianist. She is as focused on achieving that goal as the young Hurtle was in pursuing his art. She really wants to enter his personal space and see him and his work. She uses a ruse, of bringing a cat to Flint Street, pretending a cat is what he needs. This is how she gains entry to his personal space.

Hurtle sees Kathy as his spiritual child, as a way of reconnecting with his inner self. Ostensibly he wants to protect her:

> She was already so much the egotist her eyes were blind to anyone or anything but herself. He wanted to protect her from that situation. At this instant he was prepared to give himself up wholly to the salvation of Kathy Volkov: so he began walking towards her, on his knees, like the beggars he could remember outside European cathedrals; while her eyes continued blazing in a blind fury of desperation.
>
> All at once, just before reaching the island or chair on which she was stranded, his excitement over Kathy, his admiration, his own need for her, melted into an agonizing and helpless love. He almost failed to prevent himself blubbering at her, dragging her down to such a wretched level of reality, he probably would have disgusted her forever" (425).

That never happens because Kathy is in control and makes all the moves.

The near incest-seduction of his adolescence, when Hurtle was in bed with Maman, who fed him chocolate mouth-to-mouth, is repeated in the near paedophilia-seduction scene with Kathy. As she feeds him mouth-to-mouth, she is reminded of her father kissing her as a child (431), which suggests he was still around when she was old enough to have a memory of him.[23] "Then, when they were growing together like two insidious vines, she tore herself away with a force which should have reassured

---

[23] Given what we are told elsewhere in the novel, could Kathy really have memories of her father?

him."

Hurtle is not reassured by Kathy's assertion of physical and emotional independence. Both he and White know this budding man–teen relationship is dangerous. Hurtle needs to be protected. This is one of the many reasons why White reunites him with Rhoda, in the following pages, so she can be "a moral force, or booster of his conscience" against what a relationship with Kathy could grow into "if the powers over which human nature has no control established a dictatorship" (439).

White allows Hurtle to avoid moral censure, to a degree, by ensuring that Kathy initiates sex—not him—while visiting him in Flint Street and finding him lying in bed in the dark:

> Kathy had crept closer up. At least the darkness would prevent him from watching her skin burn, and the movement when those dangerously inflammable strands at the nape of the neck must catch. If she was still unaware of the fire inside him, she could only be simple, or inhuman.
>
> "What's the matter?" she asked.
>
> His mouth moved, but didn't succeed in articulating.
>
> "Oh!" she sighed. "I'd like to fall in love—with somebody appropriate."
>
> "What's 'appropriate'?"
>
> Her downy mouth was drifting over his; she seemed to have abandoned speech for touch.
>
> "Haven't you your music?" He tried to thrust her off with his thighs; but the law of nature engineered his failure; she settled deeper.
>
> "Yes, my music," she breathed. "Mr Krapovitsky says I must study harder."
>
> She was digging into his maternal, his creative entrails.
>
> "Old enough to be your grandfather," he muttered against her lips.
>
> But she didn't hear, because fire and sea were roaring through them: if only one could have halted the other.
>
> At least he was, technically, the passive one; he could console himself morally with that: he hadn't attempted.
>
> In the hot dusk, Kathy was devouring him, with sticky kisses at first, then, not with words, but a kind of gobbledegook of jerky passion. The surprising part of it was she took their behaviour completely for granted—except his passivity.
>
> "Don't you like me?" she asked between mouthfuls.
>
> From amongst the wreckage of what he had aspired to, he didn't. He had hoped to love, not possess her.
>
> "Don't you?" she gasped.
>
> "No, Kathy, I love you." That seemed to satisfy her: now she could accept the dry science of his approach.
>
> Anatomically, she was in every detail what he could have desired—or almost. The shock of discovering her only deficiency made him spill out

incontinently and without thought for the consequences.

He became as curiously unafraid of Kathy, and finally, unsurprised. She was by now half-snoozing, at the same time exploring his stubble; while he listened to Rhoda pulling her charitable cart, across the yard, up the lane, away. Had it occurred to Rhoda at any point that her charity might be needed at home?"

"Kathy," he began, swallowing hard, because since she was nothing more than his mistress, whatever he might say must sound embarrassingly trite. "I only wonder how it happened that you learned so much so soon."

"About what?"

"About men."

"Honestly," she said, "I've never been with a man. My mother would have a fit."

Honestly, she was becoming intolerable.

"Boys, though—she mumbled in her drowsiness—boys won't always leave you alone: you have to do it to have peace" (461–463).

After this, Kathy becomes preoccupied with her music practice and leaves Hurtle alone. Nearly a year later, nine days before she turns 14, she slips into Hurtle's bedroom again. It is the dawn of the day she is leaving for Melbourne for two years of study with her tutor Khrapovitsky. This time Hurtle is the active partner.

After returning from Melbourne, winning her music competition, and touring Australia, Kathy leaves to continue her studies in Europe. They do not speak again, even in the Green Room during her farewell concert, but she writes a letter to him during her flight to London:

… This was to have been a letter about *us*, full of meanings we haven't said. I realize the dangers I may run into, but because I was brought up close to the gutter I'll take the risk.

If I've learnt anything of importance, it was you who taught me, and I thank you for it. Yes, I know there was Khrapovitsky whipping me along to perfect my technique—important certainly—but I've come across several machines put together by Khrap alone—impressive except that they were never anything more than machines. It was you who taught me how to see, to be, to know instinctively. When I used to come to your house in Flint Street, melting with excitement and terror, wondering whether I would dare to go through with it again, or whether I would turn to wood, or dough, or say something so stupid and tactless you would chuck me out into the street, it wasn't simply thought of the delicious kisses and all the other lovely play which forced the courage in me. It was the paintings I used to look at sideways whenever I got a chance. I wouldn't have let on, because I was afraid you might have been amused, and made me talk about them, and been even more amused when I couldn't discuss them at your level. But I was drinking them in through the pores of my skin. There was an occasion when I even dared to touch one or two of the paintings as I left, because I had to know what they felt like, and however close and exciting it had been to embrace with our bodies, it was a more truly consummating love-shock to touch those stony surfaces and suddenly glide with my straying fingers to what seemed like endless still water (537–538).

Immediately after Hurtle first met Kathy, he was reunited with Rhoda, and White sets up a tension between Hurtle's different relationships with these two females. Ostensibly, Rhoda's presence was meant to be moral protection for him. However, when he discovered that Rhoda was the cat-lady friend of Mrs Volkov, which Kathy spoke of, he becomes suspicious of, and obsessed with, not only what Rhoda may know about Kathy and his relationship with her but also of Rhoda's secret "world". This is the small network of people within her sphere, which includes Mrs Volkov, Mr and Mrs Cutbush, Don Lethbridge,[24] and perhaps Olivia–Boo, which form the immanent or the shadow side of the transcendent symbolic Courtney order that tempted him as a child. Hurtle never fully understands or accepts these people, yet they are precisely the people he must accept if he is to achieve soteria.

There is of course a qualifier here. While Hurtle never fully accepts or understands Rhoda, the rapprochement they achieve in the novel's final chapters is poignant. In *The Solid Mandala* Waldo felt so threatened by Arthur that he had to destroy his brother and destroy himself in the process. Hurtle has a different reaction to his sister. If he always "hates" her, and often wants to strangle or vivisect her, his hate gradually turns into a mutual recognition of their human need. Particularly in the last section of the novel, their banter is priceless and their affection is real.

Hurtle wants to buy Rhoda a fur coat but she does not want one: "Expensive presents are in every way an embarrassment. Besides," she smiled, and raised her eyes, "fur coats are one of the traditional bribes women are offered by men" (464). Touché Rhoda. He *is* trying to bribe her. Because she does not take bribes, he becomes threatening:

> In the circumstances, his hands were almost throttling the brandy bottle. "I wonder you can enjoy the company of liars, and buggers, and hysterics, and Scottish prigs."
> Rhoda seemed hypnotized by his blenched knuckles. "Aren't they other human beings? Almost everybody carries a hump, not always visible, and not always the same shape."
> "But that child—I wonder how much she understands?" If he could

---

[24] The artist–academic Alan Oldfield (1943–2004), a long-time parishioner and some-time rector's warden of my parish, Christ Church St Laurence, was fond of admitting that as a youth he was White's inspiration for Don Lethbridge.

have burnt Rhoda open with the blow-lamp he was becoming, he would have done so: to find out what she was keeping locked away from him.

She only said, and that slowly: "You should know, Hurtle."

"How—I?"

"You were a child, weren't you? I think, perhaps, in many ways, you are still; otherwise you wouldn't see the truth as you do: too large, and too hectic."

Shortly after, she finished her imaginary tidying and shut herself up with her cats. He went to the back door, and chucked out the empty bottle, which exploded somewhere in the dark yard (467).

Rhoda signals a mystery, as does every other red-haired protagonist in White's fiction, but she is also highly rational. To repeat what Olivia–Boo once admitted: Yes, Rhoda was hysterical, but she was always conscious of the reasons for her hysteria. That was her great virtue and why Hurtle hated her (299). In the west, the idea of *rational hysteria* is confronting, and for the most part incomprehensible, because it blurs our traditional boundaries between logos–mythos and rational–irrational. Hysteria is widely understood as the absence of reason. If it is understood to be a manifestation of reason, then an overarching binary—upon which western self-understanding rests—is called into question.

Hurtle wants the fur coat to be nutria (river rat), probably to accentuate her rat-like features, but she wants squirrel. While they are on the tram into the city, to fit her for the coat, he tells her squirrel is a soubrette's fur. Her answer is "If I have to go through with his, I want squirrel, Hurtle." When he continues to harp on the nutria, and on his benevolent or altruistic motives for wanting to see her "warmly, presentably clothes in winter, instead of looking a fright" she shuts him up: "Oh dry up, Hurtle! I couldn't begin to compete with your vanity and arrogance" (472). Touché again Rhoda!

The bribe worked, however. On the tram home, the "glow from his recent generosity" made him ask her about Kathy. He learns about Kathy's movements. She is moving to Melbourne in a month to be with her tutor Khrapovitsky, who has retired from the Conservatorium and is moving south because his wife has inherited property there. In the following weeks Hurtle painted "several more or less abstract" versions of his "Girl at Piano" series, but is frustrated at failing to capture what he hopes to capture.

White brilliantly records Hurtle's crisis as a painter, which may mirror his own crisis as an author. There is Hurtle's failure to realize the ultimate possibilities of art. There is his highly defended personality. There is his fear or paranoia about Rhoda "knowing" things—about him; about the human condition in general—which he does not know. There is his consciousness of his past but his refusal to integrate it into his present. He searches for the truth in painting but recoils from it in himself. Especially in the novel's last three chapters, he becomes angry on being told that some people believe him to be gifted, move to Paddington to live near him, and treat his house as a place of pilgrimage.

As someone said at his final retrospective:

> "I'd like to believe in revelations. And these paintings are, for me, almost revelations. That is why I could go down on my knees, and beg, beg him for one little word which might remove the last scale from my eyes. Because I'm sure it's here in the paintings. If I could only see."
>
> "Numen" is the word I've been trying to remember all the evening. Not apropos. I'll probably die a sceptic".[25]
>
> O numinous occasion sighted in distorting mirrors of variable treachery! Now that the trap was closing in on him, what he longed for was a room of reasonable proportions furnished with a table and chair (580).

McCulloch summarizes Hurtle's dilemma vis-à-vis the Ultimate:

> To be struck by God, as Mrs Volkov says, is to be filled with an unendurable force that neither she, Mr Cutbush, nor Hurtle is able to transform into anything but a celebration of failure. When Hurtle hunches his shoulder against the truth, he is both rejecting Mrs Volkov's view of Rhoda as well as incorporating a truth of Rhoda into his own person; it is also a gesture that signifies his refusal to accept his inability to reach Godhood and infinity in his art.
>
> His final painting of Indigo is a fraud, as it attempts to rise beyond the reality that Rhoda represents. It is a painting that is pushed along by his remembrance of his "psychopomp", that is Kathy. But his "presumptuous body" reaching for the blessed blue and prickled stars is sent "crashing Dumped" to the earth. His dying, his last and most honest recognition is of Rhoda, who in being "of the earth" embodies the true infinity.
>
> O rose Rose.
>
> Too tired too endless obvi indi-ggoddd (94).

McCulloch suggests that: "Hurtle does not succeed in painting the 'real picture' because there are aspects of his life that he refuses to accept" (94). This is certainly a compelling view of his dilemma—and may even represent White's own view—but a Jewish and Christian response must be different.

Hurtle's failure is not because of his lack of integration, by any human measure—philosophical, aesthetical, psychological, sociological—but

---

[25] "Numinous" relates to divinity. It refers to the mysterious, the awe-inspiring, the arousal of spiritual or religious emotions. Hurtle's paintings have this quality. Many readers believe White's writing also has this quality.

because God cannot be realized in art. Not fully. To believe otherwise is either presumptuous or blasphemous, depending on one's theology. Even if Hurtle had undergone psychoanalytical therapy, become a self-aware or well-adjusted person, and devoted his life to divine contemplation, orthodox faith, and good works, he would still not have been able to paint a picture of God.

As for Hurtle's final painting of Indigo being a fraud, "as it attempts to rise beyond the reality that Rhoda represents", McCulloch is pointing to a compelling aspect of the transcendence–immanence debate. Rhoda is an abstract idea to which different meanings have been attached, over the centuries, over the millennia, for various purposes. Hurtle attaches meanings to her, throughout *The Vivisector*, and he is frightened of, or threatened by, some of those meanings. White is skilfully ambiguous about this, since he knows Rhoda does not attach the same meanings to herself. In fact, she usually says No to them.

For many reasons— all of them important—the question of Rhoda's identity is the necessary corollary to the question of God's identity. When Jesus was asked which commandment in the Torah was greatest, he answered:

> "You shall love the Lord your God with all your heart, and with all your soul, and with all your mind." This is the greatest and first commandment. And a second is like it: "you shall love your neighbour as yourself." On these two commandments hang all the law and the prophets (Matthew 22: 37–40).

In other words, we cannot claim to love God without loving our neighbour and we cannot claim to love our neighbour without loving God. Hurtle found that difficult. So did White. But at least they knew they did. And they were both honest enough to admit it.

CHAPTER FIVE

STORM

Nature and Civilization

In *The Eye of the Storm* (1973), White maintains a Gadamerian frame, and continues to populate it with Ricoeurean anthropology, but in a more attenuated way, and for the last time. The novel represents a turning point between his middle and late periods. After *The Eye of the Storm* he continues to explore the tension between logos and mythos but he no longer investigates the varieties of religious experience in the self-conscious way of the 12 years leading up to the Nobel Prize.

While some may argue that his "religious" phase ended earlier, with the götterdämmerung of *Mandala*, that does not account for its muted but still coherent presence in *Storm*. Also, the strong difference in the way White investigates religious experience should be acknowledged. Religious horizons are allocated to characters who are not aligned—confessionally, doctrinally, or liturgically—with their given category of myths and its metaphors. This is particularly true of Judaism, a shadow in *Storm* compared with *Riders* and *Mandala*.

The novel weaves two parallel stories into a broader or a greater narrative but whether that makes it a meta- or a grand-narrative is moot. The first story revolves around Elizabeth Hunter's relationship with her husband, son, and daughter, the four of whom represent Paglia's tension between mythos (dionysian–chthonic nature) and logos (apollonian civilization). The second story revolves around Elizabeth's relationship with her three nurses and one housekeeper–cook. These carers, which White refers to religiously as "acolytes", represent the varieties of religious experience, as he understood what they had become in the increasingly secular postwar period. Both of these stories are focused on Elizabeth, the glue that binds everything together.

Marr 1991 reminds us that Elizabeth is drawn from several people including: Ruth, White's mother; Emily, Geoffrey Dutton's mother, a friend of King George of Greece; and Victoria, Lady Sackville, the mother of Vita Sackville-West (496). Another clue comes from White himself, as he often said his characters were aspects of his psyche, imaginative projections of himself. In spite of this, when psychoanalytical criticism was de rigueur—before it disappeared into the aether—some critics insisted White's portrait of Elizabeth was misogynistic, gynophobic; and represented his attitude towards women generally and Ruth specifically.

The problem here is not only the reader's projections—since readers will always project anything they want to project upon texts—but misunderstanding how characters function in particular genres of novels. Ruth may have been wilful in the same way Elizabeth is wilful. Apart from that, Ruth was nothing like Elizabeth. Even if Ruth had been more like Elizabeth, knowing this does not help us understand how Elizabeth functions as the central character of *The Eye of the Storm*. The novel is not a fictionalized portrait of White's mother or his family life. It is something else.

Who is Elizabeth Hunter? One clue comes from the fact that her son and daughter, Basil and Dorothy, move to Europe as adults: Basil becomes a successful actor in Britain; Dorothy becomes an unsuccessful princess in France. They do this because, like many Australians of their period and their class, they suffer from the cultural cringe and are ambivalent about Australia, its people, and its landscape. Because they are conflicted characters, White uses the rhetoric of dissociation, loss, and alienation to describe them. By contrast, dissociation, loss, and alienation do not apply to Elizabeth, whose only frustration is not achieving the ultimate illumination or enlightenment.

Elizabeth never sought to leave Australia because she identified with and understood it. She knows who she is. She is comfortable being in the world. In that sense, Ruth's desire to leave Australia after the war was characteristic of Basil and Dorothy, while White's desire to return to Australia after the war was characteristic of Elizabeth. If readers baulk at associating Elizabeth Hunter with Mary Hare, Arthur Brown, and Rhoda Courtney, they all belong to the same category of archetype, or trope, which suggests the broad diversity of archetypal representation. Red hair comes in many shades including strawberry blond. It inevitably turns grey, unless it is dyed, or is covered with a wig, and lilac—like Elizabeth's lilac wig—is a shade of red.

Within Gadamerian hermeneutics, Elizabeth represents mythos prior to logos and/or nature prior to civilization. Within Ricoeurean anthropology, she represents the myths of chaos and creation (Theogonic metaphors) that are prior to—or give birth to—Basil's myths of tragic hero and Dorothy's myths of the exiled soul (Hellenic metaphors). In Heideggerian or phenomenological terms, characters who represent Theogonic metaphors feel comfortable being in the world, while characters who represent

Hellenic metaphors are aliens within the landscape and never feel comfortable being in the world. The contrast is always between apollonian civilization and dionysian–chthonic nature. In this kind of rhetoric, different creation myths influence different experiences of being, and different manifestations of art.

While this kind of rhetoric was once powerful, it is necessary to keep remembering that characters are not persons. The relationship between myths, metaphors, being, and art is speculative. White's symbolism belongs to a fictional world not to a real world. He describes this tension between literature and life in *Flaws in the Glass*:

> I sometimes wonder how I would have turned out had I been born a so-called normal heterosexual male. If an artist, probably a pompous one, preening myself in the psychic mirror for being a success, as did the intolerable Goethe, inferior to his self-abnegating disciple Eckermann. My unequivocal male genes would have allowed me to exploit sexuality to the full. As a father I would have been intolerant of my children, who would have hated and despised me, seeing through the great man I wasn't. I would have accepted titles, orders, and expected a state funeral in accordance with a deep-seated hypocrisy I had refused to let myself recognize.
>
> As a woman, I might have been an earth-mother, churning out the children I wanted of my husband, passionate, jealous, resentful of the cause and the result, always swallowing the bile of some insoluble frustration. Or I might have chosen a whore's life for its greater range in role-playing, greater than that offered an actress, deluding my male audience of one into thinking I was at his service, then flinging back at him the shreds of his self-importance as he buttoned up. Or else a nun, of milky complexion and sliced-bread smile, dedicated to her quasispiritual marriage with the most demanding spouse of all.
>
> Instead, ambivalence has given me insights into human nature, denied, I believe, to those who are unequivocally male or female—and Professor Leonie Kramer. I would not trade my halfway house, frail though it be, for any of the entrenchments of those who like to think themselves unequivocal. In fact sexuality refreshes and strengthens through its ambivalence, if unconsciously—even in Australia—and defines a nation's temperament. As I see it, the little that is subtle in the Australian character comes from the masculine principle in its women, the feminine in its men. Hence the reason Australian women generally appear stronger than their men. Alas, the feminine element in the men is not strong enough to make them more interesting. One English critic finds it a serious flaw that my women are stronger than my men. I see nothing anomalous about this imbalance; it arises from a lifetime of observing my fellow Australians, in closest detail my own parents when I was young (154–155).

Notice how White elides from the particular to the universal; from the sexual to the social; from an assessment of himself and his family to an assessment of the nation. It is easy to misunderstand what is happening here. He uses archetypes when describing male and female, because he lived in a century where archetypes were valuable currency; however, that currency is not as valuable as it once was. The reality of being male and female—like the reality of nature and civilization—cannot be confined to archetypes. That he admitted to having "unequivocal male genes" makes him cisgender. For him, archetypes are not a substitute for the reality of biology and genetics.

There are similarities between *The Living and the Dead* and *The Eye of the Storm*. Just as Kitty Goose becomes Catherine Standish and has two children, emblems of the "lost" generation between the wars, Betty Salkeld becomes Elizabeth Hunter and has two children who are also "lost". Just as Catherine Standish sees herself as a sun around which everything revolves, the Hunter household revolves around Elizabeth with varying degrees of attraction and repulsion.

This revolving does not occur simply because Betty–Elizabeth is a selfish matriarch but because she is an archetype among archetypes. She represents a force that embodies a compelling and repelling will. Her inner strength allows her to identify with the seagull speared–smeared to a tree during the eye of the storm (425); a will that enables her to survive in a chaotic universe—creative and destructive, good and evil, real and imagined—that other characters withdraw from. She is larger than life.

Once Elizabeth's larger-than-life status is acknowledged, it is difficult to judge her by human standards. While she may not be quite like the Greek gods and goddesses, she is not within the conventional human range, hence her odd capacity for vision. Because humans are not gods and goddesses, this may make some readers wonder how she can be the focus of a novel about the human condition. The arts of the ancients were comfortable with depicting the theophanies and apotheoses of the gods and goddesses in the human sphere. The contemporary arts distance themselves from such techniques, unless they serve a specific literary or rhetorical purpose, which they do in the postwar novels of White and his contemporaries. One thinks of Murdoch and Spark here. Their protagonists are seldom within the human range.

It has been hypothesized that—for the ancient Greeks—gazing at the on-stage spectacle of human suffering invoked tragic pity, promoted catharsis, and, in McCulloch's words, "embodied man's overcoming of despair" (230). The hypothetical result was an aesthetic soteria which is sometimes called transcendence through art. If this once defined tragedy's importance, tragedy's current importance is harder to define—and tragedy's future importance is harder to predict—since soteria is more than aesthetic. The whole question of art as a means of soteria is contested, as is the idea of tragedy as a hypothetical benchmark for the ultimate possibilities of art or commentary on the human condition. Even if the ancient Greeks *did* depend on catharsis and tragic pity for their soteria, we now have more options for soteria than pagan belief, including the myriad benefits of parliamentary democracy, modern medicine, superannuation, and the welfare state. Further, if one is a practising Jewish or Christian believer, there is the Torah and the Christ.

Also, some scholars of ancient Greek theatre are no longer sure that the idea of catharsis can be taken for granted, since we cannot presume upon what the ancient Greeks experienced when watching a play (Walton 2015), and neither can we presume upon the idea of tragedy as a form of religious experience. In other words, if tragedy was originally performed within pagan religious festivals, attending the Great Dionysia may not necessarily have been an act of worship or a declaration of belief; it may simply have been going to the theatre. If Nietzsche focused on the apollonian and the dionysian principles, tragedy is not only the unity of these principles. If White was inspired by Nietzsche's *The Birth of Tragedy*, particularly in *The Solid Mandala*, he was also familiar with other forms of tragedy.

In the case of Shakespeare, the similarities between *The Eye of the Storm* and *King Lear* are widely noticed and compelling. As the differences are considerable, however, the meaning of the similarities is far from self-evident. As Marr 1991 points out:

> Had White been able to act, he might not have written a word. He still dreamed of *his* Lear, *his* Hedda and the vaudeville routines he would perform—if he had the knack (494).

What White accomplished in *Storm* is unique compared with *Mandala*. It is not limited to Nietzschean questions and answers. It is broader, subtler, and more complex. *His* Lear does not have to be *his* tragedy. It can be something else.

What does White mean by *his* Lear? In *King Lear*, Shakespeare makes a range of assumptions about humanity, divinity, and nature, and the relationship between the three, which reflected a contemporary debate about fatalism and humanism, and about nature and civilization.[1] The

---

[1] Renaissance humanism and modern humanism cannot be conflated. The former was not opposed to—and did not contradict—Christianity. Today humanism is typically centred on human agency and ignores divine agency. Theoretically, modern humanism

play's overwhelmingly fatalism falls neatly within Ricoeur's anthropology of fatalistic myths and metaphors. These myths of constraint, so dominant in *King Lear*, leave little or no room for the myth of freedom. This is understandable, as the play is set in Celtic Britain—in a pre-Roman period—an age when Theogonic metaphors were dominant, before Hellenic and Hebraic metaphors crossed the Channel.

Within the Great Chain of Being (Lovejoy 1936)—the hierarchical ladder of Medieval and Renaissance thought—Lear's royal position linked the human order with the natural and divine orders. Shakespeare understood this. His play is an object lesson of what happens when the king abdicates his royal authority and retires (Manninen 2015).

On the whole, westerners no longer believe in this hierarchical ladder. After God's death, there is no divine order, there is only the physical or material world—but whether this "nature" has any characteristics of a "natural order", let alone a "natural order" analogous with a "divine order", is contested. While Elizabeth is associated with nature, if not with a natural order, she never abdicates her authority; therefore, she never suffers the consequences of abdication. This is the key difference between the play and the novel. Lear relinquished his authority at the beginning of the play. This reversed the natural order and unleashed chaos. Elizabeth clung to her authority until her death. Her will remained intact. This allowed her to die in her own time and on her own terms:

> But I shan't die—or anyway, not until I feel like it. I don't believe anybody dies who doesn't want to—unless by thunderbolts (63).

Even if humans are not divine, White still leaves more room for the humanistic adamic myth in his novel than Shakespeare does in his play. If humanism is a belief in the human capacity to change human lives—for better and for worse—it is an important concept to apply to the novel. Did Elizabeth choose to become a bitch goddess or was she made that way? Did Basil and Dorothy choose to become the novel's Goneril and Regan or were they made that way? White maintains a significant tension between nature and nurture here. If there are theories to explain every facet of this tension, each generation has adapted those theories to suit whatever it wants to believe about itself.

White's generation was focused on the mother-complex, which is why Basil and Dorothy are able to blame Elizabeth for their stunted emotional status and everything wrong with their lives. In the 20th century there was no shortage of psychological and sociological theories to support them.

---

looks to science rather than revelation, although its definition of "science" is somewhat arbitrary, selective, slippery, and often self-serving.

Even in the 21st century, we can still blame our mothers for ourselves, if we wish, but this kind of rationalizing does not hold as much water as it once did.

Basil and Dorothy return to Australia to put their mother into a home and claim their inheritance. They hate her but need her money. If this Goneril and Regan story is timeless, White gives it a twist. Elizabeth only dies when her son and daughter commit incest—an incest between archetypes not between persons—in the bed on which they were conceived. While this symbolism belongs to a fictional world—not to a real world—what does it mean?

Parents

Alfred Hunter

Stendahl's *The Charterhouse of Parma* (1839) is a significant motif in *The Eye of the Storm*. Dorothy brings her copy of the French version with her from France. The English translation is Alfred's favourite book. When Elizabeth puts her life on hold to nurse him while he is dying of cancer:

> He loved her to read to him. They were halfway through *The Charterhouse of Parma,* which he admired, he said, "almost more than anything else". Her own pleasure in it was sometimes lost in its longueurs, but she improved on those by listening to the sound of her own voice: when she made the effort, she read well.
>
> That night Alfred began staring at her in what appeared like suddenly feverish, hitherto unrealized, admiration. "Isn't she splendid?" he interrupted. "What a dazzler of a woman—the Sanseverina!"
>
> "A bit female at times." If her voice sounded dry, it was from the length of time she had spent reading aloud.
>
> "Womanly women don't much care for one another, I suppose."
>
> She herself certainly had never much counted overmuch on her women friends. "There's something else—a kind of freemasonry which brings them together, and they feel they must obey some of the rules".
>
> He laughed: they were united in a moment of such understanding she went and knelt beside his chair and started desperately kissing his hands. It was as close as they came to physical desire during those last weeks. But the hands remained cold and yellow (200).

Gina—the Duchess Sanseverina—was known for her passion, insight, and ability to exercise female influence in a male world, all while leading an unconventional life. As the parallels with Elizabeth are obvious, Alfred admires Stendahl's novel almost as much as he admires Elizabeth, who—like the Sanseverina—is also a splendid dazzler of a woman.

In *Flaws in the Glass*, White tells us the feminine element in Australian men was not strong enough to interest him. His preference for the masculine element in Australian women came from "a lifetime of observing my fellow Australians" especially "my own parents when I was young" (155). The Marr biography, which consistently advocates an autobiographical approach to White's work, notices that psychoanalytical critics have spent a great deal of energy showing how he revenges himself on his mother in his work: "But there is a parallel and perhaps overlooked ambition in White's work," Marr says, "to seek an accommodation with the memory of Dick" (513).

It is good of Marr to draw attention to this aspect of White, because too much energy has been spent on amateur, second-rate psychoanalyzing of his personality, particularly his relationship with his mother, while his relationship with his father tends to be ignored. In the latter case, there may be compelling parallels with Lawrence who admitted later in his life that he had:

> come to understand and respect his father much more than when he wrote *Sons and Lovers*. He grieved over the hostile portrait (Sagar 2003, 197).

Apart from Willy Standish and Tom Godbold, the majority of White's literary fathers are—within their ability and means—generous attentive husbands and loyal fathers. That they tend to die before their wives mirrors the reality of female longevity compared with males. If males are portrayed as weak it is because in White's period female strength was widely acknowledged; although this strength was usually explained in relation to the symbolic order.

Apollonian Alfred is the source of the material wealth that drives the engine of the novel. Dionysian–chthonic Elizabeth never loses sight of that fact. She may represent nature. This may be what gives her a strong, wilful, and seemingly indestructible personality. However, in a material sense, nature did not make her wealthy—Alfred did—and because his material wealth is more significant than her temperamental wealth, without his material wealth the novel would not be as compelling as it is.

Is Elizabeth a womanly woman? Is Alfred a manly man? What does her animus, the masculine principle in her unconscious, look like? What does his anima, the feminine principle in his unconscious, look like? White delineated his male and female characters in a generation where Jung's anima and animus had become predetermined scripts: to be looked for even when they were not there; to be imposed or assigned to reinforce whatever theories of female or male identity were in fashion. Like Freud, though, Jung is no longer in fashion.

The elephant-in-the-room question hovering over the novel is whether

Alfred's loyal and acquiescent temperament allowed its action to unfold the way it did. Had he been a more assertive husband and father, would his family have been different? This is hypothetical. We can only work within the frame White has given us. Elizabeth's temperamental and archetypal power is given:

> *I've never seen you cry, Elizabeth, unless you wanted something.* Alfred would lower his chins as though riding at an armoured opponent. And she would raise hers, accepting the challenge. *It hadn't occurred to me. But must be right if you've noticed* (15).

> *You know, Betty, you are the only one who has never called me by a friendly name.* Not "Bill": just to attempt it made her feel she was shaking her jowls like a bloodhound. *How can I? When "Alfred" is the name you've been given. I mean it's your NAME—as mine is "Elizabeth".* She raised her voice and drew down her mouth to produce a dimple she held in reserve; but on this occasion it failed to persuade him (15).

Alfred can see through Elizabeth but he is still in thrall to her:

> At his most masterful his toes would be gripping the sheets on either side of her long legs, as though he had found the purchase to impress her more deeply than ever before. Once, she remembered, she had felt, not his sweat, his tears trickling down the side of her neck, till he started coughing, and tore himself away from her: their skins sounded like sticking plaster. She tried to make herself, and finally did, ask what had upset him. His "luck", in everything, was more than he deserved; however indistinct the answer, that was what it amounted to (28).

Elizabeth Hunter

Elizabeth is not just a woman, she is a force of nature. As Paglia points out:

> The identification of woman with nature was universal in prehistory. In hunting or agrarian societies dependent upon nature, femaleness was honoured as an *immanent* principle of fertility. As culture progressed, crafts and commerce supplied a concentration of resources freeing men from the caprices of weather or the handicap of geography. With nature at one remove, femaleness receded in importance (italics added) (7–8).[2]

Since Paglia published this—in the year of White's death—it has become increasingly less fashionable to identify woman and her fertility

---

[2] The rise of monotheistic religion has been blamed for many things, including constructing female identity and suppressing female power. This idea is still powerful.

with nature. In the post-White west, fertility is no longer dependent upon nature. Instead, like gender, fertility has become an artefact—or a fetish—of social constructionism in collusion with promethean medical opportunity. As a result, any sense of nature as a created, material, spiritual phenomenon, independent of human intervention, has been diminished or lost. Fertility and gender are now subordinate within identity politics. Suggestions of biological determinism, of hetero–homo men who identify as male, of hetero–homo women who identify as female, are currently censured in academic and public discourse.

As Marr 1991 suggests: "Elizabeth is one of White's great roles, an opulent monster searching for illumination in a death scene that lasts for six hundred pages" (495). The novel is about love or the failure of love. Early in the novel, when she was around 86, Elizabeth tells Mary de Santis: "*I wanted very badly to love my husband, Sister, even after I knew I didn't—or couldn't enough*" (20). About 15 years earlier, when she was around 70, not long after the storm, Elizabeth was recovering from "a slight nervous upset" (18). At that time Mary was her companion rather than her nurse.

Elizabeth adamantly insists, here and elsewhere: "Whatever they tell you, I loved my husband. My children wouldn't allow me to love them":

> "Oh, I know I am not selfless enough!" When she turned she was burning with a blue, inward rage; but quickly quenched it, and drew up a stool at this girl's feet. "There is this other love, I know. Haven't I been shown? And I still can't reach it. But I shall! I shall!" She laid her head on her nurse's hands (162).

The family solicitor puts this differently, when Basil and Dorothy first canvass with him the idea of putting their mother in residential aged care:

> "Though Mrs Hunter's mind wanders at times, it always appears to be searching after subtleties." Arnold Wyburd was feeling his way. "I'd say she is still the most complex woman I know." He couldn't confess the rest: she terrified me as much as ever (262).

What are these searched-for subtleties? What is this "other love" Elizabeth has been shown but cannot reach? Is it a very different kind of love from eros? Is it lovingkindness, grace, mercy, forgiveness, fidelity, kinship or familiarity, or friendship? Is it agape or self-emptying divine love? Or is it simply the eye of the storm, inseparable from the storm itself?

Elizabeth is aware of her shortcomings but is unable or unwilling to do anything about them. White highlights her dilemma when admitting his own:

> Every time I say "Forgive us our trespasses as we forgive those who

trespass against us" I realize I am a hypocrite and un-Christian (Letter to
The Reverend Austin Day, 13 August 1985, CCSL Archives).

This problem, of hypocrisy and inability to forgive, is universal. It has to
do with human nature, and perhaps its "fall" and/or its "original sin", two
concepts Golding explored in depth during the 1950s (see Appendix). We
can elevate this problem to tragic heights, if we wish. We can attempt to
turn it into great art—perhaps even great tragic art—but there are
problems with this: first, the attempt presupposes tragedy is a benchmark
for the ultimate possibilities of art or ultimate comment on the human
condition; second, the attempt is not a postwar Jewish or Christian
response to the universal problem.

As McCulloch reminds us, each of the characters in *The Eye of the
Storm* is given a token experience of the "eye" or the "centre of life". For
example, "Flora's experience occurs at the climax of her cosmetic
handiwork" (114):

> Then, for an instant, one of the rare coruscations occurred, in which the
> original sapphire buried under the opalescence invited you to shed your
> spite, sloth, indifference, resentments, along with an old woman's cruelty,
> greed, selfishness. Momentarily at least this fright of an idol became the
> goddess hidden inside: of life, which you longed for, but hadn't yet dared
> embrace; of beauty such as you imagined, but had so far failed to grasp
> (with which Col grappled, you bitterly suspected, somewhere in the
> interminably agitated depths of music); and finally, of death, which hadn't
> concerned you, except as something to be tidied away, till now you were
> faced with the vision of it.
>   It was the spectre of death which brought them both toppling down.
> Mrs Hunter suddenly twitched as though someone had walked over her
> grave. Sister Manhood herself was stroked into gooseflesh (*Storm* 121).

In interpreting this passage, McCulloch suggests that: "Elizabeth Hunter is
represented here as the source and energy of life, all the more dynamic
because of its emergence in the face of death" (114).

Like all of White's novels, *The Eye of the Storm* is character-driven
rather than plot-driven. The novel is essentially hermeneutical: it
instinctively reacts against correspondence or coherence theories of
knowledge and truth. It is perspectivist in the Nietzschean sense. It is
disclosive in the Heideggerian sense. As McCulloch says:

> Each of the six perspectives of *EOS* is similarly structured around
> Elizabeth Hunter. All characters involved do have an individual vitality but
> they are ultimately subordinated to a more abstract intention. Like a
> spider's web they make up the frame of the whole, but inevitably the focus
> is drawn to the centre of the weave. At this centre there is Elizabeth

Hunter, her life and her "eye of the storm" experience (115).

For McCulloch, the ultimate meaning of Elizabeth Hunter—the "abstract intention" of her character—is inseparable from tragedy; from Nietzsche's understanding of tragedy, and from Shakespeare's understanding of tragedy, both of which seem to be linked in McCulloch's mind:

> The dominating metaphor of *EOS* is White's use of Shakespeare's *King Lear*. Elizabeth Hunter knows it is impossible to describe her "eye of the storm" experience: "You can never convey in words the utmost in experience" (414). She exists in a rational world, that precludes the expression of tragic theatre, which belongs to a pre-rational phase of history. Nevertheless, as White's ultimate poet-seer, she represents the hope for a return of that mystery in words which lies at the source of tragic poetry (115).

Here, and throughout *The Tragic Vision*, McCulloch situates her critique within an influential Nietzschean rhetoric that attaches great significance to Presocratic philosophy and aesthetics—or rather to Nietzsche's view of them—and how they supposedly changed because of socratic rationalism. Clearly, White was familiar with this rhetoric, as *The Solid Mandala* demonstrates, but there is disagreement over how much of the rhetoric can be applied to his other novels.

As far as McCulloch is concerned, Elizabeth Hunter is a hero, "but she is not portrayed as a tragic character in the mould of Lear" (116); instead, she is symbolically represented as a superman or an übermensch: as an "inscrutable power, or an 'order' that has replaced God" (117). She does not assume this state without question, however: "What one witnesses is the coming of a 'superman', but not the arrival":

> Elizabeth Hunter's failure to arrive at the "endlessness" in life, plus her failure to create one whole being, results in a picture of fragmentation. Her children are pale, weak shadows of herself … the terrible pessimism in this novel is that there cannot be a real Lear or a Cordelia without the existence of some kind of "order" or "deity" for these characters to work in relation to. Mrs Hunter's children are presented as Goneril and Regan. She is also shepherded towards death by a Shakespearean fool character and, like Lear, she is the only person to experience enlightenment and tranquillity at the heart of the storm. But the analogy drawn between Elizabeth Hunter and Lear is a complex one that will create misinterpretation if applied too rigidly.
>
> As Elizabeth is not a Lear character, it is not possible for her to reach tragic heights. At most, her final state expresses the tragic vision of White. Tragedy in its purest sense can only exist in the presence of a known, normative and revered deity, or cosmic order, or principle of conduct. There is no order that Elizabeth Hunter can appeal to beyond herself.

Unhappily, she must be a creation of a post-tragic world, which is not in the temporary disorder of an ordered universe, but is in indefinite fragmentation. She exists in what Sewell terms:

> times when for reasons internal and external, spiritual and sociological, the questions of ultimate justice and human destiny seem suddenly to have jarred loose again. Often these critical periods or "moments" come after a long period of relative stability, when a dominant myth or religious orthodoxy or philosophic view has provided a coherent and sustaining way of life.

Elizabeth Hunter's task is to combat the original terror of existence, which cannot be dispelled by old formulations. There is an essential change in the face of the universe. White attempts to combat this terror through his creation of a character who is to embody a new essence or Divinity to replace the one robbed from man with the "death of God" (118).

It is good of McCulloch to keep drawing our attention to White's philosophical and aesthetic context. This is necessary because that context—whether we call it post-Winckelmann, post-Kant, post-Sturm und Drang, romantic, or post-romantic—is easily overlooked or misunderstood.

While McCulloch is a pioneer—and one of the few 20th century critics to take White studies where it needed to go—she consistently conflates a range of separate or distinct ideas: the pagan gods, the Judaeo-Christian God, the götterdämmerung of the pagan gods, the death of the Judaeo-Christian God, the critique of transcendence and pursuit of immanence, and tragedy as a benchmark for the ultimate possibilities of art or comment on the human condition. If these ideas relate to each other at some points, as rhetorical propositions, they are not statements of fact, and they are not interchangeable. They cannot be conflated without creating a host of logical fallacies. To notice how White reacts against correspondence and coherence theories of knowledge and truth—to notice how he moves among perspectivist and disclosive theories of knowledge and truth—is to simply acknowledge his 19th and 20th century context. If he is a brilliant example of that context so are his contemporaries.

We know White critiqued transcendence, with its necessary impasses. We know he pursued immanence, with its inevitable aporias. We also know he believed in God, which challenges us to notice and discuss—in terms of what theologians call negative or apophatic theology—the God he believed in. We know he was aware of tragedy and its historical conventions—"*his* Lear, *his* Hedda"—but it is difficult to be reductionist about that awareness or dogmatic about how it appears in his work.

Elizabeth does fail to arrive at the "endlessness" in life. The superman must fail, because failure is an inevitable part of the superman's quest, and because the journey is more important than the destination. She fails because the übermensch, which is linear, will always blunder against the eternal return, which is cyclical. She also fails to create one whole being, as neither of her children is a whole character. But the reasons why she cannot be "a real Lear or Cordelia" have nothing to do with God's death, or the end of "old formulations", or an "essential change in the face of the universe". Neither the universe nor its face changed in any way, essentially or materially, once God's death was proclaimed. It continued to be what it is. It still expanded, as it has been expanding, ever since the Big Bang: the theory of which, by the way, was first proposed by a priest.[3]

There is an underlying assumption among secular literary critics that classical metaphysics—understood here as the history of philosophy prior to Kant—has been proven to be "false" and, because of this, the proclamation of God's death is "true" and proves atheism with language. This is not the case. Judaism and Christianity are still intellectually and scientifically coherent. In all mainstream Christian denominations, the theory of evolution is understood to be reconcilable with the Genesis creation story. In philosophy, it is still possible to be a pre-Kantian pluralist. In spite of what non-binary thinkers assume, Plato, Aristotle, Augustine, Aquinas, Locke, and Descartes are all still relevant.

I wonder whether McCulloch's point is that it was never possible for White to give his characters the same telos Austen gave hers. Irrespective of his beliefs, or doubts, his philosophical and aesthetic context would not allow any return to the kinds of telos we find in the novel before the proclamation of God's death. Austen's neoclassical–romantic world had passed, focused as it was on correspondence and coherence theories of knowledge and truth. White lived in a modernist–postmodernist world, focused as it was on perspectivist and disclosive theories of knowledge and truth. But if White could not be an Austen, he still worked with the archetypes or tropes he inherited from her, including the assumptions attached to concepts such as reason and feeling.

Perspectivism means human subjects bring different perspectives to their encounters with others. As this book argues, the different perspectives White attaches to his protagonists are paradigmatic, they represent the creation myths and their corresponding metaphors at the heart of different worldviews. This is why noticing them is so important. Arguably, *The Eye of the Storm* is best understood when the mythical and metaphorical associations of its protagonists are recognized, as ciphers, in

---

[3] The Big Bang theory, widely attributed to Edwin Hubble, was first proposed by Georges Lemaître (1894–1966), a Belgian priest, astronomer and professor of physics at the Catholic University of Leuven.

relation to the central protagonist Elizabeth Hunter, representing the Theogonic metaphors.

Because the götterdämmerung (the twilight of the pagan gods) and the proclamation of God's death are two different things, it is debatable whether White intended Elizabeth Hunter to embody "a new essence or Divinity to replace the one robbed from man with the 'death of God'". It is important to not conflate Athens and Jerusalem here.

To repeat part of Nussbaum's quote in Chapter One from *The Fragility of Goodness*:

> In the Greek world ... the morality of the gods' actions is regularly impugned, and it is frequently suggested that the gods lack full awareness of and sensitivity to moral norms, not being in the position of neediness and incompleteness that gives rise to the need for them. Aristotle takes this perspective to one extreme, denying that the gods have the moral virtues at all. Because it would be ridiculous to imagine the gods making contracts and returning deposits, they cannot be said to have justice. While the tragic poets do not go this far, there is a tendency, from Homer on, to portray the gods as callous and selfish in their dealings with mortals. But this means that even tragedies that are caused by divine scheming may be caused by obtuseness, laziness, and moral failure, not by mysterious necessity (xxxii).

If this line of thought is applied to Elizabeth Hunter—supposedly a substitute divinity now that God is dead—she clearly does not represent the tension between freedom and necessity, which is a central aspect of the human condition. Rather than representing some kind of necessity, or force of nature, she can be seen as simply obtuse, lazy, and immoral in her dealings with her family and servants. If this makes her a "god" in the ancient Greek sense, that has nothing to do with the God of Judaism and Christianity.

A lot depends on how the reader understands Elizabeth. If her worst crime is not being a loving mother, she is certainly not the worst mother in existence. Many loving mothers have produced children as narcissistic, solipsistic, and emotionally challenged as Basil and Dorothy. Also, many loving mothers are known to prefer their sons to their daughters, which explains why Basil gets preferential treatment, but that did not make him a nicer person than Dorothy. The worst thing Elizabeth does to Dorothy—which may stand out in the minds of many readers—is wilfully poaching her daughter's potential love interest just before the storm on Brumby Island. If mothers are not supposed to do this to their daughters, she is not the first and will not be the last.

If the novel has a moral centre, it must surely be the Hunter marriage between Alfred and Elizabeth and her regret at not loving him enough:

At least she had given him their children. She must remember that, re-create their faces: fluctuating on the dark screen, Dorothy's little mask, never quite transparent nor yet opaque, not unlike those silver medals on the dried stems of honesty; and Basil the Superb, who preferred to perform for strangers or gullible innocents like Lal Wyburd. Their children. Hardly Alfred's, except by accident of blood (28).

The children are "hardly" Alfred's because they are hers—mythically and metaphorically—and because she is a work of art. As McCulloch suggests:

> Elizabeth Hunter is White's most complex and dynamic elected character. She is a character whose "love of life often outstripped discretion". Evidently, when White failed to express artistically his perception of wholeness through the artist character, Hurtle, he rethought the make-up of his poet-seer. Whereas Hurtle "lived" only through his art. Elizabeth Hunter becomes the work of art by embracing life itself in all its forms. She is the first character in which White has condoned ruthless manipulation of others and a determined indulgence in sexuality and all possible manifestations of sensuality (128).

> Life must be lived to its fullest if death is to be meaningful. Death is not to be a signal for the end but, instead, will involve a new form of immortality or "endlessness". White's belief in the infinity of life is expressed in some or other form in most of his novels. The possibility that Elizabeth Hunter may know this infinity is glimpsed by her, just prior to this experience of the storm: "For the first time she was disturbed by the mystery of her strength, of her elect life, not that frequently unconvincing part of it which she had already lived, but that which stretched ahead of her as far as the horizon and not even her own shadow in view". Even at this stage she believed "her life had been a ceremony", involving rituals that went beyond the anointing of make-up. As White's ultimate poet-seer her indulgence in all that pertains to Love, Beauty, Fulfilment and Death is ritualized towards the ceremony of a final vision (129).

> The suggestion in this novel is that "transcendent" movement towards the core of "immanent" reality, and not beyond it, is to be achieved through an absolute indulgence in all that a physical and sensual life can offer … It is important to understand that the transcendence White attempts to identify in life and in art is a non-metaphysical one. It is a belief that in this post-Christian world transcendences must be identified as occurring within the world (133)

In this philosophical–aesthetic scheme, after God's death, the west longs not for the messiah's return but for some reification or embodiment of dionysian man.

Children

Basil Hunter

White persistently denied being intellectual, but persistently claimed to be intuitive, whatever that means; however, as Marr 1991 reminds us, his intuition was grounded in research: "In Basil Hunter, White came close to laying bare his own creative machinery" (495). Basil is not "stuffed" with "theories" and "taste" but builds his roles from flashes of intuition. When given a part that interested him, he:

> would ferret out the last refinement of lust in a Bosola, say, or just show them, wrap up a homosexual bread-carter in all the oblique motivation required by the Royal Court" (495).

So, Basil researched his roles with the same thoroughness that White researched his novels.

This begs questions. Can intuition be based on thorough research and still be regarded as intuitive or instinctive? Instead, would it not be more in the category of conscious reasoning? These questions are important, because reason, which is supposed to reside in the conscious mind, and intuition, which is supposed to reside somewhere else, are supposedly the two different rational and empirical ways in which westerners arrive at knowledge and truth.

Marr tells us White's Basil was to be:

> ... a ham actor of the Sir Donald Wolfit type preparing to play Lear. A new biography of Wolfit had just been published and White devoured it when it arrived from London. The old actor was "a fascinating, though in many ways awful character". White reread *Lear*, and read all he could about the great Lears. He wished he had seen Wolfit's: "I suspect his of being the Lear of our lifetime—anyway, so far. To read about other good actors in the part one doesn't get the impression they got anywhere near what it ought to be ... How I should love to see a great Lear, but I don't expect I ever shall" (495).

In the novel, White always distinguishes between Basil the actor and Basil the person: the former is successful, to a degree; the latter is an ultimate failure as a person, like Hurtle. The actor and painter are dissatisfied, professionally, and never accomplish what they hope to accomplish in their lifetimes. This is because creating art and living life are different things.

Basil knows he has never fully realized or performed his life in art, even as a tragic hero, in any of what Lotte Lippmann calls—paradoxically and/or comically—"all the great *German* roles" (149); a phrase he remembers later (234). This is why he wants to have "another go" at his Lear (127, 235, 350, 592), and Richard II (467). Also, as Mitty Jacka attests, the possibility of realizing his life in art is the meaning of the "unplayed I" (246). If only he can write the right autobiographical script, and perform the right autobiographical role, on stage, in front of a receptive audience. His will is so absorbed by the possibility of soteria through art that he never makes a serious attempt at soteria through a much more difficult challenge: such as trying to have better human relationships, or trying to lead what philosophers before Nietzsche called a "good life".[4]

Like her son, Elizabeth treats her family as an audience:

> If she overdid it slightly it was because she had something of the actress in her. (They used to say of Basil Hunter later, *you know where he gets it from*) (34).

In other words, the Theogonic precedes and begets the Hellenic. Later, on the same page, we hear that "Basil was at his most horrid, exploiting human harshness under cover of his beauty: like a still-ripening plum, he would have shrivelled the mouth if you had bitten into him".

The question we inevitably confront, with regard to Basil, is the degree to which his personality is a product of his parents' marriage. To what extent is Elizabeth responsible for her son's personality? Would he have been a better person had she been a better mother? While this question is at the heart of a complex and ongoing nature–nurture debate, White's characters are not persons and their fictional lives are determined in a way that human lives are not. Elizabeth is who she is. Basil never trusted her. Even as a child: "It was Basil who suspected something, nothing specific, he couldn't have. It was just that he suspected his mother generally and on principle" (100). The Hunter family is acting out what the young White saw in the *Myths of Ancient Greece*, which in his mind merely substituted "the gods' adulteries, feuds, and murders for those of the wider-ranging British social system" (33).

"I have no one," the adult Basil admits to the witch-like Mitty Jacka, on the bus to her home in London's Beulah Hill. "I ran away from my family, my country, to become an actor":

> She was waiting.

---

[4] Plato, Aristotle and Kant discussed the "good life", within classical metaphysics, as reasonable restraint and civic duty. Because the God of classical metaphysics is "dead", Nietzsche's critique of conventional morality pits the supposedly life-denying values of self-restraint, democracy, and compassion (a "slave morality") against the supposedly life-affirming values of his disruptive aristocratic "master morality".

"I've done what I set out to do," he insisted, he felt, modestly.

She didn't disagree. "You were knighted by the Queen," she reminded with appropriate gravity.

When it wasn't his achievement he wanted to recall, but his childhood, from which Macbeth, Hamlet, Lear, together with other paler apparitions, had sprung, out of the least likely drought-stricken gullies, brown, brooding pools, and austere forms of wind-tattered trees. Only the bus was not the ideal place in which to begin his invocation; and for once the sound of his famous voice would have made him wince.

"I've seen some of your performances," she was telling, "though I don't make a habit of going to the theatre. I remember your Lear—and I've been to the present thing."

This drew him. "Will you admit it isn't as bad as they said?"

"No, not bad—in fact good, in its stunted way."

He could feel himself inwardly bridling; perhaps vanity was the source of his greatest sensual pleasure.

"But might have been better if you had dared to give yourself."

"How do you mean 'give'?" He could hear the anger in his voice; and he looked at her afresh, wondering whether this old bag was leading up to what would materialize as an unmade bed.

"Nothing physical," she formed the word with almost prudish care. "I don't doubt you've given yourself physically, night after night, in the parts you've acted—to the wives you mention—mistresses probably (I know nothing about your private life because I don't read newspapers). And I don't mean creatively either, because that's unconscious where it isn't disciplined physical labour. Nor do I mean what used to be called 'spiritual' before we shed our illusions. Perhaps I should say you haven't given yourself 'essentially'" (240–241).

Soon after this, Basil tells Mitty about a memory of his, which has intriguing parallels with the *Allegory of the Cave* (Republic VII, 514a–520a) which, along with the *Allegory of the Sun* (Republic VI, 508b–509c) and the *Allegory of the Divided Line* (Republic VI, 509d–511e), is central to Plato's metaphysical framework.

Once, when he was a child, immobilized with a fractured arm, he had night fears of a back-lit screen behind his bed (244). The effect, which is permanent, has the same "fear of freedom" implications which characterize the secular or atheistic forms of existentialism. As an adult, this screen–fear keeps recurring. Now he suspects Mitty Jacka of wanting to introduce him to "the other side of that grey screen":

"This screen—now it's continued cropping up. So solid and real—as real as childhood." He laughed uneasily for his discovery. "I've built speeches round it, rehearsing parts which have worried me. It's always protected me from the draught." He sniggered, sipping the drink which had let loose his confession. "This screen thing—it materializes again when you feel you're beginning to slip—in musty provincial theatres—a piece of disintegrating silk stretched on a rickety, tottering frame. You're less than ever inclined to look behind it. And you're pretty sure that if it blows over, you're lost" (245).

Basil spends the night on an uncomfortable old sofa in Beulah Hill. Early in morning, before Mitty Jacka descends from her eyrie, he reads a reminder note she wrote to herself the previous night and tossed into an urn:

> … an actor tends to ignore the part which fits him best *his life* Lear the old unplayable is in the end a safer bet than the unplayed I … (246).

Whether Lear is really unplayable is moot, but Mitty's (and White's) point is that art is never a substitute for life, and living is always harder than acting.

If White is a rhetorician, not a philosopher, he still asks us to consider philosophical questions about life. Mitty Jacka is challenging Basil to go on a journey, to discover his "essence", but she insists the journey must be outside religion—it cannot be "spiritual", in the traditional religious sense—since God is "dead" and we have shed our "illusions". Whether he is up to the challenge is another matter, and her motivation for issuing the challenge is unknown. What does she want from this "unplayed I" collaboration? The 20th century was full of Mitty Jackas, exploring the non-religious or anti-religious possibilities of secular or atheistic existentialism, or the transcendent–immanent possibilities of art, or, using Platonic metaphors, trying to cross the divided line that separates the *Allegory of the Cave* from the *Allegory of the Sun*.

Basil is faced with a difficult choice. He can continue along the path of attempting soteria through art or he can attempt something harder: struggle to find soteria through improved social and familial relationships; through trying to lead an examined or "good" life. The omens are bad. Both his marriages failed. His "daughter" Imogen is not his child. Apart from unsuccessful relationships with his ex-wives, "daughter", parents and sister, the novel sets up a series of encounters designed to test his ability to overcome his solipsism. The most important of these other encounters—or encounters with "others"—are with Lotte, Flora, Mary, and the Macrory family at Kudgeri, the landscape of his childhood, where he believes his talent came from. In each encounter, he is challenged to be a person rather than an actor, but it never quite works out.

On the night of Basil's arrival from England–Bangkok, Lotte serves him dinner, alone, in his mother's formal dining room. The meal begins positively: "From inside, sounds of cutlery and glass transformed his hopes into confidence" until "he suddenly remembered he had to face another actress" (144). Over excellent food, while Lotte is in professional attendance, nervous and emotional, he asks about her acting career. It was mere "Tingeltangel",[5] she says. While his questions become prompts, through which the reader learns much about Lotte's story, she humbles him by reminding him that "he was not wholly actor: he was also a whole human being":

> Again this crazy Jewess was right. It is the next part which promises to bring the sum right. At the end another fly at *Lear*'s stony, perhaps unscalable mountain. He feared the prospect almost as much as Mitty Jacka's non-play. Worst of all he dreaded the sound of projecting a tattered voice into a half empty theatre. In Glasgow during that last tour someone had thrown a banana skin (149).

He ventures to ask why she left her Aryan lover:

> "What became of your German?" he hardly dared to ask.
> "I left him."
> "But others left together."
> "We were not as others. I left him because I loved him." She gave up, trying but failing at first to unlock her arthritic hands. "Or because—as your lady mother insists—I am the original masochist."
> "No one ever knew better than Mother how to rub salt into other people's wounds."
> "But I love her!" the housekeeper gasped.
> "How can you love what is evil, brutal, destructive." If he were to survive, he must persuade himself to continue believing some of this.
> "Yes. She is all you say," her housekeeper agreed; "but understands more of the truth than others." As her hands fell away from the table she added, "And if I cannot worship, I have to love somebody" (150).

Notice how Basil believes his survival depends on the existential necessity of not loving his mother because she is evil, brutal, and destructive. He then drinks two cups of Lotte's coffee—"strong enough to blow a safe let alone a human skull"—because he "must see his mother before leaving the house which, he had to remember, was only legally hers" (151).

So, he thinks the house "only legally" belongs to his mother. If his will is still strong, his understanding has become opaque, nevertheless:

> There had been a time when he saw clearly, right down to the root of the matter, before his perception had retired behind a legerdemain of technique and the dishonesties of living (273).

---

[5] Tingeltangel is a kind of cabaret, often no more than a raised platform in a bar, café, or restaurant, featuring those at the start or the end of their cabaret careers.

In other words, while Basil's mind is not as sharp as it once was, he knows he must remain focused on the reason for his trip, obtaining his inheritance, regardless of whatever personal journey he chooses to go on.

The Schepisi screen adaptation rewrote several aspects of the novel to make it unrecognizable to those familiar with it. Basil's stopover in Bangkok, where he ran into his acting chums, was transposed to Sydney, and was expanded to include several scenes that were unnecessary distractions. Basil's relationship with Flora was blown out of proportion and made into something the novel never intended it to be. For example: the first time she met him, she did not hover semi-naked in his old bedroom with the intention of seducing him. The pregnancy idea comes to her much later. She never went to the theatre or dinner parties with him. He never regarded himself as having a serious relationship with her. He never introduced her to his acting chums as both his fiancé and his mother's nurse. Then there's Basil's "unplayed I" project, a unrealized idea in the novel, which Schepisi turns into a fully-realized play-within-the-film.

Later in the novel, Flora stops taking the Pill and goes to Basil's hotel with the intention of getting pregnant. She has mixed reasons for doing this: she has heard about Basil and Dorothy's plan to put Elizabeth in a home and hopes to intercede on her employer's behalf; she is ambivalent about Col Pardoe and wants to thwart his desire to possess her; and there was a mutual attraction between Basil and Flora from the moment they met.

During sex, he asks whether she will be able to "love" him, whatever he means by that. She is confused but mutters "yes", she can, when she gets used to the idea. After sex she "felt becalmed rather than calmed, let alone fulfilled. There was nothing she needed beyond the certainty—she might even settle for the faint hope—of conceiving". She falls asleep and dreams not of Basil but of Col Pardoe (316).

Basil wakes, drooling for an Alka-Seltzer, wishing he could spread out, knowing he cannot turn on the light, because the nurse he had gone to bed with was breathing beside him. So he lay in bed flickering his eyelids and thinking, "there was no alternative in the trap in which he found himself … His thoughts began steeplechasing, spurt after spurt, a string of competitive images" (317).

There are two types of competitive images. First, images about himself as an actor in the role of Alvaro in de Montherlant's *The Master of Santiago* (1947): "Impress anybody with some of those lines—and your voice: *God neither wishes nor seeks anything. He is eternal calm. It is in wishing nothing that you will come to mirror God*" (317). Second, images about himself as a person; "What if he did fall for some pretty, healthy, but ordinary girl like this. Would her love for him survive his bitches of friends? Would he be turned by her perpetual clangers into a pillar of sullenness?"

> What he had always longed for, he now knew, was to be loved by some such normal, lovely, insensitive but trusting hunk of a girl as this Flora Nightingale beside him: he had done her twice and felt progressively younger. Then why Alvaro? at one level a rewarding part for an elderly—let's say "mature", actor of voice and presence; at another, the mouthpiece of asceticism preaching its withering gospel from the foothills of tragedy (319).[6]

Here the subject of money—and hence his mother—enters his thoughts, since "money" is interchangeable with "motherhood" in the Hunter family. The observation, which Elizabeth made earlier in the novel (123), is repeated: *I was never a natural mother—I couldn't feed. But that—you see, darling—hasn't deprived you of—of nourishment* (320). Because the cheque she had "doled" out to him—apparently for $5000; a considerable sum when the novel was published—was "only a wretched nibble":

> He dragged the sheet up, tight, sawing at his throat, then settled down to hugging his resentment. Forgetful of his love, he must have rocked his anger to sleep (320).

When Flora wakes, she thinks Basil looks frightening in his sleep, and she "did in fact feel unbearably sad":

> Here was this strange, not bad, but boring man, unconscious of the part he was playing, or the child she could conceive by him, regardless of whether he, or the child, wished it … She was the dishonest one, the deceiver. Her own child, *whom she could not help seeing with the features of Col Pardoe*, would grow up as the visible proof of her deception, and she would have to disguise her remorse as love for her boy. Whichever way she looked she could see no end to her dishonesty: a vista of mirrors inside a mirror (italics added) (321).

For many reasons, this relationship is ill-conceived and will go nowhere.

Early in the novel, although celibacy–chastity is understood to be part of Mary de Santis's "vocation", Basil's arrival is an opportunity for White to suggest sexual repression (174). Later, she visits him in his hotel, not with sexual intentions, like Flora, but because she has heard of what Basil and

---

[6] What does "the mouthpiece of asceticism preaching its withering gospel from the foothills of tragedy" tell us about White's attitude towards tragedy?

Dorothy intend to do to their mother. She intends to interceded on
Elizabeth's behalf. This never happens. Instead, they have a couple of
martinis at his hotel before driving out to Watson's Bay for a seafood
lunch on the harbour (339).

Throughout their encounter, both Basil and Mary are out of their
comfort zones. Conversation is difficult. There is no common ground for
small talk. He can only talk about acting. She knows nothing about acting.
At one point he struggles to be candid, admitting that all his life—even
when he was a "mere boy"—he wanted to be an actor. Overall, he is
pleased with his career:

> Till you reach—let's call it "the age of disgust"—when you can feel
> something taking place in your metabolism, and a change comes over the
> expression on other people's faces, and you want to reject the whole
> business of—of acting: all its illusions and your own presumption—not to
> say spuriousness."
>
> Mary de Santis would have liked to think he was not serious, but he
> was, she saw. She could not bear to witness this second death of [her
> father] the only man she had ever loved. This time she was unable to offer
> even a needle. She sat looking at Sir Basil Hunter's silken ankle.
> "To reject," he said, "before you are rejected."
> He was horrified by what he had spewed up" (344–345).

She senses he is a man who is dying in a different way from her father.

As his confession continues, he feels more and more exposed,
vulnerable, and "suddenly maddened … what infuriated him was his own
worst, or what she had seen of it. Mercifully not all … his uneasiness
increased as she continued brooding opposite. Perhaps she was preparing
to accuse him" (351). But Mary's thoughts are elsewhere:

> In fact, Sister de Santis was accusing herself of her own fall from grace
> which had begun with the arrival of Mrs Hunter's son. … She would have
> liked to substitute pity, which is one aspect of pure love. But between Basil
> and her soul's eye, hovered the face of her pitiful father whom she had
> desired to love in some way never made clear to her during his lifetime,
> only recently in the line of Basil Hunter's jaw, the veins of his temples, the
> bones of a silken ankle. Her whole vocation of selflessness was threatened
> if she offered this man her pity, grown as it was on *decomposed lust*. Now
> too, in the context of slovenliness and apathy presented by the half
> deserted restaurant, she knew she would never find the strength or
> opportunity to bear witness to her true faith and plead for the one who was
> also, incidentally, Elizabeth Hunter (italics added) (351).

Does Basil want or deserve her pity? He still has random, fleeting
thoughts about the possibilities of a relationship with Flora Manhood.
What does White mean by pity grown on decomposed lust? Why does the

idea of decomposed lust threaten the idea of Mary's selflessness?

If Hellenic Basil is still a commanding on-stage presence, off-stage he is emotionally vulnerable and cannot cope with life. By contrast, Hebraic Mary is emotionally strong and can cope with life; hence their paradigmatically different reactions to the rotting dog carcass that washes ashore near their table:

> Sir Basil appeared to take it personally. "Isn't this the ultimate in filth? This barbarism! But only what can be expected," he screeched, like an old parrot she thought, its tongue stuck out, hard and blue; like—oh no, his mother caught in what could be a seizure, at the point of aiming her deadliest insult, or curse.
>
> Unlike Sir Basil, Sister de Santis was not immediately shocked by the drowned dog; she was more passive of course, and less articulate; while most of her life she had been personally, though objectively, involved with the physical aspects of death. Till now a nameless anguish began seeping, and she put her handkerchief to her mouth to stanch it. She could do nothing about the smell: this continued penetrating, and would probably haunt her nostrils, cling to her clothes forever; or the gelatinous sockets where the dog's eyes had been: they were staring at her so intensely they gave the mask a live expression (352–353).

Basil leaves the table and disappears, to the back of the restaurant, in a somnambulant state. Mary remains and notices the wire eating into the dog's neck. So, in spite of her flaws, Mary is closer to and can cope with reality. The tragic hero cannot. After dropping off at her flat:

> His mechanical self drove off by jerks in the tinny car. Because he never felt at home in one, he knew he would be sitting upright, his shoulders narrows. *Pray you, undo this button. Thank you, sir.* Why? Only that his last performance as the old king he had never felt so personally bereft, so bankrupt; technique could not protect him from it. This last gasp; and the poverty of a single bone-clean button. In this you may have conveyed the truth, if in nothing else (356).

Where can Basil feel at home? He knows the landscape of his childhood is the source of his talent. Earlier, he admitted this to Mitty Jacka. Now that he and his sister have finally told Elizabeth they are moving her to Thorogood Village, once a room becomes vacant, he sees his trip to Kudgeri with Dorothy as a: "Return to the source of things, and in doing so, perhaps even save yourself from Mitty Jacka and the death play" (433). But why is "looking behind the screen" a "death play"? Is his avoidance of this form of "death" why he continues to hope for "another go" at his tragic roles? Does acting keep him "alive"? Is he afraid of—or is he perhaps denied—any other form of identity?

While driving to Kudgeri, coping with the long distance made it difficult for Basil to maintain a human balance: "He had to remind himself *I am Sir Basil Hunter—the actor*" (470). While physical hunger, heightened by "the crudest sentimental longing", prompted him to buy and guzzle an iconic Aussie meat pie, now "a deeper, more confused desire made him urge the car across the blinding plains towards this mythical house in which a real family was living" (471).

That night, as he nipped out of the house before dinner, to pee off the edge of the veranda:

> Basil stood listening and shivering awhile. To be passively accepted by your natural surroundings is only temporarily gratifying. What he craved was confirmation if his own intrinsic worth as opposed to possibly spurious achievement. Which might not be forthcoming, however. The darkness continued to offer the kindly indifference of nature at its domesticated fringes, while the house behind would probably never share its secrets with one who had renounced life for the theatre (477).

When Basil re-entered the house, as if he were making a stage entrance, he "waited for the recognition he was not accorded. Again he found it was not his scene" (477).

The next morning, Rory Macrory takes Basil on his station rounds. Basil asks to be left at "a brown dam framed by a stand of withered tussock" (489). This is where he confessed to yabbying as a boy: "What he did not dare confess was that he wanted to feel the mud between his toes" (490). At the far end of the dam stood a tree of tremendous girth, which triggered memories of a fall and a fractured–broken arm (100).

The memory of the fall triggers another crucial memory of his father arriving to rescue him. During the rescue, Alfred is described as frail and trembling but determined to do the right thing:

> A man's a father's hands shouldn't tremble it was frightening: if you cry you may make him worse. *Have it put right. Get you up in front of me. Shove the good arm around my neck.* Too close his breath on you like the trembling and that scalding sweat your own as cold. *Now lie back son lean against me I'll support you.* Awful bumpy hard half on the mare's withers the pommel of the saddle and half lying on Dad's stomach the bone shrieking under your skin deliciously delirious his fire dripping into your cold sea of sweat. *Won't be long Basil boy.* It was Dad trying to love. It made you want to cry, to reach up with your crooked arm. So you laughed (491).

A few lines later, the narrator calls this "Alfred Hunter offering downright love disguised as tentative, sweaty affection". Notice that what Basil sees as "trying to love" the narrator sees as "downright love".

Basil cuts his foot, wading in the dam. After he recovers, he starts frequenting the homestead's old stables, which "now fulfilled only a memorial function" (503). He becomes particularly attached to his father's old 3-litre Bentley which "stood waiting for him on flat tyres" (505). This triggers more memories:

> *What you doing Basil boy?*
> *Nothing Dd-dadd.* After defeating that slight stammer, your voice had developed what seemed like unlimited power; but the limp came to replace the stutter (505).

After this, he has a vivid memory of riding in the car with his parents, which triggers emotions:

> They drove on, and the wind started coming from another direction. She lost control of her gossamer. It flicked your eyeball.
> It was still not crying, running. Sir Basil Hunter was forced to take out Enid's Christmas handkerchief, to mop the trickling (506).

Clearly, the trip to Kudgeri has been much more significant to Basil than it has been to Dorothy—who argues that they must leave this country "where we don't belong", and in her case never did belong, as she admits:

> "To you it may mean something— something you aren't prepared to admit." She had raised her voice, to force its scorn past the knots in her throat. "I've always hated—HATED it!" (508).

After the episode in the shed "Basil took care to keep to himself" (515). He has not been given what he had hoped to receive from this journey to Kudgeri. His solution to this dilemma is to take refuge in the old orchard and start learning an old part he hopes to play again: Lear.

> Here he lay to study, if not to understand, the Part. It was foolish of him to bring it to "Kudgeri" to remind him of past failures; although better to fail in a part than as a whole: Lear rather than the Jacka's threat (516).

After the night of the incest—during which Elizabeth dies—he receives his inheritance, leaves Australia, and returns to his previous life. On the flight home, he has a stream of consciousness dream which gives us glimpses of what the "unplayed I" might look like. During the dream there is a role reversal. Elizabeth—the Lilac Fairy–Oracle he confronted on his arrival in Sydney—is now cast as Lear–Nature:

> LILAC KING opens her legs go on Bas on all fours natch it's the womb stint you've got to expect in living theatre well it happens doesn't it they pull you through beneath the lilac pubics ATTENDANTS writhing and lithing some of them jolly appetizing fruit if you had the time if

somebody's heel hadn't been put in your eye if you hadn't choked on
somebody's parts at least you are born at last MITTY blacktights JACKA
He is born our King of Kings (crack) forward Basssll *well folks here I am
this is my real role your fool* (jingle bells little soft shoe here) the audience
is loving it as for the OLD KING she yawns she is above it she wants to
get out from under and into her coffin SISTER–DAUGHTERS simmer as
FOOL hogs the scene their bearded king of a crypto brother how now
where's that mongrel? Anyone Dorothy is at liberty to at a pinch to pinch a
line she takes a fancy to and FOOL has all the plums I'll go to bed at
noonlight with my sister Dorothy will kill you for this to say nothing of
Enid Histryl Shiely Moan and all the others only Cordelia the almoner the
one who matters who might care is absent she always was whoever played
the part ought to cut it Mitty (594).

Again, here is another allusion to Freud's Oedipus complex—with the
same Ferenzian twist—similar to the one at the end of *The Letters* (1962).
To repeat part of what Paglia says of the Family Romance in *Sexual
Personae*:

> We each have an incestuous constellation of sexual personae that we carry
> from childhood to the grave and that determines whom and how we love or
> hate. Every encounter with friend or foe, every clash with or submission to
> authority bears the perverse traces of family romance. Love is a crowded
> theatre, for as Harold Bloom remarks, "We can never embrace (sexually or
> otherwise) a single person, but embrace the whole of her or his family
> romance." We still know next to nothing about cathexis, the investment of
> libido in certain people or things. The element of free will in sex and
> emotion is slight. As poets know, falling in love is irrational (4).

The Hunter family—Elizabeth, Dorothy, Alfred—are part of who Basil is.
It must remain part of who he aspires to be. Acting cannot change that. In
this sense, his need to accept the reality of Elizabeth, the Lilac King—her
purple wig a shade of red—is no different from Hurtle's need to accept the
reality of Rhoda, or Waldo's need to accept the reality of Arthur, or
Norbert's need to accept the reality of Mary. If this need has been
expressed in different ways, over the centuries, over the millenia, the
underlying principles remain the same.

Dorothy Hunter

On her arrival in Sydney, in a taxi to her hotel, before going to her
mother's house, Dorothy laments privately and tearfully: "*I have never
managed to escape this thing, Myself.*" (49). Who is this thing, Herself?
Apart from being her mother's daughter, "a horse-faced version of
Elizabeth Hunter" (51), or, as her brother later admits:

> A handsome horse: a Regan of a horse. Did it mean he was to be cast as a
> drag Goneril? (Shades of Mitty Jacka and the "unplayed I!)" (261).

Does she have an independent identity? Does she have free will—if a
protagonist in a novel can ever be said to have free will—or is she a pawn
in White's discourse? Are all protagonists pawns in whatever fiction they
inhabit?

As it did with Basil Hunter's relationship with Flora Manhood, the
Schepisi screen version of *The Eye of the Storm* also changed Dorothy's
Hunter's role significantly. Schepisi's Dorothy was portrayed as needing
and attempting a better relationship with her mother, only to be thwarted
or rebuffed at every turn. Also, Schepisi's Dorothy spends much more
time with Elizabeth than the novel records. Towards the end of the film,
Dorothy flees from her childhood home, Kudjeri, to return to the city, to
be with her dying mother, which never happened in the novel. The film
also has Dorothy putting her mother on the commode Elizabeth dies on: a
reconciling act of tenderness that never happened in the novel. It was
Sister Manhood who put Elizabeth on the commode and found her body.
White's Dorothy was not in Elizabeth's house when her mother died. She
did not find her mother's body. She was not even in Sydney. She was in
Kudgeri committing incest with Basil.

White's Dorothy escapes, after their first mother–daughter reunion:

> Dorothy de Lascabanes was in fact stumbling down the stairs ... she
> trampled and lurched. In the hall she found herself pushing at what? The
> only opposition was a void: and guilt, tenderness, desire, lost opportunities.
> She must never forget *Mother is an evil heartless old woman*. If you did
> forget, Basil would remember, himself Mother's only equal at driving the
> knife home. *Boo-hoo, poor you! If anybody ever told you they loved you
> you wouldn't believe that either now would you?*
>
> The thought that she still had to face her brother started her tearing at
> the hall door (79).

What is Dorothy desperate about? Is she free to change her life? Or is she
a victim of her circumstances?

Dorothy suffers from the cultural cringe. Until recently, this was a
characteristic of her class.[7] In her case the cringe was not inherited, as
neither of her parents suffered from it. Like many of her contemporaries,
she was ambivalent about Australia, its people, and its landscape, which is
why White uses the rhetoric of dissociation, loss, and alienation to

---

[7] Traditionally, the logic of the cultural cringe revolves around the idea that British and
Continental cultures were superior to colonial culture. This cringe changed after the
arrival of Whitlam and the resultant ascendancy of the cultural Left.

describe her conflicted character. "When the nurse closed the door" of her mother's bedroom, leaving her alone with Elizabeth during their first reunion meeting, "the princess felt imprisoned not only in the room but in her own body" (62). So, just as Basil is a perfect example of Ricoeur's myths of the tragic hero, Dorothy is a perfect example of Ricoeur's myths of the exiled soul. Both brother and sister represent Hellenic metaphors.

As a young woman, Dorothy fled Australia as soon as she could. The Hunter money allowed her to marry into an aristocratic French family but the marriage did not last. As her mother-in-law admitted, *"Mon fils adore la chasse"* (57). As Cousin Marie-Ange confessed: *"But you understand Do-rô-ti I only tell you out of frankness and—amitié. A woman can so much better hold her husband if she understands his moeurs"* (57). In the end, Hubert left her for an American margarine heiress from Cincinnati.

Some readers may wonder whether her marriage might have been a happier one—and more enduring—had she embraced her inner whore and been more like Hero Pavloussi in bed. Although that strategy did not work for "tragic" Hero and may not have worked for Dorothy either. After Hubert left her: "she clumsily rejected the four or five creaking boars and arthritic tortoises from whom she might have chosen a lover if that had been her fancy" (56).

So, she remains an exile in France, as much as Australia:

> She had never been theirs, alas. She was not *la petite Australienne*, not even, perhaps, an Australian, except on damp piercing nights at Lunegarde, or in moments of expatriate despair alone in the Paris apartment. Sometimes Dorothy Hunter suspected she existed only in the novels of Balzac and Stendhal and Flaubert, the plays of Racine (54).

Part of her problem, which her mother notices, is her secretive and closed nature:

> Dorothy's absorbed little face was specially designed for locking up accusations. If she let them out, her emotions might get the better of her words; though sometimes she saved them up for a better occasion (101).

But having a more open nature would increase her emotional vulnerability; generally, in relation to others; specifically, in relation to her mother:

> Mrs Hunter thought she detected a masochistic tone of voice; she wondered whether she might take advantage of it (67).

If emotional barriers are key to Dorothy's self-preservation, what self is being preserved? McCulloch reminds us of something important about Dorothy:

> Her need to realize herself, beyond the person her mother has created, is

constant. On her return to Australia she attempts to impress her mother
with her account of her experience within a storm. Her story is interesting
only at the point when she mentions her fellow passengers, a Dutchman,
with the "square, hard looking" hands, who speaks of his experience of a
typhoon at sea.

> For several hours we were thrown and battered—till suddenly calm
> fell—the calmest calm have ever experienced at sea. God had willed us
> to enter the eye—you know about it? the still centre of the storm—
> where we lay at rest—surrounded by hundreds of sea-birds, also
> resting on the water.

This is as close as poor Dorothy will ever be to that central experience.
The actual storm that she experiences is "paltry", and predictably her
account of it is greeted with Mrs Hunter's query "Is that all?" It is also an
opportunity for Elizabeth Hunter to mention her own typhoon experience
which torments Dorothy. "And the cyclone: why was it given to Elizabeth
Hunter to experience the eye of the storm? That too!" Dorothy, in fact, had
left Brumby Island before the typhoon or, as Elizabeth Hunter recalls, she
had run "away from Brumby and storms of her own imagining". Dorothy's
adult life is as sterile as her brother's. She too has experienced an
unsuccessful marriage and, whereas Basil hides from his barrenness within
acting, Dorothy succumbs to the fictional world of dreams, where she
indulges in the explosive release of sexual repression. The only reality in
life Dorothy concedes as an adult is: "that of the past, and more
specifically, her not particularly happy childhood" (123).

Yet there is another reality operating here too. Elizabeth *knew* she was
interfering with Dorothy's potential love interest on Brumby Island,
Edvard Pehl, even though she was not particularly interested in Pehl
herself. Did she, as a 70 year old cougar, poach Pehl from her daughter
simply because she could, as an act of selfish will, to spite Dorothy? Was
this a cultural taboo when the novel was written? Is it still a cultural
taboo? Or, in a world with no morals, are cultural taboos things of the
past?

Not long after the storm, which Pehl fled from as well as Dorothy, we
discover he wrote to Elizabeth during her "slight nervous upset":

> "Why," Sister de Santis noticed, "you haven't read your letter"; it had
> come by the morning delivery, but still lay unopened on the salver. "And
> isn't the stamp unusual. Is it Norwegian?" She could have been trying to
> encourage a patient who threatened to despond.
>
> "Yes. The letter is from a Norwegian," Mrs Hunter admitted, "who
> was in this country recently—an ecologist—by repute an intelligent man—
> but weak, it turned out, and something of a boor." She had begun tearing
> up the still unopened envelope.
>
> "Shouldn't you at least read his letter?" asked Sister de Santis, who
> seldom received one.

Mrs Hunter said no, she wouldn't, and gave the pieces to her nurse to
dispose of.
"One day, Mary, I shall tell you about it" (165).[8]

So, we never discover the contents of Pehl's letter; whether it was
declaring admiration and affection for Elizabeth; or whether it was
expressing remorse for his actions and concern for Dorothy.

Dorothy shows impressive resilience during her visit to Kudgeri,
where she makes herself indispensable: cooking, cleaning, sewing,
befriending Anne and her many children, and nursing Basil when he cuts
his foot in the dam. But here too there is a parallel with the way her
mother made herself useful to the Warmings on Brumby Island before the
storm:

> Madame de Lascabanes stuck to her pans. She often surprised in herself a
> practically mystical attitude towards the ordering of chaos, even in its more
> squalid manifestations. In different circumstances, she might have made a
> devoted and inscrutable *femme de ménage*. Strange that it was her French
> self which abounded in humility, while the Australian in her aspired to be a
> place among the "happy few" (485).

> Dorothy was still too dazed by light to assess the situation. She looked
> beautiful, he thought; almost not his sister.
>   Then the truth struck her. "Oh, darling, what have you done to
> yourself? Ohhhh!"
>   While the Macrory women were flapping their wings ineptly, Dorothy
> Hunter swam across the kitchen, to arrive, to settle herself as her brother's
> feet, and untie the dirty handkerchief. She dipped her head; for a moment
> he thought she was going to put her lips to the wound: they protruded so
> noticeably, and were besides so tremulous.
>   Basil basked.
>   "You're not feverish?" Dorothy cried. "Or are you?' She began
> tenderly exploring, while giving icy orders, which Mrs Macrory and her
> girls were glad to obey." (496–497).

However, each time we are tempted to regard Dorothy as a character with
free will, moral agency, and the ability to change her destiny, White
reminds us of her status as an archetype or trope in his highly determined
literary scheme. Hence the illuminating but disturbing incest scene:

> So she and Basil were comforting each other.
>   Somewhere in the night he rejected their drowsy nakedness. "Do you

---

[8] We ever discover why Elizabeth had a "a slight nervous upset" after the storm, during
which the term "nervous breakdown" was never discussed. Even forces of nature are
subdued now and again.

realize, Dorothy, they probably got us in this bed? Such thoughtless candour poured them back into their separate skins: to turn to ice.

Till she felt she must tear open a darkness which was at the same time stifling her.

This stick women was staggering, tripping, lashed, he could just see, before she reached the curtains and started snatching by handfuls, at last wrenching the window up.

The moon was at its highest and fullest above the ring of mineral hills. Her exertion, and the icy draught from opening the window, flung her back. She might have fallen if he had not been there behind her to support and comfort her nakedness with his own.

"You've got to admit it's beautiful." It was her brother looking over her shoulder at the landscape at "Kudgeri".

"Oh God yes, we know that!" she had to agree; "beautiful—but sterile."

"That's what it isn't, in other circumstances."

"Other circumstances aren't ours."

It rent him to touch with his hand the hair his sister had screwed up in a knob for the night.

She let him lead her back to the bed. It had become an island of frozen ridges and inky craters. They lay huddled together, and he tried to conjure their former illusion of warmth, under a reality of wretched blankets" (526–527).

The incest between Basil and Dorothy is the same as the incest between Waldo and Arthur; it is an incest of archetypes rather than persons. It was mutual comforting. It was also necessary for them to unite in this way, to vanquish or overcome their mother. Who, perhaps as a result, chose to withdraw her will and die on that same night.

From *Flaws in the Glass* we know that, early in his life, White was introduced to the *Myths of Ancient Greece*, which in his mind merely substituted "the gods' adulteries, feuds, and murders for those of the wider-ranging British social system" (33). If we look at the novels of his British contemporaries—particularly Iris Murdoch and Muriel Spark—we see other authors giving their protagonists godlike characteristics for similar but different narrative purposes. Alfred Hunter remains within the human range. Elizabeth, Basil and Dorothy do not. With White, it is always necessary to remember the context in which he writes and his fidelity to that context, philosophically and aesthetically. The Hunter children belong to their mother, in every way, and are never allowed to have independent lives. In this sense, neither of them can ever be free.

Acolytes

There are two strands in *The Eye of the Storm* and the novel gives them equal weight. First, there are Elizabeth Hunter's relationships with her husband, son, and daughter. Second, there are her relationships with her three nurses and one housekeeper–cook who White refers to in religious terms as "acolytes". In the latter case, he was exploring the varieties of western religious experience, albeit in a more attenuated way than *Riders in the Chariot* and *The Solid Mandala*.

Flora Manhood is pagan (like Elizabeth herself), Lotte Lippmann is Jewish, Mary de Santis is half-Catholic and half-Orthodox, and Jessie Badgery, noticeably omitted from Schepisi's film, is Protestant. His exploration of how these characters relate—or fail to relate—to self, world, and other is consistent with his context. Given the complexity of his discourse—and the fact that these characters function as archetypes or tropes—it is easy to understand why Schepisi ignored or downplayed this aspect of the novel. However, we should know this aspect exists, as White was frustrated by our inability to recognize it.

Mary de Santis

Mary de Santis—Mary of the Saints—is described as "probably something of a ritualist" (9); a creature of the night, perhaps an angel, with a transparent veil, under which "the wings of her hair, escaping from beneath the lawn, could not have looked a more solid black" (9). She is associated with a transcendent or other-worldly vision but remains firmly grounded in this world. She is linked with White's concern to explore the unity of matter and spirit, or transcendence grounded in immanence.[9] Her veil is made of lawn, the fine woven linen used for bishop's sleeves. This adds weight to her description as head of the religious hierarchy; an arch-priestess to whom the other acolytes defer (20):

> None of them questioned the efficiency of their superior, while some even sensed an authority of the spirit which gave her deeper access to the heart of the creature round whom they revolved, and to whom they were all, more or less, dedicated (18).

Elizabeth sees Mary as "some kind of—big—*lily*" (10), a symbol of

---

[9] There has been an erroneous assumption, for several generations now, that the "unity of matter and spirit" or "transcendence grounded in immanence" are incompatible with the Christian worldview when in fact they are orthodox beliefs. Neither Judaism nor Christianity is Platonic or Nietzschean. Both religions teach the unity of matter and spirit.

the archetypal feminine, and "the one and the many", which in the Christian imagination can signify chastity, innocence and humility, as well as the eternal cycle which revolves around the incarnation, passion, death, and resurrection of Christ. These images combine with her austere figure and "opulent breasts" (11) to suggest a spiritual motherhood not of the great mother, or of the earth mother, but of the Blessed Virgin Mary.

While Mary grew up in a mixed Roman Catholic and Orthodox household, she has evolved her own religion of "perpetual becoming" the other acolytes respect and defer to, even though they detect it to be "odd and reprehensible" (11). Her own religion is practised "in the night hours", when she would "patrol the intenser world of her conviction, to practise not only the disciplines of her professed vocation, but the rituals of her secret faith" (12). In the night Mary is transformed, and "floated, unassisted, whether up or down" throughout the house and garden because, for her, the night is comfortable:

> Doubts seldom arose at night, because love and usage will invest the most material house with numinous forms and purposes, from amongst which an initiate's thoughts will soar like multi-coloured invocations (16).

But the morning light:

> sprang at the high priestess, stripping her of the illusions of her office, the night thoughts, speculations of a mystical turn few had ever guessed at ...
> In her daytime form, Mary de Santis of thumping bust and pronounced calves, might have been headed for basketball (14).

More than the other acolytes, Mary embodies the tension of Christian mystical experience: between matter and spirit. Her life becomes a tension of what theologians call "unrealized eschatology"; a tension between the "now" and the "not-yet"; between her confinement within the material world and her experience of a spiritual world.[10] At first glance, this tension links her with the Hellenic metaphors, and their myths of tragic hero and exiled soul, but White does not think about Mary in that way. In the Ricoeurean sense, her myth is adamic and her metaphors are Hebraic.

In this imaginative world of myth and metaphor, Mary de Santis experiences guilt when forced to reflect on her lust. In the darkness and silence—as she experiences the numinous through ritual and mystery—she also experiences the torment of her desire of Sir Basil, and anger as

---

[10] In theology, unsolved or unsolvable problems tend to be consigned to the eschaton: that is, to what will be revealed at the end of time on the Day of Judgment. While this technique can be criticized—by those who want answers to all their questions in the here and now—it simply recognizes that some things are only known in faith.

she realizes she is of the flesh. Other characters are not afflicted in this way. Her response is characteristic of her myth. In sensual torment, Mary sits in a chair, enclosed by sights and smells that conjure her past and present, mingling her conscious with her unconscious: images of white lilies, of plants engaging in frottage to point of orgasm, images of smelling and sucking, because her lust for Sir Basil is proscribed by parental injunction: "*You mustn't touch the basil Maro Papa has planted*" (174).

The darkness and silence of night—the same night that brings ritual and mystery—also brings her need of penitence and mortification. To atone for the sin of being human, Mary would do housework to lighten the disabled cleaner's load. Yet:

> If Sister de Santis genuinely wished to compensate the cleaner for some of the injustices suffered by her, she was not unaware that her acts of charity could also be sly attempts to lighten her own darkness through a discipline of drudgery (207).

The austere monastic symbolism of Mary's floor-scrubbing and the language White uses to describe it, is characteristic of her alone:

> By the time Mary de Santis, still plodding on all fours, backed into the scullery, her shoulders had begun to ache, her knees were numbed, the glory had gone out of penance. She saw herself as the eternal novice, muddling around the narrow cell, thrown back off its walls whenever she blundered in the wrong direction; yet her attempts, like any of her other bursts of desperate clumsiness, would be registered as experience in the eyes of innocents (207).

Her excursions into mortification do make her pure enough to enter the garden in search for something she wants to find there: roses.

These roses are a symbol of perfection, unity and wholeness that Mary would like to give to Mrs Hunter. Yet Mrs Hunter already owns and possesses them, and the symbol of perfection also has thorns. The garden is a place where Mary is subject to the exigencies of life as she totters on heels among showers of dew with thorns gashing her. In this outside world of nature Mary is reminded of her materiality and her mortality. Only the roses bring her the temporary reminder of what she wants to believe in: a perfect spiritual realm beyond the real material world:

> the light translated the heap of passive roseflesh back into dew, light, pure colour. It might have saddened her to think her own dichotomy of earthbound flesh and aspiring spirit could never be resolved so logically if footsteps along the pavement had not begun breaking into her trance of roses (209).

Mary has an image of herself as mixture of "earthbound flesh and aspiring spirit". She offers the roses to Mrs Hunter, but the same rose-trance will not work on her mistress, for in the sick room: "the roses sparkled drowsed brooded leaped flaunting their earthbound flesh in an honourably failed attempt to convey the ultimate" (211).

Mary intends to confront Sir Basil with the moral issue of putting his mother in a nursing home. The dynamics of their meeting are a mixture of attraction and repulsion as Mary struggles with her desire to relate to him on a idealistic level that sublimates what were once her carnal feelings for him. She arrives unannounced at his hotel. Because he is unoccupied, and probably lonely, he buys her a couple of martinis before suggesting lunch at Watson's Bay. Their lunch becomes an uncomfortable date that highlights the clash of their mythical and metaphorical affinities.

Sir Basil has embraced the world of acting, its myth of the tragic hero, and all the aesthetic illusions around it, as a way of masking his true self. However, as there is nothing to his character except the actor, even the off-stage Basil Hunter is nothing but a series of disguises and personae that he slips on and off like a wardrobe. He is unhappy being with Mary and "would have recoiled from touching this statue of a goddess" (348). Why? Because she is much more comfortable with the real world than he is. This has something to do with her myth and its metaphors.

This is obvious during their lunch at Watson's Bay, as Sir Basil is confronted by the putrefying carcass of a dog "something black drenched swollen and obscene rolling slightly in imitation of life" (352). The dead dog is a "a not-too-well pickled Labrador" whose body causes "a sick stench" to rise "out of the natural smells of salt and weed". For Sir Basil it is "the ultimate in filth" and "barbarism". His myth cannot imagine that death and putrefaction are part of the lifecycle, or that, in a narrative schema in which dog is often God "turned round",[11] filth, barbarism, death and decay are all aspects of the divine nature. Thus he leaves the table in a "somnambulant condition", presumably to go to the toilet, to escape reality, to attempt a cathartic voiding, of vomit or diarrhoea; traits of White's Hellenized characters who fear the irrational.

However, Mary's imagination allows her to respond differently to the reality of the moment:

> Unlike Sir Basil, Sister de Santis was not immediately shocked by the drowned dog; she was more passive of course, and less articulate; while

---

[11] White uses the Dog–God palindrome to great effect in "A Cheery Soul" in *The Burnt Ones* (1964). At the end of that short story, Miss Docker "saw for the first time" that dog is "God turned round" (180).

> most of her life she had been personally, though objectively, involved with
> the physical aspects of death. Till now a nameless anguish began seeping,
> and she put her handkerchief to her mouth, to stanch it. She could do
> nothing about the smell: this continued penetrating, and would probably
> haunt her nostrils, cling to her clothes forever, or the gelatinous sockets
> where the dog's eyes had been: they were staring at her so intently they
> gave the mask of a live expression (353).

A moment later Mary realizes that the dog has been strangled by wire,
whether by accident or by human agency. Yet she does not, like Sir Basil,
turn and run away from this reality, rather she is able to sit "staring a
lifetime at the strangled dog", for her myth gives her an affinity with the
forces that control the world.

Mary's ability to accept, rather than deny, reality is neither morbid nor
idealistic. Her myth keeps her more in touch with the pulses and rhythms
of the real world than Sister Badgery or the Hunter children. Perhaps this
is why, at the end of the novel, she is the only living acolyte in the house.
Roaming through it "her veins, her heart, were throbbing with life as she
went from room to room throwing open the windows".

The novel closes with Mary performing "her rites" of planting seeds in
the garden, seeds that are to grow in a "prism of dew and light" that "she
could not ward off: it was by now too solid, too possessive; herself
possessed" (608). Shortly after this, she went back into the house:

> In the hall she bowed her head, amazed and not a little frightened by what
> she saw in Elizabeth Hunter's looking glass" (608).

Perhaps this frightened amazement is Mary's sense of the numinous,
her sense of the appalling strangeness of a divine power that she
apprehends and participates in. It becomes a sense of "grace"—a word
used often in this novel—that projects Mary into the future. With her
apprehension of this strange thing called "grace", Mary de Santis
continues White's tradition of closing most of his novels with a character
whose background—in an explicit or implicit way—is associated with the
Christian imagination. These Christian characters are always poised,
waiting to be launched—or perhaps thrown—into their mysterious future.

Jesse Badgery

Just as Mary de Santis is associated with the night-shift, darkness, the
unconscious mind, and mystery, Jessie Badgery is associated with the day-
shift, the conscious mind, and non-mystery. Her character, heavily
influenced by her Protestant and Puritan background, recedes about a third
of the way into the novel, after having been established with as much

detail and apparent design as her Roman Catholic–Orthodox counterpart. Given the structure of the novel, the reader may wonder whether White had originally intended to give equal weight to Badgery's character, in order to compare and contrast the novel's Protestant subtexts with its Orthodox and Catholic subtexts.

Elizabeth Hunter likes Jessie Badgery least of her nurses, perhaps because Sister Badgery represents the "dun coloured journalistic realism" which is the object of White's satire. Hence the colour of her hair that is a "neutral or sludge colour" (304), her habit of "controlling her wind" (599), and her Puritan fear that the tasty foreign food she is suspicious of (but loves to eat) will turn into distasteful flatulence. Of all the acolytes, Badgery is portrayed with the least sympathy, not because she is bad, but because her world view is so bland as to admit of no contrasts of passion, no dark side to her character. Just as she is a creature of the day-shift, so her even temper, her reasonable world view, and her Puritan fear of mystery, the irrational, and the unconscious, all combine to separate her from the ken of the other acolytes. Flora Manhood, Lotte Lippmann and Mary de Santis, who all participate in the "blood-myth" of the pagan, Jewish and Catholic–Orthodox experience which the reformed Badgery does not, and perhaps cannot, by the logic of her myth.

The logic of this myth is established at the opening of the novel as the reader learns that Elizabeth Hunter "hates" Jessie Badgery because the nurse is bossy and talks too much. Catholic–Orthodox de Santis suggests that Badgery is kind and practical because "you have to be in the daytime" (10). Immediately a link is established, Catholic–Orthodox de Santis with the mysteries of the unconscious night and Badgery with the non-mysteries of the conscious day. Later that morning she enters Mrs Hunter's bedroom with the breakfast tray; reminding the family solicitor "of a white leghorn: inquisitive, ostentatiously industrious, silly, easily outraged" (40). The Puritan Badgery does not approve of drink or cosmetics. She tells Mrs Hunter "in all my life nothing but good soap and water ever touched my face" (41). Her father was an engineer in the State public service and all her brothers are public servants, "two of them elders of the Presbyterian Church" (42). Badgery had a very strict upbringing and tells the reader "even when I started my nurse's training at P.A., my father expected a full account of my leisure activities" (42).

Whatever her religious outlook, Jessie Badgery remains associated with the Reformation and has a lifelong antipathy to things Catholic. Whatever her inner feelings, she "would never be caught out in a popish act" and would "deflect the wrath of her forebears" by displays of "down-to-earth professional skill"; certainly "she did not believe in saints, not, at any rate, those Roman Catholic ones: ugh!" (43). As Badgery is obviously not attractive to men, perhaps because of her passionless sensibility, she was forced to join what White calls the Fishing Fleet: "the Australian women who went up to cast their net in Ceylon waters" (44). She netted an older man who died soon after their marriage, and during her long widowhood she speaks of him constantly, as if they had been together for years.

In her world, emotions, especially irrational ones, are unfortunate accidents, thus on the arrival of Dorothy Hunter, the Princesse de Lascabanes, to visit her mother: "Sister Badgery had hurried to the bedside to disengage her patient from a too emotional embrace; intent on professional duties, her least concern was a princess" (50). In this daylight world she represents the Protestant marriage to the neoclassical Enlightenment, setting her apart from and contextualizing her relationship with the other acolytes.[12] She relishes eating Mrs Lippmann's food, but otherwise she regards the Jewess as having a "civilized monkey's face" that combines with Lotte's solecisms to rouse Badgery's scorn, in what is essentially "a scorn for all foreigners" (81).

When confronted with the affinity of joy and laughter that pagan Flora shares with Jewish Lotte, Jessie senses she is an outsider and notes "What's all these jokes I'm not in on?" (81). Likewise, when the Jewess becomes morbid, mysterious and elliptical Flora empathizes but Jessie does not. Badgery "did not like it at all when the housekeeper carried on like this; Sister Manhood, on the other hand, sat with her elbows on the table, her face in her hands, and felt she was experiencing life" (82). When Lotte reminds them of the horror of the Holocaust, Flora cries for human suffering "while Sister Badgery was wondering how she might slip away and release the cucumber seeds trapped under her denture" (83).

In Jessie's world Flora's emotional reaction has nothing to do with creature-feeling but "overdoing it". Indeed, Jessie suggests the Flora's only problem is not getting her "proper quota of sleep". From this well-ordered world of rational explanation Badgery looks upon the relationship between the pagan and Jewish characters and:

> sucked her teeth in sympathy or disapproval, and by doing so, managed to work out several of the pointed cucumber seeds; after which success, and the rich meal, she meditated, 'We've all of us got our job;' and swallowed the seeds (83).

---

[12] Within romantic hermeneutics, it is axiomatic but erroneous to hold the Reformation responsible for the Enlightenment, capitalism, romanticism, and the birth of the modern world. For a history of the unforeseen consequences of the Reformation, see Gregory's *The Unintended Reformation: How a religious revolution secularized society* (2012).

For Jesse there is no Holocaust to remember, it might as well never have happened. In her world there is only the Protestant work ethic, the Cartesian *cogito ergo sum*, and solipsism.

Mrs Hunter dies and leaves Jessie a legacy of $500. Over another of Lotte's meals, the only fruit of "foreignness" she simultaneously objects to and enjoys, Jessie tries to jolly along Lotte and Mary who are depressed by the loss of the object of their devotions. Jessie does not seem to be depressed, and speaks with great enthusiasm of a trip she is soon to take with the proceeds from her legacy. The fact that she is so out of touch with, or needs to deny the validity of, the emotions of her colleagues is part of her horizon. This heightens the irony when she admits to having "intuitions":

> "In fact, if I wasn't a nurse—but I wouldn't give up nursing, not for worlds—I often think I might offer my services to the police. I am always right." Laughter exposed almost the whole of the pale gums before the mouth closed abruptly; she might have overdone it, owning to psychic powers in front of a colleague (601).

Yet Jessie presses on, oblivious of the mood around her, dominated by a horizon that offers nothing beyond justifying having cream with her torte.

Jessie's world is a shallow one, even when the other three acolytes have been affected by Mrs Hunter's death, she does not want to explore the emotions this death has engendered. She rises from the table and asks de Santis to make her farewells to Lotte:

> Now that she had eaten her meal, Sister Badgery had to go: to a former patient become a friend. "Say goodbye to Mrs Lippmann, dear. I can see it's one of her moody days."
>
> The day itself was moody. Sister Badgery was thankful she had brought her brolly. Already as she opened it, big cold drops were falling out of purple clouds.
>
> "Oops!" she called as she went clicketing down the path. "Shall I make it?"
>
> She would not have stayed on though, not for anything, in that ownerless house. Spooky too. She thought of the cosy chats she would have with her friend Win Huxtable inside the coach as the New Zealand scenery went whizzing past: scenery, like silence, depressed Sister Badgery (605).

So Jessie Badgery leaves the novel, like so many other characters in White who, in their denial of their emotional centre, are consigned to a purgatory of shallow sociability. Badgery is to spend the rest of her life chatting, to avoid looking at the scenery of life which, like silence, would otherwise force her to engage with reality.

Flora Manhood

Compared with Mrs Hunter's relationships with her other "acolytes", her relationship with Flora Manhood is unique. She sees aspects of herself in Flora she does not see in the other acolytes. Like most of White's wilful matriarchs, she wants to establish Flora within the same symbolic order that allowed her to exercise so much archetypal power. That does not mean she is grooming Flora to be another version of herself. She is too self-aware to want that.

As mentioned in Chapter One, Elizabeth's marriage to Alfred Hunter was unsuccessful, as a marriage between nature and civilization, although Elizabeth regrets this, as much as nature is capable of regret, and redeems herself while nursing Alfred as he dies from cancer. Flora is being courted by the chemist Col Pardoe—a trope for logos who reads books and listens to classical music, neither of which her mythos understands—and she resents his desire to possess her. Although Elizabeth keeps her motives hidden, she wants Flora to marry Col, to demonstrate that a marriage between nature–mythos and civilization–logos can be successful, even if hers has failed.

Flora bursts into the novel like a sun, "too radiant to be dispossessed", while her perspex earrings "cunningly gyrated, and a pattern of great suns on her pretence of a dress dazzled the beholder with their cerise and purple, particularly just off centre from the breasts" (80). These reds and purples are the colours of passion and divinity. The image of light reflecting through her earrings onto her red and purple dress, and around her breasts, draws attention to her archetypal significance. Flora is "by moments something of an anarchist" (81), which links her with the myths of chaos and creation, and also with the irrational mind. She nibbles Lotte Lippmann's ear, making the Jewess laugh, and establishing the same archetypal affinity Mary and Mordecai share in *Riders in the Chariot* and Arthur and Dulcie share in *The Solid Mandala*. However, while Flora and Lotte share feelings, Flora is more self-centred.

Flora's dilemma is established early in the novel: "when you are *involved* with somebody—and can't make up your mind how deep" (83). Col wants to possess her because he believes he understands her and can give her the kind of language, form, and order she does not have. Indeed, her whole access to logos–civilization is through Col Pardoe. Without Col's horizon Flora, like Elizabeth Hunter, is focused on a more timeless realm where "two minutes can encompass aeons of rot: that was something you couldn't explain to human beings who measured time by the clock" (84). This timeless realm is thought to be "natural" and mystical, according to romantic logic, thus Flora's scent is "wych-hazel", a scent Col associates with her: "one of the sweet natural smells just what I'd expect of you Flo" (106). In this timeless realm Flora's first instinct is to resist myths that do not belong to her. She wants to "contemplate her own body" and live in a world focused upon "rich, yummy food; sleep; cosmetics; making love; not making love" (84). This gives her an "animal presence" Elizabeth Hunter's mind "craves the farther the body shrivels into skin and bone" (85).

Flora is not really interested in her job. She does not see it as a "vocation", as a calling, in the way Lotte Lippmann and Mary de Santis see their jobs. Even Jesse Badgery, locked in the straightjacket of her Puritan ideology, still manages to associate her nursing career with a system of belief. This lack of altruism is not a judgement against Flora's character, it is merely noticing a function of her character as a trope. Her main preoccupation is how to avoid, how to run away from, the relentlessly compelling, absorbing and masculine world of logos–civilization:

> But even as she ran, he (or some other) would be running after, waving his thing to bludgeon her into childbirth and endless domestic slavery. So there was no escaping: on the one hand it was snotty noses, nappies and a man's weight to increase your body's exhaustion; on the other, it was rubbing backs (grinding your knuckles into the unsuspecting tissue-paper skin) and wiping the shit off sick or senile bottoms. She wished she was a plant or something (86).

If she were a plant, Flora could stop being frightened of "the way the old witch could plug into your thoughts" (86) and stop being frustrated by what Col called her "intellectual deficiencies" for "she had never hoped, never wanted to be, clever, only to live, to know contentment, if she could discover what that was" (86).

Like Pluto, who carried off Proserpine into the underworld, so Col carries Flora off to Noammura (no + amour = no love). It is a place of no signposts and of "old neglected orchards" (108). On the journey there, Flora is lulled for the "warmth, the sound of the road, had drugged her" (108), and perhaps also she is lulled by the smoke from Col's pipe. The effect created is one of Flora being carried off into a dream world.

At Noammurra nature apparently conspires with Col's libido as he prepares to make love to Flora in this place of no love. To Flora this appears, at first glance, to be the possessiveness of a man she calls her "lover-tyrant" (112). But in fact her consent has been given: "She was part of the plan his fingers had worked out scientifically, and which, finally, was their plan. He only tore one button from where it was rooted in his pants" (112). They copulate, and as she is brought to her climax she "began to moan for something else as he drove her deeper and deeper into the yielding mattress of prickling grass", as he tries to impregnate her. In saying "I don't know what's come over us" she is being coy. Col reminds her "That's what we do know, and you won't admit it" (113).

After this Flora and Col partake of a post-coital luncheon of fried eggs, and egg tomatoes, at a place where a waitress mistakes them for a married couple and extols the virtues of marriage and "kiddies" who "make all the difference" (113). Eggs are a symbol of fertility and egg tomatoes are otherwise known as "love apples". These have a singular significance, as Col and Flora devour the fruits of love. Later in the novel the reader learns that Flora is always careful to practice birth control, so in retrospect we know she will not conceive in Noammura.

As they drive home Flora is surrounded by Col's civilized world in his car, his classical music which she cannot understand, the metaphors of his world which make her "feel empty: the paperbacks, the records, knowing what Noammura means" (114), and his displays of physical possession and dominance in putting "a hand between her thighs as though trying to show he owned her". She doesn't throw off his hand because just as she entered Noammura in a dream trance, so leaving it she was "lulled by the road" and returns to the same somnambulant state. On receding from the dreamworld of Noammura, Flora has a dream filled with:

> little children climbing on her lap kneading her breasts dabbling their lashes in her throat crimping her skin into the smiles she wouldn't allow herself to show how much she longed to take their golden cheeks between her teeth to test for love (114).

Like the goddess Kali, Flora is both sides of the pagan imagination. She would bear her children and then want to bite their cheeks to test their love. When she wakes from this dream, she is back in the real world that contains the mixed classical and romantic metaphor of the Hunter mansion. Soon Flora is looking out a window where she "might have slipped the moment before from the attitude of prayer to one of dreaming" (115). Prayer is not part of her myth. Dreaming is. Prayer is associated with civilized religion and:

> whatever else, she wouldn't like to be a nun. Better than anything she would like to be nothing, or a dream through which she let down her hair into the evening like in that opera Col told the long hair her lover tied to a tree and she was caught (115–116).

Flora dreams of being loose yet bound, free yet caught but by "what lover? Someone unknown walking out of the park at dusk, perfect to almost not existing? But wouldn't she be caught? Yes, always!" (115). She wants a knight in shining armour, she wants romance and chivalry, as a way of delivering her from the drudgery of her daily life.

Flora's link with Mrs Hunter is a tactile and cosmetic one, of touching and massaging her body, and of anointing it with make-up from a "vanity case" filled with "jars and cartridges" (117): that is, filled with cosmetics that are also weapons. This process of painting the body becomes Flora's religion, it makes her a distinctive kind of priestess who "had been prepared to give her all on a big feast day" (118) as she prepares the devouring goddess, Elizabeth, with a flowing lilac wig, which Flora drew on:

> reverently enough, over the fretful wisps of unnatural hair and meek patches of scalp. The lilac climax appealed to a religious sense Flora Manhood thought she had discarded outside the weatherboard church down the road from the banana farm: she had wanted a miracle and it wasn't granted; unless, possibly, whenever she assisted at Elizabeth Hunter's resurrection (120).

Elizabeth Hunter is the object of Flora's "desire to worship" something, and according to the logic of her myth this object is a mixture of creation and chaos, of attraction and repulsion, of great beauty and great ugliness, which are both sides of the mystery of life and death:

> In spite of her desire to worship, the younger woman might have been struck with horror if the faintly silvered lids hadn't flickered open on the milkier, blank blue of Elizabeth Hunter's stare. Then, for an instant, one of the rare coruscations occurred, in which the original sapphire buried under the opalescence invited you to shed your spite, sloth, indifference, resentments, along with an old woman's cruelty, greed selfishness. Momentarily at least this fright of an idol became the goddess hidden inside: of life, which you longed for, but hadn't yet dared embrace; of beauty such as you imagined, but had so far failed to grasp (with which Col grappled, you bitterly suspected, somewhere in the interminably agitated depths of music); and finally, of death, which hadn't concerned you, except as something to be tidied away, till now you were faced with the vision of it (121).

Because "Flora's emotions were centred on Flora" (169) she does not want to become involved, practically, emotionally or intellectually, in Mrs Hunter's death. She "simply didn't want the trouble of ringing Doctor and tidying up the body". Her Theogonic horizon makes her live in an absolute and timeless present which places her apart from the myths of tragic hero and exiled soul, both Hellenized metaphors that are non-biblical but have become associated with the Christian imagination over time. She shares this much with the more scriptural imagination of Lotte Lippmann, but Lotte and Flora both cannot see beyond the grave for quite different reasons, Lotte because through the Holocaust she has deconstructed the God of metaphysics, Flora because she never had a metaphysics to deconstruct.

Although Flora often "hated" and "admired" Mrs Hunter simultaneously, and sees her as a mountain Flora could not aspire to climb, she does not feel contempt for Mrs Hunter, for her patient "did at times break through the mists of senility" to give her "a glimpse of something else", glimpses that she hopes are never going to be too frightening a recognition for her. Mrs Hunter is the Theogonic mirror of Flora's own nature. She has apparently solved the dilemmas Flora is still running from. Largely because of her class, Mrs Hunter has already located herself within Col Pardoe's civilization, which did not destroy her identity, whereas Flora is frightened of losing herself in that civilization, frightened by the prospect of cleaning Col's "greasy old grill" while he:

> played Mahler at her, or read out from some intellectual magazine opinions which confirmed his own. Then when you had hung out the damp, stinking towels, and you were what Col like to call "mooded" by the music, he would make "love", he referred to it; and though you too, recognized it as such, you couldn't very well have admitted. Love as she tried, but failed to imagine, couldn't be so easy and cheap, or smelling of mutton fat and sweat (178).

The threat of motherhood makes her panic, as does walking down the suburban street where she lives, to the end of the street "of deadly dolls'-houses, all painted up in emulation of one another, and behind their faces, either suffocating kindliness, or variations on her own theme of chaos" (178–179). Chaos is, after all, a part of her horizon.

In trying to avoid the spectre of Col's metaphysical culture, Flora seeks out Snow Tunks, her lesbian bus conductor cousin. There are signs which suggest Flora had a youthful affair with Snow in a tropical paradise garden setting, and now she is trying to recapture that pre-lapsarian polymorphous innocence, through a relationship she once thought was "the miracle" that was not "vouchsafed" (300).

However, Snow has changed. She is no longer a pre-lapsarian or polymorphous innocent, having fallen into an unattractive mixture of obesity, alcoholism, and promiscuity. In spite of Snow's protestations of undying love, and her offer to share her life with Flora, we discover she is now living life through a gin bottle and a series of brief affairs with femme lesbians who call her "Butch". In the chaos of Snow's flat, Flora has mixed feelings.

On the one hand, Flora sees here a chance to free herself from Col, "she was so glad for what she was hearing, though melancholy in the end that these women should know better than Col" (185). On the other hand, she realizes their desire is to get her "to be the ham in their sandwich" (186). Snow and her current lover, Alix, begin to partake of their ham sandwich and "became more frantic, and would have been united in a single aim if the drink hadn't sided with Flora Manhood" (187). Soon the "half strangled chewed nuzzled Flora recovered enough of her wits to know she did not belong to this community of seething flesh" (187).

Having extricated herself from the bed to the independence of another room that was "delicious" and "unlimited" by comparison, Flora is immediately confronted again with the dilemma of how to escape from Col. Her conscious mind alights on the figure of Sir Basil, as a knight in shining armour, who brings the possibility of soteria. He becomes her next imaginary refuge (or refuge imaginary). Having glimpsed at hell through Snow's window and its view of the "fiery furnace blazing down Botany way" (188), Flora realizes that "she must end by every means the goose chase with Snow and Alix: it was her worst madness to date" (188). She leaves the flat, crosses Anzac Parade, avoids Col's pharmacy, and returns home where she finds a love-note from him. On reading the note:

> Flora Manhood sat a while on the edge of the convertible lounge her trembling fingers shielding her eyes from the gun which was neverendingly inescapably pointed at her (189).

Still fleeing Col's imagined gun and real penis, Flora "thought up her idea" of being saved by Sir Basil. Unconsciously, she is trying to live out her secret longing for a child; a child she is sure she does not want by Col but now believes she wants by Sir Basil. So she goes off the pill before visiting Sir Basil. It is never clear who is seducing whom.

Flora asks for the room to be made dark. She is more comfortable in the dark, and as Sir Basil explores her body she feels herself becoming a mountain, perhaps the same kind of mountain she once imagined Elizabeth Hunter to be (315). Her energies are focused on "this child he was going to give her: the child who would be the embodiment of unselfish love" (315). Driven by the darkness, and her instinctive desire, "now it was she who had become the guiding force. It was this desire to create something tangible, her only means of a self-justification" aimed primarily against Col Pardoe (316). However, as Sir Basil brings her to her climax she can only think of Col, "the getter of her child this pseudo-husband drove the word back into her she had wanted *oh Col Col ohh* she wanted her own flesh her child *ohhhhh*" (316).

Sir Basil is exhausted by their copulation but Flora "felt becalmed rather than calm, let alone fulfilled. There was nothing she needed beyond the certainty—she might even settle for the faint hope—of conceiving" (316). However, she drifts off into a dream in which she confronts her worst fear:

> to find herself walking it could only be with Col Pardoe amongst the green hummocks of Noammura printed up large on a hoarding A NOAM-MURRA WELCOME TO MAN AND WIFE Col if it was his arm seemed pleased to confirm what he already knew (316).

Flora's dilemma of Col is still present. Her illusions about Sir Basil are now shattered, "Flora Manhood did in fact feel unbearably sad", for "here was this strange, not bad, but boring man, unconscious of the part he was playing" (321). Whichever way she looked she could see no end to her dishonesty: a vista of mirrors inside a mirror" (321).

Flora arrives at the Hunter mansion the following morning and "if she looked good to other people, it was, to put it crudely, on account of the friction: there's nothing like the friction of one human skin against another, she had often noticed, for bringing the complexion to life" (314).[13] She hopes Mrs Hunter will not smell Basil on her body, as Elizabeth could previously smell Col Pardoe on Flora, like the buck on the doe (87). She has a cryptic exchange with Mrs Hunter, during which she is never quite sure whether Elizabeth is aware of her liaison with Sir Basil. Elizabeth tries to seal Flora's fate in the symbolic order by giving her a ring for her engagement. Flora is never sure whether Mrs Hunter, through the ring, is trying to arrange a marriage for her son, or whether she is sanctioning the relationship between Col and Flora.

The ring is from her collection of star sapphires. Elizabeth never liked them particularly. She called them "lovely trans-cend-ental" lollies (328). They represent the dominant ideology of the symbolic order into which she was nominally enslaved by her husband, Alfred. In this way Elizabeth hopes to also enslave Flora in the same symbolic order, an order which upholds a transcendent vision. However:

> because she didn't know what "transcendental" meant (she couldn't remember Col ever using the word) Flora Manhood brooded. Or sulked (328).

Elizabeth appears to be offering Flora a choice between the blue sapphire, which "is more intellectual-*spiritual*, compared with lush lollypink". Flora strokes the "lush lollypink" ring, because it is a colour she has greater affinity with, than the intellectual–*spiritual* blue. Flora resists at first, but

---

[13] White uses the phrase "rejuvenated by friction", elsewhere in his work, to speak of the therapeutic aspects of having sex.

she is tempted by the gift: "Since you had allowed the old thing to transfer the pink lolly to your hand, you were growing greedy for it: from certain angles the buried star would come alive" (329).

Later while Lotte is dancing in front of Mrs Hunter, Flora sees them as "a couple of crazy bitches" (544). She opens a window "to let in some air" on the strange dance she cannot see the religious significance of, and then shuts herself in the bathroom to contemplate the dilemma of her possible pregnancy to Sir Basil, her disillusionment, and her inability to govern the forces which seem to control her life. Yet, in this dark hour, while she is "getting a certain amount of enjoyment out of her own post-mortem", Flora begins menstruating, a sign she is not pregnant to Sir Basil after all:

> Her lovely blessed BLOOD oh God o Lord who she didn't believe in but would give her closer attention to as soon as she had the time and as far as she was capable (548).

Flora's relief and joy at this reprieve makes her reassess the rhythm and movement of her life as a woman. Or, as some readers see it, her life as an archetype for one of the myths of western religious experience.

Within minutes of the dance finishing Flora returns to Mrs Hunter and places her on the mahogany commode for the last time. When Flora returns to her patient:

> Mrs Hunter had slipped sideways on her throne while still hooked to the mahogany rails. One buttock, though withered, was made to shine like ivory where the rose brocade was rucked up. The eyes were mooning out through the mask, which was the apex of her acolyte's creative skill (552).

Flora is again confronted with a dilemma. She has fled from Col, Snow, and Sir Basil, now she must flee from the dead Mrs Hunter gazing at her out of the mouth of Elizabeth's and Flora's shared myth. After treating the body "respectfully", in spite of a drunken doctor trying to molest her in the death chamber, she flees the house and has a kind of "dark night of the soul" in Anzac Parade.

While walking towards Kingsford, Flora tells herself, "if you had been wise to yourself at the time you might have joined in Lottie's dance for Mrs Hunter" (568). She comes across a drunken Snow lying in the gutter, crying over the recent break-up of another short-term affair. At first she tries to offer assistance, but realizes she must run away from the scene "to dry her embarrassment, not to say shame: for blokey men, for her drunken dyke cousin, and worst of all, HERSELF" (570). She keeps wandering along the Parade, narrowly missing being run over by a car. She suspects Elizabeth's intervention has saved her. It might be Elizabeth's influence driving her towards Col.

Amid the smell of burning chops, which remind her of the world she always feared being enslaved in, Col admits her to his flat, and to a kitchen table where "she had never wanted so much to sit down and stay sitting" (572). She has arrived at what will be her home:

> amongst the dishes on the table, bacon rind set in waves of fat, lettuce leaves wilted by vinegar dregs, one of Col's books was lying: *Thus Spake, Zarathustra*, whoever he was to sound so certain. She who was plumb ignorant would probably remain so forever (572).

In this intellectual world she will always remain separate and silent, there will always be archetypal differences between Flora and Col, as man and woman, and as tropes for Theogonic nature and Hellenic civilization:

> She would have liked to share with him the joy she had felt when the blood had begun to run between her legs. But would not tell what nobody but herself knew. Unless Mrs Hunter had guessed. Sir Basil Hunter's misconceived, miscarried child would remain a secret: the dishonest touch is sometimes also necessary and harmless.
>
> As sleeplessness can become a virtue of sorts or stocktaking in the bed he hadn't made since when he was all around you though sleeping on the lounge in the other room never properly heard him before sleeping too close in this narrow marriage bed She is knocking on the wood with her sapphire the pink it is yours isn't it the coffin Nurse is where one sows one's last seed I can see it germinating inside you like a lot of little skinned rabbits oh Mrs Hunter how can you be so *unkind* (giggle) always hated obstets but your own flesh is different my children are human we hope Mrs Hunter if the blessed sapphire works (573).

So, Theogonic Flora accepts her fate, armed with one of Elizabeth Hunter's sapphires. It is not the blue intellectual–*spiritual* one but rather the pink one which is a mixture of the transcendent and the immanent.

Lotte Lippmann

Lotte Lippmann is one of four "acolytes" arranged schematically around and giving palliative care to Elizabeth Hunter. Along with Mrs Hunter and her children, each acolyte is given a myth, or a horizon, that suggests the acolyte's metaphorical significance. However, if the drama surrounding the Himmelfarb and the Feinstein families is a benchmark for the Hebraic horizon—or White's sense of it—in what sense is Lotte really "Jewish", compared with Mordecai or Dulcie? Is her Jewishness religious or ethnic? In some senses, following Nietzsche, she embodies the slave mentality he despised.

Lotte shares some characteristics with Mordecai and Dulcie. Like their fathers, her parents were "these liberated Jews who worship scientifically. Medicine you might say, is their religion, their rabbi a physician, when not a psychiatrist" (150). Here again White is a critic of Freud, an "enlightened" secular Jew, who influenced many Jews to abandon—to become "liberated" from—their covenant with the God of Israel.

In her youth, the enlightened and idealistic Lotte became a Tingeltangel cabaret artist and fell in love with a Gentile. This enlightened idealism obscured the real world of fascism and antisemitism unfolding around her in pre-war Germany. She was arrested for having an Aryan lover, but "the boy's family agreed to see her safely delivered into Switzerland—alone—and Mrs Lippmann had accepted for her lover's good" (88). Or perhaps because, as Elizabeth insists, Lotte is "the original masochist" (150). Or perhaps because she is a kind of "suffering servant" (Isaiah 52:13–53:12). Lotte's life experience gives her a desolate appearance that "might have looked more desolate if she had not grown used to carrying a cross of proportions such as no Christian could conceive" (543). This is the cross of antisemitism and the suffering it cause, the cross of Jewish suffering.

Her struggle in the novel is different from theirs. Her pilgrimage around the decaying shrine of the Hunter home is one of constant suffering and affliction through a foot impediment. This adds a penitential dimension to her vocation as Elizabeth Hunter's housekeeper and dancer, a vocation constantly under threat, as Jessie notes:

> Actually, what upsets Mrs Lippmann more than anything is to think she may become so incapacitated she won't be able to dance again for Mrs Hunter (367).

While Elizabeth Hunter is alive she is the human face of God in Lotte's horizon. Cooking and dancing replace worship in fulfilling Lotte's desire to witness to a divine loving-kindness so incomprehensible that—in the face of the Holocaust—it might look like hatred or evil itself. This is what makes her earthly suffering bearable. Without it she has no reason for being because her particular version of Jewish horizon has no sense of an afterlife.[14] Lotte cannot see "beyond the handful of ashes" (169), whether they be the ashes of the Holocaust, or the ashes of Mrs Hunter's death.

Living in a sparse, small room in the Hunter servants' quarters, Lotte is "a grateful soul" who would never "begrudge her services" (222), which she performs for spiritual rather than material reasons. Her lack of materialism allows her to constantly forget her pay cheques: "Money

---

[14] "The Sadducees say there is no resurrection, or angels, or spirit; but the Pharisees believe all these things" (Acts 23:8).

keeps, Mr Wyburd" (274). If her "one fault, her only luxury" (19) is sleeping, she has many psychic needs, including the need to seek and live out the logic of her own myth. Her individuality:

> had always been of secondary importance to her own enslavement; and now, with all her gods brutalized or gone up in smoke, or almost all, where else would she offer up her limbs for shackling (89).

The theme of the "suffering servant" is dominant in the Old Testament. It is an integral part of salvation history. With her parents' enlightenment gods now brutalized and annihilated, Lotte is left with the need to shackle herself in Mrs Hunter's service, and serve her, as a way of serving the God that "died" or concealed himself—whether through the Enlightenment, or the Haskalah, romanticism, science, Freud, the Holocaust—the God she has no language to describe.

In her desire to protect her mistress Lotte can become quite spirited and emotional. She sublimated her anger with the Hunter children for wanting to put their mother in a home, with a nature as fierce as a dragon, "her nostrils would have blown two streams of the fiercest smoke" (82). With similar passion Lotte can accept punishment from her angry mistress, appear to make hell her preferred heaven, as Elizabeth Hunter notes when contemplating a sought-for masochistic punishment for Lotte:

> one mouthful made things worse. But that was what Mrs Lippmann liked. If you had full command of your senses, and your strength, and could order a spectacular *bombe* for a party, and take a sword and slash it just as it was ready to be brought in, Mrs Lippmann would descend into the deepest of her infernal heavens (88).

Like Himmelfarb, Lotte travelled to Australia via what would soon to become the Jewish State of Israel. Also like Himmelfarb, she did not choose to participate in the Zionist experiment. Like Himmelfarb, her life becomes an atonement for the sins of her pseudo-enlightenment, the foolishness of which is revealed to her by the Holocaust and her providential deliverance from it. Lotte's atonement is dominated by four phrases of her credo: "something will always consume: if not the family, then it's the incinerators" (22), "My art was a tiny, satiric one—to find what in all things is ridiculous—and all things are ridiculous if you look" (82), "there is no desecration where there is love" (150), and "I do not see why I should fear what I have already always known" (448). This belief system contains much of what is distinctive about the Jewish horizon, with its rabbinic method of interpreting life, love and text.

While Lotte might always appear to be a secular Jew, in the narrative schema of this novel, she is also a rabbinic interpreter par excellence. We see this through the way she radically deconstructs her own horizon, through her ability to process her life experience, and through the logic that allows her to live her life the way she feels she must. As a rabbinic interpreter, she also functions as a fool,[15] as McCulloch suggests:

> Lotte Lippmann exists within the symbolic framework as a pseudo-Shakespearean fool. She is the fool who speaks the truth, which she knows not by ratiocination but by inspired intuition. Like Lear's fool, Lotte Lippmann is portrayed as a licensed critic who sees and speaks the real truth about people about her. Lotte is the first of Elizabeth Hunter's attendants to identify Basil and Dorothy as "murderers". Flora Manhood recognizes that Lotte has a grasp on a kind of truth that eludes others and suspects that it is Lotte who had the power to free her from her present predicament of an ill-fated non-pregnancy. Her enjoyment of living, "shackled" to the mortality of Elizabeth Hunter, involves a deeper insight and keener criticism of the nature of human pain and human "beatitude". As a pseudo-fool to a pseudo-Lear character she attends the attempted "beatification" of Elizabeth Hunter and causes Basil, a shadow of his Lear-mother, to take, if only momentarily, account of his pain.
> Like the Shakespearean fool, Lotte Lippmann falls outside the average person's expectation of normal rational behaviour, but her supposed "defects" are transformed into a source of delight. She is referred to as being "foreign and out of the running", "an old clown", and she reminds Flora of a "golliwog money box on a nursery mantelpiece". Nevertheless, Flora, upon seeing Lotte's dancing outfit, is unsure whether laughter is an appropriate response, as Lotte suggests both the "tragic" and the "funny" simultaneously. When Flora angrily accuses her of letting Elizabeth Hunter push her around and making a fool of her, Lotte replies: "She is making no fool, this is what I am." Lear's fool sees that when the match between the good and the evil is played by the intellect alone, it must end in a stalemate, but when the heart joins in the game the decision is immediate and final. "I will Tarry, the fool will stay—and let the wise men fly." This is the unambiguous wisdom of the madman who sees the truth (127).

Like Mrs Feinstein, Lotte lives to cook and feed others, initiated into this archetypal Jewish function, not by her mother, but by some "fat Swiss always smelling of the kitchen" (150), after her flight from pseudo-enlightenment had begun; at the same time, perhaps, as her parents died in the Holocaust. Unlike Mrs Himmelfarb and Mrs Feinstein, Lotte is childless and without a family to focus her energies upon, so these energies are lavished upon the other inhabitants of the Hunter home, reminding them always of her distinctive personality and horizon. She

---

[15] For an excellent discussion on the role of the fool in art—including in *King Lear*—see "The Fool", Chapter 11 of Harry Eiss's *The Joker* (2016).

does not blame anyone else for her condition, it is a fact of history, but it is an event rather than a process she feels involved in—and responsible for—hence her feelings of guilt and need for atonement.

Lotte explains her cooking in terms of creativity, as an atonement for, her "destructive" career as an artist, a career which aspires to acting the kinds of drama incompatible with the logic of her myth, a career which "ended in the gas ofens —the smoke from the Jews" (82):

> So now I cook. That too is an art—a creative one, I tell myself—though I should be doing it in some huddle of Jews—all together mortifying ourselves and remembering the smoke from the incinerators of Germany (83).

Her observation is as much a rabbinic commentary on the 20th-century Jewish condition as it is an existential remark made by a lost soul. Is soteria through cooking more tangible than soteria through art or faith?

The Jewish journey in *Riders in the Chariot* moves Mordecai Himmelfarb from his pseudo-enlightened position as a middle-class literary academic to a shack in Sarsaparilla and his humble job at Brighta Bicycle Lamps. The Jewish journey in *The Solid Mandala* moves Dulcie Feinstein from the pseudo-enlightened metaphor of Mount Pleasant to the medieval fortress of exclusive, protective Kabbalistic mysticism in Centennial Park. The Jewish journey in *The Eye of the Storm* moves Lotte from a rational and pseudo-enlightened belief in her tiny satirical art—her Tingeltangel—to servitude as Mrs Hunter's housekeeper, living humbly in the servants' quarters. Hence Lotte's truthful, but mysterious and cryptic comment to Sir Basil Hunter:

> "Cooks! Actresses! No one is all-important, unless the great artists: Mozart, Goethe, Bernhardt—Sir Basil Hunter!" Her rather Jewish compliment had him wincing; or did she intend it as a side swipe? "If I could choose—if I could begin again—I would ask to create one *whole* human being" (148).

This is one of Lotte's rabbinic riddles; a cryptic commentary on why she cannot aspire to idea of soteria through art; the aspiration of Sir Basil's horizon, with its aesthetic myths of tragic deliverance and imaginary catharsis.

Lotte needs to perform a different kind of "necessary" theatre that strives imperfectly to express her holistic vision (148), a theatre of the absurd, of the clown, of drunkenness, which aspires to be translated out-of-self, which is necessary for the complete deconstruction of self, through an atonement for her parents' delusions, and through a need to remember what the Holocaust reveals to her about the divine and human natures. She is led to dance the grotesqueness and foolishness of this mystery as a means of trying *"to create another being out of my own body"* (149).

Among the other acolytes, Lotte has an affinity with the Theogonic Flora, with whom she laughs, sings, touches, and relates in a manner absent from her relationship with the Christian acolytes. Flora "nibbled at the housekeeper's unresisting ear" (81) and they share a sense of humour that makes Jessie complain, "what's all these jokes I'm not in on?" (81). It is Lotte who several times calls Flora "Floradora", the adoration of nature. Such affinities are reminiscent of Himmelfarb's relationship with Mary Hare and Mrs Feinstein's relationship with Arthur Brown.

Flora becomes self-conscious when she is apprehended by Lotte's gaze,[16] "Something in Lotte Lippmann's eyes pierced an unhappiness at Flora Manhood's core so that it squirmed" (440). This gaze combines with Lotte's dance, forcing "inklings of transcendence" (442) to wash over Flora's consciousness and confront her conscience: "now, thanks to this crazy Jewess, she was again troubled" (442) when "like every good Australian, she must continue to believe only in the now which you can see and touch" (443).

Mrs Hunter is similarly affected by Lotte's presence, her "smile, her eyes, suggested a slight fever as she lay looking inwards at an image possibly invoked by Lotte Lippmann's song and dance: was it herself?" (445). While dancing, Lotte is armed with ammunition of white roses (446), a Kabbalistic symbol of the sun and the infinite but harmonious diversities of nature emanating from the tree of life. This makes Lotte a kind of reflection, or Kabbalistic spark, smiling "at her satellites" as she seeks to dance her way into, gather herself into, re-integrate herself with the sun Mrs Hunter represents: "I have only to learn to re-enter and I shall be accepted" (446).

Lotte fails to achieve this, for unity and re-integration are, according to the adamic myth, not possible by human agency alone. Because of this failure, Lotte loses control of her emotions, her "voice tore itself out by the roots and lashed the air with an excruciating scream" (446). So Lotte's song and dance, and any holistic revelation it might imagine, gives way to physical repulsion and embarrassment. When Lotte rushes upon her benefactress with "convulsive lips fastening themselves on the back of her

---

[16] Beginning with Sartre, the terms "gaze" has had many theoretical meanings attached to it, which have enlarged over time. Lacan theorized "the gaze" as part of the mirror stage within the symbolic order. Since then, it has become a typical manoeuvre within intersectional theory. Foucault theorized the medical and other power-tainted gazes. Feminists theorize the male gaze. Post-colonialists theorize the imperial gaze. Queer theorists theorize the queer gaze.

hands" (447), her mistress is appalled and sends her servant away.

Yet Lotte returns to dance before Mrs Hunter again, in the presence of Flora Manhood, who "had never taken part in a mystery before". During this rite, with all its dimensions of comedy and parody, Elizabeth Hunter expects or hopes for some kind of revelation to occur:

> Now surely, at the end of your life, you can expect to be shown the inconceivable something you have always, it seems, been looking for. Though why you should expect it through the person of a steamy, devoted, often tiresome Jewess standing on one leg the other side of a veil of water (which is all the human vision amounts to) you could not have explained. Unless because you are both human, and consequently, flawed (544).

This final dance is different to the rest, as Mrs Hunter seems to participate in it, and seems to spur Lotte on.

Flora calls this mock mystery the antics of "a couple of crazy bitches" (544). She tries to clear the air by opening a window, Lotte and Elizabeth again try to fuse their horizons through the dance, by which Elizabeth is given a childhood recollection where "the past is so much clearer than the purblind present. Every pore of it" (545). She wrestles with this revelation. She "fought the dance by which she was possessed", as it draws her into remembering a childhood experience of the strangeness or loving-kindness; a memory blocked out of her consciousness is now re-awakened by Lotte's horizon with its similar understanding of passibility as an attribute of the God of loving-kindness:

> You don't at first re-live the tenderness: it's the lashing, the slashes, and near murder. So Elizabeth Hunter moaned. Like a stricken cow lying on its side (545).

Lotte, too, is possessed by her dance. She is driven on by Mrs Hunter, her hair undone, her dress falling apart, dancing for "no apparent reason", but for a function and purpose, as a "ceremony of exorcism" (547) in which Mrs Hunter was both spectator and participant. Lotte finally collapses before her and pants, "What more do you expect from me?" (547). She is sent away by the forbidding and angry goddess who dismisses her coldly, "Nothing. Go! You're hurting. I don't feel like being touched"; an untouchable divinity who rejects her: "Send my nurse to me, I want to relieve myself" (547). In the narrative, Elizabeth is about to withdraw her will and relieve herself of life.

Lotte senses Mrs Hunter's death before she is told, "you need not tell me. The whole house already knows" (561), and its effect upon her is described in graphic and lengthy detail. She has put a towel over her mirror. Her identity has been destroyed. She can no longer bear looking at her reflection. Her self-understanding cannot exist without Elizabeth as the human face of a God with whom she can be an atoning suffering servant. In her grief the distinctly Jewish images of sackcloth and ashes are present; her face "the colour of damp ashes (561); her dress rent by a "wilful, passionate rending, downwards from the yoke" (562). Soon Lotte declares: "I shall be with friends" (606).

Lotte does join her friends—in death—and her suicide is performed with all the signs and symbols of the Holocaust around her, "the heater, with its permanent smell of gas and flames roaring", and the sky outside her bathroom "was more convincingly on fire, the blaze smudged by chimneys of smoke" viewed from her "suffocating" narrow maid's bathroom (606). As she slit her wrists they "were winking at her: all this time her fate had been knotted in her wrists" (607). As she floats in the water her eyes are shut, but "if she cared to look" she would be "faced with a flush of roses, of increasing crimson" (607). The white rose—a symbol of perfection and wholeness offered to others during her dance (607)—gives way to the red roseblood of the *nefesh* now flowing out of her. So Lotte Lippmann dies, soaked in her own blood, along with the human and divine blood myths.

FUTURE DIRECTIONS

In an ideal world, following the pioneering lead of Heltay 1983, and Hewitt 2002, White's work would be approached as the literary equivalent of romantic, modernist, and postmodernist art and be viewed in relation to the art of his predecessors, contemporaries, and successors. Regrettably, we do not live in this ideal world.

At the height of his career, many regarded Patrick White as a literary giant with extraordinary perception. He was welcomed as Australia's only Nobel Laureate for Literature until J.M. Coetzee emigrated from South Africa with his Nobel. Australian high school students were once taught him. The novel was usually *The Tree of Man*. At some point, however, the legend of a great literary giant was displaced by the myth of a nasty old queen, after which Australians were free to cut him down to size, while blaming him for doing so. In Australia, lopping tall poppies is a cultural virtue, a widely-accepted means of cultural participation.

White's reputation has suffered from a combination of events: the trough that often follows a writer's death, the general decline in serious reading, the influence of third-wave feminism and intersectional theory, the rise of identity and advocacy politics, the censoring of the ideas of high art or great tradition or secular canon, his suddenly unfashionable whiteness, and a general sense that—like most authors of the past—he does not matter. He disappeared from the curriculum around the same time, and for the same reasons, as Lawrence and other dead white males. He has become a casualty of what Dutschke calls the Long March Through the Institutions and what Bloom calls the School of Resentment.

The literary–cultural theory supporting all of this has had an extraordinarily powerful influence across the humanities and throughout the social sciences. Most critical methodologies in these disciplines now depend upon structuralist and/or poststructuralist assumptions about the nexus between language, worldview, and power. There is no intrinsic problem with this. Structuralism and poststructuralism have made important contributions to human knowledge. This book actively promotes the structuralist and poststructuralist aspects of White's rhetoric (content) which are inseparable from his aesthetic (form). Yet the academic relevance of structuralism and poststructuralism can never be taken for granted. When defining and defending a critical methodology, their relevance needs to be renegotiated each time they are invoked or used.

In the 20th century, the fault line among White's critics was between the minority who were sympathetic to what he was trying to achieve and the majority who were challenged by it for a broad range of reasons. In the 21st century, the fault line is more between the minority who approach him on his terms and the majority who use him as a screen upon which to project a range of critical agendas that have little or nothing to do with him or his work.

Until relatively recently, the most effective way of neutralizing White as an artist was arguing that his literary vision was false, illusory, weird, or sick. Those who attempted this neutralizing wanted us to know that going on the journey White invited his readers to go on was neither sensible nor wholesome. Their proudest achievement, apparently, was to have seen through and exposed him.

Tacey 1989 measured White's performances against a no longer influential Jungian system, only to find that his failures all pointed to a homosexuality-induced dread of the Great Mother. Following Tacey's lead, During 1996 diagnosed White as suffering from a "double Oedipus relation", as if one was not enough. In her essay "Patrick White's Götterdämmerung" (*Quadrant* 1973; XVII(3); 8–19), Kramer accused White of pointing to "a wordless revelation at the heart of which meaning might be found" (9). Apparently, his betrayal of her intellectual, artistic, or moral standards was an affront to rationalism's self-evident good sense.

Green's less-cited critique of Kramer's essay, "The Edge of Error" (*Quadrant* 1973; XVII(5–6); 36–47), argues that, in her Götterdämmerung essay, Kramer effectively disqualifies herself as a serious White critic. Green begins with the declaration:

> It is both strange and saddening to think that Professor Leonie Kramer's article on Patrick White in the May–June 1973 number of *Quadrant* could have been written and published contemporaneously with Bronowski's Reith Lectures, *The Ascent of Man*, and W.K. Hancock's Boyer Lectures 1973. It is sadder still that she should have chosen *Riders in the Chariot* as the main target of her attack, for it anticipates Bronowski's final argument by twelve years and there is a marked affinity in outlook between the novelist and the scientist. It is disturbing to find a literary critic still preoccupied with the faded problems of Victorian rationalists when theologians and scientists have long left them behind (36).

The key observation here is "faded problems of Victorian rationalists". The idea of White's irrationality is common in negative criticism of his work.

One of the more mischievous assertions of rationalist White criticism is that he lacked self-awareness and, as a result, he was never in control of his literary vision. This is nonsense. Few authors were more self-aware and in control:

> Where I have gone wrong in life is in believing that total sincerity is compatible with human intercourse. Manoly, I think, believes sincerity must yield to circumstance without necessarily becoming tainted with cynicism. His sense of reality is governed by a pureness of heart which I lack. My pursuit of razor-blade truth has made me a slasher. Not that I don't love and venerate in several senses—before all, pureness of heart and trustfulness (White 1981, 155).

As Paglia suggests in the Introduction to *Glittering Images* (2012):

> The only road to freedom is self-education in art. Art is not a luxury for any advanced civilization; it is a necessity, without which creative intelligence will wither and die … History shows that, for both individuals and nations, political power is transient. Politicians and partisans of both the Right and the Left must recognize that art too is a voice of liberty, requiring nurture without intrusion. Art unites the spiritual and material realms. In an age of alluring, magical machines, a society that forgets art risks losing its soul (xviii).

In the present populist environment, where the humanities are increasingly market-driven, ideology-driven, theory-driven, and casualized, it is difficult to promote White's relevance. Literature Departments are no longer powerful, prestigious places. Nowadays, semiotic controls are manipulated by frustrated gatekeepers fighting over their ever-diminishing slice of the academic cake.

What does the future of White criticism look like? Is it an example of herd mentality or group-think? An overview of the monographs and anthologies published since his death shows that postcolonial approaches occupy a large space, queer theory approaches are occupying increasingly more space, and metaphysical approaches are occupying increasingly less space. Clearly, the majority of White's critics are participating in the Long March and many of them belong to the School of Resentment. Clearly, I favour the metaphysical approach, which I believe meets White on his own territory, but that approach has long since lost its primacy, is hard to do well, and is not without risks.

In May 2014 I went to a performance of Mark Langham's new play *Amanda*. During the first scene I recognized the storyline and predicted how it would unfold. The central character—Amanda—had red-hair. She was dressed as a little girl—and hence infantilized—although she was an adult, an inmate of an asylum. Each scene was aimed at creating a mystery around her identity: whether she had free will, whether she was a victim, whether patriarchy had oppressed her, or whether she was an oppressor herself. Other characters represented that patriarchy. There was an impotent male priest representing oppressive religion. Other characters represented the oppressive medical establishment. The play ended suddenly. The question of Amanda's identity was unresolved. She had to remain a mystery because—more to the point—Langham had obviously exhausted the intellectual limits of his story.

To someone like myself, trained in 19th and 20th century literature, Langham was simply repackaging the rhetoric of prior generations for a new audience and presenting it as if it was original and, more than that, as if it was still relevant. I have no idea whether he is aware of the logos–mythos dialectic and how it has been performed in philosophy and aesthetics since and perhaps before Plato. While that may not be the point, it raises the questions: How did he arrive at his terms of discourse? How does any author arrive at his or her terms of discourse?

As Spark says, socially-conscious art (such as *Amanda*) can be brilliantly done, or it can be badly done, but the victim–oppressor rhetoric does not work anymore (Spark 1970, 77–82). This presents us with a problem, since Spark worked with the same rhetoric herself, although she cleverly adapted it in each of her novels to keep it relevant. White and his other contemporaries including Murdoch, Golding, and Davies also worked with variations of the same rhetoric. To me, the critical questions are, how this rhetoric relates to the human-condition novels of the middle-to-late 20th century and whether this rhetoric is still relevant to us in the 21st century.

Ultimately, it is a question of whether the various Platonic, Nietzschean, Heideggerian, Freudian, and Jungian prisms, as they have appeared in the arts, are still relevant to the arts, or whether the arts should be doing something else. Also, as far as this book is concerned, there is the ongoing relevance of Gadamer and Ricoeur to consider, since I believe Gadamer and Ricoeur frame the broader 19th and 20th century post-Kantian context. I do not offer this book's version of the metaphysical approach as the only one—or as better than anyone else's—I simply offer it as the approach that resonates in my mind, although I do believe it is closer to whatever White had in mind. Of course, many will argue that whatever White had in mind is irrelevant. After Roland Barthes warned us against making too much of the author's intention, and proclaimed the author's death—within the same critical tradition that Nietzsche proclaimed God's death—the pendulum has swung heavily towards reader response.

This brings us to the larger question of literature's function, relevance, and interpretation. The question "How should this text be interpreted?" is simply an extension of the question "Why should this text be read?" Surely the author's intention ought to figure somewhere within the hermeneutical circle. Surely reader response does not mean the reader is the sole arbitrator of meaning and can impose upon the text any meaning he or she wishes. Surely all literature academics who "teach the conflicts", or hope to teach them in the future, need to contextualize their own scholarly formation: those influential attempts to form our minds and influence our different approaches to literature. This is too large a subject to cover here. A good place to begin is Gardner's attack on Kermode in *In Defence of the Imagination* (1982), his droll reply in *On Being an Enemy of Humanity* (1991), and Crews's witty overviews of the current state of academia: *The Pooh Perplex* (1963) and *Postmodern Pooh* (2001).

Hewitt 2002 makes the point that *The Vivisector* was written "during the tail end of Sydney abstract expressionism", when the novel's romantic–modernist description of the nexus between painting and religious experience was becoming passé (83). Coetzee 2008 makes the point that *The Vivisector* was thus fated to be an elegy not only to the school of painting represented by Duffield but also to the school of writing represented by White himself (xix). McMahon 2010 suggests *The Twyborn Affair* was his "theatricalized and over-determined farewell to the novel" (77). Each of these observations is moot. Clearly, White was aware of movements within art and trends within literature. He adapted accordingly. That was his strength.

This book has chosen a small frame, limited to White's middle or religious period. Something was happening in these four novels—written in the 12 years leading up to the Nobel Prize—absent from the novels before *Riders in the Chariot* and after *The Eye of the Storm*. This something is rhetorical (related to content) rather than aesthetic (related to form), although form and content always reinforce each other and are inseparable (Randisi 1991, 18).

I have argued that, in these novels, White investigated the varieties of western religious experience as he understood them. Further, I believe he did this, perhaps unconsciously, within a Gadamerian frame described in *Truth and Method*, which he populated, also perhaps unconsciously, with a Ricoeurean anthropology described in *The Symbolism of Evil*. Further, I may be the only scholar with an interest in placing White in dialogue with Benedict XVI.

I do this because both men are central to an ongoing debate that is often said to define western civilization. They are opposite sides of the same metaphysical coin. Both are committed to evaluating the nature of logos as reason or rationality. As far as I can see, there is an obvious rightness about noticing White's persuasive post-Kantian context, which is more focused on mythos, and an equally obvious rightness about noticing Benedict's persuasive pre-Kantian critique of that context, which is more focused on logos. Admittedly, in White studies, this is a road less travelled. In the current literary and cultural climate, there are as many obstacles to promoting the rhetoric of the emeritus pope as there are promoting the rhetoric of White's novels.

I am comfortable generalizing these two contexts—the one post-Kantian, the other pre-Kantian—because Kant is widely thought to represent one of the great turning points in western self-understanding, for better and for worse. A dialogue between Benedict and White is a necessary focus for White studies and perhaps for the humanities and social sciences more generally. Perhaps placing the logos–philosopher Benedict in conversation with the mythos–poet White on the subject of reason–logos—its definition, its meaning, its scope, its limits—is the highest compliment those who take White seriously can pay him.

Some will dismiss Benedict as simply offering a latter-day version of the Church's former stance against modernism. Some will dismiss White as simply offering a latter-day version of modernism's former stance against classical telos. Both men are more nuanced than that. As they are opposite sides of an "old quarrel", which is still with us, any conversation between them would force us to reconsider—or consider for the first time—the foundational assumptions on which a lot of literary criticism is predicated.

This is not simply a matter of theorizing the text—to elicit meanings the text may or may not sanction—it is contextualizing the text in its historical moment. Whether that historical moment is relevant to our historical moment is a matter for separate reflection. It is not relevant to the contextualizing itself.

The Australian Broadcasting Corporation has a website called "Why Bother with Patrick White"—www.abc.net.au/arts/white—but why single out White for such a hypothetical question? Why not ask a broader question: Why bother with literature at all? If literature is important, how do we judge what literature is worthy of serious study and what literature should be taken less seriously? Judgments about texts are made all the time. My judgment tells me Benedict and White are important to western self-understanding. I know this is unfashionable. I also know my judgment does not in itself establish White's relevance.

In his Regensburg Lecture, Benedict admits that, in the reaction against the alleged intellectualism of Augustine and Aquinas, there arose with Duns Scotus a voluntarism which would gradually, post-Kant, undermine the rapprochement between reason and revelation. Benedict never meant this to be a criticism of Duns Scotus himself, or of the Protestant Reformers, or even of Kant, although in limiting reason to the practical sphere Kant went, or allowed his descendents to go, in a direction the Reformers could not have foreseen.

Is this observation relevant to White studies? I believe it is. Eventually, everything returns to the question: What do we mean by reason and rationality? In the Introduction, I pointed out that the terms reason or rationality, or their many variants, have never been defined objectively. Instead they are invoked as universal or self-evident givens. They are usually waved around like a fetish, or pointed like a witch-doctor's bone, at anyone westerners disagree with.

I stand by this generalization because my experience tells me it is true. However, if these terms have never been defined—objectively—there have always been descriptions of the different subjective traditions that seek to define and assert reason, which inform an ongoing conflict between contested rationalities. The best description of these traditions, which begin with Heraclitus and Homer and continue in the present, can be found in MacIntyre's *Whose Justice? Which Rationality?* (1988), the sequel to *After Virtue* (1981), and the predecessor of *Dependent Rational Animals* (1999).

In *Whose Justice? Which Rationality* MacIntyre tells us the Enlightenment was ostensibly about reason yet there is no consensus about what this means:

> In [*After Virtue*] I concluded both that "we still, in spite of the efforts of three centuries of moral philosophy and one of sociology, lack any coherent rationally defensible statement of a liberal individualist point of view" and that "the Aristotelian tradition can be restated in a way that restores rationality and intelligibility to our own moral and social attitudes and commitments" (ix).

Within modernism and postmodernism, there was an overarching concern to conduct what is essentially a Left-inspired immanent or emancipatory critique of classical metaphysics and its correspondence and coherence theories of knowledge and truth. One of the foundational Death-of-God assumptions we are habituated to—whether we realize it or not—is that all analogical theories of transcendence are illusory, and therefore false, especially if they come from Plato (Deleuze 1993), or from the Church, or if they take correspondence or coherence theories seriously (DiCenso 1991). This is a baseline assumption of contemporary literary–critical theory, whether the theorist is willing to acknowledge it or not.

Among religious theorists, an error-prone "Scotus story" emerged in a postmodern movement known as "Radical Orthodoxy". In his review of Horan 2014, MacDougall 2015 summarizes the Scotus story thus:

> Radical Orthodox theologians maintain that Thomas Aquinas's (1224–1274) analogical approach to God-talk preserved the prevailing Neoplatonic participatory metaphysics. In Aquinas, the contingent being of finite entities is held to derive from its direct, analogical relation to the non-contingent Being who is God. In this relationship, "being" must be understood equivocally, as the finite being of created entities and the infinite being of God are utterly different. By contrast, Radical Orthodox theologians maintain, Scotus's assertion that such an analogy only works if finite being and infinite Being are understood univocally as being the same kind (and so can be perceived as being authentically and reliably related), though crucially differentiated, is an illegitimate equation of finite creature's being with God's being. This makes finite being the same as and independent of divine Being in a way that was never asserted previously. Scotus's univocal idea of being, they claim, permitted the conception of a till-then unknown space standing apart from the divine, a realm that came to be called "the secular." Radical Orthodoxy's Scotus story thus positions Scotus as the anti-Aquinas, the first philosopher to separate metaphysics and theology and, because of this, as the figure who paved the way for modernity and postmodernity. This, they argue, places Scotus at the head of an intellectual line that led eventually to Nietzsche, Heidegger, Derrida, and the various nihilisms of postmodernism. Radical Orthodoxy's overall effort is aimed at defeating the line of thinking that Scotus initiated and at undoing the "secular" world they believe it legitimates (344).

In the book reviewed, *Postmodernity and Univocity* (2014), Horan argues this Scotus story is fatally wrong and undermines the movement's attempt to rescue orthodoxy from secularism. Horan says Scotus "is not a theological puppet" conveniently serving the interests of those contemporary thinkers who need a simple genealogical starting point for the emergence of modernity, or secularism, or an ontological romantic or post-romantic understanding of "being". The danger is in the "trickle down" effect of the Scotus story, which seeks credibility and academic veracity by endless repetition:

> To put it simply, the more people repeat the story and the more hegemonic it becomes, the harder it is to convince others that it is untrue. Fortunately, repeating something does not magically make something true when it isn't, but it can be difficult to speak the truth or challenge the ubiquitous Scotus story or present an alternative narrative when so many have blindly repeated what has been handed on to them about the subtle doctor.

Horan concludes his book by reminding us that:

> Scotus does not reject analogy as such but convincingly argues from the

vantage point of a logician, that a univocal concept of some sort is axiomatically necessary to maintain any analogical discourse. ... Scotus's starting point is not ontological, but epistemological and semantic. His primary concern is the correlative project that arises from the issue of natural knowledge of God, not establishing or "flattening" an ontological order that would place God and creatures under some genus *being*.[1] Finally, the doctrine of univocity is only comprehensible within the context of Scotus's entire system, which takes for granted the formal distinction and Scotus's unique principle of individuation, among other things. To lose sight of the integrated whole of the subtle doctor's project, or to misundersand any element of this incredibly nuanced system, will inevitably result in a misreading or inacurate interpretation.

This background—about how the Scotus story was invented and has been repeated—helps to explain the work of Radical Orthodoxy's secular, non-binary counterparts, such as Deleuze, who use Scotus as a puppet to further their anti-Platonic critiques.

We know that, perhaps in an unconscious way, White participated in the immanent or emancipatory critique of transcendence. That much is obvious. But he was never attached to the ideological or political agenda that goes with it. He was never a member of the Frankfurt School, or of the intellectual Left, even if he shared some of their philosophical and aesthetic concerns. Although Deleuze illuminates some of White's modernist context, he was not Deleuzean.

White's belief in a creator God who can make mistakes—a God who made us, and we got out of hand, like Frankenstein's monster—comes from Mary Shelley's reworking of the Prometheus myth, not from univocity or Scotus or Deleuze. As Benedict points out, the claim that God is free to change his mind, and do the opposite of what he has done, posits a voluntarism that allows for a capricious or fickle God who can change his mind and undo what he has done. The idea that God's freedom does not bind him to his word—or to truth and goodness—renders his covenants with humanity, on Sinai and in Christ, meaningless and undermines the idea of humanity as an authentic mirror of God. This is why our understanding of logos requires consensus. This is why the west needs a conversation between Benedict and White.

In the 20th century, White studies rarely rose above the binary of cheering

---

[1] Does God defy all attempts to anthropomorphize him in humanity's image? If God is not within the genus *being* then is he within any genus? How does that affect God's position in the Trinity, in relation to Jesus as both fully human and fully divine? For a challenging postmodern discussion of this topic see Marion's *God Without Being* (1991).

him on or tearing him down. Beginning with *Patrick White: A Critical Symposium* (Shepherd and Singh, 1978)—still one of the best anthologies of White essays—we see a tendency among some of his critics to identify his supposed flaws and insist upon his ultimate failure. The logic of this tendency is hard to locate. Do failed authors really win Nobel Prizes? Or is finding fault the first resort of lazy thinking, an example of critical poverty? Is it not counterintuitive to hold a conference about, present papers about, or write books and articles about, a failed author who, by some accident, was awarded Nobel Prize for Literature?

My own view is that in spite of the lofty insights of Morley and Beatson from the 1970s—which go far in demonstrating the ways in which White's literary vision either falls within Jewish–Christian orthodoxy or is not opposed to it—White criticism really begins with McCulloch's *The Tragic Vision* (1983). While I do not agree with everything McCulloch proposes—for reasons given in Chapter Five—she has a keen hermeneutical eye. Her reading of White shows us how the parts relate to the whole and vice versa. She believes in close reading and provides us with a baseline—a point of reference—to branch out from. She is particularly useful to those of us who wish to focus on the text, and contextualize its historicized and historicizing rhetoric, rather than impose a literary–critical theory or sociopolitical agenda upon it.

As White's work is greater than the sum of its parts, the worst a critic can do is focus on one influence and offer it as a master key. He was too clever for that. He always was and always will be several steps ahead of us. His ability to weave his way through an extraordinary range of influences is what makes his work extraordinary. So his context matters more than the individual influences that contribute to the context.

McCulloch does seem to focus on Nietzsche but never claims Nietzsche as a master key to White. Rather, Nietzsche is more of a conduit to access White's broader romantic, modernist, and postmodernist context. From Nietzsche we can trace our way back to Winckelmann, to the blessings and curses of Germany's classical and romantic reconstructions of ancient Greece (Butler 1935; Williamson 2004). From Nietzsche we can also trace our way forward to Freud, Jung, Spengler, Heidegger, and Lacan.

Perhaps we should stop there. Why? Like the majority of westerners, White was a binary thinker. He made distinctions between categories. It is therefore important to notice the many influential binaries within his kaleidoscope. Since Lacan, binary thinking has been challenged by a range of ephemeral, marxist, non-binary thinkers who have attempted to replace binary thought with populist critiques of any object-based metaphysics.

They insist upon an increasingly vague desire for immanence driven by an increasingly vague disdain towards transcendence. This destabilizing yet influential post-Kantian context, always hostile toward Plato's realm of Forms and Ideas, tends to assume, as Nietzsche assumed, that Christianity is a form of Platonism. This kind of thinking is dated and false, except among the political–cultural Left. It has become irrelevant to White studies particularly and to western philosophy and aesthetics generally.

I hope this book demonstrates that assessments of and judgments upon White and his work tend to be assessments of and judgments upon 200 years of western philosophy and aesthetics, roughly between Austen and Atwood. I believe how we feel about White is a measure of how we feel about ourselves as individuals, a community, a nation, and a civilization. White was perhaps the first great Australian author to identify and critique the narrative of colonizer and colonized. No Australian did it better than he did. That his frame is so large it absorbs all critical obsessions, without being exhausted by them, is truly epic.

White was never able, in his novels, to realize his vision of God. He was not alone in that regard. The idea that God cannot be fully represented in art, because the fullness of God is beyond art, is a fundamental Judaeo-Christian principle (Exodus 33:17–33; Acts 17:22–24). If he was never able to realize God in art, he believed God was there somewhere in the shadows. Faith *knows* God. Theology (theo + logos = words about God) describes that knowledge. Notice how, with the introduction of the term theology, we inevitably return to the "old quarrel" between philosophy and poetry. And if Whitehead is right, and we are still writing footnotes to Plato, we are also still writing footnotes to the Bible.

In White's experience of life, and the "world", Manoly was his tangible experience of God. Manoly kept him on track, and grounded, which allowed him to create great literature. White admitted this dependence regularly, in public and in private, here from *Flaws*:

> My inklings of God's presence are interwoven with my love of the one human being who never fails me. This is why I fall short in my love of human beings in general. There are too many travesties of an ideal I am still foolish enough to expect after a lifetime's experience, and knowledge of myself (145).

For White, God existed because Manoly existed. God loved him because Manoly loved him. His theology never needed to be more complex than that.

So, Manoly must be part of any dialogue MacIntyre moderates between Benedict and White. As an Orthodox Christian, Manoly's role would be limited to that of an observer, as the Orthodox never experienced an equivalent of the Enlightenment or the blessings and curses of the post-Kantian critique of logos. Therefore, the Orthodox do not have to resolve the problems the west has created around this term.

Let the dialogue begin.

APPENDIX

This book is not only about the four novels of White's middle or religious period. It is an attempt to make sense of their place within the literature once regarded as essential to the high school and university curricula. For many reasons, much if not most of this literature has disappeared from the curricula and what remains is no longer taught or studied the same way. This is because those who now design these curricula have other agendas and face different constraints. Along with the rest of the world, Australia has changed and keeps changing; however, because Australians are a historicized people—individually and collectively—remembering the texts of the past and interpreting their contexts is vital to understanding the present and anticipating the future.

I was introduced to White's novels in the 1980s as part of a once-typical English major: The British and Commonwealth novel "from the romantics to the present". The boundaries of this major—which take for granted that the romantics were an influential turning point—have influenced the way I interpret him and the other authors discussed in this book. The tutor who marked most of my undergraduate essays made similar comments on each essay, regardless of whether the essay topic was Jane Austen, Ruth Prawer Jhabvala, or any other 19th and 20th century novelist taught in the major: "This novel", she always wrote in the margin, "explores the tension between the neoclassical and romantic imaginaries." This persistent reinforcement, which borders on monomania, may explain my obsession with situating modern and postmodern literatures in relation to neoclassical and romantic literatures.

Iris Murdoch

Iris Murdoch was a philosopher as well as a novelist. Her philosophy has been called Platonic Freudianism. This makes sense, as Freud adapted Plato's model of the mind to suit his psychoanalytical theories, and the ongoing relevance of those theories depends on the ongoing relevance of Plato's model of the mind. She believed it was difficult for a philosophical novelist such as her to be "purely existential" and still "keep her head", which is why she worked with mythical backgrounds.

In *The Bell* (1958), for example, she gave each of her protagonists a horizon, which allowed her to explore "the whole question of what human nature most truly is". The ways in which these horizons relate, or fail to relate, represent the ways in which classical metaphysics continued to frame the human condition and its existential dilemma in the postwar period.

The novel is a series of frames within frames, through which Murdoch conducts her rhetoric. The first frame is, of course, the novel's beginning and end, which show the protagonist entering the story in one state and leaving it in another. In understanding how this first frame functions, notice the similarities as well as the differences between the heroes of *The Bell* and *Middlemarch*. As both the eponymous Dora Greenfield and the eponymous Dorothea Brooke must come to terms with classical metaphysics in their different ways, *The Bell* can usefully be understood as *Middlemarch* with a Freudian makeover.

The young Dorothea is in an agape-driven thrall to her sexless and passively-dominant husband, Casaubon; not only to his person but to the ideas he represents. Those ideas belong to Scholasticism and are therefore grounded in classical metaphysics, making them part of the mythology Eliot believes Dorothea must overcome because, to her at least, it is as sterile and futile as Casaubon's search for the "key to all mythologies." Casaubon dies early in *Middlemarch*, leaving Dorothea a rich widow, but his legacy is entailed and she can only keep it as long as she remains, as it were, a kind of virgin martyr to his Scholasticism. According to Eliot, Dorothea's dilemma is resolved, to a degree, when she meets Ladislaw; however, in giving up Casaubon's influential legacy to marry the insouciant and insubstantial Ladislaw, Dorothea becomes poorer financially as well as philosophically.

The young Dora is in an eros-driven thrall to her sexual and aggressively-dominant husband, Paul; not only to his person but to the ideas he represents. Those ideas belong to his career as an art historian, which can usefully be compared and contrasted with Casaubon's scholastic career. The novel begins with a nervous, bumbling, and insecure Dora travelling from London to Imber, a play on umber (shades) or umbra (shadows), where she is to visit Paul while he studies Imber's antiquities. Dora is an on-again off-again wife and art student, unable to complete her studies because she is always in a state of angst and chaos and cannot apply herself.

This is because Murdoch invests her Dora with the pathologies Freud diagnosed in his Dora. It is implied that these pathologies are the result of classical metaphysics oppressing Dora's pagan spirit; a spirit which Murdoch regards as a force of nature. According to Murdoch, Dora cannot come to terms with the conscious dilemma of Paul until she comes to terms with the unconscious dilemma of Imber. Each reader must decide whether this argument—so influential in the 20th century—is still relevant in the 21st century.

The second frame is what confronts Dora on her arrival at Imber, a Court and an Abbey, two architectural symbols dominating the landscape, which combine to form the horizon of classical metaphysics. Within Gadamerian hermeneutics, the decaying Court and its Greek façade represent an Enlightenment horizon of reason (logos) while the restored Abbey and its Norman tower represent an older horizon of pre-Enlightenment feeling (mythos). Under the sign of logos, the Court is the site of a fledgling attempt to establish an Anglican lay community. Under the sign of mythos, the Abbey is the site of an enclosed order of Anglican Benedictine nuns, established in a Tractarian spirit that, according to Gadamerian logic, seeks to restore the mythos that logos has erased.

The Court and Abbey are separated by a lake, the surface of which represents the divide between the conscious and unconscious minds. The inhabitants of the Court reach the Abbey by gliding across the lake. They do not swim and are therefore not in touch with the unconscious. Dora cannot swim either, which means she also is not in touch with the unconscious. Fortunately, at least one of the nuns at the Abbey can swim and is therefore in touch with the unconscious. At one point, this allows her to save Dora from drowning in the lake (of the unconscious).

The third frame is within the Court itself. Two ethical or moral horizons, which Anglicans hold in creative tension, are given to the two authority figures dominating the Court. The first authority figure, Michael Meade, is an effete, tired, weedy man who inherited the decaying Court from his family. Michael has a teleological horizon which appeals to natural law and uses reason to reflect on nature and what is "natural". This is how he believes the good life ought to be pursued. The second authority figure, James Tayper Pace, is a muscular Christian who has made a name for himself doing good works with the poor in the East End. James has a deontological horizon which appeals to the law of divine command and uses reason to reflect on scriptural revelation in order to arrive at a sense of duty, obligation, and commitment. This is how he believes the good life ought to be pursued.

Michael preaches the teleological horizon timidly, in a sermon at the beginning of Chapter 16, where he equivocally proposes that pursuing the good life requires one to "have some conception of one's capacities," to "know oneself sufficiently," and to "study carefully how best to use such strength as one has." James preaches the deontological horizon confidently, in a sermon at the beginning of Chapter 9, where he unequivocally asserts that pursuing the good life requires one to "live without any image of oneself" and simply obey the deposit of the faith. The novel is dedicated to disabusing Michael of his teleological horizon. The novel does not attempt to disabuse James of his deontological horizon. It is beyond Murdoch's power to do that.

The central action of the novel revolves around the first and second frames as interdependent constituents of Dora's conscious and unconscious minds. The third frame is a sub-frame within the second frame. There are other sub-frames as well: a fourth frame, the antithetical but symbiotic twins, Catherine and Nick Fawley; a fifth frame, the story of how an old bell is found and a new bell is lost; a sixth frame, the antithetical relationship of Michael and Dora who combine to represent a range of other dichotomies including: neoclassicism and romanticism, rationality and irrationality, logos and mythos, civilization and nature, conscious and unconscious, and apollonian and dionysian, etc.

The fourth frame, the twins Catherine and Nick, can be understood in many dichotomous ways: good and evil, pure reason and pure feeling, ego and id, etc. forth. Catherine is a good, beautiful, and saintly lay companion, living at the Court prior to being accepted by the Abbey as a novice. She can swim but not well. She is afraid of water and often dreams of drowning. When her brother sabotages her novitiate, physically and metaphysically, Catherine suddenly goes mad and enters the lake between the Court and the Abbey in an attempt to drown herself.

Dora tries to save Catherine but as she cannot swim she ends up nearly drowning herself; however, the two are saved by Mother Clare, the aquatically proficient Abbess. When Catherine regains consciousness she immediately seeks comfort in the arms of Michael, whereupon it becomes obvious to those gazing at her dripping body, and to the reader, that her vocation has concealed a sublimated desire for him. She is soon dispatched to London where she is treated for paranoid schizophrenia. Notice how this pattern fits the literary definition of "madness" as opposed to mental illness.[1]

Nick physically resembles Catherine but is her metaphysical opposite, being a trope for a destructive Byronic passion; a troubled troublemaker whose only service to the community at the Court is using his rifle to slaughter the fauna threatening its crops. As a youth, Nick had considerable beauty, was clever and impertinent, and was always at the centre of loves and hates. At that time, as Michael's student, Nick

---

[1] Byatt, who has studied and written about Murdoch's novels, follows this pattern in *The Virgin in the Garden* (1978). Red-haired mythos, Marcus, goes "mad" under the Platonic influence of homosexual logos, Lucas.

admitted to loving his twin sister with "a Byronic passion". He also tried to seduce Michael with what Murdoch calls a radiant desire "to beseech and to dominate." Michael had resolved to keep the relationship nonsexual, knowing his reputation was at risk. However, when Nick realized the relationship was not going to develop according to his Byronic will, he went to the headmaster and "contrived to give the impression that much more had happened than had in fact happened, and also seemed to have hinted that it was Michael who had led him unwillingly into an adventure which he did not understand and from which he had throughout been anxious to escape." Michael's teaching career is therefore ruined by Nick.

Many years later the brooding, self-destructive, Byronic Nick follows his sister Catherine to Imber, where he eventually becomes Michael's nemesis, and ensures the Court's lay religious community folds, before turning his rifle on himself and committing suicide. While at Imber, Nick seeks Michael's attention, in a pent-up passive–aggressive manner, which Michael avoids by keeping his distance and otherwise erecting a barrier between them. Towards the end of the novel, Murdoch places the idea in Michael's mind that he actually "loves" Nick, on taking note of what Mother Clare once told him as his spiritual counsellor: "all our failings are ultimately failures in love." Michael hopes that "some good" might come of trying to "love" Nick, in an agape sense. According to Murdoch, however, Michael's conscious agape sublimates an unconscious eros, which will be his undoing, precisely because she determines it will.

Indeed, it would appear Murdoch's intention is to shoot down every passing agape with a canon of eros she reserves specifically for that purpose. Like any Platonic Freudian she must invest any and every text with a sexual subtext. As Michael gives Nick no rational reason to destroy him again—apart from maintaining healthy boundaries and refusing to become physically involved with him—Nick uses another young man visiting the Court, the impressionable Toby Gashe, as a tool to fulfil his irrational desire to destroy Michael's religious dreams. Murdoch ensures Nick is successful, since the logic of her novel depends on it. Michael ultimately realizes Nick's "revenge," in forcing Toby to play the part Nick himself played 13 years earlier, could not have been "more perfect":

> Toby had been his understudy indeed. Michael had hoped to save Nick. But Nick had merely ruined him a second time and in precisely the same way.

The fifth frame, the two bells, is a further device through which Murdoch weaves together her critique of the Enlightenment and Dora's existential dilemma. On the same day Catherine is going to be admitted to the Abbey as a novice, the Court is going to present the Abbey with a new bell among great ceremony and episcopal blessing. The old bell, named Gabriel (God's messenger) is lost and has a medieval legend attached to it: an anonymous and faithless nun once broke her vows with a young man; the bishop of the day called upon the anonymous nun to confess her infidelity; when no confession was forthcoming he put a curse on the Abbey, whereupon the bell "flew like a bird out of the tower and fell into the lake." As an art historian, Paul has unearthed a medieval story about the old bell, which he has only told to Dora and Catherine. The old bell sometimes rings at the bottom of the lake. Hearing it "portends a death."

Toby discovers the old bell by accident, buried at the bottom of the lake, and confides his find to Dora, who has heard the story of the bell from Paul. She is "suddenly filled with the uneasy elation of one to whom great power has been given" which she "does not yet know how to use." She instinctively feels recovering the old bell is important to recovering her identity, and to resolving her unease with Imber, but she cannot express why or how, intellectually. With Toby to help her, Dora feels she can "do anything," as if "by the sheer force of her own will she could make the great bell rise"; in "her own fashion, she would fight"; in "this holy community she would play the witch."

Under the cover of night, with heroic effort, Toby raises the bell for Dora, and in the process he makes an important transition from being a "sorcerer's apprentice" to becoming a "medieval knight" who sighs and suffers for a medieval lady "whom he has scarcely seen and will never possess." When the bell is raised, Toby and Dora are awed by its size and notice the Latin inscription on it: *Vox ego sum Amoris. Gabriel vocor* (I am the voice of love. I am called Gabriel). Toby and Dora immediately fall into a passionate embrace, and, struggling together, roll into the mouth of the bell causing the clapper to strike violently against its side. Two things happen as a result: first, a muted boom is sent echoing across the lake, which has profound consequences for Dora and Imber, as hearing the bell portends a death; second, according to Murdoch's Platonic–Freudian logic, the natural influence of Dora's mythos rescues impressionable Toby from the unnatural influence of Michael's logos.

From this point onwards, Dora moves from "playing the witch" to feeling herself a priestess "dedicated" to a kind of pagan rite. She hatches a scheme with Toby to exchange the two bells; when the new bell is unveiled the old bell will be in its place and Imber will be given a much needed shock. Dora is unable to carry out this plan, and instead she visits the old bell the night before new bell is due to be blessed. While gazing at the old bell, Dora realizes that while she imagined herself to be its master, and able to "make it her plaything," it is now "mastering her and would have its will." Using all her strength, Dora manages to fling herself rhythmically against the old bell, with an urgent need to make it ring out: "The thunderous noise continued, bellowing out in a voice that had been silent for centuries that some great thing [perhaps some *Weltanschauung*] was newly returning to the world." From miles around, crowds come to the barn, where the astonished pagan priestess Dora is "almost annihilated" by the effort of her bell ringing and the wondrous effect it is having.

When considered against the broader logic the novel proposes, the new bell, under the Court's sign of logos, cannot be an authentic messenger for the Abbey. Murdoch suggests a pre-Enlightenment wholeness about the old bell, under the Abbey's sign of mythos, which the new bell cannot match because it belongs to the Enlightenment and must bear the full weight of her critique of the Enlightenment. Accordingly, Murdoch ensures that Nick sabotages the causeway, across which the new bell and Catherine are due to enter the Abbey the following day. As the bell and novice process over the causeway, it gives way, the new bell falls into the lake, and the postulant follows after it in her sudden, narratively convenient madness. Murdoch's image of the submerged Catherine has something of Millais' *Ophelia* (1851–1852) about it, which now seems camp, but perhaps the image is meant to be more serious than it really is.

The turning point in Dora's existential dilemma occurs at the geographical centre of the novel, during one of its shapely turns, when she flees from the combined oppression of Paul's bullying and Imber's imaginaries. She travels to London where she seeks refuge in the arms of an acquaintance, Noel Spens. On arrival at Noel's "modern" flat in Brompton Road, Dora takes a luxurious bath while Noel mixes cocktails, prepares a cosmopolitan lunch, and plays rhythm and blues on the record player. While they are having cocktails, Noel lectures her about Paul being jealous of her "creative powers", as Paul "can't create anything himself", and he is therefore determined Dora will not become the kind of creator he cannot be. Noel's most powerful harangue, however, is reserved not for Paul but for Imber, as he implores Dora to not "give in to them" and to never forget that "what they believe just isn't true"; "no good comes in the end of untrue beliefs": "there is no God."

The phone rings while Noel dashes out to buy a bottle of wine. Dora picks it up only to hear Paul's voice. She is silent, not wishing to admit her whereabouts, and in this silence she hears a blackbird calling in the background of Imber. The sound of the blackbird has a powerful effect on her. She puts the handset back on its receiver and realizes that here, too, in

Noel's "modern" flat, "she was being organized" through the "dreary apparatus" of his seduction. A newly awakened Dora is not happy with this seduction, any more than she is with Paul's persecution, because in Murdoch's terms Noel is No + El: to the Judeo-Christian, no God; to the ancient Greeks, no gods or no Good. Noel represents the existential alternative to there being no classical metaphysics: no logos of Court, no mythos of Abbey. He wants to destroy everything they represent and hopes, after their destruction as influential imaginaries, Dora will leave Paul and come to him. As far as Murdoch is concerned, Dora must flee from his seduction and "go back to Imber at once" as her "real life" and "real problems" are there.

On her way back to Imber, Dora visits the National Gallery; a place where "the pictures were almost as familiar to her as her own face." She feels these pictures "belonged to her" and she "reflected ruefully that they were about the only thing that did." They fill her heart with love, inspired as she is by their authority and generosity and splendour. Before them even her husband Paul is only a dream. They are "something real outside herself, which spoke to her in kindly and yet sovereign tones, something superior and good whose presence destroyed the dreary trance-like solipsism of her earlier mood." Before these paintings Dora realizes "something else" is in the world "after all." While she does not draw an "explicit moral" from gazing at the paintings, she feels she "had had a revelation" through them; suddenly she has the desire to "go down on her knees" before a Gainsborough and embrace it while shedding tears. The terms "gaze" and "solipsism" belong to existentialism, which Murdoch uses in *The Bell* and her other novels. In this novel, art is offered as the only thing Dora can "gaze" at and overcome the "modern" tendency towards "solipsism": the denial of any possible knowledge other than one's own existence.

Dora leaves the Gallery and returns to Imber, where she inspires Toby to raise the old bell, hatches the plot to exchange the old bell for the new bell, and, when this plot fails, makes the old bell ring, thus breaking the spell logos has hitherto held over Imber. Noel then arrives at Imber to do his best to save Dora and destroy Imber—through a reprehensible act of journalism—because he can see Dora obviously cannot or will not save herself. However, the Court is imploding anyway, while the Abbey is not. If Dora has been responsible for some of that implosion, she is enraged by Noel's interference, because she can now see the "good" of Imber. She does not wish to see this "good" destroyed, because she now links it with her experience of art at the National Gallery, but she is powerless to control what she has put in motion.

The sixth frame occurs when the lay community at the Court disbands because Michael's homosexuality has been exposed. The Abbey remains untouched across the lake. Dora is left alone with Michael. A "curious dream-like peace" descends on Imber, as Dora shows a "sudden new enthusiasm" for the classical music she once disdained and teaches herself to swim in the lake between the Court and the Abbey. (As Murdoch camply puts it: "The depths below affrighted her no longer.") During this time "a curious relationship grew between Michael and Dora," both connected but also separate and autonomous, which is not surprising as they represent dialectical opposites.

By then Michael's world of logos has changed radically. Murdoch has disabused his horizon and left him with nothing but an absent God he no longer believes in. Michael, who once wanted to be a priest, now has the "calmness of the ruined man" whose only connection with his former life is attending the Mass, which remained for him: "not consoling, not uplifting, but in some way factual. It contained for him no assurance that all would be made well that was not well. It simply existed as a kind of pure reality separate from the weaving of his own thoughts. He attended it almost as a spectator." This observation of Murdoch's is unconvincing. It denies the nature of a sacrament and the way sacraments operate in the lives of sacramental Christians.

Of her own accord, Dora now seeks some "talks" with Mother Clare, which are apparently a kind of spiritual counsel, or as much spiritual counsel the pagan Dora is capable of having as a force of nature. They "talk" on three occasions and Dora seems pleased with these "talks" although she is "reticent about what was said." Around this time, Michael suspects Dora is "a little in love with him" but he does nothing "to reduce the distance between them," encourages her to talk about herself, and quietly circumvents "her clumsy efforts to make him talk about himself." His focus is on Dora's future, which to Murdoch is more positive than his own future, because he understands that, unlike Catherine who went mad, Dora "had fed like a glutton upon the catastrophes at Imber and they had increased her substance."

Michael helps Dora obtain a small grant, which allows her to resume her studies in art. This is necessary because, although her substance has increased, Dora's mythos is still dumb. She is still Dumb Dora who requires the help of Michael's logos. While Dora has taught herself to swim, which means she is beginning to get in touch with the unconscious, her horizon still lacks the language of Michael's horizon, to the point of being unable to put pen to paper and apply for her own small grant. Thanks to Michael, with this small grant Dora can continue her studies in art and perhaps become an artist, or art teacher, who will one day mediate the truth art tells. According to Murdoch, this is the truth western religion once told, no longer being heard, which now needs to be told again by the artist, and of course by literary–philosophical novelists such as herself.

While there are signs Dora is developing a stronger but still partial sense of her own freedom, it is important to remember Dora is not a person in real life. She is a character in a novel. It is also important to notice the large degree of victimhood with which Dora enters the novel and the small degree of freedom with which she leaves it. Both are, like the dilemmas surrounding her, completely unrepresentative of Murdoch's own life as creature of logos, teacher of philosophy, intellectual novelist, and woman who orchestrates her novels and controls her life. The reader needs to take this into account when considering the way Murdoch investigates the human condition and the existential and/or mythological dilemmas she attaches to it.

Archetypes or tropes for logos and mythos appear in Murdoch's other novels. One thinks particularly of *The Unicorn* (1963), where male homosexual Gerald is logos and red-haired Hannah is mythos. For mysterious reasons, Hannah is "trapped" in Gaze Castle. Gerald is her jailer. Hannah's husband Peter has been away for seven years, like some absentee landlord, or tragic hero, or god. Apparently at some stage he was also Gerald's lover. Murdoch's story revolves around the idea that Hannah and Gerald are trapped in Gaze. Any attempt to rescue Hannah fails. She cannot exist apart from Gaze. Finally, for mysterious reasons, she shoots Gerald, whereupon the reader is told:

> The sphere was shattered now and the open sky looked in. Hannah had brought the day of judgment upon them" (230).

The judgment by whom and for what? Murdoch never explains. But it has something to do with the gap left by God's death, and the literary author's role as someone attempting to re-enchant the disenchanted world.

Muriel Spark

The dialectic of logos and mythos was not a feature of Spark's first novel *The Comforters* (1957); however, she was setting the scene for it. Early in the novel, we are told the much loved and mysterious matriarch, Louisa Jepp:

> was half gipsy, the dark one and the youngest of a large red-haired family, which at the time of her birth owed its prosperity to the father's success as a corn dealer. The success was owing to good fortune in the first place, his having broken jail while waiting to come before the Bench, never

afterwards returning to his gipsy tribe. It was a hundred and thirty years after this event that Louisa was sitting down to breakfast with Laurence [her grandson] (12).

Like similar archetypes or tropes—one thinks particularly of Maria's gipsy mother Oraga and uncle Yerko in Davies's *The Rebel Angels* (1982)—Louisa knows a few secrets about life and how to break the law without getting caught.

Spark began using archetypes or tropes for logos and mythos in Miles and January in *Robinson* (1958) and continued to use them in different ways until her last novel. Consider Frederick and Annabel in *The Public Image* (1968), Paul and Elsa in *The Hothouse by the East River* (1973), Hubert and Maggie in *The Takeover* (1976), Harvey and Effie in *The Only Problem* (1984), Lucky and Hildegard in *Aiding and Abetting* (2000), and Rowland and Chris in *The Finishing School* (2004). Red hair is often a clue.

Red-haired Margaret Damien in *Symposium* (1990) deserves special mention, with her sinister pre-Raphaelite affectations and the way she uses the existential philosophy of *les autres* to mask the pure evil she represents. Spark understands the truth of lies and the lies of truth better than any other author in this book. In some of her novels, she presents logos and mythos as opposites, reverses their roles in others, and makes them indistinguishable from each other in others. Her theology is rich in paradox without ever becoming unorthodox.

Spark and Murdoch are often compared but it is more useful to contrast them. Where Murdoch turns the Platonic model of mind into a place where civilized reason (logos) oppresses and suppresses natural feeling (mythos), Spark has a much more orthodox sense of their dialectical relationship within classical metaphysics. To read *Robinson* (1958), published the same year as *The Bell*, is to realize Spark has her own take on her hero's free will and moral agency. It is easy to imagine her regarding the existential dilemma Murdoch gives to Dora Greenfield with a mixture of amusement and disdain, since her own hero, January Marlow, is much stronger and more intelligent. Unlike Murdoch, Spark was not a Platonic Freudian. She had recently converted to Catholicism and her thinking about the Platonic model of mind, and to classical metaphysics generally, owed more to Cardinal Newman than to Freud. Newman was crucial to Spark's conversion.

Robinson

As an explicitly Catholic novel, *Robinson* should be read as a religious commentary on modernism, much in the same way as Greene's Catholic novels, although Spark and Greene are as intellectually different as their commentaries. Also, Spark's literary economy is legendary. Where Murdoch needed six frames in *The Bell*, Spark only needed three in *Robinson*. Also, her three frames are set against four backgrounds, which intriguingly match the four metaphors Frye associates with the biblical imagination and its influence on western literature: mountain, garden, cave, and furnace. In *Words With Power* (1990) Frye analyzes these metaphors in order to relate the Bible and literature more closely within "the cultural history of the western world" and "the myths we live by." Spark does the same thing in her second novel, published 32 years before *Words with Power* and 24 years before *The Great Code* (1982). Her novel anticipates not only Frye's ideas but those of hermeneutical philosophers such as Ricoeur who, in the wake of World War II, made a conscious decision to re-evaluate the symbolic content of classical metaphysics once the failure of literary modernism and philosophical modernity became widely evident.

Like *The Bell*, the first frame of *Robinson* is the opening and closing scenes. There is an essential difference between the two novels, however. Murdoch adapted the *Middlemarch* theme. Within her first frame, her heroine moves from one degree of immaturity to another. Spark adapted the *Robinson Crusoe* theme. Within her first frame, her heroine becomes a more mature version of the mature woman she already is.

Because of a plane crash, January Marlow is stranded on an eponymous man-shaped island in the North Atlantic called Robinson. The island, owned by a meditative hermit, Miles Mary Robinson, is a topos: a "time and landscape of the mind" both "dangerous and lyrical" where "all things are possible." It is the landscape of January's mind, as opposed to her real life back in Chelsea, where she is a single mother with a teenage son, recently converted to Catholicism, who leads an otherwise unremarkable life among her two sisters and their antithetical husbands.

The second frame is what happens to January after her plane crashes into the island. On this topos, she becomes a trope for mythos and has a dialectical relationship with a trope for logos, Miles Robinson, who owns and governs the island's mental and physical landscapes. The third frame is good and evil; Jimmy Waterford, another crash survivor, is a trope for good; Tom Wells, another crash survivor, is a trope for evil. To summarize the allegorical scenario so far: there is a plane crash on an apocryphal island owned and governed by logos; only mythos, good, and evil survive; the plot unfolds against four backgrounds associated with the biblical imagination and its influence on western literature: mountain, garden, cave, and furnace. Also, there is a child on the island, Miguel,

Robinson's adopted son, whose mind is tabula rasa (a blank slate). Each protagonist tries to influence Miguel's mental development in a different way, according to the logic of his or her horizon.

Robinson represents January's eldest brother-in-law back in Chelsea, Ian Brodie. Wells represents her younger brother-in-law, Curly Lonsdale. Miguel represents her son, Brian Marlow. The novel contains many paradoxes: January likes Robinson but dislikes Brodie, dislikes Wells but likes Lonsdale. She believes Wells is a bad influence on Miguel but Lonsdale is a good influence on Brian. Also, Waterford has no counterpart in her real life, an admission that, in the modern world, good is hard to find but evil is everywhere. In this allegory, what is positive in January's conscious mind is negative in her unconscious mind and what is negative in her conscious mind is positive in her unconscious mind. Like Spark's habit of exposing the lies of truth and the truth of lies, her hallmark is to give everything, physical and metaphysical, a double face in which nothing is what it appears to be.

As the trope for logos, Robinson was born into a wealthy family in Gibraltar, where his mother was a devout Catholic. He nearly completed seminary training but refused to be ordained. Instead, he travelled through the more Latin parts of Europe and South America to observe Catholic practices. He eventually left the Church, objecting to what he believed to be its heretical and superstitious character, while still maintaining a personal belief in the logos aspect of its faith. Robinson attributes this superstitious character to Marian devotion as a kind of mythos. This is significant, as his middle name is Mary. He is so obsessed with Marian devotion that he writes a book linking it with earth mythology, superstition, and evil. Brodie, his counterpart in January's real life, is less sophisticated and more contemptuous in declaring Marian devotion a "materialistic" heresy "eating the Christian heart out of the Catholic faith."

As the trope for mythos, January's moods are "not stable at the best of times." While her grandmother's pagan tendencies once embarrassed her as a child, on Robinson she experiences sudden longings to worship the moon as her grandmother once did. She finds this strange, as she is a Christian. While on the island her perceptions are more acute than they are in the real world. She is touched by "a pre-ancestral quality", "an enchantment, a primitive blood-force". She accepts that logos is in charge but this does not mean she always agrees with Robinson; in fact, her existential dilemma is not so much voicing her disagreements with him but the difficulties she faces when trying to put her beliefs into practice.

As the trope for good, Waterford is related to Robinson as logos. January is "quite charmed" by Waterford as he "appealed to a quality" in her mind that she "considered the most advanced" she possessed, which was also "slightly masculine". He is as attracted to her as she is to him; however, although he is handsome and well-intentioned he is also weak, vulnerable, and easily manipulated, which is why Robinson does not approve of his budding relationship with January. In spite of this, Waterford is still Robinson's relative. Along with January, he is allowed to accompany Robinson to some of the novel's metaphorical landscapes (the mountain and the furnace), but he is not allowed access to the secret place only Robinson knows about (the cave).

As the trope for evil, Wells sees life as a matter of chance rather than design. He has a portable emporium of fake spiritualism which he uses as part of a confidence trick to steal from the gullible. On a superficial level, he appears to be someone January can identify with, much in the same way Dora thought she could identify with Noel in *The Bell*, through their shared interest in rhythm and blues, and the dancing and drinking afforded by London's nightlife, but these dionysian affinities do not reflect his real character. Because Wells is evil, Spark restricts his movements. He seldom walks "beyond the vicinity of the house". He turns back from his only attempt to visit the mountain and the furnace, and he has never been to the cave. He is occasionally found lurking in the garden, like the serpent in Genesis.

Much to January's chagrin, Robinson turns out to be right about most things, even if her mythos manages to score a few points against his logos by the end of the novel. Also, it must be admitted, she owes her life to logos. Robinson saved January, Waterford, and Wells from the plane crash, nursed them back to health, and endured their invasion of his cherished privacy.

As soon as January regains consciousness from the crash, Robinson can see she is intelligent and persistently encourages her to think, describe, and above all to be reasonable. He lets her have the run of his extensive library. He gives her a notebook and suggests she makes a journal of her observations of the natural world around her. He insists she should "stick to the facts" as the "healthiest course" and not let her imagination wander. In spite of January's intelligence, however, things fall apart on the island after Robinson goes missing. According to Spark, this is inevitable when logos departs and mythos, good, and evil are left to their own devices.

Robinson has a casual and negligent relationship with nature which January finds incomprehensible. While his island is fertile, his garden lies in ruins. Most of his food is dried or tinned, being imported once a year from the outside world. While he does not grow food in the garden, he has planted a field of mustard next to a lake, purely for the aesthetic effect. He does have a pomegranate orchard on part of the island. It is run as a business, does not need to be tended, and does not provide him with fruit to eat. He encourages formality among his guests, determined to keep control over any development that might lead to an outbreak of the irrational (Dodds 1951). Also, while Brodie is sexually impotent, Robinson is "not a man for the ladies."

During the first half of the novel, Spark describes the differences between logos and mythos, along with January's spirited objection to Robinson providing her with a list of things to do and not do. He strongly advises her against the "depressing habit" of "gazing" at the sea in the hope of finding a rescue boat or plane, and he encourages her to "stick to the facts" when writing up her journal. There is a qualitative difference, however, between what they both regard as factual. Spark insists that not all facts springing from January's fertile imagination are wrong. For example, she intuitively knows, even before being told, that Robinson is neither Miguel's biological father nor a "man for the ladies". As she reflects:

> There is easily discernible in some men a certain indifference, not to women precisely but to the feminine element in women, which might be interpreted in a number of ways. In Robinson I had detected something more than indifference: a kind of armed neutrality. So much for his attitude to me. And I thought it likely that he could be positively hostile to the idea of women in general.

That said, Robinson is never the misogynist Brodie is in January's real life, and she finds Robinson's anti-Marian fervour "far more interesting" than Brodie's. As she admits: "whereas I could never really dislike Robinson, I hated Ian Brodie's guts."

When Robinson warns January to avoid Wells and his pagan charms, and quietly tries to discourage her from forming a relationship with Waterford, she does not understand why she ought to be prevented from either. When he discovers she is not writing up her journal regularly he encourages her to do so, to keep her "mind" off things, to prevent her imagination from getting the better of her, but she objects to being told what she should or should not do and why. She has emotions and cries, which Robinson would rather she did not do. She likes to wear makeup, which Robinson says, "simply and factually", is not essential, although he has no objection to it. She is superstitious about wearing clothes and using makeup taken as salvage from the plane crash. Because they are possessions of the dead, she has constructed a pagan taboo around them.

Ultimately, logos and mythos clash in a battle of wills over Marian devotion and Miguel. January lost her rosary during the plane crash but several weeks later she discovers it in a drawer in Robinson's desk. She keeps it and remonstrates spiritedly with him when he admits to having taken it from her because he does not want Miguel to see it or be influenced by it: "That sort of thing can easily corrupt the Faith," he says. "What bloody rot," she says, "What a fuss to make about a rosary." Soon after this exchange she discovers the rosary missing again. When she confronts him and asks him to return her property, stolen from her bedroom, he reminds her it is actually his bedroom, as she is a guest on his island. She can have the rosary back as long as she promises not to teach Miguel how to recite it. She promises nothing and keeps demanding the return of her property. He repeats his wish that Miguel should grow up "free from superstition", whereupon she tells him to go to hell, as there is nothing superstitious about the rosary: "It's a Christian devotion," she says, "not a magic charm."

Finally, January admits defeat and lets Robinson keep the rosary, telling him she "can do without it". She comes to believe that, in withholding the rosary, he "was not simply attempting to make small difficulties, or to exercise his authority on an island simply from a need for power," but that he "was constitutionally afraid of any material manifestations of Grace". That evening, Wells tells her his briefcase, containing his emporium of fake spiritualism, has disappeared. The next morning it becomes apparent that Robinson has also disappeared, along with all the superstitious objects he objects to. So, logos, the only force capable of preventing total chaos, has departed. From this point onwards, things slowly fall apart on the island.

The implications of Robinson's absence only gradually dawn on mythos, good, and evil, as they discover blood soaked garments scattered everywhere along a trail between the house, the mountain, and the furnace, which they take to be clues that Robinson has either met with an accident or was murdered. At the end of the novel it is revealed that neither of these conclusions is true, Robinson simply left without telling them, without providing a reason for doing so, but while they were searching for him they "saw blood smeared everywhere." The idea of murder over accident takes hold, and, because they believe themselves to be alone on the island with Miguel, they conclude the murderer must be one of them, although it suits Wells's pagan, pseudo-spiritualist purposes to propose death by supernatural force rather than human agency.

The events of the following weeks unfold in two broad spheres. First, as mythos, and therefore as the natural successor to logos, January keeps her journal, uses her intuition and imagination to help her understand the truth of what has happened to Robinson, and endeavours to deal with the consequences of this truth. Second, there is a struggle between good and evil in which evil tries to blackmail good, and nearly succeeds because good, in its 20th century disguise, is weak in the face of evil. Spark is clear that mythos, in the absence of logos, is the only thing standing in the way of evil, but mythos can only challenge evil so far while good remains ineffective.

When writing up her journal, January makes several observations, all assuming Robinson has been murdered and the murderer is among them. In arriving at these observations, January admits to judging people by their appearances (facial expressions). She knows judging the human character by appearances is misleading; however:

> The misleading element, in fact, provides the essence of my satisfaction. In the course of deciphering a face, its shape, tones, lines and droops as if these were words and sentences of a message from the interior, I fix upon it a character which, though I know it to be distorted, never quite untrue, never entirely true, interests me. I am as near the mark as myth is to history, the apocrypha to the canon.

In this way her journal becomes a "murder dossier" through which she moves well beyond the observable facts Robinson asked her to stick to. While some of her observations are not factual, and some of them are false, Spark knows some of them reveal a kind of truth. The more January ponders the murder the more she is convinced of Wells's guilt. Her journal becomes the vehicle through which Wells nearly kills her.

Also, January comes to think of Robinson as a legendary figure; a religious man who, in his desire for spiritual advancement, adopts a son as a child disciple and leaves the world, only to have ungrateful intruders, whom he rescued and nursed, try his god like patience and sabotage his elected solitude. As January suggests:

> That he should have met his end at the hands of one of his beneficiaries seemed the essence of his tragedy. And in this interesting light he took on the heroic character of a pre-Christian pagan victim of expiation.

January increases in stature during Robinson's absence. In addition to writing up her journal, she takes the key to the gun room, hides it, and appropriates a pistol for protection. Also, she overcomes her superstitious fear of using salvage from the plane crash and appropriates frocks, and a string of amber beads to make a rosary for Miguel. She appears to be on her way to full control of events, setting out to fight the forces of evil; like Sigourney Weaver in *Alien* (1979), complete with red hair, gun, and orphan. Wells steals both her journal and the key to the gun room. She makes an astute guess as to where he may have hidden the journal and takes it back, resolving to hide it in one of the island's secret tunnels where he cannot find it. While she is leaving the tunnel where she has hidden the journal, Wells, who has just learnt about the existence of the tunnel from Miguel, confronts her with a knife. He apparently intends to kill her, in order to obtain the journal, but she manages to escape by momentarily blinding him with torchlight and winding him in the guts. The next day she tells Waterford what happened in the tunnel, whereupon good is finally roused into action and prepares to battle evil. As the first blows are struck between Waterford and Wells, however, Miguel suddenly arrives and announces that Robinson has returned.

Everything returns to a controlled normality, now that logos is back. Mythos, who has explored the boundaries of her power, is once again second fiddle to logos, but something has changed in their relationship; something that is not possible in the relationship Dora and Michael develop at the end of *The Bell*. January's fury rises whenever Robinson tells her he does not have to explain his disappearance: He went by his own choice; his actions are "beyond the obvious range"; it is not up to her to understand but simply to accept his "system". Her reply is sarcastic. She tells him she "chucked the antinomian pose" at the age of 20. To her there is "no such thing as a private morality". She believes any "system" that does not "allow for the unexpected and the unwelcome is a rotten one." His final justification for his actions, which is classically Greek, is: "Things mount up inside one, and then one has to perpetuate an outrage."

Whenever January tells Robinson about what occurred during his absence, his reply is usually: "It was only to be expected." January finds this phrase "unendurable" as it implies that Robinson "had foreseen all the consequences of his action to the last detail" and that "he more or less held the wires that made us move." When she tells Robinson she believes Wells to be a professional blackmailer and a criminal, he tells her she is full of suspicions and some of her suspicions have been fundamentally wrong: for example, in believing Wells murdered him. When she tells him she was "not far wrong," as Wells had tried to kill her, he rehearses the same answers as before: it was only to be expected, people act in this way, human nature does not vary much.

Robinson presently gives his motives away, however, in admitting: "It was to be expected that a man like Wells would turn a situation to his own interests. It was to be expected that a woman like you would, in the circumstances, withdraw very rapidly from a man like Jimmie." When his true motives sink in, January expresses outrage over those motives, his need to separate mythos from good and withdraw mythos from evil, he continues to fuel her outrage by saying: "Motives are seldom simple. I find no call upon me to go into my motives. Of course you are annoyed. It is only to be expected."

Spark gives the last laugh to her heroine. January tells Robinson she made Miguel a rosary and taught him how to recite it. He is upset and admits he did not think she would do this to him, to which she replies: "It was only to be expected ... I see no call to tear myself to bits over motives. They are never simple. I am happy to say I have taught the child the rosary." When he asks her "What else have you taught him?" and notices Miguel has not been the same towards him since his return, her answer is "You are full of suspicions." Robinson finally admits defeat, when January tells him Miguel wants to go to a Catholic school when he returns to Portugal for his education. Robinson then announces that he shall be "glad to see the pomegranate boat" which will soon arrive to take them all away from his island and leave him alone.

Spark is clear about one thing, however. Robinson is kind, good, and forbearing. He always tells the truth and never lies. At the centre of the novel he even gives them clues as to where he would go should he ever leave them. January recalls these clues in hindsight but at the time they did not listen to his Scheherazade-like storytelling:

> even now I keep remembering new facts which Robinson gave us then, night after night, as if compelled to do so lest we should run amok.

Robinson told them the story of the island, its history and legends, and even the location of the inaccessible cave he will hide in when has he finally had enough of them and becomes exhausted by their presence. So logos was the teller of the story even though, in the Platonic scheme of things, storytelling is traditionally the lie-telling role of mythos. They either did not want to listen to the story or they were not capable of interpreting its message. The reasons for this are many; one being the failure of literary modernism and philosophical modernity to prevent the horrors of the 20th century.

In all her novels, Spark reminds us that logos and mythos are canonical tropes in the landscape of the western mind, true and untrue, real and unreal. Their dialectical relationship is never an end in itself. It is a vehicle for a higher reality. What then of good and evil? As a Catholic, Spark is clear, much clearer than the Freudian Murdoch. While mythos is able to take a stand against logos, make him feel threatened, and witness to a truth of her own, she cannot compensate for the weakness of contemporary good and cannot protect herself—or the world—from the problem of contemporary evil. If Spark does not give logos the final say in the dialectic—the nature of the dialectic being endlessly dialogical—she does give him a pre-eminent position within the dialectic, which makes her theology orthodox.

It has been said no author of the 20th century was more aware of the many forms evil takes than Spark. This awareness had something to do with her conversion to Catholicism after the World War II—inspired by the Church's teaching about the unity of spirit and matter—which also gave her a particular perspective of what the morally-responsible author should do about evil. In "The Desegregation of Art", her 1970 address to the American Academy of Arts and Letters, she descried the literature of sentiment which, however beautiful in itself, however striking in its depiction of actuality, cheats the reader into a sense of social involvement but is in fact a segregated and segregating activity. She wanted to see:

> a less impulsive generosity … a more derisive undermining of what is wrong … less emotion and more intelligence in these efforts to impress our minds and hearts.

Because she believed the victim–oppressor complex of socially conscious literature had itself become cliché and ineffective—and because "we have come to a moment in history when we are surrounded on all sides and oppressed by the absurd"—she advocated satire and ridicule as "the only honourable weapon we have left".

Most importantly, Spark wanted her writing to give pleasure; perhaps believing that, when it comes to fiction conveying a moral message, it is better to use satire and ridicule. In her well-known *The Prime of Miss Jean Brodie* (1961), contemporary evil takes comic form through a schoolteacher who attempts to shape the identities of her students. In her lesser known *The Only Problem* (1984), contemporary evil of biblical proportions is visited upon the protagonist, in a reworking of the Book of Job, a story in which God permits evil as a way of testing human endurance and faith.

The Hothouse by the East River

During the 20th century, Freudians and Jungians tried to understand and cure evil in the mind. Were they successful in their attempt to systematize the mind into ego and id or conscious and unconscious? Did psychoanalysts ignore evil outside the mind: evil among people and in society; evil within local, national, and international communities? What of the archetypes psychoanalysis inherited from Greek mythology and Hebrew scripture? Are they true or false? Can they be both? These are questions Spark explores in *The Hothouse by the East River*, a novel that moves between her characters' mortal lives in England during 1944 and their immortal lives in Manhattan in the early 1970s.

The mortal strand of the novel occurs in rural England in the months before D-Day, in an intelligence compound engaged in black propaganda and psychological warfare. Spark describes as "the propagation of the Allied point of view under the guise of the German point of view," which involves a "tangled mixture" of damaging lies, flattery, and plausible truths. Spark is qualified to write about life in such a compound, having been an intelligence officer in one herself. In fact, her autobiography says she was hired by Sefton Delmer, author of *Black Boomerang* (1962), and notes that his account of the Allies' black propaganda and psychological warfare is "well worth reading".

This is an understated way of saying Delmer's book helps us understand the literary style of *The Hothouse by the East River* and many of her other novels. The compound's inhabitants are English intelligence officers and German prisoners of war who chose to "leave their camps and work for their enemy." The central on-stage characters are Paul and Elsa, both intelligence officers. The central off-stage character is Kiel, a German prisoner with an eponymous name, an anagram of l-i-k-e, who might be involved in an eternal triangle with Paul and Elsa. The truth about the off-stage Kiel, and his relationship with Paul and Elsa, is a mystery. Who is Kiel? What is he like? Does he represent disembodied evil or does he simply mirror human evil? Spark is ambiguous here.

Paul is 28. Now British, he was born into impoverished nobility in Montenegro. His knowledge of Serbo-Croat affairs means that, when not at the compound, he is an aide on trans-Atlantic trips whenever the Balkan situation is to be discussed. Elsa is 23. When walking about the countryside with German prisoners, she is fond of sharing stories about her family life in Kent and her education at boarding school. She refuses to share a room at the compound, something all women under 30 are expected to do, explaining that it "wouldn't be comfortable for the other girl", as she sees things, is uncanny, and has supernatural communications. A senior officer tells Elsa she is out of her element at the compound and does not understand the value of what is being accomplished there. She has even declared the compound to be ridiculous. All of this suggests she is also a security risk. Kiel arrives a few weeks before Paul. Soon after they meet, they have a fight in a field behind the compound, which starts with a trivial argument over their work, but is really over Elsa.

Kiel is a double agent who arranged to have himself taken prisoner before getting a job with the intelligence compound on the pretext of being anti-Nazi. Elsa, already seen as a security risk, gets herself into difficulty and is suspected of having an affair with Kiel. Paul gets her out of that difficulty. But after Kiel had been broadcasting for their compound for six months, he picks a fight with another man and gets himself sent back to his prison camp. Three days later Kiel goes on air, in a prisoner exchange-of-greeting program, and sends a coded message that betrays the compound's identity. This results in a major breach of security. Paul and Elsa are investigated but, as they close ranks and tough out the investigation, it leads nowhere.

There are other intelligence officers at the compound: Poppy Xavier, Miles Bunting, and Colonel Tylden. Each contributes to the ambiguity Spark creates around the relationship between the on-stage Paul and Elsa and the off-stage Kiel. In the final chapter, at the end of the mortal strand, we learn that in the late spring of 1944, not long before D-Day, all the intelligence officers are attending a conference of other intelligence units and are staying at the same hotel in London. Given their friendly off-duty alliance, "which disappears when they are back in the country, hemmed in with their German collaborators," the reader wonders whether the eternal triangle is a quadrangle, or a pentangle, or more. How culpable are these intelligence officers, wittingly or unwittingly? Does each of them represent mortal evil? Spark is ambiguous here as well.

The immortal strand of the novel occurs in Manhattan. After the war, Paul and Elsa marry, migrate to the United States, and have two children. Pierre their son is gay, avant-garde, and unable to empathize with Paul's anxious memories about the war and Kiel. "What does it matter?" Pierre says to his father. "There isn't any war or peace anymore, no good and evil, no communism, no capitalism, no fascism. There's only one area of conflict left and that's between absurdity and intelligence." Katerina, their daughter, is promiscuous and takes drugs. As adults, both children live independently of their parents but remain financially dependent on them; especially on Elsa, who is inexplicably a source of immense wealth.

Elsa spends most of her days in their old over-heated apartment gazing out a picture window that frames her view of the East River and the United Nations. She sees things no one else can see. Her shadow falls at unnatural angles in relation to her body because, in Paul's words, she "gets light or something from elsewhere". In this way the uncanniness of her youth is elevated to a metaphysical plane. Paul is busy pathologizing Elsa, and tries to manage her as a problem, as if his life depends on it. In this way the jealousy of his youth is also elevated to a metaphysical plane.

In Manhattan, Paul and Elsa have become metaphysical extensions of the physical man and woman who were two points of the eternal triangle in England during the war. They have become Greek archetypes: Paul is classical and represents, among other things, the masculine, the ego, the conscious mind, rationality, light, order, and the apollonian; Elsa is pre-classical and represents, among other things, the feminine, the id, the unconscious mind, irrationality, darkness, chaos, and the dionysian–chthonic. Are these archetypes real or imaginary? Are the dichotomies they represent true, or false, or both? Spark is not sure but acknowledges the normative role they have played in the western imagination, as idea and as art. The third point of that triangle, the eponymous Kiel, a Hebrew archetype for Satan, still figures in their lives in an off-stage way. Paul imagines his life is threatened by Kiel. Elsa cannot make up her mind whether Kiel is really in Manhattan, but, even if he is, she does not feel threatened by him, because the archetypes she represents can embrace the reality of what he represents.

Paul and Elsa's overheated apartment is hell; and, according to western iconography, hell is simultaneously a place of eternal punishment for the wicked after death and the forces of evil that reside there. So, given this archetypal framework, the reader is invited to ask: What is hellish about Manhattan in the early 1970s? What is evil about the archetypes which inhabit the hothouse by the East River? What did Paul and Elsa do in those months before D-Day to earn this damnation? Finally, in this surreal part of the novel, who is Kiel and what is he like? The reader is never sure, since Spark is a master at disguising her moral among the satire and ridicule of her fable. But there is definitely a moral.

As two halves of one whole, like Waldo and Arthur in *The Solid Mandala*, Paul and Elsa cannot live without each other, just as logos cannot live without mythos, but their antithetical relationship is difficult. As logos, Paul's existence seems to depend on coping with the "problem" of Elsa, while Elsa gets on with the uncanny mystery of her own existence, while humouring or eluding Paul as much as she can within the limits of her mythos. Paul's fear of Elsa is archetypal; it is the Greek fear of the irrational; greatly written about over the millennia; often translated into paradigms, theories, and psychoanalytical methods; much investigated in philosophy and literature. The classical Paul once had the romantic Elsa committed to an asylum but she bought her way out. He would have her committed again, if their son Pierre had not insisted on psychotherapy as a conscience salving alternative.

In several of Spark's novels, sending up psychoanalysis is a favourite theme. Elsa's relationship with her psychoanalyst, Garven, is a hilarious example of that theme. The more Garven analyzes Elsa the more elusive and paradoxical she becomes, and she reminds him that he may have a problem rather than her. Eventually Garven moves in with Paul and Elsa and becomes their butler. When Elsa's behaviour becomes too distracting for Paul, and too exasperating for Garven, they conspire to have her committed for observation. Elsa will have none of this. It is eventually revealed that Paul is also seeing a psychoanalyst, Annie, who forms a partnership with Garven so the two of them can try to understand both Elsa and Paul. Elsa sends up this partnership: "They will have to come to an agreement," she says. "Fifty-fifty on the proceeds of my shadow."

At the end of the novel, we learn that back in 1944, not long before D-Day, the conference in London is over and the intelligence officers are all boarding the same train to return to their compound. As the train pulls out of the station, a V-2 bomb makes a direct hit and the novel's mortal characters are all killed. So, in the Manhattan of the 1970s, the Greek archetypes representing the ego–conscious and id–unconscious, Paul and Elsa, are no longer physical, mortal, and real. They have become metaphysical, immortal, and surreal. As far as Spark is concerned, psychoanalyzing them has become a local preoccupation: "New York, home of the vivisectors of the mind, and of the mentally vivisected still to be reassembled, of those who live intact, habitually wondering about their states of sanity, and home of those whose minds have been dead, bearing the scars of resurrection." Outside the consultant's office, though, a different city is "heaving" with myriad problems, social and economic and moral, which psychoanalysis ignores.

Spark wants us to notice these myriad problems without ignoring those influential archetypes living in their contemporary hell. At the end of the novel, after spending all night out on the town, Paul and Elsa return home to find their old apartment building torn down to make way for a postmodern structure. "Now we can have some peace," says Elsa. But that is not true. Poppy Xavier, Miles Bunting, Colonel Tylden, and Kiel too, are waiting for them nearby in a Rolls Royce. "Come Elsa," Paul says, "we can go back with them," wherever "back" may be. He follows her, "watching as she moves how she trails her faithful and lithe cloud of unknowing across the pavement," towards the Rolls that drives them to their next hellish residence.

The Abbess of Crewe

During the 20th century John XXIII called the Second Vatican Council (1962–1965) with the goal of renewing the life of the Church, bringing its teaching, discipline, and organization up-to-date, unifying Christians, and promoting inter-faith dialogue. We are only just beginning to appreciate and understand the ways in which Vatican II has been successful. However, at the time, did those who negotiated and promoted Vatican II underestimate the potential for evil within the process of renewal? This is a question Spark explores in *The Abbess of Crew* (1974), a novel set in a fictitious Benedictine abbey, which uses the scenario of the Watergate scandal to satirize the struggle between conservatism and liberalism during a period of ecclesiological change. The struggle focuses on the election of a new abbess and the direction the successful candidate will take the order. To highlight their equal potential for evil, Spark caricatures conservatism and liberalism by making them much more extreme than they would ever be in a real religious order.

The forces of conservatism revolve around Sister Alexandra and a trio of nuns committed to her election: Mildred, Walburga, and dim but serviceable Winifrede. Narcissistic, materialistic, and self-entitled, Alexandra represents a kind of ancien régime, with 24 generations of ruling ancestors in England and France behind her. She is fond of the pre-Christian Roman poet, Sextus Propertius. During daily offices, instead of the Psalter, she prefers to recite English poetry quietly to herself: Marvell, Milton, King, Pope, Yeats, Hopkins, Pound, and Auden. She follows the political philosophy of Machiavelli's *Discourses* and *The Art of War*. If elected, she intends to ignore the latest ecclesiological reforms, return the order to an ancient and rigid rule, reinvent a system of double monastery with the Jesuits, and use Cistercians as discreet domestic servants. She knows it is absurd in modern (or postmodern) times to reinstate the seven canonical hours, but she believes modernism (or postmodernism) exist in a historical context, and, as far as she is concerned, history does not work. She wants the abbey to discard history and enter the sphere of mythology. She assumes every nun in the abbey yearns to be part of a myth, whatever the price in comfort. She feels this mission is her destiny and she uses the language of predestination, including the Felix Culpa, to justify that destiny.

The forces of liberalism revolve around Sister Felicity and any impressionable nuns and novices influenced by her. Felicity's lineage is as noble as Alexandra's, but she shows no trace of that lineage, as her function in the novel is to represent a bourgeois threat to Alexandra's old order. She knows the Psalter by heart, and can chant it without the aid of an office book, but otherwise she is ignorant of the high culture Alexandra represents. She believes the abbey, being too prosperous and materialistic, should follow the teachings of Francis of Assisi, a saint who understood total poverty and sacrificial love, but her liberal vision is in fact a perversion of Francis's radical vocation. If elected abbess she would turn the abbey into a love-nest in the heart of England. She leaves the abbey every night to copulate with her lover, Thomas the Jesuit. The reader is left in no doubt that if Felicity is elected chastity will be abolished and the entire rationale for the religious life will be abolished with it.

Spark presents this stark choice, between Alexandra's extreme conservatism and Felicity's extreme liberalism, but she sends them both up since the dichotomy between them may be false even if the evil they each mask is true. Felicity will usher in a period of chaos, a new reign of terror, if Alexandra's new version of the ancien régime, which masks its own hypocrisy and moral corruption, is prevented from materializing. In exploring this dilemma, between freedom and necessity, Spark is covering similar ground as other philosophers and authors of her generation, such as Murdoch. It is a well-trodden path that defined what was literary in many postwar novels.

There is another nun protagonist apart from Alexandra and Felicity, who remains off-stage. Sister Gertrude, a German, is a kind of Secretary of State for the abbey, a satire of Henry Kissinger, a member of Nixon's administration who emerged unscathed from the Watergate scandal. Gertrude is always overseas, studiously refusing to be drawn into the abbey's politics, contactable only by a secure green phone, while conducting a broad variety of missionary negotiations: in the Congo reconciling witch doctor's rituals with a specially adapted rite of the mass; in the Andes converting cannibals with dietary concessions and suppressing the zeal of vegetarian heretics; in the Himalayas preaching birth control. Alexandra defers to Gertrude, because of her popularity and gravitas, while finding the Teutonic logic of her realpolitik suspect. Gertrude is a master of not hearing what she should not hear, pushing ecumenical boundaries to absurd limits, and surviving.

An extraordinary amount happens in this novel of scarcely thirty-five thousand words. The narrative weaves back and forth, from the three week period before the new abbess's election, to the two year period after the election. Alexandra's agenda is to fulfil her destiny by winning the election. The polls favour her but she is taking no chances. She arranges surveillance, for the abbey to be bugged, aurally and visually, while appearing to distance herself from the surveillance. She summons two senior Jesuits to a secret conference with Mildred and Walburga, instructs them to do something about the affair between Felicity and Thomas, and to leave her out of it. They arrange for two Jesuit novices to break into the abbey one night to steal Felicity's love letters, hidden in a secret drawer at the bottom of her workbox. But Felicity discovers the intruders, locks them in the embroidery room, and calls the police. No charges are laid, though, as Alexandra convinces the authorities that this is an internal church matter. The Jesuit novices are expelled from their order, Alexandra goes on to win the election, and Felicity flees the abbey "to join her Jesuit lover and to tell her familiar story to the entranced world."

From that point onwards the eyes of the Vatican and the media, on both sides of the Atlantic, are on the abbey. Felicity becomes a perpetual media event, attacking Alexandra from outside the abbey and lobbying for a police investigation. But there is no evidence and the police would prefer the affair remained within the Church. None of this deters Alexandra from implementing her austere reforms while simultaneously renovating her apartments in a lavish style. She feeds her nuns tinned cat food and boiled nettles while her inner-circle dines on pâté and fine wine. She increases audio and video surveillance, bugging every room and hallway, the trees in the garden, everywhere except the chapel and the confessional. In her office an Infant of Prague conceals the abbey's central transmitter: "The infant is adorned with its traditional robes, the episcopal crown and vestments embedded with such large and so many rich and gleaming jewels it would seem they could not possibly be real. However, they are real." Alexandra used the nuns' dowries to buy them.

Alexandra is not worried about the publicity. "The more scandal there is from this point on the better," she tells Mildred and Walburga:

> We are truly moving in a mythological context. We are the actors; the press and the public are the chorus. Every columnist has his own version of the same old story, as it were Aeschylus, Sophocles or Euripides, only of course, let me tell you, of a far inferior dramatic style. ... the facts of the matter are with us no longer, but we have returned them to God who gave them ... let Felicity tell it like it was as she may. You cannot bring a charge against Agamemnon or subpoena Clytemnestra, can you?

Like Richard Nixon, her contemporary among the elected, and the elect, Alexandra is out of touch with reality. She behaves as if she is unaccountable. She is wholly within the world and yet beyond the world. She acts like God, looking at what she has created and declaring it to be good.

Meanwhile, the expelled Jesuit novices have started blackmailing. Alexandra is now forced to sell the jewels adorning the Infant of Prague one by one to prevent them from telling their story. Winifrede, the dim but serviceable go-between, eventually gets caught, dressed as a man, in a gents lavatory at the British Museum, hugging a plastic bag packed with thousands of pounds. She is released without charge on Alexandra's assurances that this internal church matter is being intensively investigated.

The headlines on both sides of the Atlantic finally force the Vatican to act. Alexandra is delated to Rome to face possible excommunication. Unfazed, she allows edited versions of the surveillance tapes to be released. She takes confessions with her to Rome, extracted from every nun in the convent. These confessions, though, are simply printed and signed copies of the confiteor from the mass, through which every penitent, including the Pope, acknowledges a personal fault that is also universal. The novel's final scene is of Alexandra sailing to Rome, unperturbed, standing on an upper deck:

> straight as a white ship's funnel, marvelling how the wide sea billows from shore to shore like that cornfield of sublimity which never should be reaped nor was ever sown, orient and immortal wheat.

Here Spark reminds us of the parable of the wheat and the tares. The sun shines on both of them, which means God allows good and evil to grow together. It is not up to humanity to winnow them, just to recognize them. They should be left to God, who will separate them on the last day.

The Takeover

During the 20th century the term "paradigm shift" was first used to describe a change in the assumptions (or paradigm) that underpinned the ruling theory of science. Since then the term has been widely used beyond science and is now a cliché that applies more broadly to any change of thinking. Modernism, an ideological and aesthetic movement that attempted to diverge from classical metaphysics, is one example of paradigm shift. One of the concerns of modernism, as Gadamer reminds us, was the restoration of a pre-classical vision or power (mythos) that classical metaphysics (logos) is supposed to have either suppressed or erased.

Did those who advocated modernism, within and without the Church, lose sight of the fact that evil continues regardless of any paradigm shift away from classical metaphysics? This is a question Spark explores in *The Takeover*, a postmodern novel set within the panorama of Lake Nemi: "the scene which had stirred the imagination of Sir James Frazer at the beginning of his massive testament to comparative religion, *The Golden Bough*," a book which proposed that human belief evolved or progressed through three stages: first magic, then religion, then science. If Nemi stirred Frazer's imagination to search for what Casaubon was also searching for in *Middlemarch*, the key to all mythologies, Spark is doing her own stirring of a different kind here.

The novel is about the evils of neo-paganism in the 1970s. The story revolves around Maggie and Hubert, two characters through which Spark satirizes Frazer's theory of evolutionary progress, for much the same reason she satirizes psychotherapy through Elsa and Paul. The symbiotic love–hate relationship between the archetypes Maggie and Hubert represent is distracting the west from something far more serious: the "complete mutation" in the meaning of property and money occurring at the time. Spark suggests the mutation is: "not merely to be defined as a collapse of the capitalist system, or a global recession, but such a sea-change in the nature of reality as could not have been envisaged by Karl Marx or Sigmund Freud." This sober observation is conveyed within the rich and comic plot of Spark's subversive satire. Given the global financial crisis of the early 21st century, that satire of paradigm shift is as relevant today as it was when the novel was first published.

The beautiful and elegant Maggie, an American, is the contemporary reworking of a literary archetype; its pre-classical status often represented by red hair and an association with the feminine, the id, the unconscious mind, irrationality, darkness, chaos, the dionysian. This archetype owes something to *The Golden Bough* but it existed before Frazer and appears in a variety of positive and negative ways in 19th century iconography: for example, in the idealized women of the Pre-Raphaelites, and the pathologized women of the Victorian novel such as Estella's natural mother in *Great Expectations*. In the second half of the 20th century, it was a sort of literary apprenticeship for the aspiring author to consider what this archetype represents and to explore the limits of its power. They used it in similar ways but arrived at different positions on the relationship between imagination and reality, logos and mythos, and freedom and necessity. Spark had been using the archetype since *Robinson*; Murdoch used it *The Bell* and other novels; Patrick White used in several novels, pre-eminently so in *The Solid Mandala* where the archetype is a dionysian male, Arthur. Even Margaret Atwood used it in *Alias Grace* although her heroine in that novel a historical person, Grace Marks.

The handsome and sophisticated Hubert, a Briton, is the contemporary reworking of an opposite literary archetype; its classical status often represented by its attitude towards women and an association with the masculine, the ego, the conscious mind, rationality, light, order, the apollonian–socratic. This archetype owes something to *The Golden Bough* but it existed before Frazer and appears in a variety of positive and negative ways in 19th century iconography: for example, in the omnipresent, panoptic lawyer, Jaggers, who dominates and controls Estella's natural mother in *Great Expectations*. The archetype does not always fear or hate women, though, as Spark noted 18 years earlier in *Robinson*. In Hubert's case his homosexuality is more than a sexual preference for men. It is a metaphor for the classicism that is ironically dependent on Maggie's pre-classicism; they are two sides of the same

Greek coin. But now Maggie wants Hubert out of her life, and his subversion of her every attempt to get rid of him is the basis of Spark's satire of the paradigm shift that had been occurring, in many ideological and aesthetic ways, since neoclassicism morphed into romanticism, which in turn morphed into realism, naturalism, modernism, and postmodernism. For Spark, it is useless to take sides in the struggle between Maggie and Hubert, since they are immortal as well as immoral and the forces of evil can use either of them to great advantage.

As Maggie has become immensely wealthy through her previous husbands, she belongs to an international set of the incredibly rich that treats the world as their playground. Her current husband, Berto, an Italian nobleman with a famous Palladian villa, is romantic and chivalrous. During a previous marriage, before she became a Marchesa, Maggie fell under the influence of Hubert, who believes he is directly descended from the goddess Diana. Hubert convinced Maggie to buy land around Lake Nemi, one of Diana's sanctuaries, and build a house for him with pre-eminent views of the lake.

For the first half of the novel, Maggie is obsessed with moving Hubert out of her house and out of her life. She is ambivalent, though; she wants to protect him as much as destroy him; her attempts to get rid of him are half-hearted. In the second half of the novel, more urgent socioeconomic realities overtake her, once she places her financial affairs in the hands of a swindler who produces a "global" plan for her financial affairs: "so intricate that it might have been devised primordially by the angels as a mathematical blueprint to guide God in the creation of the world." The plan is unfathomable and mysterious, because it uses "the new crisis-terminology introduce by the current famous American Secretary of State" Henry Kissinger.

Under this unfathomable and mysterious plan: "money of Maggie's sort was able to take lightning trips around the world without ever packing its bags or booking a seat on a plane," from "Switzerland to the Dutch Antilles and the Bahamas, from the distilleries of Canada through New York to the chain-storedom of California, and from the military bases of Greenland's icy mountains to the hotel business of India's coral strand" before it ultimately disappears without trace. Spark's point is that, because Maggie's money is stolen during the financial crisis of the mid-1970s, she is forced to attend to other realities than Hubert, but in the process of trying to recover her money, she draws upon an indestructible archetypal power she did not know she had. In the meantime, Hubert is busy arranging a replacement for Maggie in his life: a lucrative neo-pagan religion, devoted to the worship of his supposed ancestress Diana, with himself at its head. While this central theme of the novel unfolds—how the paradigmatic relationship between pre-classical Maggie and classical Hubert distracts the world from more urgent social and economic realities—Spark weaves three supporting themes into her rich and comic plot, accomplishing an extraordinary amount in scarcely 70,000 words.

First, the novel is full of masters and servants whose relationships mirror satirize Hegel's theory of a master–slave dialectic in the development of consciousness. It is not over-reading to notice this, since the psychology of consciousness was a major theme in the 19th and 20th century novel, and interrogating the Hegelian dialectic was part of the literary apprenticeship of authors who explored the human condition. Hubert's servants were once young men, or "secretaries," the original meaning of which was "one who keeps secrets." They massaged his ego as well as his body, drink his alcohol, take his drugs, maintained his curia, and protected his paradigm. But they left Hubert once Maggie started the process of evicting him, and were replaced by Pauline Thin, a young Catholic woman, a kind of Vatican II figure who is the antithesis of everything Hubert is attracted to. Worst of all, because Pauline is a loose cannon who cannot be counted on to keep Hubert's secrets, he is forced to use his wits to protect his paradigm.

While that comic theme is unfolding, one of Hubert's former "secretaries," Lauro, becomes a servant in Maggie's household, where he wields immense power because he knows its secrets and also because he copulates with Maggie and most of her family regardless of their sex. Hubert's household is pagan and homosexual, in the classical sense, and he struggles to remain master of his new female servant. Maggie's household is pagan and bisexual, in the pre-classical sense, and she struggles to remain master of her new male servant.

Second, the novel explores the issue of title and entitlement, particularly to land. The American Maggie buys acreage above Lake Nemi, builds a new house for the British Hubert, which gives him pre-eminent views of the lake, and restores two other houses nearby. One is for her American son and daughter-in-law, Michael and Mary. Another is rented by a wealthy Italian businessman, Emilio, whose daughter Letizia resents foreign ownership without realizing that it suits her father to rent from a foreign landlord.

Who really owns this land? During the lengthy and comically fraught eviction process, a lawyer engaged by Maggie, who eventually acts for Hubert instead, discovers that Maggie bought the land from a fake lawyer who told her it was Church land, now on the market, and issued her with fake title deeds. So Maggie does not really own the land. The house she built for Hubert is *abusivo*, it does not really exist under Italian law. For at least five generations, the acreage above Lake Nemi has belonged to an Italian family, some of whom live overseas among the Italian diaspora, and the irony here is that Lauro, Maggie's bisexual servant, is about to marry into this family. Once he does, Lauro will have a greater claim to the land than either Maggie or Hubert.

Third, the novel sends up the way in which, in the wake of Vatican II, the Church flirted with paradigm shift, in the form of two pesky American Jesuits, Fathers Cuthbert and Gerard, who function on the level of gossip rather than academic rigour. They have come to Lake Nemi to study ecological paganism, including the paganism that was absorbed into, and remains within, the legends and beliefs of local Christians. First they try to insinuate themselves with Hubert and his classical paradigm, but when he brushes them off, as politely as he can, they try to insinuate themselves with Maggie and her pre-classical paradigm. Finally, they return to Hubert's classical paradigm, once his new religion becomes popular among the locals. Cuthbert and Gerard start attending Hubert's pagan services. They give out charismatic smiles in all directions. They wink at, whisper to, and nudge each other. They become ecstatic whenever they see syncretic possibilities between Hubert's pagan religion and their version of post-Vatican II Catholicism. During these pagan services, Cuthbert occasionally becomes so excited he jumps up and down in his seat.

At the end of the novel, Hubert has transferred or sold all the possessions Maggie left in his care and is preparing to leave Nemi for Rome. Maggie is preparing to move into the empty house she built for Hubert on land she does not own. On his last night in Nemi, Hubert takes a walk in the forest, towards the ruins of Diana's temple, under a moon three-quarters full, almost on the wane. He meets Maggie in the forest, disguised as an old gipsy or hag or crone, which is the disguise she used to recover her fortune. They resume friendly relations, for a brief while, before going their separate ways. Maggie explains how she has recovered her fortune by kidnapping the man who stole it and blackmailing his family. Hubert asks her whether the man can be trusted to not report her. Maggie points out that the man cannot indict her, since he is too indictable himself. Her final words to him are: "There are times when one can trust a crook." His final words to her are: "There's something in that."

William Golding

If Ricoeur is right in suggesting the myth of the fall is non-biblical or extra-biblical, how do we explain it within our contemporary intellectual frame? If it is not only a mythical first family eating forbidden fruit, and being expelled from the garden of paradise as a result, then what does it look like? Did it happen once? Is it still happening? Does it only happen to humans or does it happen to all creation? These questions were important to literary novelists in the second half of the 20th century; who were exploring the human condition in their similar-but-different ways; who were questioning what the fall means as they reflected on a century of unprecedented man-made horror, which revolved around the fact of being human.

The fall stands at the centre of William Golding's literary vision. His novels of the 1950s were informed by his experience of World War II, and his fresh memory of the unholy alliance of modernity and evil, which revealed to him the truth of the fall. His first novel *Lord of the Flies* (1954) was about the fall, as were his three subsequent novels: *The Inheritors* (1955), *Pincher Martin* (1956), and *Free Fall* (1959). In each novel, Golding presents a fall, physical and metaphysical, located within language, consciousness, free will, or a combination of these. The power of Golding's presentations of the fall comes from his gift for mimesis rather than diegesis : that is, his ability to show rather than tell, for the way he embodies rather than narrates. Each novel is a virtuoso performance. Also, *Free Fall* (1959) should be read alongside White's *The Vivisector* (1970). Both novels are similar, rhetorically, but different.

The Inheritors

Does the fall occur within language? Humans are distinguished from other genera by our capacity for language, and, among other things, language gives us the capacity for good and for evil. In *The Inheritors* Golding presents the fall in relation to language, or the absence of language, by reworking the story of Genesis through an anthropological or evolutionary prism. The novel is about a fatal encounter between two isolated remnants of different species within the Homo genus; H. neanderthalensis, who do not have language and are associated with nature, and H. sapiens, who do have language, are associated with civilization. The difference between them is anthropological and evolutionary. The former, H. neanderthalensis, are being destroyed by H. sapiens because they do not have the language that allows the latter to adapt and survive.

While Golding uses the nature–civilization dichotomy to describe these two species, his story does not pretend to be an accurate or complete history of either species or of the encounter between them. In spite of the limitations of the dichotomy, and inevitable criticisms of his approach, his story is not out-of-date, any more than the story of Genesis is out-of-date, even if science has added to our understanding of the history and the encounter. We are now told that, perhaps, both species coexisted for tens of thousands of years. Perhaps H. neanderthalensis were more advanced than Golding describes. That does not diminish the underlying truth of his allegorical snapshot of the innocence of a vulnerable species living in harmony with nature and the guilt of a less vulnerable species, which is able to adapt to nature's challenges and tribal threats. Most of the novel embodies the perspective of H. neanderthalensis through a mimesis of its communicative and conceptual limitations. The last chapter embodies the perspective of H. sapiens. Each page advances Golding's mimetic genius, as he takes the reader into the minds of two species of humans which, according to the most recent data available, did not interbreed but did share similar lineages.

There are eight persons among the remnant Neanderthals, which Golding calls "the people": an aged patriarch (Mal), an aged matriarch (Old Woman), two men (Ha and Lok), two women (Nil and Fa), a female child (Liku), and a male infant (New One). Hal and Nil are partners, as are Lok and Fa, but their relationships are neither monogamous nor jealous. The people's pre-language, proto-religion, and gender identity are precursors of what evolved in modern humans. Their pre-language is made up of mental pictures and a few words to communicate their limited understanding of what those pictures mean. Their proto-religion is a theistic precursor of animism, with its own high-god ethics, which revolves around a female creator, Oa, two letters which frame the Greek alphabet, alpha and omega, representing monotheism's sense of God as beginning and end. Their gender identity is constructed by their pre-language and proto-religion—Old Woman describes that identity in non-negotiable terms: a man is for pictures (pre-language); a woman is for Oa (proto-religion)—and the constraints of their pre-language, their proto-religion, and their gender identity frame their fallenness at one period of human evolution.

At the beginning of the novel, the people are nearing starvation as they return earlier than usual from their winter home by the sea. They are unable to approach their summer home because a log, which usually bridges a marsh, is missing and they are frightened of water and cannot swim. They do not know how the log was moved but believe it may have crawled away on business of its own. Mal has a mental picture of something similar happening in his youth, but since no one shares his picture, even though they struggle to, he signals to them to find another log. The new log makes an unstable bridge. All cross successfully, except

Mal who falls into icy water. The people rescue him but, because he is already frail and sick, he catches the chill which hastens his death.

The people's summer home is within an overhang, on a rock terrace, near a cliff, by thundering misty falls. It overlooks a river they have never crossed. It looks towards an island they have never been to. On their approach, Lok slips over a precipice, during a moment of "extreme perception" while struggling to identify a new smell: the mixture of mist coming from the falls and smoke coming from the island. The people rescue him; however, as they cannot share his mental picture of something unknown to them, it is disregarded.

On their return to the terrace, Old Woman builds a fire, which kindles hope. The next day the younger people search for food, by way of gathering and scavenging rather than hunting: they will not shed blood, as that would cause blame. During the search, Fa struggles with an idea that does not correspond with any known picture: growing food near the terrace. Lok laughs at her attempt to convey this idea, which is a precursor of gardening, since "No plant like this grows near the falls." They both see smoke rising from the island but, as they are unable to find "any picture they could share," they cannot find words to give the smoke meaning. When it is discovered that Ha has disappeared, Lok tries to find him. Because Lok has an acute sense of smell, he tells the people that Ha's scent has dissolved into the scent of others. But as Mal cannot see this picture he denies the possibility that others—"new people"—exist.

Mal dies and is given a proto-sacramental burial. This leaves an immature and unprepared Lok to lead the people. He soon sees a new person, so he now knows new people do exist, but he does not perceive them as a threat, as the people have never experienced human threat and therefore have no fight-or-flight response. Soon a party of the new people arrive at the terrace, kill Nil and Old Woman, and kidnap Liku and New One. From that point onwards, Lok and Fa are alone and become the Neanderthal equivalent of Adam and Eve on the edge of the falls: or the fall. As they explore ways of rescuing Liku and New One, so they can escape and start a new life elsewhere, Golding describes the drama of evolution—and the role language may have played in the ancient descent from monotheism to animism, or from religion to mythology—in a handful of events that occur within a couple of days.

If they are to survive, it is obvious to Fa—who has recently struggled with many ideas—that in spite of Lok's acute sense of smell he needs direction because he has "fewer pictures" than an infant. She tries to lead him but he is consistently sidetracked and fails to follow her directions not because he wants to control her but because he does not really understand what is happening around them. Their shared frustrations, missed opportunities, and failures are acted out among their shared misery at having lost their people. Their encounter with the new people, whose "many pictures" seem to them like the water they are afraid of, simultaneously horrifies and dares them.

The more the reader views H. sapiens from the Neanderthal perspective, as Lok and Fa gaze at them through the dense forest canopy, the differences between the two species as a dichotomy of nature and civilization become starker. H. sapiens have a social system of totem and taboo which includes: an animistic religion of human sacrifices and scapegoats, masters and slaves, a culture of dominance and submission, sophisticated brutal sexual gratification, relatively advanced technology, and a culture of substance use and abuse.

Lok and Fa notice Liku is tethered but otherwise appears well and New One is even being wet-nursed. At first this sends mixed messages about the intentions of the new people, but when Liku disappears Fa realizes something is amiss and the reader suspects Liku is being prepared to be offered as a sacrifice, or to be eaten, or both. In addition to being afraid, the new people are also emaciated and starving. They are in a frenzy to repair or build the boats that will enable them to get away from the island. They clearly want to distance themselves from whatever they are fleeing from, whether they are experiencing a threat of nature or a tribal threat—and make progress towards wherever they are going. Finally, Fa indicates to Lok that the new people, H. sapiens, have not come from Oa; her admission that the two species cannot coexist in harmony. She indicates that the new people are frightened of something in nature that is not real, something that does not frighten the people. Soon after this, Fa is killed and her body is swept over the falls. Golding now describes Lok as a creature rather than a human. He loses his will to live. Soon after struggling unsuccessfully to give Fa what is, apart from proto-language, that other sign of humanity—proto-sacramental burial—he dies near her body, above the people's burial mound, unable to bury her or himself.

In the last chapter H. sapiens have struggled overland, successfully carry their belongings and their boat, to avoid falls and rapids. They can now continue their flight from whatever they are fleeing and their migration towards wherever they are heading. In an exchange between two clansmen, Tuami and Marlan, who are about to engage in a slay-the-king leadership struggle, we are told why "the devils" (the people) were killed: "What else could we have done? ... The devils do not like water ... If we had not we should have died ... They keep to the mountains or the darkness under the trees. We will keep to the water and the plains. We shall be safe from the tree-darkness." The H. sapiens thought the Neanderthals were evil gods in human form, which needed to be killed because they perceived them to be a threat to their progress. They never understood the people were harmless.

Fa was right. The H. sapiens are afraid of the dark forest, an environment they have not adapted to and therefore cannot control. But they have more to fear than the dark forest. They have come a long way, over ocean or sea, and, for some unknown reason, they are frightened of being pursued by their tribe. Also, there is an eternal triangle, something that would never occur among Golding's Neanderthals. Vivani, the woman nursing New One, plays her lovers Tuami and Marlan against each other. Vivani lost a child, fathered by Marlan, in a storm on the salt water. Tuami saved New One's life as a joke and gave him to Vivani as a plaything. But the joke has backfired as H. sapiens now find themselves both loving and hating New One: an infant devil who represents what they fear most. The novel ends with unanswered questions: What will happen when the infant devil grows up? What will happen if it becomes necessary to once again offer sacrifice to a world of darkness and confusion? Both Tuami and the reader are unsure:

> He peered forward past the sail to see what lay at the other end of the lake, but it was so long, and there was such a flashing from the water that he could not see if the line of darkness had an ending.

Pincher Martin

Does the fall occur within consciousness? Apart from our capacity for language, humans are distinguished from other genera by our degree of consciousness: our awareness of self and world, of facts and phenomena, which determines our actions, and, along with language, our capacity for good and evil. Up to and including the neoclassical Enlightenment, western discourse about consciousness tended to be framed by the Platonic model of the mind as a tripartite structure of reason, feeling, and base appetite, analogous with the head, the heart, and lower abdomen. This is the model—inherited from the classical Enlightenment of ancient Greece, described in *The Republic*—upon which the influential Cartesian dualism of mind and body rests. For the last 200 years, that model has been critiqued. As part of that critique, in *Pincher Martin* Golding describes the fall within consciousness, or within the limits of consciousness.

The story is deceptively simple. A British seaman serving in World War II, Christopher Martin, falls from a ship in the North Atlantic. He is struggling in the sea. His ship is exploding and sinking near him. His lungs are filling with "air and water mixed," dragging his body down "like gravel." While being buffeted about on icy swells, in panic, vomiting water and taking in more, he has an image of a little world he once saw, which was "quite separate but which one could control." It is a jam jar, nearly full of water, with a tiny glass figure of a floating man "delicately balanced between opposing forces." The top of the jar is covered with a membrane of rubber. If you put pressure on the rubber, you can make the man rise or fall in the water, so the glass man's life is wholly within your power.

Christopher relates the glass figure to his body and the delicate balance to his situation. He thinks of his lifebelt. Once he puts it on he thinks he can control his life, and once the belt is on, his consciousness struggles between rationality and irrationality—those two Greek prisms which underpin classical metaphysics—while he alternately makes plans for survival (because he thinks he is now in control) and screams for help (because he really is helpless). Within this overarching struggle, between freedom and constraint, he thinks he will not die, because his life is precious, and because reality is something his consciousness has always constructed.

Eventually "hardnesses under his cheek" become "vicious in their insistence" and begin to "pull him back into himself." Christopher is now vaguely conscious of being on land. There follows a very slow and painful process as his consciousness struggles to ground itself and summon the will to move and act. The capacity to think eludes him during this struggle. When it finally returns he is inspired by the idea of his intelligence, by his version of the still influential Cartesian *Cogito ergo sum*—I think, therefore I am—and its capacity to save him. Once he becomes mobile, the novel unfolds in two broad spheres: his flashes of memory, of life before his physical fall, and his moment-to-moment struggle to survive in an environment hostile to human life. These spheres unfold in a real yet surreal frame, embodied and disembodied, as his consciousness simultaneously looks out at the world from within and looks in at himself from without.

Through Christopher's flashes of memory, Golding gradually assembles a picture of a man whose profession was acting, and whose life has been an act, without any sense of loyalty or morality to recommend him. He struggles through life, a failed second-rate übermensch. He has an ambiguous sexuality, cuckolds his employers and colleagues, takes women by force if they do not submit to him willingly, and trades sexual favours on the casting couch.

This is during the 1930s, a decade in which individual desires gave way to communal concerns. As the decade unfolds, Christopher reaps what he sows. First, his career does not go his way, as his producer, whom he has cuckolded, no longer gives him the roles he wants, telling him instead that he would be good at playing most of the seven deadly sins (and could play Pride without a mask, just with stylized makeup). Second, when war breaks out, his producer refuses to protect him from conscription. He is desperate to avoid conscription, and begs for loyalty and support, from his producer, from his producer's wife, but none is forthcoming. When he is conscripted he lies. He tells everyone he has volunteered for noble and altruistic purposes.

Christopher has a kind of antithetical twin, Nathaniel, who shadows him throughout the novel, right up until his fall. Nathaniel represents everything Christopher is not. He never notices his bad character, he is aware of the unhappiness at his core, he is sensitive and loyal, and he is always, with a perceptive naïveté which Christopher patronizes, holding out the prospect of redemption to a friend who consistently refuses it. Nathaniel is a spiritual person, although his religion is gnostic and dualistic, and he prays to his aeons as often as he can. He ends up marrying a woman Christopher once raped. He asks Christopher to be best man at their wedding, to honour the fact that he brought them together. Nathaniel preaches against the sort of heaven "we invented for ourselves after death, if we aren't ready for the real one"; he reminds Christopher about human mortality and the need to be prepared for death. Golding repeats this religious vision twice during the novel, verbatim: "Take us as we are now [in our dark state] and heaven would be sheer negation. Without form or void. You see? A sort of black lightning destroying everything that we call life."

Christopher's struggle to survive focuses on his ability to think, and through thought to reason, and through reason to mastering nature and therefore survival. Golding has chosen an extremely inhospitable place for Christopher's struggle to take place, which may have been modelled on Rockall, a remote islet in the North Sea, 300 kilometres west of Scotland.[2] Nature is not as kind to Christopher as she is to Robinson Crusoe, and *Pincher Martin* is a very different kind of allegory from *Robinson Crusoe*, both in its discourse and its style and the greater demands it places on the reader's imagination. Like *The Inheritors*, this is an immensely rewarding novel but not an easy one to read.

Christopher focuses on how to meet his physiological needs (water, food, shelter, warmth, excretion) and emotional needs (safety, security, wellbeing), all basic to Maslow's hierarchy, and, because all this depends on his state of mind, he is conscious of the need to remain sane. There are

---

[2] A Google search for Rockall will reveal how inhospitable to human life the islet is.

periodic assertions of rationality, as Christopher tells himself he must "use his loaf" to create shelter, find water and food, and do as much as he possibly can to participate in his rescue. Affirming but irrational exclamations of identity—I shall live! I am what I always was! I am awake!—are balanced by more rational assessments of his situation: I shall never get off this rock. The overall effect is of increasing despair and mental decline, as he tries to control his environment by naming it, as he builds unsuccessful monuments to attract the attention of passing ships or planes, as he exists on fetid rain water and seaweed and raw limpets, and as he gives himself a symphonic enema, comical and classical.

Golding signals this despair and decline with increasing surrealism. After a shapely turn, halfway through the novel, he begins to describe Christopher more as creature than human, as he did with Lok near the end of *The Inheritors*. Christopher is still the centre of his universe, his consciousness being the only universe he knows, but in fact he has become decentred: "There was still the silent indisputable creature that sat at the centre of things, but it seemed to have lost the knack of distinguishing between pictures and reality." He becomes more aware of his insanity, sees flying lizards, and eats red lobsters that could be his own bleeding hands. His final moments of consciousness are during a sea storm that, prophetically, brings the black lightning of negation Nathaniel spoke of. Christopher is convinced supernatural forces are trying to end his life. As he is meant to be the antithesis of Job, he rails against them:

> The lightning crept in. The centre was unaware of anything but the claws and the threat … Some of the lines pointed to the centre waiting for the moment when they could pierce it. Others lay against the claws, playing over them, prying for a weakness, wearing them away in a compassion that was timeless and without mercy.

There is a twist in the final chapter. A naval officer arrives on an island, not the islet of Christopher's consciousness, to claim his body, whereupon it becomes obvious to the reader that Christopher actually died at the beginning of the novel not long after falling into the sea. Most of the novel, then, is an extended exploration of the relationship between time and consciousness, and consciousness and the fall, where Golding presents in thirteen chapters what may have occurred in the final seconds of Christopher's life.

When the novel was first released, many critics thought this ending gimmicky, but later critics are more sensitive to its importance. To say the ending is a gimmick is to suggest that, without it, the reader is already aware that Christopher died at the beginning of the novel rather than the end, already aware that the novel is about Christopher's life flashing before him moments before his death, that Golding's mimesis of consciousness was a failure because it took thirteen chapters rather than a few seconds. Fiction is fiction, however, and no mimesis is perfect. As Christopher is a kind of everyman, Golding should be allowed to narrate a moral greater than Christopher's personal story. That moral is explained by the man whose job it is to guard Christopher's putrefying body until the navy arrives to collect it:

> They are wicked things, those lifebelts. They give a man hope when there is no longer any call for it.

Christopher died just after putting on his lifebelt. Whether during war and peace, then, Christopher's consciousness was never really in control, and his fall, which is a fall within the Cartesian cogito, is also ours.

Free Fall

Does the fall occur through free will? Apart from our capacity for language and consciousness, humans are distinguished from other genera by the ways in which our rationality, as opposed to irrationality, its antithetical twin, influences our decisions and actions. The question of free will tends to be framed within a debate that focuses on whether the laws of nature are determined, whether freedom is compatible with determinism, or ultimately whether freedom is an illusion. In science, free will implies that the actions of the body, including brain and mind, are not wholly determined by physical causality. In ethics, it implies that individuals are morally accountable for their actions. In religion, it implies that divinity has given humanity free will.

In *Free Fall* Golding presents the fall in relation to free will, or the loss of free will, through a mimesis that weaves the story of one man with the metahistory and metanarrative of his civilization, to the point where the personal story, the metahistory, and the metanarrative cannot be separated. Sammy Mountjoy is an artist, born in 1917, and raised between the wars, who later in life tries to locate precisely when he lost his freedom; a free will that could not be debated, he says, but only experienced, like a colour, or the taste of potatoes, along the journey from a happy childhood in a poor slum (Rotten Row) to an unhappy adulthood in a wealthy neighbourhood (Paradise Hill). This journey is not an ascent to Paradise. It is, paradoxically, a descent to somewhere else: from infancy, where nature and myth are competing influences; to boyhood, where science and religion are competing influences; to adolescence and young adulthood, where Sammy acts out the contradictions of modernity as a romantic communist; to the postmodern reflections of his maturity. Paramount in Sammy's story are his relationships, mainly with women, some of whom are tropes as well as persons. At the end of his reflection on each relationship, Sammy asks the rhetorical question of himself, or perhaps of the reader: Did I lose my free will during this relationship?

Sammy's first relationship is with his Ma, like Hurtle's Mumma in *The Vivisector*, a person and a force of nature, whom he can only remember as earth or ground, not drawn on canvas or outlined in words "ten thousand years younger than her darkness and warmth." His second relationship is with Evie, a girl who brings knowledge and myth to his life. As an adult Sammy remains grateful for these two relationships, with Mother Nature and Eve; the first a whore, the second a liar. Their memory tempts him into an aphorism, "love selflessly and you cannot come to harm," until he remembers what came after them. His memory of what came after them, his personal dark ages, his personal medieval period, his personal enlightenment, his personal modern period, begins with a disabled girl at infant school, who howls and pisses on the shoes of a visiting (perhaps royal) lady and is taken away. To Sammy and his classmates:

> Minnie had revealed herself. All the differences we had accepted as the natural order drew together and we knew she was not one of us. We were exalted to an eminence. She was an animal down there as we were all [human] up here.

Sammy moves out of Evie's orbit, enters boyhood, and befriends Johnny and Philip. This period of his story parallels the Dark Ages, where the boys are described as barbarians who bully and terrorize other students. Sammy and Philip are caught trying to invade a local parish and desecrate its altar. The verger catches them and boxes Sammy around the ears, which gives him mastoiditis, a serious condition in the age before penicillin. Ma dies during his admission to hospital, and he is adopted by the vicar of the local High Church parish, the eponymous Father Watts-Watt, an ascetic reclusive celibate who represents logos and is apparently paranoid and struggling with sexual demons. This clerical prototype, by now a clerical cliché, is a stock character in the postwar novel of ideas that parallels the history of ideas.

Golding shifts suddenly to Sammy's young adulthood but returns to his boyhood later in the novel. The shift is necessary because Sammy's first experience of romance is medieval and closer to his personal dark ages than his personal enlightenment.

In his young adulthood, around the time of the phony war, Sammy is both a promising artist and a member of the communist party. He has fallen madly in love with Beatrice, an art student: "Part of me could kneel down, could say as of Ma and Evie, that … if she would be by me and for me and for nothing else, I wanted to do nothing but adore her." He idealizes her, places her on a pedestal, as Dante did his Beatrice, but Sammy's Beatrice is chapel, a conventional and moral woman of her period, with the pragmatic expectations of her class. He tells her he will go mad without her. She warns him against saying such a thing. The more Sammy pursues her, the more she resists him, but once he has seduced her with a promise of marriage, once she lets down her barriers and plans a future with him, once the ideal gives way to the real, once their relationship becomes like millions of others, he no longer desires her.

Sammy then becomes "wildly and mutually" involved with Taffy, a beautiful fellow communist. He rationalizes their passion as appropriate, since the world "was exploding" and neither of them "would live long" anyway. They get married, for expedient rather than romantic or idealistic reasons, she has a baby, and they fade out of the party. The moral dilemma of running away from Beatrice is easy for him to rationalize, once she begins to bore him and he sees her as needy and pathetic. More rationalizations assist him: "I had lost my power to choose. I had given away my freedom. I cannot be blamed for the mechanical and helpless reaction of my nature. What I was, I had become." He then welcomes the destruction, death, and terror of war:

> There was anarchy in the mind where I lived and anarchy in the world at large, two states so similar that the one might have produced the other.

He enters the army where, because of his artistic talent, he becomes a war artist rather than a soldier.

The novel shifts again suddenly. Sammy is a prisoner being interrogated by German intelligence. His interrogators want him to inform on fellow prisoners, to prevent further escapes from the camp. The reader is never sure how much Sammy knows, or how strong his resistance is, for Golding is determined, as he is with Christopher in Pincher Martin, that Sammy never achieves heroic status. He is blindfolded, stripped, and thrown into a "cell" where he experiences his dark night of the soul. He is frightened of the dark. A whole chapter explores where his fear may have come from. He wonders whether it began when Ma died and he was adopted into the cold repressions of Father Watts-Watt's classical or logos religion; he wonders what kind of person the priest might have become had he given in to the same passions Sammy has. But later he admits that blaming the priest is an excuse and settles for a simpler admission: "Once upon a time I was not frightened of the dark and later on I was." Another chapter explores his existential panic, during this ultimate deprivation of freedom in his dark "cell." Later, at the end of the novel, the possibility emerges that Sammy's "cell" was merely a broom cupboard. While in that cupboard, was he tortured by his interrogators or by his consciousness?

After the war, Sammy continues to reflect: "Somewhere, some time, I made a choice in freedom and lost my freedom." He reflects on two normative influences at school, Rowena Pringle, a spinster who taught him Enlightenment religion, and Nick Shales, a bachelor who taught him Enlightenment science. He remembers Miss Pringle as an irrational theist, mentally and sexually frustrated, who probably disliked him, and was cruel to him, because of her repressed desire for Father Watts-Watt. She was still a good teacher, though, even if she "achieved the apparently impossible" by bowdlerizing Bible stories while "keeping their moral implications" clear, and even if she took the magic out of the scriptures by demythologizing them. He remembers Mr Shales as a rational atheist, but as there was no place for spirit in his cosmos "consequently the cosmos played a huge practical joke on him." He too was a gifted teacher, who loved humanity, and was a selfless and kind "homeland for all people," even if he "preached the gospel of a most drearily rationalistic universe."

To the boy Sammy, neither of these prisms of the neoclassical Enlightenment is real, but both were coherent, suggesting that the real universe "does not come so readily to heel." He did make a choice, though. Miss Pringle did not convince him, not by what she said but because of what she was. Mr Shales did convince him, not by what he said but because of what he was. Having made his choice, Sammy slammed the door shut on revealed religion and would not knock on it again until he was in a Nazi prison camp "half crazed with terror and despair."

On leaving high school, Sammy has a final meeting with the headmaster, who makes perceptive observations and asks cogent questions: You will go a long way from Rotten Row but only partly because of the patronage of Father Watts-Watt. If you want something enough, you can get it provided you are willing to make the appropriate sacrifice, but what you get is never what you thought, and sooner or later the sacrifice is always regretted. Is your artistic gift for portraiture important to you? Is anything important to you? You have not been happy for some years now, have you? Towards what end are you working? Sammy is too immature to understand, as he is consumed by a Byronic passion for red-haired Beatrice; his only desire is to consume her, even though, as the headmaster tells him, she dislikes him and thinks him depraved.

The novel ends with three visits, each with a twist, in which Sammy seeks reconciliation: with Beatrice, with Mr Shales, and with Miss Pringle. He visits Beatrice in the institution where she has lived since he abandoned her. She behaves exactly as Minnie did. She howls, pisses on his shoes, and is taken away. He is shocked and wants to know whether she would have become mentally ill anyway, or whether his abandonment tipped her over the edge. The doctor, who knows their history, tells him no one knows. But Sammy sees her illness as an example of cause and effect. This gives him an epiphany that reconciles the science and religion of the Enlightenment.

As a result of this epiphany, he visits the atheist Mr Shales, dying of a tired heart in hospital, but leaves before speaking to him, on seeing, from the edge of the ward, that his teacher is struggling with what science never gave him. He visits the theist Miss Pringle, intending to forgive her, but forgiveness needs to be received as well as given. She is now delighted to see him; she wants to take some credit for his success. His flesh crawls and he wants to get away: "She was still this being of awful power and now her approval of me was as terrible as her hatred and I knew we had nothing to say to each other."

Deprived of reconciliation—whether because it is impossible or simply because he is wilful and still wants it on his terms—Sammy continues to live with the mystery of his fall, without the pre-lapsarian wholeness he experienced with Ma and Evie:

Love selflessly and you cannot come to harm.

Is this true?

Robertson Davies

Robertson Davies writes about the distinction between knowledge and wisdom, fundamental to any journey of self-discovery, and about an invisible immaterial world alongside the visible material world, which is terrifying but beautiful and full of wonder. He believes humans can discover this other world through religion, and many do, but he also believes the arts—visual, performing, fine, and literary—are other paths too. He has a proviso, though, which each of his trilogies reworks in its distinctive way. He takes the view, typical among his contemporaries, that a rupture occurs whenever the western mind focuses on reason as its primary means of verifying truth claims, ignores symbolic communication—particularly the signposts of allegory, metaphysics, myth, and legend—and avoids the realm of feeling. The goal of self-discovery is wholeness—soteria—which is achieved through a right balance of rationality and irrationality, or sense and sensibility, or conscious and unconscious.

This territory isn't unique to Davies. Since western civilization began, it has been explored through many ideological discourses and aesthetic styles, whenever philosophers and storytellers enter into dialogue and occasionally make rival truth claims.

The 1950s Salterton Trilogy

In his first novel, *Tempest-Tost* (1951), Davies portrays a cross-section of contemporary Canadians living in a small provincial city. Salterton has seen more history than most Canadian cities, its tranquillity is not easily disturbed, its real character is beneath its surface; its collective self-conscious belies its collective unconscious. The protagonists are involved with an amateur theatre company, which decides to stage *The Tempest* on the grounds of a local estate. Davies gives many of them an emblematic horizon, chosen from among the normative secular and religious horizons which form the western imagination. The story is about how these protagonists interact, and how their emblematic horizons clash, as they struggle to stage Shakespeare's play. The novel and the play are both meta-fictions which throw light on each other in interesting ways.

One protagonist is a maths teacher, Hector, who is portly, single, and approaching middle age. Hector's father, a depressing failure of a Presbyterian minister, died poor when his son was fourteen. Hector's mother, as steeped in failure as his father, with little character of her own, made motherhood an unnecessary ordeal. While Hector respected his mother, and always cared for her, he found it hard to place her on any pedestal of motherhood or womanhood. He lapsed from his parents' religion (the Protestant Reformation), embraced the gods of planning and common sense (the neoclassical Enlightenment), and became a self-disciplined and self-controlled stoic with no time "to be young" or to "invite his soul". As a result, many important things were driven "down into the cellarage of his mind" where they were forgotten.

Hector, for many years treasurer of the amateur theatre company, has never acted. For some reason, which belies an unacknowledged feeling, he uses planning and common sense to secure the role of Gonzalo, the honest old counsellor, without understanding why he wants to act, now, in his middle age. Once cast, he falls in love with Griselda, a rich young woman of eighteen, eldest daughter of the estate, who has been cast as Ariel. For the first time in his life, he dreams that a beautiful woman, lightly clad, leans towards him tenderly and speaks his name.

For much of the novel, Hector behaves like a chivalrous knight who remains in the background, nursing an unrequited love for his beautiful lady. He senses danger when he sees another man, Roger, who has been cast as Ferdinand, using planning and common sense a different way: to seduce Griselda. Hector cannot see that Griselda is neither a victim nor an idealized woman on a pedestal. In spite of her youth, she can take care of herself.

The play comes together quite well, under the direction of Valentine, an archetypal wise-woman, who grew up in Salterton but spent many years as a professional actor and director in New York. Hector's emotional crisis comes to a head on opening night. He moons about and his acting is atrocious; half-way through the performance he sneaks away to a shed, on another part of the estate, where he hangs himself. The rope snaps and the suicide fails; he is eventually discovered unconscious on the shed floor. When he regains consciousness Valentine comforts him and arranges for him to be taken into the estate's mansion where the only available bed for him is Griselda's.

Valentine asks Griselda to visit Hector in her bedroom, so they can discuss what has happened. Griselda doesn't love Roger and was never aware that Hector loved her. Now that Hector knows Griselda is safe from Roger, he is happy to move on, knowing he will never love her in the same way again. He does not need to, though, since this stage of his journey into self-discover no longer requires it; but his romantic vision is not abandoned altogether, as the novel's ending makes clear. Griselda begins their final exchange:

> "I'd better go now. But I don't want you to think I don't know what a lot of trouble I've made for you."
> "It was nothing."
> "But I couldn't know, you see."
> "Of course not. You couldn't know."
> "And it wouldn't really have done, would it?"
> "No: I see that now. It wouldn't have done at all."
> "Well, goodnight, Mr Mackilwraith."
> Hector looked up into her serious face, and for the first time in weeks, he laughed. After a puzzled moment, Griselda smiled.
> "Good-night, Hector."
> She leaned forward as she had done in that first dream, and kissed him. Then she turned out the lamp, and closed the door behind her.
> Hector slept.

What will he discover in his dreams?

Shakespeare's *Romeo and Juliet* is the leitmotiv of *Leaven of Malice* (1954), Davies' second novel. That thought did not occur to me until Prokofiev's ballet score started playing in my head, halfway through reading it, and would not stop. The novel begins with a false engagement announcement published in the Salterton newspaper on Halloween. The announcement, that Veronica Vambrace will marry Solomon Bridgetower on November 31st, a day that does not exist, stirs an enmity between two families that are, in an understated way, the Montagues and Capulets of Salterton.

Veronica is the daughter of Professor Vambrace, head of the classics department at the local university. The professor is Canadian–Irish. During periods of stress his histrionic temperament bounces between two roles: the well-born Celt and the wild-and-romantic Celt. At other times, he is a secular creature of the rational Enlightenment, deeply opposed to his wife's Catholic faith which he never allowed his daughter to be raised in. To the casual onlooker, Veronica's life appears unendurable; however, as it is the only life she has, she would not exchange it for another. Although she is vaguely pleased to be of Irish blood, from both parents, she finds it increasingly difficult belonging to such a psychologically divided family as she negotiates young adulthood and embraces thoughts of independence and marriage.

Solomon Bridgetower, a young literature academic trained in Cambridge, is the son of the late Professor Bridgetower, an eminent geologist, who died when Solomon was twelve. His mother, the elderly invalid Mrs Bridgetower, is an educated but xenophobic, anti-communist, anti-fascist woman, who would have benefited from a professional career had she not become a wife. The Bridgetowers are wealthy. The Vambraces and the Websters represent the closest thing to an Anglo-Celtic establishment in Salterton. Although Solomon is Cambridge trained, and from loyalist stock, he is not an anglophile, does not suffer from the cultural cringe. He hopes to make a name for himself in the emerging discipline of American and Canadian Literatures (AmCan).

The enmity between the Vambraces and Bridgetowers began many years earlier, when Professor Bridgetower was elected dean of arts; an office Professor Vambrace felt was his by right, especially since Bridgetower was a scientist. Vambrace has always been convinced the election was a plot—on the part of a considerable number of unknown persons, to do him out of his rightful dignity, mock him, and bring him into disrepute. When the false wedding announcement is published, he sees it as another attempt to disgrace him through his family. Much of the story is devoted to his paranoid and comic–tragic attempt to sue the newspaper for libel, and uncover the plot against him, but the leaven of malice that drives the novel, which is in fact the malice in every human heart, is a moral dilemma beyond the power of the law.

Veronica is a dutiful daughter. Her problem is her father's patriarchal Canadian–Irish hold over her. Solomon is a dutiful son. His problem is his mother's matriarchal Canadian–English hold over him. They are not in love with each other. Indeed, Solomon has been carrying a torch for Griselda for several years, while Griselda does not love him and has always mocked his relationship with his mother. Veronica and Solomon are thrown together as unlikely allies: struggling to manage the fallout of the false announcement, coping with their emotionally needy parents, and working around the enmity between their families.

They do fall in love eventually, which may never have happened without the false announcement, but they face another dilemma. How can they get married, with no money, and no prospects, in the face of so much parental opposition? Well-wishing friends channel what may be the author's sentiments:

> Put first things first. Get married, and plunge into all the uproar of baby-raising, and loading yourself up with insurance and furniture and all the frowsy appurtenances of domestic life, as soon as you can. You'll survive. Millions do. And deep down under all the trash-heap of duty and respectability and routine you may, if you're among the lucky ones, find a jewel of happiness. I know all about it, and I assure you on my sacred honour that it's worth a try. Come on! You know how all this will end up. You'll act on instinct anyhow; everybody does in the really important decisions of life. Why not get some fun out of it, and forget all the twaddle you'll have to talk in order to make it seem reasonable, and prudent, and dull."

And that is what they do.

The newlyweds do suffer for taking that plunge. In Davies' third novel, *A Mixture of Frailties* (1958), they are manipulated into living with Mrs Bridgetower until she dies from a bad heart a few years later. Their problems do not end with her death, though, as she rules them from beyond the grave. Under the terms of her will, Solomon is given a one-off legacy of one hundred Canadian dollars, and, according to the terms of the will, not only must he live in his mother's mansion, he is required to maintain it out of his salary as a junior lecturer.

The rest of Mrs Bridgetower's capital, over one million Canadian dollars, a lot of money in the 1950s, is used to establish a Trust to educate young Salterton women who want to follow a career in the arts. Under the terms of the trust, the young woman is not to be more than 21, her scholarship is to last until she is 25, when another young woman is chosen. She is to be trained in Europe, and be maintained in the best circumstances, so she may bring back to Canada the intangible treasures of

European tradition. The trustees are the dean of the Anglican cathedral, an old spinster friend of Mrs Bridgetower, and Solomon. The Trust can be only be wound up if Veronica gives birth to a male heir, who is to be baptized Solomon. Mrs Bridgetower's grandson shall inherit her estate; although her own son, the boy's dutiful, long-suffering, and studiously overlooked father, will have a life interest in it.

Most of the novel is about the Trust's first venture, and a young woman's journey into self-discovery. Monica Gall, a play on Gael or Gaelic, is working class, belongs to a non-denominational sect, and sings in the sect's gospel choir. Like the sect's message, the choir's repertoire is "pseudo-religious twaddle", or "music in the service of cant", which "primes the pump of sweet self-pity, mingled with tremulous self-reproach and a strong sense of never having had a square deal from life". She has a good voice, which needs to be trained before it suffers irreparable harm; she also needs to get in touch with her Celtic roots.

Monica is sent to England to train under a celebrated conductor, Sir Benedict. He begins by suggesting to her an essential distinction between *bardic* singing, under the sign of Eros, which once distilled life and captured the beauty and delight people once found in life, and *sexual* singing, under the sign of Thanatos, which has become a substitute for life by churning up emotions people hadn't felt before. Some of the romantics are to blame, he says, although not all romantics are, and he convinces her to train as a bardic singer. She needs to get in touch with her feelings without becoming swamped by her feelings. That's not as easy as it sounds. (Jane Eyre had to find out about that, early in her life, before she could mature.)

In the following years, Monica becomes a Celtic phoenix, rising from the ashes of the Reformation and the Enlightenment in their most dissociated forms. She is transformed under a range of tutors and blossoms into a very good singer. She falls in love with one of those tutors, Giles. An undiscovered composer of genius, he is also an ungrateful user, self-destructive, and incapable of mature love. He produces *Lantern*, a journal that criticizes critics of literature, theatre, painting, and music—who are without exception men of mean capacities and superficial knowledge—but he cannot cope with criticism himself.

Monica becomes his mistress, although he treats her badly. She creates a stable environment which allows him to compose an opera, *The Golden Asse*, and she bankrolls its production from her large scholarship. It is a success, and is compared with *The Magic Flute*, but when he is criticized for poor conducting, he is consumed by an unfocused desire for revenge and gasses himself. Her first thought, on finding his body, is that she drove him to suicide, but her instincts are for self-preservation rather than guilt. Sir Benedict becomes her confessor, and proposes to her, although he is old enough to be her father.

The novel ends with Monica's return to Salterton, where Solomon reflects on what's happened:

> Mother cared too much about having her own way; result—a remarkable artist gets her start ... an extraordinary opera gets its first production. Neither of them things Mother would have foreseen or desired, to be truthful. She just wanted us to feel the weight of her hand.

Veronica gives birth to a healthy son, prematurely, after wrestling with her mother-in-law's malicious spirit in the middle of the night. Monica's return and the birth of an heir both occur around Christmas: the memorial of another incarnation. The will is fulfilled. The spell is broken.

The 1970s Deptford Trilogy

The consequences of another premature birth dominate Davies' fourth novel, *Fifth Business* (1970), an allegory of 20th-century Canada, which could also be an allegory of 20th-century Australia. The novel begins in the village of Deptford, with a quarrel between two boys. Percy's new sled will not go as fast as Dunstan's old one. Humiliated and vindictive, Percy hides a stone the size of a hen's egg in a snowball and throws it at Dunstan, who ducks. The snowball hits Mary in the head and sends her into labour. Her premature son, Paul, struggles for life. His childhood is lived in the shadow of his mother's progressive madness, until he is abducted by a child-molesting drug-addicted magician, Willard, passing through Deptford with a travelling circus. Dunstan, Percy, and Paul are of "the company of the twice born". Each rejects his beginning and becomes something his parents could not foresee.

Dunstan's life is devoted to exploring the individual and collective unconscious, the relationship between history and myth, and the lives of the saints. He keeps the memory of the snowball alive, regards Mary as a fool saint, and eventually becomes her guardian. He watches over Paul, until the abduction, and is the first person to teach the boy magic tricks. He loses a leg in the trenches during World War I and is awarded a Victoria Cross for heroism. He loves Leola, the town beauty, for many years, but eventually loses her to Percy. He never marries. His career is teaching in a boarding school, and, although he fills the role of headmaster with distinction during World War II, he is never promoted to the position. He is the only Protestant contributor to *Analecta Bollandiana*, a prestigious quarterly review of critical hagiography.

Percy's life is devoted to himself. He operates purely on the conscious level. He forgets hiding the stone in the snowball, or throwing it, and would not have cared about the consequences had he remembered. A rich young ruler on the rise, he becomes an officer during World War I but never goes to the Front. In peacetime he greatly increases his family fortune and eventually becomes immensely useful to both Canada and Britain economically, politically, diplomatically, during and after World War II. He marries Leola and they have two children, a boy David and a girl Caroline, but Leola cannot keep up with his social aspirations and eventually dies a broken and lonely woman. His second wife, Denyse, is a social climber. Together they scheme to have him appointed Lieutenant-Governor of their Province.

Paul's life is devoted to becoming a master of illusions. He's the son of Amasa, a failure of a Baptist minister, and Mary, who is unsuited to be a clergy wife. The stone in the snowball brings him into the world prematurely, he struggles to live, he is an outcast who is never accepted by the locals, apart from Dunstan. He never dwells on his abduction, though, since he naïvely initiated it. He remains loyal to Willard, who teaches him the tricks of the magician's craft. When Willard dies, Paul matures as an artist, assembles his own troupe, changes his name to Magnus, and becomes an international celebrity. In Europe he meets Liesl, an ugly but rich bisexual woman who is an archetype for something important in Jung's theory of the shadow or dark side of the unconscious mind. Magnus and Liesl meet and befriend Dunstan in Mexico on one of his hagiographical pilgrimages.

At the end of the novel, Percy meets Magnus for the first time. They are in Dunstan's study, during Magnus's first tour of Canada. Mary's ashes are brought down from a shelf. The stone is on the desk; it is used as a paperweight. Dunstan tells the story of the snowball. When Percy objects, Dunstan explains:

> I'm simply trying to recover something of the totality of your life. Don't you want to possess it as a whole—the bad with the good? I told you once you'd made a God of yourself, and the insufficiency of it forced you to become an atheist. It's time you tried to be a human being. Then maybe something bigger than yourself will come up on your horizon.

Humiliated and vindictive, Percy attacks Dunstan, but makes the tactical error of referring to Paul's "miserable mother", thus dismissing the reality of Mary and her son. Magnus calms them down and asks Percy for a lift to his hotel. Percy is found dead the next morning. Magnus and Liesl leave the country. Dunstan finds his paperweight missing and has a heart attack. When he recovers, he receives a postcard from Liesl begging him to join them in Switzerland, where his journey into self-discovery continues.

The focus of Davies' fifth novel, *The Manticore* (1972), is Percy's son, David, a hard-drinking middle-aged celibate barrister, who is called to the scene of his father's drowning in Toronto. Percy's car is dragged from Lake Ontario, he is sitting in the driver's seat, his eyes are wide open, his hands are on the steering wheel in a vice-grip, the stone is hidden in his mouth. Traumatised by the mystery of his father's sudden death (he suspects murder, the authorities conclude suicide) David seeks help.

Part One, "Why I Went to Zürich", explores David's motives for Jungian analysis: "The Jungians had two negative recommendations," he says, "the Freudians hated them, and Zürich was a long way from Toronto." He is shocked to discover his analyst is a woman, Johanna, who encourages him to talk about the events around his father's death. As his story unfolds, we discover how hard it was for him to cope with identifying the body, managing his step-mother's desire for a pseudo-state funeral, and being executor of his father's will, which he has been left out of, since he was a disappointment, as far as his father's dynastic ambitions are concerned.

As in *A Mixture of Frailties*, the family money will return to David's legitimate son and heir, should he ever have one. Once his need for anamnesis is established, he enters the next phase of psychoanalysis: looking at people he knows, looking at people he does not know but who are portions of himself, looking at what he has remembered, looking at things he thought he had forgotten, looking deeper into that part of him which is not unique but is part of humanity's common heritage.

Part Two, "David Against the Trolls", explores the scope and limit of Jungianism as a prism for exploring David's unconscious and persona. Through his journal, and Johanna's observations on his anamnesis, he learns he is a thinker not a feeler, and he gradually identifies the way his ego has projected the "comedy company of the psyche" onto others: his shadow onto the brother of his lifelong family retainer, his friend onto the stuffed bear of his childhood, his anima onto the Jewish girl he loved as a young man, his magus onto his blind genius of a law tutor at Oxford. The only archetype missing is his great mother, who remains hidden, since his inner-conflict is with his great troll, his father, who did so much conscious good and caused so much unconscious harm, between throwing the stone hidden in the snowball and dying with the stone hidden in his mouth. Eventually, Johanna feels David no longer needs to be guided in his anamnesis, can continue his analysis himself, and become stronger and more independent. David, who is still a rationalist, is not convinced and wants their relationship to continue.

Part Three, "My Sorgenfrei Diary", accomplishes what Jungian analysis cannot. David leaves Zürich for a holiday in St Gall, where he meets Dunstan and Leisl, who invite him to her magnificent enchanted castle, Sorgenfrei, which means "free of care". Dunstan is Leisl's permanent guest, and Magnus, the master of illusions, is also there preparing for another world tour. David is still burdened, he still wants to know how Percy died, the individual and collective damage Percy has caused is still unresolved.

Three important things happen at Sorgenfrei. First, Liesl takes him deep into a hidden cave, where our ancestors once experienced awe and the numinous in bear worship, and where she now worships. When he tries to escape from the hidden cave, he is possessed by the spirit of his forebears and shits himself, literally—that is, he gets in touch with his shit—which gives him the strength to move on. Second, the next day, Dunstan gives him a gingerbread bear, so he can eat his father's sins. Third, later that day, Dunstan takes him for a walk to a nearby precipice and asks whether he still has the stone found in his father's mouth. David takes the stone from his pocket and gives it to Dunstan, who:

> raised his arm high, and with a snap of the wrist threw it far into the valley. In that instant it was possible to see that he had once been a boy. We both watched until the little speck could no longer be seen again the valley dusk.

This happens on Christmas Day, Jesus' birthday. David is now free to return to Canada and try to grow into the fullness of his humanity.

The sixth novel, *World of Wonders* (1975), is the story–history–myth of Paul the boy, who became Magnus the man, which unfolds in the genre of magic realism, rather than the genre of psychoanalytical fiction, as it is a philosophical commentary on freedom and constraint not a psychological commentary. Whenever we are tempted to cast Paul as a victim, Magnus reminds us of Paul's ego and his agency. As Davies is a hermeneut, framing is important: 19th century versus 20th century, romanticism versus modernism, vaudeville and proscenium arch versus cinema and camera lens. The text is a film about the life of a famous 19th century magician, Robert-Houdin, whom Magnus portrays, which is being made at Sorgenfrei. The sub-text, which gives Magnus's performance depth, is his personal story–history–myth, which he tells to the director, producer, cameraman, Dunstan as historical consultant, and Liesl their host who remains in the background.

During Part One, "A Bottle in the Smoke", Magnus tells the story–history–myth of Paul's ten years with the travelling circus between 1918 and 1928. Some of his listeners assume he is not telling the truth as they believe autobiography is self-serving: at best faction; at worst fiction. "I did not run away with the show; the show ran away with me," Paul says, which means his obsession with the Bible, the focus of his childhood indoctrination, conspired with his obsession with the magician.

If his decade with the travelling circus was a period of hellish abuse, perhaps it was no more hellish or abusive than his life as Mary's son back in Deptford. His relationship with Willard can be read as a magic realist representation of Hegel's master–slave dialectic, and his relationship with Happy Hannah, the bible-bashing fat lady, can be read as a magic realist representation of the Protestant worldview in the western imagination. These influences are powerful forces to be reckoned with and Paul reckons with them quite well. A gypsy fortune teller prophesies bad luck for the travelling circus, which will be good luck for Paul, provided he is smart and keeps his eyes open.

At the beginning of Part Two, "Merlin's Laugh", the film is in the can. Magnus and Dunstan and Leisl travel to London to see it. On arrival, Magnus continues with the next stage of his story–history–myth. After Willard died, Paul joined the theatre company of Sir John and Lady Tresize, the first persons he admits to loving. Sir John was the most popular romantic actor of his day; an egoist with a Celtic surname, who fought against modernism to maintain a 19th century idea of theatre in the 20th century: "He believed devoutly in what he did; he believed in Romance, and he couldn't understand that the concept of Romance was changing." Paul eventually becomes Sir John's double, which means getting inside him, learning his rhythm, and becoming him rather than simply imitating him. This movement beyond mimesis—and ongoing loyalty to the romantic tradition—is the source of Paul's creative power. Although it is the twilight of their career, the Tresizes take their theatre company on a long winter tour of Canada with their successful repertoire. On this tour Paul encounters his native land and is reconciled to all of it except Deptford. On their return to London the Tresizes retire and eventually pass away. Paul moves to Switzerland, where he is absorbed into Leisl's world and becomes a famous magician.

Part Three, "Le Lit de Justice", takes place in a large bed at The Savoy, as a bed is the best place "for a philosophical discussion, an argument, and if necessary a show-down". Dunstan and Magnus and Leisl are nicely tucked up. Dunstan wants to know how Percy died; he has always suspected Magnus killed Percy for revenge. Magnus admits to owing everything he has become to Percy throwing the stone in the snowball, and makes the counter accusation that Dunstan had the real motive for killing Percy.

According to Magnus, Percy took his own life, once he realized that being Lieutenant-Governor meant the end of his freedom of choice. His only real choice was to abdicate, as his friend and hero Edward VIII had abdicated, since he believed Edward's abdication "took guts". So Magnus did not murder Percy, but neither did he stop Percy from committing suicide, as he says:

> Was I the man to fret about the end of his life when he had been so cavalier about the beginning of mine?"

Even Magnus, the egoist, the master illusionist, believes God is not dead, and God not mocked.

The 1980s Cornish Trilogy

In his seventh novel, *The Rebel Angels* (1982), Davies gradually moves another eponymous Maria away from a pursuit of knowledge towards a pursuit of wisdom. Knowledge, refracted through the prisms of the Renaissance and the Reformation, is associated with the university, an institution that "retains a strong hint of its medieval origins". Wisdom, refracted through the prisms of whatever the Renaissance and the Reformation are supposed to have subjugated or erased, is associated with a realm beyond the university. In Maria's case, the pursuit of wisdom begins when she embraces her gypsy heritage, from which she had been trying to escape, and falls into the orbit of Arthur Cornish, a rich and powerful man whose first and last names have Celtic associations.

Maria is a doctoral candidate whose subject is Rabelais. Her middle name is Magdalena, which suggests she is possessed by devils, and her surname is Theotoky, which suggests she is a potential God bearer (theotokos). But she cannot become a theotokos, or represent the Divine Sophia, until she comes to terms with the rebel angels in her life, all of whom are associated with the university. Hollier, a paleo-psychologist who is vicariously interested in what motivated the ancients, represents the positive aspects of secular humanism. He is supervising Maria's doctoral research and she is in thrall to him. McVarish, a Renaissance historian who is also vicarious, in a narrower and more limited way, represents the negative aspects of secular humanism. Darcourt, a priest–academic, represents Anglo-Catholicism, which to Davies is the most holistic expression of Anglicanism. He is also vice-warden of a residential college within the university.

Near the middle of the novel, he hosts a dinner in its senior common room. At this dinner, eighteen professors, plus Arthur Cornish and a representative of the Canadian government, eat at a high table shaped like a coffin. Two rebel angels are absent. Froats is a controversial academic who is conducting ground-breaking research into human excrement, which may bridge the gap between the sciences and the humanities and recover subjugated knowledges. Parlabane (parla + bane = speech + evil) is a failed philosopher–monk–genius with a dissolute and destructive but seductive character. If the fall is from the word—a fall that keeps occurring within language; the knowledge that makes humans human— Parlabane is the most fallen, most rebellious, and most human.

Parlabane represents the Devil. He is a character of fundamental importance within the human psyche, a character in Jung's quaternity, the fourth person of the Trinity (Jung 2009). He has something important to teach Maria: about how to be herself, not someone else, about the tree of her life, about how the roots of her tree are larger than its crown, about how her roots should nourish her crown. Maria's roots are revealed to us in her mother, Oraga, and her uncle, Yerko, gypsies who run an eccentric boarding house in one of Toronto's wealthier suburbs. They also run a smelly secret business in the basement, as luthiers, restoring old and sick violins, by encasing them in dung, and making new violins, which they invest with the romance of age and sell as authentic old ones. They are the romantic counterparts of Froats.

Hollier, McVarish and Darcourt are co-executors of the late Francis Cornish's will. He was Arthur's rich uncle, an eccentric patron of the arts, who owned an unknown, undiscovered manuscript by Rabelais. McVarish has hidden the manuscript, for petty egocentric reasons, and denies having it. Hollier wants it, for noble altruistic reasons, so it can become the focus of Maria's doctoral research, launch her on a significant academic career, and contribute something significant to Renaissance scholarship. Parlabane, who has been secretly servicing McVarish's sexual fantasies, murders him one evening, during one of their nocturnal sex rituals, and retrieves the manuscript before killing himself. But Darcourt prevents Hollier from appropriating the manuscript for Maria, and for Hollier himself, as it forms part of the Cornish bequest.

At the end of the novel, Maria and Arthur marry in Darcourt's college chapel. Hollier toasts her health at their reception:

> She is surrounded at this moment by her two families. Her mother and her
> uncle, who so clearly represent the splendid tradition of the East and of the
> past, and by Father Darcourt and myself, who are here as devoted servants

of that other tradition [the university] which she has claimed as her own
and to which she has brought great gifts ... Those of you who know of
Maria's enthusiasm for Rabelais will understand why I wish her happiness
in words for his: *Vogue la galère—tout va bien!*"

Darcourt puts it another way: "Maria. Let your ship sail free."

The frame of Davies' eighth novel, *What's Bred in the Bone* (1985),
shortlisted for the 1986 Booker Prize, is a biography of Francis Cornish,
which Darcourt is writing to support a cultural foundation that grew from
Francis's will. Arthur, with celtic affinities in his unconscious, is the
Foundation's head; Maria, with gypsy affinities in her unconscious, is a
wise background presence. Tensions emerge in the first chapter, once
Darcourt voices misgivings about the authenticity of old master drawings
Francis left to the National Gallery; he has a hunch Francis drew them
himself. The rest of the novel tells Francis's story: his history, his myth,
what is bred in his bones.

Francis's story begins in the small town of Blairlogie. His maternal
forebears, the McRorys, are poor Catholics who migrated from Scotland in
the 1850s and did well in the New World. His maternal grandfather,
Hamish, makes his fortune in lumber and finance, maintains strong links
with the Liberal Party and the Roman Catholic Church, and is what we
now call aspirational. He is made a life senator, and, after much
diplomatic to-ing and fro-ing, he arranges for his eldest daughter, Mary-
Jacobine, to be presented at Court in London. After the presentation,
feeling elevated but depressed, she orders a bottle of champagne, shares it
with a footman, and becomes pregnant.

The footman is a respectable Englishman from Cornwall, Major
Francis Cornish, who has a good name but no money, and is looking for
an advantageous marriage. He offers to marry Mary-Jacobine in return for
a financial settlement, an executive role in the McRory family business,
and an agreement that all children with his name will be raised Anglican.
After the child is born, the Cornishes move to Blairlogie where the Major
becomes an asset to the McRory empire and a good husband to Mary-
Jacobine. The child fathered by the footman is retarded and develops
microcephaly. A gravestone in the family plot tells the world he died
young but in fact he is hidden away in the attic where he is cared for by
trusted servants. Another son, Francis, grows up among this potent
mixture of reforming, counter-reforming, and deforming influences,
during which the McRory empire is re-branded with the Cornish name for
the sake of social expediency. How can Francis construct a mythology of
wholeness from all this?

Francis begins by observing the real world, and teaching himself to draw it realistically, using Furniss's *How to Draw in Pen and Ink* (1914). In the words of the omniscient narrator:

> You must develop an eye; you must see everything in terms of line and form. Andrea del Sarto was no Raphael, but he could correct Raphael's drawing; you could aim at drawing like del Sarto even if you hadn't a hope of being anything better than a Harry Furniss—which wasn't the easiest thing in the world to be, either.

Francis's subjects are wide ranging, and include corpses being prepared for burial, but one thing is uppermost and demandingly powerful in his young mind: he wants to draw his older brother, hidden in the attic, who is part of what is bred in his bones.

Francis eventually leaves Blairlogie to study at Oxford, where he is recognized as an authentic aesthete, and where he comes under the influence of Saraceni, the world's foremost restorer and authenticator of old masters. He tells Saraceni of his desire to become a painter, although he is not inspired by Modern artists. Saraceni encourages him to find his legend, his personal myth, rather than imitate Moderns who are not right for him.

Like his father, Major Cornish, Francis becomes an intelligence officer during World War II. His cover is working for a wealthy German aristocrat, in her castle, restoring her collection of old masters. Saraceni is there too as his master and fellow co-restorer. During his time in Germany, Francis paints an allegorical painting in the mannerist style, *The Marriage at Cana*, eventually accepted as the work of an old master, which is actually a representation of Francis's myth of wholeness. His retarded and microcephalic older brother is portrayed as the angel hovering over the figures in the painting:

> Thus it was, when Francis came to die, he had pretty well made up his accounts with all the principal figures in his life, and although he seemed to the world, and even to his few close friends, an eccentric and crabbed spirit, there was a quality of completeness about him that bound those friends tighter than would have been the case if he had been filled with one-sided know-nothing sweetness and easy acceptance.

Finally accepting that Uncle Francis was a master copyist, not a forger or faker, Arthur and Maria begin accepting applications from needy geniuses, and give Darcourt the go-ahead to complete the biography.

The central theme of Davies' ninth novel, *The Lyre of Orpheus* (1988), is the Cornish Foundation's first venture: bankrolling the completion and production, faithful to the early-19th century style, of an incomplete opera score, *Arthur of Britain, or the Magnanimous Cuckold*, which E.T.A. Hoffmann was composing when he died. The novel weaves four sub-themes together: first, the completion of the score by a damaged music student, as her doctoral project, and her resultant healing; second, the writing of an appropriate libretto, faithful to the period, and true to Hoffmann's intentions, as he hated the preliminary sketches proposed by his librettist Planché; third, the cuckolding of Arthur in the novel, which parallels the cuckolding of Arthur in the legend; fourth the deliverance of Hoffmann from Limbo, where he has been since 1822, following the successful staging of the opera more or less as he originally conceived it. The action of the novel is dedicated to vindicating Davies's belief in transcendence through art, and in an authentic romanticism over and above a superficial romanticism.

The completion of the score occurs under the sign of the unconscious and its realm of feeling (mythos). The doctoral candidate, Hulda, is a filthy, anorexic, and slightly crazed genius, whose personality has been damaged by her mediocre and ultra-conservative Lutheran parents, who see themselves as victims, but are in fact psychological manipulators. She has abandoned this damaging environment, which represents the worst features of the Reformation, but is rudderless. She has been exploring a modern path in composition but has become interested in the romantic tradition of the early-19th century. The Foundation arranges a special supervisor, a musical midwife from Stockholm. Gunilla—the Liesl of this novel—is a female bisexual archetype who represents something important in the unconscious. She exerts a positive influence over Hulda.

The writing of an appropriate libretto occurs under the sign of the conscious and its realm of reason (logos). Music can give life and feeling to an opera but cannot tell its tale. The task devolves to Darcourt—as priest, academic, and biographer—who represents the best features of the Reformation, and whose instincts and detective work unlocked the mystery of Francis's history and myth. So he is simultaneously the Merlin of the novel and the Fool of its Greater Arcana. He now needs to unlock the mystery of what kind of libretto will be faithful to Hoffmann's intention and deliver the composer from Limbo. After discarding unhelpful suggestions from knowing but uninspiring academic experts, he keeps his own counsel and turns to Sir Walter Scott for inspiration.

The opera is realized (directed) by Geraint, a man with a career to make in the theatre, a Welshman who is handsome, egocentric, Celtic, and Byronic. Arthur likes Geraint and has appointed him to produce and direct the opera, through which he hopes to launch the mission of the

Foundation. Maria's dislike of Geraint coincides with a crisis of identity, as Arthur's loving wife, as one of the Foundation's trustees, and as a stalled doctoral student unable to progress her thesis on Rabelais. Who is she? What is her role? Thus the Excalibur and Grail themes, and the romantic relationship of Arthur, Lancelot and Guinevere, are reworked in a contemporary way: Arthur gets mumps and becomes infertile; while he is away on a short business trip, Geraint steals into Maria's bedroom in the middle of the night, wearing Arthur's robe, and silently gets her pregnant; both men have a crisis; the woman has an epiphany; they all learn important lessons about the mystery of life and move on.

From an audience perspective, *Arthur of Britain, or the Magnanimous Cuckold* is a huge success. E.T.A. Hoffmann has been watching everything from Limbo. He has been observing the struggle to complete and produce his final unfinished opera. On the whole he is satisfied with the result. He believes it is a musical drama performed with a unity of style and intent impossible in his time. But he is not jealous. He does not sense a true romantic fervour in Hulda: "as we knew it who first felt its pain and beauty; we, of whom it was my luck to be among the foremost." He is a creature of his time. He misses elements in this production "that were familiar, rather than good."

> I have watched *Arthur* brought into being, I have watched the complexities
> it has introduced into so many lives, and, as an artist, it becomes me to
> know when enough, even of one's own art, is enough.

A piece of unfinished work brought Hoffmann to Limbo. Now that *Arthur* is done, and, as far as he is concerned, is sufficiently well done, he can finally move on from Limbo.

Margaret Atwood

Atwood studied literature as an undergraduate at the University of Toronto, as a postgraduate at Radcliffe College, and as a doctoral candidate at Harvard who chose to not complete her dissertation. She understands literary genres and philosophical movements, the novel that critiques the metanarrative of colonizer and colonized, and the national novel that is simultaneously international in scope. She also has a broad and impressive knowledge of the sacred canon, other writings from the classics, the humanities, the sciences, and the history of ideas, all of which she wears lightly and gracefully. From this we know she is aware of, on a range of conscious and unconscious levels, the tradition movements in literature share with movements in philosophy.

After *The Handmaid's Tale* (1985), Atwood continued to push her literary boundaries, as she entered the period of her literary maturity, which coincided with her middle age. For example, as far as ancient Greece is concerned, she decided Homer's *Odyssey* needed to be rewritten from a different perspective, since the traditional story, which is male-centred, does not hold water, and contains too many inconsistencies. Operating on the principle that mythic material was originally oral, local, and would have been told one way in one place and differently in another, she used non-traditional material to re-tell the story from her reconstruction of Penelope's perspective. In *The Penelopiad* (2005), she used the details of Penelope's parentage, her early life and marriage, and scandalous rumours about her, to answer a question any close reading of *Odyssey* must pose: What was Penelope really up to? As Atwood is aware of hubris, the novel is, to a certain extent, a response to questions about precursors and historicity. In *Negotiating with the Dead* (2002), she acknowledges the pitfalls of the romantic image of the artist as inspired by the muse. This is why she avoids the "often drastic mythologies" of the author as self-dedicated "priestess of the imagination" devoted to creating a perfect work. But even she admits: "In truth, if you do not acknowledge at least some loyalty to this ideal ... you are unlikely to achieve more than mediocrity, and perhaps a 'glaring insignificance'" (96). From this we can assume that, as far as she is concerned, not all literary works are equal. Also, she associates writing fiction with functions once reserved for religion, such as bridging the gap between the living and the dead, the gap between this life and the afterlife.

According to Atwood, what happens during the process of writing is primordial; narrative is motivated "deep down, by a fear of and a fascination with mortality—by a desire to make the risky trip to the Underworld, and to bring something or someone back from the dead" (156). Thus the author, although not a romantic priest, is still likened to an ancient shaman, who descends into forbidden places, and struggles with dark forces, wresting something important from them, while trying not to be killed in the process. This important something is a story, the final quality of which is a proxy for the nature of the struggle. She emphasizes the religious function of this special kind of story by retelling the story of the first shaman–author, Gilgamesh:

> He wants the secret of life and death, he goes through hell, he comes back, but he hasn't got immortality, all he's got is two stories—the one about his trip, and the other, extra one about the flood. So the only thing he really brings back with him is a couple of stories. Then he's really, really tired, and then he writes the whole thing down on a stone (176).

Being a shaman, descending into the dead, negotiating with them, wresting something from them, and ascending again to write up what you have wrested from them, is exhausting, but tremendously important.

Why does Atwood question her precursors? Is it because, as a student of literature and life, she recognizes the ways in which romanticism has influenced her own historicity? Is it because, like all historicity, her historicity is a mixture of lies as well as truths? Is it because one of her mottos, expressed by the female narrator her second novel, *Surfacing* (1969), is:

> This above all, to refuse to be a victim. Unless I can do that I can do nothing. I have to recant, give up the old belief that I am powerless and because of it nothing I can do will ever hurt anyone … withdrawing is no longer possible and the alternative is death (77).

As Atwood's career progressed, she became more interested in the future than the past, as she explains in *In Other Worlds: SF and the Human Imagination* (2011). Incidentally, in this work, SF means "speculative fiction", not "science fiction", since she confesses to no longer knowing what "science fiction" means, and she is always reminding her readers of the underlying realism of her speculative fiction. In other words, the future that interests her is not far-fetched.

While Atwood is not a literary theorist, her mature novels do question the traditional roles of neoclassicism and romanticism, and their traditional relationship with modernism, especially those written after *The Handmaid's Tale* (1985). In *Cat's Eye* (1988) and *The Robber Bride* (1993) she questions the historicity of her generation. In *Alias Grace* (1996) and *The Blind Assassin* (2000) she questions the historicity of the previous generations that constructed Canada's historicized metanarrative. In the 21st century, she returns to the future, where her heart seems to be, in the MaddAddam Trilogy—*Oryx and Crake* (2003), *The Year of the Flood* (2009), and *MaddAddam* (2013)—and in *The Heart Goes Last* (2015). More recently, she has published *Hag-Seed* (2016), her marvellous retelling of Shakespeare's *The Tempest*.

Alias Grace

The central mystery of *Alias Grace* is based on a true story, never solved, which Atwood brilliantly describes. Grace Marks was one of the most notorious Canadian women of the 1840s, convicted of murder at the age of 16. In the novel's Afterword, Atwood tells us Grace's trial was widely reported in Canada, the United Kingdom, and the United States because the combination of sex, violence, and the "deplorable insubordination" of the lower classes was "attractive to the journalists of the day" (461).

As opinion about Grace was divided from the start, her death sentence was commuted to life imprisonment. During an incarceration of nearly 30 years, she continued to polarize public opinion, and contemporary attitudes towards her reflected an ambivalence about women. Was she "a female fiend and temptress, the instigator of the crime" or "an unwilling victim, forced to keep silent" by threats from her co-accused for fear of her own life (Atwood, 1996: 461)? In searching for the true character of the historical (and historicized) Grace, as a biblical scholar searches for the true character of the historical (and historicized) Jesus, Atwood confronted the same problem they did: All the textual evidence portrays a constructed person.

Contemporary constructions of Grace's identity are aliases traceable to the master–slave dialectic (Hegel 1807) which originates in the Greek myths of rationality and irrationality, emblematically located in Plato's "old quarrel" between philosophy and poetry. Accordingly, Grace's peers choose from two possible choices; or from one choice with antithetical aspects: she can be a slave embodying the heart's noble feeling (a Madonna) or she can be a slave embodying the lower abdomen's base appetite (a whore). Her peers never allow her a master's reason, although she may have a great deal of reason she is forced to conceal. While she is aware of her aliases, as aliases, she still acts them out. Why? Is it because she has no alternative?

Depending on who you were in the 19th century, you might assign Grace an alias according to the logic of what, at the time, passed for science, or the alias might be located in the opposite of science, somewhere between spirituality and spiritualism. Those who believe Grace is evil are identified with classical reason (logos). They need to invoke their contemporary definition of "rational" science to demonize and control her because they supposedly fear the irrational, as the classical Greeks supposedly feared the irrational (Dodds 1951). Those who believe she is good are identified with romantic feeling (mythos). They are a party of strange bedfellows—religionists, spiritualists, mesmerists, hypnotists, and con men—who supposedly do not fear the irrational.

Atwood's purpose was not to write a historical novel about Grace. It was to write a novel through which she could achieve something she could not have achieved in nonfiction. This does not mean *Alias Grace* is untrue; any more than the portrayals of Jesus in the canonical gospels are untrue. Atwood interpreted her sources with wisdom and integrity. In answering the "Who do you say I am?" of Grace's humanity she complements the "Who do you say I am?" of Jesus' divinity (Matthew 16:15).

There are four themes in *Alias Grace* central to Atwood's exploration of Grace's identity. First, her experience of being a constructed woman in the 19th century, without a voice to describe herself. Second, her relationship with Simon Jordan, a doctor who wants to use her as evidence for his "scientific" theory of metapsychology which prefigures Freud, Jung, and Lacan. Third, her relationship with Jeremiah the Peddler, who has many aliases of his own; a con-man who appears to have an affinity with her but turns out to be another constructor of her identity Fourth, her relationship with Enoch Verringer, a clergyman who represents western religion, who supports her throughout her incarceration, against a great deal of institutional opposition, and who—by the way—is ultimately responsible for her pardon.

The neoclassical Simon Jordan hopes to "penetrate" Grace's unconscious, recover her repressed memories, and discover the truth about her innocence or guilt. One of his motives is to validate his "scientific" theory of mind,[3] which would give him fame for having contributed something important to "modern" medicine; although we must now admit that, like Freud's theories of the mind, Jordan's proto-Freudian theories are neither scientific nor modern. Another motive is hidden and only emerges as his relationship with his neurotic, desperate, and manipulative landlady evolves from something harmless to something as dangerous and transgressing as the relationship Grace is supposed to have had with her alleged accomplice and lover.

Doctor Jordan takes his proto-Freudian experiment seriously because he is a male and "science" is essentially a male thing. Grace pretends to take it seriously, because she has a vested interest in it, and because she has no other options. Atwood sends up the experiment. One comic sign, which bemuses Grace, is Jordan's attempt to use associative objects to trigger repressed memories. He begins with a red apple but no memory is evoked. She simply sees it as a reminder of a fruit she is deprived of in prison. Her response, when he leaves the room, frustrated, is to press the apple against her forehead, signalling to the reader that he is trying to transpose the myth of the apple, hence the myth of Eve, from one side of her cranium to the other. Then he tries a range of root vegetables (pun intended) that all grow underground; tuberous vegetables which will hopefully lead Grace's conscious mind into the underworld of her unconscious mind. That comic attempt also fails.

As the novel progresses, and each new phallic attempt to systematize

---

[3] Every age has its own definition of what is "scientific", which has the status of objective fact at the time, but is often discredited as "myth" in the future.

Grace's unconscious fails, Jordan interrogates her in an increasingly forensic manner. As he becomes more aggressive she becomes more opaque. Whatever truth she possesses is packaged within dreams or is simply forgotten; at times she covers her eyes with a hand and says, somewhat camply: "All that time is dark to me, Sir". When he attributes motives that place her in an unflattering light she points out to him that thinking about a criminal act is not the same as doing it, as she says: if "we were all on trial for our thoughts, we would all be hanged". Their relationship becomes a "contest of wills" in which Jordan wants to know what she "refuses to tell" or what she "chooses perhaps not even to know". His intention is to pry the truth out of her. He sees himself as a fisherman who has got "the hook in her mouth". He hopes he can "pull her out" of "the deep blue sea". He thinks of this mission "as a rescue" but she does not appreciate being likened to a fish. That is why she evades his hook.

During these masculine, phallic, proto-Freudian endeavours, representing the science of the mind before Freud was born, Jordan maintains an appalling and arrogant insensitivity to the social, economic, and moral dimensions of Grace's reality. Atwood is clear about his lack of humanity towards her, his ambition for himself, and the abusiveness of his experiment. Ultimately, Jordan fails to discover the truth about Grace. He becomes afraid, abandons Grace, escapes from his dangerous landlady, and flees. Later, Grace writes him a letter reminding him that he was going to "write a letter to the Government" on her behalf, to set her free, and she is now afraid he will "never do so". The power he had over her life, as a doctor and a man, explains her complicity in an experiment indistinguishable from any other treatment she has received from men throughout her life.

Jeremiah the Peddler has an apparently romantic affinity with Grace. Atwood describes an attraction between them and weaves a mystery around their friendship. From the moment Jeremiah meets Grace he wishes her luck, warns her of "sharp rocks ahead" and tells her she is "one of us", which means he sees her as a fellow romantic. He occasionally disappears and reappears in her life, each time in a new disguise: as Jeremiah the Peddler; as the noted medical practitioner Jerome DuPont; as the master of neuro-hypnosis Geraldo Ponti; as the celebrated medium Gerald Bridges. He often makes prescient observations about the reality around her and the dangers before her. She once asked him about this prescience. His reply is: "the future lies hid in the present, for those that can read it". But is he simply reading the signs for what they are? Is his supposed clairvoyance just common sense?

When they first meet, Jeremiah asks Grace to "come away" with him.

When she asks whether they will be married, his answer is: "Marriage never did any good … if the two are of a mind to keep together, they will". She is alarmed. If she is surrounded by present dangers there will still be future dangers with him on the fringes of respectable society. These are similar to the dangers facing the romantic Marianne in Austen's *Sense and Sensibility* (1811) should she become too involved with Willoughby, or those facing the romantic Jane in Bronte's *Jane Eyre* (1847) should she marry Rochester before his first wife dies. Life with the handsome, sexy, and basically decent Jeremiah may well be better than any other life available to Grace at the time. But she has been chosen for a crucible of suffering, just as Jesus was, and the life she is eventually given provides her with rewards Jeremiah could not give her.

The turning point in Jeremiah-Jerome-Geraldo-Gerald's clairvoyant ability comes when he hypnotizes Grace as part of another experiment, in the presence of Simon Jordan and Enoch Verringer, in an attempt to discover the truth about the murder. Jerome does the hypnotizing, and the reader suspects he has coached her in what to say while she is under; however, he is either a good actor or he is confronted by what the hypnosis reveals, since it reveals something unexpected even to him. While she is under, a voice issuing from her admits to being present when the murder was committed. But the voice is ambiguous about who committed it:

> The kerchief killed her. Hands held it … The wages of sin is death. And this time the gentleman dies as well, for once. Share and share alike.

The voice claims to be another servant, the dead Mary Whitney, whose spirit entered Grace's body while she was unconscious. The voice admits to telling the murderer "to do it", making the murder a proxy not only for any motive Grace may have but for the motives all female slaves may have against all male masters who abuse them.

Atwood lets the reader suspect Jeremiah-Jerome-Geraldo-Gerald is just another constructor of the historical Grace. After the hypnosis, when he realizes she is a mystery even to him, he disappears from her life for good. She has challenged romantic Jeremiah in the same way she has challenged neoclassical Jordan.

Without Enoch Verringer, the novel's moral recognition would never eventuate. While both the neoclassical Jordan and romantic Jeremiah eventually abandon Grace, the Reverend Verringer stands by her because he knows that to abandon her is to abandon Christ. He is committed to the social gospel and he is the only protagonist who sympathizes with her cultural context. As he explains to Jordan early in the novel, there is "a widespread feeling against Grace" in this "most partisan" country, from

Tories who confuse Grace with "the Irish Question", even though "she is a Protestant". In the public mind, "the murder of a single Tory gentleman" was the same as "the insurrection of an entire race" of Irish immigrants.

Verringer puts the case succinctly: "we are caught between the notion of a possibly innocent woman, whom many believe to be guilty, and a possibly guilty woman, whom some believe to be innocent". He is interested in the truth, which the Lord says will set us free (John 8:32), even if this truth is uncomfortable and an affront to positivism and scientism. Witnessing to this truth means recognizing the social, economic, and moral dimensions of Grace's dilemma. He eventually encounters evil during her hypnosis, which leaves him "somewhat shaken" and needing to pray for the strength to make the "leap of faith" required to maintain her innocence in the face of the possibility of her guilt. The strength that allows his leap of faith comes from a belief in a God who "must have his reasons, obscure though they may appear to mortal eyes".

Over time, Verringer keeps working towards Grace's pardon, against the weight of public opinion, institutional authority, vested interests, and above all against the fear of the irrational (Dodd's, 1951) that was being repackaged as science in the 19th century. If Jordan eventually fears what she represents, and Jeremiah eventually avoids her, Verringer never fears or avoids her. Why? Because he accepts that Christ can be known through Grace. This knowledge does not depend on her innocence or guilt. It depends on the broader social, economic, and moral truth of her life as a poor female slave, not simply on hegemonic male constructions of her identity. It depends on the call to repentance and forgiveness through which the fullness of divine and human love are known. Only Verringer, the novel's representative of western religion, understands the religious significance of her name: Grace Marks = the Marks of Grace. According to Verringer, Grace is not Jesus but we can know Jesus through Grace.

At the end of the novel, Grace is released from nearly 30 years of imprisonment and Verringer's pastoral care. Now in her late forties, she marries Jamie Walsh, the son of her murdered employer's overseer, who had shown her a boyish love in his youth and yet testified against her during her trial. Whenever she recalls "a few stories" from her previous life of "torment and misery" he repeatedly asks for her forgiveness. She is annoyed at first, although she does not admit it, because she knows that "few understand the truth about forgiveness". She does not believe it is the culprits who need to be forgiven, it is the victims:

> … because they are the ones who cause all the trouble. If they were only less weak and careless, and more foresightful, and if they would keep from blundering into difficulties, think of all the sorrow in the world that would

be spared.

The reader may regard this as a strange take on forgiveness, unless they account for Atwood's literary–philosophical habit of questioning traditional formulas. Just as she loves female villains, and the example of female evil, she is fond of subverting the romantic theme of female victim. She is not alone. Since Austen, female novelists have given their female heroes varying degrees of disadvantage to overcome. This literary–philosophical pursuit is not simply a matter of describing and inscribing female victimhood, it is a matter of maturity, and the literary–philosophical author knows maturity is not easy (Giffin 2013).

The Blind Assassin

In *The Blind Assassin* (2000), Atwood calls one of her heroes Iris: the muscle that controls what the eye can see; the messenger of the gods. In her youth, Iris chose between classicism and romanticism; preferring to be "upright and contained", an "urn in daylight", while her younger sister Laura becomes a romantic prototype and all that implies in the literary–philosophical tradition Atwood is questioning. The chronology is correct; neoclassicism is the older sister of romanticism; they coexist within the same classical metaphysical paradigm; also, both Iris and Laura are "like bookends" framing the character of Alex Thomas, the revolutionary or anarchical face of literary modernism and philosophical modernity. At this point, a question needs to be asked: Why does *The Blind Assassin*—which is simultaneously a history of Canada's story and a fictional reflection on the lives of two sisters within that story—conceal references to neoclassicism, romanticism, and modernity?

The question is interesting because the novel subverts the traditional roles of neoclassicism and romanticism within Canada's story. Iris ends up being different from a typical neoclassical trope. She had the clandestine affair with the modern Alex not the romantic Laura. She wrote the novel within the novel famously attributed to Laura. She remained silently in the background and allowed the world to regard her sister as a tragic hero. Conversely, Laura's identity remains a mystery. She committed suicide because of an excess of feeling—a romantic thing to do!—while Iris the neoclassical survivor lives on to tell their story, which is also Canada's story, similar to Australia's story, and the broader story of the Anglosphere. Is Atwood making a similar point about reason that many of her contemporaries make? Why does Iris have the strength of character to tell Canada's story rather than Laura?

The MaddAddam Trilogy

At the beginning of *Oryx and Crake* (2003), we find Snowman living in a tree by the seashore. He believes he is the last human alive after a global pandemic. A gentle humanoid species live nearby, the Crakers, bioengineered by Crake, Snowman's one-time best friend and rival for his beloved, the beautiful and enigmatic Oryx.

Snowman (Jimmy) first met Crake (Glenn) at high school, where they bond over internet porn and complex online games. They lose touch when Glenn, who has barely perceivable neoclassical attributes, is accepted at the prestigious "scientific" Watson-Crick Institute, while the less intellectually endowed Jimmy, who has barely perceivable romantic attributes, makes do in the "humanities" at the shabby Martha Graham Academy of Liberal Arts. When they reconnect years later, Glenn-Crake is in charge of Paradice dome, where he is gene-splicing the Crakers and slowly but deliberately creating the pandemic that will destroy humanity.

Once neoclassical Glenn-Crake unleashes the pandemic, he kills Oryx and himself, leaving romantic Jimmy-Snowman alone with the Crakers. The logic Atwood proposes here is something like this: When neoclassical reason is left to its own devices, it destroys civilization and nature. When romantic feeling is left to its own devices, it is helpless to prevent neoclassical reason from doing whatever it wants to do. Romantic feeling cannot fix the mess neoclassical reason makes. This makes Atwood sound a lot like Austen.

Oryx has an interesting relationship with her past and her present. Atwood tells us the story of her childhood in a remote and impoverished part of Asia, where her family sold her into sexual slavery. Not long ago, life as a child sex slave would have been considered harrowing and we would have constructed a narrative of victimhood around it, but Atwood does not, because her focus is female agency not female victimhood. Clearly, neoclassical Glenn-Crake and romantic Snowman-Jimmy have different kinds of relationships with her. They do different things to her. They want different things from her.

While Oryx responds to each of them differently, like Grace Marks, she keeps her true identity to herself. When Snowman-Jimmy learns about Oryx's past, he wants to construct a myth of victimhood around her, and wants to rescue her. She never buys that myth. She does not want to be rescued. When Glenn-Crake unleashes the pandemic, he murders Oryx and kills himself. What is Atwood telling us about female freedom and constraint in these different relationships?

In *The Year of the Flood* (2009), which takes place during the same timeframe as *Oryx and Crake*, the focus is on the God's Gardeners, a green sect which has reconciled science and religion while prophesying the man-made pandemic. Their dilemma is whether to remain pacifists, who pray and forgive their enemies, or become militants who pray and try to stop the pandemic. The prevailing view, promoted by their charismatic celibate leader, the trace of a neoclassical trope, Adam One, is to remain pacifists, since meeting threat with threat would violate their integrity. Significant opposition comes from one of the male elders, the charismatic non-celibate trace of a romantic trope, Zeb, who favours strategic militancy and becomes a kind of freedom fighter. When their intelligence suggests the pandemic is approaching, sides are taken. What does Atwood favour: Adam One's pacifism or Zeb's militancy? We do not know, as she is even handed, and always pragmatic, but Zeb is a sexy man.

The novel has two female protagonists, Ren and Toby. Ren was brought to the Gardeners as a young girl, and assimilates Gardener values, but she is eventually forced to leave the sect. After graduating from a liberal arts college, she becomes a pole dancer in a high-end club, Scales and Tails, where she survives the pandemic, while locked away in quarantine for several months. Toby also lived with the Gardeners, assimilated their values, gradually became indispensable to the sect, and was eventually elevated to the status of elder. She was forced to leave the Gardeners, however, as a sadistic Painballer is pursuing her. She is given a new physical identity and finds work in a luxury spa for women, eponymously named AnooYoo. She survives the pandemic, quarantined in the spa.

After several months of isolation, she discovers Ren on her doorstep, near death, and nurses her back to health, but they are also driven by necessity to leave the deserted spa, to seek other humans, and to try to rescue their friend Amanda, captured by the sadistic Painballer.

While the novel gives us little sense of Ren and Toby being historicized by neoclassicism or romanticism, their different perspectives are best read alongside the perspectives of other female protagonists in Atwood's earlier novels. While they are not tropes in the same sense Grace, Iris, Laura Glenn-Crake, Snowman-Jimmy, Adam One and Zeb are tropes, or traces of tropes, they are still on a journey into their freedom and their constraint. Who is out there in what is left of the world? Can they save Amanda? Or will they need to be saved themselves? The omniscient narrator makes a poignant observation, near the end of the novel, just as Toby feels certain she and Ren are about to die: "The Human moral keyboard is limited, Adam One used to say: there's nothing you can play on it that hasn't been played before. And, my dear Friends, I am sorry to say this, but it has its lower notes." They do not die, at least not then;

although how long they can survive is another story, which Atwood tells in the next and last volume of her trilogy.

MaddAddam (2013) is not about the end of the world but the beginning of a new world. There are a few humans. There are a few genetically-modified humanoids. There are the genetically-modified flora and fauna. There is the permanently-altered ecosystem quietly absorbing the ruins of what passed for civilization before the pandemic. It sounds dark and pessimistic but is curiously optimistic. This is a redemption story, subversive but salvific, in the tradition of North American religious allegory.

Atwood salvages the religious vision of the God's Gardeners, "saves" Toby, and gives her the central role of narrating the next creation story. It is a creation story which the romantic Snowman–Jimmy could not have narrated, because romantic tropes have never been high on Atwood's list of storytellers, and because he spends most of this novel in a comatose state before dying near the end. Instead, she makes Toby a new Hesiod, one of ancient Greece's first known teller of creation stories, and Toby's creation story is a new version of *Theogony* (c.700 BC), Hesiod's story of the birth of the ordered world. This new creation story is necessary because the ages of the more recent creation stories—chaos and creation, tragic hero, exiled soul, adamic—described by Ricoeur in *The Symbolism of Evil* (1960), are now over. Toby's new creation story is composed of her experience, which she is trying to make sense of, and putting into an oral form, so it can be passed on to the Crakers and become the basis of whatever kind of religion it might become. Poignantly, Atwood also develops the relationship between Toby and Zeb, which is easier to understand if the reader has been keeping up with relationships in her earlier novels, between Grace and her men, between Iris and her men, between all women and all men, each of which has elements of pain about them.

Unpredictable things happen, when humans attempt to usurp the gods, or God, or try to be anything more than human. Another poignant moment in the novel is when the malevolent pigoons, ultra-powerful and ultra-smart pigs genetically-modified with human DNA, stop being enemies and become allies. They speak telepathically to the remnant humans through a young Craker named Blackbeard. They say they are concerned about their future. They want the killing of their genetically-modified species to stop. We can no longer call this an appeal to a common humanity, since it has become something else, something different: perhaps a common genetic mutancy.

Ultimately, Atwood subverts Crake's legacy. We know he was a genius, in an über kind of way, but even über genius has its limits, and all übermenschen are bound to fail. Did Crake think he could predict the form his legacy would take and control how it would evolve? Did he know the Crakers would go on to develop their own language and evolve their own religion through Toby and Blackbeard? Did he know they would eventually interbreed with the remnants of the God's Gardeners, and the remaining MaddAddamites, who helped to genetically-design the Crakers, in Paradice dome, before Crake launched the pandemic? And did the MaddAddamites have any idea that they would eventually become part of the genetic experiment, outside Paradice dome, after the pandemic?

While we can only speculate about Atwood's speculation, one basic principle is certain, which is not speculative, since Atwood constantly reminds us of its reality. Her speculative future is our real present, as she says in her acknowledgments:

> Although *MaddAddam* is a work of fiction, it does not include any technologies or biobeings that do not already exist, are not under construction, or are not possible in theory (Atwood, 2013: 393).

In all these novels, Atwood provides a highly nuanced critique of how the evolution of post-romantic literature has historicized human identity. Why the critique? Could it be that, while we are historicized subjects, still processing our historicity, the future is not always in the past? Is our historicity a mixture of truths and lies? Do the prisms of neoclassicism and romanticism, or logos and mythos, need to be challenged, consistently, as they cannot be categorized as easily as they have been? Has post-romantic literature reached its expiry date? Or do we need to debate its claims more thoroughly than we have? We have Plato. We have the footnotes on Plato. We have the non-binary anti-Plato movement. We have the 'old quarrel' between philosophy and poetry. Throughout the ages we have quarrelled about the quarrel.

How helpful is the quarrel when only two things really matter, Civilization is under existential threat. Nature is under environmental threat? If we have our precursors, and we are obliged to identify and dialogue with them, are we obliged to hand them on, or can we determine the direction of our philosophical and aesthetic evolution?

Atwood is an excellent example of the options open to us.

BIBLIOGRAPHY

White's Novels

White, Patrick. *Happy Valley (1939)*. Melbourne: Text Publishing, 2012.
—. *The Living and the Dead (1941)*. London: Eyre & Spottiswoode, 1962.
—. *The Aunt's Story (1948)*. New York: The Viking Press, 1948.
—. *The Tree of Man (1955)*. North Sydney: Vintage Books, 2009.
—. *Voss (1957)*. New York: Penguin, 2008.
—. *Riders in the Chariot (1961)*. New York: New York Review Books, 2002.
—. *The Solid Mandala (1966)*. Harmondsworth: Penguin Books, 1983.
—. *The Vivisector (1970)*. London: Penguin Books, 2008.
—. *The Eye of the Storm (1973)*. New York: Picador, 2012.
—. *A Fringe of Leaves (1976)*. North Sydney: Vintage, 1997.
—. *The Twyborn Affair (1979)*. New York: The Viking Press, 1980.
—. *Memoires of Many in One (1986)*. London: Jonathan Cape, 1986.
—. *Three Uneasy Pieces (1987)*. London: Jonathan Cape, 1988.
—. *The Hanging Garden (2012)*. London: Jonathan Cape, 2012.

White's Short Stories

—. "The Twitching Colonel" (1937). In *Patrick White: Selected Writings (1994)*, by Alan Lawson, 3–11. St Lucia: Uni of Queensland Press, 1994.
—. "A Cheery Soul." In *The Burnt Ones (1964)*, by Patrick White, 145–180. New York: The Viking Press, 1964.
—. "Miss Slattery and Her Demon Lover." In *The Burnt Ones (1964)*, by Patrick White, 199–216. New York: The Viking Press, 1964.
—. "The Letters." In *The Burnt Ones (1964)*, by Patrick White, 217–232. New York: The Viking Press, 1964.
—. "The Night The Prowler." In *The Cockatoos* (1975), by Patrick White, 120–168. New York: The Viking Press, 1975.

White's Plays

—. "The Ham Funeral" (1947). In *Four Plays* (1965), by Patrick White, 11–74. London: Eyre & Spottiswoode, 1965.

—. "A Cheery Soul" (1962). In *Four Plays* (1965), by Patrick White, 179–264. London: Eyre & Spottiswoode, 1965.

—. "Night on Bald Mountain" (1962). In *Four Plays* (1965), by Patrick White, 265–356. London: Eyre & Spottiswoode, 1965.

White's Nonfiction

—. *Flaws in the Glass (1981).* New York: Viking, 1981.

—. *Patrick White Speaks (1989).* Sydney: Primavera Press, 1989.

Other Authors

Abrams, M.H. *The Mirror and the Lamp: Romantic Theory and the Critical Tradition (1953).* New York: Oxford Uni Press, 1953.

Ali, Ameer. "Negotiating Otherness: The Muslim Community in Australia." In *Patrick White Centenary: The Legacy of a Prodigal Son*, by Cynthia vanden Dreisen and Bill Ashcroft, 486–495. Newcastle upon Tyne, Cambridge Scholars Publishing, 2014.

Alomes, Stephen. "Flaws in the Glass: Why Australia did not Become a Republic ... after Patrick White." In *Patrick White Centenary: The Legacy of a Prodigal Son*, by Cynthia vanden Dreisen and Bill Ashcroft, 470–485. Newcastle upon Tyne, Cambridge Scholars Publishing, 2014.

Alonso-Breto, Isabel. "The Shift from Commonwealth to Postcolonial Literatures: Patrick White's The Twitching Colonel and Manuka Wijesinghe's Theravada Man." In *Patrick White Centenary: The Legacy of a Prodigal Son (2014)*, by Cynthia vanden Dreisen and Bill Ashcroft, 302–318. Newcastle upon Tyne, Cambridge Scholars Publishing, 2014.

Aristotle. *Poetics (c.335 BC).* Oxford: Oxford Uni Press, 2013.

Aschheim, Steven. *The Nietzsche Legacy in Germany 1890–1990 (1994).* Berkeley: Uni of California Press, 1994.

Atwood, Margaret. *The Edible Woman (1969).* Toronto: McClelland and Stewart, 1969.

—. *The Handmaid's Tale (1985).* London: Vintage, 1996.

—. *Cat's Eye (1988).* London: Virago Press, 2011.

—. *The Robber Bride (1993).* London: Virago Press, 2002.

—. *Alias Grace (1996).* New York: Anchor Books, 1997.

—. *The Blind Assassin (2000).* London: Virago Press, 2001.

—. *Negotiating with the Dead: A Writer on Writing.* Cambridge: Cambridge Uni Press, 2002.

—. *Oryx and Crake (2003).* New York: Nan A. Talese, 2003.

—. *The Penelopiad (2005).* Edinburgh: Canongate, 2005.

—. *In Other Worlds: SF and the Human Imagination (2011).* New York: Doubleday, 2011.

—. *The Year of the Flood (2009).* New York: Nan A. Talese, 2009.

—. *MaddAddam (2013).* New York: Doubleday, 2013.

—. *The Heart Goes Last (2015).* New York: Penguin Random House, 2015.

—. *Hag-Seed (2016).* New York: Penguin Random House, 2016.

Auerbach, Eric. *Mimesis: The Representation of Reality in Western Literature (1953).* Princeton: Princeton Uni Press, 2003.

Austen, Jane. *Sense and Sensibility (1811).* Cambridge UK: Cambridge Uni Press, 2006.

Bakhtin, Mikhail. *Rabelais and His World (1968).* Bloomington: Indiana Uni Press, 1984.

—. *Problems of Dostoevky's Poetics (1984).* Minneapolis: Uni of Minnesota Press, 1984.

—. *The Dialogic Imagination (1981).* Austin: Uni of Texas Press, 2011.

Barclay, John. *Jews in the Mediterranean Diaspora.* Berkeley: Uni of California Press, 1996.

—. *Negotiating Diaspora (2004).* London: T&T Clark, 2004.

Battye, Greg. "Looking at Patrick White Looking." In *Patrick White Centenary: The Legacy of a Prodigal Son*, by Cynthia vanden Dreisen and Bill Ashcroft, 164–180. Newcastle upon Tyne, Cambridge Scholars Publishing, 2014.

Bauman, Zygmunt. *Modernity and the Holocaust* (1989). Ithaca: Cornell University Press, 2000

Bauman, Zygmunt. *Wasted Lives: Modernity and its Outcasts* (2003). Cambridge: Blackwell, 2004

Beatson, Peter. *The Eye in the Mandala (1976).* London: Barnes & Noble, 1976.

Beckett, Samuel. *Waiting for Godot (1949).* New York: Grove Press, 1954.

Ben-Bassat, Hedda. "To Gather The Sparks: Kabbalistic and Hasidic Elements in Patrick White's Riders in the Chariot." *Literature and Theology*, 1990: 327–345.

Benedict XVI. "Faith, Reason and the University: Memories and Reflections." Vatican website. 12 September 2006.

http://w2.vatican.va/content/benedict-xvi/en/speeches/2006/september/
documents/hf_ben-xvi_spe_20060912_university-regensburg.html.

Berlin, Isaiah. *The Roots of Romanticism (1999).* Princeton: Princeton Uni
Press, 2013.

Bevis, Matthew. *Comedy: A Very Short Introduction (2013).* New York:
Oxford Uni Press, 2013.

Blake, William. "All Religions Are One (1794)." In *The Complete Poems*,
by William Blake, 77–78. London: Penguin Books, 1977.

Blake, William. "The Marriage of Heaven and Hell (1790–1793)." In *The
Complete Poems*, by William Blake, 180–193. London: Penguin
Books, 1977.

Blake, William. "There Is No Natural Religion (1794)." In *The Complete
Poems*, by William Blake, 75–76. London: Penguin Books, 1977.

Bliss, Caroline. *Patrick White's Fiction: The Paradox of Fortunate
Failure (1986).* New York: St Martin's Press, 1986.

Bloom, Harold. *Ruin the Sacred Truths (1987).* Cambridge Mass: Harvard
Uni Press, 1991.

—. *The Western Canon (1994).* New York: Harcourt Brace & Company,
1994.

Boyarin, Daniel. *A Radical Jew: Paul and the Politics of Identity (1994).*
Berkeley: Uni of California Press, 1997.

—. *Sparks of the Logos: Essays in Rabbinic Hermeneutics (2003).* Leiden:
Brill, 2003.

—. *Border Lines: The Partition of Judaeo-Christianity (2004).* Philadelphia:
Uni of Pennsylvania Press, 2004.

—. *Socrates and the Fat Rabbis (2009).* Chicago: Uni of Chicago Press,
2009.

—. "Logos, A Jewish Word: John's Prologue as Midrash." In *The Jewish
New Testament (2011)*, by Amy-Jill Levine and Marc Zvi Brettler,
546–549. 2011.

—. *The Jewish Gospels: The Story of the Jewish Christ.* New York: The
New Press, 2012.

—. *A Traveling Homeland: The Babylonian Talmud as Diaspora (2015).*
Philadelphia: Uni of Pennsylvania Press, 2015.

Brettler, Marc Zvi. "The New Testament between the Hebrew Bible
(Tanakh) and Rabbinic Literature." In *The Jewish New Testament*, by
Amy-Jill Levine and Marc Zvi Brettler, 504–506. New York: Oxford
Uni Press, 2011.

Brontë, Charlotte. *Jane Eyre (1847).* London: Penguin Books, 1996.

Brown, John. *The Riddle of the Pacific (1924).* Kempton Illinois:
Adventures Unlimited, 2003.

Brown, Norman. *Life Against Death: The Psychoanalytical Meaning of History (1959)*. Middletown CT: Wesleyan Uni Press, 1985.

—. *Love's Body (1966)*. Berkeley: Uni of California Press, 1966.

—. *Apocalypse and/or Metamorphosis*. Berkeley: Uni of California Press, 1991.

Bulman-May, James. *Patrick White and Alchemy*. Melbourne: Australian Scholarly Publishing, 2001.

Butler, Christopher. *Modernism: A Very Short Introduction (2010)*. New York: Oxford Uni Press, 2010.

—. *Postmodernism: A Very Short Introduction (2002)*. New York: Oxford Uni Press, 2002.

Butler, E.M. *The Tyranny Of Greece Over Germany (1935)*. Cambridge UK: Cambridge Uni Press, 2011.

Byatt, A.S. *The Virgin in the Garden (1978)*. London: Vintage Books, 1992.

Clements, James. *Mysticism and the Mid-Century Novel (2012)*. New York: Palgrave Macmillan, 2012.

Cobb, John. Pantheism and Panentheism. In *A New Dictionary of Christian Theology*, by Alan Richarson and John Bowden. London: SCM Press, 1984.

Coetzee, J.M. Introduction. In *The Vivisector (1970)*, by Patrick White. New York: Penguin Books, 2008.

Coleridge, Samuel Taylor. "Kubla Khan (1816)." In *The Complete Poems*, by Samuel Taylor Coleridge, 249–251. London: Penguin Books, 1997.

Collins, John. *Between Athens and Jerusalem: Jewish Identity in the Hellenistic Diaspora (2000)*. Grand Rapids: William B. Eerdmans, 2000.

Cornford, Francis. *From Religion to Philosophy: A Study in the Origins of Western Speculation (1912)*. Mineola NY: Dover Publications, 2004.

Crews, Fredrick. *The Pooh Perplex (1963)*. Chicago: Uni of Chicago Press, 2003.

—. *Postmodern Pooh (2001)*. Evanston: Northwestrn Uni Press, 2006.

Critchley, Simon. *Continental Philosophy: A Very Short Introduction (2001)*. New York: Oxford Uni Press, 2001.

Culp, Andrew. *Dark Deleuze (2016)*. Minneapolis: Uni of Minnesota Press, 2016.

Davey, Nicholas. "Gadamer's Aesthetics." In *The Stanford Dictionary of Philosophy*, by Edward Zalta, http://plato.stanford.edu/archives/sum2015/entries/gadamer-aesthetics. Stanford: The Metaphysics Research Lab, Stanford University , 2011.

Davies, Robertson. "Tempest-Tost (1951)." In *The Salterton Trilogy (1986)*, by Robertson Davies, 1–248. New York: Penguin Books, 1991.

—. "Leaven of Malice (1954)." In *The Salterton Trilogy (1986)*, by Robertson Davies, 249–478. New York: Penguin Books, 1991.

—. "A Mixture of Frailties (1958)." In *The Salterton Trilogy (1986)*, by Robertson Davies, 479–808. New York: Penguin Books, 1991.

—. "Fifth Business (1970)." In *The Deptford Trilogy (1983)*, by Robertson Davies, 1–257. New York: Penguin Books, 1990.

—. "The Manticore (1972)." In *The Deptford Trilogy (1983)*, by Robertson Davies, 259–515. New York: Penguin Books, 1990.

—. "World of Wonders (1975)." In *The Deptford Trilogy (1983)*, by Robertson Davies, 517–825. New York: Penguin Books, 1990.

—. "The Rebel Angels (1981)." In *The Cornish Trilogy (1992)*, by Robertson Davies, 1–311. New York: Penguin Books, 1992.

—. "What's Bred in the Bone (1985)." In *The Cornish Trilogy (1992)*, by Robertson Davies, 313–737. New York: Penguin Books, 1992.

—. "The Lyre of Orpheus (1988)." In *The Cornish Trilogy* (1992), by Robertson Davies, 739–1136. New York: Penguin Books, 1992.

Davies, W.D. *Paul and Rabbinic Judaism (1948)*. London: S.P.C.K, 1965.

de Soyza, Anne. "Aboriginal Progress in the Native Title Era: Truth and Substantive Equality in Terra Nullius." In *Patrick White Centenary: The Legacy of a Prodigal Son*, by Cynthia vanden Dreisen and Bill Ashcroft, 400–412. Newcastle upon Tyne, Cambridge Scholars Publishing, 2014.

Deleuze, Gilles. *Essays Critical and Clinical (1993)*. Minneapolis: Uni of Minnesota Press, 1997.

Delmer, Sefton. *Black Boomerang (1962)*. London: Secker & Warburg, 1962.

Derrida, Jacques. "White Mythology: Metaphor in the Text of Philosophy." In *Margins of Philosophy (1972)*, by Jacques Derrida. Chicago: University of Chicago Press, 1982.

Detweiler, Robert and Doty, William. *The Daemonic Imagination: Biblical Text and Secular Story (1990)*. Atlanta: Scholars Press, 1990.

DiCenso, James. *Hermeneutics and the Disclosure of Truth (1990)*. Charlottesville: Uni Press of Virginia, 1990.

Dodds, E.R. *The Greeks and the Irrational (1951)*. Berkeley: Uni of California Press, 1951.

Dolin, Keiran. "Rewriting Australia's Foundation Narrative: White, Scott and the Mabo Case." In *Patrick White Centenary: The Legacy of a Prodigal Son*, by Cynthia vanden Dreisen and Bill Ashcroft, 413–428. Newcastle upon Tyne, Cambridge Scholars Publishing, 2014.

During, Simon. *Patrick White (1996)*. Melbourne: Oxford Uni Press, 1996.

Eagleton, Terry. *Sweet Violence: The Idea of the Tragic*. Oxford: Blackwell Publishing, 2003.

Eiss, Harry. "The Fool." In *The Joker*, by Harry Eiss, 420–448. Newcastle upon Tyne: Cambridge Scholars Publishing, 2016.

Eliot, George. *Middlemarch (1871–1872)*. Harmondsworth: Penguin Books, 1983.

Feiner, Schmuel. *The Jewish Enlightenment (2002)*. Philadelphia: Uni of Pennsylvania Press, 2004.

Ferber, Michael. *Romanticism: A Very Short Introduction*. New York: Oxford Uni Press, 2010.

Frazer, James. *The Golden Bough (1890)*. New York: Oxford Uni Press, 2009.

Freud, Sigmund. "Five Lectures on Psychoanalysis, Leonardo Da Vinci and Other Works." In *The Standard Edition of the Complete Psychological Works of Sigmund Freud: Volume XI (1910)*, by Sigmund Freud, 165–175. London: Vintage Books, 1957.

Freud, Sigmund. "Jensen's Gavida and Other Works." In *The Standard Edition of the Complete Psychological Works of Sigmund Freud: Volume IX (1906–1908)*, by Sigmund Freud, 237–241. London: Vintage Books, 1959.

Freud, Sigmund. "Moses and Monotheism." In *The Standard Edition of the Complete Psychological Works of Sigmund Freud: Volume XXIII (1937–1939)*, by Sigmund Freud, 7–16. London: Vintage Books, 1964.

Frye, Northrop. *The Great Code: The Bible and Literature*. San Diego: Harvest Books, 1983.

—. *Words With Power: A Second Study of "The Bible and Literature"*. San Diego: Harcourt Books, 1990.

Gadamer, Hans-Georg. *Truth and Method (1960)*. New York: Bloomsbury Academic, 2013.

Galambush, Julie (2005). *The Reluctant Parting: How the New Testament's Jewish Writers Created a Christian Book (2005)*. New York: HarperCollins, 2005.

Gardner, Helen. *In Defence of the Imagination (1982)*. Cambridge Mass: Harvard Uni Press, 1982.

Giffin, Michael. *Funny Little Things: Perceptions of Childhood in the Novels of Patrick White*. Uni of New England: Master of Letters Thesis (unpublished), 1989.

—. *The Religious Imagination in the Fiction of Patrick White: Arthur's Dream: (1996)*. Lewiston NY: Edwin Mellen Press, 1999.

—. *Jane Austen and Religion (2002)*. Basingstoke: Palgrave Macmillan, 2002.

—. *Female Maturity from Jane Austen to Margaret Atwood: When Bildungsroman Meets Zeitgeist (2013)*. Charleston SC: CreateSpace Independent Publishing, 2013.

Gillespie, Michael. *The Theological Origins of Modernity (2008)*. Chicago: Uni of Chicago Press, 2009.

Golding, William. *Lord of the Flies (1954)*. New York: Perigree Books, 1954

—. *The Inheritors (1955)*. London: Faber and Faber, 2005.

—. *Pincher Martin (1956)*. London: Faber and Faber, 2005.

—. *Free Fall (1959)*. London: Faber and Faber, 1959.

Goodman, Martin. *Rome and Jerusalem: The Clash of Ancient Civilizations (2007)*. New York: Vintage Books, 2008.

Gottleib, Anthony. *The Dream of Reason: A History of Philosophy from the Greeks to the Renaissance (2016)*. London: Penguin UK, 2016.

Graham-Smith, Gregory. "Against the Androgyne as Humanist Hero: Patrick White's Queering of the Platonic Myth." In *Remembering Patrick White: Contemporary Critical Essays*, by Elizabeth McMahon and Brigitta Olubas , 163–179. Amsterdam: Rodopi, 2010.

Green, Dorothy. "The Edge of Error." *Quadrant*, November–December 1973: 36–47.

Green, Garrett. *Theology, Hermeneutics, and Imagination: The Crisis of Interpretation at the End of Modernity (2000)*. Cambridge UK: Cambridge Uni Press, 2000.

Gregory, Brad. *The Unintended Reformation: How a Religious Revolution Secularized Society (2012)*. Cambridge Mass: Harvard Uni Press, 2015.

Grieves, Vicki. "Patrick White, Belltrees and the Station Complex: Some Reflections." In *Patrick White Centenary: The Legacy of a Prodigal Son*, by Cynthia vanden Dreisen and Bill Ashcroft, 429–442. Newcastle upon Tyne, Cambridge Scholars Publishing, 2014.

Griswold, Charles. *Self-Knowledge in Plato's Phaedrus (1986)*. University Park PA: Pennsylvania State Uni Press, 1996.

Halliwell, Stephen. *The Aesthetics of Mimesis (2002)*. Princeton: Princeton Uni Press, 2002.

Handelman, Susan. *Slayers of Moses: The Emergence of Rabbinic Interpretation in Modern Literary Theory (1982)*. New York: State Uni of New York Press, 1982.

Hardy, Thomas. *Jude the Obscure (1895)*. London: Penguin Books, 1998.

Harris, Jocelyn. *A Revolution Almost beyond Expression: Jane Austen's Persuasion (2007)*. Newark: Uni of Delaware Press, 2007.

Harrison, Jane. *Prolegomena to the Study of Greek Religion (1903)*. Princeton: Princeton Uni Press, 1991.

Havelock, Eric. *Preface to Plato (1963)*. Cambridge Mass: Harvard Uni Press, 1963.

Hegel, Georg. *The Phenomenology of Mind (1807)*. Mineola NY: Dover Publications, 2003.

Heidegger, Martin. *Being and Time (1927)*. New York: HarperPerennial, 2008.

Heltay, Hilary. *The articles and the novelist: reference conventions and reader manipulation in Patrick White's creation of fictional worlds*. Tubingen: Gunter Narr Verlag, 1983.

Henderson, Ian. "Knockabout World: Patrick White, Kenneth Williams and the Queer Word." In *Patrick White Beyond the Grave*, by Ian Henderson and Anouk Lang, 181–192. London: Anthem Press, 2015.

Hesiod. *Theogony and Works and Days (c.700 BC)*. London: Oxford Uni Press, 2008.

Hewitt, Jennifer. *Patrick White, Painter Manqué (2002)*. Melbourne: Miegunyah Press, 2002.

Hollier, Gordon. *The Rocks and Sticks of Words (1992)*. Amsterdam: Rodopi, 1992.

Honour, Hugh. *Neoclassicism (1968)*. London: Penguin Books, 1991.

—. *Romanticism (1979)*. New York: Westview Press, 1979.

Horan, Daniel. *Postmodernity and Univocity: A Critical Account of Radical Orthodoxy (2014)*. Minneapolis: Fortress Press, 2014.

Horkheimer, Max and Adorno, Theodor. *Dialectic of Enlightenment (1944)*. Stanford: Stanford Uni Press, 2002.

Hughes, Robert. *The Shock of the New (1980)*. London: Thames and Hudson , 1991.

Ingersoll, Earl. *Waltzing Again: New and Selected Conversations with Margaret Atwood (2006)*. Princeton: Ontario Review Press, 2006.

Inwood, Michael. *Heidegger: A Very Short Introduction (1997)*. New York: Oxford Uni Press, 2000.

Jacob, W.M. *The Clerical Profession in the Long Eighteenth Century 1680–1840 (2007)*. New York: Oxford Uni Press, 2007.

Jarratt, Susan. *Rereading the Sophists: Classical Rhetoric Refigured (1991)*. Carbondale: Southern Illinois Uni Press, 1991.

Jaspers, Karl. *Tragedy Is Not Enough (1952)*. Hamden CT: Archon Books, 1969.

Johnston, Adrian. "Jacques Lacan." In *The Stanford Encyclopedia of Philosophy*, by Edward Zalta, http://plato.stanford.edu/archives/sum2014/entries/lacan/. Stanford: The Metaphysics Research Lab, Stanford University, 2014.

Joyce, Clayton. *Patrick White: A Tribute (1991)*. North Ryde: HarperCollins, 1991.

Jung, Carl. *Psychology and Alchemy (1953)*. Princeton: Princeton Uni Press, 1993.

—. *The Red Book (2009)*. New York: W.W. Norton & Co., 2009.

Kamesar, Adam. *The Combridge Companion to Philo (2009)*. New York: Cambridge Uni Press, 2010.

Kaufmann, Walter. *Translator's Introduction to The Birth of Tragedy and The Case of Wagner (1966)*. New York: Vintage Books, 1967.

—. *Tragedy and Philosophy (1968)*. Princeton: Princeton Uni Press, 1992.

Kaur, Ishmeet. "Establishing a Connection: Resonances in Gurugranth Sahib and Works of Patrick White." In *Patrick White Centenary: The Legacy of a Prodigal Son*, by Cynthia vanden Dreisen and Bill Ashcroft, 339–353. Newcastle upon Tyne, Cambridge Scholars Publishing, 2014.

Kermode, Frank. *Romantic Image (1957)*. London: Routledge Classics, 2002.

—. *The Genesis of Secrecy (1979)*. Cambridge Mass: Harvard Uni Press, 2006.

—. *The Sense of an Ending: Studies in the Theory of Fiction (1966)*. Oxford UK: Oxford Uni Press, 2000.

—. "Freedom and Interpretation" (1993). In *Freedom and Interpretation: The Oxford Amnesty Lectures 1992*, by Barbara Johnson. New York: Basic Books, 1993.

—. "On Being an Enemy of Humanity" (1991). In *The Uses of Error*, by Frank Kermode. London: Collins, 1991.

Knox-Shaw, Peter. *Jane Austen and the Enlightenment (2004)*. Cambridge: Cambridge Uni Press, 2009.

Kramer, Leonie. "Patrick White's Götterdämmerung." *Quadrant*, May–June 1973: 8–19.

Krieger, Murray. *The Classic Vision: The Retreat from Extremity in Modern Literature*. Baltimore: Johns Hopkins Uni Press, 1971.

—. *The Tragic Vision: Visions of Extremity in Modern Literature (1960)*. Baltimore: Johns Hopkins Uni Press, 1973.

Lacan, Jacques. *Écrits (1966)*. New York: W.W. Norton & Co., 2006.

Laing, R.D. *The Politics of Experience and The Bird of Paradise (1967)*. London: Penguin Books, 1990.

Lang, Anouk. "Queering Sarsaparilla: Patrick White's Deviant Modernism."
    In *Patrick White Beyond the Grave*, by Ian Henderson and Anouk
    Lang, 193–204. London: Anthem Press, 2015.
Lawrence, D.H. *Psychoanalysis and the Unconscious (1921) and Fantasia
    of the Unconscious (1922)*. Mineola NY: Dover Publications, 2005.
—. *The Rainbow (1915)*. Harmondsworth: Penguin Books, 1981.
Leane, Jeanine. "White's Tribe: Patrick White's Representation of the
    Australian Aborigine in A Fringe of Leaves." In *Patrick White
    Centenary: The Legacy of a Prodigal Son*, by Cynthia vanden Dreisen
    and Bill Ashcroft, 257–268. Newcastle upon Tyne, Cambridge Scholars
    Publishing, 2014.
Ledbetter, Mark. "An Apocalypse of Race and Gender: Body Violence
    and Forming Identity in Toni Morrison's *Beloved.*" In *Postmodernism,
    Literature and the Future of Theology*, by David Jasper. London:
    Macmillan, 1993.
Levenson, David. "Messianic Movements." In *The Jewish New Testament
    (2011)*, by Amy-Jill Levine and Marc Zvi Brettler, 530–353. New
    York: Oxford Uni Press, 2011.
Levine, Amy-Jill. *The Misunderstood Jew: The Church and the Scandal of
    the Jewish Jesus (2006)*. New York: HarperCollins, 2006.
—. *Short Stories by Jesus: The Enigmatic Parables of a Controversial
    Rabbi* (2014). New York: HarperCollins, 2014.
Litvak, Olga. *Haskalah: The Romantic Movement in Judaism (2012)*. New
    Brunswick: Rutgers Uni Press, 2012.
Llewelyn, Robert. *With Pity Not With Blame (1982)*. Norwich: Canterbury
    Press, 2013.
Locke, John. *An Essay Concerning Human Understanding (1690)*.
    London: Penguin Books, 1997.
Locke, John. "The First and Second Treatises of Government (1689–
    1690)." In *The Selected Political Writings of John Locke*, by John
    Locke. New York: Norton Critical Editions, 2005.
Lovejoy, Arthur. *The Great Chain of Being (1936)*. Cambridge MA:
    Harvard Uni Press, 1964.
MacDougall, Scott. "Daniel P. Horan Postmodernity and Univocity: A
    Critical Account of Radical Orthodoxy." *Anglican Theological Review*,
    Spring 2015: 343–345.
MacIntyre, Alasdair. *After Virtue (1981)*. Notre Dame: Uni of Notre Dame
    Press, 2007.
—. *Whose Justice? Which Rationality? (1988)*. Notre Dame: Uni of Notre
    Dame Press, 2014.

—. *Dependant Rational Animals: Why Human Beings Need the Virtues (1999)*. Chicago: Open Court Publishing, 2014.

Malpas, Jeff. "Hans-Georg Gadamer." In *The Stanford Encyclopedia of Philosophy*, by Edward Zalta, http://plato.stanford.edu/archives/sum2015/entries/gadamer/. Stanford: The Metaphysics Research Lab, Stanford University , 2015.

Manninen, Alisa. *Royal Power and Authority in Shakespeare's Late Tragedies (2015)*. Newcastle upon Tyne: Cambridge Scholars Publishing, 2015.

Marckie, Peter. "Rationalism vs. Empiricism." In *The Stanford Encyclopedia of Philosophy*, by Edward Zalta, http://plato.stanford.edu/archives/sum 2015/entries/rationalism-empiricism/. Stanford: The Metaphysics Research Lab, Stanford University, 2015.

Marion, Jean-Luc. *God Without Being (1991)*. Chicago: Uni of Chicago Press, 2012.

Marr, David. *Patrick White: A Life (1991)*. Sydney: Random House Australia, 1991.

—. *Patrick White Letters (1994)*. Sydney: Random House Australia, 1994.

—. *The High Price of Heaven (1999)*. St Leonards NSW: Allen & Unwin, 1999.

Maurin, Anna-Sofia. "Tropes." In *The Standford Encylopaedia of Philosophy*, by Edward Zalta, http://plato.stanford.edu/archives/fall2014/entries/tropes. Stanford: The Metaphysics Research Lab, Stanford University, 2014.

McCrone, John. *The Myth of Irrationality: The Science of the Mind from Plato to Star Trek (1994)*. London: Macmillan, 1994.

McCulloch, A.M. *The Tragic Vision: The Novels of Patrick White (1983)*. St Lucia: Uni of Queensland Press, 1983.

McKirahan, Richard. *Philosophy Before Socrates: Second Edition (2010)*. Indianapolis: Hackett Publishing, 2010.

McMahon, Elizabeth. "The Lateness and Queerness of The Twyborn Affair: White's Farewell to the Novel." In *Remembering Patrick White: Contemporary Critical Essays*, by Elizabeth McMahon and Brigitta Olubas, 77–91. Amsterdam: Rodopi, 2010.

Mehta, Harish. "Violent Aboriginals and Benign White Men: White's Alternative Representation of the Encounter in Voss." In *Patrick White Centenary: The Legacy of a Prodigal Son*, by Cynthia vanden Dreisen and Bill Ashcroft, 241–256. Newcastle upon Tyne, Cambridge Scholars Publishing, 2014.

Mehta, Julie. "Smelly Martyrs: Patrick White's Dubbo Ushers in Roy's Velutha and Malouf's Gemmy." In *Patrick White Centenary: The*

Legacy of a Prodigal Son, by Cynthia vanden Dreisen and Bill Ashcroft, 368–381. Newcastle upon Tyne, Cambridge Scholars Publishing, 2014.

Miller, Arthur. "Tragedy and the Common Man and The Nature of Tragedy." In *The Theater Essays of Arthur Miller (1978)*, by Arthur Miller, 3–11. New York: Da Capo Press, 1996.

Milton, Giles. *Paradise Lost: Smyrna 1922: The Destruction of Islam's City of Tolerance (2008)*. London: Hodder & Stoughton, 2009.

Mitchell, Adrian. "Eventually, White's Language: Words and More Than Words." In *Patrick White: A Critical Symposium*, by Ron Shepherd and Kirpal Singh, 5–16. Adelaide: Centre for Research in the New Literatures in English, 1978.

Morley, Patricia. *The Mystery of Unity (1972)*. Montreal: McGill-Queen's Uni Press, 1972.

Morreall, John. *Comedy, Tragedy, and Religion (1999)*. Albany: SUNY Press, 1999.

—. *Comic Relief: A Comprehensive Philosophy of Humor.* Oxford: Wiley-Blackwell, 2009.

Murdoch, Iris. *The Bell (1958)*. New York: Penguin Books, 2001.

—. *The Unicorn* (1963). London: Penguin, 1966.

—. *The Sovereignty of Good (1970)*. London: Routledge Classics, 2001.

Neusner, Jacob and Chilton, Bruce. *In Quest of the Historical Pharisees (2007)*. Waco: Baylor Uni Press, 2007.

Nielsen, Cynthia. *Foucault, Douglass, Fanon, and Scotus in Dialogue (2013)*. New York: Palgrave Macmillan, 2013.

Nietzsche, Friedrich. *Beyond Good and Evil (1886)*. New York: Vintage Books, 1989.

—. *On the Genealogy of Morality (1887)*. Indianapolis: Hackett Publishing, 1998.

—. *The Birth of Tragedy and The Case of Wagner (1872)*. New York: Vintage Books, 1967.

—. *The Pre-Platonic Philosophers (1872-1876)*. Chicago: Uni of Illinois Press, 2006.

—. *Philosophy in the Tragic Age of the Greeks (1962)*. Washington DC: Regnery Publishing, 1962.

Nobbs, Alanna. "The Idea of Salvation: The Transition to Christianity as Seen in Some Early Papyri." In *The Idea of Salvation*, by R.G. Tanner and D.W. Dockerill, 59–63. Auckland: Uni of Auckland, 1986.

Nussbaum, Martha. *The Fragility of Goodness (1986)*. New York: Cambridge Uni Press, 2013.

Ong, Walter. *Orality and Literacy (1982)*. New York: Routledge, 2012.

Osborne, Catherine. *Presocratic Philosophy: A Very Short Introduction (2004)*. New York: Oxford Uni Press, 2004.

O'Sullivan, Moira. "Salvation is a Chameleon." In *The Idea of Salvation*, by R.G. Tanner and D.W. Dockerill, 43–58. Auckland: Uni of Auckland, 1986.

Paglia, Camille. *Glittering Images: A Journey Through Art From Egypt to Star Wars (2012)*. New York: Vintage Books, 2013.

—. *Sexual Personae: Art and Decadence from Nefertiti to Emily Dickinson (1990)*. New York: Vintage Books, 1991.

Pailin, David. "Enlightenment." In *A New Dictionary of Christian Theology (1983)*, by Alan Richardson and John Bowden, 179. London: SCM Press, 1985.

Pellauer, David and Dauenhauer, Bernard. "Paul Ricoeur." In *The Stanford Encyclopedia of Philosophy*, by Edward Zalta, http://plato.stanford.edu/archives/fall2016/entries/ricoeur/. Stanford: The Metaphysics Research Lab, Stanford University, 2016.

Plato. "Phaedrus (c.370 BC)." In *Complete Works*, by Plato, 506–556. Indianapolis: Hackett Publishing, 1977.

Plato. "Republic (c.380 BC)." In *Complete Works (1997)*, by Plato, 971–1223. Indianapolis: Hackett Publishing, 1997.

Randisi, Jennifer. *On Her Way Rejoicing: The Fiction of Muriel Spark (1991)*. Washington DC: Catholic Uni Press of America, 1991.

Ricoeur, Paul. *The Symbolism of Evil (1960)*. New York: Beacon Press, 1967.

Rutherford, Jennifer. "Homo Nullius: The Politics of Pessimism in Patrick White's The Tree of Man." In *Remembering Patrick White: Contemporary Critical Essays (2010)*, by Elizabeth McMahon and Brigitta Olubas , 47–64. Amsterdam: Rodopi, 2010.

Saldarini, Anthony. *Pharisees, Scribes, and Saducees in Palestinian Society (1988)*. Grand Rapids: William Eerdmans, 2001.

Sanders, E.P. *Paul: The Apostle's Life, Letters, and Thought*. Minneapolis: Fortress Press, 2015.

Satran, David. "Philo of Alexandria." In *The Jewish Annotated New Testament (2011)*, by Amy-Jill Levine and Marc Zvi Brettler, 572 575. New York: Oxford Uni Press, 2011.

Schäfer, Peter. *The Jewish Jesus: How Judaism and Christianity Shaped Each Other (2012)*. Princeton: Princeton Uni Press, 2012.

Schwartz, Daniel. "Jewish Movements of the New Testament Period." In *The Jewish New Testament (2011)*, by Amy-Jill Levine and Marc Zvi Brettler, 526–530. New York: Oxford Uni Press, 2011.

Scrunton, Roger. *Fools, Frauds and Firebrands: Thinkers of the New Left.* New York: Bloomsbury, 2015.

—. *Kant: A Very Short Introduction (1982).* New York: Oxford Uni Press, 2001.

Seidel, George. *Martin Heidegger and the Pre-Socratics (1964).* Lincoln NE: Uni of Nebraska Press, 1964.

Sewall, Richard. *The Vision of Tragedy (1959).* New York: Paragon House, 1990.

Shakespeare, William. *Hamlet (1599–1602).* London: Methuen, 1984.

—. *King Lear (1606).* London: Methuen, 1984.

—. *Macbeth (1606).* London: Methuen, 1984.

—. *Richard II (1597).* London: Methuen, 1984.

Shelley, Mary. *Frankenstein: or The Modern Prometheus (1818).* New York: Dover Publications, 1994.

Shepherd, Ron and Singh, Kirpal. *Patrick White: A Critical Symposium.* Adelaide: Centre for Research in the New Literatures in English, 1978.

Shepherd, Ron. "An Indian Story: The Twitching Colonel." In *Patrick White: A Critical Symposium,* by Ron Shepherd and Kirpal Singh, 5–16. Adelaide: Centre for Research in the New Literatures in English, 1978.

Southwell, Gareth. *A Beginner's Guide to Nietzsche's Beyond Good and Evil (2009).* Oxford: Wiley-Blackwell, 2009.

Spark, Muriel. "The Desegregation of Art" (1970). In *The Informed Air,* by Muriel Spark, 77–82. New York: New Directions Publishing, 2014.

—. *The Comforters (1957).* London: Penguin Books, 1963.

—. *Robinson (1958).* New York: New Directions, 2003.

—. *The Prime of Miss Jean Brodie (1961).* New York: HarperPerrennial, 2009.

—. *The Public Image (1968).* London: Penguin Books, 1970.

—. *The Driver's Seat* (1970). New Directions, 1994.

—. *The Hothouse by the East River (1973).* New York: The Viking Press, 1973.

—. *The Abbess of Crewe (1974).* New York: The Viking Press, 1974

—. *The Takeover (1976).* New York: The Viking Press, 1976

—. *The Only Problem (1984).* New York: G.P. Putnam's Sons, 1984.

—. *Symposium (1990).* London: Penguin Books, 1991.

—. *Territorial Rights (1979).* New York: Coward, McCann & Geoghehan, 1979.

—. *Aiding and Abetting (2000).* London: Penguin Books, 2001.

—. *The Finishing School (2004).* London: Viking Penguin, 2004.

Spengler, Oswald. *The Decline of the West: Abridged One Volume Edition (1932).* New York: Oxford Uni Press, 1991.

Stark, Rodney. *Bearing False Witness: Debunking Centuries of Anti-Catholic History (2016).* West Conshoshocken PA: Templeton Press, 2016.

Steiner, George. *The Death of Tragedy (1961).* New Haven CT: Yale Uni Press, 1996.

Stendhal. *The Charterhouse of Parma (1839).* London: Penguin Books, 2007.

Stern, David. "Midrash and Parables in the New Testament." In *The Jewish New Testament*, by Amy-Jill Levine and Marc Zvi Brettler, 565–569. New York: Oxford Uni Press, 2011.

Steven, Laurence. *Dissociation and Wholeness in Patrick White's Fiction (1989).* Waterloo ON: Wilfred Laurier Uni Press, 1989.

Tacey, David. *Patrick White: Fiction and the Unconscious (1988).* Melbourne: Oxford Uni Press, 1988.

Tanner, Michael. *Nietzsche: A Very Short Introduction (1994).* New York: Oxford Uni Press, 2000.

Tonner, Philip. *Heidegger, Metaphysics and the Univocity of Being (2010).* London: Continuum International, 2010.

Turner, James. *Philology: The Forgotten Origins of the Modern Humanities (2014).* Princeton NJ: Princeton University Press, 2014.

vanden Dreisen, Cynthia. *Writing the Nation: Patrick White and the Indigene (2009).* Amsterdam: Rodopi, 2009.

Vermes, Geza. "Jewish Miracle Workers in the Late Second Temple Period." In *The Jewish New Testament (2011)*, by Amy-Jill Levine and Marc Zvi Brettler, 536–537. New York: Oxford Uni Press, 2011.

Walton, Michael. *The Greek Sense of Theatre (1984).* New York: Routledge, 2015.

Waterfield, Robin. *The First Philosophers: The Presocratics and the Sophists (2000).* Oxford UK: Oxford Uni Press, 2000.

Whitehead, A.N. *Process and Reality (1929): Corrected Edition.* New York: The Free Press, 1978.

Williams, Margaret. *The Jews Among the Greeks and Romans (1998).* Baltimore: Johns Hopkins Uni Press, 1998.

Williams, Mark. *Patrick White (1993).* New York: St Martin's Press, 1993.

Williams, Raymond. *Modern Tragedy (1966).* Peterborough ON: Broadview Encore Editions, 2006.

Williamson, George. *The Longing for Myth in Germany (2004).* Chicago: Uni of Chicago Press, 2004.

Winckelmann, John. *The History of Ancient Art: Volume II (1764)*. Boston: James Munroe and Company, 1849.

Winton, Tim. *The Riders (1994)*. New York: Scribner, 2003.

Witham, Larry. *The Proof of God: The Debate That Shaped Modern Belief*. New York: Atlas & Co., 2008.

Young, Julian. *Nietzsche's Philosophy of Art (1992)*. Cambridge UK: Cambridge Uni Press, 1999.

—. *Heidegger's Philosophy of Art (2001)*. Cambridge UK: Cambridge Uni Press, 2004.

—. *The Philosophy of Tragedy: From Plato to Zizek*. New York: Cambridge Uni Press, 2013.

Zimmermann, Jens. *Hermeneutics: A Very Short Introduction (2015)*. New York: Oxford Uni Press, 2015.

INDEX

A

The Abbess of Crew (Spark), 309
  characters
    Jesuits, 323, 324
    Sister Alexandra
      (conservatism),
      236, 323, 324–5
    Sister Felicity (liberalism),
      323–4, 325
    Sister Gertrude (Kissinger
      satire), 324
    Winifrede, 323, 325
  conservatism and liberalism,
    struggle, 323
  evil within renewal, 323, 324, 325
  plot, 324–5
  Watergate scandal, 323, 324
  wheat and tares parable, 326
Aborigines
  character, Alf Dubbo, 53, 54, 82,
    88, 93, 106, 107–15,
    126, 178
  White's engagement with, 3, 60,
    107
Abrams, M.H., 11
Acts
  17:22–24, 297
  17:23–25, 32
adamic myth
  Hebraic metaphors, 88, 93, 94–5,
    103, 264, 284
  humanistic, 235
  Ricoeur, 45, 103, 177, 264, 370
Adorno, Theodor, 26, 43, 57
After Virtue (MacIntyre), 5fn, 293
Aiding and Abetting (Spark), 309
Ali, Ameer, 53
Alias Grace (Atwood)

aliases, constructions of Grace,
  362
characters
  Derringer, Enoch, 363, 365–6
  Jeremiah the Peddler
    (romantic), 363,
    364–5, 366
  Jordan, Simon, 363–4, 365,
    366
  Marks, Grace, 327, 361–2,
    361–6, 363
forgiveness, 366–7
pre-classicism archetype, heroine,
  327
psychoanalytical theory, 188
purpose in writing, 362
religious significance of Grace,
  366
themes, 363
Alice in Wonderland (Carroll), 154
Alien (1979) (film), 315
All Religions Are One (Blake), 83
Allegory of the Cave (Plato), 97, 248,
  249
Allegory of the Divided Line (Plato),
  98, 248
Allegory of the Sun (Plato), 98, 248,
  249
Alomes, Stephen, 53
Alonso-Breto, Isabel, 53
Also Sprach Zarathustra (Nietzsche),
  78
*An Essay Concerning Human
  Understanding* (Locke),
  125
analogical theories. *see* coherence
  theories; correspondence
  theories
ancient Greece

Athens and mind of ancient Israel
    (Jerusalem), 12, 13, 19
and German romanticism, 13–14
logos and mythos, 17
pagan imagination, 12–13
Antiphanes (408–334 BC), 75, 76
apocalypse, struggling with mimesis,
    9, 10
Aquinas, Thomas, 10, 62, 243, 292,
    294
Aristotle
    comedy, 91
    correspondence theories, 10
    empiricism, 13
    evidence base, 18
    logos and mythos, 16, 17
    tragedy, 91
art
    function of, 14
    Gadamer's perspectives, 41
    and God, 197, 229
    Paglia's perspectives, 188, 289
    questions, 28–9
    as religious activity (Nietzsche),
        127
    soteria through, 67, 79, 102, 177,
        226, 233, 247, 249,
        283
    in White's religious vision, 126–7
The Articles and the Novelist (Heltay),
    28, 287
artists
    White's fiction
        Dubbo, Alf, 53, 54, 82, 88,
            93, 106, 107–15,
            126, 178
        Duffield, Hurtle, 178, 183,
            197, 198–9,
            201–2, 204, 218,
            220, 221–2, 227–9
    wholeness, 245
Atwood, Margaret, 31
    Alias Grace (1996) see Alias
        Grace (Atwood)
    apocalypse, 9, 10

The Blind Assassin (2000), 361,
    367
Cat's Eye (1988), 361
The Edible Woman (1969), 30
education, 359
Hag-Seed (2016), 361
The Handmaid's Tale (1985), 10,
    360
The Heart Goes Last (2015), 361
historicity, critique, 361, 371
Homer's Odyssey, 360
literary maturity, 360
MaddAddam (2013), 9, 361,
    370–1
MaddAddam Trilogy see
    MaddAddam Trilogy
    (Atwood)
Negotiating with the Dead (2002),
    360
Oryx and Crake (2003), 361, 368
In Other Worlds: SF and the
    Human Imagination
    (2011), 361
The Penelopiad (2005), 360
pre-classicism archetype, 327
and Ricoeur, 370
The Robber Bride (1993), 361
romantic failings in the face of
    neoclassical
    destructiveness, 368
'shadow of romanticism,'
    comment, 7, 9, 82
Surfacing (1969), 361
writing process, 7, 8–9, 360–1
The Year of the Flood (2009),
    361, 368–9
Auerbach, Eric, 11, 29
Augustine of Hippo, 62, 67–8, 243,
    292
The Aunt's Story (1948), 3, 25, 28, 32,
    41, 60, 76–7, 89
Austen, Jane
    classical formula, 29
    reason–feeling dialectic, 125, 130
    romanticism, 31

autobiography *(Flaws in the Glass)*, 1, 13, 30, 55, 72, 78, 129, 184, 232, 237, 262, 297

B

Babylonian Talmud, 96
Bacon, Francis, 28, 183, 198–9
Bakhtin, Mikhail, 67
Barclay, John, 20
Barth, Karl, 80
Barthes, Roland, 290
Battye, Greg, 60
Bauman, Zygmunt, 31
Beatson, Peter, 25, 55, 73, 296
Beckett, Samuel, 32, 33, 90
Being and Time (Heidegger), 94
The Bell (Murdoch)
   characters
      Frawley, Catherine, 302, 303–4, 305, 307
      Frawley, Nick (Byronic trope), 302–3, 305
      Gashe, Toby, 303, 304, 306
      Greenfield, Dora, 89, 300–1, 302, 303, 304–6, 307, 308, 309, 312, 316
      Meade, Michael, 301, 302, 303, 307, 316
      Mother Clare, 302, 303, 307
      Pace, James Tayper, 301–2
      Paul, 300, 304, 305, 306
      Spens, Noel, 305, 306, 312
   classical metaphysics, 300
   conscious and unconscious dilemmas, 300–1
   frames (in order)
      beginning to end, state (Dora), 300–1, 310
      classical metaphysics horizon (Dora at Imber), 301
      Court's ethical horizons (Michael/James), 301–2

antithetical, symbiotic twins (Catherine/Nick), 302–3
bells, old and new (Dora's existential dilemma), 302, 303–6
antithetical relationship (Michael/Dora), 302, 307–8
Freudian pathologies, 300–1
Gadamerian hermeneutics, 301
Imber (place), 300, 301, 303, 304, 305, 306, 307
logos (Enlightenment horizon of reason), 301, 302, 305, 306, 307, 308
"madness," 302
Middlemarch comparisons, 300, 310
mythos (pre-Enlightenment feeling), 301, 302, 304, 305, 306, 307, 308
Platonic Freudianism, 300, 303, 304
symbolism
   bell, 302, 303–4, 305, 306
   blackbird, 305
   lake, 301, 302, 304, 307
   National Gallery, 306
tropes
   destructive Byronic passion, 302–3
   logos and mythos, 308
Ben-Bassat, Hedda, 94, 96, 97, 100
Benedict XVI
   comparison to White, 61, 67, 291–2
   dialogue with White, 297–8
   God and voluntarism, 62, 83, 184fn, 292, 295
   Kant interpretation, 63, 293
   logos, positive view, 61, 62–3, 64, 66, 68
   and religious authority, 88

romanticism in White's fiction, 86–7

Berger, John, 46

Berlin, Isaiah, 11

Berlin Wall, fall, 23

Bevis, Matthew, 75

Bible, 19, 31, 85, 114, 177, 181, 297, 310, 342, 353

binaries in White, 46–7, 49

binary thinking, Marxist challenge, 296

The Birth of Tragedy (Nietzsche), 77, 79, 94, 126, 127, 128, 129, 130, 134, 136, 234

bisexuality, 54, 329
    female tropes, 58–9, 210, 214, 350, 358

Black Boomerang (Delmer), 319

Blake, William, 18–19, 82–5, 86, 94, 104, 107, 108, 193
    ideas in White's work, 20, 28, 102, 107, 109, 172, 177
    God's contrary nature, 83
    solitary poetic genius, 18, 19, 110, 219

The Blind Assassin (Atwood), 361, 367

Bliss, Caroline, 47, 124–5

Bloom, Harold, 21–2, 95–6, 186, 257, 287

Boyarin, Daniel, 20, 21, 95, 96

Brettler, Marc, 21

Brontë, Charlotte, 125, 126, 365

The Brothers Karamazov (Dostoevsky), 138, 140, 154, 155

Brown, Norman O., 67, 68

Bulman-May, James, 26

The Burnt Ones (1964), 69

Butler, E.M., 11, 13, 27, 32, 70, 71–2, 296

C

Campion, Edmund, 3

Cartesian mind body dualism, 335, 336, 339

Cat's Eye (Atwood), 361

Chilton, Bruce, 20

Christ as the logos, 53

Christ Church St Laurence, 1, 3fn, 5, 226fn

Christchurch St Lawrence. *see* Christ Church St Laurence

Christianity, 20, 21
    de-Hellenization of, 62–3
    logos, 62
    symbolic language, 103

christology, 53, 78, 170, 175

classical metaphysics. *see also* immanence; transcendence
    critique, 11
    end of, 13 (*see also* God's death)
    "good life," 247fn
    "immanent" ("emancipatory" critique), 13, 14, 60
    post-war re-evaluation, 310

The Classic Vision (Krieger), 74

Clements, James, 38–9

The Cockatoos (1975), 69

Coetzee, J.M., 184–5, 287, 291

Cogito ergo sum—I think, therefore I am, 336, 339

coherence theories, 10, 40, 41, 80, 84, 240, 242, 243, 293

Collins, John, 20

colonialism, White's critique, 53–4, 192

comedy
    tragedy, contrast, 75–6
    White's work, 76, 80, 91–2

Comedy, Tragedy, and Religion (Morreall), 76

The Comforters (Spark), 308–9

Comic Relief (Morreall), 75

1 Corinthians
    1:22– 23, 18
    13:12, 181

2 Corinthians 12:10, 104

Cornford, Francis, 30, 94

Cornish Trilogy (Davies), 59, 67, 135
    The Rebel Angels (1982), 354–6

What's Bred in the Bone (1985), 356–7
The Lyre of Orpheus (1988), 59, 357–9
correspondence theories, 10, 40, 41, 80, 84, 240, 242, 243, 293
Crews, Fredrick, 291
Critchley, Simon, 27
criticism of White, 7, 48, 60–1
 Freudism, 51, 55
 homosexuality in fiction, 51
 Jungian, 51
 post-Lacanian assumptions, 52
 postcolonial, 53–4, 107
 psychoanalytical, 237
 rationalist, 288–9
 religion, 20
 White's "visionaries" (poet-seers), 88
Culp, Andrew, 65–6

D

The Daemonic Imagination (American Academy of Religion), 9
Dauenhauer, Bernard, 37
Davey, Nicholas, 41
Davies, Robertson
 contemporary of White, 7, 38, 89, 290
 Cornish Trilogy see Cornish Trilogy (Davies)
 Deptford Trilogy see Deptford Trilogy (Davies)
 emblematic horizons, western imagination, 344
 evil, 355
 female bisexual trope, 58–9, 210
 Fifth Business (1970), 349–51
 Jungianism, 135, 350, 351, 352, 355
 knowledge and wisdom distinction, 343–4, 354
 Leaven of Malice (1954), 345–7
 logos (reason), negative view, 67
 The Lyre of Orpheus (1988), 357–9

The Manticore (1972), 351–2
A Mixture of Frailties (1958), 347–9
The Rebel Angels (1982), 309, 354–6
Romeo and Juliet leitmotiv, 345–7
Salterton Trilogy see Salterton Trilogy (Davies)
Tempest-Tost (1951), 344–5
What's Bred in the Bone (1985), 356–7
World of Wonders (1975), 352–4
Davies, W.D., 21
Day, Father Austin, 1, 240
de Bono, Edward, 75
de Burgh, Una, 4, 5
de Maistre, Roy, 27, 59, 184, 199
de Soyza, Anne, 53
The Death of Tragedy (Steiner), 72, 74
The Decline of the West (Spengler), 30, 31, 49, 128
Deleuze, Gilles, 86
 critics of, 65–6
 immanence, 65, 66
 madness, 90
 modernism, effects, 29–30, 60, 79
 negative view of logos, 64
 Plato, 64, 65
 transcendence, 64–5, 66, 293
 transcendental empiricism, 47, 66
Delmer, Sefton, 319
Dependent Rational Animals (MacIntyre), 293
Deptford Trilogy (Davies), 59, 67, 135
 Fifth Business (1970), 10, 349–51
 The Manticore (1972), 351–2
 World of Wonders (1975), 59, 352–4
Derrida, Jacques, 23, 58, 294
desoulment idea, 15–16
Detweiler, Robert, 9, 175
DiCenso, James, 10, 36, 42, 293
Dickens, Charles, 31
Dodds, E.R., 18, 40, 130, 143, 162, 313, 362, 366
Dogwoods, Castle Hill, 1, 3, 4, 182

Dolin, Keiran, 53
Dostoevsky, Fyodor, 31, 154, 156
Duns Scotus, John, 36, 62, 63, 292–3
*Duns Scotus's Doctrine of Categories
    and Meaning,* 36, 62,
    292–3, 294–5
During, Simon, 51, 132
Dutton, Emily, 230
Dutton, Geoffrey, 230

E
Eagleton, Terry, 74
"The Edge of Error" (Green), 288
The Edible Woman (Atwood), 30
Enlightenment (European). *see also*
        Greek Enlightenment;
        Haskalah (Jewish
        Enlightenment); logos;
        neoclassicism
    and 9/11, 23–4
    and ancient Greece, 13
    Anglican Church, 26
    Bloom, 96
    Gadamer, 37, 136
    reason, meaning, 293
    White's critique of reason, 19, 27,
        40, 63–4, 67, 74, 95,
        96, 97, 109
    White's Jewish characters, 97, 98,
        124, 158–9, 160, 167
eponymous names, 33, 88, 100, 133,
        181, 195fn, 217, 272, 297,
        306, 355
evil, 45, 48, 80, 85, 92, 94, 103. *see
        also* good and evil
    Atwood's fiction, 362, 366, 367
    Davies's fiction, 355
    Golding's fiction, 331, 335
    Spark's fiction, 309, 310, 311,
        312, 315, 317, 318,
        319, 320, 321, 323,
        324, 326, 328
    White's characters, 92, 94, 103,
        123, 191, 250, 258,
        280
Exodus 33:17–33, 297

The Eye of the Mandala (Beatson), 55
The Eye of the Storm (1973)
    characters
        Badgery, Jessie, 263, 267–70,
            272
        de Santis, Mary, 172, 239,
            249, 252, 253,
            254, 260, 263–7,
            268, 270, 272
        Hunter, Alfred (logos), 50,
            236–8, 244, 245,
            255, 262, 271, 277
        Hunter, Basil, 50, 79, 231,
            235, 236, 239,
            244, 245, 246–57,
            259, 260, 261,
            262, 264, 265,
            266, 267, 276–7,
            278, 282, 283
        Hunter, Dorothy, 79, 231,
            235, 236, 239,
            244, 251, 253,
            254, 256, 257–62,
            264, 269, 282
        Hunter, Elizabeth (mythos)
            character and role, 68,
                231, 233,
                238–44
            family relationships, 50,
                79, 230,
                236–61
            non-family relationships
                (acolytes), 50,
                51, 230,
                260–1,
                263–86
            Theogonic metaphors,
                50, 231–2,
                244, 247, 275
        Jacka, Mitty, 247, 248–9,
            254, 257, 258
        Lippmann, Lotte (Jewish),
            246, 249–50, 263,
            268, 269, 270,
            271, 272, 275,
            278, 279–86

Macrory family, 249, 255,
        261
Manhood, Flora (mythos), 50,
        51, 240, 249, 251,
        252, 253, 258,
        263, 268, 269,
        271–9, 282, 284,
        285
Pardoe, Col (logos), 50, 79,
        251, 252, 271–3,
        275, 276, 277,
        278, 279
Pehl, Edvard, 260, 261
The Charterhouse of Parma,
        motif, 236
exiled soul (Hellenic metaphor),
        79, 231, 259, 264, 274
Gadamerian frame, 177, 230, 231
God's death, 243, 244
Holocaust, 286
incest of archetypes, 236, 262
Jewish horizon, 280, 281
King Lear, similarities, 234–5
The Living and the Dead,
        similarities, 233
marriage and civilization, 50, 79,
        233, 234, 271
mother blaming, 235–6
narrative structure, 230
nature and civilization, 50, 79,
        233, 234, 271
nature and nurture, 235
perspectivist, Nietzschean, 240
psychoanalytical criticism, 231
red hair symbolism, 50, 231, 257
religion, present, 230
Ricoeurean anthropology, 177,
        230, 231, 235
soteria through art, 233, 247, 249,
        283
tragic hero (Hellenic metaphor),
        79, 231, 246–7, 254,
        259, 264, 266, 274
The Eye of the Storm (2011) film, 251,
        258, 263

Ezekiel
        1:4–28, 87
        (1:4–28), 108
        10:1–22, 87

F
the fall, 43, 44–5, 240, 330–1, 335,
        338, 339, 355
Family Romance, 238, 257, 289
Fantasia of the Unconscious
        (Lawrence), 35
fatalism, 48–9, 51, 55, 234
Feiner, Schmuel, 19, 95
feminism, 51, 52, 56, 287
Ferber, Michael, 11, 27
fertility and nature, 238
Fifth Business (Davies), 349–51
The Finishing School (Spark), 309
First and Second Treatises of
        Government (Locke),
        125–6
Flaws in the Glass (1981), 1, 13, 30,
        55, 72, 78, 129, 184, 232,
        237, 262, 297
Forms and Ideas theory (Plato), 13, 60,
        65, 134, 221, 297
Foucault, Michel, 89–90, 197
The Fragility of Goodness
        (Nussbaum), 68, 75, 244
Frankfurt School, 16, 295
Frazer, James, 30, 94, 326, 327
Free Fall (Golding), 331
        characters
            Beatrice, 340, 341, 342, 343
            Evie, 340, 341, 343
            Father Watts-Watt (clerical
                prototype), 112,
                340, 341, 342
            Johnny and Philip, 340
            Ma, 340, 341, 343
            Minnie, 340, 343
            Mountjoy, Sammy, 178fn,
                339–43
            Philip, 340
            Pringle, Rowena (theist), 342,
                343

Shales, Nick (atheist), 342
Taffy, 341
the fall, 338, 339
free will, 339, 340
mimesis, 339
neoclassical Enlightenment, 342,
    343
free will, 178, 182, 186, 258, 261, 289,
    309, 331, 339, 340
Freud, Sigmund, 23, 33, 327, 363
ego, 44, 45, 92
Family Romances theory, 180,
    185–6, 257
influence on White, 49, 67, 69
in Murdoch's fiction, 300–1, 303,
    304
on Nietzsche, 128
Plato's model of mind, 90, 299
psyche model (ego, id, super-ego),
    44, 125
unconscious, 52
White's view on theories, 35
From Religion to Philosophy
    (Cornford), 30, 94
Frye, Northrop, 310

G
Gadamer, Hans-Georg
aesthetics, 40–1
art, 41
critique of reason, 141
Enlightenment (reason) critique's
    irony, 136, 141
history and conditioning, 23, 37–8
language and conditioning, 23,
    37–8, 42
logos and mythos (frame), 38, 50,
    58, 87–8, 109, 326
metaphysical approach, 290
modernism, 326
prejudices, 23, 37–8
romantic hermeneutics (frame),
    36, 41, 52, 82, 87, 109,
    230, 290, 301
symbol, 41
Galambush, Julie, 21

Gardner, Helen, 291
Genesis 38:8–10, 207
Gilgamesh, 360
Gillespie, Michael., 23, 24
Glittering Images (Paglia), 289
God
as logos, 62
as *the* Other, in White, 190
transference of attributes, 24
White's beliefs, 24, 63
God's contrary nature, 83
God's death, 235, 243, 245, 308
Nietzsche, 13, 14, 290
White's fiction, 14, 80, 86, 243,
    244
God's freedom, 62
God's Gardeners, 368–9, 370, 371
The Golden Bough (Frazer), 30, 94,
    326, 327
Golding, William
contemporary of White, 7, 38, 290
the fall, 240, 330–1, 335, 338, 339
Free Fall (1959) see *Free Fall*
    (Golding)
The Inheritors (1955) see *The
    Inheritors* (Golding)
Lord of the Flies (1954), 331
original sin, 240
Pincher Martin (1956) see
    Pincher Martin
    (Golding)
and Ricoeur, 330–1
Goneril and Regan story, 235, 236,
    241
good and evil, 43, 84, 87, 130, 233,
    282, 302, 326, 335
Goodman, Martin, 20
Gorgias (Plato), 17
götterdämmerung (twilight of pagan
    gods), 133, 134, 135, 156,
    157, 175, 176, 230, 244,
    288
Gottlieb, Anthony, 7
Graham-Smith, Gregory, 55, 56
Great Chain of Being (Lovejoy), 235
Great Expectations (Dickins), 327

The Great Code (Frye), 310
Greek Enlightenment, 15, 40, 129
Greek Orthodoxy (Eastern), 2, 5, 26, 298
The Greeks and the Irrational (Dodds), 40
The Greek Sense of Theatre (Walton), 68, 74–5
Green, Dorothy, 288
Green, Garrett, 128
Greene, Graham
    contemporary of White, 38
    religion, 38–9, 309–10
Gregory, Brad, 26
Grieves, Vicki, 53
Griswold, Charles, 42

H
Hag-Seed (Atwood), 361
Halliwell, Stephen, 29
The Ham Funeral (1947), 32–5, 76, 77
Handelman, Susan, 21
The Handmaid's Tale (Atwood), 10, 360
The Hanging Garden (2012), 41
Happy Valley (1939), 27, 30, 41, 59
Hardy, Thomas, 11, 34, 48
Harris, Jocelyn, 29
Harrison, Jane, 30, 94, 187
Haskalah (Jewish Enlightenment), 19, 95, 281
Havelock, Eric, 18
The Heart Goes Last (Atwood), 361
Hebraic metaphors, 124, 177
    Christianity, 103, 119, 136
    de Santis, Mary *(The Eye of the Storm)*, 254, 264
    Himmelfarb, Mordecai *(Riders in the Chariot)*, 93, 94–5, 99, 114, 118
    Ricoeur's categories, 45–6, 49, 77, 88, 103, 109, 124, 235
Hebraic mind, 99
Hegel, Georg, 10, 11

master-slave dialectic, 69, 70, 125, 126, 329, 353, 362
    objective spirit, 189
Heidegger, Martin, 30, 42, 69, 294
    disclosure theories, 10, 77, 240
    God concealed, 16, 24, 32, 181
    metaphysics, 13–14
    nature of "being," 36, 231
    Presocratic wholeness, 141
    White's zeitgeist, 72, 94
Hellenic metaphors, 77, 235
    Christianity, 22, 62, 63, 103–4, 113, 114, 274
    The Eye of the Storm
        Hunter, Alfred, 50
        Hunter, Basil, 79, 231–2, 247, 254, 259, 266
        Hunter, Dorothy, 79, 231–2, 259
        Pardoe, Col, 50, 279
    Judaism, 20, 21, 62, 95, 99
    Ricoeur's categories, 45–6, 49, 77, 88, 103, 109, 124, 235, 259
    Riders in the Chariot
        Hare, Norbert, 88, 90–1, 91–2
    The Vivisector, 177, 181
        Duffield, Hurtle, 195
        Pavloussis, Hero, 181
    Winckelmann's homoerotic, 70, 71
Heltay, Hilary, 28, 287
Henderson, Ian, 55, 56
Heraclitus, 16, 61, 293
Hesiod, 10, 370
Hewitt, Jennifer, 27, 28, 59–60, 108, 184–5, 198–9, 287, 291
History of Ancient Art (Winckelmann), 13
Homer, 17, 43, 71, 75, 244, 293, 360
homosexuals
    and identity politics, 55
    males, 38, 50
        function in White's fiction, 50
        tropes, 54, 56, 57

reading perpectives of White's,
        54–5, 59
Honour, Hugh, 11
Horan, Daniel, 36, 294–5
Horkheimer, Max, 26, 43
The Hothouse by the East River
        (Spark)
    characters
        Annie, 322
        Bunting, Miles, 320
        Elsa, 309, 319, 320, 321–2,
                326
        Garven, 321, 322
        Katerina, 320
        Kiel (l-i-k-e), 319, 320, 321,
                322
        Paul, 309, 319–20, 320–1,
                322, 326
        Pierre, 320, 321
        Tylden, Colonel, 320, 322
        Xavier, Poppy, 320, 322
    evil, 318, 319, 320, 321
    hell, 321, 322
    immortal strand, 320–2
    mortal strand, 319–20, 322
    psychoanalysis, 321, 322
    questions explored, 318
Huebsch, Ben, 82
humanism, 48–9, 55, 234
Humboldt, Wilhelm von, 17, 23, 28,
        36, 42
Huxley, Aldous, 30

I
iconoclasm, 25–6, 124
iconography, 24–5, 26, 124, 131, 321,
        327
immanence. *see also* transcendence;
        transcendence-immanence
        debate
    after Kant, 70
    Deleuze, 65, 66
    Marxist critique, 61, 70
    relationship to transcendance, 68
    secular critics, 86

shift to, from transcendence, 13,
        14, 60
    and transcendence in White, 64,
        66, 67, 68, 204, 221,
        229
In Defence of the Imagination
        (Gardner), 291
*In Other Worlds: SF and the Human
        Imagination* (Atwood), 361
incest, 132, 236, 262
Ingersoll, Earl, 8
The Inheritors (Golding), 331
    character species
        H. neanderthalensis, 331,
                332–4
        H. sapiens, 331, 332, 334–5
    evolution, 331
    the fall
        in evolutionary terms, 331,
                332, 333
        and language, 331, 332, 333
        nature–civilization dichotomy,
                331–2, 334
intersectional theory, 107, 284fn, 287
Inwood, Michael, 10

J
Jane Eyre (Brontë), 125, 126, 365
Jarratt, Susan, 18
Jaspers, Karl, 72
Jewish characters in White's work,
        19–20, 95, 124
Jewish Enlightenment (Haskalah), 19,
        95, 281
Jewish horizon, 45, 94, 158, 159, 280,
        281
Jewish thought. *see also* Judaism
    contrasts to Greek thought, 21–2
    influenced by Greek thought, 95
John
    1:1 (92), 16
    1:1–4, 23
    8:32, 366
    20:25–28, 22
John XXIII, 322
John's Gospel, 52–3, 113

Johnston, Adrian, 23, 52, 180, 189, 191, 194
Johnston, Heather, 199
Joyce, Clayton, 3, 94
Judaism, 20–1, 62
    Hellenic metaphors, 20, 21, 62, 95, 99
    logos, 62
    Theogonic metaphors, 94
Jude the Obscure (Hardy), 34–5, 48
Julian of Norwich, 68
Jung, Carl, 52, 85
    archetypal masculine and feminine, 79
    conscious and unconscious mind, 23, 33, 44, 45, 125, 134, 154, 350
    individuation, 58, 130, 132, 134, 156
    influence on White, 26, 35, 49, 69, 130–1, 237
    Trinity as quaternity, 85, 209fn, 355

K
Kabbalah, 82, 101, 102, 116, 160
Kant, Immanuel, 11, 27, 42, 189, 196
    coherence theory, 10
    "practical" reason, 63
    turning point, philosophy, 292–3
Kaufmann, Walter, 74, 128, 129
Kaur, Ishmeet, 53
Kermode, Frank, 8, 176, 177, 192, 291
King Lear (Shakespeare), 79, 140, 234–5, 241
Kissinger, Henry, 324, 328
Klee, Paul, 28, 60
knowledge and truth
    correspondence-coherence theories, 10, 40, 41, 80, 84, 240, 242, 243, 293
    perspectivist–disclosure theories, 10–13, 41, 240, 242
Knox-Shaw, Peter, 29
Kramer, Leonie, 25–6, 51–2, 232, 288
Krieger, Murray, 74

L
La symbolique du mal (Ricoeur), 23, 42, 93
Lacan, Jacques, 190, 191, 194, 284fn
    on Freud, 55, 56
    Symbolic Order, 180
    three registers theory, 153fn, 189
    unconscious, 23, 52, 190
Laing, R.D., 90
Lang, Anouk, 55–6
Langham, Mark, 289–90
Lascaris, Manoly, 1, 3, 130, 289
    and God's existence, 297
    Greek Orthodoxy (Eastern), 2, 5, 26, 298
Lawrence, D.H., 30, 33, 34, 35, 51, 90, 128, 192, 237, 287
Leaven of Malice (Davies), 345–7
Ledbetter, Mark, 9
lesbian tropes, 50, 58, 210, 275
Levenson, David, 20
Levine, Amy-Jill, 20
liberation, 43–4
linguistic worldviews theory, 28, 42
literary fathers, 237
Litvak, Olga, 19, 95
The Living and the Dead (1941), 28, 30, 39, 41, 95, 163, 193–4, 233
Llewelyn, Robert, 68
Locke, John, 125–6, 243
logos. *see also* logos-mythos dialectic
    ancient Greece, 17
    Benedict's positive view, 61, 64, 66, 68
    Christ as the, 53
    critiques' irony, 136
    definitions, 16, 61–2
    Heraclitus, 16, 61
    as higher authority (over mythos), 136
    liminal place between mythos and, 53, 54
    male homosexuals, 53, 58–9
    Patristic, Trinitarian understanding, 26

post-Enlightenment critique,
  25–6, 109
protagonists (postwar period), 38,
  39
replacing mythos (desoulment),
  15–16
romantic hermeneutics, 62–3, 130
subjugation of mythos, outcomes,
  35
tension with mythos, 230
White's negative view, 61, 63, 66,
  67
White's protagonists, 39–40
logos–mythos dialectic, 15, 17, 130,
  290
The Longing for Myth in Germany
  (Williamson), 17, 43
Lord of the Flies (Golding), 331
love, 130, 152–3, 204, 297
Lovejoy, Arthur, 235
The Lyre of Orpheus (Davies), 357–9

M

MacDougall, Scott, 294
MacIntyre, Alasdair, 5fn, 293, 297
MaddAddam ((Atwood), 9, 361, 370–1
MaddAddam Trilogy (Atwood)
  apocalypse, 9–10
  characters
    Adam One, 369–70
    Crake (Glenn) Glenn–Crake,
      9, 368, 369, 370–1
    God's Gardeners, 368–9, 370,
      371
    Jimmy-Snowman, 9, 368,
      369, 370
    Oryx, 368
    Ren, 369
    Toby, 10, 369, 370, 371
    Zeb, 369, 370
  MaddAddam (2013), 9, 361,
    370–1
  Oryx and Crake (2003), 361, 368
  The Year of the Flood (2009),
    361, 368–9

madness, 78, 91, 302, 305
  as social construct (Foucault),
    89–90, 197
Madness and Civilization (Foucault),
  89–90
magic realism, 352
Malouf, David, 57
Malpas, Jeff, 36
mandala symbol, 108, 124, 130–1, 144
Manninen, Alisa, 235
The Manticore (Davies), 351–2
Marckie, Peter, 27
Mark 5:1–17, 9
Marks, Grace, 327, 361–6
Marr, David, 1, 2, 3, 6, 7, 14–15, 30,
  31fn, 35, 51fn, 52, 59, 60,
  67, 78, 82, 127, 128, 130,
  182, 183, 184, 188, 230,
  234, 237, 239, 246
marriages, archetypal, 40
The Marriage of Heaven and Hell
  (Blake), 82–3, 87, 94
Marx, Karl, 11, 70, 327
Matthew
  5:39, 104
  16:15, 362
  22: 37–40, 153, 229
Maurin, Anna-Sofia, 89
McCrone, John, 13
McCulloch, Ann, 69–70, 240–2, 243,
  245, 259–60, 282, 296
  purpose and rational method, 196
  religious vision of White, 126–7
  romanticism in White's fiction, 86
  tragedy in White's fiction, 74, 196,
    207, 220, 233
  The Vivisector, 178, 204–6, 209,
    210, 213, 218, 220,
    228, 229
McKirahan, Richard, 18
McMahon, Elizabeth, 56–8, 291
Mehta, Harish, 53
Memoirs of Many in One (1986), 15,
  41, 86
metaphors of biblical imagination

mountain, garden, cave, furnace,
        310, 312
metaphysics, post-Kantian alternatives
        in White, 14
Micklem, Philip, 3–4
Middlemarch (Eliot), 300, 310, 326
Millais, John, 89, 305
Miller, Arthur, 73–4
mimesis, 9, 10, 29, 134, 135, 331, 332,
        339, 353
Mitchell, Adrian, 25
A Mixture of Frailties (Davies), 347–9
Modern Tragedy (Williams), 74
modernism
        Deleuze, interrelated effects,
                29–30, 60, 79
        as paradigm shift, 326
        relationship to romanticism, 29
modernist theologies, 63
modernity, 23–4, 36, 294
Morley, Patricia, 35, 85–6, 130–1
Morreall, John, 75–6
Morrice, Gertrude, 30
Murdoch, Iris
        The Bell (1958) *see The Bell*
                (Murdoch)
        contemporary of White, 7, 38, 89,
                132, 170, 262, 290
        as creature of logos, 308
        existentialist thinking, 36fn
        logos tropes, 308
        morality, 64
        mythic backgrounds, 42fn9, 299
        mythos tropes, 308
        philosophy (Platonic
                Freudianism),
                299–300, 303
        pre-classicism archetype, 327
        protagonists, 233, 262, 299–300
        realism, 42fn
        rhetoric, nature of, 49
        The Sovereignty of Good (1967),
                36fn, 64
        transcendence, 64
        tropes (logos and mythos), 308
        The Unicorn (1963), 308

Muslim "other," 53
The Mystery of Unity (Morley), 85
Mysticism and the Mid-Century Novel
        (Clements), 38
mythos. *see also* logos; logos-mythos
        dialectic
        ancient Greece, 17
        and pre-Enlightenment wholeness,
                136
        protagonists (postwar period), 38,
                39, 49–50
        victims, 58
        White's protagonists, 39–40
        White's religious experience, 170
myths. *see also* adamic myth
        ancient Greek, 42–3
        chaos and creation, 43–4, 45, 93,
                103, 177, 231, 271,
                370
        exiled souls, 44, 45, 76, 77, 79,
                91, 92, 103, 133, 177,
                181, 231, 259, 264,
                274, 370
        tragic hero, 44, 45, 77, 91–2, 103,
                133, 177, 181, 231,
                259, 264, 266, 274,
                370
Myths of Ancient Greece, 30, 247, 262

N
names, eponymous, 33, 88, 100, 133,
                181, 195fn, 217, 272, 297,
                306, 355
naturalism, 328
        White's hostility, 11, 24–5, 27, 59
nature and civilization, 50, 79, 233,
                234, 271, 334
nature–nurture debate, 247
"The Nature of Tragedy" (Miller),
                73–4
Negotiating with the Dead (Atwood),
                360
neo-paganism, 326
neoclassicism, 10, 18, 29, 32, 37, 71,
                84, 126
        Atwood, 361, 367, 369, 371

Murdoch, 302
Spark, 328
White, 27, 95, 125
Neusner, Jacob, 20
Newman, Cardinal, 309
Nietzsche, Friedrich, 84, 156
   apollonian–dionysian dialectic,
      44, 125, 127, 129
   art as religious activity, 127
   Christianity, 20, 85, 104, 297
   critique of socratic reason, 74
   God's death, 13, 14, 16, 290
   ideations, perspectives, 23
   influence on Freud and Jung, 23,
      125, 131, 136
   Judaism, 20, 279
   logos, 16, 37, 130
   mimesis, 134, 135
   perspectivist–disclosure theories,
      10, 36, 77, 240
   Presocratic wholeness, 141
   tragedy, 69, 74, 77–8, 234, 241
   White influenced by, 20, 30, 33,
      49, 69, 94, 126, 127–8,
      129, 130, 296
Night on Bald Mountain (1964), 77
9/11 World Trade Center attack, 23
Nixon, Richard, 324, 325
Nobbs, Alanna, 22
non-binary thinking, 47
Nussbaum, Martha, 68, 75, 90, 244

O
Odyssey (Homer), 360
Oldfield, Alan, 226fn
On Being an Enemy of Humanity
    (Kermode), 291
Ong, Walter, 18
The Only Problem (Spark), 309, 318
Ophelia (Millais), 89, 305
Oryx and Crake (Atwood), 361, 368
Osborne, Catherine, 16, 61, 62
O'Sullivan, Moira, 22

P
Paglia, Camille
   art, 188, 289
   biological determinism, 51
   civilization, 40, 44, 45, 112, 131,
      192
   Family Romances, 180, 186–7,
      257
   logos and mythos, tension, 230
   nature, 40, 44, 73, 238–9
   tragedy, 79
paradigm shift
   meaning, 326
   Modernism movement, 326
Paradise Lost: Smyrna 1922—The
    Destruction of Islam's City
    of Tolerance (Milton), 53
Patrick White (During), 51
Patrick White (Williams), 46
Patrick White: A Critical Symposium
    (Shepherd and Singh), 296
Patrick White: A Life (Marr), 2, 7
Patrick White: A Tribute (Joyce), 3
Patrick White: Fiction and the
    Unconscious (Tacey), 51
Patrick White and Alchemy
    (Bulman-May), 26
Patrick White, Painter Manqué
    (Hewitt), 27
Patrick White's Fiction (Bliss), 124–5
"Patrick White's Götterdämmerung"
    (Kramer), 288
Patristics, 21–2
Pellauer, David, 37
The Penelopiad (Atwood), 360
perspectivism, 36, 243
perspectivist–disclosure theories,
    10–13, 41, 240, 242
   Gadamer, 41
   knowledge and truth in White,
      242
   Nietzschean, 10, 240
Phaedrus, myths, 42–3
The Phenomenology of Mind (Hegel),
    126

philosophical–aesthetic binaries
          (White's), 46–7
*Philosophy in the Tragic Age of the
          Greeks* (Nietzsche), 128–9
Pincher Martin (Golding)
     characters
          Christopher, 336–7, 337–9
          Nathaniel, 337, 338
     contrast to *Robinson Crusoe,* 337
     the fall within consciousness,
          336–7, 338
     story, 336–7
     time and consciousness, 338
Plato
     analogical theories of
          transcendence, 293
     correspondence theories, 10
     evidence base, 18
     Forms and Ideas theory, 13, 60,
          65, 134, 221, 297
     logos and mythos, 17
     model of the mind, 12, 29, 33, 34,
          38, 60, 84, 90, 135,
          299, 309, 335
     philosophy
          influence on European
               tradition, 12
          and poetry, quarrel, 13, 34–5,
               38, 61, 84, 125,
               126, 137
     rationalism, 12–13
     in White, 70, 97–8, 131
Poetics (Aristotle), 9, 29, 91
*The Politics of Experience and The
          Bird of Paradise* (Laing),
          90
The Pooh Perplex (Crews), 291
post-Vatican II, 78, 170, 175, 330
postcolonial critics of White, 53–4
postcolonial theory, 56
postmetaphysical and
          anti-metaphysical, 14
Postmodern Pooh (Crews), 291
Postmodernity and Univocity (Horan),
          294
poststructuralism, 23, 52, 74, 289

pre-classicism archetype, 327
The Pre-Platonic Philosophers
          (Nietzsche), 128
Presocratic scholarship, 18
The Prime of Miss Jean Brodie
          (Spark), 318
Process and Reality (Whitehead), 12,
          94, 297
*Prolegomena to the Study of Greek
          Religion* (Harrison), 30, 94
Protestantism, 18–19
Psychoanalysis and the Unconscious
          (Lawrence), 35
Psychology and Alchemy (Jung), 130,
          132, 154
The Public Image (Spark), 309

Q
queer modernism, 55–6
queer theory, 51, 55–8

R
Rabbinics, 21–2
Rabelais, 67, 68, 354, 356, 359
The Rainbow (Lawrence), 33, 34, 192
Randisi, Jennifer, 27fn, 291
Raphael, 13, 357
rational hysteria, 227
rationalism
     Aristotlan empiricism dialectic, 13
     Platonic, 13
rationalism–empiricism debate, 13, 14,
          67, 83–4, 87, 204
     post-Kant, 13, 27, 60, 291–2 (*see
          also*
               transcendence–immane
               nce debate)
     in White's fiction, 27
rationalist White criticism, 288–9
realism, 328
     Atwood, 361
     link to romanticism, 29
     and metaphysics, 39
     White's hostility, 11, 24–5, 27
reason, 125, 130
reason and feeling, 19

dialectic in Austin, 125, 130
revealed religion, after Kant, 12
reason and revelation, 19
after Kant, 62
The Rebel Angels (Davies), 309, 354–6
red hair symbolism, 49–50, 89, 180,
    195, 227, 231, 257, 289,
    309, 315, 327
Redon, Odilon, 28, 108–9, 113
Regensburg Lecture (Benedict), 61,
    62, 63, 292
The Republic (Plato), 12, 17, 90, 335
Ricoeur, Paul
    adamic myth (humanistic), 45,
        72fn, 103, 177, 264,
        370
    anthropology of myth and
        metaphor, 43–4, 95
    categorisation of myths, 43–6
        sub-categorisation into
            metaphors, 45
    chaos and creation myths, 43–4,
        45, 103
    contemporaries, 42, 43, 95
    creation myths, 45–6, 370
    exiled soul myths, 44–5, 77, 103
    the "fall" story, 45
    fatalistic and humanistic
        categories, myths, 49
    language, symbolic, 23, 42, 103
    metaphors, categories, 45
    metaphysical approach, 290
    romantic heremenutics, 42
    subjective self and language, 36–7
    symbols, 124
    tragedy, 72, 77, 196
    tragic hero myths, 44, 45, 77, 103
Riders in the Chariot (1961)
    art and White's religious vision,
        126
    characters
        Calderon, Reverend Timothy,
            52–3, 54, 110,
            112, 113
        Chalmers-Robinson, Mrs,
            105, 106, 120, 123

Dubbo, Alf (artist), 53, 54,
    82, 88, 93, 106,
    107–15, 126, 178
Godbold, Ruth (Christian),
    88, 93, 103–7,
    114, 118, 172
Hare, Mary (mythos), 77, 88,
    89–94, 104, 106,
    108, 109, 180,
    195, 196, 231, 284
Hare, Norbert (logos), 88,
    90–1, 91–2, 196,
    257
Himmelfarb, Malke (Jewish),
    98, 99, 100
Himmelfarb, Mordecai
    (Jewish), 82, 88,
    93–103, 104, 106,
    114–15, 116,
    117–18, 118–19,
    121–2, 158, 159,
    183, 195, 279,
    281, 283, 284
Himmelfarb, Moshe (Jewish),
    98, 99, 100
Himmelfarb, Reha (Jewish),
    100, 101–2
horizons, 87, 88
Jew, portrayal, 82
Jewish horizon, 94
Jolley, Mrs, 92–3, 94
Mortimer, Humphrey, 54, 114
Pask, Mrs Emily, 53, 110–11,
    111–12, 113, 114
Rosetree, Harry (apostate
    Jew)
    (Rosenbaum),
    115–19, 120,
    121–2, 123
Wolfson, Sheila (secularized
    Jew) (Rosenbaum
    and Rosetree),
    119–24
chariot, 87, 91, 93, 102, 106,
    108–9, 112–13,
    113–14, 115

colour symbolism, 110–11, 113
Gadamerian frame, 41, 77, 82, 89,
        93, 109, 177
Hellenic logos, 91
logos Christianity, 109–10
mythos and religious experience,
        87, 88
places
        Sarsaparilla, 88, 94
        Xanadu, 91, 92, 93, 94,
                106–7, 195
Ricoeurean anthropology, 52, 77,
        89, 93, 177
romantic hermeneutics, 82, 83, 84,
        94, 95, 96, 97, 103
soteria, 104, 106, 107, 115,
        118–19
sparks, symbols, 96, 100, 101,
        102, 113
Theogonic mythos, 91
tragedy, 77, 91
The Riders (Winton), 216
The Robber Bride (Atwood), 361
Roman Catholicism, 19, 116, 119
Romans 8:22, 104
romantic hermeneutics. *see also Riders
        in the Chariot* (1961)
in Austens's work, 125
Gadamerian frame, 36, 41, 52, 82,
        230, 290, 301
Gadamerian horizons in White's
        works, 37–8
logos, 61, 62–3
logos fear of mythos, 130
paradox, 37
in White's fiction, 137, 141, 150,
        159, 170, 173
Romantic Image (Kermode), 8, 192
romanticism
as emancipating literature, 29
and modernism, 60
relationship to neoclassicism, 29,
        86
shadow of, 82, 86–7, 130, 185
White's, 10–11, 59–60, 86
Ruin the Sacred Truths (Bloom), 21

Rutherford, Jennifer, 48, 53–4

S
Sackville, Lady Victoria, 230
Sackville-West, Vita, 230
Said, Edward, 53, 57, 58fn
Saldarini, Anthony, 20
Salterton Trilogy (Davies)
        Tempest-Tost (1951), 344–5
        Leaven of Malice (1954), 345–7
        A Mixture of Frailties (1958),
                347–9
salvation
        Christian, 22–3, 85, 103
        denial, 102, 119
        history, 119, 281
Sanders, E.P., 21
Satran, David, 20
Schäfer, Peter, 21
Schepisi, Fred, 251, 258, 263
The School of Athens (Raphael), 13
Schwartz, Daniel, 20
science, 18
science–religion binary, 18
Scotus story. *see Duns Scotus's
        Doctrine of Categories and
        Meaning*
Scrunton, Roger, 27, 65
Scrutiny, 30
The Search for Meaning, ABC Radio
        (1993), 2
Second Vatican Council (1962–1965),
        322
secularism, 24, 36, 64, 294
Seidel, George, 36
Self-Knowledge in Plato's Phaedrus
        (Griswold), 42, 90
Sense and Sensibility (Austin), 11,
        125, 132, 365
Sewall, Richard, 74
Sexual Personae (Paglia), 51, 188, 257
"The Sin Eater" (Atwood), 9
The Slayers of Moses (Handelman), 21
Socrates
        correspondence theories, 10
        evidence base, 18

impact, 78, 129
logos and mythos, 16, 17
myth in Phaedrus, 42–3
The Solid Mandala
    The Birth of Tragedy, commentary
        on, 126–7, 136
    "blood myth," 140
    characters
        Brown, Anne, 147, 152, 154,
            159, 167
        Brown, Arthur (dionysian
            archetype -
            mythos)
            asylum, his future, 176
            contrast to Waldo, 132
            love, 140, 152, 162
            mythos half, 137, 141
            relationship with
                Feinsteins,
                164–9
            relationship with Mrs
                Poulter,
                148–52,
                175–6
            relationship with Waldo,
                140–1, 156–7
            role, 133
            tragedy, 130
        Brown, George, 116, 132,
            133
        Brown, Waldo (apollonian to
            socratic - logos),
            78, 124, 125
            contrast to Arthur, 132,
                141–2
            death, 139–41, 169, 174
            failure as a writer, 135,
                137–8, 157–8,
                162
            logos half, 134–5, 135–6,
                137, 140, 141
            love, 139–40, 152, 154
            relationship with Dulcie
                Feinstein,
                159–62
            tragedy, 130, 133

Brown family, 132–58
Dun, Mrs, 170, 171, 172, 174
Feinstein, Dulcie (Jewish),
    78, 147, 148, 151,
    152, 158, 159,
    160, 161, 162,
    163, 164, 165–7,
    168–9, 174–5,
    279, 283
Feinstein, Mr (Jewish), 158,
    160, 161, 162,
    163, 164, 166, 168
Feinstein, Mrs (Jewish), 158,
    159–60, 161,
    162–3, 164, 165,
    166, 282, 284
Feinstein family, 158–69
Poulter, Mrs (Christian), 78,
    148–50, 151, 152,
    153, 154, 169,
    170–7
Poulter family, 169–76
Saporta, Leonard, 137, 159,
    163, 166–7
soteria, 133, 160
two halves of one whole, 125
Gadamerian frame, 124, 177
Götterdämmerung, Wagner's, 133
götterdämmerung (twilight of
    pagan gods), 134, 135,
    156, 157, 175, 176,
    230
Jewish horizon, 158, 159
logos and mythos, psychic
    conflict, 137–9
love, 139–40
mimesis, 135
paradoxes, 124–5
pre-classicism archetype, 327
Ricoeurean anthropology, 124,
    177
symbols
    dogs, 158
    mandala, 124, 130–1, 144,
        147, 148, 150,
        153–4, 163, 165

quaternity, 130–1
Terminus Road, 133, 139, 148,
    150, 160, 170–1
tragedy, 77–8, 130, 146
transcendence to immanence, 78,
    136
Wagnerian opera, 130, 132–3, 142
Sons and Lovers (Lawrence), 35, 237
Sophists, 17–18
soteria, 22, 26, 44, 45, 58, 104
    through art, 67, 102, 177, 226, 233
Southwell, Gareth, 36, 84
The Sovereignty of Good (Murdoch),
    36fn7, 64
Spark, Muriel
    The Abbess of Crew (1974) see
        The Abbess of Crew
        (Spark)
    Aiding and Abetting (2000), 309
    Catholicism, 309–10, 317–18
    The Comforters (1957), 308–9
    contemporary of White, 7, 38, 89,
        132, 170, 262, 290
    evil, 309, 310, 311, 312, 315, 317,
        318
    existential philosophy, 189fn4
    The Finishing School (2004), 309
    good, 310, 311, 312, 315, 317
    The Hothouse by the East River
        (1973) see *The
        Hothouse by the East
        River* (Spark)
    logos and mythos tropes, 309,
        311, 317 (*see also*
        individual characters
        under novels)
    moral message, 318
    The Only Problem (1984), 309,
        318
    paradoxes:, 311
    Platonic model of mind, 309
    The Prime of Miss Jean Brodie
        (1961), 318
    The Public Image (1968), 309
    red hair symbolism, 309, 315, 327
    religion, 38–9

and Ricoeur, 310
Robinson (1958), 309
Symposium (1990), 309
The Takeover (1976) see *The
    Takeover* (Spark)
"The Desegregation of Art"
    (1970), 318
unconscious, 33, 35, 215fn20
victim–oppressor rhetoric, 290,
    318
White's postwar contemporary, 7,
    33, 35, 38, 39, 49, 89,
    132, 169–70, 262, 290
Spengler, Oswald, 31, 128
    cyclic model of civilization, 30,
        49, 76, 79
Spinoza, Baruch, 10, 65
St James King Street, Sydney, 3, 4, 5
Stark, Rodney, 3, 19
Steiner, George, 72, 74
Stendahl, 236
Stern, David, 21
Steven, Laurence, 35
structuralism, 23, 52, 190, 289
Sturm und Drang movement, 15, 16,
    70, 77
Surfacing (Atwood), 361
Sweet Violence: The Idea of the Tragic
    (Eagleton), 74
Swift, 67, 68
The Symbolism of Evil (Ricoeur), 42,
    43, 72, 95, 291, 370
Symposium (Plato), 55, 65, 189fn
Symposium (Spark), 309

T
Tacey, David, 51, 288
The Takeover (Spark)
    characters
        Father Cuthbert, 330
        Father Gerard, 330
        Hubert (classical archetype),
            309, 326, 327–8,
            329, 330
        Lauro, 329, 330

Maggie (pre-classicism archetype), 309, 326, 327–8, 329–30
Thin, Pauline, 329
evil
of neo-paganism, 326, 327–8
regardless of paradigm shift, 326, 327, 328
homosexuality, 327–8
Lake Nemi, 326, 328, 329, 330
Middlemarch comparison, 326
plot, 327–8
satire of Frazer's evolutionary theory, 326–7
themes
Church flirting with paradigm shift, 330
distraction of paradigmatic relationship, 326, 327, 329–30
master–slave dialectic, 329
title and entitlement, 329–30
Talmud, 82, 96, 117
Tanner, Michael, 10, 128, 129
Tempest-Tost (Davies), 344–5
The Tempest (Shakespeare), 344, 361
Tennant, Kylie, 1
Theogonic metaphors
Christian imagination, 103
The Eye of the Storm, 50
Hunter, Elizabeth, 50, 231–2, 244, 247, 275
Manhood, Flora, 274, 275, 279, 284
Judaism, 94
King Lear, 235
MaddAddam Trilogy, 10
Ricoeur's categories, 45–6, 49, 77, 88, 103, 109, 124, 235
Riders in the Chariot, 77
Hare, Mary, 88, 90–1, 92, 93, 108
The Vivisector, 177
Courtney, Rhoda, 195
Theogony, 104

Theogony (Hesiod), 370
The Theological Origins of Modernity (Gillespie), 23, 24
There Is No Natural Religion (Blake), 83–4
Three Studies for Figures at the Base of a Crucifixion (Bacon), 199
Three Uneasy Pieces (1987), 41, 86
throne–chariot visions, 87, 102, 108–9
time, influencing how writers write, 6
Tonner, Philip, 36
Torah, 14, 80, 95, 116, 117, 153, 160, 234
tragedy. *see also King Lear* (Shakespeare)
ancient Greek, 72, 74–5, 78
apollonian and dionysian principles, unity, 78, 234
approaches, 68
Christian, 72
comedy, contrast, 75–6
importance, 233–4
modern, 72, 73–5, 77
in White's work, 69–70, 76–81, 220, 234
Tragedy and Philosophy (Kaufmann), 74
"Tragedy and the Common Man" (Miller), 73–4
Tragedy Is Not Enough (Jaspers), 72
The Tragic Vision (Krieger), 74
The Tragic Vision (McCulloch), 69, 74, 241, 296
transcendence. *see also* immanence; transcendence-immanence debate
analogical theories, 293
and immanence in White, 64, 66, 67, 68, 204, 221, 229
Marxist critique of false, 64
Plato, 64, 65
relationship to immanence, 66, 68
secular critics, 86
shift to immanence, 13, 14, 60

through art (*see* soteria)
transcendence–immanence debate, 14,
        60, 67, 70, 204, 221, 229
The Tree of Man (1955), 25, 28, 41,
        88, 170, 287
Trinity as quaternity (Jung), 85, 209fn,
        355
Truth and Method (Gadamer), 23, 37,
        38, 291
Turner, James, 7
"The Twitching Colonel" (1937), 9
The Twyborn Affair (1978), 25, 41, 49,
        54, 55, 56–7, 79–80, 86,
        132, 215, 291
The Tyranny of Greece over Germany
        (Butler), 70–1

U
The Unicorn (Murdoch), 308
universal problems, 240
universal truth, 191

V
Vatican II, 170, 322–3. *see also*
        post-Vatican II
Vermes, Geza, 20
The Vision of Tragedy (Sewall), 74
The Vivisector (1970)
        characters
                Courtney, Alfreda, 180, 181,
                        182, 193–4, 195,
                        197, 200, 203,
                        205, 206
                Courtney, Harry, 183, 184,
                        191, 192, 194,
                        195, 200
                Courtney, Rhoda
                        (pythoness oracle;
                        dionysian–chthoni
                        c archetype), 58,
                        78–9, 231
                discovering, 191–9
                losing, 199–206
                absence, 206–19
                finding, 219–29

Cutbush, Cecil (homosexual),
        54, 180, 206–10
Duffield, Hurtle (apollonian),
        78, 79, 108
art (painting), 178, 183,
        197, 198–9,
        201–2, 204,
        218, 220,
        221–2, 227–9
creative, destructive
        forces, 177
between logos and
        mythos, 178
Lightfoot, Nance (dionysian–
        chthonic), 179,
        180, 182, 198,
        200, 201–6
Mothersole, 217–18, 218–19
Olivia–Boo, 78, 177, 210,
        212–13, 215, 226,
        227
Pavloussis, Cosma, 78–9,
        181, 213, 214,
        216, 218
Pavloussis, Hero, 78–9, 180,
        181, 182, 209,
        213, 214–17, 218,
        219, 221, 259
Volkov, Kathy, 78, 196, 199,
        219, 222–6, 227,
        228
fatalistic Theogonic metaphors,
        177
Gadamerian frames, 177
God and art, 197, 229
Hellenic metaphors, 177
love, 201, 204, 221–2, 229
narrative structure, 178 9, 180
red hair symbolism, 195, 227, 257
rhetoric in shadow of
        romanticism, 185
soteria through art, 79, 177, 226
suicide theory (McCulloch),
        204–6
tragedy, 78–9, 181, 213–14

transcendence–immanence debate,
204, 221, 229
voluntarism, 62, 63, 292–3, 295

W
Waiting for Godot (Beckett), 32
Walton, Michael, 68, 74–5, 234
Waterfield, Robin, 15, 16, 17, 62
Weaver, Sigourney, 315
Weltanschauung, 15, 37, 67, 305
What's Bred in the Bone (Davies),
356–7
White, Patrick
20th century critique of his work,
6, 7
anti-Catholic Protestant agenda,
18–19
archetypes and reality, 233
Australian critics after the Nobel,
6
authorship, concepts, 28
autobiography see *Flaws in the
Glass* (1981)
belief in God, 1
Brown brothers as self, 129–30
Christian Brothers visit, 3
Church, relationship with, 2
critique of reason, 63–4, 74, 95,
96
excremental vision, 67, 68
faith, 1, 2
family's Church relationship, 2
fiction, 28
fortunate failure, 47–8, 125
Gadamerian frame, 291
German influences, 13–14, 70–1
Greece, 214
historicized rhetorician, 7–10
homosexuality, 52, 55, 57
literary influences, 30, 49, 69, 128
literature and life, tension, 232–3
middle or religious period, 124,
291, 299
Nobel Laureate statement, 6
performances, 7, 14–15, 25–6, 50,
61, 63–4, 66, 288

and postcolonialism, 54, 88, 107
pre-classicism archetype, 327
religious (formative) experiences,
3
religious performances, 25–6, 64,
66
religious period, 124, 291, 299
religious problems, 26
religious revealings, 3–4
religious themes and symbols, 15
religious vision, 73, 86
reputation, 287
revelatory experience at
Dogwoods, 4–5
Ricoeurean anthropology, 291
self-awareness, 289
shortcomings, 239–40
tribal anti-Catholicism, 2
unconscious, 35
unity of aesthetics and rhetoric, 27
Virgin Mary devotion, 2
World War II, 30–1
White, Ruth (mother), 230, 231
White family's Anglican patronage, 2
Whitehead, A., 12, 16, 94, 297
wholeness
artist, 245
Christian definition, 22
loss, 33, 35, 40, 59, 66, 67, 137,
156, 181, 182, 186
Nietzsche, 136
pre-classical, 37
pre-Enlightenment, 136, 305
pre-lapsarian, 343
Presocratic, 141
self-discovery, 343, 357
symbols, 144, 150, 265, 286
withdrawal, 101
Whose Justice? Which Rationality?
(MacIntyre), 293
Williams, Margaret, 20
Williams, Mark, 46
Williams, Raymond, 74
Williamson, George, 13, 17, 43, 296
Winckelmann, John, 13, 70, 71, 126,
127, 136, 242, 296

Winton, Tim, 216
Witham, Larry, 36
Words With Power (Frye), 310
World of Wonders (Davies), 352–4
writers, metaphysical dimension of
        western consciousness, 7
Wynne, Mariamne, 30

Y
The Year of the Flood (Atwood), 361,
        368–9
Young, Julian, 10, 72

Z
Zimmermann, Jens, 37, 42
Zionism, 95